Rebels in the Making

Rebels in the Making

The Secession Crisis and the Birth of the Confederacy

WILLIAM L. BARNEY

OXFORD
UNIVERSITY PRESS

Oxford University Press is a department of the University of Oxford. It furthers
the University's objective of excellence in research, scholarship, and education
by publishing worldwide. Oxford is a registered trade mark of Oxford University
Press in the UK and certain other countries.

Published in the United States of America by Oxford University Press
198 Madison Avenue, New York, NY 10016, United States of America.

Library of Congress Cataloging-in-Publication Data
Names: Barney, William L., author.
Title: Rebels in the Making : The Secession Crisis and the Birth of
the Confederacy / William L. Barney.
Description: New York : Oxford University Press, 2020. | Includes index. |
Identifiers: LCCN 2019034327 (print) | LCCN 2019034328 (ebook) |
ISBN 9780190076085 (hardback) | ISBN 9780190076108 (epub) |
ISBN 9780190076092 (updf) | ISBN 9780190076115 (online)
Subjects: LCSH: United States—History—Civil War, 1861–1865—Causes. |
Slavery—Economic aspects—Southern States. |
Southern States—History—1775–1865.
Classification: LCC E441 .B339 2020 (print) | LCC E441 (ebook) |
DDC 973.7/11—dc23
LC record available at https://lccn.loc.gov/2019034327
LC ebook record available at https://lccn.loc.gov/2019034328

1 3 5 7 9 8 6 4 2

Printed by Sheridan Books, Inc., United States of America

For Elaine,
who never left me

CONTENTS

ACKNOWLEDGMENTS

The genesis of this book goes back to my graduate days at Columbia University in the 1960s that awakened in me a career-long fascination with secession. The book was made possible by the legions of scholars who have explored the roots of secession and by the manuscript keepers across the South whose assistance in locating manuscripts was both helpful and unstinting, especially the staff at the Southern Historical Collection at the University of North Carolina at Chapel Hill. It has been enriched by insightful conversations with colleagues and graduate students at Chapel Hill and speeded along by a research leave from the UNC history department in the spring of 2019 for which I am most appreciative. Special thanks are due to two outside reviewers for Oxford University Press whose critiques were spot on for strengthening the narrative and sharpening my analytical perspective. Susan Ferber, my editor at Oxford, was everything an author could hope for with her discerning stylistic eye and mastery of clear, concise prose. Her suggestions were invaluable for smoothing out the narrative flow of the manuscript.

Above all, I owe a debt I can never repay to Elaine, my late wife and mother of my two wonderful children, Kristina and Jeremy. Her love and unwavering encouragement sustained me as a graduate student, a teacher, and a scholar and made me a better person. In her name this book is dedicated with eternal gratitude.

Rebels in the Making

Introduction

As the rumbling of cannon fire rolled down the Cape Fear River valley in the early hours of April 12, 1861, a carriage carrying two white men came to a stop. The men became noticeably pale and agitated. After proclaiming "It's come," one of them, Joseph Cowens, a merchant-planter from nearby Wilmington, North Carolina, hastily scribbled a note, placed it in a sealed envelope, and directed William, the young slave driving the carriage, to hurry directly back to his master's Summer plantation and hand the message to Cowens's wife.

William took a detour on his way back. He drove first to the Five-Mile plantation and gave the note to Tom, the black overseer who had taught William how to listen in on the conversations of the white folk in the main house. Tom could read and write and served as a source of information on the outside world for the other slaves. William had often brought him newspapers to examine and then carried them back to the house early the next morning before they were missed. When Tom opened the envelope, its message confirmed the hopes that had been aroused when those on the plantation had also heard the sound of cannon—the war over slavery anticipated by the slave owners was about to break out. Cowens wrote that the Confederates had fired on Fort Sumter and he likely would be leaving "to help whip the Yankees." Cowens also instructed his wife to inform their white overseers to tighten up surveillance of the slaves and to prevent any private meetings among them.

After reading the note, Tom gave it back to William with directions on a round-about way to the Summer plantation that would take him by a large mud puddle in the middle of the road. Upon reaching that spot, William was to smear the envelope with wet mud so as to conceal that it had already been opened. The ruse worked. When William handed the envelope to his mistress with profuse apologies and tears for having accidentally dropped it into a muddy pool, she unsuspectedly tore it open in her rush to read its contents. To eliminate any signs of his deception, William picked up the envelope dropped by Mrs. Cowens as she hurried into the house. He tore it up, chewed it into a pulp, and stuffed it into a hole in a wall of the barn.

Cowens came home that night and met with a group of men from Wilmington. William eavesdropped on their conversation and was overjoyed when he heard one of them heatedly say, "If the Yankees whipped [us], every negro would be free." He was now certain, as he put it, that "the negro was the bone of contention and that the light of liberty was probably about to dawn." When Cowens left for the war on the morning of April 15, he took William with him.

This interchange between a master and his slave laid bare the paternalist ethos based on the belief that the master understood the enslaved, whose affection and loyalty could be assumed. In fact, Cowens understood little of William's thinking and likely actions. Cowens had assumed that his command to rush home with his message would be faithfully carried out. Instead, William took advantage of what openings the master–slave relationship offered him. While his master rushed off to a war that would destroy slavery and in the process cost him his life, William acted on his own self-interest and that of his fellow slaves to learn more about the unfolding crisis that would ultimately free him.[1]

This firsthand account of how enslaved people reacted to hearing of the outbreak of the Civil War and how they interacted with masters is rare. What little we know usually has to be filtered through the accounts of whites. The great strength of William's story is the immediacy it brings to a slave's perspective on the climax of secession, the seminal event in Southern history.

* * *

Solid, state-centered studies of secession, heavily political in orientation, first appeared in the 1930s.[2] Major works in the 1970s pushed research on secession in new directions by focusing on race and class, including pervasive fears over slave insurrections, concerns that the Republicans would shut down profitable outlets for slavery, and worries by planters over a looming crisis of control within the South.[3] Also examined were the unsettling effects of rapid internal change that led the yeomanry to fear a loss of their liberties to dark, sinister outside forces, best represented by the antislavery North.[4] The cultural turn of the 1980s produced an influential analysis of how the Southern code of honor demanded a rejection of the shameful degradation of submitting to a Republican administration that defamed Southerners and their way of life.[5] A study on the cultural dynamics of lowcountry South Carolina argued for the primacy of patriarchy, the exercise of authority and power of white heads of household over their family members and, in some cases slaves, as the bond that united whites in defense of their local worlds. A methodologically innovative work linked divisions in the Upper South over secession to competing cultural attitudes toward the direction of future economic development.[6]

More recent research has stressed the point that anxieties over the loss of slavery and racial control, rather than a defense of states' rights, drove the

South to secession.[7] The doctrine of state's rights was always a tactical means for protecting slavery, and revealingly the Confederate Constitution did not recognize the right of secession. The last major work on secession emphasized that planters, especially those in South Carolina, feared that the erosion of slavery in the border slave states and its stagnation in the Upper South were a prelude to emancipation within the South. They defied rule by Northern majorities at the national level in an undemocratic bid to ensure their future control over slavery in an independent South. To gain popular support from doubting Southerners, they justified secession less in the dry, legalistic language of exercising a constitutional right to leave the Union and more as the same revolutionary right of a free people as that exercised by the patriots of the American Revolution in overturning British tyranny.[8]

Rebels in the Making offers, for the first time, a one-volume narrative history of secession in all the fifteen slave states.[9] Grounded in the deepening strains within Southern society as the slave economy matured in the mid-nineteenth century and Southern ideologues struggled to convert whites to the orthodoxy of slavery as a positive good, it focuses on the years 1860–61 when the sectional crisis exploded into secession and civil war. Organized chronologically, it details the election of 1860 and the events in the summer and fall of 1860 that resulted in fears readily exploited by secessionists as they launched a movement in South Carolina that spread across the South in a frenzied atmosphere Southern whites referred to as "the great excitement." The middle chapters explore why secession stalled in the Upper South and how and why moderates and former conservatives pushed aside the original secessionist radicals in laying down the foundations of the Confederate States of America at a convention in Montgomery, Alabama, in February 1861. It concludes with the final crisis over Fort Sumter that precipitated war and a second phase of secession in the Upper South when Lincoln sent a relief expedition to the fort.

This book makes several contributions to understanding secession. First and foremost, it affirms the centrality of slavery in the coming of the crisis, the failure to reach a compromise, and the founding mission of the Confederacy. Many whites may have had moral doubts over slavery, but they were united in their opposition to any outside interference with the institution. More than previous studies, it documents the initial caution of older, established planters and identifies the main impetus for secession in the rising middling ranks of younger slaveholders who saw their aspirations for planter status blocked and denigrated by the Republicans. New evidence is presented on slave resistance in the form of targeted arson in the fall of 1860 and the political consequences of that resistance. The understudied economic crisis resulting from Lincoln's election is also shown to have been one of the secessionists' greatest assets. The findings and insights of the new history of slavery as the driving force behind American nineteenth-century capitalism are qualified by showing how the South's version of slave capitalism was a distinctive one incapable of generating the broad-based economic diversification, social specialization, and innovation that increasingly set it apart from the free-labor North and provoked the opposition of capitalists in the North and Europe.[10] The commitment to economic advancement and social mobility spawned by the North's free-labor values set the North's form of capitalism on a collision course with the South's version. When Southerners brought their ethic of mastery to the halls of Congress in escalating demands to ensure slavery's future and to the towns of the North as they tried to recover fugitive slaves, they confronted mounting opposition. By 1860, most Northerners denounced the slaveholders' belligerence and rejected their ultimatum on secession.

Finally, *Rebels in the Making* presents secession as a slaveholder-driven movement from the top, unfolding incrementally over time on a state-by-state basis, heavily influenced by the progressive narrowing of options as the number of seceded states increased. In so doing, it isolates the contingencies and reactions that predisposed whites to favor or oppose disunion. In short, secession was not inevitable but the end result of events and decisions, many of which were not foreseen, which built momentum over time and culminated in the final crisis over Fort Sumter. Extensive archival research in period sources has recovered the voices of a broad range of Southerners, free and enslaved, men and women, caught up in that momentum as political and economic storms buffeted their lives. All of them had stories to tell as they experienced secession as a kaleidoscope of events and emotions that synergistically propelled whites out of the Union and into a war that fulfilled the slaves' dreams of freedom.

The crisis that engulfed them had been simmering ever since the delegates at the Constitutional Convention in 1787 struck a Faustian bargain between slavery and liberty that made possible the new federal Union.[11] The key protections granted to slave property and the power of masters included the clause about counting slaves as three-fifths of "all other persons" for apportioning representation in Congress and an explicit provision calling on the states to return "persons held to Service or Labour" in any other state. Issues related to slavery, however tangentially, became enmeshed in national politics from the earliest sessions of Congress.[12] Northern opposition to the expansion of slavery west of the Mississippi River touched off the first major sectional crisis in the Missouri debates of 1819–21. In the resulting Missouri Compromise, the South gained the admission of Missouri as a slave state and the organization of Arkansas as a slave territory, but in return slavery was prohibited in the remaining unorganized area of the Louisiana Purchase north of the 36^0 30' parallel. Planters in South Carolina, obsessed with the specter of federal power encroaching on their rights as masters, soon incited the nullification crisis of 1832–33 when they resorted to extremist state's rights doctrines in a bid to veto federal legislation they deemed threatening to their interests.[13]

The emotional and cultural stakes in the sectional disputes over slavery escalated dramatically with the emergence of abolitionism as an organized movement in the 1830s. At the core of that emergence was the activism of Northern free blacks and escaped slaves who fused their hatred of slavery with support for slave resisters in the South. They launched a multi-faceted campaign in pamphlets, newspapers, speeches, community- and church-based protests, the testimony of former slaves, legal assistance to blacks claimed as slaves in the North, and networks dominated by free blacks who assisted slave runaways on their journey north. Their unstinting goals were to free the slaves and gain full equality for African Americans. "We go for the largest liberty—for reform— radical reform, in every ramification of society, especially among that part of the community with which our destiny is immediately connected," proclaimed the *Mirror of Liberty*, an abolitionist newspaper, in its inaugural issue in July 1841.[14]

An inspiration to many of these black abolitionists was David Walker's electrifying *Appeal to the Colored Citizens of the World*, published in 1829. Born a free black in North Carolina, Walker witnessed firsthand the terror unleashed by whites on blacks in Charleston after a failed slave plot in 1822. He traveled throughout the South before settling in Boston in 1825. There he joined black civic institutions, related his tales of slave courage and resistance to the city's black abolitionists, and expressed his own rage in the *Appeal*. In demanding an immediate end to slavery, he urged all blacks to throw off white-imposed shackles of physical and psychological dependence, organize on their own behalf, and, if necessary, resort to violence. Learning from Walker's radicalism, William Lloyd Garrison, a white antislavery reformer, committed to a new position of uncompromising abolitionism and in close collaboration with the black community, launched a movement that unnerved whites in both the North and the South.[15]

Earlier antislavery efforts had focused on a gradual end to slavery and accepted the need for colonizing free blacks in Africa as the best, if not the only, response to the white prejudice which seemingly rendered impossible the assimilation of African Americans into American life on any terms approaching equality. In a radical departure from this view, the Garrisonian abolitionists made immediatism and racial equality the defining features of their movement. In doing so, they drew on the militancy of free black leaders in the North and embraced what African Americans had known all along—racial prejudice underlay the colonization movement and stymied any efforts at ending slavery, gradual or otherwise. For their model of reform and conversion, the abolitionists turned to their own evangelical Protestant backgrounds. They relied on moral suasion to convince slaveholders of the sin of holding slaves and of the need to confront their guilt and seek God's cleansing grace. They turned to the pulpit, schoolhouse, printing press, lecture circuit, handwritten petitions, and the mass distribution of pamphlets to spread their message of the utter immorality of slavery.[16]

This unsparing attack on slavery as a sin put Southern whites on the defensive and enraged many of them. To have accepted the abolitionist indictment—that holding slaves in and of itself was sinful—would have made a mockery of Southern religious institutions and the self-respect and moral standards of any slaveholder. Politically, it would have been an entering wedge in a debate over the continued existence of the institution in a society where non-slaveholders comprised a decided majority and slaveholders often harbored moral misgivings over slavery. Duff Green, the proslavery editor of the *United States Telegraph* in the 1830s, revealingly wrote that the great danger from the abolitionists was not the fear that they would stir up a slave insurrection. Rather, "we have most to fear from the organized action upon the consciences and fears of the slaveholders themselves; from the insinuations of their dangerous heresies, into our schools, our pulpits, and our domestic circles."[17] In insisting that "slavery is right, in itself," the Oxford (Miss.) *Intelligencer* stressed that "it is only upon that ground that the institution can be successfully defended."[18]

The abolitionists, in striking the defense of slavery at its weakest point, had to be denied a hearing in the South. The mails were censored and civil liberties suppressed, often by mob violence. In the Lower South the open expression of ideas hostile to slavery was virtually eliminated. The abolitionists were vilified as wild-eyed fanatics scheming to entice the slaves into bloody uprisings. And their central doctrine of immediatism, by which most abolitionists meant the absolute need for an immediate moral commitment to begin the work of dismantling slavery by whatever pragmatic steps were possible, was distorted into an utterly unreasonable demand to end slavery with a single blow.[19] Although the abolitionists succeeded in building an organizational infrastructure in the North, most whites there denounced them as meddling fanatics. Their call for racial equality before the law was a direct challenge to white prejudice, entrenched about as deeply in the North as the South, and virtually assured that the abolitionists would be a despised minority movement in the free states. Anti-abolitionist mobs roamed the streets of Northern cities in the mid-1830s targeting abolitionists and free blacks.

Apart from suppression, Southern politicians reacted to abolitionism with an increasingly aggressive assertion of the right of slavery to expand and be shielded from any criticism. They pushed the so-called Gag Rule through Congress in 1836 (renewed through 1844) to table antislavery petitions and silence any debate. Over Northern opposition, they set their sights on adding the large slave Republic of Texas to the Union and succeeded in doing so in 1845. In a war widely interpreted in the North as an immoral act of aggression fought to secure more slave territory, the United States acquired an immense amount of land from Mexico that Southerners wanted left open for the introduction of slavery. Northerners, taking their cue from the abolitionists, began to talk of a Slave Power, a conspiratorial force that had taken over the federal government, intent on expanding the reach of slavery and subverting any free institutions that opposed it.

The stage was set for an antislavery movement more broadly based than abolitionism. It began to coalesce in the North in the 1840s around the issue of preventing the expansion of slavery into the federal territories. This movement said nothing about immediatism or racial equality. Its focus was not on the plight of black slaves in the South but on the threat that slavery posed to the economic advancement, social mobility, and civil liberties of white labor. A solid Northern majority formed in Congress committed to keeping slavery out of the lands acquired in the Mexican War. The Free Soil Party organized in 1848 around the same issue and captured about 15 percent of the popular vote in the North, an impressive showing for a new third party. As Congress remained in a sectional deadlock, secession movements began to mobilize across the Lower South.

The crisis fitfully petered out when a settlement of sorts was worked out in the Compromise of 1850, a series of bills tailored to meet the most pressing demands of each section. Chief among its features were the admission of California as a free state, the organization of the territories of New Mexico and Utah with the implicit understanding that their territorial legislatures would decide the status of slavery within their boundaries, and a substantially strengthened Fugitive Slave Act.[20] Fears of disunion faded, but the wounds opened by the crisis never fully healed.

The most contentious feature of the Compromise was a new measure that placed the law and federal enforcement machinery on the side of Southerners seeking to reclaim fugitive slaves on Northern soil. The law ignored the prohibition of slavery in the Northern states, rendered every citizen liable to assist in the recapture of slaves, and disregarded community concerns for due process and individual liberties. By challenging the law, runaway slaves emerged as political actors who forced Northerners to confront first-hand the often brutal thuggery of Southerners and their agents intent on returning runaway slaves to the South. Open defiance of the law led by black men and women, often with the support of local whites infuriated by the flouting of their communities' standards of fair play and human rights, spread by the late 1850s from New England and the upper North to the broad belt of states from Iowa to the east. Only in the lower North, where large numbers of upland Southern whites lived, was the law routinely enforced as the decade ended. In trying to extend their mastery over Northern whites, Southerners succeeded only in alienating them and deepening the sectional divide.[21]

Any good feelings engendered by the Compromise of 1850 fell by the way-side in 1854 with the passage of the Kansas-Nebraska Act. Aiming to unify his Democratic Party on a platform calling for white settlement of the entire West, spurred on by a transcontinental railroad, Senator Stephen Douglas of Illinois introduced a bill to organize a large bloc of territory west of the Mississippi River. All this territory lay north of the Missouri Compromise line of 36°30' and hence was closed off to slavery. Not wanting to call attention to the issue, Douglas intentionally avoided any reference to slavery in his original bill. His evasion ploy failed when Southern congressmen, whose backing was necessary for the passage of any bill, demanded a repeal of the Missouri Compromise pro-hibition in exchange for their support for the bill. Southern radicals had decried the admission of California as a free state as a sell-out of slave interests symp-tomatic of what John Palmer, a lowcountry planter in South Carolina, saw as a pattern of "humiliation and degradation inseparably associated with the sys-tematic aggressions of the north."[22] Thanks to Douglas's predicament, at least the stigma placed on slavery in the Missouri Compromise territorial prohibition could be removed. In its final version the bill organized the territories of Kansas and Nebraska with the status of slavery to be governed by popular sovereignty, that is, the decision of the people who settled in the territories.[23]

Douglas got his bill, but it was a costly victory. Antislavery congressmen im-mediately branded the act as the latest and most monstrous outrage of the Slave Power, nothing less than a conspiracy to overturn the commitment to freedom in the trans-Mississippi West pledged in the Missouri Compromise. Northern outrage over the Kansas-Nebraska Act and the supposed proslavery con-spiracy behind it was the catalyst for the formation of the Republican Party. Its founders declared that they would protect the North from the encroachments of the Slave Power and halt the expansion of slavery. Its more radical members followed the lead of the black abolitionist Frederick Douglass in refashioning the Constitution into an antislavery document. After competing for two years with the anti-immigrant, anti-Catholic Know-Nothing Party, the Republicans emerged in 1856 as the major opposition party in the North to the still nation-ally organized Democratic Party. They had replaced the Whigs, Henry Clay's old party, which had brought together commercial interests across sectional lines to promote economic development with governmental assistance.[24]

In a surprisingly close election, the Democrats, with James Buchanan of Pennsylvania as their candidate, retained the presidency in 1856. The primary lesson of the election was that American politics was polarizing around the sec-tional axis of the free and slave states. The Republicans were a Northern, not a national, party. The Democrats were still organized across sectional lines, but the party was tilting heavily toward the South. Two-thirds of Buchanan's electoral votes came from the slave states and the party's share of the popular vote in the

North had dropped to 45 percent. The major Protestant denominations—the Methodists and Baptists—had already split apart in the 1840s over the slavery issue, and the Democratic Party, the last major national institutional structure, would do the same under Buchanan's ill-fated leadership.

Contrary to Buchanan's expectations, the Supreme Court's decision in the Dred Scott case further inflamed rather than dampened the sectional divide over the slavery issue in the territories. Missouri slave Dred Scott sought his freedom on the grounds that a former owner had taken him into free territory north of the Missouri Compromise line. In 1857 the Court rejected Scott's claim, ruling that Congress never had the constitutional authority to prohibit slavery in the territories. Slavery, as a form of property recognized in the Constitution, fell under the protection of the Fifth Amendment, which stated that no citizen could be deprived of life, liberty, or property without due process of law. Slaveholders were citizens and Congress had no right to single out and prohibit their form of property. The Court further declared, in an opinion written by one of the five Southern judges, Chief Justice Roger Taney, that Scott, as an African American, was not a citizen of the United States. He belonged, according to Taney, to a race specifically excluded by the writers of the Constitution from consideration as potential citizens. Blacks were entitled only to those rights a given state might decide to grant them. Taney had twisted the historical record, but his position reflected the prevailing racial prejudices of the vast majority of contemporary whites.[25]

Rather than fatally weakening the Republicans, as Buchanan had hoped by depriving them of the issue that defined them as a party, the Dred Scott ruling solidified the party by convincing more Northerners of the ever-spreading reach of malignant proslavery forces in the federal government linked to the Democratic Party. They saw those same forces at work in the violence-wracked Kansas territory. Popular sovereignty, the centerpiece of the Democrats' efforts to take the issue of slavery's expansion out of national politics, took a beating on the Kansas prairies when the settlement of Kansas turned out to be anything but normal. Because Kansas shared a long border with slaveholding Missouri and was a potential gateway to the Pacific, proslavery advocates were intent on winning the territory for slavery. Conversely, to lose the territory ran the risk of exposing the entire western flank of slavery to the advances of free soil. In a move widely publicized in the South, antislavery forces in Massachusetts provided some funding to subsidize free-soil settlement in Kansas. In an emotionally charged atmosphere punctuated by sporadic outbursts of low-level guerrilla warfare, a race quickly developed between free-soil and proslavery men to gain formal control of the territorial government. Ballot stuffing by Missourians and the entrenchment of proslavery territorial officeholders appointed by the Democratic administration in Washington resulted in the Lecompton Constitution being pushed through in an election boycotted by the free-soil majority. This document protected the slave property already in the territory (never more than few hundred) and could not be amended for seven years. The only choice offered about slavery was whether to admit more slaves.

Convinced that agitation over slavery in the territories was a dire threat to the Union and desperate to eliminate that issue in Kansas, Buchanan threw the full weight of his administration behind the admission of Kansas under a constitution that had made a travesty of popular sovereignty. Douglas, the unquestioned leader of the Northern Democrats, was up for reelection in 1858. Already under attack by Northern voters for his association with the Slave Power after his championing of the Kansas-Nebraska Act, he had to oppose the administration on the Lecompton issue in order to shore up his political base in the North. He rallied enough Northern Democrats to force a compromise that sent the Lecompton Constitution back to Kansas for another popular vote. When the constitution was rejected, everyone knew that Kansas would be a free state.[26]

While Buchanan declared open party warfare on Douglas and his followers for abandoning the administration on Lecompton, Southern Democrats began to doubt if they could ever trust Douglas on the slavery issue. Their worst fears were confirmed when, during their debates in Illinois in the summer of 1858, an obscure politician named Abraham Lincoln maneuvered Douglas into a statement that became known as the Freeport Doctrine. Douglas declared that, regardless of the Supreme Court's ruling in the Dred Scott case on the constitutional rights of slavery in the territories, the settlers could shut slavery out by failing to pass the local police legislation or slave codes necessary for the protection of the institution. For Southern Democrats, Douglas's attempt to salvage his doctrine of popular sovereignty was tantamount to a disguised form of abolitionism, a deceitful version of the openly expressed Republican stand on prohibiting slavery in the territories.

In what amounted to an ultimatum laid down to Douglas early in 1860, a few months before the Democratic National Convention was scheduled to meet in Charleston, Southern Democrats, led by Senator Albert G. Brown of Mississippi, called on Congress to pass legislation protecting the rights of slaveholders in future territories. Brown's resolution made such legislation, known as a federal slave code, mandatory if the need for the protection of slave property was not addressed by the territorial legislature. Brown's political rival, Jefferson Davis, Mississippi's other senator, countered with a more moderate proposal that called on Congress to act only if at any time it became apparent that the courts lacked the means of providing adequate protection. Further evidence of Southern opposition to Douglas and what was scornfully labeled his "squatter sovereignty" came out of the Alabama Democratic state convention in January. It demanded that the party endorse in its national platform the need for a federal slave code. Should it fail to do so, Alabama's delegates were commanded to walk out.[27]

The demand from the delegates from the Lower South for federal protection of slavery in the territories, "when necessary," split the party at Charleston.[28] The odds of the Douglas Democrats acceding to such a demand were virtually nil. Why then was the issue pushed? William L. Yancey, the noted Southern fire-eater from Alabama, laid out the reasoning in his celebrated speech at the convention. The fatal error of the Northern Democrats, which effectively ceded the moral high ground to the abolitionists, was their admission that "slavery was wrong." From that admission, according to Yancey, followed all the unconstitutional aggressions of the North upon the South. By not acknowledging that slavery was a moral good that could "exist anywhere by the law of nature or by the law of God," they had allowed abolitionism to infect the entire political landscape of the North until the South faced a "great antislavery army." The major divisions of that army—abolitionists, free-soil Republicans, and squatter sovereignty Democrats—all represented "the one common sentiment upon which the Abolitionists commenced their war, that slavery was wrong." Still, Yancey assured the Northern Democrats that by agreeing with their Southern brethren that slavery was a positive good, they could atone for their heretical stand on slavery. He called upon them to acknowledge their error and unite with the South on a platform that guaranteed equality for all forms of property and reassured Southern whites that their property and their lives would no longer be endangered by remaining in the Union. The issue had to be faced squarely. Once Northerners grasped the great constitutional principle that was involved and were made aware that the fate of the Union hung in the balance, the result would be "a healthy state of public opinion at the North as well as the South." Only with such a bold approach could the onslaughts of the antislavery forces ever be turned back and harmony restored in the Union.

In his uncompromising assertion of Southern rights, Yancey provided a rallying cry to arouse the Southern masses to a final reckoning with the antislavery North should the Republicans win the presidential election in November. Only bold leaders who placed principle above personal success could unite the people behind the defense of their honor and equality. Yancey issued a thinly veiled warning to Southern politicians not to "demoralize your own people" by backing down now. Those who did "ought to be strung upon a political gallows higher than ever erected for Haman."[29]

It was quite a performance. Yancey had laid down the ideological and emotional foundation for future Southern resistance and had gone to the heart of the sectional dispute in a rhetorical flourish that Cowens's slave William would distill into the observation that slaves and their future were "the bone of contention." The speech, however, moved few Douglas Democrats onto the Southern position on slavery in the territories. Failing to gain a slave code provision in the party's platform, fifty delegates from the Lower South walked out. Efforts to reunite the party at Baltimore in early June proved futile, and the Republicans behind Lincoln swept to a victory in November.

Prophets without much of a following until Lincoln's election, the secessionists masterfully exploited their best, and likely last, opportunity to precipitate disunion and reach their goal of an independent South. During the secession winter, they channeled their rage and anger over Northern condemnation and Lincoln's triumph into a compelling vision of a South permanently safe, powerful, and morally respected. They gained the support of the Upper South when Lincoln ordered a military response to enforce federal authority. Whites across the South rallied to secession once they were convinced the existence of slavery was at stake. They agreed with the firebrand Lawrence Keitt of South Carolina when he declared that "even if slavery be the product of rapine and violence, even if it be the hideous wrong the Abolitionists declare it to be, still the South is wedded to it in eternal union." War with the North might well result, but let it come. "Would the horrors of a civil war be greater to the South than the loss of the institution of slavery?" asked the *Anderson* (S.C.) *Intelligencer.* The answer would come in the war that secession unleashed.[30]

1

Uneasy Rest the Masters

Strains from Below in the 1850s

The prosperity of the South in the 1850s bypassed most Southern whites. That prosperity was built on slaves, fertile land, and an expanding global demand for cotton, the antebellum production of which peaked in 1859. By then, good land and slaves were increasingly beyond the reach of the bulk of the white population. Slave prices more than doubled in the 1850s, and only the wealthy or those with substantial lines of credit could afford to purchase them. Decades of soil depletion and degradation had reduced the amount of cheap, fertile land for new plantations. A growing underclass of white poor found themselves reduced to working as farm tenants, sharecroppers, or hired laborers for the farmers and planters who did own slaves. Depending on the agricultural sub-region, 20 percent to 40 percent of the farm household heads owned neither land nor slaves. As a result, the color line blurred as more whites were forced into economic competition with slaves and free blacks.[1]

Anger and frustration over shrinking opportunities for economic independence and advancement produced challenges to the established rule of planter elites and widened the cracks in the façade of white unity planters presented to the outside world. As the threat of the antislavery North loomed increasingly, planters grew uneasy over their mastery at home. Here was a potential crisis that Southern radicals promised secession would resolve.

Agricultural Wastelands

Vast swaths of the South were a graveyard for farming by the mid-nineteenth century. "No thoughtful, intelligent man can survey the old fields from the Chesapeake to the Mississippi, and not bear witness to the fact that there is something fundamentally wrong in Southern agriculture," wrote Virginia lawyer-planter George Fitzhugh in 1858. More alarmingly, the *Jackson Semi-Weekly*

Mississippian two years later pointed to "those vast tracks of worn-out lands, now lying everywhere as useless as the bills of spurious and broken banks" as evidence that "improvident agriculture has already ruined millions of the best acres of our soil, and if persisted in, will ultimately turn the whole country into a wide, measureless waste."[2]

Soil exhaustion first emerged as a major problem in the early nineteenth century in the old tobacco belt of Virginia and North Carolina. Heavy rains from summer storms and the light, acidic soils common in the Piedmont region of the Southeast made it difficult to grow fodder crops as feed for the cattle and other livestock that could have served as a source of nutrient-rich manure to help restore depleted soils. Parasitic infections spread by ticks also stunted the size of cattle herds. Marl (fossilized seashells) was abundant and a good source of calcium to neutralize overly acidic soils, but it added no critical nutrients and could bear transportation costs only up to a distance of about fifteen miles. Nitrogen- and phosphorous-rich guano (bird-droppings imported by the ton from Peru) was touted as the answer at mid-century for barren soils, but the massive quantities required and rising costs in transporting rendered it impractical for most planters.[3]

Above all, the economic logic of slavery perpetuated wasteful agricultural practices. Slaves were more valuable than the land they worked. Aiming at the highest rate of return per slave, planters worked their slaves as hard and constantly as was possible in the production of a cash crop—tobacco, rice, sugar, and increasingly cotton. There was little incentive to divert expensive slave labor to restoring soil fertility when cheap, fresh land could be had farther west. A frustrated Alabama planter put the issue succinctly: "The opinion is generally prevalent among our cotton planters, that it is cheaper to purchase new lands than to manure old ones; and hence like the locust, they settle only to destroy." And destroy they did.[4]

Given the logic behind using up land and then discarding it, the plantation economy had to recreate itself on new cotton frontiers in order to maintain itself. Rice and long-staple cotton, named after its long, silky fibers, were ecologically limited to the sea islands and tidal flats of the coast of South Carolina and Georgia. They also required, as did sugar cane, a second major cash crop, huge capital investments in labor, drainage systems, and specialized equipment. None of these constraints limited the spread of upland or short-staple cotton. Apart from needing about 200 frost-free days and twenty inches of rainfall, it could be grown across most of the South. From its original heartland in Piedmont South Carolina, new cotton regimes were carved out in Middle Georgia and northern Florida, the black belt of central Alabama and Mississippi on lands seized from Native Americans, eastern Texas on lands secured in the Texas War of Independence, and the river valleys of southeastern Arkansas before the last great cotton frontier was opened up in the 1850s in the lush Mississippi Delta.[5]

Except for the most recent, all the areas opened up for cotton production after 1800 were showing signs of serious economic decline by the 1850s. Since the 1820s, worn-out lands in Piedmont South Carolina, compounded by the competition of newer cotton fields to the west, resulted in a mass exodus from the state. By 1850, over 40 percent of South Carolina–born whites had left, and those who returned for a visit were often saddened by what they saw. "Dear wife," wrote Smith Lipscomb, who had moved from upcountry South Carolina to Calhoun County, Alabama, "you cant draw no idy how old & desolated this country looks[;] it is nearly all cut down & in old Broome straw fields." Barren red clay hills, deeply washed gullies, and fields covered with young pines and broom sedge greeted those returning for a visit to Middle Georgia in the 1840s. Migration out of Georgia was very high in that decade except for an inflow into the southwestern section of the state where fresh lands had been opened up. Just ten years later, there were signs that the light, sandy soils were showing signs of exhaustion there as well. In what had been the booming counties of the Alabama and Mississippi black belt, which derived its name from its rich, dark soils, planters on worn land at mid-century were anxiously checking out prospects in Arkansas and Texas.[6]

The goal of slaveholders was to seize the main chance before diminishing returns set in. Non-slaveholding farmers, the dominant group in the country-side except in established plantation districts, set their sights lower. Without the labor services of slaves, they had no choice. They worked the poorer land, planted mainly corn as a food crop, kept hogs that ran free on the open range, and generally placed the economic security of their families above the risk of losing everything by going into debt to purchase slaves. Nonetheless, they were at least as wasteful of the soil as the planters, and corn was more demanding of soil nutrients than cotton. They lacked the inclination and the means to keep up with improved agricultural techniques. Their slash-and-burn method of cultivation produced a fertilizing ash that initially led to bountiful yields but was quite land-extensive. In areas of good land, they were quickly pushed aside when settlers of more substantial means arrived. In many counties, two-thirds to three-fourths of non-slaveholders left within a decade.[7]

Unlike the newer states in the free-labor West, the states of the new South settled after the War of 1812 quickly became net exporters of population. Most of the planter's capital was fixed in the value of his slaves, who were worked as steadily as possible throughout the year. He aimed for self-sufficiency in foodstuffs and could meet most of his manufacturing needs with slaves trained in artisan skills. The most significant economic exchange, exporting cotton, took place in international markets and was handled by factors, specialized commission merchants, in Charleston, Mobile, and New Orleans. Little of the planter's agricultural operation fostered local economic development or commercial interactions between town and countryside that was characteristic of farming communities in what became the Midwest. There, in a rural setting of small family farms, aspiring businessmen and land speculators had an ongoing incentive to promote towns and attract settlers to drive up land values. Bustling towns with marketing ties to the countryside sprang up. In the South, such towns were conspicuous by their absence. An influx of newcomers did not enhance the value of slaves and always carried the political risk of opposition to slavery itself.

The South had plenty of land for agricultural development in the 1850s and much of it could be had for $2 to $4 per acre. The issue was not the availability of land per se but the amount of land suitable for commercial agriculture with increasingly expensive slave labor. Land under cultivation rose by a third in the 1850s as some 3,000,000 acres were developed, much of it in areas newly opened up to commercial agriculture by the spread of railroads. The demand for good land, however, outstripped the supply and prices rose. In Mississippi, a cotton frontier state a generation earlier, good land that was available for $5 per acre as late as the early 1850s was going for $10 to $20 by the end of the decade and prime alluvial land for up to $35 per acre. Despite rising costs as well for slaves and provisions, slavery remained profitable in cotton growing regions, though some evidence suggests that rates of return were declining in the 1850s. The most successful planters were those with large holdings of slaves on fertile bottomlands. They maximized profits by curbing soil erosion and washouts with horizontal plowing on hillsides; employing more efficient and disciplined means of managing the plantation workforce under the supervision of overseers; and utilizing the latest improved varieties of cotton that produced higher yields with larger cotton blossoms that enabled faster and more thorough picking by the slaves at harvest time. By all appearances, these planters, most of whom belonged to the planter elite who owned more than fifty slaves, were fabulously wealthy. Yet much of their gross wealth was offset by large debts, and the problem of indebtedness was reaching dangerously high levels across much of the Cotton South in the 1850s.[8]

Debts, More Land, and More Debts

"All that I am worth . . . is invested in land and slaves," wrote rice planter William Allston, "the annual income from which is pledged before it is realized." "Python," writing in *De Bow's Review* in 1860, observed that "almost every estate at the South now valued at two hundred thousand dollars, equally divided between lands and machinery on the one side, and negro slaves and live stock on the other side, is encumbered with a debt, by way of mortgages or otherwise, of at least twenty thousand dollars." A committee in the Mississippi legislature appointed early in the Civil War to investigate the problem of debts concluded that the proceeds of two years of a bumper cotton crop would have been needed to pay off the debts of the state's planters.[9]

Most planters were chronically in debt, but as long as their debts could be rolled over year after year and their main collateral in slaves was rising in value, they could both bemoan their indebtedness and blithely ignore it. Old debts were rarely paid, and new ones were frequently added in order to finance the purchase of the additional land and slaves needed to maintain and expand production. Slaves were periodically sold to pare down particularly onerous debts or to placate an incessant creditor, but that was at best a stopgap measure since it cut into the future plantation output needed to pay off the bulk of the debt. Even after the depressed years of the 1840s had given way to the prosperity of the 1850s, planters were groaning under debt burdens that only seemed to get heavier. Writing from his Somerset Place plantation in eastern North Carolina in 1860, Charles L. Pettigrew described to his wife how he was laboring with "the care of unreasonable and troublesome negroes. I cannot help it, my own sweetest. It is a duty I owe to you, to my children, to my creditors, and to the character of my family to use every effort to pay off the really heavy debt that hangs over my estate."[10]

Cotton planting was capital intensive and required cash outlays that few planters possessed. Slaves, a highly liquid form of wealth that could readily be transferred from one area of the South to another, and, to a lesser extent, land were mortgaged to raise the necessary funds. Factors beyond the planter's control—drought, flooding, an early frost, crop infestations, disease epidemics among the slaves, bad timing in committing to a price to sell a crop—resulted in uneven incomes from year to year. A bad year often necessitated taking on more debt to cover losses, whereas a good year stoked the optimism to take on more debt for plantation improvements or to acquire more land and slaves. Good year or bad year, continual indebtedness made possible the ongoing operation of the plantation and what prosperity the planter did enjoy.

The much higher capital requirements of sugar planting were met in the same way. As of 1860, at least one-quarter of the slaves in St. Landry Parish, Louisiana, had been pledged as collateral for loans. Mortgages backed by slaves equaled 85 percent of the value of the parish's cotton crop and amounted to three times the value of the sugar crop. In East Baton Rouge Parish, capital raised by mortgages on slaves was over five times the value of the cotton produced in the parish in 1859. In the lowcountry of South Carolina, another area of very capital-intensive plantations, slaves alone accounted for 75 percent of the collateral pledged for mortgages. Sheriffs' sales and court-ordered probate settlements of estates raised additional cash and credit when slaves were sold to meet the claims of creditors.[11]

Rising demand in the 1850s for the staples of cotton and sugar resulted in increasing income streams produced by slave labor. Planters capitalized the value of that income stream when they put their slaves up for collateral in the debt market. However rational and economically sound was the decision to go into debt, it assumed a steady, even rising, flow of income that in actuality could be reduced or cut short for any number of reasons. High profits, high costs, and high risks—it was all a huge gamble, "as much trusting luck as betting on a throw of dice," as sugar planter Richard Taylor put it.[12]

Sugar planters in the 1850s benefited from favorable prices and demand for their cash staple. The same could not be said of the rice and sea-island cotton planters in the South Carolina lowcountry caught up in that region's long stagnation and decline. Declining yields and growing competition from Georgia and East Asia cut into the profits of the rice planters. Conditions were more favorable for sea-island cotton, but the main beneficiaries of better prices in the 1850s were the planters on higher-yielding acreage opened up in coastal Georgia and Florida. By 1858, Florida was on the verge of overtaking South Carolina as the leading producer of sea-island cotton.[13]

With debts outweighing his ability to pay them in a period of flat to lower profits on land far past its productive peak, Nathaniel Russell Middleton was one of the lowcountry planters who felt trapped in a financial morass. Born into great wealth, a pillar of Charleston society, and the holder of a number of prestigious political and economic offices, Middleton seemingly was one of the last Carolinians likely to be beset with financial problems. Yet, over the years, his debts had grown faster than his assets. Already forced by financial difficulties into selling his plantation Bolton-on-the-Stono in 1852, he wrote his wife Anna in March 1860 that "as to our funds, my condition is just as it always has been, I have never been otherwise than anxious on that account." He had received an offer of $15,000 for their Charleston house but was reluctant to sell until he had time to see if some good investments in planting might surface. The problem, as he explained to Anna, was that "[plantation] property is now so high that $15000 would be like a drop in the bucket towards establishing us. It would take at least double to make us in any way comfortable."[14]

The Elliotts, another of the lowcountry's long-established, prestigious families were also feeling the pinch of financial stringency by the 1850s. William, the head of the family, inherited rice and cotton plantations from his father and added more with his marriage in 1817 to Ann Hutchinson Smith. He had great wealth and great expenses—the bills for the Harvard education of two of his sons, frequent travels to Europe and Northern spas, fine foods and liquors, and plantation costs to offset the inefficiencies of relying upon overseers to manage the plantations he rarely visited. Market conditions improved in the 1850s, but decades of single-crop planting had taken their toll on Elliott's once-fertile lands. Worried about low prices for sea-island cotton in early 1858, he warned his wife that they were "on the road to impoverishment with such crops at such low prices" and had to eliminate all wasteful household spending. The bills and debts coming due "will absorb every dollar of the proceeds of last year's crop. My own wages and the allowance of my children must come out of my *capital*, since they cannot be provided out of the *income of my property*." He began selling more slaves, in part to pay the bills for guano, his largest plantation expense.[15]

For twenty years Elliott had sensed that his economic fortunes were slipping, but he never experienced the desperation that by the 1850s gripped the King family of St. Simons Island, Georgia. Retreat, the family estate, was a showpiece plantation for long-staple cotton back in the 1820s when Anna Matilda Page inherited the plantation two years after her marriage to Thomas Butler King. The soil was rich, profits high, and prospects for the planter-politician King seemingly unlimited. He borrowed heavily to purchase more slaves and expand into rice and cotton planting on the mainland. The Panic of 1837 ruined all his grandiose plans. Forced to sell off his holdings, he still remained mired in debt from which he never recovered. Anna was able to retain Retreat only because of the foresight of her father in setting up a trust that made it and fifty (named) slaves and their increase exclusively Anna's and beyond the control of her husband and his creditors. Despite a large family of nine children who needed him at home, King spent most of his time on extended trips trying to raise funds and secure allies in an effort to pull himself out of debt. He became increasingly obsessed with dreams of regaining his fortune with convoluted financial schemes and speculations for a Southern transcontinental railroad. Until her sons were old enough to run Retreat, the major responsibility fell on Anna.

Debts that slowly mounted and falling yields on overworked soil that Anna fretted seemed "*almost tired*" consigned the family to genteel poverty. "We have been living beyond our means which unfortunately most planters (who have nothing but their crops [to] depend on) do," Anna lamented to her absentee husband in 1855. She felt compelled to tell her son Richard Cuyler "to give a full warning when *money* is *absolutely wanted*. I have not a cent *and must have time to raise it—on credit*." Georgia, her eldest daughter, spelled it out for her brother Floyd: "Now the naked facts are these. We are all dependent upon this property, which is *twelve thousand* dollars in debt. And if . . . we can get free of debt at best our property will only support singly & very moderately each of us."[16]

Although many lowcountry planters were living in the shadow of their past economic glory in the 1850s, enviable incomes could still be had in growing rice and sea-island cotton. One of the most successful planters was Charles Manigault of Charleston. The key to his success was foresight in spotting new opportunities.

He was the first of three South Carolina planters to extend part of his holdings into the new rice lands opening up along the Savannah River in Georgia when, in 1833, he purchased the Gowrie plantation on Argyle Island, a few miles from Savannah. He added an adjoining plantation in 1849. His son Louis managed the properties as one plantation after 1852. By keeping meticulous records, providing copious and specific instructions to Louis and his overseers, and sending to Georgia slaves experienced in the specialized techniques of rice cultivation from his less productive plantation in South Carolina, Manigault garnered impressive returns that still averaged over 10 percent in the 1850s.

Robert F.W. Allston and John Berkley Grimball continued to produce good returns in South Carolina. Although their lands yielded less per acre than Manigault's in Georgia, their Carolina rice usually commanded a higher price. A writer of learned treatises on rice planting, Allston applied his knowledge in the selection of superior seeds, the systematic application of fertilizer, and the rotation of fields so as to avoid overcropping with rice. Like Allston, Grimball was a very experienced planter. He devised a system of bonus incentives for his overseers that helped boost his income to over $15,000 from his rice crops alone in the 1859 growing season. He had a net worth in excess of $90,000 in 1860. In addition to his sound plantation management, a major contributor to his financial good fortune was his wife Mata's sizable inheritance in New York lands, which he used to pare down his debts.[17]

For most planters and slaveholding farmers engaged in producing upland or short-staple cotton, the key to economic sustainability was finding new acreage to supplant or replace their older, declining fields. Whatever the scale of their operations, they were constantly on the lookout for fertile, affordable land. Those priced out of good land in their immediate vicinity searched farther afield. Family members and friends passed on news of who was looking for what and advised on prices and the best locations. Mary Milling of Camden, South Carolina, wrote her husband James in the fall of 1860 that Mr. Mickie had just sent his slaves ahead to his new Mississippi lands and would himself follow in a few weeks to join them on his new place. James had moved his slaves to a plantation in Bossier Parish, Louisiana, in 1859, but he was soon scouting out land in Mississippi after a dispute with his partner in the plantation. Mary told him that her father would help out in any purchase price as long as James did not take on too much debt. John Milling advised his brother to make sure any land he purchased was open: "Settling in the woods is a tedious and laborious business and it is said a man had better pay five dollars for improved land than one dollar for unimproved." [18]

One of the most favored areas for new holdings was Arkansas. Land prices around Camden, a bustling port along the Quachita River, doubled in the late 1850s as newcomers poured into the area. On meeting a Mr. Haskell of South

Carolina at the Exchange Hotel in Richmond in the summer of 1860, Virginia planter Richard Eppes asked for advice on where to purchase a plantation for his "surplus slaves." Haskell, who had bought a plantation near Pine Bluffs, Arkansas, recommended the bottom lands along the Arkansas River. Eppes planned on going out to Arkansas within a year and hoped to buy three sections [a section had 640 acres] at around $5 per acre and some wooded land on ridges at 12 ½ cents an acre for its timber. [19]

John Kirkland, a small planter who had recently moved from Alabama to the hill country of Attala County, Mississippi, was also considering Arkansas by 1860. "Such a crop year as I have made this year & last has put me out with Attala," he wrote his brother-in-law William Otey in the fall of 1860, "and I want to go to Arkansas [;] just had enough." He hoped to convince Otey back in Alabama to join him. "Let me know immediately for I cant stay here to starve and it seems like I cant make a living here." He had given some thought to buying "the Swamp place" in Attala but feared it would not be as healthy as the hills and he would "lose more in negroes than the difference in cotton would justify." For the time being, he planned to make some income by hiring out his slaves to his neighbors as cotton pickers.[20]

The relatively fresh lands in southwest Georgia were also attracting a good many buyers. In the summer of 1860, Georgia planter Alexander Allen bought the Paramore plantation fronting on the Chattahoochee River for $12,000. He put up his Rock Pound plantation for sale to raise cash for the purchase but was forced to settle for an annual rental of $700 when he found no buyers. Very hard-pressed for money, he pressured his brother George to pay what he owed him. Likewise convinced that "a location in Southwest Georgia promises more advantages than any other," Charles C. Jones Jr. looked at several places in 1859 before agreeing to buy a 1,250-acre plantation for $4,000 in cash payable in February 1860, with three equal installments of the reminder due annually starting January 1, 1862. The plantation needed "proper attention," as Charles delicately phrased it in a letter to his father seeking approval for the very large financial commitment he had made. The Reverend Charles C. Jones was guarded in his response. He had inherited an old rice plantation in the Georgia lowcountry and shared with many of the older, established planters a distaste for the moral crudeness of cotton frontiers and the excessive demands made of the slaves.[21]

Nearly all the smaller planters and slaveholding farmers found the most desirable cotton lands east of the Mississippi priced beyond their reach. Milledge Luke Bonham of Edgefield District, South Carolina, inherited slaves but not a plantation that was productive enough to pay off his debts. He advised his mother Sophia in 1847 that it would be best to sell off the family plantation except for what she wanted to keep, and he would see that she was provided for.

For the next decade, Bonham searched in vain for good land he could afford. Apart from what he earned as a lawyer and his salary as a congressman from 1857 to 1860, he made do by renting land in Alabama and Texas on which he could work his slaves. More representative of the land poor than Bonham, who owned sixty slaves in 1860, was A. F. Burton of Kemper County, Mississippi. He had moved to Mississippi in the 1850s to farm some of the land that his relatives in Caswell County, North Carolina, had bought with their pooled resources. He owned, in his words, "a few slaves" and worked them in the fields along with hired white hands. Burton's land, however, was "thin," and he felt "bound to leave here or buy more land where I am." While Burton stayed put on his marginal farm, thousands of small slaveholders and farmers moved onto land generally shunned by the planters—the uplands of Arkansas and the backcountry of Texas.[22]

Far fewer but exponentially wealthier planters moved into the slave South's last bonanza cotton frontier, the Yazoo Delta, with its nearly inexhaustible alluvial soils. Not developed until the 1850s, the Delta, or more precisely the flood plain of the Yazoo and Mississippi rivers stretching from Memphis to Vicksburg, was a lush, nearly impenetrable wilderness of hardwoods and tangled undergrowth subject to frequent flooding. Less than one-tenth of its acreage had been cleared by 1860 and slaves outnumbered whites by five to one in the counties along the Mississippi. The lack of roads or levees, a reputation for unhealthiness, and, above all, the very high costs of up to $100 an acre to clear and drain the land kept the region an isolated backwater until wealthy planters seeking to extend or improve family fortunes began investing the capital and slaves to clear the land and outfit large-scale plantations. To begin planting in the river counties of the Delta entailed huge start-up costs of at least $150,000. At least half of the planters in these counties operated absentee plantations managed by overseers.[23]

The largest Delta plantation was owned by Steven Duncan, who had moved from Pennsylvania to Mississippi in the early nineteenth century and amassed through banking and planting one of the greatest fortunes in the South. More than 800 slaves worked it in the river county of Issaquena. Philip St. George Cocke, whose family plantation was in Powhatan County, Virginia, had been diversifying away from a reliance on tobacco since the 1830s with fresh cotton lands in Mississippi. He added new plantations for himself and his son John in the Delta counties of Yazoo and Washington in the 1850s. Another Virginian, James A. Seddon of Goochland County, followed a similar strategy with an emphasis on land speculation. Paul Cameron of North Carolina, who had shifted part of his slave workforce onto cotton lands he acquired in Alabama in the 1830s, moved into the Delta in the late 1850s and incurred debts of $31,000 in doing so. Too much rain and too early a frost kept his first year's production far below his estimate, but he had the resources to double down on his bet by sending more slaves and livestock from his home plantation in North Carolina to Mississippi.[24]

Cameron's new debt was quite modest compared to that of the Hamptons of South Carolina. The family began buying Delta properties in the 1840s. The showcase purchase was Wade Hampton II's Walnut Ridge estate in Issaquena with its slaves, 2,700 acres, and $400,000 mortgage. Wade's son, Wade Hampton III, went on a buying and borrowing spree in the 1850s when he acquired four plantations with a total of over 4,000 acres in Washington County to add to his Mississippi hunting preserve of 2,085 acres. When Wade Hampton II died intestate in 1858, his daughters received Millwood, the home mansion near Columbia, South Carolina, with its slaves, while his three sons divided up the rest of the estate with its debts of half a million dollars. Kit settled for his father's landholdings in Wisconsin, which came with no debt; Frank took over most of the South Carolina plantation properties and $100,000 in debt; and Wade, who inherited the Walnut Ridge property in Mississippi, wound up with the most land and the most debt. Despite the unrivaled productivity of his Delta plantations, Wade was in danger of being dragged down by his debts. His returns in 1858 and the following two years, cut short by flooding and frosts, were sufficient to meet most of the carrying charges on his huge debt load but not to reduce it. Like most planters, he was banking on a continuation of the economic good fortunes of the 1850s.[25]

Frustrated Sons

Much was expected of the sons born into the planter class. George W. Mumford, the son of a Virginia planter, passed on to his son in 1860 his own father's advice: "May this my Son transcend his father's fame—for Virtue, for talent, for position, for religion, for patriotism, for service to Country, for everything ennobling & great." Such ideals, however, were hard to achieve when sons raised in wealthy families were treated as dependent children subordinated to their fathers' commands. They had few responsibilities and little incentive to learn habits of personal industry and perseverance that would equip them to become successful planters. As they waited for their share of the paternal inheritance, many of them lapsed into habits of indolence and carefree pleasures. Common were such complaints as those in 1860 of J. L. Pennington of Arkansas: "When I look around & see the sons of so many rich men going down the road of ruin and destruction . . . I say these things are enough to make one pause and ponder well their faith. Place money plenty into the hands of a young man now a days & the chances are 100 to one against him." James M. Wilcox, a planter in Charles City County, Virginia, struck a bitter tone when he wrote of his son Lamb. He still had hopes that his son Hamlin, a law student in Philadelphia, would do well professionally, but he had almost given up on Lamb. "Your Brother Lamb," he told his daughter Susanna, "is yet in idleness, indulging in frolic and glee, helping others do nothing, bent on his own ruin, causing me trouble and finally to bring me to my grave in sorrow. I never have seen his match and if I am ever to have another son to pursue the same course I pray God to take him young and spare me the pain."[26]

Major Coe, a planter in Ochessee, Florida, might have said the same of his son Jesse. A bright lad, he was sent off to Transylvania College in Kentucky and the University of Virginia. Described by a local doctor as "full of life & fun, but unfortunately with a strong appetite for drink," he began using opium and became addicted. By the time he married Alice, a first cousin from Memphis, he had grown enormously fat and his eyes bulged out of a florid face. Within a few years of his marriage, he had two children by Celia, a house slave of his father's. Alcohol and opium sapped his health, and he died from a sudden chill in the late 1850s.[27]

Dutiful sons who steered clear of debaucheries had their own problems in establishing their independence when fathers refused to relinquish the reins of patriarchal control. Louis Manigault was in his early thirties and had been married for three years when he wrote his father Charles in January 1860 with a plea for independence. Louis spent half of the year on the Gowrie plantation outside Savannah, which he had been managing for his father since 1852, and the rest with his wife in his father's house in Charleston. He was in chronic need of money, forever in debt either to his father or to the family's factor. At the beginning of 1860 he owed them $1,000 and, as he sourly noted, had "no better prospects than last year" to pay it off. If he could afford to, he would move out of his father's house and into the house opposite, also owned by his father who had told Louis that one day the house would be his. Assuring his father that he was "certainly trying to economize in every way," Louis asked for his assistance when he and his wife finally established their own household. Specifically, he wanted Charles's permission to take the "silver, sheets, & towels" from Gowrie. Hoping to avoid "a disturbance," he reminded Charles that he had always said when his son married "he must leave the house."

Louis had stopped just short of being obsequious, but his father did not bend. He insisted that his son stay in the Charleston house with him at least through the summer. Louis then repeated his request, adding that "although poor I feel that with a little assistance until this plantation [Gowrie] should do better I would prefer living opposite for *many reasons*." He also asked to have the use of the slave Martha as a nurse for his family. After flatly rejecting his son's request for Martha, Charles announced that he was not about to lose the good rental income from the house across the street by allowing Louis and his family to move in. His parting shot was a demand that Louis stop his whining: "Don't talk too much about your poverty, it will bring you & the plantation into ridicule." Charles paid some of Louis's bills and gave him some money for his personal expenses. A chastened Louis admitted defeat in the battle of wills with his father and conceded that it made little sense to push for greater independence when he had so many debts he could not repay.[28]

Unlike Manigault, Robert Massie, a large planter in Virginia, was quite generous in trying to set up his son Thomas in a position of secure independence. Yet Thomas squandered it all. William advanced him $23,200, more than to his wife and all his other children. In 1839, when Thomas was twenty-two, his father went into debt to purchase the Red Hill property for his son and slaves to work the land, fully expecting that Thomas could live on this for the rest of his life. Instead, as William wrote Thomas in 1860, "I have my son been in constant discomfort on you since 1840." His son clearly lacked the talent and the inclination to manage Red Hill, and by 1860 his debts had ballooned to over $20,000. When he wrote his father in early 1861 pleading for additional help, Thomas was hounded by creditors, his health was shattered, and he had overdosed on pain-numbing drugs prescribed for him by a local doctor. William replied that he had six heirs to provide for, and he calculated that once his own considerable debts were taken out of the estate, the shares of his heirs would be worth little and certainly considerably less than what Thomas had already received. He gloomily informed his son that "there is no superabundance of anything here but misery."[29]

Even many planters' sons with caring fathers who made more of an effort than the wayward Thomas Massie had difficulty succeeding as planters. Among his three sons, William Elliott had the highest hopes for Ralph, though he told him this in a rather backhanded way. "I know that you are not stupid—that you can be taught if you are earnest to learn," he wrote Ralph in 1851 when he was a student at the University of Virginia, "and I really hope that I have one son, who will not shrink from the effort which everything in life requires which is worth the effort." Eight years later Ralph admitted to his father that he had failed in trying to grow good crops on "undrained rice lands." Wanting very much "to make a mark in the world," he sought his father's assistance. William put up $7,000 and purchased the Pon Pon plantation for his son. Within a year, William realized he had made a bad investment. Ralph tried his best, but his rice yields were very disappointing. The problem, as William deduced, was the nature of the soil at Pon Pon—it was not firm enough to maintain the high embankments that were necessary to keep out the river water, and hence the embankments were constantly being breached. He advised Ralph to find a buyer for the plantation at once.[30]

At least Ralph had a father who could afford to try to establish him as an independent planter. The sons of planters on older plantations encumbered with debt faced a considerably more uncertain future. Malachi Bonham, Milledge's brother, spent the better part of the 1840s and 1850s trying to make a living by growing corn on rented land. He was out in Texas in 1860 and, as a family friend informed Milledge, "his condition is far from comfortable. I think the land he cultivates is very poor and he has to pay about as much rent for his land as it has produced." He suggested that Milledge, a congressman, secure a patronage job for his brother delivering the mail. It would be hard work "yet it is less [work] than ploughing in the fields."[31]

Thomas Butler King's sons had grown restless and despondent while waiting at Retreat for their father to return home with the financial windfall he long claimed would be his for his promotional work for a southern railroad to the Pacific. Henry Lord, the most ambitious of the four, left for college in 1848. An indifferent student and a bit of a dilettante, he frittered away the next decade with little to show for his haphazard efforts to make something of himself. "This you know is the 28th anniversary of my birth day," he wrote his mother Anna on April 25, 1859. "I do not refer to it with pride, and very properly, for I have done little or nothing of which to be proud." Thomas Butler Jr., the eldest son, had died in 1859 leaving the responsibilities for managing Retreat for his mother to Mallery. Georgia felt terrible that her brother Mallery was tied down to the money-losing plantation and urged the youngest sons, Floyd and Tip (Richard Cuyler), to learn a profession to gain their "independence." [32]

Planters passed on their estates in roughly equal shares to all their children, with a preference for the best land to pass on to the older sons. Aware that not all their sons had the skills or aptitude for plantation management, planters by the 1850s were sending more of their sons to college to prepare for professions and placing them in mercantile houses as clerks to learn good business habits. Just over 35 percent of the sons of planters with an occupation co-residing in their fathers' households in Charleston, South Carolina, were clerks. Medicine, followed by law, was the favored professions for these sons. Those intent on becoming planters in their own right tended to remain at home awaiting their inheritance in the 1850s. This was the case for about one-third of the at-home sons in Charleston and in Dallas County in the Alabama black belt.[33]

The career paths of the sons of South Carolina rice planter John Jenkins illustrate the patterns emerging by mid-century. Only the eldest of the three sons, John, born in 1824, followed his father into planting. After studying classics at Princeton and then training for the law, he took over the management of the family's Edisto Island plantation in the late 1840s when his father grew ill, and he remained in charge after his father's death in 1854. Edward, the middle son, attended South Carolina College, studied medicine at the new state school in Charleston and then abroad, and by the mid-1850s married and began his career as a physician in upstate Yorkville. Micah, the youngest son, attended military school in South Carolina, graduated from the Citadel, and then co-founded the

Kings Mountain Military Academy in Yorkville in 1855. Using loans from John and disbursements from his share of his father's estate, he financed a rapid expansion of the school and was soon its superintendent.[34]

Fathers like William Elliott could argue that it was hard "to make any youth in this Southern country feel that he needed any instruction—or require the least restraint." The problem facing so many of the sons, however, was not so much their irresponsibility or headstrong temperaments as a tightening of opportunities to do as well as their fathers in a slave economy that was maturing and stabilizing. An outlet for their ambitions and thirst for fame would have to await the formation of the Confederacy.[35]

The Problem of the White Poor and Free Blacks

Although landed, non-slaveholding farmers, the yeomen, comprised the largest single group in the rural South, an underclass of whites who owned neither land nor slaves was growing. By 1860, some 30 to 50 percent of Southern whites were landless. This range of landlessness held across rural regions, whether in the lowcountry, the Piedmont, or the upcountry. In Southern Appalachia, a region often romanticized as one dominated by sturdy, independent farmers, nearly 40 percent of farm operatives were landless, half of whom were sharecroppers.[36]

The numbers of white poor were rising in the 1850s. Suits for debt collections rose sharply in South Carolina Courts of Common Pleas in the mid-1850s, and small farmers with too few assets and too many debts were thrown into the ranks of the landless. In the Burkes Garden neighborhood of Tazewell County in the southwestern mountains of Virginia, households of farm laborers, desperately poor families who had moved into the area in search of work, made up the fastest-growing social group. With little or no cash reserves, the landless in the older seaboard states had scant chance of acquiring land in the southwestern slave states where the sales were controlled by speculators and well-connected families. Poorer farmers who did purchase land from land speculators routinely fell behind in their payments. The agent of one land company in Mississippi told Frederick Law Olmsted, an astute Northern observer of life in the South of the 1850s, that he offered farmers 160 acres of land on credit at 6 percent with full payment due in three years. "It is very rare that the payments are made when due," he noted, "and much the largest proportion of this class fail even to pay their interest punctually. Many fail altogether, and quit their farms in about ten years."[37]

The persistent stereotype of poor whites depicts them as a lazy, shiftless, and degraded group squatting on undesirable land, surviving by hunting and fishing, and lacking a sense of community involvement or responsibility. As seen rather vividly in the case of Edward Isham, the stereotype did have some basis in fact. Born in northern Georgia in 1827 into an impoverished family intermittently headed by a father described by Isham as "dissipated," Isham learned at an early age from his father that men never backed down from a fight and resorted to whatever means were necessary to win. His father abandoned his common-law wife when Isham was still a youth and took his son with him farther west into the backcountry of Georgia. With no skills and but five days of schooling, as he recalled, Isham soon set off on his own into a life of constant moves that would take him to five states before his early death. The only work available to him required hard physical labor, and his job experience was sporadic and short-lived given his heavy drinking, frequent brawling, and ongoing scrapes with the local legal authorities. He joined one church but was soon expelled for fighting. Winnings from gambling provided much of his irregular income. By a generous definition of the term he was married to three women and had sexual relations with countless white and black women. A dangerous drifter, he killed three men before his execution for murder in 1860. Isham left behind an infant daughter who was raised by a couple that had testified against him in the trial that cost him his life.[38]

Isham's violent, short existence was an extreme case of how poor whites struggled to make something of their lives. Without their own land, they cobbled together a bare to marginal existence as tenants, sharecroppers, or day laborers for farmers and planters. Landholders needed the landless for their labor, and they in turn needed patrons for access to jobs, goods, and credit. Competition with slave labor kept wages low and jobs scarce and resulted in frequent moves. Many of the moves were local ones, but within a decade most of the landless had moved out of their county of residence.[39]

In Georgia, tenants made up 20 to 40 percent of all farm operatives and generally farmed less than fifty acres. They were most prevalent on land poorly suited for staple crops. Rather than allocate capital in the form of slave labor to such unproductive land, planters preferred to rent it to tenants requiring little in the way of direct supervision. The number of tenants was quite high on the edges of the freshest and best cotton lands where they worked the poorest soil and cleared forests for their landlords. With very little if any cash, they relied on a local barter economy where the wages for their temporary labor were paid in food crops, especially corn.[40]

Above all, the rural poor met the need for supplemental or seasonal labor on many plantations. George Barnsley managed a plantation for his father in north Georgia with only seven adult slaves and six slave children, so he was always on the lookout for additional hands. He employed a mix of whites and rental slaves until the late 1850s when he turned almost exclusively to poor white families as a result of the rising cost of renting slaves. Though frustrated in the past by white hands' insistence on setting their own schedules and putting in only a partial day's work, he hired several in January 1859 for sowing rye and sawing and hauling timber. Two soon left, finding the "rules being too stringent." Others took off for half a day or walked off and then came back to be rehired. Two of his hands were a young couple who had just married. "All their fu[rniture] and household goods consist of a st[one] jug," Barnsley noted in his plantation journal, "no bed, nor any thing else." They left after three months. Barnsley rented out land that he could not work directly with slaves or white hands and was paid in bushels of wheat or bundles of fodder.[41]

Barnsley's complaints over the unreliability and stubborn independence of his white hands were mild compared to the contempt with which most planters and "respectable" whites held the white poor. In the fall of 1859, Lettie H. Gordon remarked of her visit to Arkansas: "I have seen some of the poorest, dirtiest beings since I entered this state that could be found any where on earth, I know. Indeed I venture the Arkansas people *live* on *filth*, for many of them seem to have nothing else in their possession." A planter disdainfully concluded that the poor whites in the sand hills of South Carolina were "for the most part . . . the most wretchedly inert, and therefore continually stunted people to be found anywhere."[42]

However much looked down upon by the planters, the white poor were quick to physically challenge them over any perceived slight. Alfred Davis, a plantation handyman, leveled a double-barreled shotgun at his employer, Duncan McKenzie, in a dispute over $2. Davis had dug a well on McKenzie's Mississippi plantation in the summer of 1860, and the planter proposed to pay him by returning a note for $2 that Davis had given him to cancel a debt. Demanding instead to be paid in cash, Davis refused to accept the note. The argument escalated and both men drew weapons before they backed down. Poor whites were not to be trifled with when they felt their honor was at stake. Most planters knew well enough to show them due respect and to make a show of welcoming them when they came calling rather than sending a servant to the plantation gate to ask what they wanted.[43]

Nothing bedeviled planters more about their poor white neighbors than their chronic trafficking with slaves for goods pilfered from the plantation. According to Tryphena Fox, the wife of a planter in Plaquemines Parish, Louisiana, a nearby Creole overseer made a handsome profit in the 1850s by accepting stolen goods from the slaves, "for which he pays them a mere trifle and which he sells after getting a sufficient quantity of each kind, at a good profit in N.O. [New Orleans]." In the old cotton belt of Middle Georgia, "cock-eyed Johnson" was notorious for selling liquor to slaves. After he was successfully defended in court by noted Whig politician Alexander H. Stephens, he returned to his notorious ways in the winter of 1860 "dealing out jugs full at Mrs. Terrill's Plantation to a crowd of 20 or 30 negroes." After one of the slaves passed on the information that Johnson would be at Jack Lane's plantation the following Saturday night, a number of white men, including one who "blacked himself," mingled in the crowd of slaves at the plantation and arrested Johnson yet again.[44]

Those illegally trafficking liquor to slaves, like Johnson, were often readily identified but when arrested were more often than not acquitted in court by a jury of local whites. Even vigilante action against them was often thwarted by their friends in the neighborhood. When a group of men in Buckingham, Virginia, called on D. W. Kendrick and notified him to leave the county immediately, another party of men met at Kendrick's house armed with double-barreled guns to protect and allow him to stay.[45]

The trading for liquor and clothes from poor whites in exchange for pork, corn, and other goods stolen from plantations by slaves defied all attempts at suppression. It constituted an underground economy that was advantageous to both parties. Planters sent numerous petitions to state legislatures demanding that the trade be suppressed, but it continued to flourish, in large part because of the growing economic desperation of the poor whites. For all their condemnations of the trade, planters had to be careful not to antagonize the local whites who played a critical role in enforcing slavery. The liquor dealers came out of the same pool of poor whites who worked as overseers, served on slave patrols, and hunted down slave runaways for a reward. Without their active complicity in disciplining the slaves, the institution of slavery would have been gravely weakened.[46]

The failure of planters to crack down on trading with slaves revealed that marginalized whites were placing their self-interests above racist appeals to maintain a strict racial hierarchy. Calling upon the white underclass to defend slavery by invoking the specter of their losing everything—property, status, liberty, and independence—lost much of its credibility for those whites like Edward Isham who could not claim the status of independent household head with dominance over a wife and children and who were already competing, interacting, and cooperating with African Americans, free as well as enslaved. Scratching out an existence when they could find work, legal or otherwise, these whites were frequently in fractious as well as cooperative relationships with blacks. However, poor whites tactically invoked their white identity and quickly turned on their former black allies when both groups were facing legal charges.

Non-slaveholders who still had hopes of improving their economic standing and who enjoyed the manly white status of independent household heads with dependents to protect and land to provide for their families were more responsive to calls to keep all blacks in their assigned positions of degraded inferiority. As became clear in the late 1850s, these whites wanted to push back against any signs of black achievement and competition that threatened their white identity.

Egged on by politicians, they demanded the expulsion of all free blacks who would not voluntarily submit to being re-enslaved.

The movement for black exclusion drew on many sources, but at its core was non-slaveholders' growing resentment over the class-based prerogatives and pretensions of the planters. When a slave was accused of raping a white woman, he stood a good chance of being cleared of the charges. The court records of twelve Southern states reveal that nearly half of the accused avoided conviction and the prescribed sentence of execution. Slaves were very valuable property and planters had every incentive to save them from the hangman's noose. Just as poor whites put their economic interests above racial solidarity in their trafficking with slaves, so too did planters put notions of class and gender above racially supporting the poor white women who brought most of the charges of being raped by a slave. In the eyes of the planters, lower-class white females were un-deserving of the protection extended to elite white women for they were prone to lascivious behavior and sexual come-ons that attracted slaves. By employing legal counsel skilled at character assassination, planters saved their slaves at the expense of alienating poor whites.[47]

Few issues angered the town and city component of the white underclass— non-agricultural, manual workers—more than being thrown into competition for jobs with free blacks and slave mechanics. Despite numerous petitions to legislatures calling for an end to the practice of allowing slaves to hire their own time, planters continued to evade laws against self-hiring. Apart from the eco-nomic benefits they derived from the wages the slaves returned to them, planters found the practice a useful tool in curbing the employment of the urban Irish. The same was the case for the planters' persistence in renting out their slave me-chanics. Critics of the practice argued that the unchecked competition of slave mechanics with white workers would undermine the racial and social order. Under no direct supervision in the cities, the slaves would be corrupted by their quasi-freedom and grow impatient with all restraints, while the hard-pressed white mechanic would lose both his racial respectability and his means of supporting his family. Planters and their allies angrily responded that any effort to bar the use of slave mechanics amounted to a disguised form of abolitionism. They insisted that the practice had to continue for it is "our bulwark against ex-tortion and our safeguard against the turbulence of white mechanics as seen in the great strikes, both in England and the North, and it is the only protection we have in any possible struggle between capital and labor."[48]

Poorer whites also had to compete against free blacks and a growing number of mulattoes fathered by males in the planter class. The federal census reported a sharp jump of 67 percent of mulattos born into slavery. Planters liked to think that morally loose poor whites, including itinerant Irish laborers, were the fa-thers of all these racially mixed slaves, though evidence makes clear that planters and their sons bore most of the responsibility. Over three-fourths of the free blacks in Mississippi and the lower Mississippi Valley were mulattos, the off-spring of local planters, their sons, or their overseers. Before manumissions were all but shut down by state laws, planters, whether out of a sense of guilt or in response to their wives' demands, freed many of their offspring, who merged into free black communities.[49]

Free blacks comprised only 3 percent of the South's total free population, but their numbers were much larger in the Upper South, home to four-fifths of all free blacks. Although most lived in abject poverty, a very small, but highly visible, minority were better off than the mass of poor whites. They accumulated property, often had specific marketable skills, and had earned the grudging respect of many of their white neighbors. White immigrants in the cities were pushing free blacks out of many trades, though in Charleston free black males were still 50 percent more likely to be in a skilled labor position than a white immigrant. In rural St. Mary's County, Maryland, a higher percentage of free blacks than whites had a craft skill and blacks dominated certain crafts, such as blacksmithing and carpentry.[50]

Heightening the anxiety of poorer whites as they were pushed down into a racially mixed underclass of cheap laborers was the blurring of "whiteness" itself. White status, it turned out, was whatever a local community decided it was. In a case in South Carolina in 1843 involving the claim of three mulattos that they were free men and hence should not be subject to a tax on them as mulattos, white witnesses testified the men were "colored" as a consequence of descent from a "colored" great grandfather. The judge instructed the jury to weigh reputation at least as much as color in reaching a verdict. He stressed that "Color . . . was sometimes a deceptive test; that it ought to be compared with all the circumstances . . . and if the jury were satisfied that the color, blood, and reputation in society, would justify them in rating the relators as free white men, they had a right to do so." The jury found the three to be free white men. A suit by Abby Guy, a mulatto Arkansas woman in the late 1850s seeking her freedom and that of her children on the grounds that she was white, revealed just how indeterminate the notion of whiteness was. The jury ruled in their favor after determining they had "less than one-fourth of negro blood in their veins" and thus met the state's legal definition of being a white. The verdict was quickly reversed in an appeal brought by a Mr. Daniel, who claimed to be the owner of the Guy family. The judge hearing the appeal ruled that the term mulatto in Arkansas law referred not to gradations of "negro blood" but to any mixture of white and black blood. Thus, the Guys could not claim free status on the basis of being white. Abby Guy again sued for her family's freedom in January 1861. On the basis of a close physical examination of their features, especially their feet, the jury concluded that the Guys exhibited none of the characteristics of the "negro" race and should be considered free. Daniel failed to win a retrial. The Guys were finally free.[51]

As the courts wrestled over defining the status of light-skinned mulattos, slaves were visibly becoming lighter and lighter, a phenomenon often noted by purchasers of slaves. In the spring of 1860, Thomas Watkins of Mississippi bought several slaves in Missouri as a replacement for those who had recently died of disease on his plantation. His wife Sarah noted that one of the slaves, a woman about twenty years old, had "a white child four months old. Her master sold her for it. It was his son-in-law's child." Sarah added in a letter to her daughter that most of the slaves under the age of twenty were "yellow," a common reference to light-skinned mulattos. The young slave woman "Yellow Mary" posed quite a problem for the Cartmells of Tennessee when she gave birth in 1859 to an infant who easily could have passed as white. Thomas Cartmell had purchased Mary as a sixteen-year-old house girl to assist his wife, Mary Jane. He found the slave Mary to be "very smart and headstrong," but from the start Mary Jane did not like her, was infuriated by the slave's fondness for white men, and pressured her husband to sell her. Neither Thomas nor his wife had any desire "to raise a gang of white children [who were] negroes too," so Thomas sold Yellow Mary and her near-white child in December 1859.[52]

As Southern whites realized just how unstable and indeterminate their whiteness was becoming and that it could no longer be taken as a badge of guaranteed privilege or even free status, the conditions developed in the 1850s for an offensive against free blacks. Driving them out had the appeal of squaring social reality with the proslavery ideology that insisted blacks were fit only for slavery and that free blacks were utterly incapable of supporting themselves with their own labor. The mere existence of free blacks contradicted rationalizations for slavery and the fact that some of them, no matter how few, were outcompeting poorer whites in bettering themselves was an unacceptable outrage.

With the exception in 1859 of Arkansas, planters, farmers, and urban businessmen dependent on the cheap labor of free blacks, and motivated in some cases by a sense of moral and social justice, succeeded in blocking the movement to force free blacks to leave. Arkansas, where the free black population totaled less than 1,000 and was but a tiny minority of the state's population, stood as the exception because of the negligible labor role of free blacks. The major battles over exclusion were fought in the northernmost slave states, home to the majority of the South's free blacks. Free blacks comprised nearly one-quarter of Maryland's population in 1860, and they played a major role in keeping down labor costs as planters transitioned away from producing tobacco with slave labor to a more diversified agriculture geared to producing grain and fodder crops and relying on abundant seasonal labor.[53]

Slaveholders All: Reopening the African Slave Trade

With beguiling simplicity, a movement emerged in the mid-1850s to reopen the African slave trade that had been prohibited by Congress in 1808. Its basic premise was clear enough: make abundant, cheap slaves available to all Southern whites and thereby short-circuit any class-based threat to slavery from within the South. From that premise developed an audacious vision of breathing audacity in the claims it made for the South to revive the foreign slave trade and fulfill its historic destiny of spreading the benefits of slavery worldwide.

Sporadic calls for reviving the African slave trade began to coalesce into a movement once Governor James H. Adams of South Carolina endorsed reopening it in his message to the legislature in November 1856. Mounting pressure against slavery from the North, he stressed, made it incumbent on planters "to do all we can to fortify it within." The surest way of doing that was to enable more non-slaveholders to purchase slaves. At an average price in 1860 of $1,000, slaves were much too expensive for most Southern whites. As slave prices doubled in the 1850s, the percentage of slaveholding white families fell from around 31 percent to 25 percent. With rising numbers of whites being shut out of acquiring the labor needed for economic and social advancement, slavery was in danger of being denounced as an "aristocratic" institution whose benefits were monopolized by the wealthy. Citing that danger, Adams called for diffusing slave ownership as widely as possible in order to buttress the support for slavery with "the motive of self-interest." Additionally, he recommended the passage of a law exempting at least one slave from sale for payment of debts.[54]

For Adams and others seeking to reopen the African slave trade, the future of slavery hung in the balance. Without an abundant supply of slaves from Africa, the tensions in Southern society would intensify; its worn-out lands would never be restored; slavery in the older states would further weaken as slaves were drained away to the newer states of the Southwest; and the South would continue to be shut out of the federal territories and denied the opportunity to spread slavery and plantations across the Caribbean and Central and South America. The stakes could not have been greater. As the *Yazoo* (Miss.) *Democrat* starkly put it: if "the only practical means of perpetuating our present system of labor is by importing Africans" and if the South "has not the courage to procure that labor at any hazard, then let her perish as ignominiously as her cowardice deserves."[55]

The agitation for reopening the trade was strongest in the lowcountry of South Carolina and the lower Mississippi Valley. Obsessed since the 1830s with fears over the safety of slavery in the Union and the inability of the state to retain, let alone add to, its white and slave population, Carolina planters envisaged cheap African slaves as the source of their political and economic salvation.

The slaves would provide the labor to restore the state's wasted fields, expand the number of slaveholders, and stanch an annual net loss of slaves minimally estimated at 5,000 a year. Unless slave prices came down, warned Colonel W. P. Shingler, South Carolina would become a slave state in name only and would soon be "a barren waste for the want of labor to cultivate her soil." [56]

The focus of Carolina planters rarely strayed farther than Charleston and its lowcountry environs. In contrast, sugar and cotton planters in the Mississippi Valley had a more expansive vision of the world, one that looked out to the Caribbean and across the Americas. New Orleans merchants, locked out of rail connections to burgeoning markets in the Midwest, hoped to develop new trade routes across the Caribbean and were major financiers and outfitters for filibustering expeditions to seize Cuba or Nicaragua for Southern interests. In the late 1850s those merchants were also sending ships to Africa to buy slaves to be sold in Cuba or Brazil. J. D. B. De Bow, editor of a well-known eponymous New Orleans journal, was the leading publicist for these and other expansionist schemes. An early convert to the cause of the reopeners, he foresaw an influx of African slaves spreading to the west and south and forever ensuring the South's "monopoly on that production which has given us wealth and consequence, and the power and the spirit in the enjoyment of them." He gained the backing of planters chafing under high slave prices and politicians with dreams of imperial glory.[57]

Edward A. Pollard, a Virginia journalist and one of the relatively few advocates of the foreign trade in the Upper South, especially emphasized how adding more African slaves would restore the pride of the dignity of poor whites, whom he described as "debarred from [the South's] social system, deprived of all shares in the benefits of the institution of slavery, condemned to poverty, and even forced to bear the airs of superiority in black and beastly slaves!" The poor white had become "the scorn and sport of the 'gentlemen of color,' who parade their superiority . . . and thank God they are not as he." Acknowledging his own insecurities in declaring that he had "the most repulsive feelings toward negro gentlemen," he insisted that it was high time that they were pushed back down into abject degradation by submerging them in a tide of fresh, uncivilized African stock. In addition to having an opportunity to acquire a few cheap slaves, poor whites would be elevated in status by the very lowering of blacks to a condition of brute savagery.[58]

No one propagandized more incessantly for the African slave trade than Leonidas W. Spratt of South Carolina. Deprived of much of an inheritance when his father left most of his assets, including his slaves, to Leonidas's older brother, he attended South Carolina College and then moved to Florida to establish himself as a young lawyer. Much as the young Pollard, another frustrated son of a planter, had gone off to California in the 1850s to seek his fortune, only to return home to Virginia disillusioned by his failure to make much headway in a free-for-all scramble for wealth, so too Spratt soon left Florida with little to show for his efforts. He returned to Charleston and refashioned himself as the prophet of a glorious Southern civilization unapologetically committed to the fullest use of slave labor.

Marriage provided Spratt with the funds to purchase the *Charleston Southern Standard* in 1853, which he used as a springboard for touting the virtues of reopening the African slave trade. In editorials and regular attendance at Southern Commercial Conventions, which went on record in the late 1850s in favor of reopening, Spratt insisted that the trade was the test of the moral legitimacy of slavery. "If that be right, then slavery be right, but not without." He extolled Southerners as a "chosen people" with a God-given duty "to work out the real regeneration of mankind." With a near pathological hatred of the North's free-labor society, he spread the message that slavery anchored the order, stability, and racial hierarchies of the South. For Spratt, the slave South was the world's only hope of escaping the licentiousness and impending anarchy into which the North and the rest of Western civilization was about to be plunged by the heartless conflict between capital and labor. Once the South attained greatness with an influx of more slaves, the rest of the world would admire and seek to emulate its achievements.[59]

If Spratt was the most persistent reopener, then Charles A. L. Lamar was the most flamboyant and reckless. Born into a very wealthy Savannah family in 1824, he was involved in a fire aboard the steamer *Pulaski* on a voyage in 1837 from Savannah to Baltimore. His mother and five siblings were killed and he spent five days clinging to floating debris before being rescued. In 1857, after financing filibustering expeditions and dabbling in the illegal African slave trade, he purchased and outfitted the *Wanderer* to bring in slaves from Africa. In doing so, he openly defied his father Gazaway who admonished that "an expedition to the moon would have been equally sensible, and no more contrary to the laws of Providence." Boasting that he was "right," Lamar forged ahead both for the "grandeur" and the "dollars." His father had set him up financially in several business ventures, but Lamar lost much of his fortune in ill-advised speculative ventures and an overindulgent lifestyle. By 1857, he was in need of cash and had burned through his credit lines in Savannah.[60]

The *Wanderer* took on over 400 slaves in Africa. Only about 300 of them survived the voyage across the Atlantic to be unloaded in November 1858 on Jekyll Island, Georgia, where they were distributed and sold up and down the Georgia-Carolina coast. As reports of the landing spread, federal officials arrested Lamar and the crew members, but they were all acquitted by sympathetic juries in Savannah. A similar case the same year involving the *Echo*, another illegal slaver, produced the same outcome in the federal court in Charleston.[61]

In the rabidly anti-Northern lowcountry of Georgia and South Carolina, the slave traders had defied federal laws with seeming impunity, but their very success damaged a cause that had yet to secure any political victories. The pathetic and brutalized condition of the newly arrived slaves shocked whites, particularly many planters and evangelical ministers, who were otherwise staunch defenders of slavery. The Reverend Charles C. Jones of Georgia, a leading exponent of uplifting slaves by Christianizing them, was "disgusted" by the degree of support Lamar and the crew of the *Wanderer* received in the lowcountry.[62]

Fearful that the abolitionists would be handed a political windfall, James Henry Hammond of South Carolina predicted that unless the guilty parties were arrested and punished, Northerners would flock to the abolitionists and Southern whites would waver in their commitment to slavery. Even former governor James Adams changed his mind about the slave trade when he learned in 1860 of the threat of dangerous political divisions in upcountry South Carolina as the result of protests of Baptists and non-slaveholders against the *Wanderer* affair.[63]

The slave traders had overplayed their hand. Their program was designed to reduce, if not eliminate, the strains appearing in Southern society by the 1850s, but it had the opposite effect. The mutual interests of the Upper and Lower South in which the former shipped slaves to the more fertile acreage of the latter, an internal slave trade that totaled nearly a million slaves from 1800 to 1860, threatened to unravel with a presumed plunge in slave prices with the arrival of large imports of African slaves. Such a decline would crimp the flow of capital into the Upper South that was invested in internal improvements, economic diversification, and agricultural reform. Besides, if prices dropped significantly, the most likely beneficiaries would be planters with the means of adding to their slave forces. Since slavery was a profit-driven institution, why would planters in South Carolina and other older states use any additional slaves to restore their worn-out lands when it was more profitable to continue the wasteful agricultural practices of the past by using them to produce cash staples? As the critics grasped, internal strains and problems produced by slavery could hardly be resolved by adding yet more slaves.

Above all, a large influx of African slaves, frightening savages in the minds of most Southern whites, would require harsher disciplinary measures that would shatter the planters' illusionary view of themselves as benevolent patriarchs. "Every semblance of humanity would have to be blotted from the statute-book," opined Walter Brooke, a Mississippi planter with large holdings, "and the slaveholder would become—instead of the patriarchal friend and master of his slaves—a bloody, brutal, and trembling tyrant." No wonder most evangelical divines were opposed to the reopening movement. Their attempts to reform slavery in accordance with Christian standards, including educating slaves so that they could read the Bible, prohibiting the breakup of slave families in slave sales, and legalizing slave marriages, would come to a halt. What would be ratcheted up was the most visceral of all Southern white fears—being slaughtered in a slave uprising. The mother-in-law of noted secessionist Edmund Ruffin of Virginia confided to her daughter that she had such an abiding fear of being killed by savage slaves that "we thinks we had better be Black Rep. Abolitionists, any thing than abetting the reopening of the slave trade." As for the moral ambiguity inherent in branding the African slave trade as a sin while accepting the morality of the domestic slave trade, most whites were content to live with what the reopeners saw as a contradiction fatal to the future of slavery.[64]

Populist Stirrings

By the late 1850s signs of dissent from planter rule were bubbling up in several slave states. Planters found themselves on the defensive as they fought off ad valorem (based on assessed values approximating market value) taxation on slaves and working-class opposition in the South's largest cities. Younger politicians from outside the established planter class were mobilizing voters against the old guard and making a successful case for new leadership.

From the beginnings of the republic, slaveholders had been alert to any threat that democratic majorities, either in Congress or in Southern states, could pose to slavery via taxation. The newer slave states formed after 1820 inserted clauses in their constitutions requiring that different kinds of property—land, slaves, livestock—be assessed at uniform valuations and taxed at identical rates. Any political majority of non-slaveholders that might form would thereby shrink from trying to tax slavery out of existence because they would be imposing prohibitive taxes on their own property. Older states, such as South Carolina and Mississippi, with large concentrations of slaves and relatively broad distribution of slave ownership among whites, had no need for uniform clauses on taxation. The exceptions were North Carolina and Virginia, both of which had increasingly restive non-slaveholders in their extensive western backcountries.[65]

The movement for ad valorem taxation of slaves was strongest in North Carolina. The state's constitution of 1835 prohibited any taxes on slaves under the age of twelve and over age fifty and pegged any increase in the tax on slaves to the white poll tax. As the state debt nearly tripled in the 1850s to pay for internal improvements, property taxes and the poll tax rose in tandem. Taxes on slaves were going up but not nearly fast enough to satisfy small farmers and laborers who felt that slaveholders were benefiting at their expense from an inequitable tax system and should shoulder more of the tax burden. The issue quickly became a partisan one. The Whigs, long a party championing the demands of the state's western farmers for better transportation outlets to markets, positioned themselves as the party of equal taxation and made ad valorem taxation the main plank of their platform in the 1860 gubernatorial election. They lost the election but outraged many planters who complained they were the victims of "an attempt to array the poor against the rich." For J. M. Jordan, the passage of ad valorem taxation would "effect the abolition of slavery in many states. It would be playing into the hands of the fanatics of the North." In Virginia, where the tax on slaves was fixed at the same rate as that on $300 worth of land, the ad valorem issue was just one of many that distanced the non-slaveholders in the trans-Allegheny counties from the planters in the eastern tidewater. Despite gaining suffrage reforms and the adoption of the white basis (i.e., not taking the slave population into account) for representation in the House of Delegates at the state constitutional convention in 1851, the westerners fell short of securing the state funding for internal improvements and education they wanted. As in North Carolina, the call for ad valorem taxation would later reemerge.[66]

Adding to planters' concerns was the political militancy of urban workers in the 1850s. Two sources had fed the development of the Southern working class in the 1830s and 1840s: skilled workers, many from the North, connected with mining, foundries, and textile mills, and unskilled laborers, mostly Irishmen who worked on canals and railroads. By mid-century, broader alliances began to form in the border states of the Upper South and the coastal cities that merged into regional unions. Workers then began engaging more directly in politics and various national organizations such as the Workingmen's National Association.[67]

In the 1850s the South's metropolitan areas were pulling away from the countryside as a result of their growing integration into the Northern market economy, the declining importance of slavery in filling urban jobs, and an in-flux of foreign-born workers, mainly Irish and Germans, who rankled the sensibilities of native whites by ignoring racial norms in housing, trading with slaves, and inter-racial sexual relations. In the South's largest cities—St. Louis, Baltimore, and New Orleans—slaves made up only 3 percent of the combined population by 1860, and in St. Louis, close to two-thirds of the residents were immigrants. Planters were quick to grasp the ominous implications for slavery. As early as 1849, Henry W. Connor of North Carolina noted with alarm that in New Orleans the draymen (teamsters) and laborers were overwhelmingly white immigrants who would mob or kill any blacks who threatened their jobs. Unless corrective measures were taken, he envisioned that "the issue of the Free labourer against slave labour will soon be made at the South."[68]

Connor's fears gained heightened credibility in the 1850s when Southern cities were growing at twice the rate of the countryside and workers turned to urban politics to push their agenda. Free blacks in Baltimore, driven out of most of the trades, still dominated at ship-caulking. To protect their jobs, they

formed a trade union that offered dependable skilled labor to their employers in
return for protection from the wrath of native-born white workers. Their white
patrons accommodated them as a means of blunting the possibility that an all-
white working class would gain the voting power to launch a class-based urban
politics challenging slaveholding interests. Determined to smash the alliance of
white patrons and their black clients, young industrial workers, dubbing themselves the Tigers, flocked to the Know-Nothing Party, a nativist party formed
largely out of the Whig Party that had collapsed in the Lower South for being
too pro-Northern. The Know-Nothings were particularly strong in Southern
cities. The party served as a new political home for middle-class business men
and professionals who favored an expanding use for slave labor in industrial
pursuits. Joining these former Whigs among the Know-Nothings were renegade
Democrats from the working class. Initially, this unlikely alliance was held together by a mutual interest in restricting immigration and backing urban public
improvements that would expand business opportunities and create jobs. The
alliance soon split over different conceptions of reform. For the middle class,
reform involved elevating moral standards through sabbatarianism and temperance, curbing corruption at the polls, and slashing government patronage. For the
native-born white workers, reform was a matter of pursuing their own economic
self-interests. They wanted a larger share of patronage jobs, a ten-hour work day,
an end to competition from blacks, and a hands-off policy by city officials during
strikes. When necessary, the workers enforced their demands by thuggery in the
streets against their opponents. Finalizing the split were divisions over public
assistance to workers thrown out of jobs by the Panic of 1857. The disillusioned
middle class bolted from the Know-Nothings and turned to "nonpartisan" reform in which control over municipal policies was placed in the hands of the
rural slaveholder-dominated state legislature.[69]

Know-Nothings in New Orleans also used violence against immigrant workers
at the polls and on the docks as a political weapon. They built a winning coalition
of native-born whites, nativist ex-Whigs, and businessmen anxious to extend construction on the New Orleans, Jackson, and Great Northern Railroad. In 1858 they
placed Gerald Stith, a member of the city's printers' union, in the mayor's office
after beating back a Democratic-supported Vigilance Committee that had armed
in an effort to seize control of the police force. A key to their victory was their
success in splitting the ranks of the wealthy Democrats by championing Southern
nationalism and defending the exclusion of blacks from well-paying jobs. By the
end of the 1850s, rural slaveholding interests that dominated the legislature had
effectively lost control of the state's major port and urban center.

In Missouri, where slaves were only 10 percent of the state's population, the
slaveholding minority lacked the political means to block the growth of an antislavery alliance in St. Louis between workers and businessmen. White laborers

in the city had little fear of direct competition from enslaved or free blacks and, driven by the antislavery convictions of a large class of German artisans, they bonded with free-labor entrepreneurs in the South's strongest Republican Party organization. The city delivered a plurality of its votes to Lincoln in 1860. A German editor could accurately state that "St. Louis has the character of a free state, a virtual enclave in this region of slavery."[70]

Elsewhere, in the South's mid-sized cities merchants remained in control. The Tredegar Iron Works and tobacco-processing industry in Richmond continued to rely heavily on the hiring of slaves and free blacks, who were about half of the entire workforce. Native-born whites were a minority of the free laborers and the American Party here emphasized the threat of immigrants to slavery more than to the jobs of native whites. In Mobile, Savannah, Memphis, and Charleston, in-dustrial growth was accompanied by greater reliance on foreign-born workers. Labor militancy aiming at excluding black competition occasionally flared up but was easily contained as jobs held by slaves and free blacks steadily dropped. Still, the very predominance of immigrant labor portended a dangerous future. Spratt cited that predominance as a major reason to reopen the African slave trade. He warned that the foreign-born would inevitably "question the right of masters to employ their slaves in any works that they may wish for" and by their voting power convert even Charleston, "at the very heart of slavery," into "a for-tress of democratic power against it." [71]

Although by the mid-1850s the states of the Lower South had joined South Carolina in a virtual one-party system of politics controlled by the Democrats, political competition continued, freed from the needs and discipline of a regular party organization. Politicians shut out of the ruling political cliques began to mobilize Southerners left behind in the cotton prosperity of the 1850s as the maturing slave economy funneled more of the wealth upward, leaving small farmers struggling to hold onto their land.

Rising demands from the upcountry for a larger voice in state politics shaped the National Democratic movement in South Carolina, a new political faction that wanted to cooperate with Northern Democrats and gain access to federal patronage. Since the days of Calhoun, the planters had shunned the national Democratic Party for placing the spoils of office over the protection of Southern rights. The National Democrats also sought to democratize state politics. South Carolina's government, in the telling phrase of James Henry Hammond, was "that of an aristocracy." Although the state provided for universal white male suf-frage, high property qualifications for serving in the legislature and a system of apportioning seats for the legislature that heavily over-weighted the lowcountry parishes that paid the largest share of state taxes kept political power tightly in the hands of the old planter elite. Whites could vote only for state legislators and congressmen; the planter-dominated legislature appointed the governor, presidential electors, and state and local officers. Led by James L. Orr, a congressman, and Benjamin F. Perry, a newspaper editor, the National Democrats gave voice to the small farmers and workers in the upcountry in their call for greater access to political power and economic opportunities. They demanded the popular election of presidential electors and funds for internal improvements for the backcountry and a common-school system. Planters saw a dual threat in Orr's movement. Not only did it challenge their control of state politics, but its support for Northern Democrats, whose tenet of popular sovereignty amounted to abolitionism in the eyes of the lowcountry elite, also threated the institution of slavery itself. The planters fell back on appeals to pride in the state's maverick independence and warned that the proposed political reforms would sweep aside enlightened planter leadership and destroy "the stability and permanence of the whole constitutional structure of the State Government," but they failed to quell their upcountry opposition.[72]

In Alabama, battles over how best to defend Southern rights were no longer channeled into rival party positions in presidential canvases but flowed unchecked into all political discourse. Former Whigs argued that they were the truest guardians of slavery because they had no need to compromise in a national party with their Northern counterparts. Younger politicians, drawn primarily from lawyers and businessmen in towns linked to the state's expanding rail network, tied economic development and greater opportunities for all whites to an increasingly extremist stance calling for the South to break free of all ties to a Union controlled by Northern greed and tyranny. These state's rights purists were suspicious of all parties as engines of corruption that betrayed white liberties. In danger of being pushed aside by the more radicalized politicians in his own state, Yancey felt ever greater pressure to demonstrate that the national Democratic Party could be made into a safe vehicle for protecting Southern rights, including the right to federal protection of slavery in the territories.[73]

Politics in Arkansas were undergoing a similar transformation. Thomas C. Hindman, an ambitious young lawyer, overthrew the state's ruling families by exploiting anxieties over widening wealth disparities in appeals that blended calls for internal improvements with a militant stance in favor of Southern rights. Born in Tennessee in 1828, Hindman moved first to northern Mississippi and then to Helena, Arkansas, a rapidly growing town on the Mississippi that served as the state's communications hub to the outside world. Marriage in 1856 to the daughter of a planter secured his financial security. After first gaining political prominence by attacking the Know-Nothing Party as a front for abolitionism, he took on the political dynasty known as the "Family," an interlocking network of kinship relations and business associates that had enriched itself through land dealings and control of federal patronage appointments. Once the Know-Nothings were routed in the election of 1856, the Family could not rely on calls for party unity to defeat an opposition that no longer existed. Calling for economic progress through railroad construction, lowering of state taxes, and defense of Southern rights, including the right to reopen the African slave trade, Hindman and his followers took control of state politics by 1860. A forceful orator whose invective against the entrenched interests played especially well among the state's small farmers, he had positioned himself as Arkansas's most popular politician. He was also its most uncompromising fire-eater.[74]

In Georgia and Mississippi, new political "types" espousing a neo-populist economic appeal and resistance to Northern aggressions against slavery also emerged in the late 1850s. Joe Brown, the son of a yeoman farmer, and John J. Pettus, a self-made planter with an undistinguished pedigree, won election as governors. Brown's strongest support came from the non-slaveholders in the mountains of northern Georgia, and Pettus's from poor whites in the piney woods of central and eastern Mississippi. Brown championed state-supported free public schools for white children and Pettus the need for internal improvements. Neither governor was embraced by the planter elite.[75]

All the new political groupings tapped into the discontent of those left behind in the prosperity of the 1850s. The South was no more immune to internal change than the North, and signs of that change—shrinking opportunities, a rise in a white underclass, and calls for greater democratization and economic benefits for slaveless whites—posed a challenge to continued planter hegemony. Looming over unsettling change from within was the external threat from the North of stifling the expansion of slavery. Tensions were building that the secessionist vanguard was poised to exploit with its vision of a stable, prosperous, and independent South firmly under the control of planters.

2

Getting Right with Slavery

The Drive for Unity

Evangelical ministers were in the first line of defense against abolitionist attacks on slavery as an unconscionable sin. Articulating with greater depth a moral case for slavery that had always been implicit in the acceptance of the institution by Southern churches, they preached that slavery was a morally righteous institution ordained by God. Despite their efforts, an undercurrent of unease remained among many Southern whites. For Southern leaders, the great danger was that the morally squeamish, joined by non-slaveholders, would begin to dismantle slavery through programs of gradual emancipation and colonization abroad of freed slaves. As outside condemnations of slavery increased, so did the suppression of any antislavery dissent within the South. For secession to succeed, white unity on the permanency and morality of slavery was essential.

A Holy Mission: Evangelicals and Slavery

The evangelical defense of slavery moved beyond the rationalizations of slavery as a necessary evil that had sufficed when the Western world first turned against slavery in the mid-nineteenth century. Humanist philosophers of the Enlightenment proclaimed a new faith in human progress grounded in the expression of virtuous self-interest, and Quakers and Wesleyan Methodists preached a new ethic of moral sensibilities in identifying and sympathizing with the sufferings of others. Both Northerners and Southerners of the Revolutionary generation entertained moral doubts over slavery, an institution that historically had been accepted as an immutable fixture of society in which the most dishonored and dependent were compelled to labor for the greater social good. The jarring and disturbing juxtaposition of human bondage with the Revolution's ideals of liberty and human happiness magnified those doubts all the more. When abolitionism arose in the 1830s with its blistering indictment of slavery, Southerners needed a more aggressive defense of the institution. A moral case had to be made not just to protect the immense wealth tied up in slaves but also the moral standing of Southern Christians, for if slavery stood damned, then so did they. "It is only upon this ground that the institution can be successfully defended," declared Colin J. McRae of Alabama on the floor of Congress in 1860. He proclaimed slavery "a universal institution of God and man, nature and Christianity, earth and heaven" that had been ordained "in the word of God, sustained by all history in all parts of the world."[1]

McRae's paeans to slavery provoked laughter from the Northern congressmen present, but there can be no doubt of the earnestness of the clerical defenders of slavery. They were steadfast in their conviction that the Bible was on their side. Abraham and the patriarchs of the Old Testament were slaveholders; Jesus had not condemned slavery; and Paul had enjoined servants to obey their masters. Understandably, the Bible became the anchor of their proslavery defense and served as the focal point of their counterattacks against the abolitionists. The South's strategy, advised Robert Dabney, a Presbyterian minister in Virginia, must be to "push the Bible argument continually, drive Abolitionism to the wall, compel it to assume an anti-Christian position." This approach opened the abolitionists to the charge leveled by Thomas Smyth, another Presbyterian minister, of having "perverted or prostituted the Bible" and blasphemously using it to preach the "licentious and atheistic spirit of a liberty which knows no restraint and no authority, human or divine."[2]

In fact, the biblical defense of slavery was riddled with inconsistencies and contradictions, and one of the most egregious was the use made of the biblical curse of Ham. As related in Genesis, 9:18–27, Ham came upon his father Noah lying naked and asleep in a drunken stupor. Ham then informed his brothers Jepheth and Shem who, averting their eyes, covered up their father's nakedness. Upon awakening, Noah cursed Canaan, Ham's son, and decreed that he and his descendants were to be slaves. The account said nothing about race, and whatever Ham did that deserved such a drastic punishment and why that punishment should be perpetual and visited on Canaan and his progeny are not at all clear. Nonetheless, by quite a stretch of unbiblical racism Southern whites relied on Noah's curse to identify Africans as the descendants of Ham and to make an argument that the Bible sanctioned race-based slavery.

As antislavery Northerners knew full well, the servitude depicted in the Bible was neither hereditary nor tied to race. Except when formulaically citing Noah's curse, clerical defenders of slavery elided these disquieting facts by focusing on slavery in the abstract and not on the concrete ways in which slavery was commonly practiced in the South. By doing so, Calvinist theologians were able to place the defense of slavery at the center of an epic struggle unfolding on a global scale between time-honored hierarchical traditions for ordering society and the radical heresies unleashed by the twin forces of democracy and capitalism. Dangerous new ideas of inalienable rights and calls for reforming society along egalitarian lines regardless of race or gender threatened to unleash a maelstrom of destruction that would sweep away property rights and godly morality. For the Reverend Thomas Smyth, most Northerners were not just fanatical abolitionists but "atheists, infidels, communists, free-lovers, rationalists, Bible haters, anti-Christian levelers and anarchists."[3]

Clerics approached the issue of slavery not just as theologians but as slaveholders in their own right concerned about the value of their property and their status as patriarchs over dependent women. At the founding convention of the Southern Baptists in 1845, most of the clergy present were slave owners, each of whom held an average of twenty-four slaves. Of the 112 active Episcopal ministers in Virginia in 1860, eighty-four owned slaves. Many Southern churches also owned slaves as investment property. The Briery Presbyterian Church in Prince Edward County, Virginia, annually hired out its slaves at auction in the 1840s.[4]

In the eyes of clerics and Southern society, wives, like slaves, were to be treated as patriarchal property. The Methodist clergyman Frederick A. Ross of Alabama made the comparison explicit: "The slave stands in relation to his master precisely as the wife stands in relation to her husband." Some plantation women seethed at their subordination. "I belong to that degraded race called woman," wrote Frances Peters, "who whether her lot be cast among Jew, Turk, heathen, or Christian is yet a slave." While elite women fumed in private over the legal and cultural restraints imposed on them, poor women were more likely to defy rigid codes of conduct, especially by crossing the racial line in their sexual lives, and they were rebuked for it. [5]

In the context of Southern angst over egalitarian movements, clerics joined in the defense of slavery as an indispensable social stabilizer. Proponents of slavery exalted it for removing workers with their threats on property rights from any political role and keeping what James Henry Hammond famously described as the "mud-sill" of menial workers contented with their lot. Combining labor and capital in the person of the slave, the South's social system shielded it from the escalating demands of workers empowered with the vote for equal treatment with capital. Indeed, slavery was celebrated as the model for the rest of the world to follow.[6]

For all its elegant system-building, the proslavery argument was brittle in its self-imposed isolation and hollow at its core. Its racial justification of slavery was at odds with the growing class of racially mixed slaves, some of whom were indistinguishable from whites. Defending "mere negro slavery," noted George Fitzhugh of Virginia, "will, nay, has involved us in a thousand absurdities and contradictions." He insisted that the defense had to be moved to a higher plane, one acknowledging that the Bible sanctioned slavery in the abstract with no distinction of race. Anything less, he warned, would be to "yield our cause, and to give up our religion; for if white slavery be morally wrong, be a violation of natural rights, the Bible cannot be true." He then pressed his case home with a bit of rhetorical overkill: "How can we contend that white slavery is wrong, whilst all the great body of free laborers are starving; and slaves, white or black, throughout the world are enjoying comfort?" Fitzhugh had scored some debating points, but his near glorification of white slavery was political anathema in the South's democratic political culture that celebrated the independence of white manhood. His condemnation of free-labor capitalism won him praise, but he had no great following in the South.[7]

Most proslavery clerics occupied a middle ground that stopped short of defending perpetual slavery as a positive good. As Calvinists, they knew that masters were no more immune to angry fits of passion than others of the human race. Try as they might, they could not ignore the central reality of how slavery functioned: "Cruelty is inseparable from slavery, as a system of forced labor," emphasized John Brown, a former slave; "for it is only by it, or through fear of it, that enough work is got out of the slaves to make it profitable to keep them." The cruelties—the violence inflicted on slaves, the breaking up of their families, the failure to recognize their marriages, the denial of access to scripture, and the sexual exploitation of their bodies—were what William Pendleton, an Episcopal minister in Virginia, called "the manifold evils of slavery." Yet, as the Reverend Ross lectured a Northern audience in 1857, "*Slavery*, like *all evils*, has its *corresponding* and *greater good*" as an agency of God's will for uplifting the African race and preparing it for eventual freedom "in the fullness of Providence."[8]

The role of clerics then was to ameliorate an imperfect institution by enjoining masters to practice Christian principles of benevolent stewardship, bring the gospel to the slaves through plantation evangelicalism, and sweep away secular laws that perpetuated the degradation of fellow souls thirsting for God's grace. As for the slaves to be saved for Christ, what they often remembered of religious masters was that they beat them with a Bible in one hand and a whip in the other.[9]

Missionary efforts among slaves began in earnest in the 1830s when South Carolina planters co-opted evangelicalism for their own ends. Their goals included curbing slave rebelliousness, improving labor productivity, undercutting the influence of black exhorters, and shoring up the planters' moral standing in a world hostile to slavery. Above all, as stressed by N. R. Middleton, a planter in St. Andrew's Parish in the Carolina lowcountry, even "when every good motive may be wanting, a regard to *self-interest* should lead every planter to give his people religious instruction." Sometimes the interest to be served was simple survival.

Methodist minister Whiteford Smith was prompted to ask Wade Hampton II to contribute to the cost of employing a missionary on the river plantations below Columbia, South Carolina, by the "recent melancholy murder on Mr. Singleton's plantation." The cost to each planter would be minimal, he added, but the benefits great—the improved morals of the slaves and their supervision in a congregation on each plantation free from the "danger of corruption by being bro't together with those on the neighboring plantations."[10]

Out of a profound sense of religious and moral duty, some planters embraced the missionary movement. Richard Griffin believed that slaveholders, more than any other group, had a fearful responsibility entrusted to them by God for the care of human souls. Robert W. Barnwell was passionately committed to imparting to his slaves the "righteousness not my own" he had felt in his conversion experience. Another South Carolina planter, William H. W. Barnwell, wrote his Northern friend Edgar B. Day in 1832 that the "hearts of masters are turned in a wonderful degree to their slaves, and we are in this neighborhood striving to give them that Freedom which alone can make them happy—Freedom from Sin & Hell by the blood of the crucified Savior." In assuring Day that planters were more concerned with the souls of their slaves than their monetary value, he called on Northern critics to stop their attacks so that planters could silence those among them who associated "religious instruction of the blacks with insurrection." But for every Barnwell there was at least one Catherine Edmonston who dismissed teaching religion to the slaves as a waste of time. She resented spending her Sundays "preaching, teaching & missionizing," for her slaves paid "mere lip service & then they are just as profligate, lie & steal as much as their neighbors."[11]

Slaves had little positive to say about the planter-initiated efforts to Christianize them. The message they received from the white ministers was akin to platitudes they had often heard before. They understood that the ministers were trying to disabuse them of what one of those ministers called "the fruits of their negro-preaching" and to convince them that their enslavement was divinely ordained. Even the planters describing white preaching made it sound like a bribe. "Rev. H. Middleton preached to negroes, in relation to their duties to masters, & their rewards from their Maker if they did their duty," jotted E. G. Baker in his diary. Most slaves recognized a con job when they saw one. "Talk to me about human slavery being a 'Divine Institution!' As well tell me the devil is a merciful God," was the contemptuous judgment of the former slave Isaac Johnson. Whites preached to the slaves that "they are always to remain slaves, and bear with patience and humility the unjust punishment they receive on earth, that it may be to their glory hereafter," recalled Henry Watson. "So is it not an unpardonable sin for man thus to defile the holy sanctuary, and pollute the sacred word of God by using it for such base purposes?"

No amount of white preaching could dissuade the slaves from their faith in Jesus as a prophet of liberation and not servitude.[12]

Efforts to use religion to render the slaves content in their bondage served the interests of both ministers and planters. As Southern evangelicalism became institutionalized after 1830 and developed ties to planter elites, its growth and influence depended on an ever-closer accommodation of slavery. Regardless of their personal views, clerics had to make themselves safe on the slavery issue or risk losing their congregations. After he embraced Methodism in the 1820s and became a minister, Mississippian John G. Jones preached of slavery as "a great moral evil." Publicly expressing those views in Mississippi after the uproar over the abolitionist mailing campaign of the mid-1830s would have precluded any ministerial career for Jones in the state. He either changed his critical stance on slavery or kept it to himself as he preached a gospel of Christian stewardship to slave owners. Doing so gained him the trust of the planters and by the 1840s they were supporting his mission work among their slaves.[13]

Even several clerics identified with strong proslavery views had their doubts over slavery as young men. Basil Manly Jr., the son of a preeminent Baptist preacher-planter, had a crisis of faith after reading an antislavery tract on the eve of embarking on his own ministry in 1847. He told his father that he yearned for the "cessation of slavery for the south & negroes & for our selves" and prayed that God would make possible "a way of escaping from it." With the help of his father, who himself had harbored such doubts in his youth, Manly Jr. righted his moral ballast, was ordained in 1848, and went on to be instrumental in the formation of the Southern Baptist Theological Seminary, a bastion for spreading the word of a proslavery gospel.[14]

Charles Colcock Jones, the Southern divine most noted for calls to bring Christianity to the slaves, harbored deep reservations over slavery before beginning his career as a planter and missionary. While a student at Princeton in the early 1830s, his exposure to abolitionist doctrines left him spiritually conflicted, so much so that he admitted that he was "undecided whether I ought to continue to *hold slaves*. As to the *principle* of slavery, it is *wrong!*" His family was a pillar of both plantation society and the Presbyterian Church in lowcountry Georgia. Torn between all he held dear in Georgia and his very real doubts over the morality of slavery, he resolved his spiritual crisis by deciding to return home as a reforming missionary. Telling himself that the slaves were not ready for freedom, he would devote his life to giving them religious instruction to prepare them for eventual freedom. With these mental gymnastics, he converted his moral desire to do what was right into a self-satisfying rationalization for continuing a system of oppression.

Jones saw himself as a model Christian master ministering to both the material and spiritual needs of those whom he deemed his "people" placed under his care by God. What he could not see was that he was living a life of self-deception. Vague hopes for freeing the slaves receded ever further into the future, and their religious instruction became ever more elusive. Jones's self-image was that of a Christian paternalist with the best interests of his slaves at heart, but he reacted in 1856 as would any other slave owner with rising debts when dealing with recalcitrant slaves defying his will—he sold them. Long bedeviled by what he interpreted as the defiant behavior of Cassius and his wife Phoebe, Jones decided to sell them when they refused to reveal the whereabouts of their runaway daughter Jane. Although he set down the condition that Cassius and Phoebe be sold as a family unit and accepted a lower price for them than if they had been sold individually, he also stipulated that they be sold to a buyer in the distant upcountry, thus guaranteeing that they would be separated from their kin and friends. The upcountry planter to whom he sold them took advantage of a booming market for slaves and soon sold them to a speculator in Savannah, who in turn realized a quick profit by shipping the couple to the slave markets in New Orleans where they were sold separately. After the first sale, Jones had written his wife in a self-congratulatory tone that "conscience is better than money." Phoebe and Cassius knew full well that their sale was a punitive measure, and they set the record straight when they wrote a white trader that they had been sold "for spite."[15]

Missionary work enabled Jones to feel morally good about holding slaves and to repress the brutal, profit-driven reality of slavery. For other clerics, abolitionism served as a convenient scapegoat for explaining away their own inability or unwillingness to push for emancipation. Robert L. Dabney all but thanked the abolitionists in 1840 for producing a positive shift in Southern attitudes toward slavery. With little in the way of supporting evidence, he argued that Virginians would have been well on their way to enacting a program of emancipation had abolitionist meddling not revealed the error of their thinking. Forced to examine slavery more closely, he reasoned, "we find emancipation more dangerous than we had before imagined. Who knows but that this uproar of the Abolitionist . . . may have been designed by Providence as a check upon our imprudent liberality" that might have resulted in "irreparable injury" to the slave.[16]

Consistent with their paternalism and reliance on the Bible, the clerical reformers were nearly unanimous in their opposition to two new positions staked out in the 1850s by the secular defenders of slavery. The first was polygenesis, a theory of separate racial origins associated in the South with the writings of Josiah Nott, a Mobile physician. Drawing from the emerging field of scientific racism, Nott held that blacks constituted a distinct and hopelessly inferior race. He attributed the loss of four of his children to yellow fever in 1853 to the uniquely sickly race of African Americans and their mulatto descendants, who he blamed in his racist reasoning for outbreaks of yellow fever. From this pathologizing of the black race he concluded that the biological survival of Southern whites was contingent on being separated, in effect quarantined, from disease-ridden blacks. Although he detested slavery, he viewed the institution as an essential shield for protecting whites from the contaminating presence of blacks. Nott earned the contempt of the evangelicals for his dismissal of Christian stewardship of the slaves as sheer sentimentalism and his open rejection of the teaching of Genesis that all humankind descended from the same set of parents. Nott might rant—"Just get the dam'd stupid crowd safely around Moses and the difficulty is at an end"—but the evangelicals were unmoved.[17]

Most evangelicals also lined up against the movement to reopen the African slave trade. Loudest in their denunciations were ministers such as James Henley Thornwell of South Carolina, closely identified with a slaveholding ethic of Christian paternalism for the slaves. For Thornwell, the reopening of the trade would destroy what he called the "*humanizing element*" in slavery, the ameliorating influence of the domestic and patriarchal features of the institution in the South. Inundated with dangerous and savage heathens from Africa, the South would have to resort to draconian police measures to ensure the safety of whites. World opinion would be shocked as the South morally regressed and endorsed what the Bible condemned as "manstealing." John Adger, a fellow Presbyterian minister who had undertaken missionary work abroad as well as in the South, fully agreed with Thornwell. He added that Southern participation in the trade would worsen tribal warfare in Africa and result in the separation of countless children from their parents.[18]

By a generous estimate, half a million slaves were church members by 1860, one in eight of the total slave population, and evangelical strictures undoubtedly left many religious masters with troubled consciences when they felt they had been overly harsh in disciplining their slaves. Still, aside from establishing themselves as an undeniable force in Southern public affairs, the evangelicals had fallen far short of achieving their idealized conception of a Christianized slave society. Their greatest failure was their inability to curb the power of slaveholders through effecting laws mandating the teaching of literacy to bring the Bible directly to slaves, prohibiting the breakup of families by sale, and recognizing slave marriages. Planters blocked such steps by arguing that they would reform slavery out of existence by undercutting their near absolute prerogatives in controlling and disposing of their slaves as they saw fit. It was not at all clear where to draw the line between meaningfully "reforming" slavery by correcting individual abuses and setting the institution on the road to extinction. As a result, the acknowledged evils of slavery remained, and Christian reformers increasingly feared they were failing to carry out God's will.[19]

Doubts, Rationalizations, and Self-Interest

The weakest link in the defense of slavery, and one the clerics could not directly address, was the claim that the institution promoted the material well-being of all whites. While the enslaved worked in the hot sun to produce cash staples and were assigned menial, degrading labor, all white men had the opportunity to achieve an economic independence that was denied to the mass of the population in the Northern free-labor system that pushed them down into the dependent status of "wage slaves" beholden to others for their survival. As rates of slave ownership and landholding fell and a white underclass forced to compete with free and enslaved blacks grew, that claim rang increasingly hollow.

Wilson Lumpkin, a former governor of Georgia, had no doubts in the late 1840s that slaveless whites viewed slavery differently than planters and that the South "has many, very many, antislavery people in her bosom. People whose sympathies are with our vilest enemies." Governor William Mosely of Florida believed some of these antislavery people were Southerners who looked favorably upon the Wilmot Proviso, a Northern-backed measure in Congress that called for closing off the Mexican Cession to slavery, "as tending to promote the prospective welfare of the poorer or non-slaveholding portion of the Southern people." John M. McHenry of Kentucky fretted in 1850 that "the boys up in the hollows and the brush . . . are not to [be] relied on in any contest against the Union." The small farmers, artisans, and mariners in the coastal counties of North Carolina likewise valued the Union over the slaveholding interests. According to James W. Bryan, the coast harbored "a large population in favour of the abolition of slavery & they prefer the destruction of the slave property to being made rebels & traitors."[20]

Southern nationalists opposed to the Compromise of 1850 for its failure to openly protect and extend slavery to federal territories forced the calling of conventions in South Carolina, Georgia, and Mississippi to consider secession. South Carolina provided the leadership and the defeat of their bid to unilaterally leave the Union crippled the movement. Cooperative secessionists, whose main support was in the upcountry, wanted to avoid isolating the state and favored secession only in agreement with other states. They were a majority at the convention, and when no other states committed to leaving, the best the separate secessionists could secure was a resolution justifying the need for secession but declaring as impolitic a push for it at the moment. Committed secessionists were embittered that the people had not rallied behind their cause. Charles J. Colcock, a South Carolina planter, despaired of ever achieving success: "The whole world is against us, and I fear it will not be very long before we find numerous abolitionists in our midst who have kept silent heretofore, but will now be emboldened to advocate their sentiments." Benjamin Shields of

Alabama repeated what was becoming a recurrent theme among planters when he predicted in 1852 that within ten years "an emancipation party will boldly stalk forth in the South!"[21]

More galling to the secessionists than their failure to gain the undivided support of non-slaveholders was the defeatism settling over planters, many of whom were ambivalent about defending slavery as an unqualified good. "A Slave holder then or Southern man who falters, who apologizes, much less who denounces Slavery & regards abolition as inevitable is in my opinion *our very worst enemy*," wrote James Henry Hammond, "the man who saps our strength at the core & does more to destroy us than a brigade of abolitionists could."[22]

What Hammond viewed as demoralization eating away at the defense of slavery was the recognition by most planters that owning slaves was simply a matter of making money. As planter Robert W. Barnwell argued in 1844, the "greater part of the slaveholders in other states [except South Carolina] are mere negro-drivers believing themselves wrong and only holding onto their slaves as something to make money off." David Outlaw, a Whig congressman from North Carolina, exposed the hollowness of the argument that slavery was a positive good when he declared in 1848: "To expect men to agree that slavery is a blessing, social, moral, and political, when many of those who have all their lives become accustomed to it, and so far from believing it, believe exactly the reverse, is absurd." As far as he was concerned, most Southerners were as opposed to slavery as most Northerners but, like the Northerners, had no "desire to interfere [with] it, as it exists in the Southern States." [23]

The self-interest promoted by owning slaves was the institution's greatest strength. Frightened when exposed to the physical abuse that was integral to maintaining slavery, white children usually identified with the victims. But when sons of planters became slaveholders themselves, they suppressed their traumatic childhood memories as they learned to become masters. "All children hated the institution before self-interest got in its plea," recalled Letitia D. Miller, the daughter of a Mississippi planter.[24]

As a child, John M. Nelson burned with the hatred Miller noted. Born and raised in Augusta County, Virginia, where his father was an elder in the Presbyterian church and owner of twenty slaves, he often saw his father whipping the slaves, especially those who had tried to run away. His most vivid memory was of watching while they were "stripped naked and suspended by the hands, sometimes to a tree, sometimes to a post, until their toes barely touched the ground, and whipped with a cowhide until the blood dripped from their backs." He tried to intervene "with tears on their behalf, and mingle my cries with theirs, and feel almost willing to take part of the punishment." His father rebuked his son for his childish ways and as a young adult Nelson administered "without remorse" the discipline that had so terrified him as a youth. The intergenerational transfer of the master's authority was complete until Nelson came under the tutelage of an abolitionist minister whose prayers on behalf of the enslaved stirred up memories in Nelson that he had tried to forget. He moved to Ohio and committed to abolitionism in 1835.[25]

Far more typical than the experience of Nelson was that of Edward Pollard. As a boy, Pollard felt guilty when he contrasted his soft life with the hardships inflicted on his father's slaves. "Then would I become gloomy, embittered, and strangely anxious to inflict pain and deprivation on myself; and with vague enthusiasm would accuse the law that had made the lots of men so different." As an adult, Pollard purged himself of his guilty feelings. He defined happiness as "a singular law of compensation which adjusts our natural and original approach of the gifts of fortune, precisely in inverse proportion to what we have of them." By this definition, the slave was perfectly happy with what "little of fortune he has" for that is all that he has ever known. In contrast, Pollard had left home, experienced pains and reversals, and learned that each man must bear his own burdens. A slave, taken care of his whole life by his master, knew nothing of the real struggles of life. By such reasoning Pollard came to the morally reassuring but preposterous conclusion that "I have suffered more of unhappiness in a short worldly career than ever did my 'Uncle Jim' or any other well conditioned slave in a whole lifetime." In other words, he projected onto his slaves the sense of security he yearned to have for himself.[26]

Charles Blackford reconciled himself to slavery with his own elaborate rationalizations. Born in 1833 into a Virginia slaveholding family that had long decried the wrongs of slavery, he was nineteen when he rejected his mother's advice to leave Virginia and pursue a legal career in the North where he could take a stand against slavery. He agreed with his mother that slavery was "an evil" but remonstrated that he could best work against it by remaining in the South. He insisted that only slaveholders could be entrusted with the task of moving toward the emancipation and removal of slaves out of the South. In the North, he reasoned, he would be in no position to improve the lot of the enslaved. Working with the abolitionists was out of the question, for their misguided and affected sympathy for the slaves only drove infuriated slaveholders to tighten the fetters of slavery. No, he told his mother, the morally correct choice was to stay in the South and accept the "mission" given him by Providence to work with other Southerners in alleviating the miseries of slavery. Besides, he added almost as an aside, his chances of succeeding as a lawyer would be much better in the South among friends than as a stranger in the North.[27]

Any lingering compassion for slaves from their childhoods had to be suppressed by young slaveholders were they to take their place in the ranks of elite white manhood. To do so they unconsciously deployed a variety of defense mechanisms to shape a reality that protected them from feelings of anxiety.

The most common defense was to deny any individual responsibility for the institution with the claim that it was inherent to Southern society. "Slavery has always existed about me," explained a Southern friend of Olmsted's, "and without reasoning, I have accepted it as the natural condition of the black population." By "naturalizing" slavery, planters were also disclaiming the South's role in the institution taking hold there. That responsibility was laid at the feet of Northerners and the British. A. B. Longstreet, a Georgia lawyer and college president, set forth the South's case in a public letter in 1860. The South's "slavery is a heritage, not a creature of her own begetting," he stressed. It was the British, who introduced the African slave trade in the colonial period, and the Northerners, who reaped a fortune from the trade and subsequently dumped their slaves on Southerners when slavery was no longer profitable for them, who "forced" slavery on the South "against her wishes, her prayers, and her protestations; screwed down upon her, pressed into her, until it has become so completely incorporated into her very being, that it is now impossible to eradicate it."[28]

In this version of history, Southern whites were the victims, as the masters were forced to care for those who could not provide for themselves. It followed as self-evident that it would be inhumane to free the slaves, since they would be condemned to misery, abject poverty, and most likely extermination as they attempted to compete with the superior white race. In a verbal duel with a British abolitionist, John C. Calhoun declared: "I liberate a slave! God forbid that I should ever be guilty of such a crime."[29]

For proof that blacks were unfit for freedom, Southerners pointed to Jamaica, where the British had introduced emancipation in 1833, and Haiti, the independent black republic forged out of a massive slave insurrection in the 1790s. Ignoring evidence of black achievements compiled by the abolitionists, proponents of slavery caricatured the condition of the former Haitian and Jamaican slaves and their descendants as one of chronic shiftlessness and unproductive labor. They were no better than "semi-savages," insisted V. Moreau Randolph, an Alabama planter. Closer to home, free blacks in the South as well as the North were similarly disparaged as pathetic failures who were better off when slaves. Once again, ideological needs to justify slavery predetermined the conclusions. While most free blacks did live in poverty, they more than held their own against whites when given a chance to compete. Well over half of free blacks in Charleston practiced a skilled trade; in Wilmington, North Carolina, and other cities, they dominated the trades that were open to them. The greater availability of free white laborers in the North resulted in more limited economic gains for free blacks, but restrictions on social and political liberties were less severe than in the South. African American communities in towns and cities were strong enough to offer support and protection for fugitive slaves, promote abolitionist organizations, and sponsor annual black conventions that set forth an agenda for racial justice.[30]

As with the existence of slavery itself, wrongs under slavery that were acknowledged were blamed on outsiders or lowly, poorer whites. Suspected slave uprisings had nothing to do with the desire of contented slaves to be free, it was claimed, but were the result of abolitionists planting dangerous ideas in the minds of gullible blacks. Harsh control of slaves was justified by the necessity to protect Southern communities from the unrest stirred up among slaves by abolitionist agitators. "I tell these Abolitionists, you are the men who have 'riveted the chains,'" insisted Edward Stanly on the floor of Congress in 1850. "But for your efforts, thousands of slaves would have been educated and emancipated, would have been returned to Africa, and Liberia, under the influence of the Christian religion." Overseers, under constant pressure from planters to maximize the labor output of the slaves, took the blame for excessive disciplining of slaves. Often the whippings were blamed on the slaves themselves. Apparently with no intended irony, North Carolina planter Willis Williams wrote his wife while on a trip: "Tell the negroes to behave themselves if they have any love for me and if they have no affection I shall cause them to be punished when I return."[31]

Convincing themselves that they were loved and obeyed unconditionally confirmed for masters their self-image as benevolent caregivers. Any self-directed behavior or awareness on the part of a slave threatened to dispel this comforting, self-gratifying fantasy and elicited a sense of betrayal and often a forceful, violent response. One South Carolina planter informed his slaves that if they behaved badly, "I shall conclude you don't love me & will sell you." Allison Ross of Mississippi whipped to death a slave accused of being a part of an insurrectionary plot. His remorse was limited to declaring that he "hated it very much . . . and had no idea he was whipping him so much." In his rage over this act of "disloyalty" he most likely did lose his self-control as he savagely sought to blot out his slave's self-will.[32]

Violence toward slaves was also accompanied by feelings of genuine affection toward a few favored slaves, usually trusted household slaves who played a prominent role in nursing or caring for members of the planter's immediate family. "I felt as if one of the family were dead, so greatly did I regard her," wrote John L. Manning of South Carolina upon hearing of the death of Telia, his mother's servant. How exceptional such affection was can be judged by his reaction to the news that Betsy, one of the hired-out slaves, had been sent to the workhouse for disobedience. "I shall let her reside there until I can dispose of her to get out of the State. My only desire to have her at home would be to make her a memorable example to other servants."[33]

The vaunted paternalism in which planters took so much pride, the claim that slaves were part of an extended family and treated as such, was a morally comforting, indeed necessary, rationalization fashioned in the imagination of planters. The rationalization shielded them from confronting who they were really were—the profit-maximizing owners of a sullen, resigned, and depressed workforce that required frequent beatings to be kept in line. In fact, planters were in no position to know much about the majority of their slaves or have any relations with them. Most of their slaves were under the daily management of overseers and were often housed on absentee holdings that planters rarely visited. When William Elliott paid his first visit to his Chee-ha plantation, the slaves played their assigned role of welcoming "Ole Massa," but the meeting between master and slaves was strained. Elliott was quite uncomfortable among those he described as "greasy-looking rogues" and left as soon as possible.[34]

When market conditions were favorable or estate debts had to be paid, planters sold off their fictive children, often breaking up families in the process. Here, Northerners again served as convenient scapegoats. According to the *Dallas* (Tex.) *Herald*, "the most cruel and unrelenting of all buyers and sellers of negro property are the Northern men who attend to sales of negroes in the South" to satisfy the claims of a Northern creditor against a Southern debtor. "They shrink not from the separation of man and wife, master and child . . . while the Southern master, with true patriarchal tenderness, has ever revolted from the violent separation of the mother from the infant." When it came to slave sales, however, few slaveholders were in a position to put matters of conscience above financial imperatives or anger against an openly defiant slave. Typical was the response of James Bryan when confronted with the disobedience of his slave Sarah. "We were compelled to sell Sarah in consequence of her misconduct to Mr. B. Gardner," he informed his son James.[35]

Antislavery Consciences and Their Limits

Slave narratives often included deathbed scenes of guilt-stricken masters. John Brown recalled his owner Thomas Stevens "calling old Aunt Sally to him, and begging and praying of her to get the devil away from behind the door, and such like." Brown added that it was a common belief among the slaves that "all the masters die in an awful fright, for it is usual for the slaves to be called up on such occasions to say they forgive them for what they have done." Deathbed scenes were a stock theme in Victorian literature, and Brown's recollections might well be viewed as a projection of the enslaved's bitterness toward his tormentor, but at least some slave owners wrote of nightmares that spoke to fears of retribution. Daniel Cobb, a Virginia Methodist, recorded a nightmare in which, as depicted in the Book of Revelations, a terrible apocalypse ripped open the earth. He was much "alarmed" by the vision, yet Holcum Davy, one of his father-in-law's slaves who was present in the dream, seemed "not to be alarmed at all." It is an open question whether in his subconscious Cobb feared he was about to be punished while God allowed Davy to remain calm. Johnson Olive, a young North Carolinian struggling to commit himself to the church and the ministry, often had dreams in which he was being chased by the devil. "Sometimes he would come in the form of some hideous mammoth dog," he remembered, "but more frequently like a giant of a negro, ragged and filthy, generally with a chain in his hand or somewhere about him. It mattered not in what form or shape he came. I always knew and understood his errand. He was after me, and many a hard race I have run in my dreams in trying to get away from him."[36]

Whether to rid themselves of such nightmares, adhere to the Revolution's ideals of liberty and equality, or, most likely, to shed unprofitable property, large numbers of slaveholders in the Upper South freed their slaves in the late eighteenth century through acts of manumission. In the states along the South Atlantic seaboard, the number of free blacks nearly doubled between 1790 and 1810. Had this pace continued in the succeeding decades, all the slaves in these states would have been freed well before 1860. But the increase in the free black population slowed sharply after 1810 as legislatures passed laws curbing manumissions.[37]

Fears over the destabilization of the racial order with the addition of so many freed slaves provoked the newer, tougher laws on manumission. Although it was easily suppressed, Gabriel Prosser's insurrection of 1800 in the Richmond area alarmed white Virginians and helped make the case for a harsher manumission code in 1806 that required slaves freed after its passage to leave the state. In the newer states of the Southwest, whose economies were tied directly to slave labor, stiff laws against manumissions were in place at the time of statehood. By the mid-1830s, nearly all the Southern states had so restricted manumissions that masters could free slaves only with the permission of their state legislatures or the courts, and those freed were prohibited from remaining in the state. Arkansas (until 1858), Delaware, and Missouri were the only states where slave owners were left unchecked to liberate slaves who were then not forced to leave.[38]

In the 1780s, Delaware passed a law weakening slavery that other states refused to copy. The act prohibited the out-of-state sale of slaves. Stripped of its portability, one of its greatest economic assets, slave property here quickly lost much of its value, and by 1810, prices for slaves in Delaware were significantly lower than in neighboring Maryland and Virginia. Unable to invoke the threat of a sale southward and quite aware that free states lay just to the north, masters were forced to yield to demands from their slaves for labor arrangements that promised immediate or future freedom. In Delaware, a total of just under 9,000 slaves in 1790 had shrunk to fewer than 2,000 by 1860 and comprised less than 2 percent of the state's population. [39]

The only other Southern state in which the number of slaves declined after 1810 was Maryland. Manumissions increased markedly after 1830, so much so that state authorities largely gave up attempts to enforce the restrictions against them. In Baltimore, as well as other Southern cities, slaves were more difficult to control than in the countryside where they were confined to plantations and small farms. Urban slaves tended to live apart from their owners, often arranged for their own hiring, and interacted with working-class whites and free blacks in ways that would have been unthinkable in the plantation belts. Despairing of exercising effective mastery, urban slaveholders increasingly gave in to black demands and either freed their slaves outright or agreed to emancipate them after a set period of faithful service.

Manumissions were closely tied to colonization to Africa, which, in turn, focused on the removal of free blacks from the South. For Southern whites the only other alternatives to the "problem" of freed blacks were eventual amalgamation through interracial marriages, a hideous prospect rejected out of hand, or a catastrophic race war. The strongest support for colonization came from the Upper South. Women, ministers, planters hoping to remove a major obstacle to gradual emancipation, and non-slaveholding businessmen looking toward an all-white, free-labor South made up the backbone of the movement. Aligning with Northern philanthropists and conservative reformers, they formed the American Colonization Society in 1817. State legislatures in the Upper South officially endorsed colonization, and by the 1830s, Maryland, Tennessee, and Virginia were offering public funds to expedite removals. The program in Maryland was easily the most generous—$200,000 to be spent over twenty years.[40]

Despite these efforts to underwrite part of the costs of colonization, the movement required massive federal subsidies if it ever was to make much of a dent in the steadily growing size of the slave population. The closest Congress came to providing the needed funds consisted of bills debated in the early 1820s that called for setting aside a percentage of the proceeds from public land sales to finance colonization. Solid opposition from planters in the Lower South dependent on the purchase of slaves from the Upper South to fill out their labor supply blocked the bills. Robert J. Turnbull of South Carolina starkly set out his region's position: "Discussion [of colonization] will *cause death* and *destruction* to our negro property. Discussion will be equivalent to an act of emancipation, for it will universally inspire amongst slaves, the hope."[41]

However much they stressed the conservative nature of their intent as "the best defence against the rash attempts of *abolitionists*," the colonizationists made little headway in the Lower South. The only state colonizationist organizations in the Cotton South were in Mississippi and Louisiana, and their support came almost entirely from wealthy Whig planters clustered in the Natchez area who

wanted to remove free blacks. The Mississippi Society sent about 600 blacks to
Liberia, overwhelmingly recently manumitted slaves. Roughly half this number
was shipped out of state by the Louisiana Society. Removals in Mississippi nearly
ceased with the passage in 1842 of a state law banning manumissions by wills.[42]

Opposition from the enslaved also hampered colonization efforts. Slaves
learned through their communications networks that Liberia was a very unhealthy place. One in six of the North Carolina blacks sent to Liberia by the
Manumission and Colonization Society died from malaria, sickness, poverty,
and warfare against native Africans. With little genetic resistance to the disease
environment of West Africa, American-born blacks had frightfully low life
expectancies. What support slaves did give colonization was contingent on the
freeing of kin and all family members, a policy opposed by planters and local non-
slaveholders leery of releasing too many freed blacks into their neighborhoods.
Free blacks everywhere spoke out against being expelled from their native land.
A mass meeting of free blacks in Baltimore in 1831 defiantly proclaimed: "We
consider that land in which we were born our only 'true and appropriate home'
and when we decide to remove we will reprise the public of the same, in due
season."[43]

The results of colonization fell far short of its intended objectives. By 1860, at
which point the slave population had risen to close to four million, the American
Colonization Society had transferred about 6,000 formerly enslaved blacks to
Liberia. A total of some 15,000 African Americans were colonized, the majority
of whom had been free-born. Virginia, which accounted for about one-third of
the total, outpaced the other slave states in promoting colonization.[44]

Rejecting colonization as cruel and heartless, some slaveholders navigated a
middle ground between immediate emancipation for all slaves and the blocked
paths to gradual emancipation. Given the obstacles, a surprising number of
them exploited loopholes in the legal restrictions against manumission. One approach was to petition state legislatures or courts for approval of private acts
of emancipation. Even in cotton states such as Alabama and Louisiana, such
petitions were so numerous that the legislatures delegated decisions on them to
local courts. The familiarity of members of the courts with local planters usually
resulted in a ruling in favor of the request for manumissions, often to the alarm
of other planters. "Where is this practical abolition of slaves to stop," wailed a
Louisianan in 1841, "and what are the consequences likely to follow if the law
[permitting such manumissions] is not speedily repealed?" Rather than going
through legal channels, other slaveholders evaded them altogether. While still
alive or in their wills, they deeded ownership of the slaves they wished to free
to a family member or trusted friend with the stipulation that the designated
slaves be allowed to live as if they were free. By making such arrangements, the
masters not only relieved their consciences but also avoided the financial costs

of a legal manumission. Most states required that the manumitter transport any freed slave out of state and post a bond ensuring that those manumitted did not become public charges. These illegally freed slaves joined a growing number of quasi-free blacks; in the Lower South, where laws against manumission were tighter than in the Upper South, they might have comprised a majority of the free black population. Defying laws mandating that they leave the state, they overwhelmingly accepted the constant risk of re-enslavement and chose to remain close to their friends and families.[45]

In a racially based slave society whose leaders were committed to the spread and permanency of black slavery, for a white master to free a slave was bad enough. To also bequeath him or her property amounted to blasphemy. And yet that was just what some slaveholders persisted in doing. Those most prone to do so were the fathers of slave children who made their wishes known in their wills or special trusts set up to achieve that end.

Bequests of freedom and property to enslaved women and their racially mixed children typically were contested by the white relatives of the deceased and creditors of the estate. Judges hearing cases involving contested wills had to weigh community standards committed to limiting the number of free blacks and preserving slavery against the right of individual slaveholders to dispose of their property as they saw fit. Judicial rulings varied but in general the testators' wishes were more likely to be upheld in the courts of the Upper South.

In 1831, Francis Foster, a Virginia slaveholder who had children by several of his enslaved women, brought his children and their mothers to New York City where he emancipated them. Foster and his manumitted slaves returned to Virginia where they lived together as a free family. Upon Foster's death twenty years later, the executor of his estate seized the former slaves, claiming that Foster had never secured the necessary approval of the local court to manumit them and allow them to remain in the state. In a unanimous decision rendered in 1853, the Virginia Supreme Court recognized the freedom of the slaves Foster had taken to New York on the grounds that his intent was known and clear and that failure to acknowledge it "would be an unjust interference with his right to [relinquish] property."[46]

Another strategy resorted to by family members to receive what they viewed as their rightful inheritance centered on claims that the testator was unduly influenced by a scheming slave. Shortly before his death in 1837, W. B. Farr of South Carolina stipulated in his will that his entire estate of some $50,000 be passed on for the benefit of the slave woman Fan, the mother of Henry, his only child. Farr's white relatives challenged the will, claiming that a confused and stroke-ridden Farr had succumbed to the bullying of Fan and was in no fit state of mind when he wrote his will. A jury sided with the white claimants, but the verdict was overturned on appeal to the high court of South Carolina. The justices agreed that Farr had degraded himself in his sexual relations with Fan, yet they based their ruling on the sanctity of property rights and the impartial rule of the law.[47]

The white relations of Elijah Willis were also stymied in laying claim to his estate. A lifelong bachelor in Barnwell District, South Carolina, Willis wrote a will in South Carolina in 1846 leaving his property to his extended white family. He then had a change of heart and in 1854 drew up a will in Ohio freeing Amy, his enslaved partner who lived with him as a wife, their children, and Amy's mother. All his property in South Carolina was to be liquidated to pay for their support in Ohio. He took his racially mixed family to Ohio a year later but died within minutes of arriving. Nonetheless, his Ohio will, when contested by his disinherited white relatives, was declared valid in South Carolina. Justice Thomas J. Withers expressed "disgust" at Willis's behavior but conceded that he had legally evaded the statute of 1841 prohibiting manumission in South Carolina.

Willis's relatives filed a series of appeals aiming to overturn the court's decision. Witnesses testified in 1858 that Willis had transgressed boundaries of race and class and had been guilty of "assailing the institution of slavery through a tolerated amalgamation." They further swore that Amy had the effrontery to spend money and strut around as if she were his white wife. Outnumbered by blacks in the district and fearful that the status and privilege associated with their whiteness was slipping away, these whites privileged white supremacy over any ruling by the state's high court. When the last appeal was denied in 1860, fifty white men in Barnwell signed a petition asking the legislature to overturn the court's decision. The petition called for criminal penalties against any white man known to be living openly with a black woman. The legislature tabled it.[48]

Only a very small minority of slaveholders in the Lower South circumvented the law of slavery by successfully granting freedom and passing on property to their black families. Still, their numbers were large enough to provoke a South Carolina judge in 1844 to declare: "This is another of those cases, multiplying of late with a fearful rapidity, in which the superstitious weakness of dying men . . . induces them, in the last moments, to emancipate their slaves, in fraud of the indubitable and declared policy of the State." He was referring to a case in which a planter directed his executor to hire out his enslaved children until their wages had paid the estate's debts and then apply to the legislature to free the slaves and approve their removal to a free state or to Liberia. The court voided the planter's will for violating the South Carolina statute of 1841 prohibiting any testator from directing slaves to be carried out of the state for the purpose of freeing them.[49]

The cases involving manumission and transfer of property to the enslaved produced a legal maze of decisions that fluctuated between upholding the wishes of the testators and enforcing standards of rigid racial rules. Despite clamping down on manumissions in the Lower South by the 1850s, the courts were powerless to stop a slaveholder from taking slaves to a Northern state and freeing them there. What the courts could do was to formulate a new public policy refusing to recognize in a slave state any rights of freedom conferred upon a slave in a free state. This was the policy announced by Chief Justice Wiley P. Harris of the Mississippi Supreme Court in 1859. The case centered on Nancy Wells, who had been freed in Ohio in 1846 by her father, planter Edward Wells, who subsequently left her a legacy of $3,000 in his will. When the executor of the estate refused to release the legacy, Wells sued in the Mississippi court for her inheritance. Speaking for a majority court Harris ruled that Wells had no legal rights the state of Mississippi was bound to respect, no matter where she was manumitted. For good measure, Harris blasted Ohio for being "forgetful of her constitutional obligations to the whole race and afflicted with a *negro-mania*, which has inclined her to *descend*, rather than elevate herself in the scale of humanity."[50]

Regardless of Harris's ruling, masters could still take their slaves out of state and free them, and throughout the 1850s, masters continued to do just that. Southern editors might try to explain away manumissions by blaming them on "the force of Northern opinion and teaching brought to bear on our people and young men sent there for education," but no amount of rationalization could deny the fact that not all slaveholders were committed to slavery as a benevolent institution.[51]

Plantation Mistresses: Privileges Trump Unease

Women in the planter class often privately expressed deep moral misgivings about slavery but still clung to the institution for the privileges it provided them. They had close, even intimate, ties to many of the household slaves yet were singled out in the accounts of slaves as the cruelest of masters in doling out punishments. In their ambivalence they wavered between denouncing slavery to themselves and berating slaves for bringing out the very worst in them. They were neither unquestioning supporters of slavery nor closet abolitionists. Rather they were equivocal and contradictory in their views as they made daily compromises with an institution that demanded moral compromises in exchange for material benefits.[52]

Women almost uniformly described slavery as a burden that saddled them with responsibilities that were unfathomable to Northern women. In comparing the lot of planters' wives with their "Northern sisters," "Filia" noted with a touch of envy the greater material comforts, conveniences, and cultural opportunities available to women in the North, including hiring household servants. Unlike their Northern counterparts, who could simply discharge and replace any unsuitable servants, Southern mistresses were responsible for managing a household of lazy, near helpless slaves who required constant care and direction. "Would you like to struggle and wrestle with ignorance, stupidity and the fearful tendency to immorality—alas! Almost inherent in the negro?" she rhetorically asked. In coping with such an indolent, ignorant, and semi-savage workforce, Southern wives had to labor away as health providers and caregivers dispensing clothing and food rations.[53]

For all the complaints over their workloads, the tasks of the mistress were primarily supervisory ones. For Tryphena Fox of Louisiana, one of the great virtues of slavery was the leisure time it made possible for her. She spent most of her time "sewing, reading & writing," she explained to her mother back in Massachusetts. "Having two servants to do the work, I do very little myself . . . but I have to watch them and tell them every little thing to be done, for a negro never sees any dirt or grease." When domestic work was not done promptly or up to the standards expected, mistresses interpreted such behavior not as a form of resistance to enslavement but as confirmation of black stupidity and irresponsibility. "The negroes are disposed to give all the trouble they well can," complained Anna King on her Retreat plantation, "as is always the case when they see a chance to impose."[54]

Mistresses wielded all the coercive power of slavery in their households and demanded faithful service from the slaves under their direction. "I believe it my duty, as long as I own slaves to keep them in proper subjection and well employed. So come what may, I intend to make mine do service," proclaimed Miriam Hilliard, the wife of an Arkansas planter. When that service was not forthcoming, a whipping was the usual consequence. Maud C. Fentress viewed this as her only recourse in dealing with her slave woman: "Surely Barb is the most stupid woman living, which nothing will cure, but every day whipping." A savage beating could be administered for the slightest of perceived offenses. A slave mistress used some soot from the fireplace as eyeliner, and her young slave girl, Delia Garlic, copied her "jes' for fun." Feeling mocked when she noticed what the slave had done, the mistress flew into a rage and beat Garlic unconscious with a piece of firewood, later remarking: "I thought her thick skull and cap of wool would take it better than that."[55]

If the whippings did not have the desired effect, the auction block awaited. For Mahala P. Roach, the slave Clarissa was a constant problem. "Ashamed" when Clarissa was sent back from the woman who had hired her, Roach decided to sell her off. She sent Clarissa to the local auction room, asking $1,800 for her and her baby. Especially vulnerable to being sent into the slave market or subjected to brutal treatment were female slaves whom the slave mistress believed had engaged in sexual relations with her husband. At the age of twenty, J. D. Green was ordered by his owner to marry the slave Jane. Within five months she gave birth to a child fathered by the master. Soon thereafter, as related by Green, the master's wife died, and his second wife consented to their marriage only on the "condition that all female slaves whom he had at any time been intimate with must be sold." One of the enslaved women sold was Jane. When Roswell King Jr.'s wife discovered that he had fathered mulatto children by his slaves Judy and Scylla, she had them removed from the plantation infirmary where they were confined and then flogged and banished to the estate's penal colony.[56]

Despite the need to petition the state legislature to gain a divorce and the shame that they would incur for a failed marriage, women in slaveholding families disproportionately initiated suits for divorce. Along with claiming verbal and physical abuse, they often cited their husbands' fornication with female slaves as grounds for divorce. Lucy W. Norman of Virginia had put up with such behavior by her husband James for four years before she petitioned for a divorce in 1848. A white witness at the circuit court hearing the case testified that while living with the family she became aware that the husband was "strongly attached to a servant girl . . . with whom he habitually had illicit and criminal intercourse. He frequently slept with her . . . sometimes in a pallet in his wife's chamber & at other times in an adjoining room of the house." Two other witnesses testified to the same effect and the divorce was granted. Wanting to avoid community censure and the public admission of the failure of the marriage, most white women in a similar situation did not seek divorce, especially if the husband did not flaunt his affections for a slave concubine and openly challenge his wife's position within the household.[57]

Some women tried to keep their mortification private, only to hear gossip about their husband's infidelity. "Poor Sallie Hardaway is still weathering the storm of discontent," reported Maggie Copeland in Montgomery, Alabama, to Mary Bailey. "He, I am told, gives decidedly more of his attention to his colored family than to his white. You probably heard that he was raising a colored family by Press Venice." When an angry wife went public about her husband's fornicating with a slave woman, she ran the risk of being branded by men in the neighborhood as a sexual temptress herself. A young Mississippi doctor recorded in his diary that a Mrs. Dunn had told an audience of gentlemen and ladies that "she had caught her husband having intercourse with negro girls, more than once." He hastened to add, however, that she had not actually used the word intercourse but rather spoke in lewd language that no proper lady ever would have used. He maliciously concluded that Mrs. Dunn "was only prompted by a lustful desire after some of the gentlemen present, hoping that such language would induce some of them to make such a proposal and had they, no doubt, with all her Methodist religion, she would gladly on her back yielded up to them what the negress did to her husband."[58]

Most of the betrayed women tried to keep knowledge of their husbands' sexual transgressions inside the immediate family circle as they plotted their revenge. Ann Archer had her husband's two slave children removed from her home in the spring of 1860 and taken to another plantation. She instructed her son, who was charged with the move, to make certain that the children be "made to work in the field and do good work and regular work as any of the hands on the place." As for the mother of the children, Archer told her son that she was "so insolent she shall feel *her* place the rest of her life as long as I live, or one of my children who love me as they ought." Archer remained with her husband, one of the wealthiest planters in the Mississippi Valley, despite his ongoing attraction to the slave Patty.[59]

Henry Watson recalled that when he was a slave in Vicksburg, Mississippi, his mistress discovered that her husband had made "a wife of one of his slaves." She left him to live with her mother and refused his pleas for reconciliation. He then, according to Watson, "became a perfect tyrant, lashing his slaves without mercy." Another former slave remembered one extreme case in which a wife caught her husband in bed with a mulatto slave girl. He followed his wife into the house, where they had "a big fuss" and "den marster Shaw started towards her. She grabbed de gun an let him have it. She shot him dead in de hall."[60]

When a slave woman felt that she had been rejected after having been sexually exploited, the results could be as tragic. E. G. Barker, an evangelical who habitually berated himself for losing his temper with his slaves, sat on a jury of inquest in Mississippi investigating the apparent suicide of a slave woman. Evidence was uncovered that the owner, Lewellen Cole, had had carnal relations with the woman. It was also learned that for two nights before the woman was found hanging from a tree, Cole had whipped her for allegedly failing to obey his orders. Barker gave as his opinion that the woman, feeling "set aside & imposed upon . . . preferred to die than live—thence the rash act." A slave in Alabama was so distraught when the white father of her infant child refused to stop his wife from abusing the infant that she killed the child to end the torture.[61]

The extent of the miscegenation was apparent even to the casual observer, and slaveholding women saw evidence of it on a daily basis. They deplored it in their diaries and journals but could hardly do so publicly without giving the lie to heading households of domestic purity. Mary Chesnut bitingly proclaimed that "every lady tells you who is the father of all the mulatto children in everybody's household, but those in her own she seems to think drop by the clouds, or pretend so to think."[62]

Reacting to seeing the child of a female household slave who was "as white as any white child," Ella Thomas, a planter's wife in Georgia, in the privacy of her journal blamed the rampant miscegenation not on sexually charged slave women, the standard Southern explanation, but on white men. She admitted there were exceptions, among whom she cited her husband. Taking care to stress that she was "no Woman's Rights Woman, in the northern sense of the term," she decried the double standard in sexual matters. A sexual offense that would destroy the reputation of a woman, she noted, only "slightly lowers" that of a man and "in the estimation of some of his own rather elevates." She was so disgusted by the thought of lascivious white men bidding for "fancy girls" at slave auctions that she went so far as to assert that "Southern women are I believe at heart abolishionists." Realizing she had gone too far, she fell back on the opinion that slavery degraded white males more than blacks and had a damaging effect upon white children. Still, for all her moral doubts concerning slavery, she acknowledged that she was "not so philanthropic as to be willing voluntarily to give all we own for the sake of principle." Meanwhile, both her husband and father continued to have sexual relations with their slaves behind her back.[63]

Women who wrote about their moral unease over holding enslaved people (decidedly few) were mostly of the elite planter class. They resigned themselves to accepting an institution they felt defiled all whom it touched. In dealing with the moral onslaughts of the abolitionists and their own doubts, they consoled themselves with the belief that they were doing their godly duty of caring for and Christianizing a people utterly unfit for freedom. Lucila McCorkle, the wife of a Presbyterian minister, admitted in her diary that "I should myself feel a natural repugnance toward slavery if I did not find it existing & myself an owner lawfully & scripturally." She prayed for divine guidance for help in coping with what she labeled the "natural depravity" of her enslaved charges.[64]

The dread of financial ruin, the conviction that their slaves were better off in bondage than if freed, and comforting thoughts of Christian stewardship kept mistresses safely within the folds of slavery's defenders. The few who were genuinely morally anguished vaguely hoped that a solution could be found for their dilemma. Feeling that slavery was "a great sin," Mary B. Carter, a member of one of Virginia's most distinguished planter families, could offer nothing more specific than the thought "it could be gotten rid of if all would unite hand and heart to do so." Judith P. Rives, another Virginia mistress, put her hopes in colonization. She and her husband freed many of their slaves in the 1850s and sent them to Liberia. A program of gradual emancipation enacted by the federal government was the answer of Martha Bradford of Florida. Mary Johnstone in the South Carolina lowcountry would have been overjoyed had her husband been able to find a buyer for his rice plantation to free themselves from "such a disagreeable business in a *private* way."[65]

As slavery remained entrenched, so too did women's greatest fear, that of being murdered or, worse yet, raped by their slaves in an uprising. Rogene Scott, a Northern teacher on a Louisiana sugar plantation in the late 1850s, fully shared those fears. She was terrified by the thought of what could happen if a rebellion occurred where she was. "If the servants at such a time would content themselves with simply taking the lives of the whites in a *humane manner*, it would not be so bad," she wrote to her mother. But she expected the slaves to resort to "every form of cruelty and torture" and that white women would be "ravished on the spot," a fate "worse than instant death, a thousand times worse." The specter of rebellious slaves so frightened Amanda Edmonds, the daughter of a Virginia planter, that she felt no punishment was too horrific for them: "I would see the fire kindled and those who did it singed and burnt until the last drop of blood was dried within them and every bone smolder to ashes."[66]

The vaguest rumors of slave unrest triggered the dread. Marion Harland could not "recollect when the whisper of the possibility of an 'insurrection' (we need not to specify of what kind) did not send a sick chill to my heart." All age groups shuddered when they heard the rumors. The girls at a female academy in Murfreesboro, North Carolina, were "very much excited" in 1854 when reports circulated of possible trouble among the local slaves. Christian Bell wrote her parents that she was "afraid to go to sleep" and very much wanted to be at home.[67]

Fears peaked in presidential election years when slaves were exposed to campaign rhetoric in which the rival parties accused each other of abolitionist sympathies. The widow Mary Sims, living with her four slaves in the Arkansas delta, noted in her journal how frightened she had been during the election of 1856. The election featured the first Republican presidential candidate, John C. Frémont, and party feelings were especially heated. Sims recalled that "there was so much talk of insurrections among the slaves of the South that I felt I was in danger all the time and for three months I do not think I slept sound a single night."[68]

Unprepared for managerial responsibilities they resented but could not avoid, slaveholding mistresses found themselves daily surrounded by domestic slaves who refused to play the role of docile and loving servants. When the slaves abandoned plantation households with the coming of freedom, all the pejorative stereotypes of the black race were confirmed in the minds of the mistresses. Some were relieved to see their "ungrateful" slaves leave, since at last they were freed of a responsibility that had been a constant source of bedevilment to them.[69]

The Persistent Dissenters

Judged by its message to the outside world and the positive praise for slavery by its politicians and the press, the South was solidly proslavery by 1860 and had moved well beyond its slavery-is-a-necessary-evil position of the pre-1830 period. In private, however, many Southerners were sending a different message: they were morally uncomfortable with slavery but considered it an economic and social necessity that absolutely had to be shielded from outsider interference. Only they could ever be entrusted with dismantling the institution.

In the Upper South, the Whig Party continued to provide a political home for those whites who looked forward to the day when they would be rid of both slaves and free blacks through programs of gradual emancipation coupled with colonization. Henry Clay, the South's most influential Whig, pushed such a vision until his death in 1852. He had no doubts that slavery was wrong: "That slavery is unjust & is a great evil are undisputed axioms. The difficulty always has been how to get rid of it." Robert J. Breckinridge, a fellow antislavery gradualist and an Old School Presbyterian minister in Kentucky, denounced slavery at the 1849 Kentucky Constitutional Convention as "this most atrocious of all human institutions."[70]

As a result of the great conservative reaction after Nat Turner's 1831 rebellion in Virginia, politicians in the Upper South backed off from publicly advocating colonization. Preachers assumed leadership of the movement. In the 1850s, Baptist and Old School Presbyterian ministers in Tennessee and Kentucky continued to take public stands against slavery and to condemn it as a moral evil. One of the most outspoken was James M. Pendleton, a native Virginian who pastored Baptist churches in Kentucky before his appointment as professor of theology at Union University in Murfreesboro, Tennessee. In twenty articles he wrote for the *Examiner*, an antislavery newspaper in Louisville, he boldly declared himself "A Southern Emancipationist." He called for gradual emancipation through an expanded use of manumissions and the subsequent colonization of the freed slaves in Liberia. The editor of the *Alabama Baptist* denounced him in 1855 as a dangerous abolitionist utterly unfit to teach the young men of the South.[71]

Elsewhere in the Upper South, clerical critics of slavery, including some who once had been uncompromising defenders of the institution, continued to be heard in the 1850s. Richard Fuller, a slaveholding Baptist minister in South Carolina, had defended slavery in 1845 as an expression of divine will in a published exchange of letters with Reverend Francis Wayland, president of Brown University. Rejecting Wayland's assertion that slavery was a sin, Fuller proclaimed that "what God sanctioned in the Old Testament, and permitted in the New, cannot be a sin." Perhaps because his views on slavery were beginning to change, Fuller left South Carolina in 1847 to assume the pastorship of the Seventh Baptist Church in Baltimore. Speaking before the American Colonization Society in 1851, he called upon slaveholders to recognize that "slavery is not a good thing, and a thing to be perpetuated." In due time, he believed, God's grace would dissolve the master-slave relationship and prepare the way for freed slaves to carry the gospel to Africa. An apostate in the eyes of his former followers in South Carolina, Fuller never regained the stature he had enjoyed in that state before his apparent change of heart regarding slavery.[72]

The Reverend William A. Smith, one of Virginia's most outspoken proslavery advocates, reported back to Governor Henry A. Wise from a speaking tour in 1857 that "a secret suspicion of the morality of African slavery in the South bothered many of our best citizens." Most worrisome of all were the white mechanics in Portsmouth and Norfolk, "nine-tenths" of whom, according to Smith, were "abolitionists" who "would vote the slaves out of Virginia tomorrow" if they could be assured that the slaves would be expelled from the state.[73]

Despite Smith's concerns, most of the dissenters from proslavery orthodoxy remained silent in the Upper South and elsewhere. Some, like Virginia Presbyterian Benjamin Mosely Smith, reserved their thoughts for their diaries. As he lamented in December 1858: "Oh what trouble, running sore, constant pressing weight, perpetual wearing, dripping, is this patriarchal institution! What miserable folly for men to cling to it as something heaven descended." Others, like the Northern-raised heiress to slaves in Kentucky, who intended to free her human chattel upon reaching her legal majority, found themselves frustrated by laws that forbade emancipated slaves from remaining in the state or by their own refusal to separate family members held by multiple owners. In making what she believed to be the humane choice for her slaves by keeping them together, she found that she could not "rid myself from the horrid crime to which, by accident of inheritance, I have been accessory." Caroline Pettigrew, mistress of her husband's Bonarva plantation in eastern North Carolina, recognized that "instances occur of horrible oppression & crime at the South . . . that could only be in the midst of slavery," but she was no crusader against slavery. Young men troubled by slavery had to stifle their views or else forfeit any chance of a successful public career. A wealthy planter in Kentucky admitted to a friend that "if it was not for his political aspirations, he would openly free every slave he owned, and relieve his conscience from the weight of the 'perilous stuff' that so opposed it." Of course, he added, "were I to do it in Kentucky, I should be politically dead. It would, besides, strike a blow at my law practice, and then what could I do?"[74]

Olmsted met a number of planters in the heart of the Lower South who freely said they believed slavery was wrong. One of them was Richard Taylor, a Louisiana sugar planter and future Confederate general. Slavery, he thought, was "a very great evil, morally and economically. It was a curse upon the South. . . . [N]othing would be more desirable than its removal if it were possible to be accomplished." A Creole neighbor of Taylor's agreed on the moral wrong, but, in the slaveholders' typical mixture of fatalistic acceptance and self-interest regarding the institution, he stressed that "we could not do away with it if we wished; our duty is only . . . to lessen its evils as much as we could do." After decrying slavery as wrong and a heavy burden, John Watson, a Mississippi cotton planter, reckoned that Olmsted "never saw a conscientious man who had been brought up among slaves who did not think of it pretty much as I do—do you?" When Olmsted replied that he had indeed met such men, Watson's response was "Ah, self-interest warps men's minds wonderfully, but I don't believe there are many who don't think so, sometimes—it's impossible, I know, that they don't."[75]

Among those referenced by Watson were the slaveholders who tried to free their slaves in wills contested by their white heirs. For these renegades, a Georgia judge had nothing but scorn. After invoking the curse of Ham to show the folly of expecting freed slaves to exhibit any capacity for self-government, the judge proclaimed: "Let our women and old men, and persons of weak and inferior minds, be disabused of the false and unfounded notion that slavery is sinful, and that they will peril their souls if they do not disinherit their offspring by emancipating their slaves!"[76]

One of the few Southern whites who flatly denied the racist dogma which held that blacks were incompetent of being productive citizens was William Cecil Duncan, the son of a Scottish immigrant and a Baptist minister in New Orleans. As the publisher of the *Southwestern Baptist Chronicle*, he reviewed positively in 1848 a recent talk by the Reverend Robert S. Finley, a colonizationist and itinerant preacher. He agreed with Finley that the question of "whether the negro is capable of self-governing himself" had been "forever settled" by the example of Liberia where Africans had demonstrated that, if left to their own devices and freed from debilitating restraints, they were "as capable of making their own laws, and managing their own affairs, internal and external, as other nations." Along with the Methodist minister Holland Nimmons McTaire, a fellow editor of a religious newspaper, Duncan was an outspoken critic of slavery. Both ministers promoted colonization, missionary work among the slaves that allowed for a free expression of black spiritual practices and a semi-autonomous black clergy, prohibitions on slave sales except under extraordinary circumstances, and the conferral of matrimonial rites for slave couples. In a particularly strongly worded editorial in 1850, Duncan denounced slavery "as deleterious both in a moral and social point of view" and urged each state to implement a program of gradual emancipation and cooperate with other states in backing colonization.[77]

Only the religious and racial pluralism of New Orleans, a product of its blend of Catholicism and a creolized Protestant culture with long-standing international roots, permitted such an open defiance of the orthodox proslavery establishment in the Lower South. Nonetheless, this bold experimentation in drawing on religion to hasten the end of slavery could not survive the clamping down on all forms of dissent in the late 1850s with the emergence of the antislavery Republican Party in national politics. Lacking funds and supporters, a discouraged but unbowed Duncan left New Orleans for the North soon after the secession of Louisiana.

The Impending Crisis of the South, a book by Hinton Rowan Helper, a hitherto unknown North Carolinian, soon became linked to the Republicans after its publication in 1857. Raised in yeoman-dominated Davie County on the western edge of the North Carolina Piedmont, Helper gave a voice to the yeomanry and other non-slaveholding whites concerned with declining economic opportunities that threatened their claims on personal liberty and independence. His core thesis was bluntly stated: "The causes which have impeded the progress and prosperity of the South [and] sunk a large majority of our people in galling poverty and ignorance, rendered a small minority conceited and tyrannical, and driven the rest away from their homes . . . may all be traced to one common source . . . *Slavery!*" He proclaimed himself an abolitionist and called on all non-slaveholders to join him in a collective effort to end an institution that benefited only a privileged few at the expense of everyone else.[78]

Armed with reams of statistics drawn from the federal census of 1850 pointing to the economic and social poverty of the South compared to the North, Helper more forcefully than previous secular critics of slavery laid bare all the contradictions in orthodox Southern thinking that assigned a position of universal equality to all whites. As elegantly formulated by John C. Calhoun, this ideology held that "the two great divisions of society are not the rich and the poor, but white and black, and all the former, the poor as well as the rich, belong to the upper class, and are respected and treated as equals, if honest and industrious." For Helper, the fundamental divide in Southern society was not between whites and blacks but between those who owned slaves and those who did not. Although he surely exaggerated for polemical impact, his charge that a "cunningly devised mockery of freedom is guaranteed to [non-slaveholders], and that is all" was closer to the mark than Calhoun's idyllic portrayal of common whites enjoying equality with planters. He bitterly denounced planters for degrading manual labor as fit only for slaves when toilsome labor was the lot of all non-slaveholders, including white women and children who worked in the fields. No matter his deportment or moral standards, every white man forced to labor "by the sweat of his brow" was "treated as if he was a loathsome beast, and shunned with the utmost disdain." In calling special attention to the plight of white women, he exposed the class bias of gender conventions that celebrated women as paragons of moral purity and cultural refinement.[79]

Abolition, Harper asserted, would dramatically raise the price of land, the major asset of yeoman farmers, as capital no longer tied up in slaves flowed into a more diversified economy of profitable factories and flourishing cities. Farmers would benefit as demand rose for their food crops and the meat from their livestock. Mechanics, day laborers, and surplus workers in the countryside would find remunerative employment in new manufacturing pursuits. Planters would be more than compensated for the loss of their slaves by the increased value of all the other property they owned. Competition with black labor would vanish as colonization programs financed by taxes on slave property rid the South of despised African Americans. Like the North, whose wealth Helper trumpeted in his statistical tables, the South would be a progressive society that funded public education, dignified honest labor, and provided incentives for economic and social advancement.

Helper's polemic was simplistic and overdrawn. For example, he ignored the non-slaveholders who had a stake in the institution by annually hiring slave labor and said nothing of those who at one point had owned a few slaves before selling them to raise cash to pay off debts. Still, its diagnosis of Southern backwardness in an age that worshipped material progress was difficult to refute. And the persistent opposition of white mechanics to competition from skilled slaves and the growing push for ad valorem taxes on slaves suggested at least a potential nucleus of support for a Helperite movement. However, the chances of a successful collective crusade against slavery were virtually nil in a society where most non-slave owners lived in isolated, self-contained rural communities where strong ties to family and kin snuffed out even an incipient sense of class consciousness. Aware of the barriers against organizing in the South, Helper called for an alliance with the Republican Party. The Republicans were not abolitionists and were pledged only to stopping the expansion of slavery, but Helper was confident that their end goal of eventual emancipation would commit them to backing his call for collective action against slavery.

It took the uproar in Congress in December 1859 over the election for Speaker of the House of Representatives to directly link the Republicans with Helper. Southerners were still seething over John Brown's raid at Harpers Ferry, Virginia, in late October. Brown, a Northern abolitionist, veteran of the guerrilla war in Kansas, and successful slave raider into Missouri, proved to be surprisingly inept after his band of men captured the federal arsenal at Harpers Ferry. He passively sat back seemingly waiting to be captured while federal and state forces quickly mobilized against him. The raid was a total failure in sparking a slave insurrection but, in what may well have been Brown's objective all along, it raised the fears of Southern whites to a fever pitch, and his execution in December gave the abolitionists a martyr for their cause.[80]

The Impending Crisis, which hitherto had largely been ignored in the slave states gained an instant notoriety and was lumped with other "incendiary" publications as a totally unacceptable threat to the lives of whites. In December, Southern congressmen seized on the fact that John Sherman of Ohio, the Republican candidate for the speakership, had been one of sixty-eight Republican congressmen who had signed a circular seeking funds for the distribution of a

condensed version of *The Impending Crisis*. Unbeknownst to Sherman and most
of the other signatories, Helper had not edited out of the shortened version his
call for the abolition of slavery in the states. After months of bitter debate, a compromise candidate for the speakership was finally agreed upon, but no amount
of backtracking by the Republicans or denunciations of Brown could ever convince Southerners that they were not out-and-out abolitionists.

The winter of 1859–60 saw the expulsion of any whites in the South bold
enough to speak out against slavery, even in the Upper South. Minister John
G. Fee, who had defied years of threats and menacing mobs in Kentucky, was
finally forced to abandon his preaching against slavery and flee to Ohio. Daniel
Worth, an antislavery minister who had returned to his native state of North
Carolina to distribute copies of Helper's book, was arrested in December for
circulating an incendiary work. Through two trials and an appeal to the North
Carolina Supreme Court, his judges were unsympathetic. One of them ruled
that it was immaterial whether the offending material reached a slave or free
black, for the assumption was that "its corrupting influence would inevitably
reach the blacks [and] the inevitable tendency . . . would be to make blacks dis-
contented" and set them in "hostile array" against slave owners. Worth forfeited
his bond of $3,000 when he fled the state in the spring of 1860 to avoid a jail
term of twelve months.[81]

John Brown's raid, a psychological blow from which the South never recovered,
had badly shaken confidence in the permanence of slavery in the Union. Adding
to anxieties was the persistence of moral qualms over slavery by many whites,
especially in the Upper South. The secessionists were determined never to allow
those qualms to become the basis for any systematic movement against slavery.
Thus, it was no accident that Yancey privileged the need to recognize the morality of slavery as the cornerstone of his speech at the Democratic national convention at Charleston. With the ensuing split of the Democratic Party, the first
stage of the momentous election of 1860 was about to unfold.

3

Waiting for Lincoln

The Election of 1860

By the late summer of 1860, the election of Abraham Lincoln at the head of the antislavery Republican Party appeared a near certainty. His chances of victory had been greatly enhanced by the breakup of the Democratic Party at its national convention in Charleston in April 1860. Panic and fear gripped the Cotton South in the summer as the result of food shortages amid a prolonged drought and reports of slave insurrections plotted by abolitionist emissaries. Prominent Southern politicians announced as the election approached that only secession could save the slave states from impending doom. Promising to avert disaster and usher in a glorious future of prosperity and security for slavery, the secessionists were poised to strike as soon as Lincoln's election was confirmed.

Creating a Southern Rights Party

As the year 1860 opened, many Southern whites were expecting the worst and their mood was ugly. Franc M. Carmack began his diary on January 1 by prophesying that "1860 may see the last page of the history of the United States and begin to record—perhaps in letters of blood—the annals of the disunited States of America." From Kentucky, Jane Allen Stuart wrote in January that "people here now reckon a breach of the Union as probably an unfolding event." A committee of Mississippi legislators considering a bill in February to prohibit marriages between first or second cousins reported against the bill on the grounds that the South needed to increase its white population by any possible means given "the present threatening aspect of our public affairs." If the offspring of marriages between cousins turned out "to be lacking in sense," then so much the better. After all, in any war "a fool will stop a bullet as well as a man of sense and may even save the life of a smarter and better man, and in that way become of great use, and in these times we cannot afford in the South to dispense with any who may be able to perform so useful an office, fools though they may be."[1]

Repressive measures against free blacks increased. The Georgia legislature authorized judges to sell into temporary slavery any blacks convicted of vagrancy. A second conviction was to be punished by perpetual slavery. A presentment of the Charleston Grand Jury expressed alarm at the "nuisance" of free blacks and slaves riding in public vehicles driven in many cases by whites. To stop such a violation of the South's caste system, the grand jury called for a law fining the owners of such vehicles and subjecting the occupants, whether slave or free, to corporal punishment. At sentencing in January, South Carolina judge T. J. Withers brushed aside the jury's recommendation for mercy and sentenced to death Francis Michel, a young Irish porter convicted of assisting a runaway slave who had stowed away on the steamer ship *Marion*. Declaring that Michel had corrupted a slave into an enemy of the South, Withers spun a conspiratorial web stretching back to abolitionist ministers who had converted Michel into an "ignominious" tool "to execute purposes of blood and of death and desolation upon and among an unoffending and confederate people, which purposes they are too cowardly to execute with their own hands." Ignoring Withers's diatribe, the governor of South Carolina commuted the sentence.[2]

"A Vigilant" in lowcountry Carolina referred ominously to the "vermin in our midst." For its safety, he argued, the South had to be purged of the infectious virus of incendiarism implanted in its slaves by its enemies. These foes included not just abolitionists but all loafers and vagabonds, anyone without a fixed place in the local community. Unrelenting vigilance was necessary, for, as explained by the Vigilance Committee organized in St. John's Berkley on January 3, abolitionist emissaries "come among us in various disguises and under manifold pretexts." These masked strangers might be itinerant preachers, teachers, book agents or peddlers, ditchers, and other day laborers. Any of them "may leave the germ of insubordination and insurrection among our domestics." Citing a primal law of self-preservation, vigilance associations wielded unrestrained extralegal powers.[3]

And so, the "vermin" were rooted out. Two men in Enterprise, Mississippi, were hauled before the Vigilance Committee in early February on suspicion of spreading antislavery notions. Their offense was distributing Appleton's *New American Cyclopedia*, a work judged by the committee to be "incendiary." They barely escaped being tarred and feathered before they were handed over to civil authorities. A blacksmith was ordered out of Edgefield, South Carolina, for having been "discovered drinking late at night with a parcel of negroes." The citizens of Rome, Georgia, expelled a Northern sales agent for a dry-goods firm who had just arrived on a train from Marietta. Passengers on the train informed the citizens that he had been uttering "heretical sentiments upon the subject of negro equality."[4]

Spurred on by fears of invading abolitionists, a host of volunteer military companies sprang up. "We must fight or give our consent to be plundered now of our Slaves & our rights in the Territories, and it will not be long till we have to submit to being plundered in our homes," an anxious A. C. McEwen of Holly Springs, Mississippi, wrote Governor Pettus in February. By the beginning of May, Mississippi was reported to have the most volunteer companies in its history. The most prestigious companies, such as the Governor's House Guards of Milledgeville, Georgia, publicized the high social standing of its members. The uniforms for the company, manufactured by special order in New York City, were dark blue, festooned with gold lace and gilt buttons, and came at a hefty price that only planters or their sons could afford. Seeking to gain civil honors to enhance their vote-getting appeal, the politically ambitious, as well as planters, rushed to join the companies.[5]

Exploiting the alarm over John Brown's raid, the South Carolina legislature in December 1859 issued a call for a convention of the slaveholding states to propose remedies facing the South. Christopher G. Memminger, a Charleston lawyer and a moderate by South Carolina standards, was sent to Richmond to gain the state's participation in the convention movement. Memminger's "moderation" was anything but that to the Virginians. Before leaving for Richmond, Memminger was annoyed that the *Richmond Examiner* had represented his mission "as one to preserve the Union." Instead, it was his belief that "the Union cannot be preserved. . . . New terms, fresh constitutional guarantees might make another Union desirable. But in this, we will soon be deprived of every defence against the Northern section."

Wanting nothing to do with a plan that smacked of disunion, the Virginians rebuffed Memminger. The most they were willing to consider was a convention of all the states in the Union. D. H. Hamilton, the federal marshal in Charleston, denounced Memminger's mission as a farce, adding that any conference he could have arranged would have ended "in smoke after a declaration of rights." A disgusted Memminger concluded that in the absence of collective resistance, "we shall finally be brought to the point of making the issue alone and taking our chance for the other States to join us, whenever a Black Republican has the rub over us."[6]

In the buildup to the Charleston Convention in late April, South Carolina radicals and their allies in the Lower South outlined a vision of how to redeem the South and rally the masses to secession. If South Carolina were to act alone and pull the states of the Cotton South into a secession movement, the first step had to be breaking free from the national Democratic Party. As far as the radicals were concerned, the Democrats under the leadership of Douglas were indistinguishable from the Republicans in threatening the future of slavery. If slavery in the territories were made contingent on the will of the majority, the radicals believed it never could expand. Free of the need to compromise, the Southern Democrats could appeal directly to whites to join them in a crusade to secure the rights and security of the South. The upcoming Charleston Convention offered a perfect opportunity to orchestrate a sectional split of the Democrats and lay the groundwork for a Southern state's rights' party. Triggering the split would be an ultimatum laid down to the Douglas majority at the convention to abandon popular sovereignty and endorse the Southern position that it was the constitutional duty of the federal government to protect slavery in the territories whenever it was threatened. Once the Democrats refused, the walkout of the Southern delegates would begin.[7]

Jettisoning a Democratic Party tethered to Douglas would serve many ends. Closest to home for the South Carolina radicals, it would derail Orr's National Democratic movement in the upcountry that sought an end to the lowcountry planters' stranglehold on state politics. William Henry Trescott, an absentee lowcountry planter serving in the State Department, wrote from Washington in February that the Orr movement had divided political sentiment in the state with those favoring the National Democrats almost as strong as the states' righters. He had no doubts that Orr and his followers would go along with Douglas and his popular sovereignty platform in hopes of gaining patronage and support in the event that Douglas won the presidency. Planter and longtime Charleston postmaster Alfred Huger warned Congressman William Porcher Miles in early April that Orr was aligned with Douglas and would barter away South Carolina's rights. Sharing this view, D. H. Hamilton was concerned that if Douglas prevailed at Charleston, "a pretty strong party" on his behalf would develop in the state.[8]

On the eve of the Charleston Convention, Edward Spann Hammond wrote his father that while Douglas would be the strongest candidate against a Republican, the South was quite divided over him. Unity in defeat, he felt, would be a more favorable outcome for the South than any victory under Douglas. Convinced that the lure of offices would draw ambitious politicians in the South to Douglas, S. D. Moore of Alabama wanted what he dubbed a "States Rights Resistance party." The new party would decry "the honors & instruments of the Union Govt. as 'forbidden fruit' to the true men of the South." He concluded that "the Union has to be dissolved or the South has to be subjected."[9]

The Charleston Convention met in a city seething with secessionist fervor. The star of the convention was William Lowndes Yancey, the "prince of the fire-eaters," whose oratory played masterfully to his adoring followers in the galleries, one-third of whom were women. Yancey's melodious voice was a valuable commodity in the rural South, where illiteracy was high, life hard, and pleasures few. A gifted speaker, whether at a revival meeting or a political barbecue, was a source of both information and entertainment. A successful politician needed the physical stamina to deliver dozens of speeches for hours on end while on the campaign circuit. No wonder so many of them had florid complexions flushed by the whiskey they drank to combat the rigors and fatigue of campaigning. Yancey's speeches were rich in imagery, biblical allusions, and reiteration of simple themes that appealed to the prejudices and aggrieved sensibilities of his Southern audiences. Above all, his rhetoric hammered away at the need of Southern whites to assert their absolute equality in the Union and reject all moral aspersions cast on slavery.[10]

Yancey's traumatic childhood had shaped his adult personality in which he acted out the psychosocial role of the victimized Southern white demanding from Northerners a recognition of the inherent goodness of the South's slave society. A native of Georgia, whose father died of yellow fever when he was three, he was uprooted from his childhood home when his stepfather, Presbyterian minister Nathan Beman, moved the family to Troy, New York. As an adolescent, Yancey stood by helplessly as Beman beat his mother and on more than one occasion locked her in a closet. A convert to abolitionism, Beman represented for Yancey the North writ large—hypocritical, piously rigid, and cruelly self-righteous in denouncing slavery.

Yancey moved to South Carolina in the 1830s, studied law, and acquired instant planter status through a marriage that brought him thirty-five slaves. His future seemed assured when he purchased a plantation near Cahaba, Alabama. On a return visit to South Carolina in 1838, he became entangled in a family feud with his wife's uncle and killed him in a street brawl. After serving a three-month prison term, he returned permanently to Alabama only to see some of his slaves accidentally poisoned in a feud between overseers. Strapped for cash when cotton prices plunged in the Panic of 1837, he sold off most of his remaining slaves.

While the income from his law practice enabled him to support his family and slowly restock his slave holdings, Yancey served briefly in the Alabama legislature and in Congress in the 1840s, where he stamped himself as a fire-brand political moralist protecting the innocent, wronged South from the malignant assaults of the abolitionists. Having neither the temperament nor self-discipline to engage in the politician's role of compromising and cutting deals, he resigned his congressional seat in 1846 but continued to play the role of the agitator.

In 1848, he authored the Alabama Platform demanding federal recognition and protection of slavery in the territories, including those recently acquired in the Mexican War where slavery had been prohibited under Mexican law. When the Democratic nominating convention rejected the platform, Yancey walked out, joined by only one other delegate. Yancey left the party and was a key figure in the organization of the Alabama Southern Rights Party. In 1860, he convinced

the Alabama legislature to back his platform of 1848 and to instruct the state's
delegates to bolt the Democratic Convention if the platform was not accepted.
Governor A. B. Moore was also pressured into calling for a secession convention
in the event of a Republican victory. This time Yancey would no longer be an
isolated provocateur.[11]

The delegates from the cotton states went to Charleston determined to rule or
ruin. Part of their intransigence stemmed from the disturbing electoral map. The
slave states combined had 120 electoral votes, and some Northern states had to
be carried to reach the needed majority of 152. To have a chance of gaining support in any of the free states, a softening of the stance on slavery in the territories
was needed, but that would have destroyed hopes of Southern unity and played
into the hands of the Whig-Americans in the South who were already attacking
the Democrats for supporting popular sovereignty. Second, these delegates were
out on a limb in that their legislatures had instructed them to accept nothing less
than the Alabama Platform. Breaking up the Democratic Party was preferable to
splintering Southern ranks and betraying Southern codes of honor.

In his speech on April 28, Yancey passionately appealed to Southern pride.
Just as Lincoln had done in his Illinois debates with Douglas, he zeroed in on the
morality of slavery as the issue that had to be resolved. Turning Lincoln's logic
on its head, he insisted that a generation of Northern actions based on the false
premise that slavery was wrong had demoralized Southerners and drained their
will to stand up for their rights and equality in the Union. Only a direct, open
acknowledgment of the moral soundness of slavery could purify poisonous
Northern opinion, stop further aggressions against slavery, and steel Southerners
for the defense of their rights and property. To drive home his point, Yancey
played on Southern fears that slavery was a ticking time bomb as a result of outside meddling. "Ours is the property invaded—ours the interests at stake. . . .
Bear with us, then, if, as we stand on what is but a sleeping volcano, we say to
you, to you we will not yield our position." And they did not. When the Douglas
majority endorsed a popular sovereignty platform on April 30, the Alabama contingent led a walkout of delegates from the Lower South. Charleston erupted
in celebration. "There was a Fourth of July feeling in Charleston last night—a
jubilee," observed a convention reporter. A joyous Yancey told a well-wisher
that "even now, the pen of the historian was nibbed to write the story of a new
Revolution."[12]

That revolution got off to an uncertain start. The seceders assembled in a
nearby hall with many of them expecting that their show of resolve would force
the chastened Douglasites into fresh negotiations resulting in a compromise
candidate and a platform acceptable to the South. They obtained neither. For the
Douglas managers, the withdrawal of the Southerners had seemingly left them
with a clear path to nominate their man, but they were in for a rude shock. As a

result of parliamentary maneuverings by the New York delegation headed by the pro-Southern Fernando Wood, the convention ruled that a two-thirds majority of the original delegate body, and not of the quorum left after the defections, was necessary for the presidential nomination. After fifty-seven rounds of balloting, the convention adjourned with an agreement to meet again in Baltimore in three weeks.[13]

While the radicals worried that a meaningless compromise might entice the bolters to return to Baltimore, the ranks of the Southern Democrats were divided. L. Q. C. Lamar of Mississippi, one of the Southern congressmen who signed an address urging the seceders to give the Democrats one last chance, outlined the position of the conservative Democrats. His views and those of Jefferson Davis were that the Southerners should not have left over the platform, "a mere verbal symbol," but should have secured a more solid victory over Douglas by uniting behind a nominee who agreed with "our principle."[14]

Southern Whigs were appalled by the whole affair. "Perfectly disgusted with the politicians, who will probably set fire to the Country so that they may be conspicuous by the illumination" was Georgia King's summary of her father's response to the Charleston walkout. Many Whigs believed that disunion was what the split at Charleston had been about from the start. F. L. Claiborne of Mississippi flatly stated that the "seceders were wrong." He could not fathom how the Democrats' Cincinnati Platform of 1856 on popular sovereignty, once viewed as "a Holy political Bible," could now be found wanting. Besides, he noted, a majority at the Charleston Convention had adopted a platform pledged to accept any ruling by the Supreme Court on the rights of slavery in the territories and expected that any ruling would favor the South unless the Court were abolitionized in the meantime. It was obvious to Claiborne that only the national Democratic Party could defeat the Republicans in the presidential election and that dividing it would virtually ensure a Republican victory. "The Election of such a President would result in breaking up the federal Union—therefore the Seceders at Charleston are disunionists."[15]

Before the Democrats reconvened in Baltimore, two candidates entered the presidential race. Whig-Americans, mostly from the Upper South, met at Baltimore in early May and nominated an old Whig, John Bell of Tennessee. Advanced years, along with respectability, were the distinguishing features of the Bell supporters who formed the new Constitutional Union Party. They came from an older generation of politicians pledged to preserving the Union. As journalist Murat Halstead noted, though "somewhat stale in politics," they were "fully resolved to save the country." Convinced that scheming politicians caring only for the spoils of office had recklessly agitated the slavery question to the brink of destroying the Union, they offered a voice of nonpartisan reason that would restore sectional harmony by upholding the Union, honoring the Constitution,

and trusting the courts to settle the issue of slavery in the territories. Their platform amounted to little more than that.[16]

The Republicans gathered in Chicago at the Wigwam, a specially constructed
convention site. Somewhat surprisingly, they rejected the party's best-known
leader, William Seward of New York, for Lincoln of Illinois. Seward was more
conservative than Lincoln, but his "Irrepressible Conflict" speech of 1858 had
saddled him with the label of a radical. He had argued, as had Lincoln in his
"House-Divided" speech, that the nation must commit to freedom or slavery,
and that he was confident that the superiority of free-labor values and productivity would triumph over the slave-based society of the South. He envisioned
the Northern victory to be a peaceful, inevitable one, but his phrase "irrepressible conflict" conjured up a violent confrontation for his critics. The seemingly
more moderate Lincoln had the additional advantage of being the favorite son in
a critical swing state that the Republicans had lost in 1856. Though toned down
from 1856, the platform retained its antislavery bite with its demand that slavery
be kept out of the territories and freedom enshrined as a national principle. To
broaden the party's appeal, the platform offered subsidies—free homesteads, a
protective tariff, and a Pacific railroad—to stimulate a Northern economy still
not fully recovered from the financial Panic of 1857.

The Bell and Lincoln nominations increased the pressure on the Douglas
Democrats and the Southern defectors to yield nothing in their party feud.
Lincoln would be a formidable candidate and the Douglas Democrats wanted
to go with their most popular leader in the free states. Bell, likely to do well in
the Upper South, presented Southerners with a conciliatory figure sure to brand
popular sovereignty as backdoor abolitionism.

Save for the South Carolinians, who remained in Richmond, the bolting
delegates returned to the Democrats' convention at Baltimore. A second walkout
quickly resulted when the convention refused to seat the seceding delegates
from Louisiana and Alabama and accepted the pro-Douglas delegates chosen
in those states. It was all shadow boxing, for there was no reason to believe that
the gulf over the platform on slavery in the territories could be bridged. While
the convention nominated Douglas, the bolters at another site in Baltimore
nominated John C. Breckinridge of Kentucky Buchanan's vice-president. The
South Carolinians in Richmond duly seconded the choice.

As the rupture of the Democrats was finalized, the setting in Baltimore revealed that the secessionists' fervor would meet a cool reception outside the
Cotton South. Hundreds of spectators left in the middle of Yancey's speech at
Baltimore out of boredom. More ominously for the future, the Douglas men,
especially those from the present-day Midwest, went home embittered. After
having stood up to the bragging, taunts, and arrogance of the slaveholders, they
were furious that the seceders had alienated their best friends in the North and

hoped the Southerners would suffer the consequences of treating those friends like they were their slaves. One of the Westerners told Halstead that he wished the "South . . . would sweat under an Abolition President." Another said that "if there was to be a fight between sections, he was for his own side of the Ohio." Committed Southern radicals, however, could hardly have been more pleased. A party of and for the South was finally in place. Rhett's *Charleston Mercury* crowed: "The great object was accomplished. The South was united in the vindication of her rights."[17]

The Campaign in the South: Seedtime for Disunion

Given the exclusion of the Republicans from the ballot box in most of the slave states, the campaign in the South was a three-cornered affair. The Breckinridge forces were dominant in the Lower South, where they controlled the local machinery of the majority Democratic Party. They buttressed this organizational strength with appeals to the voters that galvanized white anxieties and hopes in an ideological stance that amplified the thrust of slave society in the late 1850s. At the core of that ideology was a sense of crisis.

With imagery that spoke directly to white frustrations over shrinking opportunities for advancement in the 1850s, the Breckinridge press sketched out an apocalyptic vision of what would result from a Republican administration. Lincoln was labeled an abolitionist who headed a party of fanatics who would unceasingly attack slavery. They would begin by prohibiting the expansion of slavery and then shut down the internal slave trade. Confined to its present limits, slavery would become unprofitable and then "ferment—and last be abolished." No amount of reasoning could sway the Republicans from what Jefferson Davis called their "fiendish plot" of starving out the slaves by penning them up in a space too small to allow them to be cared for by their masters. Rather than fashioning themselves as philanthropists, the Republicans, said Davis, should be manly enough "to seek to exterminate [the slaves] by the sword rather than in this slow process to confine them until, steeped in misery, they should at last be exterminated."[18]

The alternative to this hellish scenario was, of course, to give slavery free rein to expand. Posing as the champions of constitutional liberties, the Breckinridge Democrats insisted they were seeking only the equal treatment granted them by the Supreme Court in the Dred Scott case. By declaring the Missouri Compromise to have been unconstitutional, the Court gave Southerners, especially the radicals, a tremendous moral boost. When that victory was eviscerated by Douglas's use of popular sovereignty to secure free status for Kansas, the radicals claimed the right to federal protection of slavery in the territories. In so doing, they shrugged off the justifiable complaints of many Southerners that such a demand violated Calhoun's cardinal tenet that the admission of any congressional control over slavery was an unacceptable risk to the institution.

Convinced (as were Republicans) that the confinement of slavery meant its destruction, Breckinridge Southerners demanded its expansion. "How are we to preserve the institution of slavery?" asked O. R. Singleton, a Democratic congressman from Mississippi. "There is but one mode [and that] is by expansion, and that expansion must be in the direction of Mexico." Even more alluring were the lush tropics. Resolutions demanding the acquisition of Spain's slave colony of Cuba were passed by Democratic county conventions in the late 1850s, especially in eastern Mississippi, the stronghold of Senator A. G. Brown. "I want Cuba, and I know that sooner or later we must have it," thundered Brown on the Senate floor. "I want Tamaulipas, Potosi, and one or two other Mexican States, and I want them all for the same reason—for the planting or spreading of slavery." With such a glorious tropical empire, the South would have room for all its slaves as they continued to multiply, access to valuable minerals, a monopoly on the world's production of tropical goods, and a guarantee of ongoing control over international cotton markets.[19]

The Breckinridge men tried to persuade Northerners that the extension of slavery was also to their economic advantage. The slave-produced staples of the South, they reasoned, were indispensable to the national economy, for not only did those staples form the basis of US exports, but planters, by specializing in them, created a home market for the surplus agricultural production of the West. This appeal for a political alliance of agrarians in the South and West fell flat except in the lower Ohio Valley, an area settled predominantly by upland Southern whites who still relied on the Ohio and Mississippi rivers to ship their goods to Southern markets. By the 1850s, the farm economies elsewhere in the Midwest were being integrated with the manufacturing centers of the Northeast as the railroads shipped an ever-higher volume of grain and meat eastward for consumption or export. In turn, the prosperous West absorbed a growing amount of manufactured goods. These economic linkages took the mutually advantageous political form of calls for homesteads, land grants to railroads, some tariff protection, liberal immigration policies, and free soil. By opposing all these measures, the South had only increased its political isolation.[20]

The Bell and Douglas forces retorted that the Breckinridge Democrats had driven away the Northern friends of the South over a territorial issue that was a "humbug and a cheat," a cheap device of demagogues to court votes. They had broken up the Democratic Party over an issue "wholly destitute of any practical meaning," charged the pro-Bell *New Orleans Bee*. Whether slavery ever became established in a territory would be settled not by granting powers to a changeable Congress but by laws of climate and soil that had always decided where slavery would go. A Douglas supporter in North Carolina felt that the principle that precipitated the walkout at Charleston "amounted to nothing in the end. There is no more territory fit for slavery and as for squatter sovereignty if free soilers are in the majority in a territory it will be a free state after its admission into the Union, anyhow." John A. Campbell of Alabama, one of the Southern judges on the Supreme Court who ruled against Dred Scott, repeated a common refrain of the Douglasites that the South's greatest need was more slaves, not more territory. By his reasoning, it would take twenty-five years to fill up Louisiana, Mississippi, Arkansas, and Texas with slaves. *"If men must extend slavery, let them come out for the African slave trade,"* taunted the *Memphis Daily Appeal,* "but do not be quarreling about the miserable twaddle of slavery protection by Breckinridge, or of intervention to destroy it on the other hand by Lincoln."[21]

The Bell camp argued that the Breckinridge movement was putting slavery at risk by needlessly threatening to break up the Union. They admitted that there were inevitable antagonisms between the free North and the slave South but insisted they were not irreconcilable. As proof that conservatives of both sections could work together amicably based on common interests, they pointed to the representatives of Northern capital many of whom were among the parties' leaders. Surely the Boston textile manufacturer or the New York cotton exporter had a vital stake in the preservation of slavery. Besides, not all Republicans were guilty of antislavery prejudices. Many, they said, were drawn to the party by its promises of promoting economic growth. Others joined out of disgust with the recently exposed corruption in the Buchanan administration.[22]

The moderates conceded that the South would have to expand eventually, but they believed this would not be imperative for at least a generation and counseled patience. They asserted that southern California could still be won for slavery and noted that the anarchy in northern Mexico made these states easy prey for Southern expansionists. The passage of proslavery legislation by the territory of New Mexico was held up by the Douglas press as a success story for popular sovereignty. If such an area not especially attractive for slavery could be gained, "cannot the South afford to trust the same principle when we acquire more Territory from Mexico *still further South,* and with slavery already established in the North and East so that fugitives cannot escape to free territory?"[23]

The Breckinridge men dismissed this defense of popular sovereignty as mere cant and hypocrisy. New Mexico, they pointed out, was hardly a fair test of the Douglas doctrine. Very few settlers had moved into this sparsely populated territory and many of the slave owners were transient army personnel who happened to own a few slaves. No amount of special pleading in their view could change the fact that "if slave property be not adequately and sufficiently protected in the Territories, by statutory law, it will not go to them." Slave interests, they argued, were too endangered in the present to place any faith in vague hopes for the future. The South needed immediate guarantees of equal access to the current and, most certainly, future territories before the Republican menace became too powerful. As for the claim that the demand for protection was an abstraction, William P. Miles retorted that "if that be so, it is most extraordinary that our Northern brethren should be unwilling to yield to us this purely abstract prin-ciple of Constitutional right." For Miles, it was "too practical a question to yield." The South faced "the crisis of her future. If she does not stand now, she is ruined forever."[24]

The Bell Whigs joined the chorus of condemnation of popular sovereignty. Benjamin H. Hill, long a power in the Georgia Whig Party, branded Douglas as unacceptable as any Republican and warned that popular sovereignty was "as aggressive and unconstitutional dogma as any ever enunciated by the New York agitator at Rochester or in the Senate chambers." Parson Brownlow, a feisty Whig editor in Knoxville, denounced "Squatter Sovereignty" as "an abolition heresy which threatened to destroy the South." When it came to slavery, popular majorities just would not do.[25]

In contrast to the uproar over slavery in the territories, the reopening of the African slave trade was a muted issue. Future Breckinridge Democrats were in the forefront of the movement at the Vicksburg Southern Convention in May 1859. Aware of the divisiveness of the issue at a time when the need for Southern unity was paramount, the Breckinridge men tried to keep it in the background in 1860. In explaining to Jefferson Davis why he had voted with Whig opposition at Vicksburg, Democrat H. J. Harris stressed that "I honestly thought the demo-cratic party would be destroyed by the agitation of the question *at this time.*" Still, reopening was favored in the Carolina lowcountry and the lower Mississippi Valley, and when the Breckinridge Democrats did bring up the slave trade, they invariably linked it to the acquisition of more territory in a program that would restore the South to its former glory in the Union and eventually enable it to eclipse the North in power and prestige.[26]

The territorial and slave trade demands inevitably raised the question of the value of the existing Union to the South. So closely identified was the Breckinridge party with these issues and so unlikely was their attainment within the Union that the Bell and Douglas parties argued that campaigning on them was merely a pretext for disunion. This charge provided conservatives with their most effective campaign appeal. In announcing for Bell, the *Hayneville* (Ala.) *Watchman* positioned his party as a safe alternative to the mad designs of the Breckinridge camp that would culminate in fomenting a revolution in the cotton states. The *Natchez Daily Courier* tied the territorial question to the Breckinridge candidacy as part of the same plan that "originated in the mad scheme of certain ambitious, disaffected, would-be leaders, who hope to bring about a dissolution of the Union."[27]

The sequence of events in 1860 lent credence to the charge of disunion—the ultimatum to the Northern Democrats at Charleston, the ensuing walkout of the Southern delegates, the confirmation of a divided party in June, and by the summer a drumbeat of calls for secession from Breckinridge politicians if the Republicans won the presidency. An indeterminate number of states' righters were hoping for, even expecting, Lincoln's election to precipitate secession. That was Rhett's plan all along and he had plenty of company from lowcountry planters in South Carolina. One of them, William M. Lawton from Rhett's Beaufort District, boasted in May that *"my man for the Presidency* is the most ultra Black Republican abolitionist to be found, hoping that in the event of his election, the Southern States may be forced or kicked into an organization of such a Government as I wish to see established."[28]

No evidence, however, reveals that many of the Charleston bolters viewed their actions as the first step in a deliberate effort to form an independent Southern nation. Most of them walked out in frustration over their inability to dictate policy to a Democratic Party they had lost control of. Many of them, such as Powhatan Ellis from the Mississippi delegation, believed that if they were unable to reunite with the Northern Democrats at Baltimore, Lincoln would nonetheless fail to win an electoral majority and secession would not be necessary. In May, Ellis viewed Lincoln as a weak candidate, "not known to public fame," whose unpopularity in the mid-Atlantic states would produce a divided vote in the North and deprive Lincoln of an electoral majority. Such an outcome was just what Miles and most of the bolters expected if four candidates were in the field. "In all probability," Miles thought, the election would be thrown into Congress. If, as he assumed, the House failed to make a selection from the three highest vote getters, the Senate would choose an acting president from the two highest vice-presidential candidates. Since the Senate was safely Democratic, Southern interests would not be abandoned.[29]

In response to being labeled disunionists, the Breckinridge party launched a counteroffensive. Their slogan—"Disunion which follows a perverted Union, is the work of the perverters"—epitomized this approach. Northerners, they proclaimed, were the aggressors who had violated the Constitution and threatened the very existence of the South. In a choice between their liberties or their debasement, Southerners would make the same choice as had their patriotic forefathers in the American Revolution. When the Breckinridge press, usually in the Upper South, did acknowledge the gravity of the disunionist charge, they dared their opponents to produce solid evidence of treasonable plotting. Assuring its readers that no such evidence existed, the *Louisville Daily Courier*

dismissed the accusation as the reckless tactic of those who suffered from a
"want of faith in their own principles."[30]

The Breckinridge forces were confident of victory as long as they could hold
onto the support of non-slaveholders, who had returned large majorities for the
Democrats in the Lower South since the days of Jackson. The fear was that non-
slaveholders would be drawn to Douglas and his call for popular majorities to
rule. To prevent that, the Breckinridge press continued the usual Democratic
practice of posing as the special friend to the common whites. "As a class, there
are no men [in] the South truer to her institutions, more zealous in defence of
her rights, or more jealousy of any encroachments upon her interests than the
non-slaveholding population," gushed a Breckinridge paper. Such hyperbole,
however, opened up the party to the charge of fostering abolitionism with its
"miserable demagoguery." As the *Vicksburg Whig*, a spokesman for the wealthy
Delta planters, gleefully noted: "It is criminal and wicked—aye, it is anti-
Southern and free-soilish—thus to encourage persons not to purchase slaves.
It is the most direct and certain method of limiting the number of slave-owners,
and thereby lessening the interest in the perpetuity of the institution which only
the master can feel." Such lauding of slaveless whites as the prime beneficiaries
of slavery was tantamount to rallying public opinion against the slaveholder
and calling him an abolitionist if he professed his property to be safe within the
Union. In this Whig critique, the real abolitionists were those who so slandered
their fellow citizens. True statesmanship required an emphasis on the virtues of
slave ownership as the proper reward for diligence and ambition.[31]

The Whigs also targeted the Douglasites for unconscionable appeals to non-
slaveholders, and the Breckinridge men were concerned as well. As the pro-
Breckinridge *Montgomery Advertiser* noted, to do well in the South, Douglas had
to attract the non-slaveholders' vote. If he succeeded, "it will raise up throughout
the South—what has never been there before—a political party composed
mainly of non-slaveholders, and arrayed in opposition to that supreme control
over the politics of Southern States, which the slaveholding interest has always
enjoyed."[32]

The rumored existence of a mysterious poor man's abolitionist society known
as the Friends Z Society offered further proof that planters had to be vigilant.
Centered in southwestern Alabama and across the state line in Mississippi, the
society was reported to have more than a hundred members who had taken
an oath against fighting to protect the property of the rich. The Breckinridge
editor Isaac Grant shuddered at the sentiments expressed in a letter that originally appeared in a Mobile newspaper. Identifying himself only as a National
Democrat, the letter writer was a non-slaveholder. He bitterly complained about
having to hire slaves at exorbitant prices and warned the planters and their
"dupes" that men such as himself valued the Union over slavery. If secession ever

occurred, he predicted the outbreak of class warfare. Grant labeled the letter "about as first-rate a specimen of abolition sentiment and incendiarism as could be found in the wigwam of Chicago or the Tabernacle in New York."[33]

In the last month of the campaign, South Carolina congressman Laurence Keitt warned Miles that if a Union party were to form in the South, it "now means an abolition party—not at first, it may be—but through quick transitions." From the perspective of the radicals, the outlying areas of slavery bordering the free states were crumbling, and emancipation was just a matter of time. Of greatest concern were the nascent Republican parties that had organized in the border states of Missouri, Kentucky, Maryland, Delaware, and even the northwestern region of Virginia.[34]

The collapse of slavery had already occurred in what some Southerners had expected would be its new outpost of Kansas. Although victory seemed to be within reach when the proslavery Lecompton Constitution was sent to Congress in 1857 with Buchanan's backing, planting slavery on the Kansas prairies was always a chimera. Jonathan Worth, a North Carolina Whig, spoke for his party and many Democrats when he wrote in 1858: "I have no idea slavery will long exist in Kansas and think we are fighting for a shadow." The South, as advocates for reopening the African slave trade ceaselessly preached, lacked the slaves to colonize the area. Planters seeking new lands had far more economically attractive places to send their slaves.[35]

Radicals such as Robert Barnwell Rhett Jr., editor of the *Charleston Mercury*, valued Kansas as "a great sectional issue," which, win or lose, would bolster their cause by exacerbating sectional tensions and arousing "a progressive Southern feeling . . . through the Southern States." But in the end, the effort to gain Kansas backfired. Hopes were raised that no amount of bullying could fulfill, Whigs and Democrats in the Upper South opposed the Lecompton swindle, and Southern pride was wounded. Worse yet, the violence spawned in Kansas by the Missouri Ruffians, proslavery activists who crossed the border and attacked free-state settlements, recoiled back against Missouri as the Kansas Jayhawkers invaded the state in 1860 and carried off slaves.[36]

In the border states a durable network of free-soil newspapers appeared in the early 1850s that laid the groundwork for the organization of Republican parties. The major papers came out of manufacturing cities, such as Wheeling in the Virginia panhandle, St. Louis with its diversified manufacturing and river-based economy, and Wilmington, Delaware, with its light industry and port facilities close to Philadelphia. These papers proudly proclaimed, as did the *Wheeling Intelligencer*, that they represented "those slave States where freedom of speech is not wholly stifled." Common to all of them was a working-class constituency receptive to their Helper-like indictment of slavery for pitting free laborers against slaves, stunting public education, and suppressing free speech. Their stand against slavery was generally quite conservative, saying little of taking active steps against the institution or in favor of black rights and instead stressing the need for gradual emancipation accompanied by colonization.[37]

Beginning in the 1840s, another long-range approach to emancipation involved Northern-sponsored free-labor enclaves in the upper portions of the Border South. In 1846, John C. Underwood, a New Yorker, established a string of dairy farms in the Shenandoah Valley on land his Virginia wife, a cousin of Thomas (later nicknamed Stonewall) Jackson, had brought into their marriage. A decade later, Underwood, now a Republican, co-founded with Eli Thayer of Massachusetts the American Emigrant Aid and Homestead Society. Their plan was to entice Northerners to move to the Border South by offering them land at far cheaper prices than prevailed in the North. When the Panic of 1857 made it difficult to raise capital, they changed their business plan to a commission-based matching of land sellers in the South with Northern buyers. Underwood's efforts attracted perhaps as many as 5,000 settlers to the uplands of Appalachia and another 500 to a separate colony of Thayer's in northwestern Virginia. Emancipation was soft-pedaled in favor of demonstrating the superiority of a free-labor economy. If their plans materialized, thrifty, efficient free-labor farms would push out wasteful slave agriculture, accelerate the drain of slaves to the Lower South, and enable a rapidly whitening Upper South to make a seamless transition to emancipation.[38]

More openly political in their emancipationist designs were the two leading Republicans who emerged in the Border South by the late 1850s. Cassius M. Clay, the son of a planter and a cousin of the illustrious Henry Clay, was the best-known Republican to come out of Kentucky. He also was one of its most tepid antislavery crusaders. Chastened by his defeat in 1849 when his Emancipation Party failed badly to place gradual emancipation without colonization in Kentucky's revised constitution, he dropped any references to justice for blacks, backed colonization, and redoubled economic appeals to non-slaveholders. When the Republican Party formed in 1854, he found the ally he needed in his battles against Kentucky's entrenched slaveholding interests. Attaching himself to the moderate wing of the party, Clay hoped that access to federal patronage if the Republicans ever captured the presidency would propel him to the governorship at the head of a party that could offer tangible benefits to Kentuckians willing to work against slavery.[39]

Francis P. Blair Jr. of Missouri promoted the same colonization effort with a direct racist pitch to whites. Seeking to live up to the political fame garnered by his father, Francis P. Blair Sr., a key adviser to Jackson in the 1830s, he won two terms in Congress in the late 1850s as the South's only congressman opposed to slavery. In a speech at the Cooper Institute in January 1860, he called for the removal of all free blacks in a federally sponsored program to purchase land in the

American tropics that would be economically redeemed by the labor of a race biologically suited to working in a hot, sticky climate. The removal of free blacks would spark an economic boom. Those who agreed to freeing their slaves would reap fabulous profits from the tropical staples produced by the freed slaves and with these windfall gains would be more than handsomely rewarded for having manumitted their slaves, who then would be both free men and landowners far removed from the continental United States. At home, the lands of slaveholders would skyrocket in value as more efficient white labor replaced the displaced slaves who had "deprived them of employment." Surely, Blair reasoned, slave owners would choose this peaceful path to emancipation and an all-white society over the class-driven "danger of convulsion" looming over the slave South.[40]

This conservative antislavery position, like that of Clay and most of the border state Republicans, was precisely what planters in the Cotton South feared most. By offering a gradual end to slavery made painless by eliminating freed blacks from the labor market, it promised to be attractive to the South's white majority of non-slaveholders.

Except for Missouri, the voting base of the Southern Republican parties was minuscule, but the very existence of these parties terrified Southern radicals. Evincing absolutely no confidence in the loyalty of slaveless whites to slave interests, the *Charleston Mercury* foresaw "thousands" of those obsequious to power and desirous of personal gain flocking to the "Abolition Government" in the event of Lincoln's victory. They would organize at first into a Union party and in short order become an "Abolition Party in the South." Once that happened, the struggle over slavery would no longer be confined to the North against the South but would be fought out "between the people of the South." The pro-Breckinridge *New Orleans Delta* was just as alarmed when it stated as a certainty that Republican parties would form in every Southern state soon after Lincoln's election. What better reason, asked the radicals, could the South have for secession?[41]

A South in Crisis: Drought and Insurrectionary Panics

The Breckinridge campaign fed off deepening white Southern insecurities as a prolonged drought in 1860 and a flood of rumors of plots for slave uprisings resulted in food shortages and images of bloody slave violence. Worsened by the searing heat that dried up wells, creeks, and groundwater tables, the drought decimated the corn crop, the staple of the Southern diet along with pork.

Southerners could not recall a summer that had ever been so blisteringly hot and dry. "The heavens are as brass and the streets are as a sea of molten lead" was one paper's description of the intense heat. The drought was particularly devastating in the cotton belt stretching from Piedmont South Carolina through Middle Georgia and across central Alabama and Mississippi into Louisiana. It was here that the cries of distress were the loudest, as common whites faced a collapse of their economic security.[42]

Judge John B. O'Neal of South Carolina reported from Greenville that most of the upcountry would not have "enough corn for home consumption." Letters in the *Savannah Republican* in July detailed the almost ruin of the corn crop in Middle Georgia, with yields down by over half of normal production. "The poor people of this section of Georgia will be compelled to suffer," warned "H. L. M." from Marion County, "if they can't get assistance from the rich men of our country until they can make another crop." An Augusta paper insisted that starvation was not too extreme a term "to use as crops shriveled and cattle died from lack of water." "Is the Corn being made anywhere?" the editor asked. "If this state of things is general, God help the poor this year."[43]

J. J. Williams of the Mississippi Agricultural Bureau described the corn crop in the state as generally "an entire failure." Only the watersheds of the Yazoo and Big Black rivers and the northern tier of counties saw a semblance of normal crops. Conditions in neighboring Alabama and Louisiana were just as bad. As early as May, reports were coming out of Randolph County, Alabama, a hilly area of small farms, of persons "actually starving." By late July, the citizens in Coffee County, a coastal county with poor soil, were talking of petitioning the legislature for debtor stay laws aimed at preventing the levy and sale of property for payment of debts until the next harvest was in. At the same time the *Montgomery Weekly Mail* was ominously noting: "We do not see how a scarcity, approaching famine, is to be avoided in the middle eastern counties, next year." August saw letters pouring into the governor's office demanding a plan from the legislature "by which the people can secure something to live on." The same pleas were coming out of Natchitoches Parish in Louisiana, where the short crops and the suspension of navigation along the Red River cutting off incoming supplies put the poor at risk of starvation.[44]

The worst conditions were in the Lower South, but none of the slave states were spared significant losses. A hurricane hit southern Louisiana in late September, and early frosts in October in the Gulf states ruined much of what was left to be harvested. No matter the cash crop—cotton, tobacco, rice, or sugar—planters were stunned by their losses. Indicative of the shortfalls among cotton planters, Philip Henry Pitts of Alabama recorded in his diary on November 12 that his harvest amounted to only fifty-six bales of cotton. He had made 175 bales in 1859 and expected in the spring to make 125. December brought an end to what one planter pronounced as "perhaps, the most disastrous season that Southern planters ever passed through."[45]

The damage inflicted by the drought rippled through the economy. By July, country merchants were complaining they were unable to make any collections for dry goods sold on credit "because all the money of their customers is necessarily expended on buying provisions." The wealthiest planters, those most likely to have holdings in the Delta or in more than one county, were cushioned against major losses. Most planters and small slaveholders were caught in an economic bind, as their poor crops generated insufficient revenue to pay off the prior year's debts, and the need to purchase foodstuffs forced them into greater debt. The non-slaveholding farmers who had expanded cotton production at the expense of food crops in the 1850s fared the worst. They had no credit cushion to fall back on and no means of buying food supplies.[46]

Planters retained for home consumption what corn they produced and drew on their accounts with factors to finance large purchases of western corn. As a result, supplies of this basic food staple were scarce in the open market and expensive. Railroads reduced their freight rates for corn and, along with steamers and river schooners, brought in large quantities of grain from the West with the bulk consigned for transshipment to the interior. Corn was available in the Mobile market during the summer at 90 cents per bushel, but freightage costs increased its price to well over $1 in the interior. In Montgomery, an important trading center for central Alabama, the seasonal drop in corn prices never occurred. Corn had rarely cost more than 50 cents a bushel in previous summers, but in late July suppliers were getting from $1.25 to $1.30, and the price was expected to rise throughout the fall. Grain and food provisions of all sorts had never been scarcer or more expensive in most areas of northern Georgia and Alabama. Asked the *Blountsville Pioneer*, speaking for an isolated hill county in north-central Alabama where corn was selling for over $2 per bushel, "What will become of us poor devils who have neither corn, or money to buy with?" [47]

Planters in Barbour County, Alabama, where food shortages had cropped up back in March, feared that some of those "poor devils" might take up arms to seize food supplies. In July, the county newspaper cited "reliable authority" for its understanding that "the poorer classes who have not the means of providing themselves with the wants of life . . . will take them by force of arms from those who happen to have them." To head off such confrontations between the haves and have-nots, as well as for humanitarian reasons, planters in the worst hit areas organized Relief Clubs. With contributions of $100 from each of its members, the clubs purchased western grain for distribution by local officials to the poor free of charge. More substantial assistance drawing from state funds had to await the winter.[48]

The severity of the drought had made a food crisis inevitable, but many were quick to blame the overproduction of cotton for making a bad situation worse. Although planters came in for special blame, the same criticism could have been leveled against small slaveholders and many of the ambitious yeoman farmers for getting caught up in the cotton mania. Southern agriculture was less diversified in 1860 than a decade earlier. Advocates of reform had made little headway in the face of the strong global demand for cotton, the cash crop that promised the fastest relief from debts. It was planted on the best land and received the most care, and many planters were loath to divert land and slaves into food production.

As the presidential campaign wore on, the drought became enmeshed in politics. The Breckinridge press assured its readers that the South could draw on the bountiful harvests of the West for the food supplies and animal feed it needed and that any shortages would be short-lived. The political corollary to this economic need was self-evident to the opponents of the Breckinridge party. "Never had there been a more practical argument in favor of binding still closer the bands which hold together the North and South," reasoned an anonymous planter from drought-ravaged Lauderdale County, Mississippi. The leading Douglas paper in Alabama's Tennessee Valley reminded Southerners that the very western Democrats whom the Breckinridge delegates had berated at the Charleston Convention were now those feeding the South in its time of need. Bell papers argued that "a worse time for precipitating the cotton States into a revolution than the present, could not have been selected." What the moderates overlooked was that good times hardly offered the best setting for stirring up a revolution. As the Virginia Whig William Henry Tayloe noted back in January 1860, "Prices are too high & [the] country too prosperous to apprehend disunion & revolution." But by the fall of 1860 those conditions were reversed.[49]

Only a barrage of reports from July through election day in November of abolitionist-inspired slave uprisings unsettled Southern whites more than the drought. Ruined crops, raw politicized emotions, and lurking incendiaries came together in a contagion of fear. As Thomas Gray noted from the drought-plagued Red River country bordering Louisiana and Texas, "Short *crops incendiaries* and *Politicks* form a very [com]bustible mixture or at least carry flame along." Concerns over internal security, always a powerful impulse in a slave society, reached pathological proportions during 1860. Georgia planter J. A. Turner warned in a public essay: "What we are called on to guard against now—this very day, this very hour—is the host of abolition emissaries who are scattered abroad throughout the length and breadth of our land, who permeate the whole of Southern society, who occupy our places of trust and emolument."[50]

The prior election year panic in 1856 began with industrial slaves in Kentucky and Tennessee in the early fall, spread into Missouri and Arkansas, then the Gulf states, and hit Virginia and Maryland by December. The flashpoint setting off fears in 1860 came out of Texas in early August. Newspapers across the South published reports of a fiendish and well-organized conspiracy planning to lay waste northeastern Texas. The instigators and leaders were said to be two Northern preachers, upon whose order the slaves were to strike on the first Monday in August, an election day when the men would be away at the polls. Provisions were to be destroyed, communications cut, arms and ammunition seized, and entire towns burned to the ground, until the whites were helpless and at the mercy of avenging blacks.

The sensational accounts of an apocalyptic slave uprising cited the fires in several towns as evidence that a conspiracy was afoot. The first major fire on July 8 destroyed much of the business district of Dallas. Austin escaped a fire scare in late July, but Henderson went up in smoke on August 5, and a number of smaller towns burned. Initially, no one talked of a conspiracy, since it had not rained in northern Texas since April and temperatures routinely broke 100° so fires could be expected. In a letter home to family in North Carolina, John Hull wrote of the miserable conditions: "Oh! Ingram! It would make you shuder to see Texas at this particular time. . . . The corn is all twisted into shoe-strings & this is the greatest place just now for selling *powder* of any kind I have ever seen." Wooden structures in the towns were a tinderbox. When the fires began, local residents attributed them to the new and very unstable phosphorous matches that many merchants were stocking.[51]

More than anyone, Charles Pryor, the ambitious young editor of the *Dallas Herald*, fit the fires into a conspiratorial framework that created an abolitionist scapegoat for the sufferings of white Texans in their summer of troubles. In a series of letters to Texas newspapers in early August, he purported to lay bare the particulars of the abolitionist plot. He related how the "negroes" of Crill Miller, whom Miller blamed for the burning of his house, confessed "in the course of the examination" to the conspiracy and how it was to unfold.

The Dallas fire was aimed at the destruction of major supplies of arms, ammunition, and provisions warehoused there. Next came the torching of country stores with their lead, powder, and grain. Once the country had been reduced to "helplessness," unable to defend itself, Indians would join Northern abolitionists in the destruction. The conspiracy would run like clockwork, for each county was under the command of a white superintendent who controlled the activities of his sub-lieutenants in command of each of the county's districts. The black conspirators knew only of the actions planned for their districts. The uprising was scheduled to explode on election day and the result would be the slaughter of the whites, with the exception of attractive young women to be saved for ravaging by the black males.[52]

Pryor's account was widely believed, and from August into September, vigilance committees worked to ferret out alleged conspirators. Over 1,200 slaves were reportedly arrested by mid-August and there is no way of knowing how many were whipped and tortured to extract "confessions." The most thorough study of the panic put the minimal number of those executed at thirty, the best known of whom was Anthony Bewley, a minister in the Northern Methodist Church. After he fled to Missouri, a posse out of Fort Worth tracked him down, returned him to Fort Worth, and released him into the hands of a waiting lynch mob. As in all conspiratorial fantasies, the absence of proof became proof itself. After a Vermonter was arrested by a vigilance committee in Springfield, Texas, and soon released for lack of any proof against him, Mary Starnes worried that the committee had acted prematurely and that "somehow our committee got wind of him before he got fairly to work." She felt that the committee should have waited him out, intercepted his mail, and "given him a little more rope." Now that the Northerner was on the alert, he likely would not attempt anything in the area, but, Starnes fretted, "he may go to another county where he is not known and do mischief."[53]

Not a shred of hard evidence was ever produced to support the conspiracy thesis. A clumsily written letter purportedly penned by the plotters outlining their plans was found to be almost certainly a forgery. What passed for evidence were confessions extracted "under the lash." Stockpiled caches of arms and poison were never found. Yet, conditioned by a generation of Southern denunciations of fiendish abolitionists, whites were prepared to believe the worst regardless of the facts. For Breckinridge editors such as Pryor, the Texas slave plot was further confirmation of the terrible fate awaiting the South if Lincoln was elected.[54]

News of the events in Texas quickly filtered into every corner of the South. In the Alabama black belt, Sarah R. Espy was convinced the "country is getting in a deplorable state owing to the depredations committed by the Abolitionists especially in Texas [and that] the safety of the country depend[s] on who is elected to the presidency." She could not have been comforted when reports surfaced of abolitionist plots in the surrounding area. The *Sumter Democrat* cited the discovery of hidden arms in Greene County, the arrest of an itinerant abolitionist in Wilcox, and the rumor of an abolitionist soap dealer in Sumter. The "enemy' was everywhere, according to the *Montgomery Advertiser*, "prowling about our very doors, and the torch of the incendiary lights up the whole Northern horizon in the onward march of the enemy."[55]

Nothing short of paranoia gripped whites in Mississippi and Alabama. The Mississippi panic was centered in a belt of counties in its east-central region where drought conditions most resembled those in Texas. One plot was discovered in Leake County in which five whites and forty slaves were arrested. That was soon followed by reports of a Texas-style plot in a string of eastern counties. The alleged ringleaders, said to have been allies of John Brown, were "an old man named Gilbert and the preacher McDonald." The most detailed account, and one that followed a pattern of self-fulfilling expectations, came out of Wayne

County near Plattsburgh. In late September, while undergoing "a pretty severe" punishment for some infraction, a cook revealed "an important secret to [her owner] Mr. Kelly, if he would desist." The secret concerned plans for a "general uprising" of local slaves and those "of the whole adjacent county, in concert with certain white men." The signal for the uprising was to be the poisoning of the planter families by their cooks. The alarmed Kelly rounded up half a dozen men and went around to plantations indiscriminately whipping slaves. His neighbors then organized a vigilance committee to meet weekly and pass judgment on the suspected culprits. The committee's executive council of twelve was authorized to render whatever judgment it saw fit since the law was "too tardy in its course, even if it could be effectual in its process, to obviate the dangers and punish the offenders in troubles of this character." A week later, the slaves "induced to make confessions" were said to have substantiated the cook-woman's story. On the basis of that evidence, thirty slaves and a white man were arrested. The latter was G. Harrington, a traveling ambrotypist from the North, who had aroused suspicions since his arrival in May because of his frequent conversations with slaves. At least one slave and a white, identified only as "an abolition artist," and probably Harrington, were hanged.[56]

By mid-October, reports surfaced across Mississippi of a number of contemplated insurrections, but the *Oxford Mercury* dismissed them as "wholly groundless, or magnified from a mole-hill into a mountain." In commenting on a rumored plot in Warren County, the *Vicksburg Whig* noted that every presidential election saw "reports of negro insurrections . . . gotten up for party purposes." As an example, it cited the uproar set off earlier in the month when a German traveler stopped at a house to ask for a drink of water. Finding no one home, he went around to the back and asked a servant. The mistress saw him talking to the slave, assumed the worst, and ran off to the local school to spread the news of an insurrection. The students in turn ran to the precincts where local elections were being held. A hastily arranged committee interrogated the German and then released him.[57]

Apart from a bizarre tale of a band of gypsies burying a coffin filled with arms, the major slave scare in Alabama was in the black belt towns of Talladega, Selma, and Greensboro. The leaders of the Talladega plot were vaguely described as "abolition emissaries from the North, and low graded citizens of the South." The vigilance committee arrested two local citizens on charges of inciting the slaves to burn down the town and murder the inhabitants. Lem Payne, one of those arrested, was hauled out of the jail and lynched at three in the morning. The slaves were said to be restless because of their belief that a Black Republican (the standard label in the South for a Republican) was a black man. Despite many arrests, only one slave was convicted and sentenced to be hanged. Nonetheless, whites had succeeded in terrorizing the slaves. As the wife of a Presbyterian minister in Talladega observed: "None of them knew but that the gallows wld be their end." George Miller, home from the University of Virginia to visit his parents, was swept up in all the talk of "a heinous plot on the part of the slaves" and soon was "standing guard almost every night."[58]

The panic spread throughout the black belt. The mayor of Selma issued a call for a citizens' meeting to consider emergency measures. In Greensboro, slave hands on the railroad were tagged as the instigators. Sereno Watson, the brother of a Northern planter in Greene County, took a jaundiced view of all the commotion. He noted there were numerous accounts of the uprising, "no two alike," and believed they had little foundation. One of the slaves caught up in the dragnet of the local patrols was Archy Peck, whose crime consisted of leaving his plantation and "having been caught in bed with his wife without a pass." "This is a great people" was Watson's sarcastic commentary on his white neighbors.[59]

Outbursts of spontaneous white fears also erupted in the older slave states along the Atlantic seaboard. In Georgia, they clustered around Rome and Dalton in the north and in the southern counties along the Florida border. In the Carolinas, fears were most intense in the Abbeville District of South Carolina across the Savannah River from Georgia and in the isolated lowcountry counties of Washington and Tyrell in North Carolina. The Pettigrew family had extensive plantation holdings in both of these hotspots. Speaking for many of the large, established planters, William and Charles Pettigrew attributed the insurrectionary scares to nothing more than white panic. "The timidity that exists among whites in the Southern country is almost inconceivable," William wrote fellow planter James C. Johnston. Some even talked of being "ready to slaughter the negroes immediately," he added. Charles was just as contemptuous of the poor whites. "Pray do not apprehend as these miserable cowardly people have in this country, any danger from the negroes," he assured Caroline Pettigrew. "The poor negro is in infinitely more danger than you are. At Plymouth, it was necessary to put 17 negroes in jail to keep them from being killed by the negroless people of Washington County."

The main scare in Virginia erupted in early October along the state's southeastern border with North Carolina in Princess Anne County and the Norfolk area. Before the white fright faded over the "rising" allegedly set for Sunday night, October 6, 1860, dozens of slaves were arrested, and an Irish canal worker was killed when vigilantes descended on his work camp. All the slaves on one farm were jailed, and the entire workforce on two other farms had fled, it was said, "of guilty consciences." Dick Smith, a free black, was shot but not killed by the patrolers. An arrest warrant was issued for a white man, Thomas Carroll, and an indictment was found against another white whose inciting of the slaves, "almost verbatim," was somehow accurately recounted when he was overheard through the cracks of a slave cabin. He was said to have told the slaves that Northerners would come to their assistance and that 500 men in the county were prepared to help them as well. It was little wonder that many were dubious of the entire affair. The paper approvingly passed on a report from a local "gentleman" that "the negroes seem to be more alarmed at the consequences which may befall themselves, than the white population are of a negro insurrection."[60]

The slaves had every reason to fear the frenzy of enraged whites. A white mob on the morning of June 11 burned at the stake a slave accused of killing his owner in Oglethorpe County, Georgia. In August, a group of twelve men removed a "negro boy" accused of killing a white man from a jail near Augusta, Georgia. After posting bonds for his return to the custody of the sheriff, the men took the prisoner out to station No. 11 on the Southwestern Railroad, held a kangaroo trial, and burned him at the stake. They returned his ashes to the sheriff. Mulattoes thought to be aiding runaway slaves came in for terrible retribution. On August 3, a vigilance committee in the lowcountry of South Carolina drove off Melvina Knight and her "dark family" for tampering with slaves. The vigilantes tore down the Knights' cabin and outbuildings and rained down twenty-five lashes on the bare back of the elderly mother, thirty-nine for each of her daughters, and "a number too great to be counted" for her son.[61]

The venom of vigilantes, who came from the middling ranks of rural society, also spread to planters, whose status and wealth they both envied and resented. In the summer and fall they were policing the planters, whom they accused of not keeping their slaves in check. An irate citizen informed Samuel M. Meek, district attorney for Mississippi's sixth district, of an outrage committed near Buckhorn on July 24 and 25. A group of men self-identified as a vigilance committee entered the home of a Mr. Hastings in his absence and carried off John, one of his slaves. The following day, without any formal legal proceedings, John was hanged. The same fate awaited the slave of J. E. Taliaferro, who wrote Governor Pettus complaining of that slave's brutal murder while he was absent from his plantation. He suspected the culprit was in the vicinity of Huntsville and asked Pettus to requisition the Alabama governor for a writ to extradite the man back to Mississippi. "The shooting of negroes by overseers, and other irresponsible men of the country," he stressed, "is becoming too common a thing among us, and I deem it nothing more than right that an example should be made of this man Mooney."[62]

In upcountry South Carolina, Michael Buzzard publicly called out his neighbors for daring to mount a campaign demanding he send off his troublesome slave Simon to the West. Buzzard would not "be whipped into a pale [figure] of the slave by the proscriptive opinions, in the way of resolutions, which they have seen power to adopt." William Pettigrew, whose wealth was bitterly resented by his swamp-dwelling neighbors, suffered the indignity of having his plantation visited while he was away by those neighbors. They carried off his guns and powder to keep them out of the hands of the slaves whom they ex-pected to rise up in rebellion at any moment.[63]

Even when their actions degenerated into mob rule, the vigilance committees had the support of the Breckinridge press. Frequently these editors whipped their readers into a frenzy and then demanded even more violence to sup-press the abolitionist threat. The *Montgomery Mail* argued that the South was infested with abolitionist agents because Southerners had been too slow to hang the fiends as soon as they were caught. "The whole South needs a *thorough ex-purgation*," the editor shrieked. "Let a stout search *everywhere* reveal them—it *will* bring them to light—and let **THE ROPE** do the rest." Accepting as a given that stealthy abolitionists were torching Southern towns and just waiting for Lincoln's election to commit worse horrors, the *Clayton Banner* urged voters to back Breckinridge for their own safety: "Think of this, men of the South before you consent to divide the vote of the Southern States in November."[64]

Moderates in the Bell and Douglas camps were disturbed by the growing reign of terror and correctly ascribed some of the blame to the Breckinridge forces. As the campaign wore on, they increasingly discounted the stories of abo-litionist plots and refused to print them. The pro-Bell *Montgomery Post* had only "loathing and contempt" for those exploiting these troubles for political gain. J. J. Seibels, a Douglas editor, pointedly asked, "In what way a dissolution of the Union is to prevent the evils complained of?"[65]

And so, the recriminations reverberated throughout the campaign. Bell and Douglas supporters were labeled quasi-abolitionists for making light of the abo-litionist outrages and not coming out for secession in case of Lincoln's election. They answered in kind by stigmatizing the Breckinridge Democrats for leading the slaves to believe that hordes of abolitionists were fighting for their freedom, that they had an invincible political friend in the North who would set them free, and that even some Southern whites harbored abolitionist sentiments. "There is a law in this State against inciting slaves to rebellion," declared the *Vicksburg Whig*. "Every man who charges a portion of his fellow-citizens with being abolitionists, violates it, and deserves to be arrested and trotted off to jail."[66]

Priming for Secession

Whites in the Cotton South were on edge as the presidential election approached, caught up in an almost unbearable foreboding over their safety and what lay ahead. Anna Young confessed her fear to her brother Robert Gourdin in October that the "whole South" would soon experience what had already befallen whites in some sections when they found themselves in "as in-secure a home as though it were situated at the base of some ever-threatening

& never-to-be trusted volcano." Many whites were caught up in the belief that the South was an organic body infected with a malevolent virus categorized as abolitionist assassins. R. S. Holt of Yazoo City, Mississippi, put that fantasy into words in early November when he referred to the "hellish work" of an "army of assassins [that] must number thousands and they have at their command strychnine and arsenic in such quantities as show that special factories have been established to suit their demand."[67]

Whites wrote of the "excitement" in the buildup to the election. All agreed that the result would be momentous, marking an inflection point in which their fate and that of the Union hung in the balance. What Bell and Douglas voters dreaded would be a signal for secession, many Breckinridge supporters were ready to hail as a liberating event that would free the South of Yankee rule and abolitionist machinations.

Adding to the excitement was a propaganda campaign launched by Charleston secessionists in September that luridly spelled out what would be the horrific consequences of a Republican triumph. The ringleaders were, by all appearances, an unlikely group of revolutionaries—suave, urbane, lavishly wealthy businessmen and planters. They organized the 1860 Association, a bland name for a fear-inducing propaganda machine. Through the widespread distribution of their tracts to influential leaders in other cotton states, these Charlestonians aimed at generating enough enthusiasm for secession to remove any doubts that if South Carolina took the lead, it would soon be joined by other states. Cooperative secessionists in the crisis of 1850–51, they had abandoned their former caution in the face of the Republican threat. Contemptuous of the scorched-earth tactics of the state's prominent secessionist firebrands—the Rhetts, father and son—an approach they felt would drive away the very men they wanted to court, these Charlestonians positioned themselves at the forefront of secession.

Heading the association's executive committee was Robert Gourdin. Trained as a lawyer, he grew rich in the commission business of marketing sea-island cotton. He, along with his brother Henry, handled the group's out-of-state correspondence. The chief polemicist was John Townsend, owner of a couple of hundred slaves and a showcase plantation on Edisto Island. His most attention-grabbing tract was *The Doom of Slavery in the Union: Its Safety Out of It*. In vivid detail framed by a sense of inevitability, he outlined how an utterly helpless South would face the collapse of one outpost of slavery after another before the frenzied, unrelenting onslaught of the Republicans. Wildly exaggerating the size of the Northern-born population in the South, he depicted them as proto-abolitionists just waiting to move against slavery. His account climaxed with the declaration: **"THE 'UNIONIST' OF THE SOUTH IN 1860, IS THE 'SUBMISSIONIST,' NOW . . . AND WILL BE AN ABOLITIONIST OF**

THE NORTH IN 1870!" He ended the tract with accounts of the abolitionist depredations in Texas. For all his hyperbole, Townsend had captured perfectly the planters' sense of a hostile world closing in around them.[68]

Townsend's screed was pitched to slaveholders. To rally slaveless whites to the cause, J. D. De Bow was commissioned to write a pamphlet. *The Interest in Slavery of the Southern Non-Slaveholder* lacked the dramatic fire of Townsend's piece, though it was not as turgid as the tracts justifying the constitutionality of secession and the sanctity of state's rights. Apart from the standard appeals to white status that only slavery could guarantee and assurances that the thrifty non-slaveholder could hope someday to own slaves, De Bow's most original contribution was the strained argument that the working classes in the cities were shielded from direct competition with slave labor by the high price of slaves that kept them in the countryside producing cash crops.

In just two months, the 1860 Association churned out over 200,000 pamphlets. In the process, Gourdin established a network of well-placed correspondents that would be activated during the secession crisis. However, not all Gourdin's incoming correspondence was reassuring. Savannah planter E. C. Anderson, who characterized himself as "not a disunionist per se," preferred to put off any move toward secession, especially given the military unpreparedness of the South. Citing the lack of military measures that concerned Anderson and others, the *Charleston Mercury* pressured South Carolina's governor, William Gist, to be more aggressive in spending the legislature's appropriation of $100,000 for defense.[69]

Prompted to be more pro-active, Gist initiated a clandestine correspondence with the governors of the cotton states. He was hoping to stiffen the resolve of secessionists in his own state. South Carolina had a well-earned reputation for reckless bravado and empty gasconading, and its radicalism was openly scorned in the Upper South and suspect everywhere. What the secessionists feared was plunging into secession only to be left dangling in the wind. To allay that fear, Gist informed the governors that it was "the desire of South Carolina that some other State should take the lead, or at least move simultaneously with her." Once another state committed to secession, South Carolina would immediately follow it. If no other state was willing to be first, then South Carolina, in Gist's opinion, would still secede "alone, if she has any assurance that she will soon be followed by another or other States; otherwise, it is doubtful."

Gist's letter went out on October 5 and the replies, save that of Florida's governor, came in by October 26. Gist could not have been heartened by the responses. Not a single governor said his state was prepared to act first, and only the response of Milton S. Perry of Florida on November 9 pledged his state to follow South Carolina if it acted alone. What the governors did favor, including those from Alabama and Mississippi, was a convention of the Cotton states, if not of all the slaveholding states. The purpose of such a convention, in the words of Governor Thomas O. Moore of Louisiana, would be "to consult as to the proper course to be pursued, and to endeavor to effect a complete harmony of action." He hastened to add, however, that "I fear that the harmony of action, so desirable in so grave an emergency, cannot be effected." In other words, as in the past, secession was likely to be stymied by the conflicting interests and priorities of the slave states, most notably those between the Upper and Lower South. The only encouraging news Gist received was from Governor A. B. Moore, who had no doubt that Alabama would "immediately rally" to the "rescue" of any seceded state confronted with the use of military force against it.[70]

Frustrated by the apparent consensus of even secessionist-minded governors behind a general Southern convention, an approach that had always sunk secessionist hopes in a morass of indecision, South Carolina's secessionists made one final attempt in late October to gain a commitment from another state to lead off. Robert B. Rhett Jr. sent out more inquiries to leading Southern politicians. The only extant reply is that from Jefferson Davis. As a canvasser in Mississippi for Breckinridge in mid-September, he had declared that the South would have no choice but to resist a Republican victory. He viewed secession, however, as a last resort and one to be undertaken only through a cooperative approach of the Southern states. His reply, though written when news of Lincoln's election was filtering in, counseled patience and delay. Mississippi's governor had called a special session of the legislature, but Davis considered it "doubtful" that it would issue a call for a state convention. Even if such a convention did assemble, it was unlikely to favor the state's independent withdrawal, regardless of what South Carolina did. He then hedged with a number of "collateral questions." Mississippi lacked a port and needed assurances that a cordon of Gulf states running through Georgia was ready to leave the Union. The federal response was a great unknown. If South Carolina seceded alone, Davis thought the most likely federal move would be to collect tariff duties offshore for goods coming into its ports, thus isolating the state without resorting to military force and leaving other states powerless to counteract the Union navy. Only if the federal government provoked a clash of arms did Davis feel that Mississippi and other states would come to South Carolina's assistance. He closed by recommending consultation among the Southern states as the safest course.[71]

Perhaps it was this caution that sowed the seeds of the subsequent enmity of the Rhett secessionists to Davis as the Confederate president. In any event, the Carolinians were not to be palsied by the timidity of the other slave states. All their plans hinged on Lincoln's election, and by October all signs were signaling it.

Economic conditions in the North helped swell the enthusiasm for the Republican ticket. In contrast to the dismal growing season in the South, western farmers were enjoying a bountiful harvest. Western businessmen benefited as farmers flush with cash were eager buyers of eastern goods. This confirmation of mutually advantageous economic interests running along an East-West axis was further highlighted by the falling off of orders from the South and a mounting pile of Southern bills; these were left unpaid because Southern banks suffered losses in reserves as too little cotton was coming to market to maintain bank balances. Meanwhile, manufacturing interests, especially in the key battleground state of Pennsylvania, were being pulled into the Republican fold by the prospect of higher tariffs on iron and steel goods.

In keeping with the nineteenth-century practice of presidential candidates, Lincoln, Bell, and Breckinridge had run stay-at-home campaigns. Justifiably reasoning that anything he said would be twisted and used against him, Lincoln said nothing save for a brief, noncommittal speech at Springfield on August 8. He relied on the Republican platform and a printed version of the Lincoln-Douglas debates to carry his message to the voters. What was novel about his campaign was the emergence of the Wide-Awakes, young party enthusiasts drawn from clerks and professionals. They became a staple of Republican rallies, marching in military formation with their distinctive attire of oil-cloth caps and long capes. In the South, they were sensationalized as the military vanguard of the Republicans who would finish what John Brown had started. The Breckinridge press inflated their numbers to between 100,000 and 400,000. Aiding them in their intended invasion of the South "for pillage and murder" were "buck Negroes," a reference to the small number of free blacks in Massachusetts in their ranks.[72]

The only active campaigner was Douglas. Breaking with all precedent, he embarked on a grueling speaking tour of the North. He shifted his attention to the South after the state elections on October 9 in Ohio, Indiana, and Pennsylvania resulted in impressive Republican victories. Barring the success of last-minute fusionist efforts among the presidential electors of Lincoln's opponents in New York and Pennsylvania, Republican victory in November loomed as a near certainty. In the South, Douglas promoted himself not so much as a candidate but as a defender of the Union. Hoping to persuade Southern moderates from joining the fire-eaters in a possible bid to leave the Union, he delivered his most celebrated speech at Norfolk on August 25. He stated that Lincoln's election, if not followed by an open act against slavery, was no cause for secession. Furthermore, he pledged full support for any president confronted with lawless resistance against the Union. His views infuriated the Breckinridge forces. Typical was the invective of the *Mississippi Free Trader*, which denounced his statements as "the culmination of his treachery and his alliance with the Black republican party."[73]

Yancey, after hearing Douglas speak in Montgomery in front of a hostile audience, decided that he, too, would take his message into the enemy's camp. He was hardly so naïve as to believe he was going to win over many Northerners for Breckinridge. Rather, he was throwing Douglas's unionism back in his face and defiantly, even triumphantly, reminding Northerners that secession was a distinct possibility come November. He condemned the Republicans, defended slavery, and demeaned the black race as unfit for freedom. His tour finished back in the South in late October at New Orleans, where a throng estimated at 20,000 feted him for standing up for Southern rights.

Quite apart from the scheming of the secessionists, the widespread expectation of Lincoln's election was priming more Southerners to anticipate secession as a likely response. At the very least, they were bracing for a great national crisis that would settle the slavery issue once and for all. "We are," said Linton Stephens of Georgia, "on the verge of a precipice." Philip St. George Cocke wrote his father that unless Republicans retreated from their "war" against slavery, he was certain "that the whole South[,] first two or three States—then more—then more & finally all Virginia included—will withdraw from the Union & form an independent confederation." [74]

Bucking the tide was a conservative minority that was quite sanguine over what the future might bring. The *New Orleans Bee* felt that the number of Southerners favoring secession upon Lincoln's election "is exceedingly small." The partners in the Richmond commission firm of Hunt & James had "no fear of a dissolution of the Union even if Lincoln should be elected, though we might have some trouble." A few states would probably go out, predicted rice planter William Elliott, but the Upper South would block any drive for an independent Southern confederacy. The result, he thought, would leave Southern Democrats weakened and in disarray.[75]

Much more prescient was the observation of the Northern outsider, schoolteacher Rogene Scott, based on her reading of the election excitement in Nashville in late October. From what she saw, the "whole south are for war if Lincoln is elected, and in a month from now, our peaceful country may be deluged in blood. God help us then." South Carolina's secessionists ensured that her prophesy rang true by the spring.[76]

4

Verdict Rendered

Lincoln Is Elected

Although Lincoln's election was widely anticipated, Southern whites reacted to it with shocked humiliation. The forebodings expressed during the campaign now erupted into a full-blown crisis. The economy ground to a near halt as marketing mechanisms for crops dried up in a severe credit crunch. Moderates and conservatives, found mostly in the Bell and Douglas camps, counseled patience and firm resolve, but the momentum rested with the Breckinridge Democrats whose leaders had always been prepared to view a Republican victory as a signal for secession. And, as always, the silent and hovering slaves conditioned the behavior of whites. Assumptions regarding what they were thinking and calculating were fundamental to the white response that drove forward the political drama.

A Divided Electorate: The Returns in the South

Breckinridge swept the states of the Lower South where slavery was most entrenched, but he garnered only a plurality of the popular vote in the entire South. He lost the Upper South states of Virginia, Tennessee, and Kentucky, which went for Bell, and Missouri, carried by Douglas. He won handily in Texas, Florida, and Mississippi, but elsewhere his victories came in the face of opposition. The combined Bell-Douglas vote exceeded his by 110,000. In an alarming signal about the future of slavery, the vilified Republicans received an impressive 24 percent of the vote in Delaware and, thanks to a very strong showing in St. Louis, 10 percent in Missouri.

Measured by the election returns, a majority of whites favored a moderate approach to the South's relations with the federal Union. This was nowhere more apparent than in the political preferences of the upper levels of the slaveholding class. Except for South Carolina, where no popular election for the president was held before the Civil War, Bell was the preferred choice of medium-to-large slaveholders in the Lower South. Indeed, an estimated 80 percent of slaveholders with more than nine slaves in the cotton states voted for Bell, and by a wide margin. In the Upper South, the larger slaveholders split their vote between Bell and Breckinridge. Solid support from non-slaveholding farmers, a bastion of Democratic strength, accounted for Breckinridge's majorities in the Lower South. He also ran well among the evangelicals—Baptists and Methodists—who resented the Whigs as the party of wealth and class pretensions.[1]

In addition to the wealthier slaveholders, urban and town voters also rejected the Breckinridge ticket. Breckinridge ran especially poorly in the South's larger cities, winning just 29 percent of the vote in Mobile, 27 percent in Richmond, 26 percent in Norfolk, 24 percent in New Orleans, 11 percent in Memphis and Louisville, and slightly over 2 percent in St. Louis. The exception was Baltimore, which he carried with a plurality of 49 percent. His success was attributable to the close identification of Bell Unionists with the Know-Nothings, a linkage that enabled the Breckinridge Democrats to retain their support among foreign-born workers.[2]

Irish Democratic supporters, nearly all of whom were nonslaveholders clustered in seaport cities or larger interior towns, typically found the more temperate stand of Douglas more acceptable than the strident, proslavery emphasis of the Breckinridge campaign. Efforts at stemming the defection were largely unsuccessful because of divisions in the party machinery in the cities and the writing off by Breckinridge leaders of working-class naturalized citizens as pro-abolitionist. John Slidell, the head of the Breckinridge campaign in Louisiana, concluded that in New Orleans "seven eighths at least of the votes for Douglas were cast by the Irish & Germans, who are at heart abolitionists."[3]

The towns and cities, with their ties to Northern capital and business groups and a work ethic that was not directly related to the use of land and slave labor, shied away from the agitation of issues that stressed the rights of slaveholders and the acquisition of more slave territory. The Whiggish and pro-Bell support of the factors and merchants and the Douglas leanings of the foreign-born shopkeepers and workers reflected both the cities' middleman function in the Southern economy and uneasiness over demands from which the countryside stood most to gain. Whatever their discomfort with the Breckinridge campaign, however, voters in the cities and towns were too few to alter the ideology of a party which, by speaking for and dominating the countryside, could command state politics.

The rural vote for Breckinridge was impressive, and it drew on two main sources. The yeomanry, notably in the Lower South, embraced the Breckinridge party as the custodian of the majoritarian, pro-Union Democracy of Jackson's day and were openly leery of what they resented as the aristocratic haughtiness of pro-Bell, former Whig planters. The Breckinridge ticket also won by large majorities in counties where plantation agriculture and slaveholdings were expanding most rapidly. Typically, these were counties where the spread of rail networks opened up new opportunities in commercial agriculture with the use of slave labor. This was especially evident in a swath of counties in east central Mississippi where the coming of the railroad in the 1850s triggered an influx of whites and an explosive growth in the slave population.[4]

Georgia and Virginia, two states representative of the major regional subdivisions in the South, illustrate the main outline of the voting patterns. In Georgia, Breckinridge won half of the black counties—those in which slaves outnumbered whites. His vote was concentrated in the newer plantation belt carved out of the southwestern section of the state and in the rice regions along the coast. The black areas he lost comprised the old plantation belt of central Georgia. Whether measured by flows of white and slave populations, cotton production, or land usage, the Breckinridge counties experienced significantly higher rates of economic growth than the Bell strongholds. The same pattern appeared in the counties of middling cotton production where slaves made up about one-third of the population. Breckinridge gained his heaviest majorities in counties dominated by the yeomanry and poor whites; he ran weakest where urbanization and industrialization had begun to make inroads. Aside from Savannah, he lost the cities, and of the nineteen counties with a manufacturing output in excess of $200,000, he carried only four.

With allowance for the greater economic diversification of Virginia's economy, the same voting model held there. Breckinridge lost the larger cities and the ten leading manufacturing counties. Tobacco planters did well in the 1850s as prices rose, and the Breckinridge black-belt vote was centered in the areas where tobacco production expanded the most. The moderately prosperous, general farming counties, where about 40 percent of families owned slaves and where tobacco was a second crop, were Whig strongholds. Breckinridge's rural strength was in southwestern Virginia where new rail lines in the 1850s led to an influx of whites and a spike in the slave population.

The Breckinridge campaign succeeded in appealing to newer social groups aggressively engaged in acquiring land and slaves. Their party activists encompassed the highest percentages of lawyers and of young planters and slave-holding farmers. For those not born to wealth (land and slaves), law, aside from a favorable marriage, was the customary means of climbing the social ladder. Since the profession was unstructured, with the most rudimentary licensing procedures, virtually anyone with a smattering of education could hang out a shingle. County seats had a surfeit of lawyers, and competition was fierce. Most lawyers survived by serving as debt collectors. Still, an ambitious lawyer had several options. He could enter politics and use an array of local offices to publicize his name and learn of his area's best economic opportunities. He could seek out patronage or, by moving to a frontier region, assist in the sale of the public lands and, with an insider's knowledge, amass land for himself. Politics was a key to lawyers' advancement, and the scramble for state offices was reflected in the volatility of membership in the Southern state legislatures. The three elections for the Alabama lower house in the 1850s produced turnover rates ranging from 76 percent to 88 percent.[5]

The young Breckinridge planters and slaveholding farmers had come to political maturity in the 1850s when escalating prices for slaves and good land hindered their chances for success and prestige. Even more galling was the antislavery crusade. The moral condemnations of the North were especially inflammatory to these young Southerners, whose recently gained slaveholding status had not yet been economically secured or encrusted with the defenses of time and tradition. The antislavery forces would never permit any additional slave territory or loosening of the prohibition against the African slave trade. As a result, no relief in the form of fresh land or cheaper slave prices was to be forthcoming. All the slaveholder wanted, so went the argument, was an equal opportunity to compete in the territories, but even this was to be denied him by the free-soil North.

Economic pressures and status anxieties were major factors in radicalizing young slaveholders in the Cotton South. They brought their vitality and frustrations to the Breckinridge campaign and helped shape an ideological appeal tailored to similar groups in the recently developed slave regions. A Breckinridge editor was engaging in no empty boast when he wrote of the attraction of young men to the Breckinridge ticket, "No other party has ever been raised up in this country that appealed so powerfully to, or so naturally attracted this class." The Breckinridge Democrats spoke to the hopes and fears of these new cotton entrepreneurs, promising them that if the Yankees refused to stop insulting them or putting a brake on their advancement, an independent South would do them justice.[6]

The Bell Whigs emphasized the need to put an end to the agitation of slavery for the sake of national harmony. Drawing its ranks from factors, bankers, and merchants in cities, planters and farmers in the mature or declining plantation areas, and hill farmers in the Upper South, the Whigs lacked a constituency with a sense of urgency on the slavery question. Their wealthiest adherents—planters in the Mississippi Delta who had too much capital tied up in cotton production to risk it by alienating the North and those in the Louisiana sugar parishes dependent for their profits on tariff protection from foreign competition—were satisfied with the status quo, as were some older, established slaveholders. Town and urban businessmen relied for their economic success on outside capital, much of which originated in the North. The Whig constituency either financed and serviced plantation agriculture, had grown accustomed to the status it provided, or had given up an active pursuit of it.

Many of the Bell areas had been weakened economically by the rapid expansion of the cotton frontier. Economic diversification, soil restoration, and the accumulation of capital in the older plantation belts were all made more difficult by the outflow of population, skills, and labor resources to new regions. Former Whigs from the Upper South were particularly concerned since their states had suffered longest and most severely from the effects of out-migration, but the same factors were at work by the 1850s in scattered Bell-Whig sections of the Lower South, such as the old plantation district of central Georgia and parts of the Alabama Black Belt. Whig congressmen had long decried the burden placed on their home districts by the availability of fresh land elsewhere. They attacked the newer cotton entrepreneurs for their cruelty and greed and denounced those who flocked to filibustering expeditions to spread slavery as young "elegant men, having nothing to live upon and doing nothing, and nothing to do anything on." The Whigs who backed Bell were both the South's economic old guard and its paternalistic conscience, neither of which made them attractive to the young insurgents in the Breckinridge camp.[7]

Douglas supporters tended to be peeled away from the normal Democratic coalition whose function and place in the slave economy overlapped that of the Whigs. Urban and town Democrats found Douglas very attractive and he typically outpolled Breckinridge in the large cities. The foreign-born small tradesmen and workers had an alternative in Douglas. Voting for Douglas enabled them to keep their party credentials without going over to the hated Whigs. What rural support Douglas received came out of upland areas with few ties to the plantation belts.

Both the Bell and Douglas voters rejected the Breckinridge claim that a crisis confronted the South. For them, any such crisis was the product more of the machinations of demagogic Breckinridge politicians than of any conflicts that could not be resolved within the Union. That conviction was to be badly shaken, if not shattered, by Lincoln's election.

White Outrage and Demands for Secession

The reverberations of Lincoln's election shook to the core Southern whites' confidence in the future and the fate of slavery. It mattered not that a close examination of the election returns would have revealed that the combined Democratic vote of Breckinridge and Douglas had increased the Democrats' share of the electorate from 45 percent in 1856 to 47 percent in 1860 and that the Democrats had picked up additional seats in Congress. All that counted was that a Republican, an abolitionist in their eyes, was about to take over the reins of the federal government in four months as the result of a sectional vote that had given Lincoln with only 39 percent of the vote a clear majority in the electoral college. Gone was the security blanket offered by pro-Southern administrations in the 1850s. The North had spoken and its verdict had seemingly condemned Southern whites as sinners and criminals.

Because the Republicans were morally and economically opposed to slavery, Southerners had demonized them since their birth as a party in 1854 as rabid fanatics and murderous incendiaries. Thus, the response to Lincoln's victory in 1860 was largely a reflexive one demanding resistance. His victory was a call to action. "We have risked all, and we must play our best, for the stake is life or death," wrote Mary Chesnut of her reaction. The choice was self-evident— submit or resist. In working out what that resistance should be, a secessionist minority down to the day of the election was quickly transformed into a majority, albeit a narrow one, across the Lower South.[8]

For some moderates, the conversion to secession, whether by separate state action or in a cooperative movement, was almost instantaneous. Proclaiming that he was "not willing to submit to a Black Republican President," William H. Ogbourne of Alabama, who had voted for Bell, went for secession. George Gilman Smith, a Presbyterian minister in North Carolina and Bell supporter, recalled that he had been "intensely devoted to the Union," but for him the election had made it "evident that a majority of the States in the North were determined to destroy slavery [and he] saw no hope of escape from absolute ruin but withdraw from the Union. I did not expect war but of course I would have taken the same course." The editor of a Bell paper in Florida had favored the Union as long as he felt there was any hope of defeating Lincoln. With that hope gone, he committed to secession as "as the only remaining remedy for our wrongs." He fully expected a terrible war but found that preferable to the "submission which cause[s] a nation or a people to lose their own self-respect." From the Alabama Black Belt, Sereno Watson observed in a tone of amazement: "This people is apparently gone crazy. . . . Union men, Douglas men, Breckinridge men are alike in their loud denunciation of submission to Lincoln's administration." This spontaneous reaction gave the secessionists their first great opening. They had the momentum, and they never lost it.[9]

Most whites were predisposed to embrace secession in some form. That secession was now a necessity was close to a foregone conclusion, what Linton Stephens in Georgia saw as the "almost *universal* expectation." The *Richmond Examiner* had taunted conservatives in October by asserting that "Virginia can no more prevent the dissolution of the Union after Lincoln's election that she can prevent that election." Since the time for talk was over, the states had to move quickly and decisively before the shock of Lincoln's election wore off.[10]

Pressing their advantage, the Breckinridge press issued incessant calls for immediate secession by separate state action. Their argument for immediate secession was straightforward and pitched to white fears. The Republicans were irrevocably hostile to slavery, and the fate of slavery and therefore the South hung in the balance. Since the Republicans were abolitionists, emancipation was just a matter of time. Some warned that slavery would end quickly in Republican-incited slave uprisings that would rival the horrors of the slave rebellion in Santo Domingo in the 1790s. In coming out for secession on December 1, a mass meeting at Bachelor's Retreat in South Carolina described the ranks of the Republicans as filled with "hordes ready by every diabolical means to excite, in our Slave States, insurrection, burning, plunder and murder." In the near future, according to the *Placquemine* (La.) *Gazette and Sentinel*, "our glorious South will become a second Jamaica—or worse, a second St. Domingo." Governor A. D. Moore of Alabama predicted that the Republicans would begin by abolishing slavery in the District of Columbia, the government dockyards, and the territories. They then would rush additional free states into the Union until they had the two-thirds majority needed in Congress to abolish slavery in all the states. As for the consequences, the "state of society that must exist in the Southern States, with four millions of free negroes and their increase, turned loose upon them, I will not discuss—it is too horrible to contemplate." Others were more direct in zeroing in on the racial consequences of emancipation. The Republicans, exclaimed secessionist lawyer David Schenck of North Carolina, sought nothing less than the "equality of the negro and the white man." [11]

On the surface, such fears seem overblown, if not preposterous, for the Republicans did not favor political and social equality for African Americans, only their right to earn their own livelihood by receiving wages for their labor. But for Southern whites, white equality and liberty depended on black slavery. Liberty was the exclusive right of all whites who were free to pursue material aspirations of acquiring land, slaves, and economic independence. To free the slaves was to degrade whites by reducing them to the level of equals in all forms of social and economic competition with a race unfit for freedom. Gone would be the shared equality whites had enjoyed on the basis of their racial superiority over enslaved inferiors. Thus, not to resist via secession was to assume the role of the slave by losing independence and cringing in servitude to Northern masters. "We will not tamely kiss the rod that smites," thundered the *Albany* (Ga.) *Patriot*. "We will not, like dumb brutes, wear the yoke of Abolition domination." The slave metaphor was constantly invoked by the secessionists. "If the South quietly submits," warned Philip St. George Cocke, "they *deserve* to become as they *will soon be made*—the *slaves* of an arrogant, turbulent & tyrannical northern majority." Susan Cornwall in Georgia defiantly wrote in her diary: "Do they think we are as degenerate as our slaves to be whipped into obedience at the demand of our self styled master." To do so was tantamount to social death, a fate worse than literal death. Alabama congressman David Clopton would "rather die a free man than live a slave to Black republicans. I would be an equal or a corpse."[12]

The slave metaphor made for a powerful argument for secession in a society in which whites internalized failure and dependency as the lot of a black slave. Washington Smith was a young Southerner who had moved to Philadelphia seeking the success that had eluded him in the South. He had to settle for running a country store for his uncle with whom he was staying. Frustrated and out of place in the North, he yearned for the glory of a soldier fighting for the South should a war ever break out with the North. "I pine for war," he wrote James D. De Bow, for his "ambition had no outlet." He wanted to cleanse his sense of shame. "I with thousands: aye! And tens of thousands of others are infinitely worse off than if our skin were black, head curly; and lot the servitude of the bondsman."[13]

Rather than adopting the degradation of the slave, the secessionists urged all white men to exhibit the manly honor and sense of duty of their illustrious forefathers who resisted British tyranny and struck for independence. Philip St. George Cocke was confident that the "men of the South . . . will feel the spirit of our [Revolutionary] fathers . . . and will proclaim to the world once more in the memorable words of Patrick Henry 'give me liberty or give me death!' " The same appeal was directed to women. "In the Revolution of 1860, their patriotism will equal that of their grandmothers in '76," W. E. Martin assured his audience at a secessionist demonstration in Columbia, South Carolina.[14]

Once Southern independence was achieved, the secessionists foretold an era of boundless prosperity. Freed from the shackles of Northern protective tariffs and subsidies to favored Northern industries and commercial interests, the South would be in control of its own economic destiny. Its merchants would establish direct trade with Europe, its manufacturers and cities would flourish, and slavery would seek its natural outlet in the Caribbean and tropics of Central America. The result, predicted John Townsend, would be "a prosperity, financial, commercial and manufacturing, which the South has never before enjoyed, and an abundant ability to defend herself against any aggressions, no matter from what quarter they may come."[15]

No longer would abolitionists be whispering murderous designs in slaves' ears and stirring up unrest, for antislavery Northerners would no longer feel a moral accountability to free the slaves of an independent nation. Pragmatic Northern politicians, with no partisan advantage to be gained by agitating the issue of slavery, would cease their provocations. For A. B. Longstreet, "domestic peace and security" would result as soon as the South withdrew from the cycle of presidential and congressional campaigning in the Union. "It is the everlasting stump speaking in behalf of rival candidates . . . , the indiscreet table-talk which it naturally suggests, the inflammatory extracts from northern speeches and editorials constantly paraded in the southern press, which brings uneasiness into our families—not the things said and done by the fanatics far off. Now, all of this ends where the separation begins." If attacks on slavery did continue, James H. Hammond declared that the South would soon "be free" of the fanatics "by the process of extermination already permanently put in operation here."[16]

Although certainly willing to fight if necessary, the secessionists insisted that secession would be peaceful. King Cotton would see to that. "The world cannot do without her cotton," contended the *Newberry Rising Sun*, "and the world would starve were it not for her productions. She is therefore safe, because she is needed." Since its economy would collapse without Southern cotton, England would never allow the North to impose a blockade on Southern ports. By March, predicted the *Milledgeville* (Ga.) *Southern Union*, England would have recognized an independent South, and its agents would be purchasing cotton with gold. As for the North, if it ever were foolhardy enough to attempt to co-erce the seceded states back, its effort would be short-lived. Such was the con-clusion of the rabidly pro-secession *Dallas Herald* when it triumphantly noted in December that the "cessation of trade with the North has in one short month turned loose an army of more than 30,000 idle and starving operatives, men, *women*, and children, who are now clamorous for bread and cursing their leaders for bringing this calamity upon them." Unless it quickly accepted secession and restored trading relations with the South, the North would be engulfed in com-mercial panics, bankruptcies, and anarchy.[17]

Conservatives on the Defensive

The intensity of the popular reaction to Lincoln's election and the skill with which the secessionists exploited it put the conservatives on the defensive from the start. Part of their problem was their mixed message. The most con-servative papers initially insisted that nothing need be done. "Lincoln will be the most powerless President ever inaugurated," declared the *New Orleans Bee* on November 12, 1860. "He will have to contend with a hostile majority in both houses of Congress. . . . Every nomination made by him will be subjected to rigid scrutiny, and if tainted by sectionalism will unceremoniously be rejected." The next day, the editor changed his tune and called for a state con-vention which, he assumed, would be controlled by deliberative, experienced men of wealth who would be governed by dignified reason. Such a conven-tion would "give direction and aim to public opinion, which is now agitated and fluctuating," and agree on a package of demands and further guarantees for slavery. The other cotton states would follow suit and then the Upper

South. By presenting a united front, the South would force the North to make concessions protecting Southern rights. Other conservative papers opted for a national convention of all the states or a cooperative approach in which the slave states would consult with each other to arrive at an agreement on going out as a bloc before any one state seceded separately.[18]

Whatever the approach, the conservatives were hoping to buy time to allow passions to cool and a unified response to be worked out that would result in a sectional settlement that precluded the need for secession. As the *Athens* (Tenn.) *Post*, put it in mid-December: "In our opinion the North will yield any *reasonable guarantee*, rather than be separated from the South and we now think that it is the only way by which the Union can be saved."[19]

Conservatives treated the notion of peaceful separation with contempt and decried the rush to secede as pure madness. James C. Johnston, one of North Carolina's wealthiest planters, saw secession resulting in either "the most wretched anarchy or the most horrible & bloody civil war that ever was recorded in history." Secession, warned Benjamin F. Perry, a leading Unionist in South Carolina's upcountry, would unleash "all the horrors of civil war and revolution." No one could accurately gauge the potential military power of the free states, and the size of the regular US Army at 16,000 men was indeed small, with many Southern officers resigning, but the Whigs had little doubt that the North would fight to save the Union. New York would not permit any shrinkage of its trade as a result of any Southern free-trade policy and would support a war to protect its interests. Western farmers would join in the war, for they never would consent to the control of the lower Mississippi Valley by a foreign power.[20]

Cotton was certainly crucial to the outside world, the conservatives admitted, but the South eventually had to sell its cotton, and England knew it. The *Augusta Weekly Chronicle and Sentinel* noted that England had sources in its empire to replace cotton cut off by the South. It would be foolhardy and economically ruinous for the South to endanger its cotton monopoly with an embargo to pressure England. The *Savannah Republican* picked up an analysis from the New York press arguing that bad harvests in England would force it to turn to the North for foodstuffs. "Cheap bread is the foundation of prosperity in British manufactures." Taunting the secessionists with an editorial entitled "Corn Will Be King," Parson Brownlow, a Tennessee Unionist, stressed that the corn and hogs of the border states would be most in demand if war broke out. "The Cotton States, therefore, instead of being *independent*, will become the most dependent and helpless Province in the civilized world." He followed up with an editorial rhetorically asking, "Is Cotton King?" Arguing that England would welcome the opportunity to free itself of its cotton dependency on the South, he predicted that the "wild schemes" of the secessionists to strengthen slavery would weaken the institution by ending the South's cotton monopoly.[21]

Those who still clung to the Union were convinced that slavery was doomed outside of it. To rip free from the Union was to abandon the protection of the Fugitive Slave Act, the US Army, and Northern friends who had stood by the South in every sectional crisis. Gone would be the prosperity the South had enjoyed in the Union, its former friends would become its "open enemies" and the North a "source of annoyance and injury to all contiguous territory." The source of freedom for escaping slaves in effect would shift from Canada far to the southern border between the Union and the South once the Fugitive Slave Act was no longer enforced. Slavery in the Border South would soon be untenable, and its planters would sell off their slaves to the Gulf states. With greater numbers of slaves confined in a shrinking area, prices would plunge, and the cost of their upkeep would become an unbearable burden. As for spreading slavery to the tropics, that was written off as empty rhetoric. For both moral and economic reasons, European powers and the North would block any effort to expand slavery.[22]

"Men of the South!" proclaimed a Virginian, "when you have accomplished disunion, you will have done the very work the ultra Abolitionists of the North desire. You will have opened up the flood gates through which will rush all the evils you so much dread." For conservatives, the surest way to protect slavery was obvious: hold onto the Union "as the very bulwark of their peculiar institution." Secession meant the end of slavery, "peaceably it may be, but in all probability through the fire and blood of a war among the descendants of those from whom we inherited liberty," exclaimed a Bell paper in Louisiana.[23]

Conservatives denounced as overstated and misleading comparisons of secession to the American Revolution. "A UNION MAN of the Old School" pointed out that Southern trade had not been cut off, taxes imposed without consent, nor the benefits of trial by jury denied. He dared the secessionists to cite one act of Congress that ever abolished the constitutional rights of the South. None of the colonies had separately broken away from England, noted "THE LAST WORD." Their delegates met together in a collective body and deliberated long and hard before declaring independence from England.[24]

Rejecting their stigmatization by the secessionists, conservatives used the same language of manly honor against their attackers. For the *Clarksville* (Tenn.) *Chronicle*, "secession is itself dishonor, a cowardly abandonment of the post assigned to every true-hearted American when his country is endangered." For the *Vicksburg Whig*, the very thought of "the South being frightened out of the Union is base, cowardly, and unmanly." Those advising it were the ones playing the role of the slave who was so servile as "to run away," not only without being whipped but not even being struck. Honor demanded that the South fight for its rights within the Union.[25]

The conservatives presented a reasoned rebuttal that undercut most of the radicals' claims, but once they conceded the legitimacy of Southern grievances and the need for some form of resistance, they played into the hands of the secessionists by feeding the very fears they were trying to quell. All the while, those fears were being fanned by the mobilization of angry whites into paramilitary groups striking out against the perceived enemies of the South, whether in their midst or in the North.

Ratcheting Up the Resistance

The most openly pro-secessionist of the paramilitary organizations were the Minute Men. They sprang up in mid-October in the Piedmont districts of South Carolina and provided a model followed throughout the Lower South. The Minute Men of Columbia, one of the first to form, pledged in their constitution "to sustain Southern constitutional equality within the Union, or, failing in that, to establish our independence out of it." Members were required "to wear a blue cockade on the left side of the hat," purchase a firearm, and when parading publicly to "carry a lantern, flambeau [flaming torch], or demonstrative implement 'appropriate' to the occasion." Their name linked them to the Revolutionary patriots and the blue cockade had been the symbol of the Nullifiers in the early 1830s. The emphasis on flamboyant public display was aimed both at proclaiming unified resolve and intimidating the undecided.

The Minute Men often functioned as glorified vigilance committees. Those in Aiken pledged to enforce "our Peace Laws" and to detain and punish "Abolition emissaries and incendiaries, and other offenders against the peace of the community." Lodged with the power to investigate and punish was a Committee of Public Safety, consisting of twelve men. Two corps of Minute Men would patrol the corporate limits of Aiken, "disperse all unlawful assemblies [and] arrest all suspected persons." The final say on punishment by death rested with the Committee of Public Safety.[26]

For all their military trappings, the Minute Men were used more as a Southern equivalent to the Wide-Awakes in Lincoln's campaign than disciplined military units. By appearing at major secessionist rallies and staging night marches through downtown streets, they whipped up public fervor and drew onlookers into the great cause of defending Southern rights. As noted by the *Columbia Guardian*, the 300 Minute Men of Richland who marched in torchlight procession in Columbia impressed all onlookers with their "very imposing and brilliant display."[27]

The Minute Men targeted for recruitment the yeomanry of the Carolina upcountry, who had opposed radicalism in the past. The *Darlington Southerner* portrayed the yeoman farmer as "he, of all others, who must suffer from the success of abolitionism in our midst." The rich would move away when slavery ended and the poor would be left to accept equality with blacks or wage a war of extermination against the thieving, savage hordes who threatened their property and the virtue of their wives and daughters. Despite such efforts, the Minute Men received only spotty support from small farmers. Recruitment in the Upper District of South Carolina correlated strongly with the extent of slave ownership, and three-quarters of the Minute Men came from slaveholding families.[28]

Across the Lower South the Minute Men played a major political role in promoting secession. Superimposed on the traditional militia or beat districts that were the basic unit for bringing together planters and poorer whites into a fraternity of citizen-soldiers, the Minute Men indoctrinated the male defenders of the local community into a bloc for secession. They also intervened directly in politics. In Selma, Alabama, they constituted the nucleus for the immediate secessionist party. The Jackson Minute Men, organized on November 13 after a resistance meeting had adjourned, were dominated by young Breckinridge politicians, disproportionately lawyers. All but two were slaveholders, most of whom owned more than twenty slaves. Exerting pressure for secession, they resolved that every member should consider himself a delegate to the county's nominating convention for delegates to the state's secession convention and feel "duty bound to attend." Among their activities, charged the *Vicksburg Whig*, was the ordering for circulation of 10,000 copies of an abolition article from the *Chicago Democrat*. The paper added that the circulators of such incendiary material should be "arrayed before the grand jury, as such proceedings are in direct and palpable violation of our excellent State Law."[29]

In vain did the *Vicksburg Whig* and other conservative papers denounce the Minute Men as fronts for secession and lawless activity. What were provocations for "mobocracy" to conservatives was "noble work" to the secessionists. The *Memphis Avalanche* lauded the Minute Men for their good work but cautioned that "still more needs to be done. There are lurking in your midst a thousand traitors. . . . Hunt up the cowardly ingrates, and, if necessary, nail their vile carcasses to their own doors, or hang them upon the public lamp posts."[30]

Further collectivizing the sense of crisis were the activities of the vigilance committees. These included efforts to tighten up the system of passes and traveling tickets for slaves, break up the illicit trading with slaves, and prohibit all meetings of blacks and slaves hiring their own time. Paradoxically, they were as much an indictment of the planters for failing to control their slaves as they were pressure to secede from the Union to protect the interests of slaveholders. A vigilance committee in the Lexington District of South Carolina summarized their purpose as "the better government of negroes and the welfare of the community." To fulfill that purpose, they would punish all suspicious slaves with thirty-nine lashes. In Panola County, Mississippi, a vigilance committee resolved to "take notice of and punish all and every person that may be guilty of any misdemeanor, or prove themselves untrue to the South or Southern rights in any way whatever."[31]

The retribution of the committees could be fearsome. In Marshallville, Georgia, a suspected abolitionist received 175 lashes "for manifesting too great a solicitation for the welfare of the negro population." J. K. Byler was taken from his chair in a Savannah barber shop by a party of men in disguise and tarred and feathered, a ritual of humiliation for all alleged Negro sympathizers. On November 7, 1980, two men charged with voting for Lincoln were hanged in Coryell County, Texas. A vigilance committee in the Carolina lowcountry arrested several free blacks as "vagrants" and sold them into temporary slavery. Another committee in Mobile served public notice on all free blacks that unless they left the city in ten days, they would be "dealt with to the extremities of the law." [32]

Northerners, whether resident in the South or visiting, were ready targets. They were marked for reprisal, ordered out, or subjected to mock trials in which they had to prove their loyalty to the South. A Memphis paper printed a letter from a local businessman detailing the lynching of three Northern carpenters at Friar's Point in the Delta for allegedly setting fire to cotton gins to avenge the death of a Northern abolitionist who had been hanged. Other Northerners in the Delta were sent upriver and warned not to come back. A produce dealer from Cincinnati was in Montgomery soliciting orders when the *Montgomery Advertiser* published an item from a Georgia paper denouncing him as an abolitionist. When a committee of citizens visited in his hotel room, he admitted he was a Lincoln supporter and was ordered to leave immediately or face severe punishment. Foreign nationality was no protection against the wrath of the vigilance committees. In Savannah, a British sea captain was tarred and feathered for "having a negro to dine with him in his cabin."[33]

The violence shocked many planters. "Christmas will soon be here & I suppose vigilant committees will be active and no doubt in many cases too active for both white & black," wrote the wife of a patrician planter. James H. Hammond accused the secessionists of acting in a "quite French Revolutionary" manner. He feared the unleashing of a "reign of terror" in which "solid men who advised caution" would be the victims of "Drunken blackguards." Mayors of several cities, after publicly denouncing roving bands of vigilantes, offered rewards for the arrest and conviction of those leading the mobs.[34]

The violence had its desired political effect. By helping to fuel an atmosphere of fear and hysteria, the vigilantes made attempts at rational debate futile at best and personally dangerous at worst. Conservatives sensed this from the beginning but were powerless to check it. The fears were too great and the excitement too intense. The *Tuscaloosa* (Ala.) *Independent Monitor* reported in mid-November that in some areas of Alabama "it is considered heretical and unsafe to utter a sentiment in favor of reconciling our differences with the North, even were such a thing possible."[35]

Wild rumors coming in on the telegraph dispatches fed the excitement. The reports announced a revolution in New York City with Republicans burning down the Astor House, their opponents destroying the offices of the *Tribune*, a leading Republican paper, and Wide Awakes storming the Customs House to safeguard public funds from Howell Cobb, Buchanan's secretary of the treasury. The street corners of Montgomery were "crowded with persons, agitated, per-plexed and maddened by the alarming news" pouring into the city. Other tele-graph reports told of the assassination of the ex-governor of Virginia, Henry Wise, and 7,000 abolitionists marching on Washington. A widely circulated rumor in December had Andrew Johnson, the Unionist senator from Tennessee, killing Jefferson Davis in a Washington street fight. The rumors were so sensational and persistent that the conservatives accused the secessionists of fabricating them to excite the public mind.[36]

In villages, towns, and cities young men rushed to join volunteer military companies determined to defend the South from all the dangers portended by a Republican triumph. Those in colorful, expensive uniforms displayed their status as the sons of slaveholders, while other uniforms spoke to rage and venge-ance. "The Defiants," a company in Memphis, decked themselves out in black uniforms with red plumes. Their banner, also black, was inscribed on one side with the arms of the state of Tennessee in crimson and on the other by a raised sword with Defiants spelled out in red letters above. The uniform was designed to be emblematic of "death and defiance."[37]

Everyone had a role to play. As the young men drilled, women provided food and vied for the privilege of sewing the company flag. Planters donated money in subscription drives to purchase uniforms and equipment. When the Rhett Guards were ordered to Charleston in January 1861, they marched through the streets of Newberry to the beat of a local band and were loudly cheered by the onlookers. The climax of their send-off was the ceremonial presentation of the company flag from the "ladies of Newberry."[38]

In clamoring for arms from their state governors, the companies emphasized their support for secession. To bolster his request for the Salem Minute Guards, T. F. Murphy pointed out to Governor Moore of Alabama that he had been a fer-vent secessionist for a number of years and that he and his friends would work "to elect Secessionists Straight." Such enthusiasm was fully exploited by the se-cessionist leaders. In Barbour County, a call went out for the eight companies in the Third Regiment of the Alabama Volunteer Corps to muster in Clayton on the day of a mass resistance meeting. A grand military demonstration in front of a crowd of some 3,000 to 4,000 preceded the meeting. When the orations were over, the president of the local Female College presented the regimental flag on behalf of its students. From the ranks of the volunteer companies came the county's secessionist candidates.[39]

By their very presence, the volunteer companies proclaimed retribution to the slaves and anyone who doubted the need for secession. In calling for companies of riflemen, infantry, and artillery, the *Newberry Rising Sun* made that intention explicit. What it praised as "a chivalric little army" would largely replace the ineffective patrol system and compel obedience with its military menace: "Their parade and imposing appearance, the martial music, burnished arms, gay plumes and graceful bearing, the uniformity of dress, would overawe that class of people who are the indirect cause of the present agitation, and, in the event of an emergency, men would be prepared to act effectively, in solid body."[40]

Hard Times and the Salvation of Secession

An economic storm accompanied and intensified the political upheaval. The speculative bubble produced by the cotton boom of the late 1850s burst upon Lincoln's election, plunging the economy into a depression. The collapse came as no surprise to astute observers who cited the political crisis as more effect than cause.

Signs of an overheating economy were apparent by 1859 when the *New Orleans Picayune* warned that the iron law of supply and demand would soon send the economy crashing. As euphoria over cotton demand sent slave prices ever upward, the *Milledgeville Federal Union* noted in June 1860 that there was "a perfect fever raging in Georgia now on the subject of buying negroes." Demand for slaves was especially rampant in the newer cotton fields of southwestern Georgia, where prices had risen 25 percent in the last two years despite a slight drop in cotton prices. "Men demented on the subject. A reckoning sure to come."[41]

Men staked their economic security on ever rising prices of slaves in the hope of gaining greater riches. High prices were no deterrent to those willing to shoulder huge debts. Brothers-in-law M. C. Fulton and Benjamin C. Yancey were rich men in 1858, thanks to a windfall from their father-in-law's estate. The men wiped out their previous debts, only to incur even larger ones in the purchase of new plantations. In early 1859 Fulton paid $75,000 for a Georgia plantation of 2,500 acres and "64 head of negroes" with $25,000 due on January 1, 1860, and two equal installments of $25,000 due on the first of January in 1861 and 1862. He had carefully studied the age and sex composition of the slave labor force. He noted that eighteen children had been born in the last three years with sixteen living at the time of his purchase, and at least six births were expected in 1859. The plantation was averaging 1,500 bales of cotton a year and, with a bale at 500 pounds and cotton at 10 cents a pound that came to $7,500. He calculated that all expenses could be covered from the profit on the sale of the plantation's corn production. Without even "counting the negroes & stock," he told Yancey that the planation was a better investment than stocks or bonds "if negroes & cotton continue at anything like current prices."[42]

A. F. Burton, a small slaveholder struggling to get ahead on a Mississippi farm with poor soil, wanted to expand his cotton output with more slaves, but the income from his farm would not even be able to pay the interest charge on a single male slave bought on credit. He settled in 1859 for buying a cheaper female slave, gambling "on the increase [of her children] provided there was any."[43]

The web of growing debt also enmeshed manufacturers, merchants, and customers for their goods. John C. James, a tobacco dealer in Danville, Virginia, sold his tobacco on consignment. His consignees sold the tobacco on credit to Southern storekeepers, who in turn extended credit to their customers. Drafts drawn on the purchasers' debts accumulated in the banks of New Orleans, Memphis, and Mobile and were usually converted to cash in September when the purchasers could draw on the sale of their cotton. By the late 1850s, James's retail buyers were overextended and fell behind in extinguishing their debts. James was owed over $15,000. In 1859, he hired a lawyer in Mississippi to collect his debts. Despite his problems in getting paid, he took on a large debt of his own in 1860 when he bought fifty-three slaves and an Alabama plantation for $65,000, $300 down in cash and the balance due in six annual installments.[44]

Spring brought the seasonal trek of Southern merchants to New York to buy clothing and other goods. New York was their main supplier because its banks offered the best credit terms for an extended period, generally six months, timed to the fall selling of cotton. With that money, the merchants paid back the New York drafts they had sold to the banks in the spring and the banks met their obligations to the New York banks. The low rates on long credit resulted in higher profit margins for the merchants than if they had purchased Southern-made goods with cash or on short credit. The merchants and their customers went on something of a spending binge in the late 1850s when cotton crops reached record levels. By the spring of 1860, according to the *New York World*, Southern mercantile houses owed from $7,000 to $25,000 to their New York creditors, a debt level the paper thought was unsustainable.[45]

Northern credit was essential to the South's cash-starved cotton economy. During the growing season, credit advanced to factors and planters served to meet their business expenses and buy supplies. The borrowers were required to have co-signees or endorsers on the promissory notes received, thus creating a network of mutually obligatory payees. When the cotton came to market, Northern (and often English) banks, cotton merchants, or their agents extended credit against its eventual sale to move the crop out of the South to its final purchaser. The advance was usually in the form of a sight draft (comparable to a modern check) payable in sixty days after presentation in New York or Liverpool. Factors discounted the drafts, that is, received cash in local banknotes which was less than the face value of the draft as a charge to cover the bank's risk of not being paid in full when the draft came due. The large fall-winter inflow of credit converted into local currencies enabled all the indebted parties to pay last year's debts to Northern creditors before beginning the cycle again in the spring. The debts involved were substantial. Generally, the proceeds of the current year's crop were needed to pay off the debts of the previous year.[46]

Debtors and creditors alike in the South were trapped in an economic nightmare when Lincoln's election triggered a financial panic. Signs of a slowdown in the Southern economy appeared in the summer when money grew tight given the drought and the grim prospects for corn and cotton. The slowdown grew more pronounced as the election approached, and by November the economy was in a full-blown depression, the worst anyone had ever known.

Business of all sorts was at a standstill. Banks refused to discount the factors' advances or did so only for a very short term for small amounts. With cotton prices depressed, planters withheld much of their cotton from market in hopes of better prices in the future. Merchants and commercial houses, unable to pay their debts to Northern firms, suspended operations and, in many cases, failed. By "common consent," as the *Montgomery Mail* put it, Northern debts were postponed, ignored, or sent back by lawyers who had received them for collection.[47]

Cotton prices fell by about 25 percent in the month after Lincoln's election and receipts as of December 31, 1860, were off by 500,000 bales from the 1859 total. The South's major economic assets, land and slaves, depreciated sharply. The slide started in the summer when investors began to anticipate Lincoln's victory. By late October their market value had declined by up to 30 percent. The market for slaves in Charleston was so depressed that traders were reporting "no sale for them" in October. In the same month, slaves were bringing so little in Richmond that the seller of slaves for an estate encumbered by debt advised the executor to hold off for the present on any more sales. A planter in the heart of the Alabama Black Belt reported in November that at a recent sheriff's sale of slaves in Eutaw the prices were "at least 40 to 50 percent below the ruling rates of last year or winter." In December, commission houses in New Orleans stopped making advances on slave property because its value kept falling in a stagnant market. Hiring prices for rented slaves fell in tandem.[48]

Property values collapsed. Noting that "property is worth but little now," Susan Currie of Woodland, Texas, wrote her father that "if I had a thousand dollars now I could make a fortune buying land, stock and property." From Virginia, B. M. Dewitt, who was out $700 in uncollectable debts, estimated that "four hundred dollars' worth of property would not command $100 in ready money, for the reason that *it is not there*." A correspondent for the *Richmond Dispatch* reported from Louisa County in December that farms were selling for one-third less than in the fall and that with money so scarce "wealthy men are nearly as destitute as beggars." In Pittsylvania County, another tobacco growing area, the circulating currency by January consisted of corn, oats, and tobacco in place of banknotes. In the sugar country of Louisiana, property and goods at estate sales were going for 25 percent less than in the summer. The bleak conditions persisted into the winter and spring.[49]

South Carolina was in economic misery. Banks suspended specie payments for their banknotes, cotton houses closed their doors, and the shipment of all crops was held up given the uncertainty of the terms on which orders would be settled. The municipal government of Charleston, along with private firms, laid off workers. Merchants in the interior towns faced ruin as few goods were being forwarded for sale. A letter from "CHAW" in Walhalla described the conditions in January as "the worst that South Carolina ever saw. . . . In fact, there is not as much business done here on any day in the week as there was done on the Sabbath a year ago."[50]

Cries of distress were heard everywhere in the South. Mary E. Thompson, the wife of a planter in Marion, Alabama, informed her son at the University of Alabama that "we have no money, nor provisions, it is almost impossible for the best men to raise one hundred Dol.[;] with all the notes I hold, I cannot raise money enough to pay my tax." Across the rural South, the flow of money to pay off debts dried up. Alexander Stephens fumed that "I am beginning to be annoyed and vexed at the way people cheat me out of three thousand Dollars & refuse to promise me to be paid this fall. I have not collected one dollar." Alabama planter William H. Ogbourne moaned: "No money, and no confidence in any one's ability to pay." All debtors could do was beg indulgence. Unable to make a payment to Benjamin C. Yancey, who himself was deep in debt after his recent purchase of a plantation on credit, T. C. Howard of Georgia pleaded that he had no money and could barely provide for his family. "I am living with my four orphan children *all of us in one room*, & only in that through sufferance. . . . My friend I belong to you body & blood & only beg yr clemency & confidence." Those impoverished in the crisis implored planters for a loan. John Cherry of Windsor, North Carolina, wrote George W. Mordecai for help with his "terrible fate." Cherry had been forced to sell off "a huge portion of all the earthly effects I have had, to pay my liabilities to the Bank in this place. This, with my own individual liabilities, sweeps away from me every thing I possess on the earth, even, *the home of my wife & children!!*"[51]

Planters had to forgo debt collections and cut back on all but essential expenses. Most of them were debtors themselves and the poor crop year and fall-off in crops going to market left them in no position to pay their debts, at least until the political crisis was resolved. Still, their plight paled in comparison to that of the rural and urban poor.

The food shortages from the crop failures worsened once the financial crisis hit. Prices for provisions soared and the prospect of famine loomed for many. A resident of Choctaw County, Alabama, lashed out in December at Mobile merchants for demanding non-existent cash to fill orders. He estimated that eight out of ten families would be out of corn in less than two months and had no means of buying any. Conditions were so dire that Governor A. B. Moore, worried that "perhaps starvation" was imminent, recommended to the legislature that the county courts of commissioners levy a special tax to pay for public relief. If that proved inadequate, he called upon the counties to mortgage public property to raise the necessary funds. In Georgia, the legislature in December gave the Inferior Courts the discretionary power to draw monies from the Public School Fund for the "purchase of food and fire wood for the poor." Similar relief measures, supplemented with funds donated by planters, were undertaken in other Southern states. Relief in the form of debtor stay laws was initially put off on the grounds that the crisis was so severe that no one was able to call in debts.[52]

The urban poor were just as badly off. "Never before have there been so many laborers thrown out of employment in Atlanta, as at this time," reported a local paper in December. The editor proposed that the jobless be put to work on the city's streets so they could earn some money to feed their families. The *New Orleans Bee* expressed concern with the "extraordinary amount of real destitution and poverty" in the city. It suggested that the mayor and city council make use of a large, vacant building to shelter the homeless and set up a soup kitchen. When no action was taken, the poor thronged the city's police stations seeking protection from the cold. Others were arrested and sent to the city's jails when the police broke up encampments of squatters on the outskirts of the city. Up the Red River in Alexandria, Louisiana, women and children were "crying in our streets for want of bread." In Richmond, and Virginia's other cities, clerks, tobacco workers, and women sewing for clothing manufacturers were laid off and public works suspended. Notices went out from grocers in the port cities of Norfolk and Portsmouth that credit for the unemployed would be cut off as of January 1. Rogene Scott in Nashville daily turned away beggars "because I can but just help myself."[53]

Conservatives argued it was the worst of all possible times to consider secession, but their appeals for moderation went ignored. The secessionists

successfully presented the crisis as the latest manifestation of the South's colonial bondage to the North. Once the South controlled its own economic
agenda, they contended, stability and prosperity would return. Georgian E. A.
Nisbet stated in a secessionist speech that "confidence [in the Union] is lost—
irretrievably lost." Only a fresh start in an independent South would bring back
"trade and prosperity."[54]

The secessionists were far more astute than the conservatives in understanding the psychology of panic. "Whilst cotton is up and times flush of cash,
you can't wake men up to revolution," noted secessionist Henry A. Wise. When
times were bad and all semblance of economic security was gone, desperation
took over. After witnessing the economic panic in New Orleans, a Breckinridge
politician, Frank Valliant, concluded that the "secession movement is if anything
stronger here than in Mississippi, everyone appearing to think that they can not
possibly be in a worse situation than they now are." J. B. Sharpe, a Memphis merchant, declaimed, "My God! We are forever ruined, unless we undo what we
have done, and institute measures to secure our Rights and protect ourselves
from Northern aggression." Sharpe had voted for Bell and the Union. The hard
times converted him to secession.[55]

Gin Houses Ablaze: Slave Defiance

Upon hearing of Lincoln's election, the thoughts of Southern whites reflex-
ively turned to the slaves. Many feared that the slaves would "rise in a bloody
insurrection against their masters." That was precisely the fear J. W. Walton of
Mississippi expressed to his granddaughter: "I have been kept very uneasy in my
mind about the blacks and the result of the Presidential election." That uneasiness pervaded the planter class and could be relieved only by promptly seceding.
So proclaimed Andrew P. Calhoun at the fair of the State Agricultural Society
in Columbia, South Carolina, on November 13. Noting with alarm that the rise
of the Republicans had infested the slaves with dangerous notions of freedom,
Calhoun assured his audience that separating from the North would "dispel the
idea and reduce the negro to unconditional quiet and submission, if the disen-
tanglement . . . is complete, thorough and radical."[56]

The planters' fears were overblown but hardly baseless. As Calhoun was well
aware, the slaves were not oblivious to current political events and debates. The
very ubiquity of slaves—serving food and drink at the master's table; delivering
messages between plantations and picking up mail in town; eavesdropping at
stump speeches and listening when newspapers were read, often aloud; working
on railroads and steamboats; and circulating through the community as rented
laborers—constantly exposed them to the concerns and political thinking of

whites. William Webb, a former slave in Missouri, wrote of the election year of 1856 as the time that "the scales of ignorance fell from [the] eyes [of the slaves]." Whites were visibly troubled by the Republican campaign and swore in their speeches that "the streets would run with blood before the North should rule. This was the first the colored people knew about another Nation wishing for the slaves to be free. . . . They put all their trust in Fremont to deliver them from bondage."[57]

In addition to what filtered down from whites, slaves had their own sources of information. Literate slaves played a vital role. Despite prohibitions in most states against teaching slaves to read and write, some 10 percent of slaves were literate, often taught by the mistress or her daughter. "A Colored man who could read was a very important fellow," recalled Henry Clay Bruce of his days as a slave in Missouri, "for slaves would come [from] miles and bring stolen papers for him to read them at night or on Sunday." Household slaves would steal away at night and tell slaves in the quarters "what they heard the master say about the policies of the country." Slaves who had accompanied their masters on a trip to the North passed on what they had heard from Northern whites upon returning. Northern travelers in the South occasionally befriended a slave and spoke of the antislavery movement. That was how Henry Watson, hired out as a waiter in Vicksburg, learned of "a subject which I was entirely ignorant of before."[58]

Information gained on one plantation traveled through a communications network. Local leaders organized secret, closely guarded meetings where they reported on what they had learned and appointed runners to carry the news to the next plantation. The runners covered about twelve miles and relayed the information to the next runners. The main corridors in the chain ran along waterways, notably the Mississippi River and the South Atlantic seaboard. Black sailors, boatmen, and pilots, free as well as slave, all played a role.[59]

Planters were aware of the information networks but unable to shut them down. An exasperated James H. Hammond in 1844 was "astonished and shocked to find that some [of his slaves] are aware of the opinions of the Presidential Candidates on the subject of Slavery and doubtless of much of what the abolitionists are doing and I am sure they know as little of what is done off my place as almost any set of negroes in the State." Olmsted heard from planters that the "spread of intelligence of all kinds among slaves is remarkable." A planter told him that his slaves knew what was going on in a town forty miles from his home where he and his wife spent part of the year, which, as far as he knew, was completely cut off from his plantation. He added that when in a local town on business, "his servants would sometimes give him important news from the plantation several hours before a messenger dispatched by his overseer arrived."[60]

Except on isolated plantations deep in the interior, slaves knew of Lincoln's election as soon as their masters. "The negroes are of [the] opinion Lincoln is to come here to free them," wrote Caroline Pettigrew from Charleston on November 7, 1860. Ten days later she noted: "I have not heard a dissenting voice to the fact that the belief is prevalent among the negroes that this election decides their freedom—even small negroes have spoken as to their approaching freedom, as to all this there is no doubt, but that any plan of insurrection had been formed seems untrue." In speeches, editorials, and private correspondence, whites uniformly recorded that the slaves hailed Lincoln as their liberator. Most of them were far less confident than Caroline Pettigrew that there was no need for undue concern.[61]

Calls went out for stepped-up vigilance and a complete ban on all meetings of slaves. With paramilitary groups forming daily, the South became an armed camp. Meanwhile, the drumbeat of reported insurrectionary plots picked up in volume. Out of Ramer, Alabama, in December came news that slaves in Montgomery County were to strike during the Christmas holidays. After coercing confessions by "whipping the negroes—taking them as they come," the whites learned that their estates and all their property were to be divided among the slaves. "They look for aid from Lincoln and the Northern people." One white and four slaves were hanged. The uncovering and suppression of the "plot" had served a useful purpose. As S. B. Brown, one of the white vigilantes, expressed it: "it has had the effect of more strongly and closely uniting our people politically, and is working a salutary influence on all the negroes of the plantation."[62]

Rushing to uncover slave plots unified whites and shored up their sense of mastery. After a "negro mechanic" in Sardis, Mississippi, was whipped into confessing the details of an uprising for the night of December 26, the whites of Panola County were assured that "at no former period . . . could it be said that the entire slave population was under better subjection than they were on Christmas day." As for the plot, a local Bell supporter, planter John C. Brahan, denounced the whole episode as a complete fabrication. For most whites, the veracity of a plot mattered less than the need to exert control. Whites in Aberdeen, Mississippi, like those in Sardis, felt reassured when the ringleaders of an alleged plot in January "were thrashed so severely that it was thought they would die." "Served 'em right," said the local paper.[63]

Every report of an insurrectionary strengthened the cause of secession. During the debate in the Georgia legislature on the night of November 12 on whether a state secession convention should be authorized, secessionist Thomas R. R. Cobb exploited the insurrectionary rumors. He singled out "the trembling hand of a loved wife . . . the indefinable dread [of] the little daughter," the suspicious slave, and the treacherous peddler and conniving Northerner talking too long with the slaves who greeted them at the plantation as the terrifying "heritage which this Union has brought to your firesides." He prompted the legislators to "hear, as I did this day, that within seven miles of this Capital, a gang of slaves have revolted from their labor, declaring themselves free by virtue of Lincoln's election."[64]

While Cobb was urging secession, whites forty miles away in Crawford County were rounding up and whipping slaves. Several were implicated in a plot for election day. After a frenzied week, an investigating committee rationalized the violence unleashed by concluding: "There was no attempt at insurrection, but there was a meaningful intention to rebel." A white Pennsylvanian, Amos V. Dreher, was put on notice under penalty of death to stop talking with slaves and reading them incendiary literature. Decades later, Rebecca Felton still had a vivid memory of the armed men in a revival tent near Rome, Georgia, on a Sunday night in 1860. They were "waiting for midnight to go out quietly to suppress a 'rising' that had been reported to them late in the afternoon." She noted that the " 'rising' was a false alarm but the terror of these risings made the Southern fathers and husbands desperate as to remedy it."[65]

In the fall of 1860 that terror hung like a shroud over the widow Keziah Brevard on her plantation near Columbia, South Carolina. She managed the plantation alone. Although she had spent her life among slaves, she readily admitted in her diary that she knew nothing of them save that they lacked any moral sense, were aware of a lot more than they let on, and harbored a murderous desire to kill her. Nightmares of fires raging out of control filled her nights of restless sleep, and she repeatedly referred to her dread of her slaves. She had no doubt that most of hers and those of her neighbors would seize any opportunity "to butcher us." Had she her own way, she never would have owned slaves or chosen to live in a slave society. Far from a positive good, slavery for her was an unsettling, endless source of anxiety. In a veiled reference to the rampant miscegenation around her, she clung to her one consolation—she "never had a son to mix my blood with *negro* blood."[66]

White panic broke out in the Upper South as well. Underlying it was the whites' belief that the slaves would strike for freedom with the Republicans about to assume power. A free black in Lancaster County, Virginia, told of a plan for the slaves to meet at the courthouse, break open the jail and seize the arms stored there, and indiscriminately slaughter whites before fleeing to a waiting vessel and escaping down the Rappahannock River. "Some miserable men" in Amelia County were blamed for putting it into the heads of the slaves that Lincoln would come to the rescue of abolitionists battling whites in Richmond on inauguration day and declare the slaves free. One slave reportedly was going to avenge himself against his master by cutting off his head and taking "his young mistress to live with him for a wife." Only the intervention of conservative lawyers prevented a mass lynching. Reports reached the mayors of Petersburg and Norfolk of an insurrection planned around the time of Lincoln's inauguration, and several blacks were jailed. Upon reading of the jailings, Daniel Cobb, who lived nearby, grimly announced in his diary that he was ready for a race war. "We got the Black poperlation to murder or to be murdered by the Blacks and the sooner it begins the better."[67]

Some slaves likely were unguarded in talking about freedom, but white assumptions regarding what the slaves were going to do drove much of the hysteria. After all, with more whites armed and on the alert than ever, the prospects of an uprising were more suicidal than under normal circumstances. A slave who boldly proclaimed a desire to be free stood a good chance of being shot on the spot. In late December, near Houston, Mississippi, a slave saying he wanted to be free refused to obey his owner. "His master," wrote a local paper, "walked into the house, got his gun, and shot the negro dead, then called up the balance of his servants, and asked them if they wanted to be free."[68]

The accounts of planters rarely mentioned open resistance during the secession crisis. Adept at role playing, a coping mechanism for self-defense, the slaves gave masters every reason to indulge in their paternalistic self-deception of shepherding loyal servants. In January 1861, the slaves of A. S. Coleman of Bolivar, Tennessee, asked to wear blue cockades as a way "they said, to show their contempt for the Abolitionists." Mary Sue, a house slave in South Carolina, according to her mistress, said of her own accord that "I never was craving to be free not when I was young much less now." "Even our slaves are becoming patriotic," proudly wrote a correspondent for a Charleston paper. As Charlestonians were celebrating the state's secession, he claimed to have overheard a conversation between a slave and a white gentleman "in which the slave declared himself a 'Minute Man,' and said *he was ready to fight for his master's rights*, and that he was only one of 'many of the same sort.'" Protestations of loyalty from some slaves were so convincing that a few whites suggested arming the slaves to help in resisting any invading hordes of Republicans. The *New Orleans Picayune* called such talk "all balderdash" when it demanded a strict enforcement of the Louisiana statute requiring all slaveowners to have at least one white person over the age of sixteen for every thirty slaves on a plantation.[69]

Despite the overall quietude of the slaves, a few did snap and kill their oppressors. In September, a slave in Columbus, Mississippi, killed his owner John T. Keely during a whipping. Kelly was "literally cut to pieces by the negro." The slave drowned in a river while trying to escape. Pursuing whites recovered his body and left it dangling from a rope on a tree. Robert Williams, the wealthiest man in Yalobusha County, Mississippi, was murdered on November 16 by one of his slaves after Williams told him he was in for a whipping for failing to split rails correctly. Early the next week, another Mississippi overseer was stabbed to death by a slave he was "correcting." In March, four slaves on a plantation near Commerce, Mississippi, killed their overseer by snapping his neck. Two of the slaves escaped and were last seen on a stolen boat crossing the Mississippi River.[70]

Mississippi was exceptional in the number of killings by slaves, but murders did occur in other Southern states during the fall and winter of 1860. After killing one of his pursuers, a runaway slave in Terrebonne Parish, Louisiana, managed to escape. A slave in Calloway County, Missouri, was not so fortunate. A white mob lynched him on November 2 for murdering his mistress. A Tennessee slave who slit his master's throat rather than be "chastised" was sentenced to death in December. The spring brought the killing of an overseer in Alabama, another in Florida, and the lynching of a slave accused of murder in Sumter County, Tennessee. Just to the southwest in Nashville, Rogene Scott heard numerous account "of slaves beating or killing their masters."[71]

Some train passengers in North Carolina had witnessed firsthand the results of what Scott was hearing. While returning on December 31 to his house from his plantation fields near Weldon, North Carolina, Lucius T. Woodruff was axed to death by four of his slaves, with the heaviest blow being struck by a female slave. The slaves were said to have mocked Woodruff by shouting that they had "got him at last." They dragged the body into the woods and buried it, but two days later suspicious whites rounded up Woodruff's slaves and singled out the four murderers, who confessed that they had acted because Woodruff had prohibited neighboring slaves from visiting his plantation during the Christmas holidays. A train on the Roanoke and Seaboard Railroad was detained in the vicinity of the murder and several passengers stepped off to view the mutilated body. Unwilling to believe that the slaves had acted on their own, local whites blamed the bloody affair on "Abolitionists."[72]

Poisoning was another form of potentially lethal resistance, one resorted to by household slaves when they added poisonous herbs and, in one cause, kerosene oil, to the tea, coffee, or milk they served at meals. Three slaves paid with their lives in Lunenburg County, Virginia, for a botched attempt in October to poison the family of M. L. Spencer. Convicted of the crime, they were sentenced to be hanged on November 9. A slave who poisoned Thomas Sacres of Caroline County in December claimed in his confession that a white man and woman had paid him $10 to commit the deed. A "negro girl" tried to poison the family of a Mr. Phillips in Harrisonburg, Virginia, but succeeded only in making Mrs. Phillips and her child violently ill. A distraught Kentucky woman wrote Lincoln in January that since the "negros have taken up the notion, or rather it has been taught them by beggars and Gipsies, that as soon as you were elected they would be all free," then it was his responsibility to tell them "if you do not intend such a thing . . . to *make* them know it." Otherwise, "their work of poisoning and incendiaryism" would continue.[73]

A much larger number of slaves resisted by running away. Although the federal censuses of 1850 and 1860 counted only 1,011 and 803, respectively, as the number of at-large escaped slaves, recent research has persuasively argued for a minimum number of 50,000 per year at any given time. Most returned or were brought in by white patrols within a few weeks or months. Still, runaways were a chronic problem for planters who had to absorb the costs of recapture and labor lost. The pace of runaways picked up after Lincoln's election, especially on the lowcountry plantations between Charleston and Savannah. From Argyle Island, just above Savannah, Charles Manigault complained in January of the "great arrogance of the negroes running away on Savh River, it is seriously the case in various sections of the country, & not far from Charleston. They have generally got the idea of being emancipated when 'Lincoln' comes in." Patrols of armed overseers and planters with tracking dogs scoured the swamps, trying to block the runaways from reaching the coast and possible freedom on a northern-bound vessel. In the same month, Robert N. Gourdin received a disturbing report from J. J. Pringle Smith in Colleton District, South Carolina, of some thirty slaves leaving the island plantations rather than being sent to Fort Pulaski to work on fortifications. Rumors had it that they were instigated into fleeing by local whites, known as "duckers," who told them they were "to be made to fight against their true friends and would be liberators [and] be put in the front of the battle." Smith discounted the rumors but was worried about the "possible effect on others" of such large-scale disobedience.[74]

Down the coast in McIntosh County, the slaves were restless and the planters concerned that they were about to run away out of fear that their children and women would be left behind when the male slaves were ordered out for fortifications work. One report blamed the unrest on a white butcher from Savannah, who had come down and told the slaves that a vessel was waiting for them on the coast to take them to the North. Closer to the Florida line in Ware County, the Minute Men were called out to hunt down a gang of armed runaways led by two men who had "promised them freedom." A similar gang in March pillaged property on the eastern side of the Comite River in southern Louisiana.[75]

According to accounts in Chicago, streams of runaways were pouring into the city on their way to Canada. By April, some 1,000 were reported to have arrived. Gangs of slave catchers were in hot pursuit, and hundreds of African Americans fled the city for Canada. Meanwhile, in an effort to stem the outflow and stamp out insubordination, slaveholders in St. Joseph, Missouri, began shipping their slaves farther south, including one group of thirty to forty in mid-December.[76]

Many slaves resorted to arson rather than trying to escape. Reports of slave plots aside, nothing unnerved whites more than the rash of fires across the South in 1860. They commonly conflated fires with slave insurrections in the term "incendiarism." Property damage was extensive, and unless caught in the act, arsonists were maddingly difficult to identify. The fires began in the spring, intensified in the early summer, and peaked in November and December.

When Aull's Steam Mills outside Newberry, South Carolina, burned down in early April, the local paper blamed it on an incendiary, "in fact, there's no room for doubt." After a series of fires erupted in Macon, Georgia, in April and continued into the late spring, a wave of unexplained fires in June and July swept through Newnan, Warrenton, Atlanta, Griffin, and Columbus, Georgia. By then, other cities and towns were reporting mysterious fires, the worst of which lit up the night sky in Natchez on May 26. The rattled residents of Mandeville, Louisiana, formed a vigilance committee "to deal with incendiaries" and instituted a nightly curfew announced by the firing of a cannon at 9 o'clock. The only arrests made through July were of two slaves, a woman in Macon and Bob in Columbus.

The sheer number of fires suggested to whites that a conspiracy was afoot. J. A. Turner, a Georgia planter, explained the fires as the work of "the host of abolition emissaries who are scattered abroad . . . throughout our land, who permeate the whole of Southern society, who occupy our places of trust and emolument." They were Northerners living in the South or passing through who harbored an "implacable hatred" of slavery and sought out every opportunity "to instill the poison of their opinions into the minds of slaves." Unless stopped, the South would face a "fire of servile insurrection." Turner's remedy—complete social and economic non-intercourse with Northerners—was utterly impractical, but by personalizing in the form of Southern Yankees the moral attacks of outsiders against slavery, he furnished a powerful rationale for heightened racial controls and constant surveillance of Northerners.[77]

The Texas fires and abolitionist plots dominated the news in August and seemingly confirmed Turner's grim prophecy. After a lull in late summer, the fires picked up in October. Natchez and Crystal Springs, Mississippi, were hit by major fires. A fire destroyed the courthouse in Lake City, Florida. Slaves, said to be instigated by a white, burned Charles Bannerman's cotton gin house at Lake Iamonia, Florida. Alfred, a slave blacksmith, was sentenced to death for setting fire to the house of General O. E. Edwards in Spartanburg, South Carolina. Five slaves burned down a planter's sugar house in St. Charles, Louisiana. Concerning the "large number of incendiary attempts" in the city, the *New Orleans Picayune* reported that "in every case, the suspicions based on circumstantial evidence, rested against slaves." Numerous accounts came in of burnings of cotton gins up and down the Mississippi River. "There appears to be a system about these burnings," concluded the *Coahoma* (Miss.) *Citizen*, "as we are inclined to believe that they are set on fire by traveling incendiaries." Opelika, Alabama, a great depot for Georgia and Alabama, lost five of its leading business establishments in a blaze on October 26.[78]

In November 1860, the fires reached epidemic proportions as more were reported that month than the total since March. Most occurred where property damage would be greatest, the business districts of cities and gin houses where sugar or cotton was stored. Among the cities hit were Williamston, North Carolina, in its commercial center; Columbus, Georgia, where a bank and several stores were destroyed; and Albany, Georgia, in a fire the local paper described as "beyond doubt, the work of an incendiary, as the building in which it was first discovered, had neither a fire-place or stove connected with it." Fires in New Orleans were almost a nightly occurrence and all signs pointed to arsonists at work. Despite a standing reward of $3,000 offered by the Board of Underwriters for any information leading to the arrest and conviction of an incendiary, no one came forward. The Reverend T. J. Henderson featured the fires in his Thanksgiving Day Sermon: "When have we been so aroused by the alarm of fire? When have conflagrations consumed such immense portions of property?"[79]

In the countryside, the fires clustered in plantation zones with their large numbers of slaves. Planter John S. Haywood in the Alabama Black Belt was alarmed by "these troublesome times when Ginhouses are burnt down." Hit hardest were sugar and cotton planters in the Mississippi Valley. James Shelton in Mississippi lost fifty bales of cotton and suspected "some of his own slaves were the incendiaries." When J. Gillion's gin was destroyed, along with his cotton, two farm wagons, and all his farming implements, he blamed it on "vile incendiaries." Similar reports and charges came out of Louisiana. Enraged by fourteen gin fires in six weeks, planters in the Delta sought out Northern workmen for retribution. In one instance, two white men were spotted fleeing from a burning gin. A slave woman, who was "sleeping in the gin" as a guard, sounded the alarm. The *Alexandria Constitutional* linked the burnings to "the position in which the whole Southern country is placed by the result of the recent Presidential election" and called for heightened surveillance security "from 'enemies without or foes within.'"[80]

The frequency of the fires fell in December, but they continued throughout the winter. Whites found the badly mutilated body of a black man in the smoldering ruins of a gin in Grosse Tete, Louisiana. A court in St. James Parish found two slaves guilty of burning a sugar house. One was bound over for corporal punishment and the other sentenced to death. A slave woman was arrested in New Orleans on the charge of setting fire to a coffee house. Two men charged with arson in South Carolina were slaves, each sentenced to be hanged.[81]

As the fires persisted in the Lower South, a new wave started in the states of the Upper South gearing up for elections for delegates to possible secession conventions. Memphis lost two blocks of buildings to a fire in mid-December. The courthouse in New Bern, North Carolina, burned and five fires in four days broke out in Charlotte in late March. "Nearly every place of business is closed," wired a correspondent to a Virginia paper, "and an organized body of 'Regulators' is at this time on duty throughout the town and its surroundings." In upper Georgia, where Unionists remained defiant after the state had seceded, a fire destroyed eight buildings in Newnan on February 22, 1861, and the business district of Newport on March 15. A large brick tobacco factory burned down in Richmond on February 20. A week later, the slave Adelaide was put on trial in February for setting fire to the Richmond house of Mrs. John Exall.[82]

Whites were convinced that revenge-minded slaves set several fires in the Virginia countryside. Bruce Gwynn of Suffolk County suffered property damages of $3,000 and two years' work when his barn burned in late December. As captain of a neighborhood patrol a few nights earlier, he had ordered slaves lashed for being out without a pass. George Crump, another member of the patrol, also had his barn torched. Concerned whites called a meeting and resolved for the patrol to be "even more vigilant and strict thereafter." A "negro girl," the slave of Thomas H. Richeson of Caroline County, was thought to be responsible for torching his stables, barn, and tobacco houses on the night of December 27. The next night, Andrew, another of Richeson's slaves, burned the house of Mr. Murry, a neighbor with whom Richeson was staying. When equally destructive fires broke out in Amelia County in January, a local resident demanded an end to any leniency for the perpetrators. He suggested that the fires were "some of the first fruits of the decision of our County Court at its November term, at which a negro was sentenced to be transported, instead of being hung, for burning a tobacco barn." Arson, he insisted, deserved "the severest punishment the law directs, especially when we remember how rarely the offenders are detected and brought to justice."[83]

The defiance of the slaves, in some cases abetted by whites, was unmistakable. A sizable, though indiscriminate, number bludgeoned and axed to death planters and overseers, attempted to poison their masters' families, ran away, pillaged property, and burned urban businesses and tens of thousands of dollars of cotton, sugar, and tobacco. The murders were likely spontaneous acts, but other forms of revenge revealed premeditation, driven by retaliation for abuse of self or family members or likely sparked by awareness of the chinks in the planters' mastery exposed by Lincoln's election. With the economy at a standstill, food shortages, unprecedented unemployment, insurrection scares, and continued reports of slave resistance, conditions could not have been more favorable for secession. Political actors by their own volition, the slaves had given whites all the more reason to break free from the Union.

South Carolina Takes the Lead

Since the nullification crisis, South Carolina's radicals had sought a catalyst to trigger a mass movement for secession. That catalyst finally arrived with Lincoln's election and calls for resistance. For the former cooperationist lowcountry planters in the inner circles of the Gourdins' Association of 1860, however, too much was at stake to allow Robert B. Rhett and his followers to lead South Carolina out of the Union. Fearful that the Rhett hotheads would overplay their hand and precipitate a war in which an isolated South Carolina faced hopeless odds against the North, the association orchestrated a movement intended to achieve peaceful, orderly secession that would pull in the other slave states, and minimally those of the Cotton South. The Gourdins and their allies were masters at mobilizing public support in a campaign that combined joyful celebrations of resistance with the suppression of dissent. They showed the way for other states.

Reclaiming Revolutionary Glory

Time had been cruel to the proud planter elite of South Carolina. Its oldest families had furnished patriotic heroes to the American Revolution and signatories of the Constitution. Charleston was the country's fourth largest city in 1790, rice and sea-island planters flourished, and the Carolina Piedmont was the first boom frontier for short-staple cotton.

After 1820, however, the state lapsed into economic decay and political isolation. As Charleston slipped to twenty-second in size among cities by 1860, the state's population lagged far behind that of the other states when heavy out-migration from the worn-out fields of the Piedmont drained off whites to the fresher lands of the southwest. The erosion of the region's soils was so severe that only one-third of its land was still in use by 1860, including that set aside for grazing and fallow. New sources of rice from Asia and the lower Mississippi Valley after 1840 took away market share from Carolina rice planters and kept prices low. A. G. Summer, in making his case in 1854 for a new, vigorous state agricultural society, painted a dire picture of the state's economic plight: "South Carolina is not even stationary in its industrial pursuits [but] actually and rapidly retrograding . . . and her sons are seeking the more remunerating fields of the southwest." Worse yet, slaves, "the true wealth of the State," would soon be sent to the southwest as well.[1]

The lowcountry elite, the core of support for political radicalism, were painfully aware of the state's economic problems and loss of prestige. The intellectuals among them turned to the American Revolution for a model on how South Carolina, and the South, could anticipate a bright, new future. By the 1850s, they relied on a conservative reading of the Revolution to construct the intellectual underpinnings of Southern nationalism. They did so by stripping away the egalitarian features of the Revolution and highlighting its call for self-government free of outside repression. In the forefront of the movement were William Henry Trescot and David F. Jamison, both planters and graduates of the College of Charleston.[2]

Despite a distinguished career in the State Department, Trescot was an avowed secessionist by 1850. In his tract, "The Position and Course of the South," he accepted the vindication of slavery as a given in his praise of God for having "solved for us in the wisest manner, that most dangerous of social questions, the relation of labour to capital by making the relation a moral one" of mutual duty. Northerners with their free-labor system, apparently unwilling to accept the will of the Maker, were openly hostile to the South's "peculiar" institution and its reverence for the Constitution and had gained the assistance of the federal government. Hence, the "only safety of the South [was] in the formation of an independent nation." Such a nation would mark the culmination, not the repudiation, of the "vital principle of political liberty" for which the Revolution was fought.[3]

Like Trescot, Jemison credited the American Revolution with "the birth of the democratic principle." He traced the roots of that principle back to the love of "personal independence" of the Germanic peoples who overran the Roman Empire, which in time flowed into the Reformation, English and American Puritanism, and the values of the settlers in the American colonies. It was productive of liberty and stability, however, only when entrusted to the "Anglo-Saxon race," and ultimately only when checked by the ordered liberty that slave society alone could provide. In Jemison's reading, majority rule in a North beset by the endemic conflict of capital and labor had debased the Constitution into the plaything of popular passions and had subjected the South to unrelenting assaults on its institutions and rights. "If the people of the South shall submit to a worse than colonial subjection to the States of the North," he concluded, they would " clothe our own foreheads with the crimson flush of shame."[4]

In drawing on the Revolution to legitimate their disunionist cause, the secessionists denied New England's claim that slavery limited South Carolina's contribution to patriot victory. To the contrary, insisted William G. Simms, the successful defense of Fort Sullivan in Charleston's harbor in June 1776 played a far larger role in winning independence than Lexington, Concord, or Bunker Hill. Meanwhile, Robert B. Rhett latched onto the Boston Tea Party as an example of the open resistance the South should follow in throwing off Northern tyranny.

Nonetheless, most Southern whites clung to the Union as the enduring accomplishment of the Revolution that should be upheld, not rejected. The *New Orleans Bee* dismissed South Carolina's calls for disunion and advised Carolinians to look at their own failures in not promoting "the enterprise and public spirit of her neighbors" rather than blaming the North for its "impoverished condition." The paper clearly saw how the state's economic malaise and political radicalism fed off each other. "The people of South Carolina have been persistently engaged in anathematizing Northern aggression, and in preaching the necessity of dissolution. Just in the same proportion has her commerce declined and her agricultural wealth diminished." Benjamin O. Tayloe, a conservative Virginian, made the same point with more bite. "S.C. is ripe for disunion .... Her glory has departed — & she knows it. That is the rub."[5]

Mocked though they were, the radicals offered the declining families of South Carolina an alluring path back to their former glory. The Pinckneys were one of the families that eagerly followed that path soon after Lincoln's election. Escaping the heat of the lowcountry, they were in the cool climes of Flat Rock, North Carolina, when the election was held. When they had left their plantation for the mountains, "nothing was further from our thoughts than our country," wrote Mary Elliott Pinckney. But on their return home in early December, they encountered such popular excitement that, as Mary expressed it, "why of course we took fire too, the dross of indifference was all consumed & (my niece) Carry and I are now very earnest newspaper readers, & I may add *able* politicians, all [in] the course of 4 weeks!" Almost as an aside, she wondered "how the ague shaken, mosquito bitten wretches who inhabit our low country in the summer can be endued with the same energy as the inhabitants of better climates, but I would prefer a poor honorable country, wouldn't you?" Then again, the lowcountry poor whites were never of much concern to families like the Pinckneys.[6]

The Pinckneys were one of the state's most distinguished families. Charles Cotesworth Pinckney, Mary Elliott's grandfather, was a signer of the Declaration of Independence along with his cousin. Cotesworth's son Thomas was a governor in the 1780s and chaired the ratifying convention in 1788 that brought South Carolina into the Union. In striking contrast, all of Thomas's sons were Nullifiers. Charles Cotesworth Pinckney II was, in Mary's words, "delighted with the state of affairs" when South Carolina surged toward secession "& is fully persuaded that we are to be the most glorious & prosperous country." In a reversal of the usual intergenerational pattern, Thomas, his son and Mary's brother, needed to be prodded by the father to commit to secession. Having recently been deeded one of his father's rice plantations, he likely was looking forward at the age of thirty-three to establishing his independence. His indecision lasted through the end of December when the planters along the Santee River were ordered to fortify their plantations and the entrance to the river in preparation for a Northern invasion. Enlisting in a Georgetown Cavalry unit on January 5, 1861, Thomas later used his family's prestige to organize his own company. Perhaps to Mary's surprise, the "ague shaken, mosquito wretches" rushed to fill in the ranks of the company. Charles C. Pinckney was too old to fight, but through his son he could vicariously relive the military glory of the Pinckneys' Revolutionary past.[7]

Launching the Movement

On the eve of the election, the atmosphere in the state was tense, edgy, ready to explode. At a public demonstration in Columbia, a crowd of some 1,000 serenaded Senator James Chesnut, Congressman Milledge L. Bonham, and members of the state legislature. Chesnut played up to their wounded pride by reminding them that "Northerners call us inferior, semi-civilized barbarians, and claim the right to possess our lands and to give them to the destitute of the Old World and the profligate of this." If the Republicans won, he went on, they would flood the South with abolitionist literature and staff the post offices with their "minions." Significantly, however, he offered only hedged support for the state's independent secession.

On election day, November 6, crowds mingled around the office front of the *Charleston Mercury*, where the bulletin board posted the latest election returns. At midnight, the paper unfurled and stretched across the street to lusty cheers a red flag with the palmetto symbol and a lone star. The following day, when the grand jury in Charleston was set to deliberate in the federal district court, the foreman, who by happenstance was Robert Gourdin, announced that with all hope of remaining in the Union now gone, "the Grand Jury respectfully declines to proceed with their presentments." Andrew Magrath, the federal district judge, then made that pronouncement more than an empty gesture. Having already challenged federal authority in an April 1860 ruling that engaging in the African slave trade was not an act of piracy, he took his defiance to a new level. Turning to the grand jury, he announced his resignation. The federal district attorney and US marshal quickly followed. The near-simultaneity of their resignations

Fig. 5.1 Great Mass Meeting, Institute Hall. Fashionably dressed women joined the enthusiastic crowd of Charlestonians at Institute Hall on November 12, 1860, to urge the legislature to call a state convention to take South Carolina out of the Union. Library of Congress, LC-USZ62-62193.

suggested a pre-arranged plan to jump-start secession. Within hours of Lincoln's election, they had shut down the machinery of federal law enforcement in the state.[8]

News of Magrath's resignation touched off street celebrations and torrents of secessionist oratory in Columbia and Charleston. In hailing it as "the strongest possible evidence of the resistance sentiment of the people," the *Charleston Mercury* elevated the resignation into the mythic status of the Boston Tea Party. "The tea has been thrown overboard. The Revolution of 1860 has been initiated." Rhett, the face of secession for over thirty years, now had to take a back seat. Magrath was the man of the hour.

The son of an Irish immigrant who had fled persecution for his role in the abortive Irish uprising of 1798, Magrath had imbibed his father's romantic nationalism. He had earned elite credentials by reading law under James L. Petigru and attending Harvard Law School, but his cooperationist past and non-planter background kept him out of the inner circle of leadership until his dramatic resignation. When serenaded at his private residence in the aftermath of a secession rally on the evening of November 7, he told the crowd just what it wanted to

Fig. 5.2 Secession Meeting, Mills House. Serenaders in front of the Mills House in Charleston call on the politicians for secession speeches. Library of Congress, LC-USZ62-62195.

hear. Viewing "the *actions of the day as the first gun of the revolution*," he hoped for a united South, "but if not, South Carolina would make the issue."[9]

Everything was falling in place for the secessionists, but one nagging doubt remained. Would the state move with the necessary speed to prevent any movement emerging in other states that would make secession hostage to a cooperative approach or, worse yet, to a call for a Southern convention in which the states of the Upper South would insist on working out a grand sectional compromise?

The early signs from the legislature in Columbia were not encouraging. Although the cooperationists, representing small farmers in the upcountry and commercial interests in Charleston, were in a decided minority, any lack of unanimity threatened to expose internal divisions and deter other states from acting. After reading the private letters solicited by Gist and the Rhetts in October indicating, but not pledging, support for South Carolina if it took the lead, the Rhett faction introduced resolutions in the House and Senate setting November

22 as the date for a convention election that was to meet on December 17. Robert
B. Rhett Jr. justified the haste by citing what he called "the moral effect of prompt
action." Such speed would settle the issue of secession, encourage other states to
cooperate after each had seceded separately, and force Southern congressmen to
take a stand for or against the South. Unconvinced cooperationists countered
with resolutions delaying any action by South Carolina until a commitment to
secede was received from another state, preferably Georgia. On November 9,
the legislature, frustrated by the interminable debates, compromised by voting
in favor of an election on January 8 for a convention to meet on January 15. The
Rhetts had been stymied.[10]

Another potential snag to speedy secession was the reluctance of US senator
James H. Hammond to go along with the rush. In replying to a request for his
views from A. P. Aldrich, Hammond restated his position in his Beech Island
address of 1858, which had been scorned for its adherence to the Union. He
still believed that a united South could dictate national policy and protect its
rights. The Republicans, he argued, would accomplish little in office once the
mad scramble for patronage and plunder took precedence over antislavery agitation. Better by far, he advised, for South Carolina to wait for positive assurances
of backing from other states before laying itself open once again to the ridicule
of outsiders for its impotency.[11]

Aldrich did not release the letter to the legislature, and the convention bill
delaying secession needed to pass three readings in the House and Senate before
it was approved, a matter of a few days at most. A small window of time existed
for jolting the legislature into accelerating the process. Two Georgians provided
the jolt.

In Charleston on November 9, the same day the 1860 Association had organized a mammoth secession rally, a delegation of Georgians in the city to commemorate the recent opening of the Charleston and Savannah Railroad were
guests of honor at a lavish banquet. After dining, Robert Gourdin escorted
selected guests to Institute Hall, where a crowd had been primed by the secessionist oratory of L. W. Spratt, Magrath, and others. As Gourdin undoubtedly
anticipated, two of the Georgians, Francis Bartow and Henry R. Jackson, played
their assigned roles to the hilt. Yale graduates, refined gentlemen, and the em-
bodiment of respectability, they personified all that the 1860 Association sought
in the leaders of a responsible revolution. Bartow and Jackson brought the crowd
to a frenzy with their fiery pledges for support from Georgia. "Every speaker was
for secession—immediate secession," rhapsodized the *Mercury*.[12]

Wasting no time, the radicals sent a telegram to Columbia around 10:00
P.M. announcing that Georgia was pledged for cooperation and that the excitement in Charleston would brook no delay in secession. The "pledge" of
support carried no official sanction—only the Georgia legislature could make

Fig. 5.3 Secession Frenzy, Johnson Square, Savannah. On November 8, 1860, the day before the Charleston banquet, Georgians in Savannah raised the first flag of independence in Johnson Square. Library of Congress, LC-USZC4-4584.

that decision—but the pressuring tactics worked to perfection. A specially commissioned train left Charleston early the next morning carrying key federal officials who had resigned—Magrath, James Conner, the former federal district attorney, and William Colcock, the ex-collector of customs. They were received in Columbia by marching Minute Men, showers of rockets and roman candles, and raucous cheers from the crowds.[13]

The delegation assured Carolinians that they stood on the brink of epoch-making vindication. "The time is not distant when a new day and a new era will dawn upon us as regenerated freemen, and we leave a rich legacy to be transmitted to our children," thundered Magrath. For Colcock, "We now stand in the presence of history, about to perform the greatest Drama ever enacted in the civilized world." The die had been cast. "South Carolina has decided—solemnly decided—that the day of deliverance is at hand, and she will decide the day, I trust, in one month from this time. And she will do more—she will decide the destiny of the South."

The legislators quickly gave in to the calls for greatness and unrestrained passion. Within twenty-four hours they reversed themselves, voting unanimously in the House and Senate for elections on December 6 for delegates to a secession convention to meet on December 17. Demands for unity silenced the few outliers. When a handful of upcountry legislators initially favored a delay to allow time for their isolated constituents to be informed of the issues at stake, John Cunningham countered with the argument that by displaying any hesitation, "we show to the South that South Carolina trembles in her shoes, that the South Carolinian is not prepared to stand up to her principles of the past." If such a feeling took hold, "they will not join us, and the cause of the South will then be eternally lost." With the contempt of a coastal planter for the upcountry bumpkins, he concluded: "Far better that we lose York District than we lose Alabama."[14]

With a show of bravado and firm resolve, South Carolinians made their bid for historical greatness. In private, many feared the worst. The pressure on the legislature to act boldly on November 10 was overpowering, and they responded accordingly. But behind their public face, their mood was somber, even depressed.

Frank Hampton's Woodlands plantation was close to Columbia and a refuge for the harried politicians. Their hostess at Woodlands was Sally Hampton, Frank's beautiful wife who was weakened by a tubercular condition. The daughter of a prominent New York businessman, she was raised amid a circle of reform-minded, mostly antislavery friends and married into one of South Carolina's wealthiest and most prestigious families. As was often the case with Northern brides of Southern planters, she made her peace with slavery when drawn into a world of social grace and privilege. She never abandoned her belief that slavery was morally wrong but characterized the institution in letters to her parents as far milder than she had ever imagined and even beneficial to African Americans, an ambivalence reflective of her emotional attachment to two different worlds.

As their charming hostess, Sally put the legislators at ease and learned that their private forebodings were far removed from their public façade. They "are glad perhaps," she wrote a friend in the North, "of a chance to open their hearts & own what every man of them feels that it is with a heavy sorrow that they see themselves so near the success of a scheme that has been the offspring of so many years [,] trials & tribulations." Yet the pangs of regret were "mingled [with] a calm self-devotion & heroic bravery one cannot but admire tho' perhaps in a mistaken cause. Men seem quite aware that they are moving towards self-destruction—that if they march it is to a certain grave."[15]

James H. Hammond relied on a visceral metaphor to satirize the dread that accompanied secession. "It reminds me of the Japanese who when insulted rip open their own bowels." He was venting his rage at Aldrich, who had kept under wraps his letter counseling staying in the Union, and all the reckless politicians forcing secession. Once the legislature advanced the date for a secession convention, no dissenters were to be tolerated. James Chesnut, Hammond's colleague in the Senate, resigned, and Hammond immediately followed.[16]

Hammond's caution had been cast aside by the groundswell of mobilization for the revolution-in-progress. Planter families in the lowcountry with their extensive kin connections led the charge. Among the leaders was John S. Palmer, a fifth-generation planter and owner of several plantations along the South Santee River. When he heard that the initial date for the secession election was not until January 8, he wrote his son James that "I began to feel immediately like going to the grave. I believe the shock almost induced a convulsive fit." Energized and with his senses restored after the date for the election was pushed forward, he rushed off to Black Oak in St. John's Parish for a meeting to organize a unit of Minute Men and nominate candidates for the convention. The meeting, like others in the lowcountry where intermarriage was the norm among multi-generations of planters, was a family affair. William Cain and Dr. Peter Snowdon, the convention nominees selected in St. John's, were blood relatives of Palmer's. In St. Stephens Parish, Palmer enrolled two nephews and two sons in the St. Stephens Volunteers.

Palmer could not have been happier that the day of redemption was at hand. "Oh how I glory in our gallant little State. Just see how every northern paper either teems with abuse or deprecation of our movement while every portion of the south is shouting huzzanahs in her praise." His enthusiasm was infectious. "When Pa can be so much excited as to feel young again," his son James wrote his sister from the University of Virginia, "what can he expect of us?" Itching for action, he mused that if there were "a Yankee near by I could make fetish of him and blow off in that way." The young daughters in the family talked of enlisting themselves, but Palmer advised them to make cockades and decorate flags for the volunteers.[17]

The sons were more than willing to do their part. Duty and family honor were at stake. When staying in Charleston, Caroline Pettigrew was surprised by how sharply Hal Lesesne rebuked his mother for not being a die-hard secessionist. Meta Grimball learned there was no holding back her son Lewis. Trapped in a medical practice that his mother described as "not worth anything," Lewis had enrolled in a military company. He "seems most anxious for a fight," Meta wrote, "a restless young man." Up in Abbeville District, Jane North observed that the "boys, dear fellows, are all good secession patriots—what else for them." Among the "dear fellows" was A. G. Guskins, who bid defiance to the rest of the world even if South Carolina seceded alone. All those who believed "S.C. was afraid to quit the Union" could now "think what they pleas of us. . . . We are prepared to take care of ourselves."[18]

Many mothers like Meta Grimball were reluctant to send their sons off to war. To counter such maternal instincts, the secessionists employed a number of strategies. One was a shaming tactic aimed directly at the men by urging them not to wait for the approval of the women in their lives before they committed to doing their manly duty. When a list was opened to enroll Minute Men at the courthouse in Kingstree on November 6, Judge Benjamin Whitner rose and sarcastically announced: "If there is any one present . . . who wishes to go home to ask the advice of his wife and children, before putting his name on the list, I will certainly relieve him from all embarrassments, by giving him permission to go." Howls of amusement greeted his remark.[19]

Another approach was to publish in the secessionist press letters purportedly from women calling on mothers to encourage their husbands and sons to rush to the defense of the state. One such letter from "A Carolina Woman" urged women to emulate the sacrificing patriotism of Carolina's mothers in the Revolution. Claiming to be a widow with three sons, the letter writer set a high bar for other mothers to attain, for if any of her sons "should be craven enough to desert their State *now . . . let him never look upon my face again!*" Indicative of a college education (and likely a male author), classical references embellished the letter. One of the references was to Volumnia, a Shakespearean heroine who joyously sent her son Coriolanus to march off as a warrior to defend a threatened Rome and who glorified in his wounds. A secessionist rally was not complete without an ostentatious show of support from women. At the conclusion of a rally at Institute Hall in Charleston, the president of the meeting accepted a large wreath accompanied by a note: "A mother and daughter send a wreath to the mass meeting of to-night. With it the mother offers four sons, living in the State to its service—the daughter, earnest wishes for the ultimate success of separate State action."[20]

To allay the fears of elite women over rampaging slaves, the secessionists lauded military mobilization as the best means of keeping the slaves in check. One of the stated purposes of the Kingstree Minute Men was to "put down insurrections [and] give security to women and timid men." Still, the fears persisted. Jane Caroline North, a descendant of the venerable Petigru (the Huguenot spelling of Pettigrew retained by the family in South Carolina) family, fled to New York to escape her dread of another Saint-Domingue. From Woodlands in December, Sally Hampton reported that Mrs. Preston and Mrs. Hampton "are in the most hideous state of alarm about insurrection — & I think believe that every servant who answers the bell will shoot them thru' the heart as he enters."[21]

Many women, especially the daughters in planter households, needed no encouragement to join the cause. Enthusiastic secessionists from the start, they had no sons to worry about, only young beaus eager to impress them with their fighting spirit and valor. Among them were the schoolmates of Harriet Palmer. "So rotten Lincoln is elected," fumed Anna Kirkland to Palmer. "I almost cried when I heard it, but it may be better (as you and many others say). It must come sometimes and it might as well be now." Leora Sims, another of Harriet's confidantes, attended the legislature in Columbia to listen to the speeches. She proudly proclaimed herself "a regular fire eater" who thought "of nothing but the dark times which hide a halo of glory from our country, if she acts worthy of her position and what infamy will sink her if she acts cowardly."[22]

The crisis was empowering for women. It brought them into public life with an openness and directness that was both new and exhilarating to them. Sally Hampton exclaimed that "people here seem electrified at a woman's daring to know & talk so much upon such [political] subjects. It is a new leaf turned in my life & oh! How grateful I am for a topic of interest in this wretched country." Like Hampton, women avidly followed the progress of secession. Young Emmie Holmes from one of the first families of Charleston was thrilled at the prospect of a "free and independent republic." She could hardly wait to attend the opening of the Secession Convention at Institute Hall in the galleries reserved for women.[23]

Women far outnumbered men in the evangelical churches where they found the sermons a source of both entertainment and moral instruction. Most of the evangelical clerics declared their support for secession and assured Southern Christians that this path was God's will. James Henry Thornwell, the most renowned of the Calvinist divines in South Carolina, presented the most theologically rigorous defense of secession in his Thanksgiving sermon on November 21, 1860. Both sections had sinned, Thornwell acknowledged, but only the North had blasphemously denied God's sanctioning of slavery as revealed in the Bible. In so doing, the North had defiled the divine duty of civil government as an "institute of Heaven." By its attacks on slavery, the Northern-corrupted Union was in "rebellion against God." Therefore, Southerners were religiously justified in creating their own state, one that embodied both "a Christian people, and a Christian commonwealth." He cautioned that "though our cause be just, and our course approved of Heaven, our path to victory may be through a baptism of blood." Victory, however, was not assured, but, as if anticipating the Lost Cause that followed in the wake of Confederate defeat, he proclaimed "we shall achieve a name, whether we succeed or fail, that posterity will not willingly let die."[24]

Secession as Public Theater

In the six weeks from Lincoln's election to South Carolina's withdrawal from the Union on December 20, the secessionists kept stoking excitement through a program of popular mobilization. The goal was to create and maintain such a show of unity as to overcome the reluctance of the "apathetic disunionists," who, according to Townsend, would have to be "lifted themselves over every mole-hill in the path." Ideally, his "Unionists *per se*," apologists for the North who merely professed Southern loyalties, would also be drawn into the movement, though in their case sterner measures might be necessary.[25]

The bulk of the audience the secessionists had to reach were poorly educated and semi-literate whites. The secessionists understood that any effective appeal to them had to consist of more than the mass distribution of the secession pamphlets. That appeal had to incite all the senses by combining the pageantry of a military parade, the speeches and hoopla of a political rally, the visual spectacle of a festival, and the emotional drama of saving souls in a religious revival. The result was a feeling of being swept along in a grand collective experience that promised an exciting, new beginning.

For days on end, public life in Charleston resembled a street festival. Almost nightly, torch-lit processions marched through the streets to the accompaniment of fireworks, rockets, and the booming of cannons. With economic activity at a virtual standstill in the downturn after the election, businessmen, clerks, and workers were a captive audience for one pro-secession speaker after another. The crowds listened, cheered, and showed their approval by nightly serenading the secessionists beneath their windows to come out and speak again. Further bonding leaders and followers was the near universal wearing of blue cockades pinned to hats and clothing as an emblem of support for secession. Outsiders attested to the intoxicating effect of such displays of mass emotion. "I knew the secession spirit was high in Charleston," wrote a visitor from Bennettsville, South Carolina, "but I had but a faint conception of the powerful, all-pervading, overwhelming, irresistible current of public sentiment in that direction, until I met and witnessed it in the streets, around the fireside, and in the stores and shops, and in fact, every place where man and mass meet and converse."[26]

Editors exhorted the citizenry to show their patriotism by displaying secession banners and flags. Not to comply was to place one's loyalty into question. So great was the demand that the making and selling of secession mementos and insignia was one of the few signs of commercial activity. The most popular symbol was the ubiquitous palmetto. W. Brower sold banners with palmetto designs and Welch, Harris, & Co. marketed palmetto badges. Osborne & Durbee, daguerrean artists, furnished views of the palmetto for use in designs and representations. Harper & Collins, job printers, made "a neat blue badge with Palmetto tree and lone star printed in gold." It could be purchased at Welch, Harris, & Company for 10 cents. State's Rights badges, printed in gold on a blue satin ribbon, were available from local merchants and shopkeepers, and for those who wanted painted palmetto banners, the palmetto paint store would provide them with dispatch.[27]

Those equipped to provide more elaborate work for banners stood to make a tidy profit. Madame Baptiste, the sister of Bishop Patrick Lynch of Charleston and head of the Ursuline Convent and Academy in Columbia, earned $65 for embroidering a banner for Mr. Radcliffe's store. She also got a fee for designing a flag and furnishing some materials for a Mr. Carson. The irony of what she was doing was not lost on her. "Is it not queer for Nuns to be engaged preparing flags for War?" she commented to her brother.[28]

By mid-November, banners and artfully designed flags were flying everywhere in Charleston and Columbia. They were posted at stations along the rail lines, and even lowly mules pulling the drays loaded with cotton from rail depots to the wharves were decked out with a flag around their necks decorated with the palmetto symbol. These politicized pieces of cloth were potent symbols for making political statements and tapping into emotions that surfaced during the crisis. Although occasionally including a wordy message, they most commonly relied on their visual details to communicate an unwritten text. Above all, their sheer number, as touted by the *Mercury*, were "all devised with one view—to express devotion to our State."[29]

The palmetto, which had become the most widely recognized emblem of the cause, grew in abundance along the Carolina coast. Its symbolic value stemmed from its successful use in the fortifications at Fort Sullivan during the Revolutionary War when its soft, spongy wood absorbed the impact of the shelling from the British Navy. A lone star often accompanied it. At the first public showing of his company's military flag pairing the two symbols, its vice-president proudly announced to the gathering: "We this day unfurl the 'State Rights Resistance Flag' of South Carolina—the Lone Star—emblematic of her unsullied name; the evergreen Palmetto, of her faithfulness."[30]

The workmen of the upper shops of the South Carolina Railroad unveiled one of the more elaborate flags on November 15. Eighteen feet wide and twelve feet long and painted in oil colors on both sides, it was meant to be visually arresting and seen from afar. It depicted a scene of the tranquil prosperity that awaited once South Carolina was out of the Union. Slaves on the left side were busy picking cotton, and on the right, chugging trains were hauling imports from Europe and carrying cotton for export to a coastal port. A palmetto with a rattlesnake coiled around its trunk ready to strike stood in the center. At the top of the palmetto was a large star embellished with a Crescent, the official state symbol since the Revolution when it was inscribed on the flag of South Carolina troops to represent the silver emblem on their caps. The emotive power of the imagery rivaled that of any speech. As soon as the flag was hoisted, a salute of fifteen guns, one for each of the slave states, was fired, and onlookers called on the workers to speak. The *Charleston Courier* enthused that the scene was "worth witnessing. Carolina blood is up, and will not get cool till the State is out of the Union."

Merchants rushed to establish their secession credentials with a brilliantly staged ceremony on November 17 for the raising of a Secession Pole. A crowd estimated at over 2,000 filled the blocked-off intersection of Haye and Meeting streets. At half-past ten in the morning, a deputation of merchants arrived

with the "Secession Gun" they had purchased for the firing of the opening salute. While a brass band entertained the crowd, the Lafayette Artillery marched
through the streets. Its arrival was the signal for the firing of the Secession Gun
to mark the planting of the Secession Pole and the raising of the palmetto flag.
Hours of secessionist oratory followed, including admissions from former
cooperationists that they had lost all faith in the Union.[31]

The flags, banners, and transparencies (a form of popular art, transparencies
were illuminations of scenes or inscriptions painted on light, translucent cloth
backlit by lanterns) provided a picture show dramatizing all the themes central to the case for secession. They ran the gamut from scenes of the defense
of Fort Moultrie down to the death of the Union, imaginatively represented
by "a painted sarcophagus, inscribed 'Here lies the Union, born July 4, 1776,
died Nov. 7, 1860.'" An open Bible next to a palmetto accompanied by the text,
"In the name of God we set up our banners!" typified the numerous religious
references. Individuals favored in the banner included William Jasper, a hero at
Fort Sullivan in the Revolution, and John Calhoun, appointed as the patron saint
of secession. Slaves were portrayed not just as docile, productive workers but as
avengers of the South's besmirched honor. John T. Milligan, the jailer, made up a
banner, highlighted by "two huge Africans" armed with burning sticks carrying
Lincoln to the Charleston jail on a split rail.[32]

Imparting a lively step to the cheering crowds were numerous marches,
ballads, and songs written for the occasion. Traveling companies of professional
actors adopted music celebrating secession into their performances. The George
Christy minstrels, Northern actors in blackface, were appearing in Charleston in
December, and they had the political savvy to feature the Lone Star flag in their
act. They also composed an original "Secession Polka" dedicated to the "Palmetto
Men of Charleston." Their minstrel song "Dixie," written by a Northerner and first
performed in New York in 1859, became wildly popular and soon was the de facto
anthem of the Confederacy. More widely heard yet was the Marseillaise, the song
of revolutionary France and then the French national anthem. "To judge from the
music heard here," wryly noted a *New York Times* correspondent in Columbia, "a
stranger would think he had landed in a French province . . . from the pianos in
hotel parlors, from private residences, from bands on parade, and from every conceivable instrument, comes the everlasting 'Marseillaise.'" Southerners ignored
or rewrote the verses looking toward universal human rights and glorified in the
song's stirring call to arms against foreign invaders.[33]

The culture of secession saturated Carolinians with the sights and sounds
of secession being enacted in their midst. It created, as the secessionists had
hoped, the impression of an unstoppable force. Secessionist planters had set it
in motion. They were the ones who called and led the first resistance meetings
within days of Lincoln's election, set up their sons in volunteer companies and

paramilitary groups, structured committees of safety with life and death powers, and furnished most of the candidates for the Secession Convention in meetings they controlled. In Charleston, the 1860 Association and its commercial allies organized and staged the endless rallies and marches that fused the local citizens and parading soldiers into one collective mass for secession.

A. P. Aldrich expressed what drove the mobilization campaign when he wrote Hammond: "I do not believe the common people understand it. In fact, I know they do not understand it; but whoever waited for the common people when a great movement was to be made. We must make the move & force them to follow." Still, just as they catered to the democratic pride of non-slaveholders on the hustings or when they came around to the plantation for a favor, the planters took care to credit the people for secession. State representative William D. Porter stopped just short of fawning when he told a Charleston rally that the "people started the ball of revolution; and they will carry it forward to the consummation that they have in view." Such posturing was good politics and a perfect rejoinder to Northern charges that secession was a plot foisted on the masses by the Slave Power.[34]

Nurtured by a generation of anti-Northern agitation, raised to a higher pitch in the presidential campaign of 1860, and unleashed once Lincoln was elected, the groundswell for secession was powerful and frightening. The moderates directing secession were playing a dangerous game. They had to balance their need for popular support and fury to drive secession forward with the concern that unchecked violence would precipitate a crisis discrediting secession as lawless mob action and cost it the backing of other cotton states. Caroline Pettigrew, as perceptive as any male politician, noted that the great fear was that the radicals would egg on the mobs to attack the federal forts in the Charleston harbor. The formerly cooperationist *Charleston Courier* warned against believing or acting upon "mischievous rumors" of federal reinforcements being sent to the forts. The rumors "in some cases seem designed only to force a premature and needless issue in violence." Aside from the issue of the forts, the moderates also drew the line at authorizing patrollers from entering "without suspicion" the homes and boats of whites in search of free and enslaved blacks. Tarring and feathering "abolitionists" was permissible, but lynchings stained the cause of secession and were condemned.[35]

In the main, however, the moderates welcomed the community enforcement of pro-secession conformity. Often the show of unanimity took the form of a celebration in which the crowd acted out secessionist ideology. On hearing of Lincoln's election, the citizens of Aiken "*en masse*" staged the burning of a Lincoln effigy complete with a parade and speeches from local Minute Men officers. Carrying the effigy on a rail and applying a torch as it hung on a gibbet were two slaves. The crowd then enjoyed food and drink prepared for them and listened to a fresh round of speeches.[36]

The good cheers turned ugly when the community was defied. Hugh Wardlaw, one of the upcountry's most esteemed jurists, came out for cooperation at a nominating convention in Abbeville. The crowd scornfully shouted him down. He was "told he had nothing to do there, was not wanted." In recording the confrontation, Jane North observed that the rattled judge somewhat appeased his critics by endorsing the immediate secessionist platform. Others leaning toward cooperation in the upcountry met the same fate or worse. When John Boozer, who favored delay, went home, he was threatened with being hanged. He always believed that his son Bayliss was killed on the streets of Lexington in February in retaliation for his Unionist stand. After the war, John Pearson recalled, "It was dangerous for a Union man to speak out his sentiments then." He took the advice of Congressman John McQueen to keep quiet or else be "mobbed." A Union military company organized in December near Spartanburg was short-lived. Its members disbanded out of fear of "being hanged."[37]

The upcountry, a stronghold of moderation in earlier secession campaigns and in favor of a cooperative approach in October, was cowed into submission by December. The white workers in Charleston potentially posed a more difficult problem. Their smoldering discontent against competing with black mechanics threatened to prevent a united front for secession. A campaign of intimidation against blacks resolved the problem.

Free Blacks and White Mechanics

The free African Americans of Charleston (and other Southern cities) faced daily reminders of their lowly caste status. Women, for example, could be arrested for wearing a veil or men for smoking a cigar in public. Strict rules of street etiquette demanded complete deference to whites. What liberties free blacks in Charleston did enjoy were at the sufferance of whites. The "free persons of color," as they were called, were only nominally free. A state law of 1820 prohibited manumissions except by a special legislative act. Creating a deed of trust, however, provided a loophole for masters wishing to free one or more of their slaves. By the provisions of the trust, the ownership of the slave passed to a trustee, who was required to allow the favored slave to live as a free person. Though still slaves under the law, such slaves were free in a de facto sense. Many slaveholders took advantage of the loophole. The result, wrote Judge Belton O'Neal in 1848, were "evasions without number." In 1822, in direct response to Denmark Vesey's rebellion, the legislature mandated that every free male person of color have a registered guardian who would attest to his upright character in the district court.

Failure to comply was punishable by being sold into slavery. As with the prohibition on manumissions, enforcement of the statute was spotty. Over time, more and more free men of color either failed to obtain a legal guardian or ignored the requirement of registering the guardian before a clerk of the court.[38]

The laws of 1820 and 1822 were a white testament to black solidarity and resistance. What first unsettled whites was the authority that black Methodist ministers were exercising over blacks in the white church they were allowed to join. Once an investigation in 1815 revealed that church funds were used to purchase and emancipate slaves, the financial autonomy of the ministers was cut off. The black congregation responded by sending two delegates to Philadelphia for training as ordained ministers in the African Methodist Episcopal Church. Upon their return, free and enslaved blacks left the white-controlled Methodist Church and built their own church in 1818. To the city fathers, this represented an open act of defiance. Harassment and arrests followed until the black church and its branches were razed to the ground when it was learned that several blacks implicated in the Denmark Vesey rebellion had been active in the church.[39]

White oppression never crushed the assertiveness of African Americans or their display of self-value, whether in dress, manners, or leisure activities. It did, however, force the city's mulatto elite to carefully distance itself from the slaves and darker-skinned African Americans. This relatively independent group comprised about 3 percent of the city's persons of color, most of whom were also of mixed racial lineage. They were set apart by their property holdings and favored status in the eyes of wealthy white men, who, in many cases, had fathered them and then freed them in their wills. They earned their money as skilled tradesmen, working largely for their white patrons. Although many owned a few slaves for use as domestics or laborers in their shops, they typically invested their earnings in urban real estate. Intermarriage and membership in exclusive social organizations kept them socially apart from the slaves and the mass of free African Americans, 75 percent of whom were propertyless.[40]

This elite occupied a tenuous position between the whites above them and the blacks beneath them. Michael Eggert, a mulatto mechanic, described that position as a "middle ground," hemmed in on one side by "the prejudice of the white man" and the other by the "deeper hate of our more sable brethren." That middle ground began to erode in the late 1850s as changes in the population of Charleston altered the political balance that had enabled the favored mulattos to enjoy their privileged position and other free persons of color to hold onto what rights they still had left.[41]

For most of the antebellum period, Charleston was an African American city with a white minority hovering around 46 percent. Planters, who lived in the city during the cooler months but fled in the summer to avoid the annual yellow fever season, rarely had to concern themselves with what the

plebeians were thinking or doing. That changed in the 1850s. The annexation in 1850 of the predominantly working-class Northern Neck, a continued
inflow of immigrants, and the loss of 6,000 slaves sold to plantations in the
Mississippi Valley pushed whites into a sizable majority of 58 percent. Slaves
still outnumbered whites in a workforce rapidly filling up with the foreign-
born, who by 1860 were a majority of all free workers. Embittered at being
pitted against African Americans in the labor market and belittled in their
minds as white men by rubbing shoulders in their neighborhoods with African
Americans who seemingly lorded it over them by dressing and acting in a
manner appropriate only to whites, the workers were especially resentful of
the wealth and status of the brown elite. Over 90 percent of the laboring class
reported no property holdings, and what wealth had been acquired by skilled
artisans was a pittance compared to that of planters, merchants, and lawyers.
Their numbers had grown to the point that their grievances found expression
in a political movement with considerable clout.[42]

The leaders of the labor insurgency were James M. Eason, a machinist and
owner of an iron foundry, and Henry T. Peake, the superintendent of the South
Carolina Railroad workshops. They pressured Mayor Charles Macbeth in 1858
to enforce the 1822 law prohibiting self-hire by slaves. The issue, as presented
by the white stevedores, involved "granting a licentious freedom to slaves,
to go out and act as white men." As "responsible men, men of family, [and]
tax-payers," the stevedores deserved better. They were as good as any other
white men, and all they asked was "equal rights and protection." Merchants
and shippers were unmoved, citing the need to keep labor costs low so as to
maintain Charleston's competitive position with other Southern ports. White
workers were also stymied in 1859 when the legislature failed to pass a bill
strongly backed by the upcountry to enslave free blacks who refused to leave
the state.[43]

In 1860, as racial anxieties associated with the presidential campaign rose, pressure across the state mounted to expel or enslave all free blacks. White mechanics
in Charleston pushed Mayor Macbeth to unleash the police for a rigorous enforcement of the slave badge and slave hiring laws. The badge law required slaves
working for hire to wear a metal badge, a legal mark of slave status. Their owners
purchased the badges from the city treasurer. The law was both a source of revenue
and a means of preventing slaves from passing themselves off as free.

Arrests for violations of the slave-badge requirement rose sharply until they
reached ninety-three by August. The cases were heard in the mayor's court.
When many of those arrested claimed they were free and hence had no need for
a slave badge, Mayor Macbeth demanded that they produce air-tight legal proof
of their freedom. Before the crackdown, payment of the capitation tax would
have been sufficient. All free persons of color had to pay a state capitation tax of

$2.75 per adult, as well as a city capitation tax ranging from $3 for young females to $5 for adults engaged in a trade or business. The tax bordered on being punitive for most free persons of color, who had little in the way of a cash income, but its payment traditionally had denoted free status. Rejecting this standard as sufficient proof, Macbeth demanded evidence of strict compliance to the laws of 1820 and 1822 designed to block manumissions.[44]

By the middle of the summer, 1860, the police were enforcing to the letter the full battery of restrictive laws. Legal proof was demanded of payment of the capitation tax, the designation and court registration of a guardian, and the validity of a trustee arrangement. Those who failed to provide it were hauled into the mayor's court and enslaved as abandoned property. Their persons and property were seized for the city by Macbeth. To avoid sale at a public auction to a stranger, many rushed to buy a slave badge and place themselves under the protection of a former owner or white friend. In a bizarre twist, a slave badge now offered them their best security.[45]

The panic spread even among the brown elite. James M. Johnson, the son of a mulatto tailor and a relative of William Ellison of Stateburg, the wealthiest African American in South Carolina, was helping his elderly father in Charleston in 1860. Until the summer, he had no inkling of the terror that would suddenly engulf all free persons of color. In August, he lost his innocence. He informed his brother-in-law Henry in Stateburg that "the agitation has been so great to cause many to leave who were liable to the law of 1822 & the panic has reached those whom that law cannot affect." He wrote of cases of free blacks who had paid the capitation tax for thirty years who were now forced to return to slavery and take out their badges. To avoid that fate, hundreds of those being "hunted down" were booking passage on steamers and railroads to carry them out of the state. Upward of one-third of the city's free blacks fled while they were still able to get out. On witnessing the arrival of the refugees in Philadelphia, a newspaper correspondent likened the exodus to "the expulsion of the Jews from their European homes." They had raised the funds for the move by selling at distress prices what property they had. As far as Johnson was concerned, Mayor Macbeth was engaged in a get-rich scheme for himself and his cronies. "The magistrates boast of the good it has done & Trusted that they did not know they [free persons of color] were so rich." Johnson had no doubt that "the movement is intended for their emolument."[46]

The white protectors of African Americans who had bottled up the exclusion bills in 1859 were powerless to stop the terror. The mayor and his working-class friends were intent on getting "rid of the cold. Population," and Johnson feared they would not stop until they had stripped the brown elite of their rights. The upcountry legislators, Johnson had heard, were doubling down on their efforts "'to sell those [free persons of color] there who are considered worthless, prior

to passing a Law for the removal of the Body." New laws introduced in the legislature or stalled old ones could well force all free African Americans to choose
between slavery and removal.[47]

Peake and Eason announced as candidates for the legislature in September. In
an election card signed "Mechanics," they promised to uphold the rights and dignity of the white workers by attacking their true enemies, free persons of color
and their white patrons. They pitched themselves as the only true friends of white
labor, for lawyers and merchants knew nothing of the humiliation of having to
compete "with *free* negros—negros free in *fact*, but held by *trustees*, and slaves
hiring their own time—plague spots in the community, affecting pecuniarly and
socially, only working men." They pledged to bring white workers into the club
of white respectability. Handily elected, they introduced under Eason's name a
bill in the legislature restricting free African Americans to menial jobs or work
as domestic servants. Despite presenting a petition in favor of the bill signed by
800 of his Charleston supporters, Eason was unable to push the bill through.
White workers had little political influence outside of Charleston, and the legislature was intent on maintaining unity among planters with secession looming.
If the crisis came to war, the skills and productive labor of the freed population
would be indispensable.[48]

In the meantime, the repression continued. Although propertied free
blacks were unwilling to sacrifice all they had worked for and chose to
ride out the storm, many of their friends were leaving. Escaping was no
easy matter. William Ellison Jr. tried to book passage for his children to
Philadelphia, but the ship's agents refused to take any colored persons unless
they were "cleared out of the custom house by some white person as their
slave." The agents' caution was understandable. If they had allowed anyone
to leave the state who subsequently turned out to be a slave, they would have
been guilty of aiding and abetting a runaway slave, the penalty for which was
death. Undoubtedly, they were aware of the case of the white porter Francis
Michel who had been convicted of that offense in the spring. Ellison had
every reason to refuse having his children claimed as slaves as nothing would
have prevented the claimant from selling them into slavery. Ellison waited
and finally secured passage for them as free persons on another steamer
bound for New York.[49]

The re-enslavement crisis ended with the outbreak of the war. Most of the
wealthier free blacks remained and professed to be loyal Confederates. They
did lose the property they had stayed to protect, but at least it was in a war that
erased any doubts over their free status.

Rushing to Deliverance

Once the secession timeline was accelerated, the outcome of the election was a given. The cooperation movement in its original meaning of waiting for commitments from other states was dead. Aiming for complete unity, the secessionists controlled the selection of candidates and blanketed dissenters in terror, the flip side of popular mobilization. Nearly everywhere, the only ticket that ran was one pledged to immediate secession. Not surprisingly, the turnout was light. In Newberry District, less than half of the eligible voters cast a ballot. Semi-mountainous Greenville District under the leadership of Benjamin Perry had been a cooperationist bellwether in 1850–51. This time Perry mounted a ticket only three days before the election, and his vote of 225 was swamped by a secessionist majority of more than a 1,000.[50]

Acceptance of a foregone outcome, lack of choices, and fear kept the voters away. Ransom P. Pigg of Chesterfield "was not permitted to vote because [he] would not vote their way," testified a fellow Unionist after the war. In Lancaster, High L. Belk, a small farmer with a few slaves, refused to vote when no Union ticket was offered. He opposed secession because he felt that were a Southern nation created, "no poor white man could live in it . . . and if the rebels succeeded poor white men would be little better off than slaves in the South." John Herndon of Marlboro, a tenant on E. W. Goodwin's land, felt compelled to vote for him, especially after Goodwin told him he favored the Union. Goodwin subsequently voted for secession in the convention.[51]

Nearly all the Unionists in the lowcountry were also poor whites. Eking out an existence in the pine barrens and backwater swamps on dry patches of land known as hammocks, they were isolated and marginalized. They often lived with mulattos and a few worked their land with some slaves. Rebels later admitted that "the poor and working men about here were for the Union" and that they "generally hated" the rich slaveholders. Ezekiel Stokes, an elderly, illiterate farmer with some land near the Coosahatchie swamp, cared little for slavery and believed the white poor "would be better off without it." Stokes's views on slavery, let alone his Unionism, could not be openly expressed except among trusted friends and slaves in his confidence. Lowcountry poor whites either did not vote in the secession election or resorted to subterfuge to avoid retaliation. Knowing that excitement in his voting precinct was running high, Richard Taylor of Beaufort went through the charade of voting by casting a blank ballot. For that, "he was cursed as a Yankee." His like-minded neighbors who owned slaves were vilified as "white niggers."[52]

Only a handful of planters remained die-hard Unionists. One of them, John Williams, on hearing shots fired outside his house by locals celebrating South

Carolina's secession, took it as a personal insult and fired into the crowd with a fowling piece. Fortunately for him, the crowd welcomed his scattered shots as another salute to secession. Allen S. Izard was more circumspect. Although he had inherited a large plantation on the Black River, he never wavered from the Unionist sentiments rooted in his birth and formative years in Philadelphia. In February 1861, he excoriated the secessionists as "Southern renegades" to a Republican attorney in New York and urged the Republicans to "snub them, grind their noses, mash their toes, & toss them to the gutter."[53]

James L. Petigru was the state's most noted Unionist and its most respected legal mind. The son of an Abbeville farmer, Petigru opened a law practice in Charleston in 1819. His family lineage and social connections were impeccable, and he soon rose to the top of his profession with service as South Carolina's attorney and codifier of its laws. What made him exceptional was his unflinching devotion to the Union and to the law as an instrument of justice for all, including abused wives and free African Americans. Any political aspirations came to an effective end when he opposed the Nullifiers and won an appeal of the test oath imposed by them for all state officials. His legal acumen, graciousness, and sense of honor earned him grudging respect as Charleston's Unionist outlier who had the courage to speak his mind. He even enjoyed good relations with Rhett, whom he had once bailed out of debt. Powerless to prevent the secession movement, Petigru scorned it as the height of madness. "A rising against authority upon pretexts as light as our Southern wrongs would be put down anywhere else without ceremony," he wrote Edward Everett, Bell's running mate.[54]

With their political influence and family name at stake, the vast majority of conservative planters reluctantly went along with the secession tide. Initially, as outlined by "Fentina Lente" in a public letter on November 3, they wanted to delay any decision until a convention of all the Southern states met and presented demands for the North to accept or reject. At the very least, they counseled waiting until the Northern response could be gauged. In Sally Hampton's reading, such old-money families as the Lowndeses, Mannings, Hamptons, and Petigrus desired secession "at a later date & greater moderation in all movements." Soon, however, like Charles T. Lowndes, they realized that speedy secession was "inevitable."[55]

Once they accepted the reality that more radical planters controlled the timing and method of secession, conservatives focused on how best to control the popular frenzy. The people were to follow, not lead, but now that axiom of planter rule appeared to be reversed. "The people are ahead of their leaders and they cannot be restrained, nor is it advisable that they should be," D. H. Hamilton, the former US marshal, informed Robert Gourdin in late November. Hamilton wanted the people to force a rush out of the Union so as to leave no "time for compromising and temporizing."[56]

The problem for conservatives, as noted by a correspondent for a Baltimore paper, was their uncertainty over "where and in what it will end." The secessionists were regaling the masses with a vision of a free, independent, and glorious South Carolina but giving no heed to the disastrous consequences of acting too rashly. The great danger was that the other slave states would dismiss secession as sheer anarchy if mobs were to seize the federal forts in the Charleston harbor. Such had been Rhett's aim back in 1851, and who was to say that he would not have his way now. If he did, South Carolina would be isolated and exposed in the war that was sure to follow.[57]

Rhett's need for a dramatic gesture to trigger secession was far less in 1860 than in 1851 when he was infuriated by the cooperationist movement forming against him. But he was still certain that any federal military deployment in response to an attack on the Charleston forts would bring other slave states to South Carolina's defense. Other secessionists had their doubts. The whole approach of the 1860 Association centered on structuring secession as a peaceful, law-abiding movement that would regain the respect of other Southerners that had been lost in the past secessionist histrionics. Typical of the state's reputation was the put-down of the Virginia state senator William Frazier: "The *crime* of South Carolina against the best interests of humanity is deep and damning," he charged. "She is evidently and madly bent on bringing on war that she may thereby *force* all the border States into her 'Palmetto' Confederacy." Another Virginian hoped that "the balance of the Cotton States will be wise enough to let her go alone, for we can do very well without her."[58]

An unprovoked attack on any of the forts would be seen as lawless violence designed to coerce support from other Southern states when the federal government retaliated. Gone would be a united Southern front for peaceful secession. In early November, Rhett's impulsiveness was not nearly the threat as that posed by the independent military companies and Minute Men keeping a close watch on the forts and impatient for a confrontation.

The forts were not just a symbol of federal authority; they were the vehicle for enforcing that authority. As long as they remained in federal hands, secession lacked any substance. In 1860, they were woefully undermanned and in need of repair. On one side of the harbor was Fort Moultrie on Sullivan's Island; directly across was Fort Johnson on Morris Island; and in the middle squatted on an extension of marshland was Castle Pinckney, a crumbling masonry fortification. Under construction on a shoal with a commanding view of the harbor was Fort Sumter. All were ripe for the taking. Efforts in the summer to begin the necessary repairs aroused suspicions in Charleston that turned hostile on November 7 when Colonel John L. Gardner, the commander at Fort Johnson, attempted to transfer munitions from the US arsenal in Charleston to the fort to prevent their possible seizure by the secessionists. An armed mob surrounded the arsenal and blocked the transfer.

The Buchanan administration followed the course it would throughout the crisis—it temporized. President Buchanan wanted to preserve the Union and he rejected secession as unconstitutional, but his sympathies were with Southerners, who included most of his close political and social friends in Washington. He blamed the crisis on Republicans and believed that if Southerners were only patient, their concerns would fade away when the Republicans self-destructed once in power. His success in politics was more a result of his Southern ties and his ruthless manipulation of patronage than any understanding of the priorities of the Northern electorate, a blind spot that increasingly divorced him from Northern public opinion as the crisis deepened. His dithering served his overriding goal of avoiding any sectional bloodshed on his watch.[59]

Buchanan's cabinet was of little help. Four of its members were Southerners, two of whom were secessionists: Howell Cobb of Georgia, the secretary of the treasury; and Jacob Thompson of Mississippi, head of the Interior Department. The third, Secretary of War John B. Floyd of Virginia, was wavering on secession but shrank from using his authority to place any check on the seceders. Postmaster Joseph Holt of Kentucky was a Unionist but stayed in the background. Of the Northerners, only the attorney general, Jeremiah Black of Pennsylvania, had much say in Buchanan's decisions. He agreed with the president that both secession and military force to put it down were unconstitutional, a stand later mocked by William Seward as arguing that "no state has a right to go out of the Union—unless it wants to."[60]

The flare-up over the arsenal in Charleston quieted when Floyd refused to back Gardner. He informed acting Secretary of State Henry Trescot that no order had been issued by the War Department to move the munitions. Floyd further placated Trescot by replacing Gardner with a Southerner, Major Robert Anderson of Kentucky. Trescot served as South Carolina's pipeline to the Buchanan administration. He was a secessionist, though he favored the disciplined approach of the 1860 Association.[61]

Once the arsenal issue was settled, Buchanan unexpectedly indicated that he would act on the advice of Winfield Scott, the commanding general of the US Army, and reinforce the Southern forts. Reprising the policy of the Jackson administration in the nullification crisis when he was an emissary to South Carolina, Scott aimed to avert an "early act of rashness" that might precipitate a war. Strengthening the forts would give pause to the Southern extremists and buy time for a settlement to be reached. Scott lacked the personnel to make any such strengthening much more than a symbolic act, but at least it would have demonstrated continuing federal resolve. Buchanan briefly agreed but quickly reversed himself when the Southern members of his cabinet strongly opposed it.[62]

With Trescot acting as an intermediary between Washington and Charleston, a truce of sorts regarding the forts was worked out in the next few weeks. Governor Gist and the South Carolina congressmen assured Buchanan that no attack would be made on the forts if no attempt was made to reinforce them. How binding the agreement was on Buchanan was a matter of conjecture, but the status quo held, to the delight of secessionists and Northern compromisers. Unionists in the North and South were outraged. William T. Sherman, then a civilian running a Southern college, was convinced that Buchanan had "made a fatal mistake" by not rushing troops and ships to the Charleston forts in the early stages of the crisis. "This instead of exciting the Carolinians," in Sherman's view, "would have forced them to pause in their mad career . . . and held South Carolina in check till reason could resume its sway." Sherman's anger was understandable, but he misjudged both the ease with which significant reinforcements could have been sent to Charleston and the single-mindedness of the secessionists.[63]

With a clear path in front of it, the secession convention met in Columbia on December 17. Rhett, who felt with some justification that he more than anyone was responsible for the gathering, wanted the honor of being its head. Once again, the former cooperationists put him in his place. Rhett had barely made the cut-off in the election for Charleston's delegates on December 6. His ham-fisted tactic of circulating a questionnaire designed to smoke out those not explicitly pledged to immediate secession backfired. Five days later, he mustered little support when the legislature chose for governor Francis W. Pickens, a late convert to secession and a clumsy politician more noteworthy for his illustrious family name than any leadership skills.

Rhett had made the *Mercury* synonymous with secession and one of the best-known papers in the state, despite its paltry daily circulation of circa 300 copies, dwarfed ten times over by its more moderate rival the *Courier*. He had a genius for whipping up the passions and insecurities of the lowcountry aristocracy he had struggled to join. Unlike those nabobs, Rhett had to make his own way. His father's two rice plantations had failed, and Rhett was largely self-educated. His own debt-ridden plantations were financially shaky, but they did give him an entry into the aristocracy. Feeling a need to boost his political stock, he dropped Smith, his father's name, in 1837 and adopted the surname of a more distinguished sounding ancestor, Colonel William Rhett. Still, unable to curb his own insecurities and quarrelsome nature, Rhett remained an embattled outsider deemed incapable of constructive statesmanship by most planters. Despite an unrivaled flair for promoting secession, he was utterly tactless when it came to cultivating personal loyalties and trust. In the crisis he welcomed as the culmination of all he had worked for, he was an unwanted guest written off as a selfish, impulsive agitator unworthy of a leadership role.[64]

The opening address of the convention's president, David F. Jemison, summarized why secession was necessary. After briefly listing Northern injustices heaped upon the South and dismissing any talk of compromise as not merely "fruitless, but fatal to the less numerous section," Jemison cautioned against allowing "too great impatience" by the people to precipitate secession before it could be accomplished by the "authority of law." Here was the great conceit of the secessionists' mindset. An unlawful revolution in the minds of most Northerners and many Southerners could be rendered lawful and peaceful if entrusted to gentlemen planters sanctioned by the people to reverse the process by which South Carolina had joined the Union. That was the whole purpose of calling an election for a secession convention. To make certain that no one doubted the zeal of those gentlemen, Jemison then offered the motto of Georges Denton at the onset of the French Revolution: "To dare! And again to dare! And without end to dare!" He seemingly was nonplussed by the fact that Denton was soon guillotined by other revolutionaries.[65]

The convention then postponed its deliberations and abandoned Columbia for Charleston. Smallpox had broken out in Columbia, and Charleston beckoned with more comfortable accommodations and a secession flame that burned hotter. Unfazed by taunts from Perry's Greenville paper for fleeing like frightened children, they set out on December 18, 1860, on the 4:00 A.M.. train to Charleston. Sleep-deprived but brimming with purpose, they reassembled at Institute Hall (now dubbed Secession Hall) at four in the afternoon.

The convention was a hybrid version of a family outing with a religious holiday, only with more wealth and solemnity. It was to be conducted with all the grace and decorum of rescuing an aged Southern belle from an unfortunate situation. "Today," John S. Palmer wrote his wife, "it is hoped we shall get the old lady South Carolina out of the crowd without damaging her hoops or tearing her dress." The patriarchs of the venerable, old families dominated, and their wealth was staggering, with 40 percent of them owning more than fifty slaves. Given the terrible acoustics in the hall, they limited themselves to appointing a few committees before adjourning to meet the next day at St. Andrew's Hall. Rather perfunctorily, the secession ordinance passed unanimously on December 20, 1860. To properly commemorate the historic decision, the delegates arranged a special signing ceremony for that evening back at Institute Hall. As they departed in the afternoon, the chimes of St. Michael's Episcopal Church added a light touch to the somber occasion by pealing forth "Auld Lang Syne."[66]

The scene at the ceremony was, in the words of the *Mercury*, "profoundly grand and impressive." The Reverend John Bachman opened the proceedings with a prayer. Then, as if at the end of a religious pilgrimage to the holy grail, the

Fig. 5.4 "Palmetto State Song." This cover for sheet music celebrating South Carolina's secession on December 20, 1860, depicts the interior of Secession Hall. The delegates are gathered around the secession ordinance, and above them with a palmetto positioned under the arc is the flag of South Carolina. Library of Congress, LC-USZ62-10917.

delegates rose from their seats as their names were called one-by-one and walked to a table to affix their signatures to the Secession Ordinance. Written on thick parchment, the regal document measured roughly two feet by two feet with the Great Seal of South Carolina stamped in silver on it. When his time came, Rhett at last had a measure of his just due. He fell to his knees and offered a prayer of thanks for his state's deliverance and his personal vindication. At the end of the ceremony, a crowd rushed to the two palmetto trees flanking the signing table and stripped off their bark as mementos of what they had just witnessed. The ensuing celebrations in Charleston and towns across the state lasted through the night.[67]

The next day, the fire-eater Keitt reminded the delegates why they were there in the first place and what had to be stressed in listing the immediate cases justifying secession. "Our people have come to this on the question of slavery. I am willing in that address to rest it upon that question." Pomp and pageantry aside, secession was all about slavery.[68]

Deadlock and a Deepening Crisis

Northerners were bemused, angry, and complacent as secession unfolded in South Carolina. Democrats and businessmen were more inclined than the rural base of the Republicans to offer compromise terms to stem the crisis. Buchanan stood back, openly backed the validity of Southern grievances, and lost credibility on all sides. The key players were the congressmen, but here antagonistic blocs worked at cross purposes. When efforts were made to fashion a Union-saving deal, the mutually exclusive positions of Republicans and Southerners scuttled any compromise. Simultaneously, events in the Charleston harbor emboldened secessionist-leaning governors in the Lower South to commit their states to secession in all but name. Secessionist South Carolina was soon to be joined by the other cotton states.

The Initial Northern Reactions

Northerners were indifferent to the first reports of defiance in South Carolina. The threat to dissolve the Union was "of so long standing, and its purposes so well understood, that of late it has failed to alarm the well-informed," noted the *Randolph County* (Ind.) *Journal*. Call the bluff was a common refrain of the Republican press. "Let South Carolina bluster," advised the *Wilmington* (Del.) *Journal*. "She is something like a pet child; the more she is coaxed the more she becomes unruly. A good spanking would benefit her greatly." The *Wabash* (Ind.) *Express* had no doubt that South Carolina would "attempt" to secede but was confident the storm would pass when "the sober second thought of her people" restrained the hotheads. Surely, its slaveholders were not so foolish as to cast off federal protection for slavery and face alone an enslaved "foe that only waits the moment to strike, and it will strike" for its freedom.[1]

The antislavery wing of the Republicans was most adamant in not yielding to what it called the Southern policy of "rule and dictate." The *Randolph County Journal* accused slaveholders of making unconscionable demands that would

Southern Ass-stock-crazy.

Fig. 6.1 Northern Satire of Southern Aristocracy. This satire spoofs the efforts of the Southern aristocracy to pull down the Union by pinning the state flag of South Carolina on the tail of a donkey. Library of Congress, LC-USZ62-91445.

turn every Northerner into a slave catcher, remove all legal protections for free blacks, "hermetically" seal all lips in speaking out against the immorality of slavery, and nationalize protection for slavery under a government founded "to protect and foster Freedom and Free Institutions." The paper then reported an incident in Chicago that it mockingly characterized as Northern "treason and disunion" in the eyes of a Southerner. On the night of November 12, 1860, a fugitive slave woman from the Nebraska Territory was arrested on a warrant issued under the Fugitive Slave Act. She was dragged off to a waiting hackney and put in the armory to keep her out of the hands of an enraged mob of African Americans. When the owner went to remove her to a jail cell on the charge of disorderly conduct, he was set upon by the African Americans and left sprawling while "the girl was borne away in triumph." The *Chicago Tribune* identified the woman as Eliza Grayson in an account that satirized the failed attempt to capture her as what to expect of any effort to appease the South.[2]

More conciliatory was the Democratic press. First and foremost, it acknowledged the severity of the crisis. Though it denied the right of secession, the *Ottawa* (Ill.) *Free Trader* warned that South Carolina was in earnest. If the

Fig. 6.2 "Down with Traitors Serpent Flag." The sheet cover of a Unionist song shows a proud Northern soldier vowing the Union will be preserved as he stomps on the palmetto flag. Library of Congress, LC-USZ62-91838.

Palmetto State did secede, let it fester in its impotence was the paper's advice. In the worst-case scenario of other states joining it, the *Free Trader* preferred a national convention be called to peaceably divide the Union rather than resorting to a civil war. The *Detroit Free Press*, which favored full enforcement of the *Dred Scott* decision and repeal of all Northern laws interfering with the Fugitive Slave Act, similarly believed "the danger [of secession] is upon us." It was confident that a Unionist majority in the South would assert itself and that anti-Lincoln majorities in the Supreme Court and both houses of Congress would restrain Lincoln. Nonetheless, it feared the worst unless Lincoln repudiated his party's stand on slavery. Admittedly, this would split the Republicans into warring factions, but such was the price that would have to be paid to keep the Union safe. As for Buchanan, this Douglas paper had "no confidence in his integrity or his patriotism."[3]

Regardless of party affiliation, the Northern press overwhelmingly held that "secession is revolution," an invitation by disgruntled losers to oppose lawful authority and the will of the majority. In stark contrast, Southern radicals had convinced most Southern whites they possessed the inherent sovereign power that gave them a right to withdraw from the Union. At the same time, patriotic pride and a host of new economic and cultural linkages had left Northerners with a broadly nationalistic reading of the Union that dismissed out of hand any right of secession without the consent of the other states in the federal compact.[4]

Legalistic appeals to state's rights struck Northerners as both hollow and hypocritical. Beginning with the Fugitive Slave Act of 1850, Southerners had used their dominance of all branches of the federal government to impose national protections for slavery and to spread the institution into the territories, culminating with the unprecedented demand for a federal slave code. The state's rights infringed upon in the 1850s were those of the Northern, not the Southern, states. The Southern presumption that all blacks were slaves took precedence over the Northern principle that slavery could exist only under the force of positive law. Congress and the federal courts restricted the efforts of Northern states to prevent free blacks from being kidnapped and to extend legal protections to their black residents or citizens accused of having escaped from slavery. The US Supreme Court in the 1859 case of *Ableman v. Booth* emphatically ruled against the Wisconsin Supreme Court's issuance of a writ of habeas corpus freeing the fugitive Joshua Glover.[5]

On the eve of secession, slavery was legal in all the territories and had been deemed by the Supreme Court a specially protected institution under the Constitution. The complaint of the South that their states' rights had been violated was a red herring to distract from the reality that Southerners were constantly pushing the federal government to suppress the civil liberties of Northerners voicing opposition to slavery. Aware of the nationalist position Southerners had taken in protecting slavery, Northerners had no reason to view the "right" of secession as anything more than a cover to enhance the power of a regional elite in rendering the rights of slaveholders sacrosanct across the nation.

Reflecting their financial and social ties to former Whig planters and merchants in the South, Republican conservatives joined Democrats in pushing for a compromise. "Mutual forbearance and concession," John G. Tappan, a Boston businessman, assured a Virginia planter, "are all that are requisite to carry us over our present troubles." Emory Washburn, an ex-Whig and conservative Republican from Massachusetts, was more explicit. Disputing the Southern claim that most Republicans were intensely antislavery, he cautioned A. A. Echols of Georgia not to be swayed by the impression left by demagogues in an election year. Rather, he insisted that Lincoln was "a safe, prudent conservative national man" who would rigorously protect the rights of both sections. Washburn further asserted that within two years Lincoln's conservative stewardship would win over the confidence of the South while dampening the radicalism of the North. He predicted that by the next presidential election Lincoln would head "a strong national conservative party." In his view, Southern secessionists foresaw the same outcome if they accepted Lincoln's administration and hence realized "they must move now or never."[6]

Washburn's position was a common one among Northerners invested in the Southern economy. It assumed that, if necessary, concessions would be granted by the North to keep the Southern states in the Union. Such concessions, however, ran counter to the uncompromising stand taken by the rural wing of the Republicans, the party's mainstay of voting support, and were also opposed by some antislavery Democrats. Writing Lincoln from Decatur, Ohio, G. C. Norton characterized himself and fellow Democrats in his district as "against *any compromise at all* at the present crisis with the institution of Slavery, and we look to you as our standard bearer in the cause of freedom."[7]

Though limited in most cases by an unwillingness to accept African Americans as social and political equals, such identification with the republic as the repository of universal aspirations for the dignity and liberties of people everywhere was not empty rhetoric. It animated the growing conviction of Northerners that their freedom was threatened by a Slave Power driven by aristocratic values of ruling over both blacks and common whites and the goal of turning the whole Union into one vast slave pen. The accusation was surely exaggerated, but there was enough truth in it to make it credible. Southern paranoia over slavery had resulted in the denial of basic rights of freedom of speech for whites, savage reprisals against suspected white enemies of slavery, and demands that Northerners ignore their consciences as to the evils of slavery. And now, because they could no longer rule the Union, Southerners wanted to destroy it. The central creed of the Republican Party was its stand against the encroachments of slavery, and most of their supporters held the party to it. "Shall history record that you too bowed to the iron despotism of the slave power?" asked P. V. Wise of Cincinnati in a letter to Lincoln. "Millions of Freemen regard you as their leader, and millions of the down trodden and oppressed of *all* the Nations on Earth look to you as the Champion of Freedom. . . . The ordeal must be gone through. It is the conflict of ages."[8]

Lincoln was in a frustrating position. The election gave him a mandate to deal with the crisis but not the power until his inauguration day on March 4, 1861. He faced a four-months' interlude during which Buchanan, a lame-duck president, had the power to act but not the mandate. Any pronouncements Lincoln might have made could not be backed up by any action and likely would set off endless speculations. Given his predicament, Lincoln chose to say nothing that was not already part of his public record. He stood firmly on his party's Chicago platform but was no rigid ideologue. He occupied the Republican center regarding slavery and, as he patiently explained to John Gilmer of North Carolina, he had no intention of moving for the end of the domestic slave trade or of slavery in Washington, DC. He would impose no political tests in dispensing patronage in the South and had no problem with the repeal of any laws in the North that conflicted with the Fugitive Slave Act. Pointedly, however, he declared that on the issue of slavery in the territories, he was "inflexible." "You think slavery is right and ought to be extended; we think it is wrong and ought to be restricted." That position was Lincoln's line in the sand, and he never retreated from it. His views, as he reminded Gilmer, were a matter of public record, and he saw no need to repeat or soften them. To backtrack "would make me appear as if I repented for the crime of having been elected, and was anxious to apologize and beg for forgiveness." Moreover, he feared that any equivocating would demoralize his party and encourage the secessionists to make more demands.

Though portrayed in the South as an abolitionist, Lincoln made it clear to his lieutenants in Congress that except for the expansion of slavery, he was willing to offer Southerners assurances on fugitive slaves, slavery within all federal jurisdictions, and non-interference by Congress with slavery in the states. Republican congressmen welcomed the guidelines, though some worried Lincoln might sacrifice all legal protections for African Americans accused of being fugitive slaves. Still, by early December 1860, Lincoln had achieved his objective of firming up his party's resolve not to surrender the antislavery principles that had brought it to power.

Congressional Stalemate

By the time that Congress convened on December 3, Northerners had rejected secession as a constitutional absurdity and invitation to anarchy but had come to no consensus as what to do about it. Nor had their congressmen. Options ranged from doing nothing on the assumption that secession would burn itself out, to agreeing to Union-saving measures, to using force to stop it in its tracks, a decidedly minority view. The combined anti-Lincoln voters in the North and Upper South comprised a moderate-to-conservative majority open to concessions.

In hindsight, it is clear that most Northerners, including Lincoln, underestimated the strength of the secessionist impulse. But hindsight also overestimates the commitment of secessionists to a separate Southern nation. An indeterminate, though not insignificant, faction of Southerners favored using the threat or reality of secession to reconstruct the Union on terms rendering it permanently safe for slavery. Most of the reconstructionists were former Whigs and cooperationists. Among them was the Mississippi planter William C. Smedes. He urged Lincoln in February 1861 to lead the way to "a reconstruction of the Union," imploring him "to sacrifice his party for the good of the country."[9]

The reconstructionists were sufficiently numerous to be an ongoing concern for the out-and-out Southern nationalists. As Rhett put it in a speech at the onset of secession, whether the revolution would result "in a final separation from our confederates of the Northern States, or in a re-union, with additional and better guarantees, is a matter for grave consideration." Arguing that no Northern guarantees could ever be trusted and that slavery could never survive in a polity with majority rule, he made the case for a complete, non-reversible break. Two months later, William P. Miles confessed to "some nervous anxiety lest after all there may be a disposition to reform the old Confederacy." A nationalist like Miles, J. L. Pugh of Alabama was so "oppressed by the apprehension that we are in great danger from the reconstructionists" that he advised provoking a war to eliminate any possibility of the Upper South halting the momentum of secession by reaching a deal with the Republicans on concessions to stay in the Union. He wrote Miles: "Now pardon me for suggesting that South Carolina has the power of putting us beyond the reach of reconstruction by taking Fort Sumter at any cost."[10]

Robert M. T. Hunter, a states' rights Democrat from Virginia, offered the most concrete plan for reconstruction in his Senate resolutions on January 11, 1861. Declaring that "it was no more a question of Union, but one of reunion," he argued that the South could be secure only in a Union in which it had veto powers conferred by new constitutional amendments. Invoking Calhoun's ideas of a concurrent majority, he wanted a dual executive, one for the North and the other the South, who would have to agree on domestic and foreign policy decisions. Neither could appoint officials in the other section without the other's approval or that of a majority of that section's senators. Rejected by the Senate on January 14, Hunter's scheme amounted to no less than a surrender by the North of its majority political power. Intended for its propaganda value of putting the Republicans on record for once again voting against a "compromise," Hunter's proposal was dead from the start.[11]

The notion of reconstruction persisted in various incarnations into the early months of the Confederacy. In the same message to the legislature in which he urged secession, Governor Pettus of Mississippi held out the hope of a return to the "benign influence of a re-united Government" after Mississippi, like the Israelites in Egypt, endured an exile before returning to their original political home, following the death of the evil Lincoln and his party. L. Q. C. Lamar, a more reluctant Mississippi secessionist, endorsed South Carolina's secession in the belief that "all will be well. We will have a Southern Republic, or an amended Federal Constitution that will place our institutions beyond all attack in the future." Giving Rhett another reason to doubt his Southernism, Jefferson Davis referred in February to "the not unreasonable hope" of many Southerners that the Union could still be safely reconstructed. Even the Carolina planters visiting Woodlands that winter were talking of the possibilities of re-union.[12]

A set of interlocked assumptions framed the reconstruction talk. As the number of states seceding presumably increased, the likelihood of federal military intervention would proportionately decrease. Then, as the reality of peaceful secession settled in, the sharp economic downturn in the North in the wake of Lincoln's election would produce ever greater demands on the Republicans to offer meaningful concessions. At some point, the Republican Party would shatter and the pro-business elements would blend into a pro-Southern conservative majority. A new, nationally oriented party would form, which, either before or soon after the establishment of a separate Southern government, would grant the South all that it asked. Breaking up the old Union would result in a new Union safe for slavery.

The operative phrase for the reconstructionists was bringing the North to its senses. "I am sure," pronounced E. A. Nisbet of Georgia, that "if the Union is to be preserved, it must be done by a determined, immediate and unmistakable Southern demonstration. Nothing short of the [secession] will bring the free States to their senses." This was the same reasoning used by the pro-Bell press in New Orleans and the pro-Douglas press in Memphis to explain why their cities converted to secession. Former Unionists, they argued, now accepted secession as the only practical means left to secure Southern equality in any Union. The *New Orleans Bee* predicted that within six months of all slave states joining a Southern republic, a North chastened by economic pain would be willing to reconstruct the Union on Southern terms. The *Memphis Appeal* agreed but with the proviso that the South could not delay until the Republicans were in power, for then they would use patronage to rapidly build a Southern antislavery party.[13]

The reconstructionists were not a coherent party, and they differed in the terms and timing of the demands they made of the North. And their case for leaving the Union in order to go back into a new one was readily co-opted by Southern nationalists for their own ends. Southern Unionists denounced this tactic as "a fatal deception . . . intended by its advocates to deceive and humbug." William A. Graham of North Carolina scorned it as "the favorite idea of [the Union's] destroyers." To most Republicans, the reconstructionists were indistinguishable from other secessionists engaging in extortion.[14]

The first test of Republican unity came when Congress met, and a policy had to be agreed upon. Frederick Douglass and other African Americans in the

North expected the worst. Accurately describing Lincoln as no abolitionist, Douglass inaccurately wrote that "the Southern fire-eaters will be appeased and will retrace their steps." Congress was as factious as it had been in the sectional debates before the election. The congressmen from the Lower South were present mainly to gloat and lobby for secession among other Southerners. "I was not sent here for the purposes of making any compromise," declared O. R. Singleton of Mississippi, "or to patch up existing difficulties." George Hawkins of Florida was in the middle of declaring his opposition to any compromise when he was shouted down by calls for order. Georgia's Alfred Iverson felt that any efforts at appeasement by the North were a waste of time. Repealing the Personal Liberty Laws, which the Republicans had suggested, would be an empty gesture, for they were just a symptom "of the deep-seated, wide-spread hostility to our institutions which must . . . end in the Union in their extinction." Let the sections separate in peace, he concluded.[15]

Douglas Democrats and old Whigs from the Upper South grimly played for time while Douglas tried to make peace between the warring factions. James Green of Missouri, one of the would-be compromisers, pinned his hopes on signs of a conservative reaction in Northern public opinion. His strategy amounted to working "to clog up the wheels of disunion [while] waiting for the reaction to occur." That, in effect, was Buchanan's approach as well. In his Annual Message to Congress on December 3, 1860, he laid out a constitutional logic that tied him in a knot. Secession was unconstitutional but so was any attempt on his part to stop it with force. Any support he gained in the North by his assertion of a permanent Union was squandered by his indictment of Northerners for their hostility to slavery, a hostility that made secession understandable. The *New York Times*, moderate to conservative in its brand of Republicanism, referred to the message as "cowardly twaddle." If there was to be any constructive, pro-active policy by the federal government, Buchanan made it clear that the initiative would have to come from Congress.[16]

Douglas's effort to supply the initiative came to naught. As in his failed presidential bid, he found that there was no firm middle ground to occupy. His unwavering Unionism earned him no friends among the secessionists and his branding of the Republicans as co-equal agitators with the fire-eaters drove away Republicans. The best he could come up with was a variant of popular sovereignty for the territories combined with the scapegoating of African Americans. Returning to the white panacea of colonization, he called on the federal government to acquire areas in Africa and South America for the forced expulsion of free blacks and mulattos.[17]

The secessionists from the cotton states, known as the Gulf Squadron, were just as frustrated. They won over few fellow Southerners. "Some of the mad and drunken spirits from the South are acting so outrageously," reported Horatio

King, a Union Democrat, "that the better-deposed Southern men are becoming disgusted." In a final attempt to pull in the Upper South, they presented an ultimatum, a wish list of constitutional guarantees to keep slavery safe and allow it to expand, to the Committee of Thirty-Three (one representative per state). Formed in the House to seek a way out of the impasse, the committee was controlled by Republicans. Its off-putting, vague response to the ultimatum was the last straw for the secessionists. They caucused on the evening of December 13 and issued a flamboyant manifesto declaring, "The argument is exhausted. . . . In our judgment the honor, safety and independence of the Southern people are to be found only in a Southern confederacy—the inevitable result of separate State secession."[18]

While the Gulf states and the rest of the South remained far apart, Republican unity held. Lincoln sealed a potential breach when he vetoed an idea floated by Thurlow Weed, the boss of New York's Republican machine and a confidante of Seward. An editorial in Weed's *Albany Evening Journal* proposed extending the Missouri Compromise line to the Pacific. Arguing that slavery would never take hold in territory south of that line, he reasoned that the Republicans could make a Union-saving concession without sacrificing anything of substance. Weed was said to be in the back pocket of Wall Street, and Republican businessmen were overjoyed at the prospect of retaining their stake in the cotton economy. Lincoln forced Weed to back down with a warning that was heeded by nearly all Republicans. "Let there be no compromise on the question of *extending* slavery," he admonished, "if there be all our labor is lost, and ere long, must be done again."[19]

What then could the Committee of Thirty-Three offer to the South? Nothing of real substance to the secessionists, the Republicans agreed, but the Upper South was a different story. These states had to be held at all costs, both as outposts of Unionism and allies in any possible civil war. To soften the image of the Republicans as implacable enemies of slavery, the committee's most forceful member, Charles F. Adams, a moderate Massachusetts Republican, dangled the possibility of admitting New Mexico as a slave state. Slavery was recognized by its territorial government, but there were few slaves, and Adams was convinced that the institution could not long survive in that region's hostile desert environment. It was a clever, not wholly transparent, stratagem that the Republicans pursued into January 1861. On other issues as well, the Republicans straddled a thin line between conciliating and antagonizing the Southern Unionists. The talk of reconstruction filtering into the North buttressed their view that a latent Unionist majority in the South would rise up and enable a peaceful restoration of the Union. The consensus of the party up until the Confederate attack on Fort Sumter was that an assertion of the supremacy of federal law combined with the absence of any provocative moves would buy Southern Unionists the time they needed.[20]

This approach was the best option open to the Republicans when they realized that compromising with the secessionists was doomed from the start. What one side saw as a compromise, the other side saw as a capitulation. The secessionists had gone too far to back down, and the Republicans rejected surrendering the antislavery principles that had brought them to power. That was the crux of the matter as compellingly set forth by John A. Campbell of Alabama, an associate justice of the Supreme Court. "The truth is that the grievances complained of by the cotton States are either not material or not remediable," he explained in early December. "What guarantee will prevent the denunciation of slavery and slave-holders in the pulpit, press and academy [and] who can give self-control to Southern members or prevent them from showing that slavery is ordained by Heaven?" No compromise could eliminate "a fundamental difference between the sections on questions of active and living interest." Campbell saw nothing tangible that secessionists could demand for the additional protection of slavery. The territories of New Mexico and Utah recognized that the institution and its constitutional right to move into all federal territories was sanctioned by the Supreme Court. The Fugitive Slave Act he dismissed as "of comparatively small consequence to the cotton States," where few slaveholders had ever lost a slave to Canada. But the secessionists were still not satisfied. They had "no respect for written law or judicial decisions nor confidence that they afford protection." They wanted what they could never secure—an end to the antislavery "agitation of tumultuous political assemblies." In reaching for the impossible, they had split the Democratic Party and secured the presidency for a Republican whom they refused to accept.[21]

It wound up nowhere, but against all odds Congress made a last-ditch effort at a settlement. It took the form of the Crittenden Compromise.

The Last, Best Hope

In late December 1860, Congress awaited the recommendations of the Senate Committee of Thirteen. The Senate had resolved the crisis of 1850 and many expected it would once again find a way to save the Union. On December 6, Lazarus Powell of Kentucky had introduced a resolution to create a special committee to explore compromise proposals. Obstructionist tactics by the Republicans delayed the appointment of the committee until December 18. What brought the Republicans around was pressure from Northern businessmen and Unionists in the border states to grant concessions.

Factored into the call for compromise from businessmen was a real fear of economic collapse. Two panics had hit the New York Stock Exchange, several banks had failed, and unemployment was soaring. Many of New York's wealthiest capitalists met at the Pine Street offices of Richard Lathers on December 15 to launch their drive to save the Union. Lathers implored them to do their duty under the Constitution to fellow citizens in the South "irrespective of the effect on abstract opinions of the government of colored persons or of Territories." In short, drop any concern for the rights of African Americans and the plight of the slaves and give the South what it wanted with an unqualified share of the federal territories. A delegation was dispatched to carry this reassuring message to the Southern states.[22]

Southern conservatives had argued since the election that a crumbling Northern economy, one that could not prosper without Southern markets, would force Northern businessmen to demand a compromise. By mid-December, that seemed to be the case. In the meantime, meetings of conservatives in the border states were passing resolutions calling for a sectional settlement. In language that paralleled that of the Pine Street meeting, they insisted on an agreement that would "put down and allay all discussion of the subject [of slavery]." Henry G. Smith, a Memphis lawyer, explained the thinking of the Southern Unionists. He was "wedded to no plan" but would accept any compromise that "withdrew the negro from Federal action totally (save the Fugitive Act)." The most likely compromise, he thought, would divide the territories between the free North and the slave South. Most important, the "negro question" had to be settled once and for all as he was "unwilling to live in a perpetual strife about the elementary & fundamental social & domestic & industrial institution of my section of country." He was not a secessionist, but he was "ready to go out rather than endure the agitation within."[23]

Others in the border states sought refuge in a middle confederacy free from both the abolitionists and the fire-eaters. Resentful over being coerced to join a new confederacy whose economic policies would favor the cotton over the grain-growing slave states, they looked to William C. Rives of Virginia for leadership. Rives's conception of a central confederacy was an elastic one that included states on both sides of the border. The same was true of a proposal published in January by the *Baltimore American and Commercial Advertiser*. Reasoning that sectional peace was impossible as long as the North continued to agitate the slavery issue, the editor set out to eliminate the border distinction by having the middle states broker an agreement among themselves to end all interference with slavery. Starting with a nucleus of Pennsylvania and Maryland in the east and Ohio and Kentucky in the west, a model republic would be established that soon would draw in all the states south of the upper North and north of South Carolina and the Gulf states. It was even possible, the editor believed, that in time the result would be "our original Confederacy—bound together by stronger ties and profiting from the memory of our present unhappy differences."[24]

Secessionists in the Upper South wanted nothing to do with any alliance of slave and free states, since that would vitiate the whole purpose of seceding to escape the North. So worried was Virginia secessionist Julius C. Ruffin about the possibility of such an alliance that he urged as a "fundamental rule . . . that the slave states will not work with any free state—not one." For all of Ruffin's concerns, attachment to the old Union was too strong on both sides of the border to allow talk of a new confederacy to gain any traction. All that was accomplished was the venting of frustrations over being caught in the middle between two implacable foes.[25]

As the Committee of Thirteen began its deliberations on December 22, 1860, Republicans were starting to waver on the issue of a compromise. The conciliators came mainly out of the party's conservative wing of former Whigs who had joined the party more from support of its economic platform on protective tariffs and internal improvements than from antislavery zeal. Slippage in the Republican vote in local New England elections, a near anti-abolition riot in Philadelphia, and mounting calls for concessions from business interests in the Northeast as well as from western farmers still dependent on the southern trade in foodstuffs all suggested the Republicans would consider a settlement. Southern Unionists scented victory. The Washington correspondent of the *Baltimore Sun* reported that all signs pointed to a rupturing of the Republicans and "a re-construction of the federal constitution" based on new amendments.[26]

John J. Crittenden, though not its chair, was the driving force on the committee, which was appointed by Vice-President John C. Breckinridge. A lifelong Clay Whig, Crittenden's Unionist credentials were impeccable. The committee adopted a motion of Jefferson Davis that required the assent of a majority of both the five Republicans and the eight other members for the approval of any recommendations. Robert Toombs of Georgia, along with Davis, represented the cotton states; four members were from the Border South; and the others were Northern Democrats, headed by Douglas. The committee's deliberations centered on the resolutions presented to the Senate on December 18 by Crittenden intended to meet all the "questions and causes of discontent" arising from the rights of the slave states in the territories and of their citizens to hold slaves. Amendments to the Constitution would provide a final settlement that was to be "permanent and leave no cause for future controversy."

Crittenden's compromise package consisted of ten items, six of which were constitutional amendments. The underlying rationale behind the amendments was the elimination of all potential points of friction between the federal government and slavery. Thus, Congress was to be denied the power to abolish slavery in forts, arsenals, and other federal property in slaveholding states; to end slavery in the District of Columbia as long as it was recognized by Virginia or Maryland; or to interfere with the domestic slave trade between states. When violence or intimidation prevented the capture and return of a fugitive slave, compensation was to be provided the claimant. The first of these amendments, which dealt with slavery in the territories, was the crucial one upon which the entire compromise hinged. In all the territory of the United States "now held or hereafter acquired," the Missouri Compromise line of 36° 30' was to be extended to the Pacific. North of that line slavery was to be prohibited; south of the line "slavery of the African race" was to be recognized and protected by the federal government during the territorial stage. The sixth amendment guaranteed the permanency of the settlement by stipulating that the sections dealing with slavery were exempt from future amendment. The resolutions endorsed the constitutionality and enforcement of all the fugitive slave laws, proposed a repeal of the Personal Liberty laws and a modification of the Fugitive Slave Act to eliminate the higher fee paid to commissioners who successfully returned an alleged fugitive from slavery, and called for a strict enforcement of the suppression of the African slave trade.[27]

Aware that his plan offered the North next to nothing while asking it to make major concessions, Crittenden urged the Republicans to view those concessions as "a cheap sacrifice" necessary to save the Union, the cherished legacy of Americans and the envy of the world. Republican businessmen and many Democrats agreed with Crittenden. Faced with massive losses in their Southern trade and investments, Northern merchants and manufacturers inundated Congress with pro-compromise petitions. The *Philadelphia Press* stressed that the Southern market for Northern goods dwarfed foreign demand. The *New York Herald*, a flagship Democratic paper, called on Lincoln to grant "the South their just rights." It noted that many had voted for Lincoln out of a general desire to unseat the Democrats "independently of the negro question." Dire warnings were voiced of voter revolt against the Republicans in the up-coming state elections unless they made an immediate commitment "to a more just and generous policy toward their Southern brethren."[28]

Most Republicans were unmoved. Despite the pressure to yield, the Republicans on the Committee of Thirteen unanimously rejected the key provision on the extension of slavery and its perpetual protection below the 36° 30' line in all present and future territories. Outside the cities, rank-and-file Republicans solidly stood behind their party's decision not to sell out its core principles. The Republicans were clear and consistent in why they would not yield. "There can be no compromise short of an entire surrender of our convictions of right and wrong," wrote Congressman Justin S. Morrill of Vermont to his wife. In a speech in the House, he argued that were it not for Lincoln's election, no Southern revolution would have occurred and no demands would have been made to grant slavery sweeping, new guarantees. But because the Republicans had won, they were expected to accept what even most Democrats had renounced in the presidential election. "Under these circumstances, the demand made is a humiliation to which no party can submit," Morrill proclaimed. "That verdict of the people [in the election] cannot be reversed, except by the people themselves, four years hence."[29]

In private correspondence, Republicans echoed Morrill's sentiments. "How does it happen," asked Abby Howland Woolsey of a secessionist cousin in Alabama in reference to the Crittenden Compromise, "that the Southern demands have increased so enormously since last year?" She pointed out that then the Senate by a vote of 43 to 5 declared that a slave code was not necessary for the territories. Then, Southerners split their party by trying to force such a code onto the party platform. That was followed, after being outvoted in the election, by a demand to place a slave code *"into the Constitution!* We can never eat our principles that way, though all fifteen of the [slave] states secede."[30]

Then, and now, critics of the Republicans' stand against compromise accused them of putting their party above the country, an indictment informed by looking back at the drastic consequences of their refusal to budge. That a war of such magnitude was on the horizon was by no means self-evident in December of 1860. The distinction between party and country ignores the belief of the Republicans that the best interests of the country would be served by holding firm to what the party stood for—the non-expansion of slavery. Republicans, as well as many other Northerners, were convinced that the indefinite existence of slavery, let alone its spread, was a moral, political, and economic threat to the ideals and material health of a just, progressive America. Privileging sectional peace as the ultimate good, as the Republicans understood, meant consigning future generations of African Americans to ongoing chains of slavery. Moreover, nothing but Northern silence on slavery would satisfy the ultra-secessionists. "When a people reach the Utopian dream of the South, where all agitation is banished," Morrill warned, "and where all criticism is silenced, they will indeed, have reached the perfect equality . . . where property in slaves will everywhere be recognized; for there all will be slaves."[31]

That agreement on the Crittenden Compromise would have resulted in sectional harmony and an end to agitation over slavery was no more than an assumption. Davis and Toombs stated that if the Republicans on the Committee of Thirteen accepted the compromise, they would have been satisfied, as presumably would secessionists in the Lower South. Only South Carolina had seceded when the committee deliberated, though secession elections in early and mid-January 1861 were to be held in the other cotton states. A case can be made that Republican capitulation and self-imposed destruction would have arrested the drive for secession, but it was far from a certainty. Even if it had, the South would have continued to push for more slave territory. That was the very reason Toombs supported the compromise, "so that the whole continent to the north pole shall be settled upon the one rule [free labor], and to the south pole under the other [slavery]." That was the rub. Republicans viewed the Crittenden Compromise as a blank check for the expansion of slavery into Mexico, Central America, and the Caribbean. The result would be, predicted Representative James Wilson of Indiana, "an empire of slavery, such as the world has never before witnessed." [32]

The empire envisioned by Wilson would have required the assent of the North to the acquisition of more territory to the south for slavery, the chances of which were virtually nil. Milton Latham, a pro-Lecompton Democratic senator from California and no friend of the Republicans, seized upon this point in opposing the 36° 30' feature of the Crittenden plan. Speaking for a state that wanted to expand into Sonora and Lower California and gain a monopoly of trade on the Pacific Coast, Latham was unwilling to support a measure that would forestall any future southward expansion. And, as he pointedly added, once "the Southern states at some future period would see the disposition on the part of the North to curtail the institution of slavery to its present limits, we would have renewal of disunion, secession, revolution, or whatever else you want to call it." Far from putting an end to sectional hostilities over slavery, the Crittenden solution was a recipe for more of the same in the future. This was the same logic behind Lincoln's directive to party leaders to reject any plan for the expansion of slavery. Apart from eviscerating the party's defining creed, any such plan would lead only to future strife. "Stand firm," he admonished. "The tug has to come & better now, than at any time hereafter."[33]

Unable to agree on plans for a settlement, the Committee of Thirteen disbanded on December 28, 1860. The apparent collapse of compromise efforts dealt a crushing blow to the cooperationists in the Lower South, who had pinned their hopes on a conciliatory North. The *New Orleans Bee*, which praised the Crittenden plan as the only one offering the South "something tangible," blasted the Republicans for "fighting the battles of all those Southern men who are for unconditional surrender." On behalf of Southern conservatives, it asserted that "the Crittenden compromise was their ultimatum." "Zed," the Washington correspondent for the *Richmond Dispatch*, now saw war as all but inevitable and accused the Republicans of choosing civil war over "their own destruction."[34]

Another tipping point on the road to war was also reached in late December when Major Anderson surreptitiously abandoned Fort Moultrie and repositioned his garrison in Fort Sumter. The beleaguered Buchanan administration faced another crisis.

Major Anderson: The Charleston Wild Card

A Kentuckian by birth and a one-time slaveholder who had never voted, Major Robert Anderson was, above all, a career army officer committed to honorably serving his country. On assuming command at Fort Moultrie on November

21, 1860, he immediately recognized that he was in a political and military trap from which there was no easy escape. The forts under his command were woefully short of men, supplies, and ordnance, a tempting target for the excited Charlestonians who monitored his every move. Buchanan and his cabinet, obsessed with the fear that any strengthening of the installations would trigger an attack on them, rejected his requests for reinforcements. Anderson, on the other hand, was convinced that the very weakness of his position invited an attack and asked for specific instructions on how he should respond to an assault. Major Don Carlos Buell arrived at Fort Moultrie on December 11 with the orders. Anderson was to refrain from any provocative actions but, if attacked, was to resist to "the last extremity." Buell, likely exceeding his instructions, authorized Anderson to concentrate his forces in any of the forts if attacked or provided with "tangible evidence" of a probable attack.[35]

The authorities in Charleston honored their agreement with Anderson to restrain armed mobs from any rash move against the forts, but they made it clear that the forts had to be delivered over once South Carolina seceded. On December 22, two days after the formal act of secession, Anderson learned that steamers were patrolling between Forts Moultrie and Sumter, presumably to block any transfer by Anderson of his garrison out to Sumter, the key to the defense of the harbor. On December 24, South Carolina sent commissioners to Washington to negotiate the transfer of the forts and other federal property in the state to what they considered the sovereign republic of South Carolina. Never informed of any gentlemen's agreement between Buchanan and the Carolinians to maintain the status quo in the harbor and convinced that Buchanan would not consent to the surrender of the forts, Anderson decided to stealthily move his men and most of his supplies out to the stronghold of Fort Sumter.

Anderson acted on his own initiative, but he felt that Secretary of War Floyd's last message to him on December 21 had in effect authorized him to make the move. Anxious to avoid a "useless sacrifice" of Anderson's men in defending against an attack, Floyd instructed Anderson "to exercise sound military discretion" in weighing his options. His request on December 22 for direct authorization to move to Fort Sumter having been ignored, Anderson reasoned that the best chance of avoiding a confrontation was to get out of his defenseless position in Moultrie and redeploy to the real prize in the harbor, Fort Sumter. By so doing, he would keep it out of the hands of the secessionists and force them to think twice about attacking. "His whole desire," as summarized by Samuel Crawford, his assistant-surgeon, was "to avoid bloodshed" and put off, at least temporarily, any violent confrontation that could touch off a war.[36]

Attention to details was always Anderson's strongest suit, and it showed in his careful planning for the transfer, originally planned for Christmas but put off for a day because of stormy weather. Informing only his staff officers in advance, he sent Lieutenant Norman Hall to charter three schooners and some barges under the guise of removing the women and children at Moultrie to safer quarters in Fort Johnson. Despite the prying eyes of civilians, the ruse worked. The move to Sumter got under way at dusk and was completed two hours later. Luck played a part as the early evening guard-steamer was too busy tugging a vessel to stop and interdict one of the boats on the way to Sumter. Before the late evening patrol-steamer left its dock in Charleston, Anderson was safely in Fort Sumter with most of his equipment and ninety days' worth of provisions. A rear guard left at Fort Moultrie spiked the guns and burned their carriages.[37]

Hailed in the North for his resolve in avoiding a disgraceful surrender of a federal fort, Anderson was denounced in the South as a warmonger. The news threw Charleston "into a state of the wildest excitement." Accusing Anderson of "an outrageous breach of faith," the *Charleston Mercury* demanded that Buchanan officially reprimand Anderson and order his immediate withdrawal from Fort Sumter. Governor Pickens was just as enraged, for he had been left looking the fool. On Christmas, he had informed Miles that he had "the highest possible evidence that no alteration is to be made or allowed as to the forts until a full *hearing* is granted the commissioners.... The strictest military guards are constantly out, and I think I am authorized to say that no change will be made at present."[38]

Excitement also reigned in Washington, especially in the inner circle of the reshuffled Buchanan administration. The previous three weeks had seen a major cabinet reorganization. The first to go was Secretary of the Treasury Howell Cobb, who resigned on December 8 to campaign for secession in Georgia. In protest of Buchanan's refusal to reinforce Anderson, Cass from the State Department left a week later. Attorney General Black replaced Cass and in turn secured for his former post Edwin M. Stanton, an antislavery lawyer from Ohio. Along with Postmaster General Holt, Black and Stanton combined for a strong Unionist bloc that was instrumental in helping Buchanan withstand the pressure exerted by South Carolina's commissioners for him to undo what Anderson had done.

Charged by the secession convention with making arrangements for the transfer of the forts and other federal property to provide "for the continuance of peace and amity between the commonwealth and the Government at Washington," the commissioners were hopeful of achieving the Committee of 1860's goal of peaceful secession. Anderson's unexpected maneuver, however, upset all their plans.[39]

The first meeting of the commissioners with Buchanan was scheduled for the morning of December 27, just hours, it turned out, after Washington had been rocked by the surprise news from Charleston. Trescot and Senators Jefferson Davis and Robert M. T. Hunter rushed to the White House, where Buchanan was still unaware of what had happened. Startled and confused, Buchanan blurted out, "I call God to witness . . . that this is not only without but against my orders, it is against my policy." He was inclined to give in to the Southerners' demand to order Anderson back to Moultrie, but in keeping with his character, hesitated and insisted he must consult with his cabinet.[40]

The cabinet meeting was loud and boisterous. A distraught Floyd, forgetting his directive of December 21 (written by Black as attorney general) authorizing Anderson "to exercise sound military discretion," raged that Anderson had violated orders and that honor required sending him back. Black, supported by Holt and Stanton, corrected Floyd and retrieved the directive to refresh Floyd's memory. Pulled in opposite directions by the Northern and Southern members of the cabinet, Buchanan put off a decision. Governor Pickens then helped him make up his mind. When Anderson rejected Pickens's demand to withdraw at once from Fort Sumter, the governor ordered the seizure of Fort Moultrie and Castle Pinckney. On December 29, he moved to take over the federal arsenal in Charleston. He next ordered the erection of batteries on Morris Island and Sullivan's Island overlooking Fort Sumter.

Just as Pickens pushed Buchanan's patience too far, so too did the commissioners when their postponed meeting with Buchanan took place on December 29.

Fig. 6.3 South Carolina's Ultimatum. Governor Pickens and President Buchanan are portrayed here as two fools squabbling over Fort Sumter. Library of Congress, LC-USZ62-17261.

Buchanan began by stating he was willing to talk with the commissioners only as "private gentlemen," not the representatives of an independent nation. Ignoring this condition, the commissioners acted as the injured party lecturing to the head of a foreign government. Accusing Buchanan of bad faith in allowing Anderson to move to Fort Sumter, they presumptuously announced that negotiations were impossible in such a treacherous atmosphere. Buchanan responded with his own accusations. Before storming out, the commissioners left Buchanan with a formal request for "the immediate withdrawal of the troops from the harbor of Charleston," declaring them "a standing menace [which] threatens speedily to bring to a bloody issue questions which ought to be settled with temperance and judgment."[41]

Despite the harsh, if not insulting, attitude of the commissioners, Buchanan still hoped to fashion a somewhat conciliatory response. Stiffened by General Scott's advice to reinforce the forts in the South and alarmed by plunging support for their Democratic Party, the Northern members in the cabinet forcefully opposed the reply to the commissioners submitted to them the next day. Under the threat of resigning, Black convinced Buchanan to strengthen his reply and follow Scott's advice. The remaining Southerners in the cabinet (save Holt) resigned in protest.

Delivered on December 31, Buchanan's reply was argued with all his lawyerly skills. Reiterating that Anderson had acted without his orders, he denied the charge of bad faith. Initially he had been inclined to order Anderson back, but, in his most telling point, stressed that he could hardly do so now after federal installations had been seized. In their parting shot, the commissioners responded with a vindication of South Carolina's actions and chided Buchanan for not sending Anderson back in the twelve hours before the seizures.[42]

During the negotiations in Washington, the governors in the Lower South pounced on Anderson's move as justification for seizing federal forts in their states. The news from Charleston reached the other Southern states "like an electric" shock and sent indignant citizens into the streets. The editor of the *Macon Daily Telegraph* wrote that Georgians could no longer have any doubts of the wisdom of secession since it was now clear the federal government was bent on coercion. Drawing on the master metaphor of the degraded slave, he declared, "There are none of us so degraded as to submit to be whipped into submission." No Georgian was more outraged than the ever-excitable Augustus L. Lamar, who somehow latched onto the idea that the Gourdins were now planning on taking Fort Sumter by force. Lamar wrote that his men were ready to seize Fort Pulaski, fifteen miles downriver from Savannah, and deliver its guns to Charleston. Aghast at the thought of the volatile Georgian in charge of any phase of secession, Robert Gourdin telegraphed his Savannah associates to direct Lamar to make no move without consulting Alexander Lawton, a sober businessman and key Gourdin ally in Georgia.[43]

Still, the momentum to seize Fort Pulaski was irresistible. A sequence of telegrams from the commissioners in Washington to the convention in Charleston and Governor Brown in Georgia warned of an imminent attack by federal reinforcements on the way to the Southern forts. On January 2, 1861, Brown ordered Georgia volunteers to occupy undefended Fort Pulaski at the mouth of the Savannah River. He then telegraphed the governors in Alabama, Florida, Louisiana, and Mississippi urging them to follow his example.

A. B. Moore of Alabama was the first to act. A South Carolinian whose path to wealth was eased by his marriage to a planter's daughter, he converted to secession under pressure from the legislature. On January 3, he ordered the Alabama First Volunteer Regiment to seize Forts Morgan and Gaines and the US Mount Vernon arsenal in Mobile Bay. Not wanting his order "to be misunderstood by the Government of the United States," he wrote to Buchanan the next day assuring him he had acted solely out "of self-defense, and the plainest dictates of prudence, to anticipate and guard against the contemplated movement of the authorities of the General Government." The Alabama cooperationist Thomas J. McClellan had a different take on Moore's actions. He had exceeded, McClellan wrote his wife, "in usurpation of force any thing that has yet been done even in South Carolina." At least the Carolinians "passed their ordinance of Secession before they took the forts in that State, but here it is done two days before the assembling of the convention."[44]

McClellan's observation held true across the Lower South. The seizures undertaken by Brown in Georgia and Madison Perry in Florida on January 6 and 7, and those of Thomas Moore in Louisiana on January 10 predated their states' conventions. The exception was in Mississippi, which had no coastal forts to seize. The takeovers were bloodless, but a major prize was missed. When Florida troops swarmed over federal installations in Pensacola on January 12, the commanding officer at Fort Barrancas on the mainland evaded them by transferring his men and supplies across the bay to Fort Pickens (named after the grandfather of Governor Francis Pickens of South Carolina) on Santa Rosa Island. Inaccessible by land and far enough out in the Gulf of Mexico to be provisioned and protected by the US Navy, Fort Pickens was held by the Union throughout the war.

Strategically positioned to shape secession, the cotton state governors left the conservative cooperationists fuming that they were the victims of conspiratorial forces. Alexander Stephens was certain that Governor Brown had seized Fort Pulaski on the advice of Toombs "and the other ultra men who are determined to precipitate us into secession. That was the object. They had no real fears of the Govt. using force."[45]

In the week of the seizures, Buchanan proclaimed January 4 as a national day of fasting and prayer. The tone of the sermons often strayed from themes of Christian comfort to scathing condemnations of Buchanan's policies and the corruption and decadence that gripped his administration and the nation. The sharpest attacks came from antislavery evangelicals. In language that coincided with Lincoln's reasoning in opposing compromise, the Reverend Joseph P. Thompson of the Broadway Tabernacle Church in New York declared that "God is rebuking our idolatry of the Union." Rather than valuing the Union as a means to promote greater freedom and Christian righteousness, too many Americans in his view "have glorified it as in itself an END, and have vaunted the Constitution above the 'higher law' of God." The source of the crisis was to be found in the endless efforts of Congress "to sanction and protect slavery."[46]

With or without the same Christian convictions, more Northerners were coming to the same conclusion that the North must stand up to Southern demands and depredations. The conservative *Cincinnati Enquirer* editorialized that the North had reached the breaking point in its forbearance. When news was received of efforts to besiege Anderson and of the seizures in Georgia, the *Enquirer* declared these "acts of hostility" that would "excite a greater sensation throughout the country than any intelligence that has been received for years." Strident calls blared forth from the rural press for "inflexibly enforcing the laws" and punishing "highhanded treason." Northerners valued the public property as a legacy of the Revolution intended for the nation's protection and ongoing prosperity. The seizure of the forts, arsenals, and custom houses struck them as outright theft. United as never before in the crisis, they began to confront the real possibility of a civil war. But that very possibility produced a new push among Northern Democrats and Republican conservatives for Union-saving measures.[47]

A Return to Stasis and a Northern Fiasco

In the wake of the uproar over Fort Sumter and assurances from the South Carolina commissioners that the fort would not be attacked were it not reinforced, Buchanan recommitted himself to doing nothing that would provoke hostilities. In his message to Congress on January 8, he acknowledged his "right and duty" to employ military force in defense of any federal officers under attack but reiterated his belief that the Constitution forbade him "to make aggressive war upon any State." Like Buchanan, senators from the Gulf states were anxious to avoid war, especially before a Southern confederacy was formed. The most immediate risk shifted to Fort Pickens, where Governor Perry was planning an assault once troops he requested arrived from Alabama. On January 8, seven

Southern senators telegraphed Perry to call off any attack. "We think no assault should be made. . . . Bloodshed now may be fatal to our cause." The senators, worried that a trap was being set, informed A. B. Moore that the Republicans were plotting to precipitate a clash before Lincoln's inauguration to absolve him of the stigma of starting a war. Though Moore agreed on the need for caution, he advised keeping the troops at Pensacola to avoid leaving the impression with the Republicans that Southerners were afraid to fight.[48]

In the meantime, compromise efforts resumed in Congress, led by Crittenden, Douglas, and the border state Unionists. The first plan came out of a committee chaired by Crittenden. The Republicans on the committee went along with the key recommendations for a constitutional amendment banning Congress from interfering with slavery in the states and extending the Missouri Compromise line with non-interference but no explicit protection for slavery south of 36° 30'. Crittenden's other constitutional amendments in his original compromise were dropped, the "hereafter acquired" clause was eliminated, and all other measures were left up to Congress. The secessionists and congressional Republicans wanted nothing to do with it. In place of guaranteed protection in present and future territories for slavery, Southerners were offered popular sovereignty, an approach long rejected in the cotton states. For their part, the Republicans were on record as opposing any possibility for the extension of slavery, and their most fiery spokesman, Owen Lovejoy of Illinois, declared that he had no intention "to kindle the fires of hell south of the celestial meridian of thirty-six thirty." The plan went nowhere.[49]

Next up was another border state proposal authored by Emerson Etheridge of Tennessee. The only significant new feature concerned the vexed territorial issue. It dealt with territories south of 36° 30' by making it nearly impossible to acquire them. A two-thirds vote in both the House and Senate would be necessary to create any of these territories and, if added by a treaty, a two-thirds vote in the Senate. Buchanan was willing to support this and any variant of the Crittenden plan, as were Northern Democrats and New York businessmen. But the Republicans did not budge. All they had offered to date were the tepid proposals of Seward to the Committee of Thirty-Three—the constitutional guarantee on slavery in the states and tighter enforcement of the Fugitive Slave Act. Seeing no value in a useless compromise, they blocked Etheridge's efforts in the House in January to bring his plan up for discussion. That evening the Gulf state senators caucused and telegraphed home that "Hope is dead. Secede at once. Today is the darkest yet."[50]

Contrary to the Northern conciliators, the Republicans did not believe that they were choosing to go to war to overturn secession. In their minds, they would not have to resort to an armed conflict. Nothing the Republicans had done had swayed moderates in the Upper South from their view that Lincoln's election was no cause for secession. Meanwhile, the cotton states appeared to be on the brink of economic collapse. The *New York Herald* cited reports of visitors to Charleston of "much distress there," especially among the volunteer soldiers in and around the city in their damp, unhealthy camps. The docks were deserted and "no business doing." Reports from elsewhere were just as gloomy. Money was nowhere to be found in New Orleans and slave and cotton prices were falling, related a Philadelphia correspondent. He depicted Southern whites as gripped by fears of an invasion and uprisings from their slave enemies within. Alabama was said to be "almost destitute of food " for both whites and slaves.[51]

Crediting these reports, the *New York Herald* concluded that "Northerners have hardly anything to do but to let self-inflicted justice have its own way [in the South]." Southerners in due time would come to their senses and realize that "their only salvation is to retrace their steps." Likewise, the *Chicago Tribune*, which reveled in puncturing Southern dreams of greatness once out of the Union, dismissed talk of the need for a war when it was apparent that communities in the seceding states were "impoverished and starving." "Let us hear no more complaints from the semi-secessionists in the North that Civil War is about to be inaugurated in the land." Any force that might be needed, bragged the editor, would amount to no more than that expended in quelling an urban riot in the North. The inference was clear: yield nothing and watch the pitiful seceders sink in their economic misery. Most Republicans would have been more restrained in their reading of the seceders' inability to pose any viable military threat, but they were equally confident that the sufferings of the Southern white masses would bring secession to a halt and reverse its gains. That confidence held even after the fiasco of the *Star of the West* expedition.[52]

Pushed by Scott, Holt, and Black, Buchanan decided on December 31 to reinforce Fort Sumter. The original plan assigned the task to the warship *Brooklyn* after picking up 200 men and ninety days' worth of provisions at Fort Monroe in Virginia. Scott, however, quickly changed his mind and commissioned the *Star of the West,* a commercial steamer, to transport the supplies. He reasoned that a lighter, faster ship would stand a better chance of slipping into the harbor and traversing the sand bar at its entrance. On January 5, Washington received Anderson's telegram of December 31 with its disturbing report that the Charlestonians were erecting a battery on Morris Island overlooking the harbor. Almost as disquieting to Buchanan was the confidence Anderson expressed in his position when he wrote: "Thank God, we are now where the Government may send us additional troops at its leisure." As far as Anderson was concerned, he could "command the harbor" until the government wished otherwise.[53]

Shaken by the telegram, Buchanan reversed himself. With Scott's approval, he telegraphed New York revoking his previous order. It was too late; the *Star of the West* had already departed. Adding to what was becoming a comedy of errors, the message informing Anderson that a relief ship was on the way did not reach him before the *Star of the West* arrived in the harbor. The same was the fate of the *Brooklyn*, which was sent on January 7 to overtake the *Star of the West* and protect it from the fire of the batteries.

The relief ship left New York on January 5, 1861, and made good time. It was sailing into a hornet's nest. Charleston had been on a war footing since the Texas senator Louis Wigfall had telegraphed on January 2 that Holt's replacement of Floyd as secretary of war meant "war." His advice was to shut off supplies to Anderson and "take Fort Sumter as soon as possible." The arrival of the *Star of the West* came as no surprise. Despite efforts at secrecy, New York buzzed with rumors of the expedition and on January 8 New York papers published a detailed account of the mission. Upon learning the news, Secretary of the Interior Jacob Thompson of Mississippi resigned and telegraphed Charleston the ship was on the way.[54]

As the *Star of the West* entered the harbor on the morning of January 9, the battery on Morris Island fired a warning shot. From his observation post on the parapet, Abner Doubleday rushed to alert Anderson, who ordered the men to the guns. Anderson had seen the report in the newspaper brought to the fort the day before announcing the relief mission, but he had discredited it. He had received no notification from Washington, and it defied military sense to send a merchant steamer to do the work of a warship. Confused and unprepared, Anderson hesitated as the battery on Fort Moultrie opened fire. Damaged by two shots, the *Star of the West* turned around and headed back to New York. Upon seeing its withdrawal, Anderson snapped out the order: "Hold on, do not fire. I will wait." If war was to erupt over Fort Sumter, it would not be the doing of this politically torn Kentuckian.[55]

Anderson immediately demanded an explanation from Pickens for the unprovoked firing, only to receive back a lecture that South Carolina was now an independent republic with every right to repel an expedition to a fort that it considered its own. When confronted with a demand on January 11 to surrender, Anderson refused but gave the governor an out by suggesting that he send his demand on to Washington. Pickens had gained some face-saving room to delay, for he was under intense pressure from the Rhett faction to take Fort Sumter by assault, a dubious undertaking for which South Carolina was not yet militarily prepared.[56]

The result was two weeks of testy meetings in Washington between Isaac W. Hayne, the special envoy of South Carolina, and the Buchanan administration. Hayne took a hard line on the question of evacuation, and the talks might well have blown up if not for the intervention of the senators in the Lower South whose states were in the midst of seceding. Acting as mediators, they made clear they wanted "an amicable adjustment of the matter" and had assurances that no hostile intent was behind the relief effort, whose only purpose was to retain what Buchanan viewed as federal property he was duty bound to protect. Backed up by the Gourdins and other South Carolina moderates, they insisted the main goal now was to work together to create a new confederacy in February in which their states would share a "common destiny" with South Carolina. The size and armed might of that confederacy, they were confident, would force the federal government to back off from any coercive threats.[57]

When Hayne tightly held to the letter of his instructions, the senators tried another tack on January 19. They wrote Buchanan seeking his pledge not to reinforce Fort Sumter in return for Pickens continuing to allow Anderson access to supplies of food and fuel in Charleston. Responding for Buchanan, Secretary of War Holt flatly refused any pledge and rehashed the non-hostile policy of the administration. He concluded that the best way out of the impasse was an agreement by both sides to embrace "the high Christian and moral duty to keep the peace" without committing themselves to any binding obligations. Hayne found the administration's response to be "entirely unsatisfactory," but he deferred to the Southern senators who were persuaded that no reinforcements would be sent to Anderson before a convention to form a Southern confederacy.[58]

Pickens, though fuming as much as Hayne over the failure of his mission, was relieved to have an honorable way out of the corner into which he had backed himself. After all, he had retreated from none of his demands. All parties could accept the return to the status quo except the Rhett radicals. Maintaining that South Carolina should not commit to joining any Southern confederacy before Anderson was driven out of Sumter, they had opposed from the start the Hayne mission as truckling to the enemy. To their thinking, only "the capture of Fort Sumter before the end of the month" could ensure the defeat of the "submissionists" in the upcoming secession elections in the Upper South.[59]

Fort Sumter remained the most visible flashpoint for the outbreak of war. Although fears of an immediate attack receded in mid-January, the crisis over the fort had reached a dangerous new level. Even the *Detroit Free Press*, a pro-compromise Democratic paper, conceded that the firing on the *Star of the West* left the federal government no alternative but to reinforce Sumter and recover the seized forts in South Carolina. "To do less will be to confess its weakness," the editor proclaimed; "indeed, it will be to abandon its own existence." South Carolina had squandered any sympathy it might have had in the North, the paper admitted, but no other slave states had so openly defied the government and could still be kept in the Union if only the Republicans would compromise. In contrast, the Republican press wanted no surrender of the party's principles and decried what the *New York Tribune* labeled "treason in the Cabinet and tremulous vacillation in the White House."[60]

As the partisan divide persisted, the Republicans floated conciliatory gestures designed to placate the Upper South. They hoped to take advantage of the outrage over the *Star of the West* incident expressed by such Southern

Unionists as Andrew Johnson of Tennessee, who accused the Carolinians of "mak[ing] war upon the Govmt." Still, what the Republicans were offering were mere palliatives. Seward, who was trying to find a middle ground between Southerners demanding territorial concessions and Lincoln, who refused to sanction any, delivered a widely anticipated speech in the Senate on January 12. The speech was long on soothing and short on substance. In addition to pleas to set aside passions for calm reasoning, Seward urged Congress to pressure the Northern states to repeal their Personal Liberty laws; take steps to prevent John Brown–like raids in the future; charter a Pacific Railroad for the North and one for the South; and approve a constitutional amendment guaranteeing non-interference by Congress with slavery in the states. He held out hope for a grand settlement of all the sectional issues in a constitutional convention, perhaps in two or three years. Seward talked for close to two hours and moved many in the audience to tears. It was an impressive but ultimately empty performance. "Mr. Seward fails to present anything practicable for the present," accurately noted the *Philadelphia Ledger*, "and he so surrounds the Territorial question with ifs and buts that nothing tangible can be got from it."[61]

Two days later, a badly divided Committee of Thirty-Three presented its proposals. At the insistence of the Republican members, none dealt with the territorial question. The most significant proposed the admission of New Mexico as a state, with or without slavery as its constitution saw fit. The other two included the now mandatory guarantee amendment and the elimination of the requirement in the Fugitive Slave Act for all citizens to assist when requested in the capture of fugitive slaves. The proposed Thirteenth Amendment, an unamendable guarantee against federal interference with slavery, was approved in the House and Senate in early March when enough antislavery Republicans relented in their opposition and was sent on by Lincoln to the states for their consideration. [62]

As Congress went around in circles in January, six more cotton states withdrew from the Union, soon followed by their congressmen. Jefferson Davis was the last to leave the Senate. "All have gone save me alone and I am called away," he wrote on January 19. "We have piped but they would not dance and now the Devil may care." Although they expressed fond memories of what the Union had once been, most left in the defiant mood of David Yulee of Florida. A first-generation sugar planter and the driving force behind the building of Florida's first railroads, he embodied the self-proclaimed mastery of secessionists unwilling to brook any Northern checks on their ruling as they saw fit. "I am willing to be their masters, but not their brothers." He expected all the slave states, save perhaps Kentucky and Missouri, to be out by March 4, 1861. He exaggerated the secessionist appeal but correctly sensed that a point of no return had been reached.[63]

Secessionist Surge

The Lower South Leaves

Before the failure of the Crittenden Compromise and Anderson's move to Fort Sumter, secession was a tough sell in the Lower South outside South Carolina. Remnants of two-party loyalties, competitive contests in the 1860 election, and anti-planter sentiments in their backcountries slowed down the rush to straight-out secession. Coalescing under the label of cooperation with its multiple meanings, moderates and conservatives had hopes for success before they lost their momentum in late December. Once their states seceded, they called for a popular referendum on the decision of their secession conventions. When that failed, they joined the separatists in presenting a united front against the North.

Mississippi and Florida: The Surge Begins

On January 9, 1861, Mississippi became the second state to secede. Along with South Carolina, it was the only state in which slaves comprised a majority of the population, and just under half of Mississippi families owned slaves, the highest rate in the South. Unlike South Carolina, a net exporter of both whites and slaves at mid-century, Mississippi was still growing from an influx of newcomers, especially slaves whose numbers increased by 40 percent in the 1850s. The fortunes of no other state were so closely tied to slavery, a fact that was front and center in the declaration of causes behind Mississippi's secession. According to the declaration, abolitionist blows against slavery were about to be consummated, and the state had no choice "but submission to the mandate of abolition, or a dissolution of the Union, whose principles have been subverted to work out our ruin."[1]

The push for secession came not from the top, as was the case in South Carolina, but from the mid-range of the social order. It was generated by young, middling farmers and lawyers striving to join the planter elite. Squeezed by rising prices for land and slaves and growing indebtedness, these men potentially had more to

Fig. 7.1 Domestic Troubles. The Union hen worriedly looks on as seven secessionist ducks with South Carolina in the lead swim down a river of calamity with a circling hawk of anarchy about to pounce on them. Library of Congress, LC-USZ62-14833.

gain than lose by cutting free of a North identified with closing off the territories to slaveholders. The planter elites, centered in the Natchez region, hedged on secession. What set them apart and defined their conservatism was their immense wealth in land and slaves, sectionally diversified investment portfolios that could cushion against bad crop years, and close social connections to the North. They were far more cosmopolitan in outlook than the typical Mississippian whose values were shaped by neighborhood loyalties and issues of local concern. The Natchez elite and the other rich planters in the delta traveled extensively, supervised commercial interests that linked them to Northern and international sources of credit, and frequently were born or educated in the Northeast. For them, Northerners were not the terrifying abolitionists caricatured by Southern editors and fire-eaters, but relatives, family friends, and business associates anxious to maintain sectional harmony.[2]

Delay and caution were the watchwords of the wealthier planters once Lincoln was elected. Had it not been for the popular excitement and clamor for secession from the Breckinridge press, most would have been content to support a redress of Southern grievances within the Union. Only if the Republicans openly violated Southern rights were they willing to risk the perils of secession, and then only after a conference of all the Southern states had agreed on a unified approach to resisting Northern tyranny. Their Unionism, however, was decidedly conditional. William S. Yerger in a Unionist speech at Greenville in November set as his condition a Southern share in the territories by a redrawing of the Missouri Compromise line and the repeal of the North's Personal Liberty laws. L. Q. C. Lamar did not oppose secession per se but insisted that to mitigate the dangers, Mississippi's departure should be contingent on the cooperative secession of eight other slave states.[3]

An issue that in hindsight appears to be semantic quibbling over how the Southern states would secede—individually or collectively—was to the hardcore secessionists a question as to whether the states would secede at all. To the secessionist David Clopton of Alabama, Lamar's cooperationism was tantamount to a disguised form of Unionism that would "defeat the whole movement." That was also the great fear of the South Carolina secessionists as emphasized by States Rights (his name was in honor of his father, a fervid nullifier) Gist in his early November correspondence with Governor Pettus of Mississippi. Resist any call for a Southern conference, advised Gist, "as the Border and non-acting States would outvote us & thereby defeat action." Having never forgiven Virginia for stonewalling Southern action at the start of the year, the South Carolinians were determined not to let it happen again. Their strategy was clear: present the Virginians with a fait accompli and let them decide if they would be ruled by Northern masters or join other states in seceding.[4]

Governor Pettus sounded out the state's top political leaders on the issue in a private meeting at Jackson on November 22, 1860. Three of them, Lamar and US senators Brown and Davis, favored cooperative action and wanted South Carolina to hold off any precipitate secession. Delay, they argued, had the advantage of providing time for a possible compromise with additional guarantees and for maximizing the chances of a dignified and united Southern front. Pettus, as was readily apparent to an English correspondent struck by the governor's tobacco-stained clothes and brusque manner, was a first-generation planter with none of the social graces of the Delta planters. He exuded the directness and raw energy of Mississippians barely removed from frontier existence. Though peppered with reports that the people were "ripe" for secession, he likely needed no prompting to move swiftly and decisively. With his backing, the legislature set December 20 for the secession election.[5]

Only immediate and significant concessions from the Republicans could have curbed the groundswell for secession. R. L. Dixon, a Washington County planter, initially was willing to wait for such concessions, but within a few weeks his position hardened. "I do not think the cotton States will now accept any adjustment," and even if granted, he thought they would "soon be overridden by a 'higher law' doctrine, & the same insecurity & depreciation of our property & its annual products." Noting that financial matters could hardly get any worse, he was ready for immediate secession.[6]

For the secessionists, the choice in the election was clear: "Recollect that you are then to choose between the alternative of living under a Northern free negro despotism, or in a confederacy of free and equal Southern States," declared the *Jackson Mississippian*. Among the many whose minds were made up was Flavellus G. Nicholson, a planter's son and lieutenant in the Quitman Light Infantry. Whites were "determined never to be the slaves of Northern despots, though the assertion & maintenance of their rights should cost them rivers of blood," read his diary entry in November 1860. Charles D. Fontaine, a fellow Democrat from Pontotoc County, estimated that the Breckinridge men would go overwhelmingly for immediate secession, as well as forming a sizable contingent of Bell men who would see the light after failing to defeat Lincoln. Though it was not necessary, the secessionists resorted to violence to keep down the cooperationist vote. John H. Aughey, a Northern-born Unionist preacher riding circuit in north-central Mississippi, heard a secessionist candidate gloating over "the glorious news from Tallahatchie. Seven tory-submissionists were hanged there in one day, and the so-called Union candidates, having the wholesome dread of hemp before their eyes, are not canvassing the county."[7]

Compared to the presidential contest, the secession election was a listless affair. Voter turnout fell 30 percent from the November balloting. Not only had the issue been settled for most, but in roughly one-third of the counties a nebulous coalition ticket also offered no clear-cut choice. Even when the choice seemed to be clear, some cooperative-Unionists were left feeling deceived. John C. Kirk, a Bolivar County planter, later testified that he had "voted against secession, that is, I voted for the co-operationist candidate [Miles H. McGehee], but when he got to Jackson he went in and voted for secession." Other Unionists of lesser standing in the community were not allowed to vote. "I came near getting whipped for wanting to vote the Union ticket," recalled James A. Brown, a sawyer in a Bolivar steam mill. "They would not let me, and talked about handling me for wanting to vote the Union ticket, and I left that part of the country." When John Aughey asked for a Union ticket in Choctaw County, he was told there were none and was advised to vote for secession. Defiantly, he wrote out a ticket and "voted it amidst the frowns, murmurs, and threats of the judges and bystanders."[8]

Those candidates openly committed to immediate secession won by a two-to-one margin as they swept the piney woods districts and newer cotton belts opened in the 1850s. Their strongest opposition came in the Delta counties, where the proximity of the Mississippi River as an invasion route for Northern forces heightened the fears of planters over the consequences of a war. The immediatists also ran poorly in the corn-and-wheat counties of northeastern Mississippi with a large minority of Tennesseans.[9]

Assembling in Jackson on January 7, 1861, the convention moved quickly on secession. The tone was set in the opening convocation by the Reverend C. K. Marshall, who reminded those present that the South was compelled to look outside the Union for the security of "the institution which Thy Providence has solemnly bound us to uphold, defend and protect." With William S. Barry, a Breckinridge lawyer-planter presiding, the convention met in secret session on January 9 to hammer out the secession ordinance. Former Whigs from the river counties, J. S. Yerger, James Alcorn, and Walter Brooke, offered amendments covering the usual conservative nostrums aimed at delaying an immediate decision. All went down to defeat by at least a two-thirds majority. With the choice narrowed down to secession or acquiescence to Republican rule, all but fifteen of the delegates signed the secession ordinance. Alcorn explained the thinking of the conservatives: "I and others agreeing with me determined to seize the wild and maddened steed by the mane and run with him *for a time*."[10]

Alcorn came to realize that he was a bit player in Mississippi politics after a younger generation of lawyer-slaveholders had assumed control of the secession convention. Their most forceful leader was David C. Glenn, a brilliant lawyer and orator who had served as the youngest state attorney general to date. A native of North Carolina, he moved to Mississippi in his teens and eventually settled in Mississippi City in the coastal county of Harrison. By 1860, he was the state's most outspoken states rights' Democrat and the prime mover in the secession convention.[11]

The most contested issue at the convention concerned the process for the ratification of the constitution for the new Southern confederacy expected to be formed in Montgomery in February. Fearing that the constitution might confer too much power on the planters, delegates from the yeoman counties in the north and the poorer farming counties in the south favored the Fontaine amendment submitting ratification to a popular referendum. In opposition were those from the Whiggish river counties and the Democratic planting regions of central and eastern Mississippi. Agreeing that unity was now essential if secession was to be turned to their advantage, the wealthy planters recoiled at the risk of another election exposing old social cleavages. As Barry cautioned, "It is wiser and safer, in times like these, not to have too many elections. . . . At this time there ought to be complete unanimity for defence; old party strifes and jealousies would be renewed." Glenn, the chair of the committee on a Southern Confederacy, led the fight against the amendment. Not wanting to open any back door to reconstruction, he saw the issue of reconstruction as "the great question of the body" and the one which "elicited all its talents and much of its violence." His committee's report on January 15 stipulated that any constitution and plan "for a permanent Government" adopted by the Montgomery convention "shall be referred back to this Convention for its ratification or rejection." Glenn had his way. Five Whigs who had backed one of the conservative amendments on January 9 voted against the Fontaine amendment on January 22, defeating it by a vote of 49 to 43. Mississippi's path to secession and a cotton confederacy was now unobstructed.[12]

On January 10, 1861, Florida became the third state to leave the Union. Though a raw, frontier state with the smallest population of any of the cotton states, it had the most rapidly growing slave regime east of the Mississippi. Its white population grew by 60 percent in the 1850s, and the number of slaves only slightly less. Responding to the lure of unbounded opportunity, slaveholders, especially from Georgia and South Carolina, poured in. The collapse of the Whig Party after 1852 gave Democrats control of the state, and young slaveholders in the party rotated in and out of the legislature. In 1860, the 55 percent majority of slaveholders was the youngest in any Southern legislature, with a median age in the upper thirties.[13]

The most settled parts of the state ran along a west to east axis in the panhandle with the divisions designated West, Middle, and East Florida. Two-thirds of the slaves lived in the former Whig strongholds in Middle Florida, the center of cotton production. Elsewhere, whites outnumbered slaves by three to one. Here, non-slaveholders raised corn, herded cattle, and identified with the Democrats as champions of their independence and white manhood. Bitter political battles in the 1840s in the wake of the collapse of the elite-controlled Union Bank of Florida politicized poorer whites and eliminated deference to planter rule. By the 1850s, planters had backed off from strong-arm tactics to control the yeomanry, but they remained a target for lower-class resentments as shown in the "Calhoun War" in the fall of 1860. The so-called war had its origins in a feud between the Durden clan and rival families on the other side of the Chipola River in West Florida's Calhoun County. After murdering Ethan Durden, the anti-Durden faction, which called itself the Regulators, raised a mob-like army of eighty men and ravaged the countryside. To provision their forces, they demanded supplies from the large planters and forcibly seized them if refused. Terrified planters turned to a federal judge, McQueen McIntosh, for protection, and the state militia was called out to quell what had become an anti-planter vendetta. Suggestive of an underlying political dimension was the subsequent staunch secessionist stance of McIntosh and the Union-leaning position of the poorer whites in Calhoun.[14]

Planters could turn to the power of the state for protection from a white mob. Black sailors and suspected abolitionists and Unionists were not so fortunate. On November 10, 1860, four free black seamen were taken from the Brig *Wingfold* in Fernandina and placed in jail "for safe keeping." Unidentified persons broke into the jail and ran the sailors off into the woods, where they were not heard of again. The rabidly secessionist *Monticello Family Friend* defended the seizure as a down payment "for some of the fugitives the Yankees have refused to re-turn to their owners." A week later, six black sailors were forcibly removed from the *N.W. Bridge*, lying in the sound of Cumberland Island. The fall of 1860 also saw vigilantes in East Florida invading homes at night and dragging suspected enemies of the South into the woods where they were blindfolded and whipped. A white convicted in Jefferson the following January of slave tampering and "using abolition language" was taken out of town, where his head was shaved, and he re-ceived thirty-nine lashes. He was shipped to Fernandina with directions that he be sent north. Northern fishermen in the waters below Jacksonville escaped that white man's fate when they were allowed to leave after a warning that abolitionist sympathizers would not be tolerated.[15]

Lincoln's election unleashed violence in a society that felt extremely vulner-able. The presentment of the Grand Jury of Hillsborough County in the fall term of 1860 virtually admitted the failure of the legal structure to provide a sense of security. It declared the patrol laws to be "a dead letter," the illicit sale of liquor to slaves rampant, and laws against self-hiring by slaves a travesty. In calling for a revamping and strict enforcement of laws aimed at policing slave behavior, the foreman stressed that "self-preservation" was at stake. Whites across the state took it upon themselves to secure their own self-preservation in a wave of vigi-lante justice that played into the hands of the secessionists arguing for the imper-ative need of the South to free itself from the threatening North. A fresh round of cotton gin burnings and reports of slave uprisings further enraged the vigilantes. Fittingly enough, one of the gins that went up in flames with its twenty-five bales of sea- island cotton belonged to the secessionist governor, Madison S. Perry.[16]

The push for secession came from the governor and the state legislature. They had the backing of three-fourths of the state's newspapers and the endorse-ment of the Baptist state convention in Fernandina. Perry declared for secession within days of Lincoln's election and papers printed variants of the message of the *Ocala Companion* that "submission and disgrace is too revolting for contem-plation." Local meetings fused the need for resistance to Lincoln with safety at home since, as the group in Alafia put it, the laws governing slaves were "lame and defective." Perry fanned that fear by warning in his message to the legisla-ture on November 26 that waiting for an overt act by the Republicans would consign Floridians to the "fate . . . of the whites in Santo Domingo." The public address of the "Ladies" in Broward's Neck, Duval County, pleaded for protection from the threat of rape. Shaming their menfolk and taking a clever dig at their misogyny, they asked why men who would cheat on their wives would never betray the Union, the source of slave unrest. Some men, they charged, "on the most frivolous pretenses, irrevocably dissolve the sacred bonds of Matrimonial

Union, which they solemnly pledged before God and their Country, to keep inviolate; but are very tenacious of the Political Union, under the most aggravated
circumstances."[17]

That charge could not be levied against physician-planter Edward Bradford.
He was happily married, presumably faithful to his wife, and pro-secession.
When his family gathered around the table on New Year's Day, 1861, the conversation revealed private divisions among planters that rarely made their way
into public debates. Bradford favored secession and believed it would not necessarily lead to war. His son Junius was a Unionist and had no doubt there would
be a war. Though certain that the North would fight to retain the Southern states,
he admitted that if the South did not secede, the family's property, mainly their
slaves, would be taken from them. But he wanted to fight the Yankees in the
Union, not out of it. Bradford's wife dared to say she wanted the slaves freed
and clung to the forlorn hope that if sectional peace were maintained, the federal government would provide for gradual emancipation. No one had a good
word to say about the Republicans. They also agreed on one other point: "If the
negroes are freed our lands will be worthless."[18]

Such an exchange of ideas was absent in the public arena. Instead, as a Union
naval officer in Pensacola observed of the crowds in the city, everyone "seems to
have gone mad. Everybody was talking secession." Ellen Call Long, the daughter
of the Unionist ex-governor, Richard K. Call, explained why. In addition to
controlling the slave menace, the secessionists were promising something to
everybody—"the merchant to be rid of paying his Northern debts; the slave
trade revived for the planter; the ambitious, a newer and nearer field of promo-
tion; and those who have nothing are to get something in the general scramble."[19]

Opposition to immediate secession was scattered and unfocused. The most
outspoken Unionist, Richard K. Call, branded secession as "treason, high treason
against our constitutional government" in a pamphlet after he was blocked from
speaking in public. For Ethelred Phillips, a physician in Mariana and a Unionist,
the lemming-like rush to secede was the march of deluded losers: "Like all men
defeated they lose their temper, and swear the south can whip all creation alone,
that cotton is king, and sixty days after the separation we will be happier than
ever." A cooperationist minority emerged, centered in the old planting counties
in Middle Florida, but it tepidly called only for waiting for Alabama and Georgia
to act. The state was already in the middle of a military buildup with $100,000 in
appropriations for arms purchases. Minute Men were rushing to offer their services to the governor for defense. With December 22, 1860, set as the election
day for the secession convention, the opposition had little time to organize. The
election was a dull contest with many not voting since opposition tickets were
scarce and secession seemed largely to be a given. According to white refugees in
1864, widespread intimidation by the slaveholders prevented the nomination of

Unionist candidates and suppressed a Unionist majority from voting. That was also the impression of a North Carolinian in Florida on a business trip in early April. He wrote his wife that "if ever the liberty of speech and the press was ever under the direct control of a despotism it is here." Whether or not they were in a majority, Unionists were put on record that if they "dare[d] preach submission to further [Northern] injustice for the sake of the Union," they would be "hanged as high as Haman."[20]

Speeches on January 7 from L. W. Spratt of South Carolina and E. C. Bullock of Alabama, commissioners sent by their respective state conventions to promote secession, fired up the Florida convention. Susan Eppes, who accompanied her father to the convention, "never heard such cheers and shouts as rent the air, and it lasted so long." The next day all the delegates wore "Palmetto cockades . . . there were hundreds of them." The only substantial debate concerned amendments proposed by George T. Ward of Leon County delaying Florida's secession until Alabama and Georgia acted and submitting the secession ordinance to a popular vote. Only about 40 percent of the delegates supported the amendments, mainly those from the older planting counties and the yeoman areas of West Florida. Ward, like Call, was a product of an older, more conservative political order that was turned aside when Democratic newcomers and their non-slaveholding allies assumed control of the state. Ward had arrived in Tallahassee in 1825, inherited his father's plantation, and added to his large holdings in land and slaves with his marriage in 1844. Like many of the established planters in Leon County, whose slave majority of 74 percent was the highest in the state, he was understandably cautious in betting his great wealth on the success of secession. Brushing aside his delaying tactics, the immediatists easily added Florida to their string of victories.[21]

Alabama: Yancey Triumphant

Yancey's moment had arrived. For years, he had preached that the South must not submit to a hostile Northern majority, and now most white Alabamians agreed. The most fervent secessionists vowed to leave the state and accept any financial sacrifice if Alabama refused to secede. "My wife and I have talked the matter over," wrote a minister in Tuscaloosa, "and she agrees with me that poverty and hardship are to be preferred to the certain vassalage that awaits our posterity if Alabama refuses to strike one manly blow for freedom." The secretary of the Baptist state convention meeting in Tuskegee informed Governor Moore that the delegates held themselves "subject to the call of proper authority in the defence of the sovereignty and independence of the State of Alabama." The leading conservative papers came out for resistance. The pro-Bell *Montgomery*

Post announced it was ready to set aside party differences to "prepare to maintain the rights and institutions of our section." In declaring for resistance, the *Mobile Daily Advertiser* touted the economic benefits of secession for the commercial interests of the city. Interior merchants, who purchased their goods in the North, would now direct their business to Mobile. Prosperity would also be ensured by Mobile's projected status as a port for direct trade to Europe, resulting in the city's becoming "the commercial metropolis of all the Gulf coast east of New Orleans."[22]

The Breckinridge press in south Alabama lined up solidly behind separate state secession. Speed was imperative, warned the *Hayneville Chronicle* in the black belt county of Lowndes, where slaves were increasing at twice the rate of whites. Northern emissaries, it was alleged, would soon tell the slaves of Lincoln's election and incite them to rebellion. Only by rapidly organizing "a military force" could the state "readily keep down any effort at rebellion." What was at stake was "the safety of the people." In this mindset, military resistance became a preemptive strike against slave uprisings.[23]

Conservatives in the Bell and Douglas camps, who combined had polled 46 percent of the presidential vote, were less worried about what the slaves might do and more about the anarchy that might be result from precipitate action. They had no choice but to advocate resistance but insisted it take the form of a cooperative movement that would, as the *Autauga Citizen* reasoned, unite "a number of States sufficiently strong to form a Southern Confederacy that would give us needful protection." Otherwise, as another Douglas paper argued, "a mere hurrah movement" would be dangerous: "all the evils of revolution will be let loose, and the demons of anarchy will riot at will. . . . [F]renzied appeals will take the place of reason, demagogues usurp the seats of statesmanship, and secret leagues supercede [*sic*] constituted authority." A splintered and weak South at war with itself would be easy prey for vengeful Northerners.[24]

The appeal of cooperationism, as well as its weakness, was its elasticity. It clung to the diminishing hopes of saving the Union by allowing time for negotiations with the North; failing that, it served as a stabilizing device for maintaining order in the South; and, at the very least, it promised conservatives a voice in whatever new order might emerge. Jeremiah Clemens, a northern Alabama cooperationist, best characterized it as a political tool, an effort to buy time. "No good may come of it, but no evil *can*."[25]

Immediatists, however, saw plenty of evil in it. In an overpowering majority in southern Alabama, where most of the slaves were concentrated, they used their numbers to disrupt and hamstring cooperationists' efforts. When John Harvey, editor of the *Alabama Beacon* in Greene County, issued a call for a cooperationist meeting, most of the handbills announcing it were torn down. After pressure was exerted on the *Beacon*'s subscribers, Harvey was forced to sell the paper to a secessionist editor brought in from Tuscaloosa. Secessionists took over the meeting Harvey had called and denounced him and his supporters as a "nest of black republicans." [26]

The cooperationists carried only Conecuh County in southern Alabama, a region of small farms where the white population was growing three times faster than that of the slaves. Their major loss was in Mobile, where Breckinridge had won only 31 percent of the vote. Slow to organize, their leadership of Northern-born merchants made them an easy target for secessionist attacks as outsiders ready to betray the South. They received only 35 percent of the vote.[27]

William P. Gould, a sixty-year-old Massachusetts-born planter in the black belt, typified the confused, reactive response of the weak cooperationist effort. On learning of Lincoln's election, which he blamed on the "Yanceyite," Gould assumed a wait-and-see attitude. Convinced that "the leading Demagogues . . . have set their hearts upon disunion," he shunned a secessionist meeting in Eutaw and joined the cooperationist faction. Though a Unionist, he admitted that "circumstances change—and I must either change with them or stand alone." He found himself retreating from one position to another. At first, he favored giving Lincoln a chance and waiting for some unconstitutional act. When that hope proved illusory, he held out for a national convention, composed of two delegates from each state, which just might be able to hammer out a compromise. Finally, he settled for a Southern convention. He would accept their decision. "Whatever it may be I shall feel bound to submit, as the best that can be expected under existing circumstances."[28]

In a striking example of the state's sectionalism, northern Alabamians overwhelmingly backed the cooperationists, who carried all but one of the counties. North of the black belt, the topography turned hilly and then mountainous in the southeastern extension of the Appalachian Mountains. Plantation agriculture was able to take hold only on the alluvial soils in the Tennessee River Valley. By the 1850s, the Valley's plantation regime had long passed its peak. The older, wealthier planters, who hung on by buying the land of their departing neighbors, lined up behind Bell and the cooperationists. The yeomanry in the landlocked mountains voted their regular (Breckinridge) Democratic ticket but rejected immediate secession, which they identified with their traditional enemies, the Union-hating cotton aristocrats of black belt Alabama. Eleven of the twelve Breckinridge counties backed cooperation.

In the north, the cooperationists had the benefit of belonging to a popular majority. With extensive newspaper encouragement, they were assured of receiving a fair hearing. Unionist editors were not forced out of business, and public opinion, though shocked and upset by Lincoln's election, had not reached the witch-hunting levels of southern Alabama. Strangers were suspect, but there were no calls for the immediate outlawing of all Northerners as were voiced in

Barbour County in the south "on the ground that *most of those who have come have more or less connection* with the criminal objects [of abolitionism]."[29]

Operating from a favorable base, the energetic conservatives in the north nominated their candidates as soon as, if not earlier than, the secessionists. In most areas they seized the initiative. Jeremiah Clemens of Huntsville drew up and distributed by November 19 a cooperationist circular signed by 100 citizens. He rallied the conservatives, made certain their case was presented to the people, and put the secessionists on the defensive. Resolutions passed at a meeting in Ashville on December 1 exemplified how the cooperationists made their case. They would ever defend Southern rights but insisted that "these Rights could be better preserved and secured in the Union than by Secession and Dissolution." Strongly opposed to separate state action, they demanded that no state secede without the previous consent of the Upper South.[30]

To shore up their minority position, the secessionists resorted to two strategies. They usually yielded the point of referring any secession ordinance back to the people, and they sought noncontroversial nominees not identified by the voters with radical demands. Their efforts gained them only Calhoun County in the lower Coosa River Valley, which, along with narrowly lost Cherokee, had easily outstripped other northern counties in the increase of cotton production in the 1850s. Still, they were much more competitive in the north with about 40 percent of the total vote than the cooperationists in the south with a paltry 15 percent. The victorious cooperationists, however, faced the same dilemma that confounded them elsewhere. As Clemens explained, "We have before us the double duty of preserving the Union, & of obtaining redress for grievances, which undoubtedly exist, & security against other aggressions which we can not fail to see are impending." He was groping for a policy that would protect both slavery and the Union, but, given the refusal of the Republicans to accept Southern demands, even his position would make secession virtually inevitable.[31]

Young, slaveholding Breckinridge lawyers were the driving force at the Alabama convention, which assembled in Montgomery on January 7, 1861. Like the secessionists, most of the cooperationist delegates were slaveholders, but they were older and wealthier. Excited crowds milled around the State House, where the convention met, and troops were everywhere. Thomas J. McClellan, a cooperationist from Limestone County, noted that the crowds and troops seemed more anxious for secession than their leaders. The enthusiasm in the streets spilled over into the convention where the packed galleries wildly cheered every pro-secession utterance. So tumultuous was the reaction on the second day to the speech from the South Carolina commissioner that one delegate cuttingly suggested that "unless the galleries should be immediately cleared,

the Convention should certainly adjourn to the Theatre." The delegates then decided to conduct most of their transactions in closed session.[32]

The secessionists took charge from the onset. They refused to seat two
cooperationist delegates from Shelby County on the technicality that their winning votes from Bear Creek precinct had not been filed with the sheriff within
the legally prescribed time. Two secessionists replaced them. In the vote for a
permanent president, the convention broke along the lines that would hold for
subsequent key decisions. William M. Brooks, a young lawyer and Breckinridge
secessionist from Perry County, out-polled by eight votes the cooperationist
nominee, Robert Jemison, an old Whig planter-manufacturer from Tuscaloosa.[33]

On the second day, Yancey amended a resolution praising Governor Moore
for seizing the federal forts in Alabama to authorize the governor to accept 500
volunteers for service under Florida's governor. The cooperationists retorted
that such a troop deployment constituted "unnecessary aggression" and would
destroy any hopes of a peaceful settlement. In the midst of the debate, a telegram
arrived from Governor Moore stressing that Alabama could be invaded as easily
from Pensacola as could Florida and warning, "It is not only the policy of the
Federal Government to coerce the seceding States, but as soon as possible to put
herself in position by reinforcing all the Forts in the States where secession is expected." Despite further cooperationist protests, the amended resolution passed
by a strict party vote of 52 to 45.

The third day focused on the Coleman resolution pledging Alabama to assist any coerced state. Jemison, while pointing out that no such invasion had
yet occurred and that the convention had no reliable information on which to
base its action, was interrupted by J. F. Dowdell, who read a dispatch claiming
that hostilities had already commenced. As they did throughout the convention, the secessionists engaged in fear-mongering by reading a timely telegram
with sensationalized news. Outraged at this tactic of intimidating the delegates,
Jemison accused the secessionists of using telegrams "to tell whatever is most appropriate for effect. They keep the public mind in a continual state of excitement,
and, for whatever matter under consideration here, we have a telegram suited to
the occasion."[34]

As the debate continued, the secessionists committed one of their few
blunders. Overreacting to a cooperationist request for a day's delay on the
Coleman proposal, Yancey delivered a fiery speech. In a show of the rash language and intemperate action that had left him personally unpopular even
among secessionists, he flayed those who questioned immediate secession.
"There is a law of Treason, defining treason against the State; and, those who
shall dare oppose the action of Alabama, when she assumes her independence
of the Union, will become traitors—rebels against its authority, and will be dealt
with as such." When rebuked for the harshness of his language, he claimed that

his remarks had not been directed against any members of the convention but only those in certain areas of the state who reportedly would resist an ordinance of secession. The effort was a clumsy one, for the cooperationists responded that he was branding as traitors the gallant citizenry of northern Alabama. Before the convention was further divided, the secessionists wisely agreed to adjourn, and no action was taken on the resolution.[35]

Buoyed by the news of Mississippi's secession and the firing on the *Star of the West*, the convention approved the resolutions reported out of a committee chaired by Yancey declaring for immediate and separate secession. Voted down by identical 53 to 45 votes were cooperationist resolutions calling for a Southern convention and referral back to the people of any ordinance of secession. The adoption of the ordinance on January 11, 1861, touched off a jubilant demonstration throughout the city. "Take it altogether it was one of the most stirring [,] enthusiastic & thrilling scenes I ever witnessed," exclaimed the Reverend William H. Mitchell.[36]

Cooperationists were resigned but bitter. Vowing that he and thirty-five others would never sign the secession ordinance, Lawrence R. Davis damned the secessionists, "Praying God with my last breath that those who brought this on our country may meet their just award." Thomas J. McClellan felt hopeless. "I have opposed this rash action of the Convention in every way I could [and] I see no other course left but to submit to it," he wrote his wife. "We must not do anything that would look like willingness on our part to submit to the policy of the black Republican party."[37]

Still, the secessionists were leery. They realized that the unpopularity of secession in northern Alabama remained a potent political force. From Huntsville came reports that "there will be a successful attempt made to excite the people of N. Ala. to rebellion *vs.* the State & that we will have a civil war in our midst." Cooperationist leaders were supposedly planning to secede from the rest of Alabama and create a new state, Nickajack. Under these circumstances the secessionists had to guard against any pretense of allowing another set of elections around which the opposition might coalesce.[38]

Accordingly, the secessionists stuffed the last gasp of the cooperationists in the Jemison resolution calling for a popular vote on any Confederate constitution. They denounced such an election as a subterfuge to rekindle party feelings and "to introduce the destructing elements of reconstruction, and other kindred questions." Declaring that the convention had full authority to ratify the constitution, they insisted that a permanent government had to be installed as soon as possible. Not only would it protect the South, but it "will put to flight, now and forever, all hopes of Reconstruction, and would prove to the world that our separation from the North is 'final, complete, and perpetual.'" Aided by the defection of a few cooperationists who now believed that the best chance of averting war lay in strict unity, the secessionists won the last battle. The constitution, described by B. H. Baker as "this great magna-charta of the rights of white men," was adopted without referral to the people.[39]

Georgia: The Secessionists' Narrowest Victory

More than any other state in the first wave of secession, Georgia encompassed the diversity of the Lower South—extensive rice and sea-island plantations along the coast, a declining old cotton belt in its east central region, an aggressive, new slave frontier in its southwestern section, and a large area dominated by non-slaveholding farmers and herders in the hills and mountains of northern Georgia and the wire grass/pine barrens in the southeast. It was the most populous of the cotton states and second only to Texas in size. The land bridge connecting the seaboard states of South Carolina and Florida with the plantation states to the west, Georgia had to be carried by the secessionists to realize their goal of a cotton confederacy.

Resistance meetings sprang up immediately, and young men, hitherto overshadowed by their elders, took the lead in shaping popular opinion. One of them was Thomas R. R. Cobb, the younger brother of the more famous Howell Cobb. Born in 1823 on a Georgia plantation in Jefferson County, he, like Howell, had to build his own wealth following their father's bankruptcies. A dutiful younger son, Thomas loyally furthered the political career of his brother. In his own right, he established himself as one of Georgia's top lawyers, authored the only full-blown legal defense of slavery, *An Inquiry into the Law of Negro Slavery*, and crusaded against immorality as an evangelical Presbyterian. His puritanical fervor was such that Linton Stephens once wrote of his legal strictures that "it is a great . . . forbearance that [he] does not proscribe rules to govern the chamber maids in the manner of carrying out the piss-pots." Order and control inspired by an evangelical quest for perfectionism informed his secessionist politics as well. For Cobb, Republican antislavery doctrines were an intolerable assault on the Christian harmony of a godly slave society. His Republicans, aside from their abolitionism, were agents of moral anarchy—"free negroes and boot-blacks, coachmen and domestics, infidels and free-lovers, spiritual rappers and every other shade of mania and folly." On November 10 in Athens, he was among those who endorsed "*summary* and *condign* punishment" for all those judged by a duly appointed vigilant committee to have threatened the public safety. Regulated violence was to be a means to his evangelical republic of slaveholders.[40]

Joining Cobb in the limelight of the debates held in Milledgeville was Henry L. Benning, a wealthy planter in Muscogee County, one of Georgia's booming cotton areas. Like Cobb, Benning had a first-rate legal record and had taken a

Fig. 7.2 The Secession Movement. This Unionist lithograph depicts the secession of the cotton states as a mad stampede over a cliff. Only Georgia seems inclined to hesitate. Library of Congress, LC-USZ62-32995.

back seat in Georgia politics until the secession crisis. A radical states' righter, who had ruled as a judge on the Georgia Supreme Court in 1854 that a US Supreme Court decision did not necessarily take precedence over that of a state, Benning had long resented the political influence of Howell Cobb, an intellectual inferior in his mind. Secession offered him an opportunity to upstage Howell and finally win acclaim for his defense of the South.[41]

The debates were held to help guide an inexperienced legislature looking for direction. In his special message to the legislature on November 7, Governor Brown had sent a mixed message. He painted submission to the Republicans in the darkest terms but did not recommend immediate secession. Instead, he vaguely talked of the need for unity among all the fifteen slave states. Not a member of the planter elite nor fully in their confidence, Brown was a shrewd politician whose success before, during, and after the Civil War resulted from his uncanny ability to sense the direction of the prevailing political winds and steer them toward his own ends. Raised in north Georgia, he soon left and, through hard work and sheer grit, earned the funds to attend Yale and gain a law degree. Northern Georgians claimed him as one of their own when he entered politics. Aware of the rumblings from the mountains of opposition to immediate

secession, he paused long enough to gauge the odds of a successful push for
secession.[42]

Uncertain if they had a mandate and leery of the state's 67 percent majority
of non-slaveholders, the legislators were jolted into action by the pressure of the
immediatists, who introduced resolutions authorizing secession by mere legislative enactment, thus avoiding the possibility of defeat in an election for a secession convention. Speaking on November 12, Thomas R. R. Cobb passionately
supported that course: "Wait not till the grog-shops and cross-roads shall send
up a discordant voice from a divided people, but act as leaders, in guiding and
forming public opinion."[43]

On the day following Cobb's speech, the legislature invited luminaries
from the political elite to debate what Georgia should do. Robert Toombs and
Henry Benning, each of whom equated Republican rule with the abolition of
slavery unless the South seceded, were on one side, and Alexander H. Stephens,
Benjamin H. Hill, and Hershel V. Johnson (Douglas's running mate) made the
case for the Union. The debates ranged from shameless demagoguery to close intellectual engagement with the issues. The Unionists more than held their own,
and Stephens emerged as the consensus choice as the most effective speaker. He
was, as Georgia King remarked, "a curious looking man." Having the physical
appearance of a mummified, emaciated possum, his misshapen body came alive
with bright black eyes and a soprano voice when he spoke. No Southern conservative had a more penetrating or logically sound mind in the service of social
order. Cleverly using the emotional outbursts of the secessionists against them,
he impressively underscored the need for reasoned deliberation.

Despite Toombs's call for an adjournment to give the secessionists time to
regroup, rasher secessionists demanded an immediate opportunity to rebut
Stephens. Denied the podium, H. T. Jackson spoke from his desk and, as Georgia
King recorded, "ranted wildly . . . said we lived under the 'blackest despotism
under the sun'! What absurdity!" Agreeing with King's assessment, and worried
that outbursts such as Jackson's would be counterproductive, legislative leaders
recommended calling a state convention to meet on January 16, 1861, with the
election for delegates on January 2. Approved on November 20, the recommendation shifted the debate to Cobb's "grog-shops and cross-roads."[44]

After the strong showing of the Unionists in Milledgeville, the secessionists
redoubled their efforts. C. W. Howard informed Robert Gourdin, who was
closely monitoring the Georgia contest, that the secessionists had an uphill battle.
He set the coastal counties down for secession, as well as most of the towns, but
the middle counties (the old Whig belt) and the upper and middle counties as
"overwhelmingly against it." He credited Stephens's Milledgeville speech as "the
fairest index of Georgia sentiment that I have seen." Unionist speakers had to
be countered, cautioned John M. Richardson, for "three out of four never think

for themselves in political matters, but pin their faith in the sleeves of some acknowledged leader." He called on Gourdin for help in the form of "a pamphlet culled from Black republican journals, abusive of the South and particularly of Georgia." On December 14, he forwarded contributions to the Committee of 1860 and asked specifically for the pamphlet, "The Terrors of Submission," for local distribution.[45]

Heading the list of those "terrors" was the unspeakable degradation of whites that would follow Republican-forced emancipation. In his public letter of December 7 emphatically backing secession, Governor Brown tailored his message to non-slaveholders and poor white laborers. With the doggedness of an accountant, he contended that non-slaveholders would bear the brunt of the economic and social burden of emancipation. Methodically, he listed the increased taxes necessary to compensate the slaveholders (the only fair thing to do) and to colonize the freed blacks in Africa. Assuming however that the Republicans had their way and the freed blacks remained in the South, what then, he asked, would become of the poor whites? Planters, not they, would have the means to invest in additional land, and former non-slaveholders would be forced into tenantry and sharecropping or, worse yet, competition with blacks for a beggar's wages. Surely, Brown concluded, "the poor, honest laborers of Georgia, can never consent to see slavery abolished, and submit to all the taxation, vassalage, low wages and downright degradation. They will never take the negro's place, God forbid."[46]

If in fact the secessionists were initially behind, they closed the gap quickly through sustained campaigning. Aided by Gourdin's flood of pamphlets, they dispatched their top leaders where they were most needed. "Tom [Cobb] spoke last Friday night by invitation of the minute men," wrote John B. Lamar from Macon on December 11, "and such a speech I have never heard before." Cobb harangued for four hours and his audience was ecstatic. "It had a great effect on everyone." Howell was urged to return from Washington and enter the fray. On his way home from Atlanta, J. B. Guthrie of Cincinnati said of Howell's speech that "he stirred up the hearts of people in a way I never saw it done before!" The secessionists, Hershel Johnson warned Alexander Stephens, "are over the State [and] are active and noisy—disgustingly blatant."[47]

Faced with the secessionists' offensive, the cooperationists settled into a fatal lethargy. Most damaging to their cause was the passivity of Stephens. In the isolation of his Liberty Hall plantation home, he distanced himself from the campaign. Entreaties by his half-brother Linton and others to get involved were of no avail. Bordering on defeatism, he wrote a friend that he was "inclined to let those who sowed the wind reap the whirlwind, or control it, if they can." Stephens's greatest fear, one shared by other conservatives, was that the destruction of the Union would unleash uncontrollable social unrest. The same passions and emotion that fueled the secessionist craze, editorialized the *Augusta Chronicle*, would, if unchecked, "finally result in civil war, loss of liberty, and the establishment of a military despotism."[48]

Conservatives had good reason to be alarmed. The papers were filled with threats of an inner civil war if Georgia submitted. Go out now, advised "Georgia," for "Delay will inevitably produce civil war in Georgia. . . . You and I will take sides, you for law and order, and I for zealous brethren, and the result is *war—civil war*—here in Georgia." "A Nullifier of 1833" declared that the Minute Men, rather than submit, would "plunge the South into its inner Civil War." Here was the root of the conservatives' paralyzing indecision. Alexander Stephens cited the concern of Judge Andrews, among others, that "the State authority will not be sufficient to keep the peace or keep down civil war [in Georgia]" as the reason he expected the state convention to come out for immediate secession. The "timid," aware of those who would "resist any how" if Georgia held back, would vote for secession out of that "fear of civil war." Better to stay on the sidelines and retain influence to moderate the revolution, Stephens concluded, than fan the flames of political divisions in opposition.[49]

Even aggressive campaigning, however, likely would not have clarified the conservatives' position. They never did agree on how cooperative resistance would work in practice. How many slave states should meet in a convention to make demands on the Republicans or how many had to agree to act collectively before seceding? What were the minimal guarantees to be exacted and when should an ultimatum be laid down? Set against the clarity of the cry for immediate separate state secession, their stand was murky and confused. And, all the while, the states bordering Georgia were going out, adding immeasurably to the pressure on Georgia to join them.

Cooperationist ranks held firmest in the Georgia mountains. Deploring the willingness of the planters in the cotton regions to cave in to the precipitators, "Observer" up in White Sulphur Springs boasted that his county of Merriwether opposed immediate secession by 5 to 1. George Hall, a legislator from Merriwether, detected a class split among the Unionists. Valuing order above all else, the planters were willing to back down to avoid any open confrontation with the immediatists. The non-slaveholders in the mountains were for bold resistance. Hall explained that "I would rather and so will the people that we have revolution amongst our selves than to be dragged . . . into an unjust and unholy collision with the General Government. . . . Rash measures should be met with rash measures."[50]

Candidates on a cooperationist platform fared best in north Georgia and generally ran well where slavery was weakest. Conversely, the immediatists appealed to those in areas where economic growth depended on slavery. Among them were the slaveholders in the rapidly expanding plantation belt of southwestern Georgia, professionals and businessmen in towns and cities whose economic livelihoods were tied to meeting the needs of planters, and small cotton farmers in east Georgia who had moved out of food production in the 1850s in favor of growing more cotton, a shift that made them increasingly dependent on the success of a slave-centered economy. All these groups were grasping at the main chance, and secession seemed to offer it. Sidney Root, owner of a dry-goods firm in Atlanta, seized a chance to join the city's elite. He was a committed secessionist from the start. After joining the Minute Men of Fulton County, he was rewarded with an appointment to the twenty-one-man committee of safety, dedicated to ridding Atlanta of "characters . . . hostile and dangerous to the rights and interests of the city and State." With heightened political clout and ample capital reserves, he embraced secession for the new opportunities it offered.[51]

For all their weaknesses, the cooperationists were quite competitive in the secession election. In fact, they might have won a slight majority. The uncertainty exists because extant newspaper reports of the returns are incomplete, and Governor Brown did not see fit to announce detailed returns until late April. He credited the secessionists with a majority of 50,243 to 37,123, a margin of victory, which, if it existed at all, was surely exaggerated. He based the tally on the final vote for the secessionist ordinance, which passed 208 to 89, and not on the initial secessionist resolution of E. A. Nisbet, which was approved only by 166 to 130, a favorable vote that included defections from delegates who had been elected as cooperationists. Brown most likely held back reporting the returns because they revealed no clear mandate for secession. The delegates ran in a virtual dead heat that registered the uncertainty of the voters over what to do. Adding to the confusion was the lack of any fixed meaning attached to the labels "secession" and "cooperation." As the *Augusta Chronicle* stressed, the labels meant different things on the seacoast and in the towns and mountains. In addition, many of the delegates took a non-committed stance that gave them the leeway to back secession once they gauged the sentiment of the convention.[52]

After opening on January 16, 1861, the convention went into secret session on January 18. E. A. Nisbet, a consistent conservative throughout the 1850s capped by his support for Douglas in 1860, introduced a secession resolution. He had converted to radicalism after Lincoln's election, which he equated with the end of slavery and the forced equality of the races. "There are dangers more appalling than death. This is one of them," he reasoned. Hershel Johnson countered with a resolution that was essentially a laundry list of cooperationist positions calling for delay. Declaring that the issue of secession had been settled by the convention election, Stephens refused to speak for the Johnson substitute, effectively dooming it. William Martin, a cooperationist from the mountains, questioned those election returns in a resolution asking Brown to provide a precise breakdown of the vote. His resolution and Johnson's were voted down the next day and the Nisbet resolution adopted.[53]

Defections from the cooperationist and non-committed delegates, mainly those from the old planting counties, paved the way for the immediatists' victory. When William Martin moved on January 22 to refer secession to the people for their approval, Nisbet deftly foiled this last stand of the cooperationists with a resolution urging all the delegates to sign the secession ordinance as a show of resolve to defend the rights of Georgia regardless of their stand on secession. By making the issue loyalty to Georgia and not the means of resistance, Nisbet's resolution was artful politics. Forty-four cooperationists signed the ordinance, but Hershel V. Johnson and Alexander and Linton Stephens were not among them. Most of the holdouts came from north Georgia and the wiregrass region. Elected by Democratic non-slaveholders, they made clear their opposition to a planter-led revolution.[54]

The leading conservative newspaper, the *Augusta Chronicle*, accepted what it could not change: "We humbly bow ourselves—not as slaves, but as free citizens—to the supreme decree of the State of Georgia." The irreconcilables came chiefly out of the mountains. The semi-literate James W. Allen angrily wrote Governor Brown that "if Suntern [Southern] Georgia wants to leave the union let her go but the people of Cherokee want to stay in the Union so I hope you will let us go in peace and we will set up for ourselves in the union." To his thinking, "the Demegoogs and office seekers," backed by those with nothing to lose, had forced Georgia out. He claimed 25,000 volunteers were in place to fight, if necessary, to stay in the Union. Only a favorable popular vote on secession, he asserted, would end the resistance. That vote was never solicited, and north Georgia remained a sore spot for Brown throughout the upcoming war.[55]

Louisiana: Securing a Latecomer

Louisiana had never identified with the extreme states' righters who had taken over South Carolina and had a major presence in Alabama and Mississippi. Its interests were bound up with the flow of goods down the Mississippi River and the marketing of those goods to Northern and international buyers. Its sugar planters, its wealthiest slaveholders, had prospered under the protection of the federal tariff on sugar. Ethnically and culturally, its urban center of New Orleans was the most diverse city in the Lower South and had none of the fixation of Charleston's lowcountry elite on regaining a past glory. Once the planters and merchants committed to secession, however, the city rode it to the end.

Louisiana's presidential vote in 1860 reflected its political moderation. Thanks to his support in the rural parishes, Breckinridge carried the state with a plurality of 45 percent. The Know-Nothings, stronger in Louisiana than elsewhere in the Lower South because of the large Catholic presence, rallied behind John Bell as the only candidate able to save the Union. Bell polled 40 percent of the vote and bested Breckinridge in commercially minded New Orleans. He also ran well in the sugar parishes. Douglas's 15 percent of the vote came disproportionately from the foreign-born workers of New Orleans.

Within a few weeks of Lincoln's election, moderates were in full retreat before the secessionist offensive. John Slidell, the most powerful political figure in the state and one who had shunned the Rhetts and Yanceys as long as a pro-Southern administration was in power in Washington, signaled that offensive when he wrote Buchanan on November 11, 1860, that "I see no probability of preserving the Union, nor indeed do I consider it desirable to do so if we could." Bell planters in the river parishes lined up for secession in some form, and street crowds in New Orleans whipped up excitement in the city. As vigilance committees lent a veneer of legality to mob action, the police arrested "suspicious" Northerners, including a Catholic priest from Indiana, on charges of incendiary language. As early as November 12, a law student wrote home that blue cockades were everywhere and "Disunion is rife." A young Northern visitor was struck by the visible anxiety and attributed it to the belief that Lincoln's victory was "a sort of declaration of hostility by the North." Crowds acted out their anxiety by hanging Lincoln in effigy on poles along the main streets and in the public squares. "When it is run up it is saluted with the firing of cannon & cheers." News of South Carolina's secession set off such a wild celebration that an outsider passing through dryly noted that "one would have thought the Messiah had come *surely*."[56]

New Orleans, with its Creole and Catholic heritage and casual disregard of Protestant strictures on proper moral behavior, was the most cosmopolitan of Southern cities. Yet its conversion to secession matched the passionate responses in other cities and in the countryside. The common thread was the ubiquitous sense of defilement by Northerners and of powerlessness in a time of economic paralysis and future uncertainty. Mocking their tormentors, raging against outsiders identified with those defilers, and cheering on secession fulfilled a need for personal empowerment in asserting self-worth.

Emblematic of New Orleans' support for secession was the setting it provided for the most influential evangelical blessing bestowed on secession, Benjamin Palmer's Thanksgiving Day sermon of November 29, 1860. A native Charlestonian and loyal disciple of South Carolina's James Henley Thornwell, Palmer had headed Presbyterian churches in Charleston and Savannah before his appointment to shepherd the First Presbyterian Church of New Orleans.

The logic of his most famous sermon flowed from his premise that slavery was a "trust providentially committed to us." Confronted by the specter of a Republican "reign of terror" led by atheistic, anarchistic abolitionists, Southern whites, he declared, must grasp secession as their only hope "of conserving and transmitting the system of slavery with freest scope for its natural development and extension." This was the duty Southerners owed themselves, their slaves, the civilized world, and God himself. As the truest and best friends of the African race, whites understood that to free the slaves now or in the near future was to condemn them to extinction. The "most helpless" of all the races, they needed the caring protection of white masters for their very survival. Palmer contended that under the South's patriarchal system, the slave was "my brother and my friend: and I am to him a guardian and a father." He concluded his sermon with a flourish by imploring the South to embrace this "sublime" moment and accept the grace given it "to save herself, the country, and the world." Here in this evangelical fantasy was an imagined view of slavery intended to reassure any Southern whites with moral qualms over slavery of their Christian goodness and to call them to action against the infidels from the North.[57]

With its fusion of Southern patriotism and evangelicalism Palmer's sermon handed the secessionists a powerful electioneering message. It was heavily excerpted in the Southern press and at least 60,000 copies were printed for distribution. The cooperationists had no effective response. Referring to the sermon and a similarly themed one by Episcopalian William T. Leacock, a Whig lawyer in Livingston Parish complained that "The influence of such . . . Partizans . . . must be potent for evil." Robert A. Grinnan, a vice-president of the State Rights Association of Louisiana based in New Orleans, exulted that the *New Orleans Delta* printed 50,000 copies of the sermons and that the city's other papers ran off an additional 65,000 copies. In sending copies of Palmer's sermon to secessionists in Virginia for distribution, he stressed that "we carried Lou. with it."[58]

To many Northerners, Palmer's sermon was a dose of realism. Ann Davison in Northampton, Pennsylvania, wrote her granddaughter in Louisiana that a local clergyman had told her the sermon had "open[ed] the eyes of the Northern people." Prior to reading it, they thought that Southern Christians viewed slavery as a moral wrong to be gradually eliminated. Now, "to hear from a representative man, that it was holy, and righteous, and that he recommended overturning the government and fighting for it [slavery] for the benefit of the civilized world was astounding."[59]

By the time Palmer stole the spotlight, the commercial powers of New Orleans were coming around to secession. All their political instincts were conservative, for stability and mutual confidence across sectional lines were essential to the long-range, credit-based networks at the heart of their financial operations. They had spearheaded the campaign of Bell, who, along with Douglas, received 80 percent of the vote in Orleans Parish. Their Unionism, however, was contingent on the intersectional trading exchanges that allowed them to perform their role of moving plantation staples from producers to purchasers in the North or abroad. Concerns over the consequences of a Republican victory were already clogging those exchanges by early October. The shock of Lincoln's election all but shut them down. Thirty factorage houses suspended operations within a month. Facing financial ruin and frustrated by the inability of their business allies in the North to force a sectional compromise, they reassessed their political loyalties. Soon, all that was left of the merchants' Unionism was a cooperationist stance they hoped would avert a civil war and pressure the North for additional safeguards for slavery. Their ultimate loyalty was to the planters, whose slave-produced sugar and cotton had enriched them. If they could not prosper in the Union, the merchant elite expected to do so out of it.[60]

The cooperationists were in full retreat by December 1860. The *New Orleans Bee* continued to favor a united approach but conceded that "co-operation" was impractical. By the time the secession convention was to meet in January, it expected all the states of the Lower South to be out but Texas. Waiting for a unified action, it worried, would only give Lincoln's interim government time to get stronger. The only form of cooperation the *Bee* advised in late December was that advocated by the immediate secessionists. As each state seceded, it should align itself with South Carolina in a growing cluster that would form a new Southern confederacy.[61]

Once Governor Thomas Moore, likely pressured by Slidell, summoned the legislature into special session, the secessionists were in charge. Thomas Pollock, a young lawyer recently arrived in Shreveport from Virginia, was one of their enthusiastic backers. He saw in the drive for secession an "exhibition of moral courage & patriotism" that was "sublime." Dazzled by the verdant lushness of the fields of sugar cane and the opulent wealth derived from that sugar, he yearned to acquire some of that wealth for himself. Assured by a local judge that Shreveport was "the very best location for a professional man in the whole South," he would use that center of steamboat commerce as his base for the bright future he envisioned in the emerging Southern republic.[62]

In issuing the call for a secession election on January 7, the legislature ignored the requirement in the Louisiana constitution of 1852 for the submission of the question of a convention to a popular referendum. A speedy election favored the immediatists. William Tecumseh Sherman, then commandant of the Louisiana Military Academy in Alexandria, was appalled by how "men of property," convulsed by the "constant feeling of danger," talked of secession as a fixed fact. Even those formerly "moderate in their opinions" gave in to the "popular current" fanned by the "mad foolish crowd." Edward J. Gay, a conservative planter in Iberville Parish, was "quite stupefied" by how the rush of events hamstrung the efforts of moderates to slow the rush to secession.[63]

The immediatists won 52 percent of the vote on January 7. Since slaves counted in apportioning the number of delegates, the secessionist majority was padded by their strong showing in the high slaveholding parishes. They had a comfortable majority of eighty of the 130 delegates. When the convention met on January 23, it approached secession as the ratification of a decision largely already reached. The rapid withdrawal of the states to the east and Governor Moore's seizure of the federal forts left Louisianans with no credible alternative. "Louisiana [is] virtually out of the Union [and] Cooperation is dead," crowed Alexander F. Pugh, a secessionist sugar planter in East Feliciana, on January 9, 1861. He was right.[64]

Many of those elected as cooperationists accepted the inevitable and added their votes to the defeat of the Rozier resolution, seeking a Southern convention in Nashville to draw up demands to the North. Joseph O. Fuqua, an East Feliciana lawyer, followed with a convoluted resolution postponing Louisiana's secession until the convention heard back from representatives sent to the Montgomery gathering on forming the Confederacy. As much conditional secessionist as anything else, the motion fared better than Rozier's but was still handily defeated by a vote of 74 to 47. The last delaying tactic was a call for a popular vote on the secession decision. Charles Bienvenu, like Joseph Rozier, an older New Orleans lawyer, so moved, only to see his resolution added to the string of failures for the cooperationists. The delegates from New Orleans, along with about half of those from the sugar parishes and a handful from the piney woods, had honored their cooperationist and, in some cases, conditional Unionist pledges. The main strength of the secessionists came from the high slaveholding cotton parishes. These delegates saw themselves as a revolutionary vanguard and brushed aside any talk of delay or constitutional niceties. "We must assert our rights and take no step backward," declared former governor A. B. Roman. John Perkins Jr., a sugar planter from a northeastern river parish, put it plainly: "We were sent here to act. . . . We are in times of revolution, and questions of form must sink into insignificance."[65]

All but seven delegates signed the secession ordinance. Three of the irreconcilables were from New Orleans, the other four from a bloc of three hill parishes in the north. Only one of them, James G. Taliaferro of Catahoula Parish, went on record with his opposition. The secessionists refused to include his fiery manifesto in the official proceedings of the convention. A Virginian by birth and the convention's oldest member, he was the editor of Catahoula's only newspaper, the *Harrison Independent*, from which he championed the cooperationist position. His secessionist opponents, led by his longtime rival, planter St. John Richardson Liddell, attacked him for stirring up class warfare by pitting the hill farmers against the planters. Taliaferro's protest registered his "opposition, unqualifiedly to [the] separate secession of Louisiana," an act he denounced as a usurpation of power in a convention with no authorization from the people and in violation of "the great fundamental principle of American government, that the will of the people is supreme."[66]

There was enough truth in Taliaferro's indictment for the secessionists to treat it as if it never existed. But by implying that secession was a slaveholders' conspiracy, Taliaferro had stretched the truth. The commercial interests of New Orleans in league with rural planters had long called the shots in Louisiana's politics and the slaveless majority, 70 percent of the free population in 1860, generally followed along, either out of indifference or a sense of their relative powerlessness. The planters did not plot to take Louisiana out of the Union. They had no need to. The stakes were magnified, but the actions of the secession convention were politics as usual.

Texas: An Unconventional Path to Secession

Texans were less ambivalent about leaving the Union than Northerners were for admitting them into the Union sixteen years earlier. The state was more Southern than Western in 1860 and each of its major sub-regions had its own reasons for opposing the federal government. The plantation districts in the valleys of the Colorado and Brazos rivers in the southeast were the centers of wealth and political control. States rights' ideology and alarm over threats to slavery found a ready audience among the planters. If planters feared the power of the federal government, Texans on a broad frontier exposed to a rash of Indian raids denounced that government for being too weak to protect them. More in the Union than of it, Texas was too sprawling and distant for Washington to give it much federal oversight. Texans were ready in 1860 to throw off that government, but first secessionist leaders had to outmaneuver their Unionist governor, Sam Houston.

In supporting secession, Texans rejected the leadership of the preeminent hero of the Texas war for independence in the 1830s and a figure whose name was virtually synonymous with the republic and then the state of Texas. Houston's devotion to the Union had never wavered from the days of his friendship with Andrew Jackson. Upon hearing of Lincoln's election, he wrote his son Sam evoking Jackson's famous Jefferson Day response to the Nullifiers in 1830: "The Union must be preserved." Foreseeing a terrible civil war if the secessionists were successful, he wanted those "Demons of anarchy . . . put down and destroyed." He soon found he was powerless to make good on that wish.[67]

Though governor, Houston had no strong institutional base of support. Only the defection of moderate Democrats to the Opposition party of former Whig-Know-Nothings provided the votes for Houston's election in 1859. Those Democrats had been alarmed by the proslavery radicalism of John Marshall, editor of the Austin *Texas State Gazette* and chairman of the state Democratic Party. A native of Virginia, Marshall entered the planter class in the 1840s with his marriage to a planter's daughter in Jefferson County, Mississippi. When he moved to Austin in 1852, he brought with him the expansionist designs of the Mississippi Democrats. By 1859 he was calling for the annexation of Cuba as the Caribbean base for a slave empire stocked by the reopening of the African slave trade. His stand was endorsed by most of the Gulf Coast Democratic editors and the radical wing of the Democrats. The incumbent governor, Hardin D. Runnels, a planter whose roots were also in Mississippi and a filibusterer like Marshall who wanted to import slaves from Africa, was Houston's opponent. An election defined by fears of disunion and defiance of the federal government played to Houston's strengths and brought out the Unionist leanings in the largely non-slaveholding counties of north Texas, settled predominantly by natives of the Upper South.

By the fall of 1860, however, Houston's coalition had evaporated. Lincoln's election radicalized moderate Democrats, and Texans on the northern and western frontiers had lost their confidence in the Union to protect them, either from abolitionists believed to be burning their towns and inciting their slaves to insurrection or from marauding Indian raids. Driving home the fears on the frontier, secessionist J. W. Ferris asked, "What confidence can we have in a Government which leaves us continually exposed and permits arms to go into the hands of savages!"[68]

Texans most prone to agree with Ferris lived in a tier of frontier counties between the 98th and 100th parallels extending from the Red River in the north to the Rio Grande in the south. The eastern frontier lacked the rainfall to grow cotton on a consistent basis but was fertile and humid enough to support a yeoman economy based on corn and wheat. The semi-desert western frontier was higher and drier and suited only for livestock raising. Common to both was a reliance on the US Army for protection from murderous raids of Comanches, Kiowas, and Lipan-Apaches, nomadic tribes of incredibly skilled horsemen who lived off the buffalo hunt and attacks on frontier settlements for horses, food supplies, and captives. Occasionally, they were joined by reservation Indians forced into raiding for economic survival. The tempo of the raids increased after 1857 in response to the ongoing encroachment of whites on their hunting lands. Heart-rending tales of mutilations, torture, and abductions of whites, especially women, were commonplace in the press.

Except in secure areas adjacent to federal forts, Texans railed against the impotence of the army and the government it symbolized. The army lacked the manpower and mobility to catch the rapidly moving raiders, who roamed over a vast, sparsely settled expanse. State-organized companies of Texas Rangers supplemented the army's efforts in frontier defense, but they often clashed with federal officials when their vengeance-seeking tactics were counterproductive. Their numbers were limited because the state treasury was empty, and the legislature was reluctant to raise taxes to fund more Ranger units. Calls on Washington to foot the bill for expanding the force were met with bureaucratic delays. As a result, what the *Weatherford News* in January 1861 described as "the panic on the Indian frontier" heightened the insecurities still felt from the abolitionist panic in the summer.[69]

Unionists such as William P. Johnson, brother of the senator from Tennessee, saw all the more reason to oppose secession in the face of this litany of fears. Johnson was one of the multitude of nearly voiceless Southerners who never found a prosperous niche for themselves in the slave South. Fifty-seven in 1860 and the father of ten children, he had moved steadily westward from his home state of North Carolina, staying in Tennessee, Georgia, and Alabama before settling in Columbia, Texas, in 1857. He had dabbled in the printing, tailoring, and carpentry trades while vainly searching for economic independence on his own homestead. Never having achieved a secure stake to protect or expand, he dismissed secessionist rhetoric of the glorious future awaiting an independent South as just another pipe dream in a life of failure. What he did have was a burning desire to wreak retribution, to see "there necks cracked" on "these dear fellows that has made the rumpus" and endangered his life and his family's. He lumped them together with the "aristokracy" that had kept him down and lorded over him. They were already, he noted, hanging good Union men like himself. Once their mad designs were forced on the people, Johnson expected the slaves, Mexicans, and Indians to rise up and "over run the country." He vowed to defend his wife and children "to the last drop of my blood[.]" He was armed and could "kill a Negrow or a mean white man with a good gun."[70]

The rage and insecurities demonstrated by someone like William Johnson were usually directed against the Union, especially by aspiring politicians who had attained a degree of success that eluded him. Roger Q. Mills, the son of a slaveholding farmer in Kentucky, belonged to a generation of rising lawyer-politicians coming of age in the 1850s and filling the seats of Southern legislatures. Moving to Texas in 1849 as a teenager, he clerked in a store, studied law under his brother-in-law, and entered politics in the mid-1850s. He established his law practice in Corsicana, a growing town in north-central Texas. The town and his legal business shared in the slave-based prosperity of Navarro County as it transitioned from a frontier region to a new outpost of cotton production. As the white population doubled in the 1850s, that of slaves jumped eightfold and the few bales of cotton produced in 1850 shot up to 2,500. The income from his thriving law practice specializing in land transactions enabled Mills to acquire his first slaves. He left his Whiggish-Know-Nothingism of 1856 for a firm states rights' stance in the Democratic Party. Elected to the legislature in 1859, he immersed himself in shoring up frontier defense and denouncing the abolitionists. He was a quick convert to secession once Lincoln was elected. Joyfully, he told his wife Carrie that Texas would secede "and thank God for it." For Mills, the Republicans threatened all he had worked for and hoped to achieve.[71]

Those who agreed with Mills dominated Texas politics and orchestrated secession in a revolt against Houston's leadership. Democratic county chieftains, who had delivered 75 percent of the state's vote to Breckinridge, organized resistance meetings demanding the speedy calling of a secession convention. Typical of the resolutions passed were those from Houston County asking Governor Houston to call a special session of the legislature so "that such measures may be adopted as the right of self-preservation now demands." Crowds gathered in courthouse squares to listen to secessionist speeches and hoist the Lone Star flag. While Houston was waiting in vain for the excitement to cool down, secession leaders forced his hand. Meeting in the office of Judge Oran M. Roberts, a South Carolinian by birth and Calhoun follower since the 1830s, they drew up an address to the people of Texas calling for an election on January 8, 1861, of a secession convention to assemble on January 28. The call was of dubious legality, but it served its purpose of lending an aura of legitimacy to their usurpation of Houston's authority as governor. As insisted by Guy M. Bryan, a sugar planter in Johnson's Brazoria County and one of the "aristocrats" William Johnson so hated, the Texas convention was "*called* by the people." If Houston hoped that the legislature, which he finally called on December 17 to meet in a special session in January, would refuse to sanction the convention, he was disappointed. The legislature swiftly gave its approval.[72]

Reports sent to Roberts foretold the ease with which the immediatists carried the secession election. R. T. Wheeler claimed that "the whole population of the East & South East, where the slave interest is, are a unit on the question [of immediate secession]." From Comanche County, N. B. Ellis put the frontier down as "almost unanimous for secession." The secessionists swept the election with 76 percent of the vote. The pro-Union majority of 1859 had shrunk to a cluster of counties in north and west-central Texas populated by wheat-growing farmers from the Upper South and German communities with free-labor sympathies. These Texans had not been drawn into or attracted to the cultural and economic values of the Lower South.[73]

The conservatives of 1859, who had been committed both to those values and to the Union, grudgingly realized that they could not serve both. Among them was William Pitt Ballinger, a Whig who had established one of the top law practices in the state after his move from Kentucky to Texas in the 1840s. Initially, he opposed secession as "unwise" and feared it "may be a fatal thing." Confronted with the overwhelming pressure for secession, he concluded that the ordered liberty he had so valued in the Union was under direct assault from the Republican-abolitionists and could be preserved only in a new union of confederated Southern states. It was a comforting rationalization, for it convinced him he was merely transferring his loyalties to a new union that would adhere to the best safeguards of the original Constitution before it had been defiled by Northern fanatics. He would serve the Confederacy faithfully.[74]

As expected, the convention moved quickly to take Texas out of the Union. Its membership was the youngest of any in the Lower South with a median age of forty, and the largest group of delegates were small slaveholding lawyers who shared all of Roger Mills's enthusiasm for secession. The only debate was over whether to strike out a requirement for submitting secession to a popular referendum, a motion easily defeated by a vote of 145 to 29. Given the shaky legality with which secession had been carried out, such a referendum was seen as essential. Besides, there was little reason to think that secession would be reversed. The secession ordinance passed in the convention on February 1, 1861, and was affirmed by a popular majority of 77 percent in a referendum on February 23. Contrary to Houston's advice to reestablish the independent Lone Star republic, Texas tied its fate to the Southern Confederacy organized at Montgomery.[75]

Young voters and slaveholders were the key to secession in Texas, as they had been in the other cotton states. Their disproportionate support accounted for the majorities in favor of immediate secession. Party affiliation was a factor. Outside of yeoman-dominated areas, Breckinridge Democrats strongly backed secession. Bell supporters were split; one-third of them voted for cooperation, one-fifth for immediate secession, and more than two-fifths did not vote at all. With just over one in ten voting for secession, the Douglasites were the staunchest Unionists. Still, slaveholding status was a much better indicator than party of one's stand on secession. Counties where slaveholders were entrenched or on the rise carried their states out of the Union. Now that they had their revolution, the question was whether the rest of the South would join them.[76]

8

The Upper South

Straddling the Divide

The wave of secession in the cotton states fed a heady optimism among secessionists that the momentum would soon carry the Upper South, including most of the border states, out of the Union as well. The optimism masked an anxious urgency. For all they had achieved, the seven states of the original Confederacy had but one-tenth the white manpower resources of the North and even less of the manufacturing capacity, both of which were necessary to convince the North that military coercion would be futile. Despite the assurances of free-trade advocates in South Carolina that the economic might of King Cotton rendered the Confederacy militarily impregnable, most secessionists understood that any credible defense of an independent South required adding a good chunk of the Upper South, notably Virginia. Thus, the decisive battleground for the ultimate success of secession shifted to the Upper South.

Virginia: The Great Prize

All eyes were on Virginia, the Southern state with the largest population of both whites and slaves. As Virginia went, it was thought, so would the rest of the Upper South. Its size and still immense prestige as the cradle of presidents in the early republic made it the prize that had to be won.

The Old Dominion was in the midst of a structural shift in the 1850s. Led by a railroad boom that had nearly tripled rail mileage, the state experienced a quickened pace of immigration, industrialization, and urbanization. Richmond became the leading industrial city in the South with its tobacco, flour, and iron factories. Improved transportation and greater marketing opportunities also strengthened the agricultural revival that gave the lie to the persistent image of Virginia in terminal economic decline. The old tobacco counties of the Tidewater had diversified into cattle, potato, and vegetable production for urban centers in Virginia and up the East Coast. It was also home to the business centers of Norfolk, Petersburg, and Richmond. In the Piedmont, the broad expanse between the fall line of the rivers in the east and the Blue Ridge mountains to the west, tobacco dominated in the southeast, the counties south of the James River. Planters there enjoyed outsized profits in the 1850s as tobacco prices rebounded. In the northern Piedmont, wheat was the major crop. The fertile soils of the Shenandoah Valley, flanked in the east by the Blue Ridge and the west by the Alleghenies, supported a diversified agriculture geared to wheat and other grains. The southwestern counties of the trans-Allegheny region were generally too mountainous for anything but raising corn and livestock, although the coming of the Virginia and Tennessee Railroad oriented the production of wealthier slaveholders around staple crops such as cotton and tied the region more closely to the slaveholding interests of eastern Virginia. In the northwest, Virginia's Panhandle, iron and coal production jumped in the 1850s as Wheeling emerged as a major industrial city with access to northern markets via the Baltimore and Ohio Railroad.[1]

By any measure, Virginia in the 1850s had a growing, diversified economy divided into regional specializations best suited to each region's soil, natural resources, and marketing potential. The major division, economically and politically, was along an east-west axis defined by the Blue Ridge. Eighty percent of the slaves lived to the east but only 40 percent of the whites. The whitest and fastest growing area was the Northwest. The concentration of slaves in the southeastern Piedmont rivaled that found in much of the Lower South while the antipathy to slavery and commitment to manufacturing in the northwest made the Panhandle more Northern than Southern in its political orientation. Maintaining a tenuous balance between these extremes were the regional coalitions comprising the major political parties, the Whigs and Democrats. In contrast to the Lower South, where the overwhelming need to defend slavery absorbed most Whigs into a super Democratic majority, the Whigs in Virginia, and elsewhere in the Upper South, remained competitive. They retained strong pockets of support in the slaveholding east, appealed to commercial and town elites with their push for moral reform of workers and state-aided economic development, and championed the demands of the west for suffrage and reapportionment reforms. The Democrats were the majority party in the high slaveholding Piedmont areas but were also backed by German farmers in the Shenandoah Valley for their laissez-faire stand on cultural and moral issues and by yeoman farmers ambivalent over rapid economic change and outside threats to their independence. Enough eastern Democrats lined up with the Whigs in the constitutional convention of 1850–51 to reform voting requirements and legislative apportionment to allay temporarily the worst of east-west tensions.[2]

Most slaveholders adapted to the changing economic landscape. Many of the old planter dynasties established new plantations in the cotton South. Others raised cash for debts or agricultural reform by selling slaves to professional traders. Additional profits were found by hiring out slaves to Virginia's growing factories. The number of slaveholders continued its slow, post-1800 decline as it slipped to 26 percent of Virginia's families by 1860, but they still dominated state politics.[3]

Confirming the state's traditional moderation, Bell carried the state, though his winning plurality of 44.6 percent bested Breckinridge's vote by only the narrowest of margins. News of Lincoln's election produced calls for secession from a vocal minority. The state's most notable secessionist, Edmund Ruffin, had spent most of his adult life craving a public acclaim that eluded him until the secession crisis. He had harbored antislavery sentiments in his youth but inherited a worn-out tidewater plantation and an aristocratic lineage he longed to live up to. As was his aristocratic due, he wanted to lead and command respect from others, but he had neither the crowd-pleasing skills nor the speaker's voice to succeed in politics. Although his agricultural work in using marl to restore acidic soils was brilliant, he never attracted a following large enough to achieve the reforms he sought. By the 1840s, Ruffin had embarked on another crusade—this one for secession when he found a scapegoat for his frustrations in the North. Not only were Northern factories and cities undermining the agrarian existence that gave order and purpose to his life, but attacks on slavery threatened to unleash a wave of ignorant, semi-savage free blacks that would sweep aside the racial order of the South's patriarchal society. Gone forever would be the idealized Southern society with which Ruffin identified, a golden age of the past when his ancestors naturally ruled and where birth, talent, and recognition naturally meshed.[4]

In part, Ruffin's passion for secession was a repudiation of earlier misgivings about slavery he had shared with other Virginians of his youth. The same was true of Philip St. George Cocke. His father, John Hartwell Cocke, was one of Virginia's most outspoken critics of slavery with his support for a program of gradual emancipation through colonization, religious instruction, and education in basic literacy. St. George, with his large plantations in Virginia and Mississippi, would have none of it, especially with the abolitionist menace hovering over the South. One of the reasons he gave for secession was his desire to pass down to his sons a heritage of honor and duty in the defense of slavery. He reminded his son John that their ancestors had played a leading role in the American Revolution and it was John's duty to "buckle on your sword [and] root [out] the Hell inspired spirit of Abolition of red & black republicanism!"[5]

Other secessionists agreed with Cocke that the core issue was the survival of slavery in Virginia. Senator R. M. T. Hunter held that Virginia had to secede to protect slavery by giving it an outlet in a Southern confederacy. Otherwise, he predicted, the seceding states would close their slave markets and use the state as a buffer for fugitive slaves escaping from the Lower South. As a result, the black population would rise in Virginia, putting downward pressure on the wages of white labor, which would then leave the state and increase even more the ratio of slaves in the population. Without any political influence in the Union, Virginia would have no choice but to emancipate its slaves. Conversely, in a Southern re-public, Virginia slaves could be sold, and white laborers would go wherever they could find the highest wages. While slavery prospered, Virginia would inherit the Southern markets long controlled by New England, and "there would rise in or about the shores of the Chesapeake a great and commanding centre of credit and commerce."[6]

This vision of a secure slave system combined with commercial and industrial greatness was an enticing one. The *Richmond Dispatch* blamed any economic problems in Virginia on its connection with the North and foresaw Norfolk in a Southern confederacy blossoming into the "New York of the South" and Richmond rivaling the industrial centers of England. Charles Bruce, a wealthy tobacco planter, saw secession not only as an escape from forced emancipation but also a means of regaining self-respect. "I had rather see the Union shivered to fragments," he told his wife, "than to look forward to a life-time of harassing agitation, and to see the people of my section treated like aliens in a common household."[7]

This sense of estrangement from Northern society was pervasive among secessionists, especially the younger generation in slaveholding families reaching adulthood in the 1850s. Most of them longed for the status of a planter but had to settle for positions as lawyers and teachers. Those who had lived or traveled in the North felt out of place in the intensely competitive race to make money. They reacted by longing for what Virginia could be: a slaveholding oasis of order and Christian rectitude that embraced a progressive future of a balanced economy with room for themselves without the Northern excesses of destabilizing mass democracy and dangerous reformist ideas epitomized by abolitionism. They cautioned their elders not to be seduced by Northern blandishments of friendship. Charles Blackford, a young evangelical lawyer in Lynchburg, mock-ingly sympathized with his mother visiting in Philadelphia for being "among strangers, aliens and enemies." In a jab at his mother's goal of ending slavery, he asked, "What would be their condition if they were now free in the Infidel State of Massachusetts?" James Holcombe, a secessionist and law professor at the University of Virginia who had watched in his youth as his parents freed their slaves and helped provide for their freedom in Ohio and Liberia, was incredu-lous that they ever could have thought well of Northerners guilty of "not infre-quent sympathy with insurrection, rapine and murder." Colonization to him was a cruel punishment for a race well cared for in the South and shielded from the fanatical abolitionists.[8]

Demands for secession failed to move most non-slaveholders. Worse yet, according to William L'Anson, a secessionist editor in Petersburg, "the classes of overseers and the like" in Nottoway County were openly declaring that "in the event of civil war, or even servile insurrection, they would not lift a finger in defense of the rights of slaveholders." He took some comfort in the organization of vigilance committees by men of property intent on providing for their safety and rooting out dissenters. F. W. Pendleton in the Northern Neck county of Orange questioned whether it was wise for county courts to raise funds for the arming of volunteers. "This thing of arming the people may prove disastrous, for the masses may turn the arms furnished them against the slaveholders." He underlined his concern with the observation that "I have never before known the nonslaveholders arrayed against the slaveholders."[9]

Unionist leadership came from the old guard, planters from distinguished families in their fifties and older. Their views were so at variance with those of the younger secessionists that they might as well have dwelled in a different political world. Writing from New York in October 1860, the elderly John H. Cocke noted that "the more I have seen of our Yankee brethren the more highly I appreciate them—and rank them beyond comparison as the best part of our Nation. As to the ultra degree of abolitionist, they are as much despised here, among the good & true men . . . as they are with us." He regarded secession as sheer "madness."[10]

Led by William C. Rives, the most prominent Whigs counseling caution came out of eastern Virginia. Sixty-seven in 1860, Rives had two sons who had married wealthy Northern women and lived in New York City and a daughter who lived in Boston with her husband. A dozen of his grandchildren also called the North their home. Though he certainly opposed abolitionist doctrines, Rives viewed slavery as a drag on Virginia's economy and agreed with the Republicans' emphasis on a protective tariff and internal improvements to speed up economic diversification in the Old Dominion. In a public letter in December, he endorsed cooperation between moderates on both sides of the sectional border to find a middle way between the extremists. Another elderly Whig statesman, Robert E. Scott, had no fear of remaining in the Union given the alternative of joining a confederacy with the cotton states. With the many disparities in climate, soil, and economic interests, such a confederacy, he predicted, would soon break apart into antagonistic elements. In the ensuing anarchy, "our own Virginia would become the battlefield of opposing hosts" as the North militarily imposed its will. Better that Virginia seek unity with other Southern states in demanding its rights.[11]

None of their adversaries rankled the secessionists more than John Minor Botts, Richmond's leading Whig. Orphaned in 1811 at the age of nine, Botts drove himself to a meteoric rise, first as a lawyer and then a politician. As blunt in speech as bullish in physique, he castigated secession as "nothing . . . but plain, bold, daring, flat-footed rebellion, against, and treason to, the rest of the States." Although his hopes in 1860 for the presidential nomination on a National Republican ticket were quashed, he still believed that the Republicans, shorn of their anti-Southern invective, could be valuable allies in prodding the South toward a more free labor–based economy. For such heresies, the secessionists singled him out for special condemnation.[12]

No one laid out the moderates' position more forcefully than Alexander H. H. Stuart, a Whig from Augusta County in the Shenandoah Valley. Secession was undemocratic and meant a civil war in which the costs would be enormous, property ruined, and "our slaves incited to insurrection." Virginia would be ripped out of a national economy in which Northern and Southern interests complemented each other and face the ruin of its manufactures as a Southern confederacy implemented free trade. The only "true policy" for Virginia was "to remain in the Union until all Constitutional means of obtaining redress for the past and security for the future shall have proved fruitless." For all their praise of the Union and anger against South Carolina in trying to force their hand, Stuart and most moderates were but conditional Unionists. They left no doubt that their continuing allegiance to the Union depended on Northern concessions regarding slavery and absolutely no coercion against a seceded state.[13]

Unionists per se came mainly out of northwestern trans-Allegheny Virginia, a region with little interest in upholding slavery. Sheppard Clemens, a congressman from the Wheeling district, highlighted the flawed logic of the secessionists. "If you fight," he told them, "you will never extort by a treaty from the North the same guarantees that you now have in the Constitution." The Upper South would be foolhardy to sacrifice its mining, manufacturing, and capital interests to satiate the "great ruling interest of the extreme Gulf States [in slavery]." Whatever grievances the grain and manufacturing states of the South might have in a Northern-dominated Union would be slight compared to what awaited them in a confederacy ruled by the slave interest. Citing census figures on the outward flow of Southern natives into Northern states and the more rapidly growing population and productive wealth in those same states, he declared that more population and capital, not more slave territory, was the only cure for the South's political inferiority in the Union. Expanding slavery, "*either in the Union or out of it*," was a pipe dream with slaves at their current prices. Rather than see slavery "crucified" out of the Union, he favored dropping all the sectional cant for patient negotiations within the Union to buy more time for slavery while "the law of population" that accounted for the surging population of the free-labor states inevitably eroded slavery, beginning with the border states.[14]

Clemens's stand had strong backing in the Panhandle, where the Republicans had gained a foothold. The *Wheeling Intelligencer*, a Lincoln paper, advised its readers to sell off their real estate if they heard that a Virginia convention laid down an ultimatum "to get our rights." Such an ultimatum, it felt, would surely be rejected and serve as a prelude to secession. Trapped in a no man's land between the North and the South, Wheeling and the rest of the Panhandle would economically atrophy. Unwilling to see northwestern Virginians violate "their interests and their conviction of right," the *Wellsburg Herald*, another Lincoln paper, came out for the secession of the northwest from the "Commonwealth" if eastern Virginia opted for taking the state out of the Union.[15]

West versus east, old versus young, non-slaveholder versus slaveholder, a divided Virginia awaited the result of the election for a secession convention called by the legislature to meet on February 13, 1861, after an election on February 4. Although outvoted on the need for a convention, the moderates won a tactical victory by requiring any change in Virginia's relations with the federal government to be submitted to a popular referendum for approval. They also followed the recommendation of Governor John Letcher, a moderate from the Shenandoah Valley, to have Virginia sponsor a national convention to meet in Washington on the day of the secession election to work on compromise proposals to submit to Congress.[16]

Unlike their counterparts in the Lower South, the moderates ran a spirited, statewide campaign that drew the bipartisan support of Bell and Douglas voters. Noteworthy was the willingness of Breckinridge non-slaveholders to defy party leaders in the east where slavery dictated political decisions. One of the secessionists' strongholds was Lunenburg County in the southern Piedmont, where prosperous tobacco planters directed a campaign more typical of what had occurred in the Lower South. They took their first steps when the justices of the peace met at the courthouse in January. Resolutions, later approved in a public meeting, called for county funding to arm three companies of locally raised troops and authorized Colin Neblett and C. T. Allen, sons of prominent planters, to begin organizing one of the companies. To help defray the costs, the justices authorized the sheriff to sell into slavery seven free blacks for failing to pay their taxes. William J. Neblett, the secession nominee, received all of the votes in the light turnout for the convention election. The *Richmond Enquirer*, the leading secessionist newspaper, congratulated Lunenburg for acting as a " 'South Carolina' of a county."[17]

Only in their plantation strongholds in the Piedmont and Tidewater did the secessionists enjoy such advantages of uncontested control. Elsewhere, they experienced a crushing defeat. The Unionists built a coalition that backed by close to 70 percent anti-secession candidates and the calling of a referendum if needed. Pro-Union sentiment was greatest west of the Blue Ridge and in counties that had gone for Bell. Contributing to the Unionist tide was the defection of many Breckinridge Democrats in the west. In making the issue the preservation of slavery, the secessionists triggered the resentments of non-slaveholders in the west over the planters' control of their party. Voters also rejected the secessionists' claim that Virginia's economy could flourish only in a Southern confederacy. Georgian Junius Hillyer, observing the election from Washington, singled out concerns over the state's manufacturing interests as having cut into the secession vote. He also raised the persistent fear of the secessionists that the border states "are influenced by their indifference to slavery and that the anti-slavery tide is rolling further South." Citing the Unionism of "the poor non-slaveholders in many parts of the state," an alarmed young Virginian labeled the election a "free soil triumph."[18]

The Unionists were jubilant over the number of Democrats who had joined the Whig-led movement. William M. Blackford declared that the presidential and secession elections had "entirely destroyed" the Breckinridge Democrats as a party. John Critcher, a Unionist delegate from the Northern Neck, spoke of "a revolution . . . in public opinion" that would overwhelm the Democrats in future elections. Their optimism was premature. The secession Democrats retained considerable power in the east. They were defeated but not demoralized, for they well knew that the Unionist majority hung by the thread of the North's granting significant concessions. Without those concessions, the Unionist majority would vanish.[19]

Tennessee: The Hinge State in the Middle South

Tennessee consisted of three distinct sub-regions of the South that had little in common apart from the institution of slavery. East Tennessee was on the southern slope of the Appalachians; more fertile and populous Middle Tennessee supported thriving agricultural operations in hemp, tobacco, cotton, and grain crops as well as a fledgling manufacturing base; and rapidly growing West Tennessee was a northern extension of the Mississippi Delta and home to the state's wealthiest planters. The parties shared voters across the state, with East Tennessee returning a slight edge to the Whigs, Middle Tennessee favoring the Democrats, and West Tennessee up for grabs. The state was key for the secessionists in that its railroad hubs in Memphis, Nashville, Chattanooga, and the beginnings of one in Knoxville provided rail connections from the Mississippi River through Tennessee to major markets on the Atlantic seaboard

and the Gulf Coast at Mobile and New Orleans. Still, it would take a greater political shock than Lincoln's election to wrench the state out of the Union.[20]

The election of 1860 was in line with the state's middle-of-the-road politics.
Strong support for Bell from slaveholding, old-line Whigs and the 8 percent
of the vote polled by Douglas gave Bell the state with a plurality of 48 percent.
Having denounced the extremism of Breckinridge Democrats as the rantings
of power-hungry demagogues, the Bell press saw no need to panic because the
Republicans had won the election. The South had friends enough in the North
"to prevent all hostilities toward the South except in the way of talk," assured
the *Athens Post*. If the talk turned to action, a united South would have sufficient
time to protect itself. Any state that seceded, argued the *Clarksville Chronicle*,
"not only abandons all its rights in the Union, but betrays the States to which
it is bound by community of interests and identity of institutions." Whatever
grievances existed—and surely they were exaggerated by the disunionists—
could be resolved in the Union. Let a Southern convention be called, advised
the conservatives, if the Republicans turned aggressive.[21]

Governor Isham G. Harris outflanked the conservatives by scheduling a
special session of the legislature to deal with what he defined as a major threat.
Harris had gained planter status for himself in a career that paralleled that of
another secessionist governor, Pettus of Mississippi. The ninth child of a small
slaveholding preacher-farmer on the frontier of Middle Tennessee in the 1830s,
Harris was left to his own devices. He moved to Mississippi in his teens, earned a
small fortune supplying goods to the newcomers staking claims to former Indian
land, and then lost it in the Panic of 1837 that wiped out his local bank. He
started over as a lawyer in Tennessee, married well, and emerged as the leader of
the state's rights Democrats. Identifying with the planter class he had struggled
to enter, he wanted to cut all ties with the Republican North.[22]

Harris stopped just short of urging Tennessee's secession in his message to
the legislature at its opening on January 7. Although he stated that Northern
hostility precluded any possibility of a compromise, he went through the formality of presenting demands more extreme than those already rejected by
the Republicans. Among them was a permanent division of the territories to
the Pacific by a line drawn along the northern border of the slave states with
all south of the line to be "forever slave." A coalition of Whigs and Democrats
scuttled Harris's more extreme demands and succeeded in linking the election of
delegates to a secession convention with a choice on whether to hold a convention. Any action of the convention, if one was held, was contingent on approval
in a referendum.[23]

The two most outspoken Unionists, Democrat Andrew Johnson and Whig
Parson Brownlow, had been bitter antagonists, but they shared an abiding hatred of the planter elite that brought them together in opposing secession. The

roots of that hatred lay in their humble origins. Both men clawed their way to positions of respectability by converting a lingering sense of shame over their impoverished beginnings into a battering ram directed at parasitical aristocrats living off the honest work and sacrifices of plebeians such as themselves. Johnson's widowed mother, so poor as to be forced into the degrading position of a domestic servant in Raleigh, North Carolina, apprenticed Andrew out to learn the tailor's trade. Johnson ran off to East Tennessee, where he crafted a political message of championing the interests of common farmers and mechanics that carried him to the US Senate. William G. (Parson) Brownlow, the son of an itinerant farmer in western Virginia, was passed around to relatives after he was orphaned at the age of ten. Before he discovered his talent for running a newspaper, he rode the Methodist circuit attacking his Baptist and Presbyterian competitors with the same vitriol that was his trademark as editor of *Brownlow's Knoxville Whig.*[24]

Johnson's and Brownlow's enemies included abolitionists, free blacks, and Southern aristocrats. Rising to the top in the secession crisis were the aristocrats, whose drive for secession was seen as bringing on a civil war that would do the work of the abolitionists for them and stamp out the liberties of common whites. For Johnson, the secessionists' obsession with protecting slave property was a red herring to divert attention from their real objective of forming a government in the South "as far removed from the people as they can get it. There is not merely a conspiracy on foot [*sic*] against the existing Govmt, but the liberty of the great mass of the people." Brown warned that in a Southern confederacy Tennesseans would "live under a villainous tyranny" in which freedom of speech and the press would be denied and crushing taxes imposed upon the same "common people [who] will have to do the fighting." As the "Slavery aristocracy" consolidated its power, poor whites would soon be worse off than free blacks.[25]

More temperate and polished than Johnson and Brownlow, though no less committed to preserving the Union, were Emerson Etheridge and Thomas A. R. Nelson, both Whig representatives in Congress with distinguished legal backgrounds. Etheridge even put in a good word for the Republicans. He praised them as having gone further than any other party in pledging not to interfere with slavery in the states, a pledge they backed up with their support of the proposed constitutional amendment permanently protecting the institution from congressional interference. They also, he noted, publicly castigated John Brown's raid "as among the gravest of crimes." Nelson pleaded with House members to shake off their near "criminal inertness" and fashion a sectional settlement. As for himself, he was willing to agree "to almost anything rather than see the land drown in blood."[26]

The straight-out Unionists were soon in a minority, for most moderates attached conditions to their Unionism. Edited by Robert Thomas, the *Clarksville*

Chronicle expressed the views of business leaders who benefited from the town's connections to first steamboat and then railroad outlets. Thomas had opposed Southern demands for equality in the territories as an abstraction with no basis in the Constitution or in the needs of slaveholders. In the week after Lincoln's election he began hedging on his Unionism. All he initially conceded to the secessionists was a willingness to favor a Southern convention if the Republicans became openly threatening. He confidently predicted that any demands that came out of that convention would readily be met given the North's need for Southern markets. He also offered tentative support for a Tennessee convention as long as it worked for a settlement within the Union. By early January, Thomas was still blasting separate state secession as "cowardly, traitorous, and utterly destructive of the ends to be attained," but he had accepted the secessionists' claim that constitutional issues of equality had been raised from which there was "no safe retreat." Convinced that "the character of the contest has been radically changed" and that only additional Northern guarantees on slavery could stem the crisis, he was surprised when the Republicans rejected the Crittenden Compromise. With that rejection, Thomas was content to blame the Republicans for any breakup of the Union.[27]

John H. Bills, a planter in West Tennessee, agonized over the same issues that the *Chronicle* was laying out for its readers. In the forty-two years since he had moved to the state from North Carolina, he had built up a considerable fortune. He owned plantations in Tennessee and Mississippi and was about to purchase another in Chicot County in the Arkansas Delta. He earned additional income as a money lender and cotton trader. Though expressing qualms over the harsh methods of his overseer, he was quite content to enjoy the wealth the overseer's methods produced. He saw no need to risk that wealth by joining the rush to secession. Why destroy the government that was "the wisest & best men ever had," he asked himself. Still, as the winter wore on and no compromise was forthcoming, he conceded that he would have "to go with my section come what will."[28]

Secession sentiment peaked in West Tennessee, where plantations held Tennessee's heaviest concentration of slaves, and was also strong in the commercial and marketing districts of Middle and East Tennessee. The secessionists hit hardest on the economic ruin and racial horrors that would result from the forced emancipation that awaited Tennesseans if they remained in the Union. William H. Sneed, a secessionist candidate in Knox County, warned that when "the deluge comes . . . of emancipation with negro equality," taxpayers would have to foot the bill for the freed slaves. All whites would suffer, economically and socially, but none more than "the humble poor man."[29]

The business hubs of Nashville and Memphis buzzed with excitement over secession. Northern teachers, some of whom had been residents for ten years, were being forced to leave. Rogene Scott in Nashville felt that formerly conservative Tennessee was "now about as eager for secession as the more Southern [states]." She took a grim satisfaction in imagining that the slaveholders "are hugging to their bosoms the viper which will sting them very soon." Fueling the excitement was the prospect of being cut off from markets to the south if Tennessee stayed in the Union. As unemployment among clerks, mechanics, and laborers soared to unprecedented levels, the *Nashville Union and American* argued in January that once Georgia and Louisiana seceded, "all our products which have hitherto found a market in the South will be hemmed in." Deprived of the money from the cotton produced by the slaves, "we should be in a worse condition than the beggars of Italy."[30]

The conversion to secession was even more dramatic in Memphis, a city that gave Breckinridge just 11 percent of its vote. Fat and sassy from its burgeoning cotton wealth on display in the stacked bales lining its riverside streets, Memphis more than doubled in population in the 1850s. Most of the growth came from an influx of Northerners and foreign-born workers drawn to the city by its expanding economy. They accounted for 56 percent of the population, slaves another 17 percent. Literally outnumbered, native-born Southern whites turned to secession to reclaim their city and reverse the sudden and calamitous economic storm that left them stunned. As in Nashville, vigilantes roamed the streets, hounding Northerners to leave. They closely watched boats arriving from Cincinnati and forced them to head back if they spotted any suspicious activity. A self-identified "Memphis Mechanic" noted in late November that nearly all conservative men and newspapers in favor of the Union three weeks earlier had now succumbed to the secessionist storm. The *Memphis Appeal* joined the parade in December. Earlier, the paper had favored the Union for economic reasons. It blamed the depression on the anxiety over Lincoln's election and the "disunion madness" that raised doubts over the credit worthiness of Southern-issued credit notes. Cotton prices, the paper estimated, had already fallen by a cent a pound, which translated into a loss of $2,000,000 on the 1860 crop. And that was only the beginning, it cautioned.

The *Appeal* expected the economic downturn to lift once Southerners grasped that Lincoln posed no threat and that Republicans would soon tear his party to pieces. Instead, the financial nightmare darkened. A "letter to Governor Harris" decried the suspension of banks, the stagnant trade, "and (worse feature of all) negro property fallen thirty per cent in value within the last three months." The letter writer demanded the calling of a Tennessee convention. Though preferring a Southern convention, the *Appeal* now agreed that "something must be done." It conceded that Lincoln's election must be "looked upon in the light of a *crisis* . . . an epoch in the insidious aggressiveness of a free-soil fanaticism, which, when calmly contemplated, is utterly alarming." It concluded that the

Union could never be saved nor the Southern economy ever revived unless the North abandoned its crusade "for the eventual overthrow of slavery" and gave the South additional guarantees for the institution.[31]

The secessionists' linkage of slavery to continued prosperity was most attractive to planters and others engaged in market relations. An Irish-born owner of a machine shop and foundry in Nashville looked upon disunion with horror, yet, as "a matter of business," he saw a silver lining in secession and the war he expected to follow. By early January 1861, he had been forced by the economic paralysis to lay off a quarter of his 100 some workers and he felt conditions would only worsen. War, with its soaring demand for cannon and shot, could prove to be the economic salvation of himself and his workers and their families.[32]

Non-slaveholders isolated from markets on small, semi-subsistence farms and town and urban mechanics were the backbone of the Unionists' supporters. They looked to Andrew Johnson for leadership. A Chattanooga hotel keeper assured Johnson that "the mountain boys—The wood choppers The Rail splitters— In fact the bone and sinew of the country back you." A pro-Union mechanics' meeting in Greenville on January 7, 1861, demanded that all businessmen exhibit a flag showing where they stood on Union or secession. Most of these Unionists had no stake in slavery and no means of entering even the bottom rungs of the slaveholding class. They feared greater domination by the planter "aristocrats" and heeded warnings that their voting rights and representation might be restricted in a confederacy that politically privileged slaveholders. They were told that emancipation, and hence greater competition from blacks, would surely result from secession. Even if Tennessee and the rest of the Upper South stayed out of a Southern confederacy, Oliver M. Temple, a Knoxville Unionist, predicted that "constant feuds, conflicts . . . and border wars" would leave slave property too insecure to be preserved.[33]

Sensing defeat on the issue of unconditional withdrawal from the Union, the secessionists pitched the theme of "Convention and Anti-Coercion" as the election approached. It was a clever ploy, but it failed as the secessionists suffered a stinging setback in the election on February 9. In a vote closely correlating with county levels of slaveholding, secession candidates and the holding of a convention were handily rejected. As slaveholdings declined from West to Middle Tennessee and then fell sharply in East Tennessee, support for secession and a convention fell. Political loyalties in the 1860 election influenced the returns, though partisanship was not as determinate of the preferences as was the extent of slaveholding. Across the state, the poorer the area, the greater the commitment to the Union.[34]

In surveying the wreckage of their hopes in the election that registered just a 22 percent vote for secession and 45 percent for a convention, the secessionists could only conclude that Tennesseans had been "wickedly, willfully deceived." The pro-Union *Nashville Patriot* congratulated the people on their sound judgment and felt that the support for the Union in Tennessee and Virginia had given the North every reason "to yield to the demands of justice and rights." Their hopes were to be dashed.[35]

North Carolina: Squeezed from Above and Below

Sandwiched between Virginia and South Carolina, North Carolina was the poor cousin of both. It lacked the aristocratic grandeur and wealth of lowcountry South Carolina and the rich political heritage of Virginia. Its nickname, "The Old North State," hinted at the staid conservatism resistant to change for which the state was known. Its position in the secession crisis would be dictated by its neighbors. Infuriated by the political extremism of the other Carolinians, it turned to Virginia for direction. As long as Virginia remained in the Union, North Carolina would as well.

Like the other seaboard slave states, North Carolina experienced heavy outflows of population after the War of 1812 as soil fertility declined and fresher lands beckoned in the Southwest. Agricultural wealth rebounded in the 1850s as a new technique for curing brightleaf tobacco brought new prosperity to farmers and planters who had struggled to produce a cash crop on their sandy soils. Brightleaf tobacco, favored by smokers for its mild taste, thrived on those soils. As tobacco output more than doubled in the 1850s, so too did that of turpentine. Naval stores—tar, pitch, and turpentine—were the South's third largest export by the late 1850s, and North Carolina was the major supplier of them. Demand for turpentine rose as camphene, one of its derivatives, replaced candles and whale oil as a source of lighting for businesses and homes. Resin, or raw turpentine, was tapped from the long-leaf pines in the forests running through the heart of North Carolina's coastal plain. The soil in the forest was too poor for money-making crops, but the resin from the pines provided a source of living for local farmers. Many of them were pushed out in the 1850s as planters moved in with their slaves. Distilleries to process the resin and labor camps filled with slaves transferred from unprofitable plantations in the old tobacco belt soon dotted the large tracts purchased by the slaveholders. Labor conditions were harsh, but the income earned by the planters gave them another incentive to defend the institution that was the source of their wealth.[36]

Bolstered by brightleaf tobacco and turpentine, slavery maintained a deeper presence in North Carolina than elsewhere outside of the cotton South. One-third of the state's population were enslaved, and nearly 30 percent of white families owned slaves. The political system was configured not just to protect

slaveholders but to give them a disproportionate influence in running the government. Under the provisions of the 1835 constitution, taxes paid were the
basis of representation in the state senate, a provision favoring the wealthier
counties in the east. The federal ratio (five slaves were equivalent to three whites)
determined the apportionment of seats in the House of Commons. Property
qualifications for officeholding (higher for the senate), the appointive power of
the legislature over county judges and justices of the peace, and limits on the
taxing of slaves rounded out the safeguards for slave property.[37]

As a result, slaveholders, including planters, controlled the legislature
at levels more in line with the plantation states of the Lower than the Upper
South. Still, the competitive nature of a two-party system built around cross-
regional coalitions of voters was a check on the slaveholders' power. The western
Piedmont and mountains, where the yeomanry held sway and the white population was growing the fastest, leaned toward the Whigs, while the eastern slaveholding counties were heavily Democratic. As demands from the mountains
heated up in the 1850s for internal improvements and a more equitable distribution of state tax monies, the Democrats were more adept in making concessions.
They took the lead in eliminating the fifty-acre requirement for voting for state
senators and in pushing through a bill for the North Carolina Railroad, projected
to run from Goldsboro to Charlotte and open new markets for western produce.
Not to be outdone, the Whigs jumped on the ad valorem taxation of slaves to
regain the votes of non-slaveholding westerners. Parlaying the issue with discontent over a steep rise in taxes and state indebtedness for the costs of the railroad,
which had reached only the foothills of the mountains when the Democrats
halted construction for lack of funds, the Whigs narrowly missed regaining the
governorship in 1860. They would rely on their strengthened electoral base to
oppose any Democratic plans to take North Carolina out of the Union.[38]

Party lines held in the election of 1860. Thanks to a large majority in the
coastal plain and counties next to the Virginia and South Carolina lines where
tobacco and cotton were major crops, Breckinridge won the state with 51 percent of the vote. John W. Ellis, the Democratic governor, favored secession on
Lincoln's election but had enough political sense not to force the issue. Ellis
shared the new orthodoxy of the Democrats in the Lower South that combined
alarm over the abolitionist menace with support for internal improvements to
widen opportunities for slaveholders and keep the slaveless satisfied. Born into
an established planting family, he had risen rapidly in the party by pushing hard
on the slavery issue. He insisted that for all the talk of slavery in the territories,
the real issue was "whether African slavery shall be abolished here in the States."
As he informed Governor Gist of South Carolina in October, entrenched political divisions in the state prevented any consensus in favor of secession regardless of whether Lincoln won the election. He pointedly added, however, that

neither he nor the people of the state would ever agree to give "aid to a practical enforcement of the monstrous doctrine of Co-ercion."[39]

As county meetings organized by eastern slaveholders were held to demand the defense of Southern rights, Ellis was careful not to take a premature step. He nudged North Carolinians toward a more confrontational stance while patiently waiting for some future secessionist tide to roll over the state. His message to the legislature in November advised the calling of a Southern convention to be followed by a state convention. In the meantime, he sought military appropriations to prepare the state for any eventuality. Secession sentiment was strongest in the coastal counties sourced by Wilmington, the chief port for the turpentine and slave-produced crops in the east. When a delegation from Wilmington on January 1 sought Governor Ellis's sanctioning for the seizure of Fort Casswell on the Cape Fear River below the city, he refused. At the head of the Wilmington delegation was William S. Ashe, North Carolina's most outspoken secessionist. A native of the Lower Cape Fear region, he combined rice planting with an entrepreneur's eye for future profits. As a state legislator in the 1840s, he scuttled any plans for rail connections from the west to ports in South Carolina or Virginia in favor of a link with the Wilmington and Weldon Railroad at Goldsboro. Fittingly, he became president of that railroad in 1854 and heavily promoted its interests. As both a rice planter and railroad executive, his economic success rested on slave labor he was unwilling to risk under a Republican administration.[40]

While Ellis was keeping a tight rein on the secessionists, he was also furnishing Robert Gourdin with the names of leading men who could make best use of Gourdin's pro-secession pamphlets. In a move that the cautious Gourdin would have approved, Ellis interceded when locally raised troops from Wilmington and Smithville acted against his wishes and took possession of Fort Casswell and the neighboring post of Fort Johnson on January 10. Although the forts were held only by a skeletal crew of caretakers, aroused locals feared that federal troops were on the way to garrison them. Ellis immediately ordered the forts returned. As he explained to Governor Brown of Georgia, their seizure with no cause "would have an injurious effect upon the cause of Southern rights in the State."[41]

When Ellis wrote to Brown, the North Carolina legislature was in the midst of a month-long debate over whether to authorize a state convention. The Whig-Unionists had great leverage since a two-thirds approval in both houses was needed. They held out until Democrats agreed to include a choice on the holding of a convention and to delay the election until February 28, 1861, and the convention until March 11, a week after Lincoln's inauguration. The Unionists had done well, but they had to pay a price. The legislature put the state on a semi-war footing by enrolling all adult white males in an expanded militia and authorizing a 10,000-man (expandable to 20,000 in case of an invasion) volunteer force. It also mandated the death penalty for distributing antislavery literature or tampering with slaves.[42]

By January, the Whigs realized their initial wait-and-see response to Lincoln's election was no longer politically tenable. The secession of South Carolina followed by the Gulf states, the failure of compromise efforts in Congress, and the unauthorized seizure of the forts in North Carolina all seemed to be dragging the state down the road of secession. A concerned Unionist from Raleigh saw the secessionists growing daily more emboldened while the conservatives were "comparatively paralyzed and depressed." From his Magnolia plantation in late December, William Pettigrew felt that "the Revolution appears to be progressing, nor does there appear to be any probability of its progress being arrested." Zebulon B. Vance, a rising star in the Whig Party from the mountains, registered the shift in Whig thinking. In mid-December he was confident that delay would yield "sober second thought [and] developments in Congress which I hope may be favorable." By January, that hope was fading, and Vance, like most Unionist leaders, concluded that doing nothing would only "precipitate us into disunion."[43]

The newly energized Whigs ran a strong campaign in the secession election. They had the backing of most newspapers, including William Holden's widely read *Raleigh Standard*, the flagship paper of the Democratic Party. Holden's support was crucial for the Unionists. His career paralleled that of Joe Brown and Parson Brownlow. Born illegitimate in 1818 and raised by his mother and stepfather in Orange County, North Carolina, he learned the printer's trade and studied by night to become a lawyer at the age of twenty-three. Briefly a Whig, he joined the Democrats in the 1840s and was the chief architect of the strategy that secured major gains for the party in western North Carolina. His own hardscrabble background had taught him how to appeal to poor mountaineers with an egalitarian message of better schools, internal improvements, and suffrage reform. By 1858, he was party chairman and its most popular editor. Yet, in an older slave state where family lineage still brought political preferment, the Democrats passed him over for nominations for both governor and US Senate. With no chance to become a North Carolina version of Joe Brown, he followed the Brownlow route and broke with his party in favoring the ad valorem tax. Punished with the loss of the state printing contract for his opposition to disunion, an unfazed Holden orchestrated the Unionist campaign in the secession election.[44]

Holden was the most important Democrat in a bipartisan coalition of Unionists. The pillars of the Whig Party—William Graham, John Gilmer, and Jonathan Worth, all from the Piedmont—played the leading roles, but anti-secession western Democrats were key to their victory. Vance, famed for his speaking prowess, gave speeches and distributed thousands of Unionist pamphlets. Though he saw no chance of the Gulf states returning if a compromise could still be negotiated, he expected Unionists elsewhere to persuade Republicans to make the needed concessions. Then, he predicted: "If we could hold the border States firm, we could finally force the Gulf States back, by simply allowing them to bear the burdens of a separate existence. With their free trade, direct taxation, and scattering white population, they would soon be forced in by their people."[45]

In the Piedmont the Unionists were quite strong in the Quaker belt centered around Randolph County. The pacifist traditions, moral repugnance to slavery, and quest for social harmony of the Quakers and Moravians who had settled the area were fertile ground for Unionism. Some 10,000 Quakers had left in the antislavery crackdown following Nat Turner's rebellion, but the 5,000 who remained had not changed their values. Rallying them was Jonathan Worth, a Quaker and Randolph Whig. His campaign circular referred to the proposed state convention as "a modern invention of South Carolina to bring about a sort of legalized revolution." Its only purpose was to "destroy" the Union. After warning that the secessionists were planning to provoke a war once Lincoln was in power, he implored the voters to hold fast to the Union and wait for a sectional settlement from the Washington Peace Conference or a possible national convention.[46]

The Unionists convinced Whig planters that secession meant the end of slavery and non-slaveholders that the Confederacy would be an engine of oppression whose sole purpose was the protection of slavery. Class resentments, already stirred up by the ad valorem issue, colored the Unionism of the poor. The struggle, Holden declared, was between "the people," who, like him, had to work for a living, and "the oligarchs" who lived off their inherited wealth and investments. In northeastern North Carolina, Kenneth Rayner was shocked in December to find "unqualified submission" and all-out Unionists. "I heard from some sources," he reported, "that the people who do not own slaves were swearing they 'would not lift a finger to protect rich men's negroes.' " At the same time, near Plymouth in the Albemarle region, planter Charles Pettigrew heard a number of men saying they would "join any force" sent down from the North to put down South Carolina. His brother William felt firsthand the wrath of the poor. A grandee from one of the east's most pedigreed families, Pettigrew expected to run uncontested for the convention as a conditional Unionist. Instead, and much to his surprise, Charles Latham, a Unionist, defeated him. Billing himself as the "poor man's" candidate, he tarred Pettigrew as a closet secessionist and aristocratic snob, who shamed his poor neighbors by refusing to welcome them into his house and requiring them first to see a house slave at the plantation gate. [47]

The secessionists insisted that the Union was already gone and only secession could keep out abolitionists. The *Salisbury Banner* rhetorically asked: supposing "the 4 millions of slaves shall be set free and made our equals, both socially and politically—is this not a sufficient cause for rebellion?" Others followed the course of William K. Ruffin, who advised Paul Cameron not to declare for immediate secession but to stress the less inflammatory issue of the need for "positive guarantees" on slavery. "This in effect is secession," he reasoned, "and is meant to be so—and will be understood by others to be so." The "d---d fanatics" would never agree to more guarantees, and what value could they have given "their constant agitation in & out of Congress—which is in fact the great grievance?" [48]

Holden's rallying cry of "Union or Disunion" proved to be more effective than its secessionist counterpart of "Equality or Submission." The secessionists ran best in the Democratic planting counties of the east and those with commercial outlets in the triangle formed by the rail cities of Charlotte, Goldsboro, and Wilmington in the south-central part of the state. Here, the secessionists often ran unopposed or faced just token opposition. In the mountains the secessionists had pockets of support, some tied to the popularity of Thomas Clingman, who had converted from a Whig to a states' rights Democrat in his drive for a US Senate seat. The small, but very influential group of planters in counties emerging from market isolation backed secession to keep open market outlets to South Carolina via Charlotte.[49]

Most Unionists came out of the upper and central Piedmont, followed by those in the poorer counties in the northeast and semi-subsistence areas in the mountain counties closest to the Tennessee line. Whigs, supported by Democratic defectors who turned out in large numbers in low slaveholding counties, built a winning coalition. They narrowly defeated the holding of a convention and elected well over 60 percent of delegates running on a Union or conditional Union ticket. Boosting their efforts was the possibility of an acceptable compromise coming out of the Washington Peace Conference. Optimism over it influenced most Whig slaveholders to stand by the Union.[50]

The Unionist victory was impressive, but, as in Virginia and Tennessee, its meaning was unclear. Had the Union been saved or its demise only postponed? In their jubilation over the results, the Republicans ignored the fact that many, likely most, Unionists in the Upper South were so on a conditional basis. If their demands were not met, what then? As shown by the rejection by John Gilmer, one of North Carolina's Whig leaders, of a cabinet position offered by Lincoln, the Unionists would not be placated by a token gesture of bipartisan sectional cooperation. For the defeated secessionists, the struggle was not over. Vowing to carry on the fight, they accused the Unionists of deliberately deceiving the voters with false reports of progress in the Peace Conference talks. Committed as ever to secession, David Schenck grimly wrote that the election's "result has changed the feeling, from one of excitement, to a deep feeling of desperation, quiet but determined." That desperation, heightened by the mobilization of a new popular majority with a defiant anti-planter stance, expressed itself in a call for the State's Rights party to meet in Goldsboro on March 22. "Come one—come all—and save your State from the clutches of the Abolitionist." That summons hardly boded well for North Carolina's future in the Union.[51]

Arkansas: Highlands versus Delta

More than most states, Arkansas consisted of two Souths—an uplands majority of poor farmers in a semi-frontier environment and a lowlands minority of enviably wealthy planters. Only Texas experienced a more explosive surge in its free and slave populations in the 1850s than Arkansas, where each more than doubled. The slave newcomers were plantation laborers in the southeastern corner of the state, a clone of the Mississippi-Louisiana Delta. As cotton production soared in the 1850s, planters tightened their grip on state politics, and the Ozark uplands were increasingly isolated, culturally and economically, from the rest of the state. Politically, that isolation expressed itself in a steadfast commitment to the Union.

Progress in the way of schools, good roads, and civility was slow to come to Arkansas. The state became a byword for backwardness and violence, known best "for a species of savage chivalry and unlettered independence." The roads were abominable; the rivers, though plentiful, were prone to extended periods of flooding and drought; and construction of the first railroad did not begin until the 1850s. The collapse of the banks in a mountain of debt after the Panic of 1837 ruined the state's credit-worthiness and left it chronically short of capital. A revival of fortunes got under way in the 1850s as the state's abundance of cheap land attracted whites from the older slave states to a new frontier. Migrants from the Upper South poured into the uplands, the north-central and north-western upper half of the state. Most were too poor to own slaves and provided for their families with grain production and livestock. The fertile lowlands in southern and eastern Arkansas were a magnet for newcomers from the Lower South, the best off of whom were planters or their sons with the slaves needed to build the levees necessary for reclaiming swampland and clearing the jungle terrain for plantations. A sixfold jump in cotton output in the 1850s was the best measure of their success.[52]

Its opportunities and lack of restraints made Arkansas a mecca for hustlers, the economically marginal desperate to strike it rich. One of them was the young Joseph W. Morris, who had originally settled in De Soto County, Mississippi. A doctor whose real passion was land speculation, he left De Soto after losing all his possessions in a fire and falling out with a fellow doctor who accused him of attempted murder. After a brief stay in Courtland, Alabama, he moved with his family to Pine Bluff, Arkansas, in 1859. Apart from acquiring land, he found little to like in the state. "I should not choose this country in which to reside was I able to do better," he confided to his sister. Its only attraction for him was its economic potential. Certain that its cotton lands would soon make Arkansas the "Banner state in the South," he wanted to get in on the ground floor by investing every spare dollar in land. Understandably, Morris was a rabid secessionist. He believed that Northerners "would enslave us if they could," coded language for displacing fears of losing his best chance of acquiring wealth.[53]

Thomas Hindman was a speculator of a different sort, a brash newcomer who took on and bested the Family, the state's ruling political dynasty. In Hindman's rhetorical onslaught of championing the poor by touting economic development and the reopening of the African slave trade, the Family became the "Aristocracy" holding down the poor by keeping opportunities limited and slave prices high. After successfully defying the Family in his bid for power, Hindman then joined forces with them in promoting Breckinridge's candidacy and pushing for secession.[54]

Arkansas adhered to its established partisan allegiances in the presidential election. Bell, a surrogate for the old Whig Party, carried the planting counties in the Delta and the lowlands of the Arkansas River valley. Breckinridge, by retaining the Democratic vote in the uplands, won the state with a 54 percent majority. Lincoln's election set off no alarm bells. The Breckinridge press even joined the Bell camp in advising moderation. In his inaugural address on November 15, the new governor, Henry Rector, ominously declared that the issue forced upon the South was the stark choice of "the Union without slavery, or slavery without the Union," but he saw no need for immediate action. An ambitious but careful politician, he was waiting for a cue as to how to lead. Though related by kinship to members of the Family, he had feuded with them in the past and jumped at the chance to exert his independence when Hindman backed him for the governorship against the Family's candidate.[55]

Rector's signal came in late November. Family member Francis Terry introduced a secession resolution in the legislature, and Hindman returned from Washington to deliver a rousing secession speech. The legislature was unmoved. Hindman's speech set off a backlash that stiffened Unionist resolve. William Watkins from the Ozarks saw no reason why "good Southern men" should not accept state positions from a Republican administration. A self-described "Union-loving Democrat," Samuel Hempstead, argued that only an overt act of Northern aggression could force Southerners "to take up arms and fight for the institution of slavery." No action was taken on the resolutions from the planting counties of Phillips, Chicot, and Desha demanding a state convention to devise a plan for action.[56]

The state remained in a holding pattern until the second week in December when Rector, prodded by knowledge of a letter about to be circulated from US senator and Family chieftain Richard W. Johnson urging Arkansas to join any Southern confederacy, came out for immediate secession. Unless Arkansas seceded, he argued, it would become a pitiful border state with no protection for slavery, without which "her fertile fields are deserts and her people penniless and impoverished." Foreseeing the speedy secession of Mississippi and Louisiana, he warned that the state's economy would wither once deprived of free access to its commercial lifeline down the Mississippi River. Its western border fronting Indian territory would be exposed to John Brown–inspired raids already infesting Missouri. In addition to military preparations, he asked for a bill preventing the entry of any slaves into Arkansas save those accompanied by their owners. The purpose was "to compel the border States to take care of and protect their own slave property, and ultimately to look to the cotton States as confederates and allies, having like institutions and common interests."[57]

South Carolina's secession on December 20, 1860, followed a day later by a joint statement by Hindman and Johnson for a state convention, broke the deadlock in the legislature. Benjamin Du Val, a Hindman ally, introduced a convention resolution that carried in the General Assembly. The Senate, where seats more closely tracked the state's 80 percent majority of non-slaveholders, delayed approval until January 15. The election, set for February 18, offered a choice on delegates and whether the convention would meet. Unionists were outraged that no provision was made for the people's approval of any decision by the convention.[58]

The possibility of secession was horrifying to poorer Arkansans dependent on their slaves for their economic survival. Mary Sims, a young widow with three children, saw no way to avoid the poverty she feared awaited her. No matter the political resolution, she felt doomed: "If the South is forced to submit [to the abolitionists] I am a beggar and if not my servants may be destroyed in the issue." At the other end of the spectrum, Isaac H. Hilliard, a large planter in Chicot County, could hardly wait for Arkansas to leave. In announcing his candidacy for the convention, he presented the choice as either slavery or freedom for the white man. He implored the voters to "act as free men should."[59]

Resolutions passed in county meetings exposed the sharp divisions between the non-slaveholders in the market-stunted uplands and the commercially driven planters in the lowlands. Along with the familiar litany of Northern outrages, secession resolutions emphasized the shame of non-resistance. Not only would whites be degraded by forced equality with blacks, their Christian faith would forever be besmirched. Northerners were accused of "unchristianizing and denouncing the Southern Christians as heretics, manstealers and hell deserving people, declaring that there must be an anti-slavery God, Bible and constitution." Baptist ministers in southern Arkansas, in part because of reports that Northern Baptist ministers were spreading abolitionism in the Indian territory, generally favored secession in their preaching. In the view of Judge John Brown of Camden, "the Baptist Church [was] a Democratic association [and] equals in extremes with the Northern fanatics."[60]

Baptists in northern Arkansas were mostly Democrats, but they did not follow the party line of supporting secession. Slaves were few in the Ozarks, as were opportunities for economic advancement beyond a small family farm. What the yeomen most valued was an independent existence they felt was under more direct attack from planters than Northerners. Only "the owner of a negro" would be allowed to vote in a Southern confederacy, charged a Unionist pamphlet. Such charges that the secessionists aimed to erect a government "founded upon property qualifications at the expense of principle" tapped into the fears of slaveless whites that the planters were plotting to strip them of their political rights. Resolutions from Benton County in the far northwest denounced the secessionists for inciting "a spirit of anarchy, which . . . will set at defiance all laws, all rights, and involve our country . . . in civil war and irremediable ruin."[61]

In the weeks leading up to the election, Rector almost stumbled into provoking the seizure of the US arsenal in Little Rock. Reports of reinforcements on their way to the arsenal triggered preparations by volunteer companies to take the arsenal by force. Fearing a setback to their cause by an unprovoked assault, secession leaders pressured Rector to work out a peaceful solution. A clash was avoided when the arsenal's commander, Captain James Totten, who was badly outnumbered and had received no orders from Washington, agreed to turn over the arsenal to Rector. The ladies of Little Rock gave Totten and his men a cordial send-off as they departed on steamboats for St. Louis.[62]

The violence that did break out took the form of community wrath against outspoken Unionists and Northerners in pro-secession areas. Disunionists in Pine Bluff, noted Episcopal Bishop Henry Lea, threatened "to hang every man who says a word against Immediate Secession." Jeremiah Harris, a livestock farmer in the cotton county of Phillips, feared for his life after he publicly opposed secession and prudently chose not to vote in the election. Thomas Barrow, one of the few Unionist planters in Phillips, relied on his slaves to stand guard in front of his house to protect him from death threats. Northerners in plantation counties were under intense pressure to contribute money for the arming and equipping of the volunteer soldiers lest they be accused of "Unionist proclivities." Milan Serl from Wisconsin, who taught school in Chicot County, had the good sense to keep his political opinions to himself and join a local home guard in January. To avoid conscription in 1862, he fled back to Wisconsin.[63]

A solid turnout by non-slaveholders enabled the Unionists to carry the election. Deflecting the charge of submission by often running as cooperationists trusting in a Southern convention to resolve the crisis, Unionist candidates won 57 percent of the seats in the convention, which was approved by a slightly higher margin. Traditional party lines were nearly obliterated, and a new alignment pitted the non-slaveholding north and west against the slaveholding south and east. Hilliard described it well: "Our state is divided into two sections, whose pursuits are totally dissimilar—the grain and stock raising portions look with no friendly eye on the cotton planter." Hindman had succeeded all too well. He had so aroused the yeomen to protect their liberties against the Family that now he could not temper their fears of a planter conspiracy arrayed against them and their interests.[64]

The seventy-seven delegates who assembled in Little Rock on March 4 were predominantly middling slaveholders in their thirties and forties drawn to the state by its economic opportunities. Only four were native Arkansans and none had served as governor or in Congress. Given their relative inexperience, the Unionist press cautioned them not to be swayed by the "sensation' rumors" that would be spread to panic them into going for secession. A. H. Carrigan recalled the taunts from the galleries hurled at the Unionists and the excitability of the politicians gathered on the streets with the "adventurers and would-be soldiers."[65]

To the surprise of the secessionists, who expected victory within three weeks, Unionist ranks held firm. In the first test vote, David Walker, an old-line Whig and former justice on the state's highest court, gained the chairmanship by a 40 to 35 vote. Unshakable in his Unionist leanings, Walker kept at bay the secessionists' pressuring tactics. A native of Kentucky raised among slaves, he saw himself as a benevolent paternalist who cared equally well for his slaves and poor white neighbors. Secession, he feared, threatened to shatter the reassuring order of his slave-defined world and unleash the black demon of retribution against kindly masters such as himself. For Walker, secession was unthinkable until every last avenue for maintaining peace had been exhausted.[66]

After two weeks of windy speeches and pro-secession efforts by commissioners from South Carolina and Georgia changed few positions, the Unionists on March 18 voted down a secession resolution. Refusing to admit defeat, secessionists in eastern and southern Arkansas threatened to secede from the rest of the state and join the Confederacy. Although denounced by the Unionists as "a trick of designing politicians" willing to provoke a "home revolution" and plunge the state into its own civil war, the tactic likely induced the Unionist delegates to agree to holding an election in August on secession. The outbreak of war in April

obviated the need for that election, but no cotton state entered the war more bitterly divided against itself than Arkansas.[67]

The Border States: A Strategic Prize

Strung out along the northern rim of the South were the border slave states of
Delaware, Maryland, Kentucky, and Missouri. Though often relegated to a minor
role in the secession crisis, they were vital to the antagonists north and south of
them. They held nearly half of the Southern white population and controlled key
transportation corridors between the Midwest and Northeast. Although slavery
in these states was in a long-term and seemingly terminal decline, its defenders
were adamant in opposing any plans to end the institution. Indeed, their support
for the Union was inseparable from their defense of slavery.[68]

As elsewhere in the South, the uneven geographic distribution of slaves
generated class and regional antagonisms. In Delaware, slaveholders in Sussex,
the southernmost county holding nearly 75 percent of the state's small population of 1,800 slaves in 1860, fought a successful rearguard action against emancipation. Bordered on the south and west by Maryland, distant from the pull of
Philadelphia, and lacking commercial development, Sussex remained frozen in
the economic and cultural moorings of the late eighteenth century. Split east
and west by the Chesapeake Bay, Maryland contained three sub-regions. The
Tidewater counties in southern Maryland held about half of the state's slaves.
Its fertile coastal plain and access to navigable rivers were the foundations for a
continued reliance on tobacco as a cash crop. Across the Chesapeake were the
isolated, farming counties on the Eastern Shore. Slaves comprised 20 percent
of their population, less than half that in the Tidewater, and general farming in
corn, wheat, and oats dominated the sluggish economy. Punctuated by mountains in the northwest, the northern counties had few slaves (less than 5 percent) and enjoyed a thriving rural economy serving markets in Baltimore and
the North. Opportunities abounded for Northern and foreign-born settlers who
shunned the slave regions in the southern counties. Many of them found work in
Baltimore: the nation's third largest city, a major port and manufacturing center,
and a hub for three major railroads.[69]

One in five Kentuckians was enslaved in 1860, the highest percentage of any
border state. The Bluegrass and Pennyroyal regions of central and south-central Kentucky with their fertile soils were home to most of them; all of them
faced the threat of being sold south down the Ohio River by slave-trading
firms in Louisville. The Ohio River counties and Appalachian Kentucky in the
northeast were the whitest in the state. Much as Virginians had brought slaves
into the soon-to-be-state after the Revolutionary War, so too did Kentuckians

along with Tennesseans infiltrate slaves into Missouri. The favored area was nicknamed Little Dixie, a belt of good alluvial soil along the Missouri River in the middle of the state, where hemp and tobacco production thrived. Here, slaveholding was well over twice the levels in the rest of the state. The major exception was New Madrid County, which fronted the Mississippi with its cotton plantations.[70]

Even had they been so inclined, slaveholders in the Border South were too few to mount a sustained campaign for secession. Though in decline, slave owning still conferred social respectability and political clout. In a dreary dialectic that played out in the 1850s, the harder Northerners pushed against slavery, the harder these Southerners pushed back and encased slavery in a protective shell. Once Delaware failed by a single vote in the state senate in 1847 to pass a bill for gradual emancipation, the issue was never seriously discussed again. In 1852, restrictions on free blacks increased with prohibitions against political activity, owning firearms, and testifying against white witnesses in criminal cases. Maryland reworked its state constitution in 1851, eliminating a legislative option to initiate emancipation if both houses of the legislature approved. In another change, apportioning seats in the lower house was to be based on the total population, not the federal ratio, thereby ensuring future dominance by the southern counties with large numbers of slaves. Moderate antislavery politics in Kentucky reached a dead end in 1849 when the legislature revoked an 1833 statute banning the introduction of slaves into the state, and a constitutional convention rejected gradual emancipation. Two years later, the legislature ordered manumitted slaves to leave the state. In Missouri, two proslavery Democrats, Claiborne Fox Jackson and David Atcheson, gained control of state politics from the followers of the antislavery Thomas Hart Benton. The Republican success in St. Louis with a base among free-labor German artisans was an anomaly in a state intent on shoring up slavery against the threat of a free Kansas along its western border.[71]

Numbers often lie, and that seems to have been the case with slavery in the Border South. Percentages of slaves were falling in all the border states in the 1850s. In Delaware and Maryland, the slave population dropped in absolute numbers; in Kentucky, their numbers rose but failed to keep pace with natural increase because of out-of-state sales. Missouri was the outlier. Its slave population increased by 31 percent, but the white population increased even more sharply. Here, despite the antislavery enclave in St. Louis, slavery was in no danger of fading away, and the state's politics were veering toward an aggressive proslavery stance. Elsewhere in the border states, a cluster of factors belied the widespread belief in the cotton states that slavery on its northern rim was doomed to extinction, probably within a few decades.[72]

Slaves made up just 2 percent of Delaware's population in 1860, but the institution was the linchpin of the political power of the state's Democratic Party that had postponed indefinitely any talk of emancipation. In Maryland, a growing number of white laborers were competing for work with the state's large population of free blacks. They were the natural allies of slaveholders in southern Maryland in protecting slavery and closing off any additional competition for jobs. In Kentucky, the defense of property rights merged with praise of slavery as a guarantor of racial peace. And all along the border, especially on the southern banks of the Ohio River, Southern communities decried the threats to their peace and property from the armed clashes over fleeing fugitive slaves. The very vulnerability of slavery made them more determined to safeguard the institution through federal enforcement of the Fugitive Slave Act.[73]

The border states prided themselves on being the great conciliators of the nation's divisions, the balance wheel between clashing sectional interests. As a blend of both, they condemned the extremism in the North and South. Extensive family ties connected border residents with the lower Midwest and the Upper South, and their labor systems melded free workers, white and black, with slaves in the cities and countryside. Partaking of elements of Seward's "irrepressible conflict," but dominated by none of them, they felt they could show the way to national reconciliation. Their politicians had played a critical role in fashioning the Compromise of 1850, and they hoped to do so again.

The would-be compromisers believed that emancipation soon awaited any of their states that seceded. The *Louisville Journal* put it tersely: "The secession of Kentucky would make her a free State as certainly as the enactment of the most effective law of universal emancipation." It mattered not if secession were peaceful. As a Marylander explained for his state, "it could only remain in the South at the price of losing her slave labor," for slaveholders no longer aided by the federal government in capturing runaway slaves would unload their depreciated property onto planters in the Deep South. In the far more likely event of war, "the Potomac must be the line of defense, & [Maryland] would bleed to death without a particle of use to any of her friends or to herself." Expecting the same, a Kentuckian wrote to Lincoln that "all the substantial property Holders in the State are on the side of the Union." He added that "the true Union [men did not] desire for themselves any concessions on the part of the North; they are perfectly satisfied as things are but they want every weapon in the hands of the traitors wrested from them."[74]

Secessionists tried to turn the tables by accusing the border states of hastening the war they wanted to avoid. "If these States had joined the South and presented a solid phalanx as an independent and sovereign nation," argued a Floridian in March, "coercion would never have been contemplated by the Northern government." Resentment tinged by envy marked the views of another Floridian.

Believing that the border states were on the verge of gradual emancipation, he felt it was "no injustice to say that they look forward to emancipation and the sale of their slaves to us as happy escape from the dangers to which all of the slave States are exposed." For good measure, he added that the vacillating states would surely lose slavery if they remained in the Union. A Lexington paper used a variant of the same reasoning. Pouncing in December on a bellicose speech by Republican Ben Wade, the editor pronounced military coercion as all but certain. Acquiescence meant subjecting Southern states to the status of subjugated provinces after "the most fearful war ever undertaken." The only road to peace lay through a united declaration by the border states that they stood "at unit with the South" in resisting any coercion.[75]

Although the secessionists kept hammering away at the issue of coercion and vowed that the border states would never allow Union troops to march across them in a war of conquest, the Unionists remained in charge. Breckinridge had won Delaware and Maryland with a 46 percent plurality, but the Democrats shunned any states' rights extremism. The Whigs had a strong organizational base in Kentucky, a Bell state, and Democratic moderates delivered Missouri to Douglas, the only state he carried. Operating from strength, Unionists launched a campaign around speeches and pamphlets produced by such prominent slaveholders as Robert J. Breckinridge of Kentucky and John Pendleton Kennedy of Maryland to expose the folly of secession. In a major speech on January 4, Robert Breckinridge, the state's foremost Presbyterian minister and nephew of John C. Breckinridge, warned Kentuckians not to follow South Carolina's "reign of lawless passion." He then outlined what they could expect in a confederacy ruled by the cotton interests: "more negroes, more cotton, direct taxes, free imports, from all nations, and the conquest of all outlying lands that will bring cotton." His central theme was that slavery could survive, as it had since the inception of the Union, only in a polity of both free and slave states. To demarcate the "slave line" as the international boundary between a free North and a slave South was to render slavery perpetually insecure and to extinguish it in the Border South. If secession carried out the cotton states, then the "great central states" should stand united to arbitrate a settlement. If their efforts failed, they could form a Middle Confederacy and begin the task of reconstructing the Union and, in time, possibly induce the seceded states to rejoin a Union with firmer guarantees for slavery. In a widely distributed pamphlet, Kennedy, known both for his plantation novels and Whiggish conservatism, focused on the same themes.[76]

Both men favored gradual emancipation and colonization but avoided any moral indictment of slavery in their Unionism. That would not only have been politically divisive, but it was also unnecessary. What Kennedy labeled "the irresistible law of nature" would doom slavery in the border states. The triumph of free over slave labor, he believed, was "remote but certain" in all these states, even more reason not to join a Southern confederacy that would soon cast them out as abolitionists. It would be far better to remain in the Union and buy time for the continuation of slavery.[77]

The Northern allies whom the Unionists counted on to work with them in securing a compromise turned out to be too few and too marginalized to determine Republican policy. The Republicans turned aside all compromise proposals extending the Missouri Compromise line, while the much-ballyhooed Washington Peace Conference found no takers for its proposals outside the Upper South and Lower North. The conference's chances of success were never very good. The seven states that had seceded, along with Arkansas and four Republican states in the upper Midwest, sent no delegates. California and Oregon were in the conservatives' camp but too far away to be represented. The Republicans in attendance were mostly hardliners with no intention of surrendering any of their party's defining principles. In membership and purpose the conference was a meeting of moderates from the Border and Upper South. As such, any agreement it reached was almost certain to be ignored by the two sides that had to be brought together.[78]

While the Mississippi secessionist R. L. Dixon fumed that the conference was a Republican ruse to lull the Upper South into a false sense of security and deprive the South of "the moral force of united action," the delegates slogged through a month of meetings to come up with the underwhelming proposal of dealing with the territorial issue by making it virtually impossible to add any new territories. They recommended an extension of the Missouri Compromise line but with no reference to federal protection of slavery south of the line and a requirement for a four-fifths vote in the Senate for any territorial acquisitions.[79]

A non-expansionist Whig like Jonathan Worth was quite pleased with the recommendation since it meant, if adopted, that "no more territory would be likely to be acquired at all" and sectional harmony could be restored. Aside from Whig conservatives, however, the de facto non-acquisition feature rendered the proposal a dead letter for most Southerners, "a mere mockery" in the language of the *Richmond Enquirer*. The secessionist leaning *Louisville Courier* denounced the plan for effectively denying the South the chance to take slavery into the Caribbean and Central America. As for the Republicans, they saw no need to yield anything. Unsurprisingly, neither house of Congress brought the proposals of the Peace Conference up for a vote.[80]

The Peace Conference was a success in bolstering the odds for Unionist victories in the February elections and keeping their hopes alive in the border states. Proslavery Unionism was deeply rooted in these states and it persisted despite the lack of any progress toward a settlement. All that had been secured was a Republican agreement to send forward to the states a constitutional amendment guaranteeing slavery in the states. Still, the Unionists had kept their secessionist minorities in check. The Unionist governors of Delaware and Maryland prevented any move authorizing a secession convention. Kentucky governor Beriah Magoffin would have welcomed secession, but Whigs and moderate Democrats controlled the legislature and blocked bills calling for a convention. Support for secession came from the slave areas in the Blue Grass and the Jackson Purchase, the counties wedged into the southwestern corner of the state shaped by the nearby Ohio, Tennessee, and Mississippi rivers. Slaveholdings were lighter in the Purchase than in the Blue Grass, but the area's economic orientation was to Southern markets reached via Memphis. Packet boats reached the Tennessee city in half the time of the trip to Louisville, and the only rails to the South ran through Memphis.[81]

Missouri alone held an election for a convention to consider secession. Citing Lincoln's election as an overt act of aggression, Claiborne Fox Jackson, the newly elected governor, called for a convention in his inaugural address. Born in Kentucky to a moderately prosperous tobacco farmer, Jackson became a self-made planter after he moved to Missouri in 1826 with three of his brothers. A hustler who pursued every economic angle for his advancement, he worked with his brothers in a store before gaining entry into an influential family headed by Dr. John Sappington, a wealthy land speculator, money lender, and purveyor of a very popular and profitable patent medicine for fevers, billed as a cure for malaria. Sappington also had three daughters, all of whom Jackson married, replacing one after another as the first two quickly died off.

The Sappington connection he forged in the 1830s was the springboard for Jackson's path to wealth and a political career that saw him serve twelve years in the Missouri House. After leading the effort to unseat Senator Thomas Hart Benton, whom he called out as soft on slavery for not pushing its territorial expansion, Jackson became something of a political pariah for his attacks on one of Missouri's political legends. By 1856, his share of his father-in-law's estate cemented his status as a planter and the uproar over Kansas gave him an issue with which to revive his political fortunes. Using his post as the state's banking commissioner in the late 1850s to knit political loyalties across the state, he built a base for his gubernatorial campaign in 1860. Shrewdly backing Douglas in a bid to court moderate Democrats, he won the race.[82]

Jackson's inaugural address spurred the legislature to action, and it soon approved a convention bill. Forced to accept a provision for a popular ratification of the convention's actions, Jackson won a larger prize when the legislature declared that the state would rush to the defense of any coerced state. Here, in his mind, was a back door to secession that could be opened when needed. Jackson gave no credence to the notion that secession could be achieved peacefully or that Missouri could long remain neutral given its location on the strategically vital Mississippi River. Indeed, he immediately began preparing Missouri for war when he sanctioned the organization of Minute Men and cast covetous eyes on the federal arsenal in St. Louis, the largest in the slave states. War would come, he believed, and in the meantime, there was no need to force the issue on a reluctant state that had given 70 percent of its presidential vote to the moderate candidates, Bell and Douglas, and 80 percent of its vote to Union delegates in the convention election on February 18. The convention overwhelmingly rejected secession, but Jackson's patience was rewarded when Missouri erupted in civil war in the spring.[83]

Unionists in the Upper and Border South kept their states from seceding, but nothing had been settled. Most placed conditions on their allegiance to the Union and were adamantly opposed to any coercive measures to deal with secession. These states might have been stuck in the middle, but their stance masked sharp individual references. As a perceptive young woman in Bowling Green observed of Kentucky, "The policy of the *state* is neutral but the people are not—goodness knows." While Kentucky and other states were in limbo, secessionists from the Lower South put in place a new government whose very existence was unacceptable to the incoming Lincoln administration.[84]

9

The Confederacy

A Slaveholder's Republic

It was as much a grand jubilee as a somber gathering of Southern leaders to fashion a government of their own, the Confederate States of America. The host city of Montgomery was celebrating in anticipation of what was to come as well as what had already been accomplished. The shackles had been removed, and the slave South could now realize its destiny. The convention delegates aimed to take the US Constitution and reshape it to form a government forever safe for slavery. By so doing, they would show a doubting world that only slavery could be the basis for a stable republican government of free white men, one that would confirm the morality of slavery and become the envy of all Christendom. It was a tall order fully in keeping with the hubris of a master class accustomed to command and rule.

Defining Its Mission: From Convention to a Congress

With a population in 1860 of 9,000, half of whom were enslaved, Montgomery served as the state's capital and a trading center for cotton, which was shipped down the Alabama River to Mobile. On the opposite side of the river were the marshes that spawned the mosquitos and periodic yellow fever epidemics. The city spread upward from the river bank with broad, sandy Main Street leading directly to the Capitol perched on a hill. Montgomery was a hard place to reach for the convention, set to begin on February 4. Heavy rains had washed out the Tombigbee River bridge on the rail line from Mississippi and were the culprit in the derailment of the train from West Point, Georgia, with convention-bound delegates from South Carolina and Georgia. City dwellers, to say nothing of arriving delegates, grumbled over the condition of the unpaved streets, which were a pasty sludge of mud. Nonetheless, expectations ran high for the proceedings, assuming, that is, the delegates could decide what it was they were empowered to accomplish.[1]

The convention originated in a resolution introduced in the South Carolina secession convention on December 20 by Robert B. Rhett recommending a meeting of seceding states "to form a Constitution for a Southern Confederacy." A week later, the convention issued a call for a meeting in Montgomery "to agree on the terms of said Confederacy." A provisional constitution, once hammered out, was then to be referred to the states that were represented for their approval or rejection. The other seceding states, however, had a broader vision of what the convention would undertake, and at Montgomery they almost immediately rallied around the "Georgia Plan." As Trescot had insisted to Howell Cobb, it was "imperative . . . to organize a Southern government immediately" and confront the incoming Lincoln administration with a government of its own. Armies had to be raised, revenue obtained, and foreign relations established. The seceding states needed direction and purpose: "Wield them together while they are hot."[2]

Such was the intent of the Georgians at Montgomery. They wanted the convention to act as a congress, a ruling body with the power to draft a provisional constitution and government, elect a president and vice-president, and enact

THE CITY OF MONTGOMERY, ALABAMA, SHOWING THE STATE HOUSE WHERE THE CONGRESS OF THE SOUTHERN CONFEDERACY MEETS ON FEBRUARY 4, 1861.

Fig. 9.1 The City of Montgomery. Elevated at the crest of a broad street leading up from the river, the Alabama state house was the site of the Confederate Convention. Library of Congress, LC-USZ62-132567.

all the laws of governance necessary to make the president an effective leader. The only other plan was that of Wiley P. Harris of Mississippi. It was simple and direct: elect a president (understood to be Jefferson Davis) for a provisional government, accept in toto the federal constitution, and designate the seceding states' congressional representatives as delegates to a convention to take up the issue of a permanent constitution and governing structure. To delay the creation of a new government left too much up in the air, and the Georgia approach prevailed.[3]

Rhett opposed both plans. As far as he was concerned, the only authorized business of the convention was to adopt a provisional constitution for the consideration of the states and give way to the state conventions to select their delegates to a new convention entrusted with forming a permanent Confederacy. What right, he asked, did the convention have to usurp the prerogatives of the states by choosing delegates to a new convention? Just as monstrous was Mississippi's plan of adopting without change the federal constitution and opening the door to what Rhett feared most, the reconstruction of the Union. Voicing his displeasure through the reports of the *Mercury*'s convention correspondent, Rhett imagined the very worst. Once the non-cotton slave states joined the Confederacy, the divisive issues of internal improvements and protection for home industries would rear their heads. The new states would continue to turn whiter and be more open to gradual emancipation as they sold off slaves to cotton planters. With the original federal constitution in force, the possibility could not be ruled out that more conservative Northern states would be added, resulting in a de facto reconstruction. Thus, "After all, we will have run round a circle, and end up where we started." The Georgia plan was even more objectionable to Rhett since it assumed for the convention powers not expressly granted by the states, the only legitimate avenue for forging a permanent Confederacy in his rigid state's rights view. However, the Georgia approach had the great advantage of pushing ahead at once with the great task at hand. With no backing from the South Carolina delegation, one dominated by the cooperationists of 1850–51, Rhett admitted defeat. He was headstrong but no fool.[4]

The stress on speed also accounted for the overwhelming consensus in favor of the Georgia plan. Few wanted to waste time by awaiting individual state approval of a provisional government. Besides, given the divisions over secession outside South Carolina, they simply did not trust a fickle electorate. The delegates were, after all, the cream of the South's leadership class with a wealth of legislative experience and intellectual training. Who, but they, were best equipped to secure the revolution by framing a new government?[5]

Once Howell Cobb was elected by acclamation as the convention's president on February 4, 1861, the delegates turned to the task of meeting, as Robert H. Smith of Alabama put it, the "common exigency" that had brought them together, the looming threat of a Republican administration intent on retaking the seized forts, enforcing all revenue laws, and coercing the "subjugation of our people." After deciding to hold most of their sessions in secret (following the model of the Constitutional Convention of 1787) and to constitute themselves as a congress with lawmaking powers, the delegates appointed a committee to draft a provisional constitution. Again, Rhett found that his revolution was being hijacked. [6]

The committee completed most of its work by February 6. They adopted verbatim nearly all the text of the federal constitution since, as the secessionists repeatedly said, the quarrel was not with the Constitution but its misuse by abolitionists and Northern economic interests. These enemies of the South had read into the Constitution powers to attack slavery and funnel taxpayers' money through protective tariffs into the hands of Northern manufacturers at the expense of the agrarian South. Patronage also had to be curbed, for it corrupted politics with a lust for office and replaced statesmen with dispensers of spoils.

Leaving aside for the permanent constitution the issue of how the Confederate Congress was to be constituted, the framers focused on the two areas of fiscal policy and slavery. To shut down special interest groups and the squandering of public monies, a lid of 15 percent was placed on import duties; appropriations for internal improvements had to originate in a request from the president or the cabinet heads. The importation of "African slaves" from any foreign country was prohibited, and Congress was required to pass laws to enforce that prohibition. Also barred, at the discretion of Congress, was the entry of slaves from states not part of the Confederacy. A slightly modified version of the Fugitive Slave Act of 1850 dealt with the issue of runaways.

The key changes made by the convention in the draft proposal pertained to finance. To impose greater fiscal restraint, a line-item veto was given to the president to eliminate what today are known as earmarks. As a concession to those who favored free trade, the 15 percent cap on import duties was dropped in favor of a revenue tariff to meet the expenses of the government. Added to the preamble was the phrase "invoking the favor of Almighty God," a bow to the religious sensibilities of an evangelical society. Anxious to move on to the election of a president, the delegates approved the provisional constitution on February 8.[7]

The choice for president narrowed down to Davis or Toombs. Howell Cobb had the credentials despite an appearance that struck one convention reporter as that of "a fat, pussy, round-faced, jolly looking fellow." He had his backers but professed not to want the post, and many still begrudged him for standing by the Union in the crisis of 1850–51. Pointedly, the delegates ignored the most noted fire-eaters, Rhett and Yancey. Unlike Cobb, Toombs wanted the presidency. Big, brawny, and bold, he was a charismatic figure seemingly cut out for greatness.

A native Georgian, he moved from law to politics and, along with his close friend Stephens, headed the Georgia Whigs in the 1840s and into the early 1850s before taking his state's rights views into the Democratic Party. Success came easily to him and fed an overweening confidence in his abilities that was his major weakness. He could be brilliant one minute and outlandish the next. He never did tame his excesses or fondness for alcohol that cast doubts on his steadiness in a time of crisis. No one doubted his commitment to the Confederacy, but they did challenge his qualifications for the presidency after his inebriated outbursts at several functions early in the convention. Stephens had "little doubt" that Toombs would have been chosen president had he not gotten "drunk to excess" two days before the election.[8]

With a steely resolve that locked him up tighter than a drum, Davis was the opposite of Toombs. A reporter aptly described him in 1861 as "a prim, smooth-looking man, with a precise manner, a stiff, soldierly carriage, and an austerity that is at first forbidding." He had not always been so stern. This son of a Kentucky farmer spent most of his youth on his older brother Joseph's plantations in Louisiana and Mississippi. Joseph had arranged Davis's appointment to West Point, where his prankish behavior led to two court-martial charges. During his six years in the army he again faced charges of insubordination that were dismissed. While stationed at Fort Jefferson in the Michigan Territory, he met and fell in love with Sarah Knox Taylor, the daughter of General Zachary Taylor. Not wanting Sarah to become an army wife, Taylor forbade their marriage. Refusing to give up Sarah, Davis resigned his commission and the couple was married at her aunt's home in Louisville. On the day of the marriage, Sarah wrote her mother that the wedding date had come sooner than expected because she had heard that "the part of the Country to which I am going is quite healthy" (and hence there was no need to wait for cooler weather). The optimism was unwarranted. Either at Davis's Briarfield plantation in Mississippi or his sister's plantation in West Feliciana, Louisiana, where they had moved in August to be farther away from the floodplain of the Delta, they both came down with a fever, malaria or yellow fever. Delirious and bedridden, Davis learned of Sarah's death only after his recovery. Davis was devastated, and something died in him with Sarah's passing. Gone was the spontaneity and joy in the simpler pleasures of life. Here was the likely source of the compulsion for order and the need for rigid self-control. Stung by the rumors of a "runaway marriage" and burdened with the guilt of Sarah's death, he became a martyr to her memory.[9]

For the better part of the next ten years, Davis retreated to the seclusion of his Briarfield home, seeing virtually no one and immersing himself in plantation affairs and weighty tomes in history and political theory. His marriage in 1845 to Varina Howell, who at eighteen was half his age, marked his return to public life, and his distinguished military service in the Mexican War sent him to the

US Senate. A defensive carapace shielded the private from the public figure. He allowed himself to relax only in the company of non-threatening dependents: his wife, children, and slaves. For all his reserve, his public service embodied just the strengths needed for the presidency of the Confederacy. Safe on Southern rights but no fire-eater, he combined military experience with a first-rate administrative record as secretary of war under Franklin Pierce. Nearly every state delegation's second choice, Davis easily gained the presidency when the favorite sons dropped out of the race.[10]

Little drama surrounded the selection of Stephens as vice-president. Georgia had to be compensated for neither Toombs nor Cobb getting the top prize, and Whigs who had opposed secession had to be assured of a voice in the administration. Moreover, Stephens could help win over still unconvinced Southern Unionists. As the *Augusta Chronicle* stated in its support of the nomination: "Disguise it as we may, the greatest danger to the new confederacy arises, not from without, not from the North, but *from our* own people." Indeed, it noted the possibility of "*armed opposition to the new order of things in . . . parts of Southern States* not vitally interested in the Slavery question." The oblique reference was to non-slaveholders in the mountains.[11]

A Permanent Constitution: Making It Safe for Slavery

On February 11, a committee of twelve began work on a permanent constitution. As had the framers of the provisional constitution, they began with the US Constitution and made what appear to be merely minor changes. But the devil is in the details. They produced a new document designed to eliminate the flaws in the original deemed responsible for the collapse of the Union.

Everyone agreed with Smith of Alabama that the late Union had "dissolved . . . because of the negro quarrel." Their paramount goal was to ensure that such a quarrel could never destroy their new republic. Where the US Constitution had approached slavery indirectly, refraining even from mentioning the word, the Confederate Constitution met it head-on, specifically and proudly proclaiming its permanent protection for slavery. Prohibited was any "law denying or impairing the right of property in negro slaves." In a speech in Atlanta, Benjamin Hill emphasized the significance of the changes for the safety of slavery. "*No State-laws can say that property in slavery does not exist or shall not be respected.*" Congressional legislation was to recognize and protect slavery in all Confederate territories. Guarantees were set down for the right of slaveholders to pass through or sojourn with their slaves in any state of the Confederacy.[12]

Retained from the provisional constitution was the prohibition of the foreign slave trade. The issue had lost its political value in agitating sectional issues,

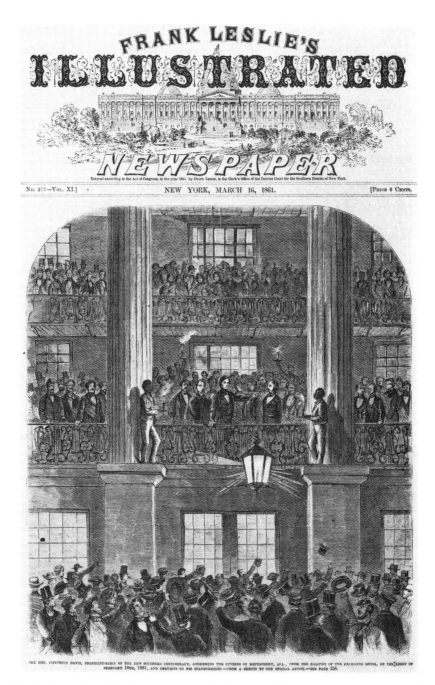

Fig. 9.2 Davis Speaks in Montgomery. A few days before his inauguration as president of the Confederacy, Davis addressed the citizens of Montgomery from the footsteps of the Exchange Hotel. Library of Congress, LC-USZ62-109704.

and most Southern whites found the trade morally repulsive. "Nine tenths of the people are opposed to it," wrote T. R. R. Cobb. The prohibition strengthened the case for secession as disinterested statesmanship, unsullied by any "goal of gain" and simultaneously helped prop up the value of preexisting slave property. With the natural increase of slaves running at about 25 percent per decade, only the most doctrinaire proslavery ideologues saw any need for fresh imports from Africa. Without the ban, the issue was sure to come up in the Confederate Congress, and that would open, in Smith's words, "a Pandora's box" that he and others did not want touched. Nor were many prepared to antagonize Britain by trying to reopen a trade the British were using their navy to stamp out. The only dissension in the convention broke out over a failed effort to lower the punishment for smuggling slaves from a felony to a "high misdemeanor."[13]

The final version of the African slave trade bill provided for the disposing of illegally imported Africans. It outlined a sequence of steps for the president to undertake. He first was to return "said negroes" to the state of entry on the condition that they were to be freed. If this was rejected by the state, he then was to seek out individuals who at their expense would transport the slaves back to Africa where their freedom would be granted. If he found no such individuals, he was to arrange the sale of the slaves at public auction to the highest bidder with the proceeds of the sale paid in equal amounts to the informer on the prohibited importation and the Confederate treasury department. Two days later on February 28, Davis issued his first veto on the grounds that the sale of imported slaves was clearly unconstitutional and evaded the intent of the prohibition on the African slave trade. Congress sustained the veto with only a radical faction centered in South Carolina, Georgia, and Florida voting to override it.[14]

In addition to specific safeguards for slavery, the permanent constitution shielded the institution from the distributive policies of protective tariffs and subsidies the delegates believed had built up the power of Northern manufacturing and commercial interests at the expense of the South. The social consequence of those policies was the rapid growth of a class of white workers and immigrants who were thought to be the ready tools of antislavery Northern politicians. To stanch the rise of class interests inimical to slavery, the Confederate Constitution forbade tariffs targeted to benefit particular branches of industry and appropriations of internal improvements "intended to facilitate commerce." The president's line-item veto was another check on profligate spending for special interests. By privileging slave-based agriculture, frugal spending was another means to keep slavery safe.[15]

For the secessionists, political parties were the vehicle that had turned class interests against slavery. They had been, in Hill's phrase, "the means by which power was to be secured." Driven by power-hungry partisans, the parties prostituted themselves by offering patronage positions in exchange for support in winning the presidency. If patronage, the life blood of parties, was shut off, then virtuous statesmen dedicated to the public good would replace corrupt spoilsmen. With that goal in mind, the Confederate Constitution limited the president to a single six-year term. Having no incentive to attract followers for his reelection, presumably he would place the country's interests above his own. Sharp limits were also placed on the vast appointive powers the president enjoyed under the old Constitution. He now had to show cause for the removal of his appointees below the level of cabinet and diplomatic ranks. In effect, tenure by good behavior would protect officeholders from partisan removals. The intended result was a purified government that left no room for antislavery parties to form.[16]

Southerners had invoked state's rights in the old Union when deemed necessary to protect slavery. In an independent South, no such necessity existed, and the Confederate Constitution treated state's rights as a handmaiden to a nation-state that had the power of the US government and then some. State's rights received only a general affirmation and a reworded preamble to the constitution specifying that each of the states was acting in its "sovereign and independent character" to form "a permanent government." When state's righters sought to insert the right of nullification and secession into the new Constitution, the pragmatists in charge easily rebuffed them. Aside from cosmetic changes in phrasing catering to state's rights and the right of a state to bring impeachment charges against a Confederate official whose duties rested entirely within that state, the framers crafted a national government equipped to defend slavery in peace or war. With a president empowered in wartime to override state's rights and call out and command a national army, set budget priorities, and initiate government support for manufacturing and transportation projects, the Confederacy had a nation-state in place for the war to come.[17]

The committee finished its work on February 24. 1861, and reported to the convention on February 27. The debates largely rehashed those in the committee of twelve, and no substantive changes were made to the committee's draft. The thorniest issue was the admission of new states. In keeping with their belief that economic self-interest ruled all, many delegates convinced themselves that the offer of free navigation on the Mississippi, coupled with the lower costs for their imports under the Confederate tariff, would draw in states from the lower Midwest. Even the Pacific Coast might be part of the Confederacy. At the Mississippi secession convention, A. M. Clayton sketched a grandiose scheme in which "the gold mines of California" and ports for trade with the Far East would add to the wealth and influence of the Confederacy. Alarmed by the prospect of any free-soil contagion, the South Carolinians backed Rhett in banning any free states. Once Stephens, with a nod from Davis, led a successful fight to keep the option open, Rhett and his followers had to settle for the requirement of a two-thirds vote for adding new states.[18]

There was no debate over how the constitution was to be ratified. That was to be taken out of the hands of the people and entrusted to the state conventions. The secessionists' margin of victory was too thin in Georgia and Alabama to run the risk of another election. The Alabama convention, the first to ratify, rejected proposals from the cooperationists for ratification either by a newly elected convention or a simple vote of the people. For James Clark from Lawrence County, the issue was the right of "the people [to] govern themselves . . . , the great fundamental law of all free governments." The majority, however, wanting to act quickly so as to prepare for a possible war, agreed with L. M. Stone of Pickens that "we have no time to delay." The cooperationist stepped aside. The vote was 89 to 5.[19]

Only in the South Carolina convention did the Confederate Constitution provoke much criticism. With its usual hyperbole, the *Mercury* warned in mid-February that the Confederate Constitution would soon saddle South Carolina "with almost every grievance except Abolition, for which she has long struggled, and just withdrawn from the late United States Government." For many lowcountry planters, that indictment rang true. Led by Leonidas Spratt, the hard-shell radicals in the lowcountry denounced the constitution for maintaining the stigma of the prohibition of the African slave trade and failing to guarantee that non-slaveholding states would be kept out. In making his case, Spratt argued that the Confederacy was setting itself up for another revolution.[20]

Spratt viewed secession as the inevitable result of what Seward had defined as an "irrepressible conflict" between two distinct and antagonistic societies. In the white "pure democracy" of the North, antislavery politicians were merely following popular will in proclaiming the equality of men. In the biracial South directed by a social aristocracy, equality was the right only of those with an equal station in life. Resting upon universal suffrage and "pauper labor with power of rising," Northern society was inherently unstable and prone to upheaval. The South with its large class of politically disfranchised slaves was a model of harmony. For Spratt, the great divergence had come with the closing of the African slave trade starting in the late eighteenth century. Though superior because of its docility, malleability, and productivity under the guidance of a master white race, slave labor lost out in the North because of the cheapness of a ready supply of nominally free workers. Northerners sold off their slaves to the South and fell prey to reform "isms" and a hatred of slavery. The Confederacy, Spratt believed, would suffer the same fate. The border slave states were slowly turning to plans of emancipation, and even South Carolina was losing slaves to newer cotton states and facing threats to the institution from a horde of immigrants in Charleston. The process of destabilizing slavery was irreversible unless the

Confederacy seized its destiny and removed the absolute ban on the foreign slave trade, thereby converting non-slaveholders, the natural enemies of slavery, into its best friend by supplying them with cheap slaves they could afford. Only by acknowledging that "slavery is the normal constitution of society" and acting on that conviction could the Confederacy hope to survive intact.[21]

Spratt was a quite logical product of proslavery thought, but he was written off as an incurable crank much like Rhett was seen as a radical rabble-rouser. The Southern press brushed aside the *Mercury's* complaints as revealing "an inordinate disposition for public notoriety." By a vote of 138 to 21, the convention ratified the Confederate Constitution over the objections of Spratt and such lowcountry holdouts as Charles Manigault and John Izard Middleton. The need for unity was too great to allow much space for doubters. Political realism ruled at Montgomery as the delegates committed themselves to bringing in all factions under the umbrella of the Confederacy.[22]

Moderates in Control: Staking Out a Middle Ground

As Stephens observed, "No body looking in would ever take that Congress to be a set of Revolutionists." Experienced in wielding power and intent on projecting an image of moderation, the delegates gave a cold shoulder to the fire-eaters and their cherished designs for the Confederacy. Thomas R. R. Cobb, a star at the Georgia convention, was ignored at Montgomery. His utopian expectation that God's hand would guide the delegates along the path of pure-minded statesmanship gave way to bitter disillusionment. "Marion it is sickening," he vented. "I had the folly to believe that there was great patriotism in this movement. God help us. It looks now as if it was nothing but office seeking." Hardest for him to swallow was the election of Stephens, a near-traitor to Southern rights in his eyes, to the vice-presidency. Although Rhett spoke out a great deal and chaired the committees on the permanent constitution and foreign relations, he lost out on what he most coveted, the presidency. Adding to his disappointment, he was passed over for an administrative position. Fearing his extremism and outbursts of anger, Yancey's legion of enemies denied him a place in the Alabama delegation.[23]

The radicals dreamed of an agrarian republic free from any threat of working-class discontent and the competing demands of manufacturing interests. To achieve it, they sought free trade as the centerpiece of the Confederacy's economic program. The privilege of duty-free imports, asserted "Mercator," would give all the European powers the strongest possible reasons to immediately recognize the Confederacy. The North would be compelled to lower its tariff, and the truth would come out that the North's vaunted prosperity rested on its protective tariff and "not the superior economy and virtue of white slavery over black." Gazaway B. Lamar, a planter, cotton trader, and co-founder of the New York Bank of the Republic, preached the gospel of free trade to Howell Cobb throughout the winter of 1860–61. "Whilst the South can rule Europe and New England by cotton," he predicted, "she can by free trade explode all the power of the rest of the Union." Europe would be bonded to the Confederacy, the revenue stream of the North blown up, and New York City sent into the lap of the Confederacy to protect its financial interests.[24]

For all its appeal, free trade defied economic and political reality. Based on the assumption of peace and foreign recognition, it ignored the costs of the military buildup under way at Montgomery. With but negligible revenue from a tariff, direct taxation was the only other major source of funds, but as Keitt noted, "Direct taxation would ruin us." Southerners "would sooner give ten dollars which they have never seen, than one they have had in their pockets." Despite Gazaway Lamar's contention that the people were intelligent enough to prefer being taxed than overrun by the abolitionists, direct taxation found few backers.[25]

Free trade also posed a fatal blow to the manufacturing base that had emerged in the Upper South and in pockets of the original Confederate states. The Whig press, which had always favored economic diversification, pointed out that the South had opposed a tariff because it benefited the North. But now the South would be the beneficiary. A tariff would promote manufacturing, the only permanent basis of any nation's prosperity; pay off the public debt; and eliminate the need to borrow from foreigners. Newcomers would be drawn to the Confederacy by factory work and slaves pushed back to where they belonged in the cotton fields. No one was completely satisfied in the end, but the adoption of the federal tariff of 1857 served as a stopgap measure (formally passed in May). In beating back efforts to significantly lower the rates of 1857, Toombs cited the absolute need to finance the military.[26]

Over the objections of the agrarian purists, the moderates kept the door open for the addition of the non-cotton slave states. South Carolina did not want them. Why import the old economic divisions and debates over slavery that had plagued the old Union asked the *Mercury*. Gazaway Lamar made the same argument, adding that the slave states still in the Union would make "a very good barrier to stand between the South and the North." Thomas Cobb felt so strongly about holding the line at the seven original states that one paper derided him for "clinging to the illusion of a pure slavocracy." Such an illusion would prove fatal in case of war, and the delegates did no more than threaten a congressional ban on importing slaves from non-Confederate states.[27]

The delegates were careful to dampen the charge that they were stripping liberties from non-slaveholders. Many planters viewed the crisis as an opportunity to wring democratic excesses out of Southern politics, but they were divided over the issue of a consolidated nation-state. George Fitzhugh, the eccentric proponent of slavery for both races, saw the "necessity of more and stronger government." However, he wanted that power entrusted to the states, including lengthening the tenure of office and blocking the masses from direct access to power, so as not to have government controlled by "their hasty, capricious impulses and seditious spirit." Simms, the South Carolina radical, hoped that the Confederate Constitution would return to the principle of absolute state equality embodied in the Articles of Confederation. For the former filibusterer J. Quitman Moore of Mississippi, the Confederacy had to be a militarized, unitary state to fulfill its mission of imperial expansion. Landed interests were to be given permanent representation, the Senate made hereditary, and the president removed from "the petty passion of politics." Fears of "old party spirits" also haunted the editorials in Georgia's premier Whig paper, the *Augusta Chronicle and Sentinel*. Dreading disorder or anarchy, the paper wistfully praised rule by monarchy, citing Brazil as an example of a successful breakaway slave country. More practically, the paper called for a chief executive elected for life and longer terms of office to deter demagogues.[28]

The delegates were certainly of a conservative bent, but they had enough sense not to roil the masses, whose support was needed more than ever. A call for full representation of slaves, a pet project of Keitt and Rhett, elicited mostly shrugs of disbelief. The delegates placed no curbs on the people's powers, and they retained the guarantee of individual liberties in the US Constitution. What was curbed was the availability of patronage to feed political parties. The citizenship features of the federal constitution were kept and a provision made for a future Congress to pass "uniform laws of naturalization." Congress never did, and the only avenue for citizenship for foreigners was service in the Confederate army. New state constitutions codified the exclusion of blacks from citizenship and nibbled away at former democratic reforms. Rebuffing both the radical state's righters and reactionary conservatives, the framers at Montgomery stressed the comfort of continuity, not the extreme measures that would raise the specter of a military despotism. That image of the Confederacy awaited the implementation of its considerable war powers.[29]

Forming a Functional Government

Davis's trip from Briarfield to Montgomery was a reminder, if he needed any, of the problems awaiting him as the Confederate president. Although Montgomery was only about 225 miles due east from Jackson, gaps in the South's rail system forced him to take a much longer, circuitous route. A steamboat carried him to

Vicksburg and then a train to Jackson. From there, he traveled north to Grand Junction, Mississippi, and then northeast to Chattanooga and south to Atlanta, approaching Montgomery from the east. It would have been more direct to go from Washington to Montgomery.

Along the way, he gave speeches to well-wishers anxious to hear from their new leader. His message was calming but firm. He expected the other slave states to join the Confederacy within ninety days, and he anticipated speedy recognition from England of the new Southern nation. Expansion into the West Indies and northern Mexico, forbidden in the former Union, was now a likely prospect. Although the Confederacy would offer peace and commercial relations with the North, if war came, the South would fiercely defend itself. Repeating the central conceit of the secessionists that Southerners were the innocent party, he regretted that they had been driven to secession by "hell bent fanaticism." On his arrival in Montgomery, he tried to put to rest rumors that he was a reconstructionist: "Our separation from the old Union is complete, no compromise, no reconstruction will now be entertained."[30]

Davis's Inaugural Address on February 18 ideologically aligned the Confederacy with the aims of the Founding Fathers. The new president was appealing to the considerable number of Southerners deeply pained by their separation from a Union they had always cherished. He assured them that the Confederate Constitution differed "from that of our fathers [only] in so far as it is explanatory of their well-known intent." Secession, in his reading, had been achieved by "peaceful resort to the ballot box" in which Southerners acted on the same inalienable right of self-government that had galvanized the overthrow of British rule. All Southerners had done was to redeem the original virtues of the Constitution of 1787 from being perverted by the North. It was only "by abuse of language that their act had been denominated a revolution." He was confident that if war came, posterity would recognize that it was not because of "wrong on our part [but] by wanton aggression on the part of others."[31]

Davis told Southern whites what they wanted to hear. Stephens told them what they already knew. Always his own man, Stephens laid to rest Davis's creation myth with his "Cornerstone Speech" in Savannah on March 21. The title comes from his unblinking stress on the maintenance of slavery and white supremacy as the foundational purpose of the Confederacy. The great error of the Founding Fathers, he said, was their belief that slavery was wrong and racial equality was right. That belief had produced Northern fanaticism on the slavery question, "a species of insanity," which had forced the South to secede. Proudly and unequivocally, the Confederacy corrected that error. "Our new government is founded upon exactly the opposite ideas; its foundations are laid, its cornerstone rests upon the great truth that the negro is not equal to the white man; that slavery, subordination to the superior race, is his natural and normal

Fig. 9.3 The Dis-United States: or the Confederacy—For all its show of unity, the Confederacy was comprised of states with disparate interests. Library of Congress, LC-USZ-92048.

condition." For Stephens, racial unity was the bond that would knit together the Confederacy. In a slightly different version of his speech a few days later in Augusta, he fretted that there were "many even in the South . . . still in the shell upon this subject." He allayed his fears over internal disunity by confidently predicting that soon these doubters, as well as the rest of the world, would recognize the "great truth" of innate black inferiority.[32]

While Stephens was promoting the politics of race, Davis was busy with organizational politics. He first turned to forming a cabinet composed of the heads of the six authorized executive departments. Attempting to soothe the wounded pride of the radicals, who had been out of favor ever since their states seceded, he offered Yancey a choice of cabinet positions. Feeling that such service in a government dominated by latecomers to the great cause he had long championed would be demeaning, Yancey followed the advice of his friends and declined. He left his meeting with Davis with an understanding that he would be first in line for a diplomatic posting to demand foreign recognition. Rhett was in Congress, and Davis was content to leave him there. For the most prestigious office, secretary of state, and the one Rhett wanted, Davis selected Robert Barnwell, who had steered the South Carolina delegation to support Davis for the presidency. In declining, Barnwell suggested Christopher G. Memminger to head the treasury. Knowing that South Carolina had to be represented in the cabinet, Davis acted on the suggestion and Memminger quickly accepted. Georgia received the state department with the selection of Robert Toombs. The war department, the other top post, went to the only pronounced secessionist in the original cabinet, Leroy P. Walker of Alabama, "an unflinching member of the States Rights party." Rounding out the cabinet were the suave Louisianan Judah P. Benjamin as attorney general, Stephen Mallory of Florida as secretary of navy, and John Reagan of Texas as postmaster general. Benjamin was the ablest of the three and became one of Davis's closest advisers. Though their selections raised hackles because of their pronounced moderation during secession, Mallory and Reagan were loyal and more than competent.[33]

Even more pressing than forming a cabinet was Davis's need to restrain the firebrands in Charleston. Governor Pickens, never graceful under pressure, was on the verge of giving in to the state militia and ordering an attack on Fort Sumter. His reasoning, such as it was, boiled down to the argument that Buchanan was powerless to respond and that Lincoln, faced with Sumter in Confederate hands, "may not attack because the cause of the quarrel will have been, or may be, considered by him as past." He informed Howell Cobb on February 12 that "I am perfectly satisfied that the welfare of the new confederates and the necessities of the State [South Carolina] require that Fort Sumter should be reduced before the close of the present administration at Washington." On entering office, Davis was alarmed by a report from John Tyler, former president turned secessionist, that the attack would occur before March 4.[34]

Counseling Pickens, who was desperate to avoid the disgrace of seemingly backing away from a fight, Davis reminded him that the Confederacy was "poorly prepared for war." It would be better by far to be patient and build up military strength "to render the inequality as small as it can be made." More sternly, he reminded Pickens that only the Confederate government, not the state of South Carolina, had the constitutional authority to decide on peace or war, and that the governor lacked the military experience and technical knowledge to make an informed decision about Fort Sumter. The dispatch of a Confederate engineer to supervise the harbor defenses and, by March 1, General Pierre G. T. Beauregard to assume command of the forces in Charleston tamped down Pickens's jitters. Also in late February, Davis appointed a three-man commission to travel to Washington to negotiate a peaceful transfer of remaining federal possessions in the Confederate states, as well as other outstanding issues between what Confederates considered two separate nations. The selection of the commissioners, moderates all, confirmed for Tom Cobb that the "best claim to distinction under the existing regime seems to be either to have opposed secession or have done nothing for it."[35]

As Davis dealt with the thankless task of trying to satisfy a swarm of office seekers for civil and military positions, Toombs, Memminger, and Walker turned to pressing issues in formulating foreign policy and raising money and troops. On February 13, the Congress authorized sending three envoys to England, France, and other European nations to gain recognition and negotiate commercial treaties. Davis had no diplomatic experience, and it showed in his appointments. Yancey, whose combustible political instincts were the antithesis of negotiating tact, headed the team. A. Dudley Mann of Virginia had served in the state department and Europe in the 1850s but was known more for his garrulousness than for securing results. The only qualification of Pierre Rost of Louisiana was his French birth. The envoys received no help from Toombs's instructions. They were told to stress the non-revolutionary nature of the Confederacy, its undeniable existence as a nation, and desire for peace and commerce. Then, in a jarring juxtaposition that claimed the mantle of the revolutionary liberalism of European nationalist yearnings, Toombs identified the Confederacy with Sicily and Naples, whose bolt for independence from the Italian monarchy had been recognized by Britain. The Confederacy's prohibition of the African slave trade was to be noted as well as the importance of Southern cotton to the British economy. Striking at what he thought was England's weak spot, he authorized the envoys to make a "delicate allusion" to the possibility of a cotton embargo. Missing in the instructions were any concrete inducements to favor the Confederacy, such as guarantees for free entry to Confederate ports and minimalist tariff duties. These were all details that had to be worked out as a precondition to any possible recognition. Toombs had put the cart before the horse.[36]

The Confederate economy was on shaky grounds in late February. In a brutal assessment of its weaknesses, the *London Times* noted that Southern securities of all kinds were badly depreciated, business was at a standstill, food scarce, and capital "flying" out. It concluded that "the Slave Confederation must commence its existence amid something like bankruptcy." Structuring a sound financial policy would have taxed anyone and broken many. Memminger fell in between. An onlooker at Montgomery fairly characterized him as "a self-made man, who had managed the finances of his State and had made a reputation for some financial ability and much common sense." His policies were generally sound but lacked the boldness to serve as anything more than a band-aid on a steadily hemorrhaging problem. Above all, he too readily assumed an extended period of peace. A loan of $500,000 in specie seized from US vaults and the custom house in New Orleans provided the treasury with its first infusion of cash. On February 28, Congress floated a loan of $15 million to fund the military and approved an export tax of one-eighth a cent per pound of cotton to repay it.[37]

Although immediate needs had been met, no provisions were made for the contingencies of war, which would necessitate a vastly expanded revenue stream for the government. Cotton could not be shipped abroad to build up reserves for loans since the Confederacy had few ships and most of the 1860 crop had already been sold. A sound basis for government credit required hard assets—specie and cotton—and heavy taxes were needed to prevent deficit financing from igniting runaway inflation. Forced borrowings from the banks to be paid back with bonds and treasury notes (paper money) would have formed a basis for a specie reserve available for purchasing cotton, beginning with the crop of 1861. Elements of such a policy, one tantamount to a nationalization of the economy, were resorted to later in the war, too late to reverse the financial death spiral. That they were not implemented in 1861 or 1862 is a stark reminder of the non-revolutionary posture of Confederate politicians fearful of the backlash taxes would provoke and of planters who viewed the new nation as serving their interests and not the other way around. Memminger knew that the Confederacy could not finance a war on the cheap, but he was not a forceful advocate of his views, which, in any event, lacked the urgency required.[38]

Secretary of War Leroy Walker had little military experience. His credentials came down to his family's power base in Alabama politics. Though his friends thought he would buckle under the pressure, he gamely learned on the fly. The organization of the war department lurched forward, with Davis constantly looking over Walker's shoulder and making many of the key decisions. After authorizing a provisional army on February 28, the Congress soon upped the number of volunteers who would be accepted to 100,000. The committee in charge of the military bill initially proposed six-month volunteers. Explaining its reasoning to Davis, Francis Bartow, the committee chair, felt confident that short enlistments would speedily raise enough men to deter any Northern aggression. Realizing that he was dealing with amateurs, Davis pointed out that six months was barely enough time to turn raw recruits into passable soldiers. He told Bartow that if war came, it would be a very long one, and he wanted three-year volunteers. They compromised at twelve months.[39]

Arming and equipping the army were formidable tasks. The first troops available were in state militia units and had to be requisitioned from the governors for placement in the national army. Walker and Davis sent agents to the North to purchase arms, but nearly all the weapons, as well as the troops, were in the individual states. Since the commissary and quartermaster departments were very slow to reach an operational stage, women had to step into the breach and supply the volunteers with food and clothing.

By early April, the army numbered, at least on paper, about 60,000 men. Its deployment reflected the strategic thinking of Davis and his top officers, most of them West Pointers who had resigned their commissions in the US Army. Troops were patrolling the Mississippi River, the Indian frontier, and the Rio Grande border with Mexico. Approaches to Mobile and New Orleans were under guard. The largest concentrations were around Fort Pickens in Pensacola and Fort Sumter in Charleston. Davis and Walker had their army in place, but its mobilization had produced the first cracks in the anticipated political harmony of the Confederacy.[40]

State's Rights Rears Its Head: The Confederacy and the Governors

In the interval between the secession of the states and the formation of the Confederacy, the state governors saw themselves as heads of sovereign nation-states whose duties included sending commissioners to Europe to seek foreign recognition of their independent republics and to negotiate trading relations. They also took seriously their duty to protect their citizens. They were loyal Confederates but not pliant tools of the central government when they felt the vital interests of their states were at stake. Protection for their citizens required raising troops and arms, and these they had under their authority in the late winter. They were not about to just hand them over to the war department and lose control of them.[41]

Beginning in the summer of 1860, Brown of Georgia and Moore of Alabama were particularly aggressive in purchasing arms with state funds. A prime source was the federal government, and Secretary of War Floyd was an all too willing seller. J. R. Powell, appointed by Moore as the state's munitions purchasing agent, procured some $46,000 worth of arms, including cannons, gun carriages, and caissons. Once the Northern press became aware of his activities, he was called back to Alabama. Many thought Floyd guilty of treason when in December he ordered (countermanded by Buchanan and Black) heavy cannons from the Pittsburgh foundry in Pennsylvania to be shipped down the Mississippi to forts in Texas. By early January, few guns were to be had in the Washington market. A disappointed buyer of Maynard Rifles for a cavalry company in Adams County, Mississippi, learned that Jefferson Davis, under Pettus's orders, had bought them up, 800 in all. The buyer asked Pettus to reserve seventy-five of them for the use of the cavalry. He stressed they were really needed "as we live where the plantations are large and the white population is comparatively small."[42]

A far larger supply of weapons, notably 125,000 smoothbore and rifled muskets, came out of the seized federal arsenals as the governors prepared for secession. Without the manufacturing capacity to produce many arms and hesitant to enter the European market for fear of being seen as warlike, the Confederate government had to turn to the states for its first arms. Walker sent a circular to the governors on March 1 requesting the arms. A. B. Moore, as did the other governors, hedged in his reply. He expected that the state would deliver the seized weapons but added that was up to the secession convention. As for the arms purchased by the state, he felt justified in withholding an unspecified number to enable Alabama "to meet any emergency and protect and defend her citizens." A report from the Georgia convention made it clear that it was "of the first importance that we make sure for the defense of our own State." Concerned for its safety, Georgia contracted for cannons from ironworks in Virginia and was offering bounties for the in-state production of cannons. Whether the heavy ordnance would be turned over to the Confederacy in the future depended, the report concluded, on negotiations undertaken by the governor.[43]

The same scenario unfolded with Walker's directives of March 8 and 9 to relinquish troops raised by the governors for service in the Confederate army. The wiliest of the governors was Brown. He informed Walker that the 2,000 volunteers requested would be forthcoming when they were properly organized. This was a clever way of eliding the point that the troops he was raising were in three-year regiments and could not possibly be ready to leave in time to meet the need for reinforcements at Pensacola. Toombs interceded on Brown's behalf and, despite Walker's pleadings, Brown refused to raise the twelve-month volunteers the Congress had authorized.[44]

Brown was easily the most obstreperous of the governors. The others complied with the troop requisitions but often with reservations. The twelve-month volunteers they had raised uniformly demanded the right to elect their own officers and prioritized the defense of their own states over any plans the Confederacy might have had for them. In late March, A. B. Moore was reluctant to transfer Alabama troops from Pensacola to Confederate authorities. The men feared losing the privilege of selecting their officers and being held in Confederate service for a full year "even if the pending difficulties should be amicably arranged in a shorter time." Pickens wrote Davis of the concerns of the officers in the state's "little army" garrisoned at Charleston; they feared that a transfer to the Confederacy might result in a loss of seniority and rank. On a more ominous note, Pickens added that if the garrison were withdrawn in the event of war, the harbors on the Beaufort coast that could accommodate large war vessels would be exposed. River access to the interior would place the enemy in "the heart of our heaviest slave districts."[45]

Issues of officers' appointments and home defense remained unresolved through March. Once again, Governor Brown was a master at frustrating the war department. The three-year regiments he was raising had a full complement of officers but were at less than half strength. He offered them to the Confederacy on the condition that all the officers be retained, arguing that it was only simple justice to the privates who had enlisted with the understanding they would serve under officers from their local communities whom they knew and trusted. Sticking to the letter of the law, which prohibited the receiving of partial regiments, Walker refused the offer. Before Stephens intervened and persuaded

Walker to be less doctrinaire, the regiments remained in limbo for two months. Disregarding the explicit language of the statute setting up the provisional army, Governor Moore of Alabama tried to make a case for appointing officers at the rank of general. When the appointment list for officers came out in late March, Pickens criticized Walker for passing over some South Carolinians of superior military ability. At his wits' end, Walker retorted that if the governors had their way, there would not be enough positions in the army for West Point trained officers.[46]

Although often dismissed as narrow-minded state's righters, the governors were under intense pressure to put their own citizens first in matters of defense. Letters and petitions to the governors conveyed widespread fears of a Union invasion, especially in coastal areas. Pickens urged Walker to station along the coast at Georgetown, Beaufort, and Charleston the South Carolina troops transferred to the Confederacy. Brown, in a speech to the secession convention on March 15, emphasized that Georgia "has reserved to itself . . . the right to repel invasion" since the Confederacy was not yet prepared to protect the state. In the meantime, Savannah, Georgia's main port, was defenseless. Although Brown had contracted with a Pittsburgh factory to supply the necessary heavy cannon, "when the guns were made, such was the prejudice of the people of that city against the seceding States" that the contract was canceled. Cannon was on the way from Richmond, and when the guns arrived, they would be under state control until Brown saw fit to negotiate their release to the Confederacy. In Mississippi, Pettus had his hand forced when a local band of insurgents commandeered Ship Island, some twelve miles out in the Gulf guarding the approach to Biloxi. Without the armaments to defend Ship Island, Pettus soon had to abandon it.[47]

In addition to undertaking their political and military duties, the governors had to honor the cultural assumptions and hierarchical relations underlying the extremely localistic nature of raising and equipping the first troops. In every county, local notables, most often planters, relied on the prestige of their names and networks of friends and acquaintances to convince men to serve. The governors acknowledged the leadership of these notables by favoring them in appointing officers in the state forces. In explaining why he had bypassed Georgians who had served as officers in the US Army, Brown noted that they "would have been strangers to our people, and could probably not have enlisted the regiments in two years. Indeed, I may say that nearly all the recruits obtained thus far have been enlisted by officers appointed from civil life." The recruits signed up because they knew these civilians and trusted their leadership. Paul Jones Semmes rejected a position on Brown's staff out of a sense of obligation to the men he commanded; they were "quite unanimous" in expecting and wishing to serve under him.[48]

The raising of troops by local elites was an extension of community norms that on most issues deferred to those elites in politics and economic affairs. Planters were money lenders, providers of corn in drought years, and cultural pacesetters. Their wealth gave them tremendous leverage to assume military roles that conferred additional status and could result in even greater political recognition. In many cases they equipped troops out of their own pockets, supplied horses for cavalry companies, and mounted campaigns to elicit funds from other planters. Most important, planters subsidized the families of poor soldiers either directly or through subscriptions to war loans. Fair warning was given to planters stingy with their funds. In lauding the spirit of giving that had "a great effect upon the poor men in the country—and especially the nonslaveholder," a Florida editor warned that a man who would "not help to advance an interest that is to prove beneficial to himself need not expect the assistance of disinterested parties." A newspaper correspondent from Montgomery cautioned the planters to remember that "his negro property mainly called our new Government into existence."[49]

Given the contributions they had made and the assumption of their right to lead, the elites expected an officer's appointment as his just due. So too did their local communities. In acting on these requests, the governors gained the political dividends of doing right by community wishes and notions of patriarchal honor. Much more than a fetish for state's rights influenced the governors' behavior.

The Confederate military establishment etched out in the acts of February 28 and March 6 was fully in keeping with a political culture that feared centralized power. Such power would be wielded once the war began, but in the period of peace in March, the Confederacy recognized in its laws the sharing of power in military matters between the states and the central government. Neither Davis nor the war department could acquire arms and troops from the states without the governors' approval. Initially ill-equipped to assume issues of defense, the Confederacy deferred to the state governors. Few legislators at the state or national levels desired a military despotism. Not only was it feared by planters and common whites alike, but it also appeared to be unnecessary, especially when such prominent figures as Toombs and Walker blithely asserted that any war would be short and virtually bloodless. Eight slave states were still in the Union, and one of the most effective arguments in keeping them there was raising the alarm of "terrorism" that would destroy individual liberties and the states' prerogatives in the Confederacy. Davis wanted more power to direct mobilization, but only the outbreak of war would give that to him.[50]

Visions of Greatness: A Model for the World

"We of the Southern American States are now masters of the Universe, because we have the power over all governments," proclaimed a Georgia editor at the birth of the Confederacy. Like other fervid secessionists, he was brimming with utopian visions of what the future would hold for the Confederacy. In instance after instance, they took a plausible premise and sent it soaring into flights of fancy that stretched, if not defied, reality. Envisioning a vast Confederate empire, J. Quitman Moore prophesized that the Confederacy would be "first among the nations" as the result of "an organized system of subordination, resting primarily on conquest, and accepting the principle of *force*, as the necessary basis of social organization." Fascinated by traits he felt Southern society shared with the feudal values of medieval Europe, he imagined Confederate armies as modern-day crusaders. He also was caught up in fanciful notions of innate racial differences between Northern and Southern whites descended from the divergent stocks of Anglo-Saxons who had settled the North and the more noble strains of Normans dominant in the South. Although most Confederates were not as reactionary as Moore, they shared his belief that the Confederacy had a special mission to right the evils of the Western world. By uplifting the African race, maintaining labor peace, and championing social and political harmony, the Confederacy would set a model for other nations to follow.[51]

Mastery would flow from the power of King Cotton. The American South supplied the world with most of its cotton, a product that provided employment for the poor, wages to feed their families, and cheap textiles to clothe them. The shock of withholding it would result in massive economic damage and social convulsions. It was a familiar argument and an immensely reassuring one, but it had been cogently critiqued by Southern Whigs who favored economic diversification. Moreover, it rested on two fallacies. It assumed that slave labor was necessary for the profitable production of cotton. Without a doubt, slaves grew and harvested nearly all the South's cotton, but not elsewhere and not in the postwar South when cotton production actually expanded over prewar levels. As the Whigs noted, England was anxious to develop alternative sources, and it would do so as the Civil War dragged on. The naïve assumption that England would do the Confederacy's bidding and break any Union blockade ignored England's self-interest as an imperial power. Its navy enforced Britain's colonial domination and repeatedly had been used to impose blockades in times of war. As Confederate leaders found out too late, they needed to sell cotton more than England needed to buy it.[52]

The secessionists' vision for the Confederacy and their rejection of the egalitarian currents flowing from the American and French Revolutions were two
sides of the same coin. They interpreted the European revolutionary movements
of 1848 and any labor unrest in the North as evidence of the endemic unrest
in free-labor societies that granted political rights to the propertyless. The
French Revolution might have been crushed, but "the sickly cant of French political philosophy" still poisoned political discourse and portended "a dark future, yet unread," warned William F. Hutson, a Presbyterian minister in South
Carolina. That future might well see the ideas of democracy, nowhere to be
found in the Gospels, "spring forth into that hideous despotism of irresponsible
slaughter, more dreadful than absolutism ever invented." George W. Bagby, the
iconoclastic Virginia physician-novelist who converted the *Southern Literary
Messenger* into a mouthpiece for secession, denounced universal suffrage as "destructive of all free institutions . . . because it opens the way by which labour may
humble and triumph over capital without raising the arm of violence." Only in
the South, where the manual and laboring half of the population had no political rights, were republican liberties safe. For Bagby, the Confederacy had "the
greatest opportunity, ever vouchsafed to any people of establishing free republican institutions upon such a basis as will guarantee their perpetuity." Other
nations would soon learn that their own stability and survival depended on imposing a class-stratified system based on some form of personal servitude for
their laboring masses.[53]

Not just social harmony but the wise and just subordination of the African
race would inspire emulation from other nations. This was Alexander Stephens's
message to the world in his Cornerstone Speech. Only Southern whites had
brought the African race into the folds of the Christian family and thereby cul-
tivated their "peculiar and remarkable genius," rhapsodized William Holcombe,
a Natchez, Mississippi, physician. In making his case for the spiritualization of
slavery from its selfish origins, Holcombe found in the Bible recognition of slavery
as "one great means and agency of human development" for Africans. Southern
slaveholders were but the appointed agents of God for this development. They
held their slave property only as *"chattels personal"* possessed of innate human
rights. These rights—food, clothing, protection, sympathy, training in obeying
rules, and instruction in the Christian religion—were all provided by the masters. In return, those in their charge owed obedience and regular work. They
were not slaves as defined by critics of the institution but apprentices for life who
were cared for much better than they ever could have cared for themselves. God
had instituted this apprenticeship for the benefit of a child-like race of perpetual
minors which, were it not for slavery, would long ago had been exterminated
in America like the Indians. In performing God's work, Holcombe's Christian

slaveholder, reviled and misunderstood though he was, might soon reveal to the world that he has "attained the sublimest point of human civilization."[54]

xxxxxUniformly, Southerners believed that their slaves were better off than the North's free blacks. Northern racial prejudice was undeniable, but it did not follow that blacks fared better as slaves. J. H. Blanks, an escaped slave, admitted that he had seen and heard of "misery" in the North, but nothing he had experienced compared in brutality to what he had seen inflicted on family and friends in his plantation youth. Limited though it was, enough equality existed for blacks in the North to raise the hackles of Southerners. A disgusted William S. Pettigrew complained of the racial "equality" he found in Ohio in 1838 such as the races eating and drinking together. A South Carolina editor was furious that "colored wide awakes" formed in support of the Republicans in the campaign of 1860. Outraged that African Americans were allowed to vote in six Northern states, secessionists demanded an absolute ban on such voting. For all the discrimination they faced, free blacks in the North succeeded in carving out a political space for themselves.[55]

As restraints tightened on free blacks in the South in the late 1850s, they fled to the North. Their main exit routes were across the Ohio River from Kentucky and Tennessee and up the Atlantic seaboard from as far south as Georgia. They faced an uncertain future as they headed to communities of African Americans in the free states, but at least they had escaped the harsh whippings inflicted on those who violated the system of passes. Richmond's mayor estimated that 1,000 free blacks were illegally in the city in the fall of 1860. He ordered the police to root them out and "punish them by the lash every day they remained." Two of the victims without passes were Jack Logan, who received fifteen lashes, and Albert, punished with thirty-nine.[56]

Worse retribution awaited slaves singled out in the insurrection panic of 1860. Whites resolved this contradiction of Stephens's paean to social harmony by denying black agency and blaming the plots on abolitionist emissaries. That was cold comfort to Southern women. Carolina Cary Harrison of Virginia was one of many who could never put her fears to rest after John Brown's raid. The nights were the worst time. "The notes of whip-poor-wills in the sweet-gum swamp near the stable, the mutterings of a distant thunder-storm, even the rustle of the night wind in the vales that shade my window, filled me with nameless dread." Military mobilization in the secession winter with companies of armed men everywhere offered temporary assurances, but the dread returned in the spring when the troops were called away.[57]

Knowing full well that the bid for independence would crumble without the support of women, the secessionists sought to quell their anxieties. Thomas Cobb proclaimed in early April that peace of mind prevailed in Southern households because the abolitionist provocateurs had vanished. They were gone, he explained, because the South's separation from the North "re-lieved the conscience of Northern Fanatics, as to their sin in connection with slavery." Evangelical preachers were particularly attentive to their largely female congregations. In a secessionist speech, Baptist minister James Furman of South Carolina described the slaves as "a tractable, docile, and affectionate class of dependents," a standard paternalist homily, before alluding to the horrors awaiting women of the Confederacy if they failed to guarantee slavery against emancipation. The greatest contribution of the ministers to the Confederacy, however, was their success in convincing evangelical laypersons that an independent South had a holy mission to purify and defend Christianity against a hostile outside world of infidels.[58]

Deo Vindice: The Confederacy's Holy Mission

The Confederate Constitution explicitly acknowledged the sovereignty of God, and the motto "Deo Vindice" inscribed on the Seal of the Confederacy declared God as the South's protector. This linkage of God to the slave republic was central to the theology of Southern evangelicalism. Blending a literal interpretation of the Bible with the providence of God that had sanctioned slavery and was present in all human affairs, evangelical ministers enjoined the faithful to do their Christian duty in glorifying God's wishes in the holy work of Southern independence.

Evangelical sermons drew on Biblical examples to explain the great threat to the South and promote resistance against it. In January, the Reverend T. L. McBryde preached in Pendleton, South Carolina. He took as his text 1st Timothy, the 6th verse, "From such withdraw thyself." He began by wishing "to dispel all doubts and misgivings from the minds of even the most timid, as to the justice and religiosity . . . of the cause in which the noble State of our nativity and other sister States are now engaged." He noted there was no denying that slavery was "the occasion" of the sectional split, particularly the question, "Is Slavery a Sin?" The answer, of course, must be found in the "Word of God." After a biblical defense of slavery, he turned to the defining theme of his sermon, Paul's exhortation to the young preacher Timothy to withdraw from all fellowship with false prophets, the modern contemporaries of which were the abolitionists, whose message was "subversive of Christianity. They were sowers of discord and political and moral warfare." Southerners owed it to themselves and their slaves to heed Paul's exhortation and cast the abolitionists aside and continue their guardianship of a race the abolitionists would condemn to death and destruction. He beseeched God for a peaceful separation, but if war came, "our appeal is to the

Fig. 9.4 Our National Anthem. From its beginning, the Confederacy claimed God as its protector. Library of Congress, LC-USZ62-33407.

God of righteousness—the God of our forefathers, who sustained them in their struggle for freedom as we are now doing."[59]

Edwin T. Winkler was among the ministers who instructed the troops on their duties as Christian soldiers. In his sermon to the Moultrie Guards in Charleston, he referenced the God who had guided the Israelites in the conquest of Canaan. So too would reliance on God prepare Confederate soldiers for their arduous duties and dispense a "most glorious deliverance" to those who died in battle. If engaged in combat, he told them they would be fighting for "a righteous cause," for both reason and religion taught that he who shrank from protecting his home and country was "something less than a man." To truly be a hero, "spiritual discipline" was necessary for obeying orders and resisting the sinful temptations of camp life. Whereas religion in the North had degenerated into fanaticism with its arraying of labor against capital and vilification of Southern Christians, it was a bulwark of strength for the "penitent and believing people" of the Confederacy.[60]

Pastors delivered a flood of politically charged sermons celebrating the cause of the South as that of civilization, religion, and God. They preached so many that Mary Nisbet, a committed secessionist in Macon, Georgia, complained to a fellow evangelical: "What times we live in! Our pastor gives us political sermons every Sabbath Day. I am weary of them now, and shall do as I used to at Dr. Smyth's in Charleston—go to some other church till he gets up a new theme." Evangelical women held daily prayer meetings in Savannah while the Georgia secession convention was in session. Mary Jones rejoiced in the hope that God "overshadow us all with the guidance and protection of His own Holy Spirit."[61]

The sectional rancor and strife of the late 1850s conditioned evangelicals to embrace secession and the formation of the Confederacy. The *Tennessee Baptist* interpreted the nation's troubles and the revolutions stirring in Europe as evidence that "we have entered the very twilight of this present dispensation—that its 'last days,' the time of its end—are at hand." The Second Coming of Christ was imminent and, as foretold in the Prophecies and Book of Revelations, divine retribution was at hand for all sinners. God's displeasure with a sinning nation was a call for repentance. The South had sinned, preached the Reverend Ebenezer Warren of Macon, Georgia, in not affirming that "Slavery forms a vital element of the Divine Revelation to man." Believing the North with its idolatrous worshipping of the Union and wealth was the most guilty party, evangelicals were prepared to accept their holy duty of inoculating the South with its divine institution of slavery from the godless North. [62]

Conservative theologians in the North were as quick as those in the South to condemn liberalizing trends in religion and calls for equality and democratic rights they felt threatened Western civilization. On all sides, they saw mounting attacks on God's authority and social order. They had no fundamental theological quarrel with their Southern counterparts. But, as always, whether in the secular or religious realm, the sectional differences circled back to slavery. Princeton's Charles Hodge, the most influential Old School Presbyterian minister in the North, was quite willing to accept the Southern position that slavery was not inherently sinful and that Southern rights should be respected and slavery left untouched. He denounced the abolitionists as fiercely as any Southerner. What he could not concede was the necessity of slavery for saving the world from social upheaval and moral decay.

James H. Thornwell, the greatest of the Southern theologians, lamented in a November fast-day sermon the corruption of God's purpose for the American nation. "We were a city set upon a hill, whose light was intended to shine upon every people and every land." The North's lust for sectional domination and its war against slavery had defiled God's charge to America. Now, only the South could salvage God's mission for his chosen people. Ignoring the depravity that Adam's transgression had imposed on the human race, Northerners profaned the very concept of freedom in their quest for worldly pleasures and wealth. Freedom came only from Christ and adjured the saved to put God before the attractions of this life and pursue rectitude in the eyes of God. The lowly slave in faithful service partook of a Christ-like freedom, just like the suffering martyr. Thornwell theologically framed slavery not only in the master-slave relationship but in socioeconomic terms as indispensable to social order. Slaves alone of all the laboring classes were the beneficiaries of cradle-to-the-grave security. The unrelenting drive of capital in a free-labor system to extract the greatest profit from the fewest workers consigned labor to a life of immiseration and insecurity. Only the imposition of an organized system of labor "so like to slavery that it will be impossible to discriminate between them" could save non-slave societies from economic unrest and revolution. Thus, Thornwell "confidently anticipated the time when the nations that now revile us would gladly change place with us." His formidable intellect in service of slavery indicted Hodge for refusing to see that free labor was the problem and not the solution to the evils that Northern and Southern religious conservatives alike condemned.[63]

With a moral righteousness forged by decades of evangelical proselytizing, Southerners plunged forward into an uncertain future. They grasped at the illusion that slavery, which had precipitated their revolution and estranged them from the world, would bear them safely to a secure refuge. Not all were convinced. Simeon Colton, who preached at Methodist and Presbyterian churches in North Carolina after leaving his native Connecticut, raised a point most evangelicals dared not to consider. He pondered whether "God may have a design in connection with slavery, to let the South know that while their purpose is to perpetuate, his is to liberate, and render their system worthless." To the manor born, Frederick Porcher of South Carolina admitted, "It may be that . . . slavery is doomed. Be it so. Everything happens for the best. All that we ask is that it may perish manfully." With his usual barbed wit, James L. Petigru concluded that the Confederacy was "formed on principles that are hollow and rotten, on the shallow conceit that all nations will pay tribute to King Cotton, and that our new reading of 'The Whole Duty of Man' will be accepted by Christendom." No one, he found, was more "full of the new-born zeal [for the Confederacy] as the clergy."[64]

At least in public, skeptics of the Confederate faith were rarely heard. For the clear majority, the caustic Petigru was surely correct in asserting that they were "as proud of their apostasy as they were sure of the verdict of history." Among the most committed were young women reared as evangelicals. Sallie McDowell extolled the military volunteers as "warriors in the cause of God." Susan Cornwell Shewmake was certain that "a faithful discharge of our duties as slaveowners will lead to a higher development of moral power and the final and universal spread of Gospel civilization." The young editor of the *Dallas Herald* was positively messianic in drawing a parallel between Christmas day in 1860 and the burgeoning drive for Southern independence. He proclaimed Christmas as "symbolical of the birth of a New and Great People, as it is the anniversary of the birth of the Savior of mankind." [65]

Among committed secessionists, confidence in the Confederacy at its birth could not have been higher. That confidence would soon be tested by continued hard times and the war that Unionists always said would come.

From Waiting Game to War

Lincoln Takes Command

Lincoln's decision to send a relief expedition to Fort Sumter in early April precipitated the last phase of secession. More precisely, his call on the states for troops once the Confederacy fired on the fort triggered the secession of four states from the Upper South. Viewed in the South as a declaration of war, Lincoln's call shattered the uneasy peace that had prevailed since his inauguration. The border slave states wavered but remained in the Union. The battle lines were drawn for the ensuing war.

The Fort Sumter Conundrum: Evacuate or Reinforce?

Lincoln was a great unknown when he began his presidency. His closest confidantes knew him as a moderate of the Henry Clay school who would be guided by a scrupulous regard for the constitutional rights of the South. To most impartial observers, however, he was a simple, somewhat uncouth prairie politician lacking the experience and depth to cope with the magnitude of the crisis confronting him. To most Southerners, who were hardly impartial, he was a vulgar abolitionist utterly unfit to assume the responsibilities of his high office. Ridiculed and scorned in the South, Lincoln was a lightning rod for Southern fears and insecurities. To a Richmond newspaper, he was "the Abolition ourangoutang that sulked to Washington the other day from the wilds of Illinois." What made him especially frightful was "something worse than slang, rowdyism, brutality, and all moral filth; something worse than all the tag and rag of Western grog-shops and Yankee factories. . . . With all that comes arbitrary power." A college student in Virginia rejoiced that at least "such an abomination was never submitted to by Southerners who boast respectability much less culture." As for Lincoln's antislavery views, a Texas politician noted that he was "a man who, if found in the State, would, by the laws governing, and of your own making, be incarcerated in the penitentiary for a term of years."[1]

Lincoln's first test of leadership came with his anxiously awaited inaugural address. He had to project an image of forceful resolve to uphold the Union and yet not cause additional slave states to stampede to the Confederacy. He also had to curb his anger over what he saw as the flagrantly illegal and blackmailing tactics of the secessionists to gain greater concessions for slavery. He aimed for a temperate tone in the balancing act of his address. Accepting the advice of Orville Browning, a close friend from Illinois, and William Seward, his secretary of state, Lincoln deleted his original phase "to reclaim the public property and places which have fallen" and replaced it with a pledge to "hold, occupy, and possess" federal installations still in Union hands. Seward also convinced him to smooth over the more forceful language to project a more peaceful intent. Nonetheless, Lincoln dismissed secession as the essence of anarchy and proclaimed the Union to be perpetual.[2]

Partisanship and ideological leanings conditioned the responses to the address. Whereas Northern Democrats panned it as unworthy of a statesman, most Republicans praised it for its unflinching commitment to the Union while keeping open the window of peace. Abolitionists and the radical antislavery wing of the party criticized it for what they feared implied a policy of appeasement.

Fig. 10.1 Lincoln the Schoolmaster. Many Northerners looked to Lincoln to act as a stern schoolmaster who would bring the unruly children of secession back into the Union without resorting to force. Library of Congress, LC-USZ62-13635.

No one was more disappointed than Frederick Douglass. He castigated Lincoln for failing to unequivocally condemn slavery as "contrary to the spirit of the age and the principles of liberty in which the Federal Government was founded." What most galled Douglass was Lincoln's pledge to enforce the Fugitive Slave Act. For this abolitionist, Lincoln was no better than the other lackeys of the Slave Power, former presidents Pierce and Buchanan. The reaction that mattered most, however, was that in the Confederacy, and here the address was branded as tantamount to a declaration of war. "To hold and occupy the property belonging to the Government, and to collect duties on imports in the Southern Confederacy are impossible achievements," reasoned the *New Orleans Bee*, "unless accompanied by beating down and overpowering all resistance." In the Upper South, Unionists were heartened by what Parson Brownlow hailed as "the temperance and conservatism" of the address.[3]

The artfulness of Lincoln's address was in its Janus-faced message. As Douglass put it: "It is a double-tongued document capable of two constructions, and conceals rather than declares a definite policy. No man reading it could say whether Mr. Lincoln was for peace or war." Charles C. Jones Jr. of Georgia described it as "a queer production. . . . What does it mean? It means this, and it means that, and then it may mean neither." By not committing himself to war or offering any concessions, Lincoln was keeping his options open and buying time to gauge the Confederate response. An alarming report that awaited him on his first day in office, however, jolted him into realizing that time was running out for a definitive policy on his part.[4]

The report was from Major Anderson at Fort Sumter. The news was bad. The buildup of Confederate artillery in Charleston harbor in recent weeks precluded the sending of any reinforcements, and Anderson's supplies were shrinking so fast he would soon be forced to evacuate. Anderson had not requested reinforcements back in January when they had a good chance of getting through to him. Now, out of the blue, he insisted that a minimum force of 20,000 men was needed. As Anderson later admitted, his paramount concern was maintaining the peace, and all along he felt that any effort at resupply would provoke a war. Surrender, which was endorsed by General Scott, now seemed to be the only recourse.[5]

Lincoln was loath to accept Scott's advice. As he later told Congress, he believed that abandoning Fort Sumter would be "utterly ruinous," a devastating blow to Union morale and an excuse for foreign recognition of the Confederacy, thus making "our national destruction consummate." Had Lincoln listened to his cabinet, Sumter would have been abandoned. Polled on March 15, the cabinet favored evacuation with the sole dissenting vote that of Montgomery Blair, the postmaster general. Instead, Lincoln delayed. He asked Scott for more information on the situation, sought out alternative assessments on the possibility of a resupply effort, sent personal emissaries to Charleston to report on conditions, and ordered immediate reinforcements to Fort Pickens, the retention of which was his fallback if he had to yield Fort Sumter.[6]

Lincoln appeared to be caught on the horns of a dilemma, and Confederates delighted in his predicament. Whatever decision he made, the *New Orleans Bee* was certain the Confederacy would gain the advantage. If Anderson evacuated, Lincoln would be forced to give up the remaining forts in the Confederacy still in federal possession. If Lincoln refrained from a coercive act, the Upper and Border South would soon join the Confederacy because their status as slave states in the Union would be untenable. On the other hand, any attempt to reinforce the forts would start a war that would gain for the Confederacy the remaining slave states.[7]

The Gourdin brothers were in contact with Anderson throughout February and knew of his pacific intent and desire to leave Fort Sumter. They relayed Anderson's views to friends in Washington and pressured General Scott to convince federal officials of the folly of coercion. Buchanan, however, kept Anderson where he was, and the Gourdins expected hostilities once Lincoln took over. In that event, the blame for the war would be squarely on the Republicans.[8]

Fears of a possible war subsided in mid-March when reports reached the South that Fort Sumter was about to be evacuated. Some secessionists such as "Ariel," the Washington correspondent for the *Richmond Examiner*, viewed the reports as a ruse to lull Virginia and other states in the Upper South into accepting Republican rule. More typically, Southerners rejoiced that peace was at hand. Accepting as "an admitted fact" the evacuation order for Fort Sumter, the *New Orleans Picayune* was convinced that conciliatory voices would prevail in Washington "over the insane plans of the rabid and fanatical ultraists." Not until early April did Southerners realize that no such order had ever been issued. They had reacted not to Lincoln's policy but the scheming of William Seward.[9]

False Hopes: Seward and "Masterly Inactivity"

Seward was the man of the hour—or so he thought. Unionists from the Upper South showered him with fulsome praise as the only Republican with the political savvy and breadth of vision to forge what could pass as a compromise. In dismissing Lincoln as a "3rd rate man," Frederick Roberts of North Carolina lauded Seward as "the Hector or Atlas of not only his Cabinet, but the great intellect of the whole north." Seward did project that image. A contemporary credited him with "a delicacy of temperament that indicated genius." A key to his influence was his ability to establish close ties with many of the very slaveholders whose institutions he roundly condemned.[10]

To fulfill his assigned role of savior of the Union, Seward pursued a policy called masterly inactivity. He assumed that time was the Union's greatest ally. Time would only worsen the economic crisis in the Confederacy, accounts of which circulated in the Northern press. In a matter of months, Seward was confident, economic distress would force a reappraisal of secession and a willingness to return to the Union. For public consumption, Confederates claimed that an economic recovery was under way. Privately and in closed sessions, they harped on the unrelenting hard times. The Lowndes County delegate at the Alabama secession convention in January bemoaned "the deplorable condition of our financial and commercial affairs." Even more reason to secede at once and restore the business confidence needed for a recovery, retorted Yancey. But secession and the formation of the Confederacy offered no economic panacea. The liquidity that lubricated the debt-bound Southern economy had dried up with the stagnation in the cotton market and the reluctance of Northerners to redeem Southern debt instruments.[11]

Business remained depressed in Alabama and elsewhere. "Cahaba is about to dry up," reported a debt-collection lawyer in March. "No business doing here." Ann Gordon Finley in Cherokee County wrote her sister in early April that "Money is as scarce as 'hen's tooth' . . . very few seem to have it at all and no one is likely to invest money in any kind of property until the country is in a more settled condition." A few weeks later, the Commissioners Court in Perry County appropriated $2,000 for purchasing corn and bacon for the "destitute of the county." The *Southern Cultivator* warned that Georgia along with the other cotton states lacked enough grain to feed its people and livestock until the next harvest. Shortfalls in years past had been met by food purchases from the western states, but Southern currencies were so depreciated that such purchases could be made only "at ruinous sacrifices." The cotton states were in the anomalous bind of having "much to sell, nobody to buy." Slaveholders anxious to raise cash faced the same problem when slave prices cratered by more than half. In the meantime, provisions of all sorts had doubled in price. Admitting in March that "uncertainty is ruinous to trade and industrial operations," "Ariel" argued that Virginia's secession would be "equivalent to a truce of peace between the two sections" and produce the assurances necessary for an economic recovery.[12]

Service in volunteer companies offered a temporary sedative for the economic pain, but boredom and restlessness were setting in among the troops cooped up in camps and engaged in endless garrison duties. Further agitating them, as noted by Robert Allston in South Carolina, was the "suffering and privations among families in town of the soldiers on duty whose revenues are materially diminish'd and curtail'd by absence from their vocations." His son Benjamin seconded that concern when he declared at the end of March that it was "high time we should have [Fort Sumter], or we shall cause much suffering, which is apt to engender discontent at home." The pressure for a resolution of the uncertainty, either by the North accepting peaceable secession or the outbreak of war, was reaching a flash point.[13]

While waiting for a political blowback in the Confederacy against economic stagnation, Seward was banking on Unionists in the Upper South to consolidate the bipartisan coalitions they had put together in the secession elections. Like Seward, with whom they kept up a steady correspondence, Virginia's Unionists felt time was on their side. "If our Federal administration will pursue a non-coercive & pacific policy—simply adopt the course of 'hands off'—secession will languish & die out," proclaimed G. W. Lewis in mid-March. "It is an evil spirit that is fed by resistance & opposition. The people of the Confederate States must be ground to earth by oppressive taxes." Led by Governor John Letcher, Union Democrats pledged to work with their former Whig adversaries in preserving Virginia in the Union. T. F. Nelson outlined the Unionists' strategy: oppose the fanatics in both sections "until we can either all remain together in the Union, gradually allowing the seceded states back to us" or go out with the other slave states if "just demands" were rejected. The Unionists confidently looked forward to the state elections in May to cement their majority position.[14]

Encouraging reports were also reaching Seward from Tennessee and North Carolina. Andrew Johnson, long scorned by the Whigs, was cooperating with Whig Emerson Etheridge in dispensing federal patronage. Unionist credentials took precedence over party affiliation. George Badger, working with the minority of Union Democrats, was pursuing the same policy in North Carolina. The grand objective was to lay the foundation for a national Union party that would include Republicans. Such a fundamental remaking of the sectional Republican Party was John Gilmer's advice to Lincoln in December. Bring your party "as far South as you can," he urged, adding that any Republican defections in the North would be more than made up by a new Southern base that would nationalize the Republicans and preserve the Union.[15]

Gilmer's thinking meshed perfectly with Seward's. Like many other Northern commentators, Seward assumed that Lincoln had to pursue a conciliatory policy to have any chance of restoring the Union. The upper and border slave states were the key to putting the Union back together, and it was essential to placate them. Lincoln's course from this perspective boiled down to merging the Republican Party into a new national organization and thereby breaking with his antislavery supporters or, conversely, holding to the Chicago platform and driving away conservative Republicans. The Washington reporter for the *New York Times* put the question plainly: "In a word, the question pending is . . . whether Mr. Lincoln shall become the head of the great 'Union party' of the country, or whether a party upon that issue shall be permitted to grow up in hostility to his Administration."[16]

Seward courted General Scott as well as Southern Unionists in trying to steer Lincoln in a pacific direction. In a letter of March 3, 1861, solicited by Seward and then forwarded to Lincoln, Scott advised against any warlike measures, which would result in a vastly destructive war that would leave embittered Southern whites to be treated as conquered subjects. Far better to stand aside, he counseled, accept the compromise demands of the Southern Unionists, and rule as a Union Party that in due time would be rewarded with the return of the departed Southern states.[17]

Seward's views were an open book to the Confederate commissioners in Washington, and they sought to use him to their advantage. Martin Crawford, a congressman from Georgia in the 1850s, arrived first on March 3, 1861. Soon joining him were John Forsyth, editor of the *Mobile Register*, and André Roman, a former Louisiana governor. Instructed to negotiate "friendly relations" and to settle "all questions of disagreement between the two Governments," the commissioners spoke for what Confederates considered an established, independent government. If Lincoln wanted to delay any decision until he consulted with the Senate or his party, it was to be granted. Time was of no concern as long as the status quo was maintained and there was no evidence of surreptitious military preparations for an attack on the Confederacy. As Davis's eyes and ears in Washington, they were to report any suspicious federal activities.[18]

Lincoln rejected any direct talks with the commissioners as tantamount to conferring legitimacy on the Confederacy. To gain access to Seward, Crawford relied on intermediaries to shuttle information back and forth. As relayed back to Montgomery by Crawford, Seward was blustering that he had built up the Republican Party and now had to save it. The "negro question must be dropped" in favor of embracing the border state Unionists, a reference to all the eight slave states outside the Confederacy. At all costs, a military collision had to be prevented. As long as peace was maintained, Seward was confident that Southerners, "unwillingly led into secession, will rebel against their leaders and reconstruction will follow."[19]

Sensing an opening he could exploit, Crawford sought a definitive statement from Seward on not upsetting the military status quo and a pledge not to reinforce Fort Pickens. Seward, of course, was in no position to sign off on a policy opposed by Lincoln, and he informed the commissioners he had no authority to agree to an interview. Still, from the perspective of the commissioners, they were in the driver's seat. Confident to the point of cockiness, Forsyth wrote Confederate Secretary of War Walker, "We are playing a game in which time is our best advocate, and if our Government could afford the time, I feel confident of winning. There is a terrific fight in the Cabinet. Our policy is to encourage the peace element in the fight, and at least blow up the Cabinet on the question." He brashly concluded, "we have the rascals 'on the hip.' "[20]

Seward had backed himself into a corner of his own making. Quite fortuitously, two Supreme Court justices, Samuel Nelson of New York and John Campbell of Alabama, offered their services as intermediaries in the muddled negotiations. Campbell, who had opposed secession, played the major role. He met with Seward on March 15, and the two agreed to treat the evacuation of Fort Sumter and the recognition of the commissioners as separate issues. In Campbell's version of the meeting, Seward authorized him to tell the commissioners and Jefferson Davis that Sumter would be evacuated within five days and that no action was under consideration for the forts in the Gulf of Mexico.[21]

For the rest of the month, Seward repeatedly assured Campbell that Sumter's surrender was imminent. As the US flag continued to fly over the fort, Davis grew increasingly wary. He never did have much hope of peace as long as the Upper South was out of the Confederacy, and he suspected that the talk of leaving Sumter was a subterfuge to deflect attention from reinforcing Fort Pickens and mobilizing the Union's naval resources. He had good reason to be worried. The time that the Confederacy was using to prepare for possible war, Lincoln was using to finalize a plan to send food supplies to Anderson. The standoff was coming to a close.[22]

End of the Waiting Game: Lincoln Makes His Decision

Almost as soon as he learned of Anderson's plight, Lincoln groped for an escape from the box of unacceptable choices in which the Confederate commissioners believed they had entrapped him. He needed to find a middle way, an approach acceptable to his party and most Northerners that avoided giving in to the Confederacy or unleashing a military strike against it. The most promising approach came from Gustavus V. Fox, the brother-in-law of the original hard-liner in Lincoln's cabinet, Montgomery Blair. Fox's plan combined the use of shallow-draft tugboats to land supplies with support from warships, stationed off the obstructed channel to the Charleston harbor.[23]

When outlined to the cabinet on March 14 by Blair, Fox's proposal failed to gain broad support. Unsurprisingly, only Blair unequivocally backed it. Failure to uphold federal authority, he argued, had emboldened the secessionists and continued to do so. To abandon Sumter would encourage them to demand the remaining forts, thus necessitating war. Only an immediate show of purpose had any chance of forcing them to rethink their insane plans and respect Northerners as their equals. Fearful of provoking hostilities, the rest of the cabinet was against any reprovisioning efforts.[24]

On March 19, Fox was on his way to confer with Anderson. A leery Governor Pickens granted Fox access to Fort Sumter after assurances that the purpose of the visit was to check on Anderson's supplies. Pickens probably assumed that Lincoln wanted the information before issuing the evacuation order. After the conference and a quick surveying of the Confederate installations in the harbor, Fox was more confident than ever that his plan would succeed. Anderson did not share his optimism.[25]

The day after Fox left, Pickens was surprised by the arrival of two more visitors from the North. Lincoln had dispatched two friends from Illinois, Stephen Hurlbut and Ward Lamon, to report back to him their firsthand impressions of the political mood in Charleston, especially whether, as Seward professed, any latent Unionism still existed. Both men were native Southerners, and Hurlbut had been a law student of James L. Petigru, the city's leading critic of secession. Posing as a disinterested party visiting his sister, Hurlbut learned from Petigru that Unionist sentiment was nowhere to be found. He had no hesitation in informing Lincoln that "separate nationality is a fixed fact, that there is an unanimity of sentiment which to my mind is astonishing, that there is no attachment to the Union. . . . There is positively nothing to appeal to." In the guise of an official agent settling up postal accounts, Lamon made his own inquiries and came to the same conclusions. His glib promises, freely given, that Sumter was on the verge of evacuation suggest that he was doing double duty on behalf of Seward.[26]

Lincoln now knew from two trusted sources that Seward's hopes of bringing back South Carolina were wishful thinking. He also had reason to believe that Fox's plan just might work. Close to making a decision, he acted quickly after Scott surprised him with a recommendation on March 28 to abandon Fort Pickens as well as Sumter. As far as Lincoln knew, Pickens was secure. He had ordered reinforcements sent on March 11, but confirmation of the mission had not been received. Since Sumter was a lost cause militarily, Scott reasoned that its abandonment would be chalked up to *"necessity."* Only withdrawing from Fort Pickens would establish the administration's peaceful intent. Furious, Lincoln lashed out at Anderson for having *"played us false"* and at Scott for his conflicting military advice and meddling in politics. He was in danger of losing control of his administration and looking like a hapless pawn in the process. This was the critical moment in his education as president, the point at which he began acting as his own man. With his anger palpable, he informed his cabinet on March 29 of Scott's memorandum and repolled them on their question of sending supplies to Anderson. With Seward the most notable dissenter, the cabinet approved Lincoln's reinforcing both Sumter and Pickens.[27]

On learning of Lincoln's decision to reinforce Sumter, Seward was appalled. His policy of peace and procrastination was about to blow up, for it absolutely depended on abandoning Sumter and maintaining an uneasy status quo that would be upset by any show of military force directed against the most sensitive symbol of Southern honor and pride. In a bold, if not reckless, move, Seward penned a memorandum to Lincoln on April 1 offering to give direction to an administration he saw drifting into a national disaster. If Lincoln felt that a show of force was necessary, then, counseled Seward, reinforce Pickens but forget about Sumter. In a separate section on foreign policy, Seward recommended demanding immediate explanations from European nations he accused of threatening American interests in the Caribbean and Central America. If their response was unsatisfactory, then war had to be seriously considered, a war that Seward argued would transform the sectional crisis into a patriotic outburst of national purpose bringing all Americans together in a common cause. Unwilling to rupture the Republican Party with Seward's dismissal, Lincoln gently reprimanded him with enough of a hard edge to make it clear that he was the president and would make the decisions.[28]

Seward's bizarre bid for power on April 1 coincided with the day the Morrill Tariff would take effect. Passed once Southerners had left Congress, the tariff fulfilled a Republican campaign pledge to grant more protection to Northern manufacturers, especially the iron and steel interests of Pennsylvania. Overall rates were double those of the Tariff of 1857, which the Confederacy had temporarily adopted. Fearing a crippling loss of orders to the Confederacy, the pro-Southern merchants and commercial interests of the Northeast were now more open to a confrontational stance toward secession.

Decidedly pro-compromise during the winter, the business press began to broach the idea in March that an end to the stalemate, even if it resulted in war, was preferable to the uncertainty that prevented any economic recovery. "Every day until the course of the Government is known," ran an editorial in a Philadelphia paper, "millions of capital lie unemployed. Any kind of decision is better for commerce, than indecision." Credit and the rights of private property, the cornerstones of a capitalist economy, ultimately depended on the authority of the federal government. Giving in to Confederate demands would shake confidence in that authority by sanctioning the use of lawless violence to gain benefits for any disgruntled group, not just Southerners but also the North's working poor. The Confederate announcement in March that debts to Northerners were to be repudiated barring prompt recognition of the new Southern government and the absence of any hostile moves against it came across to businessmen and other Northerners as blackmail.[29]

The arrival of the Morrill Tariff magnified all these concerns. Reports surfaced in late March of European producers and shippers diverting their American orders from Northern to Confederate ports. As Northern port cities faced anticipated financial collapse, the New York Times warned that the federal government would "suffer a ruinous loss of revenue" in uncollected tariff duties, its main source of income. In vain, the paper demanded a repeal of the new

Fig. 10.2 The Southern Confederacy a fact!! By late March 1861, Northern businessmen were condemning the Confederacy as a band of anarchists in league with the devil. Library of Congress, LC-USZ62-89624.

tariff. The *New York Herald*, always supportive of the city's Southern merchants, insisted that Sumter had to be evacuated and a "peaceful solution" adopted.[30]

Businessmen not directly tied to the Southern economy were more willing to risk war by enforcing federal law and collecting its revenue. Letters received in Washington from the Republicans' rural heartland registered "disappointment, shame and disgust" with the party's lack of action. Joseph Blanchard from Illinois wrote Lincoln with his concerns about all the "drifting." Westerners, he reported, were "losing confidence in the . . . government and they are beginning to look around for a Garibaldi [a general who fought for Italian unification] or John Brown to organize the hosts of freedom and lead them to victory or death." "Pardon the intrusion," wrote an Ohioan, "but Save us from Shame."[31]

Lincoln was no John Brown, but he knew he had to act. At stake was the survival of his party and the Union, one and the same cause in his mind. Northern opinion, though still divided, was hardening on the need for a decisive move, thus confirming for Lincoln the wisdom of preparing a relief expedition to Fort Sumter. Seward, faced with collapse of his peacekeeping efforts and stealth diplomacy, had two more gambits to play once Lincoln rejected his memorandum.

After baldly assuring the Confederate commissioners that Sumter was still to be evacuated, he maneuvered to make Fort Pickens the focal point of Union resolve and thereby convince Lincoln to drop his plans for Sumter.[32]

At Seward's urging, a strong naval expedition to land troops and supplies was readied for Fort Pickens. Lincoln's approval was secured, and on April 1, he signed orders in which he inadvertently assigned the navy's most powerful warship, the *Powhatan*, to both the Pickens and Sumter missions. The mix-up was Seward's doing. All along he had intended to send the *Powhatan* to Pickens. When Secretary of the Navy Gideon Welles learned of Lincoln's blunder and had him issue a new order to assign the *Powhatan* to Sumter, it was too late to undo Seward's plotting. The *Powhatan* had already set off for Pickens.[33]

Seward's second attempt to salvage his policy involved the Virginia Unionists, who he hoped could convince Lincoln to reconsider the Sumter expedition. In response to Seward's urgent request, the Virginians sent John B. Baldwin to Washington. The only account of his private meeting with Lincoln on April 4 is that provided by Baldwin in 1866. He insisted that Lincoln had offered no quid pro quo, no evacuation of Sumter for a firm pledge that Virginia would remain in the Union. Baldwin pleaded for some conciliatory gesture, such as Lincoln's backing for a national convention for further guarantees for slavery, but none was forthcoming. Unlike Seward, Lincoln was unwilling to yield on the "negro question."[34]

After the meeting, Lincoln finalized with Fox the plans for Sumter and dispatched a courier on April 4 informing Anderson to expect an attempt at resupply within a week. Any possibility that he would sacrifice Sumter for holding onto Fort Pickens (Seward's great hope) evaporated on April 6 when Lincoln learned that the Florida fort had not been reinforced per his directive on March 12. Claiming that he could take orders only from the secretary of the navy and not General Scott, the commanding naval officer refused to allow the troops to land. Although new orders were immediately issued, the status of Fort Pickens was now uncertain and the need to reprovision Sumter even more imperative. On April 6, Robert Chew, a clerk in the state department, left Washington with a message from Lincoln to Governor Pickens of South Carolina. Delivered on April 8, the message stated that an expedition was on the way "to supply Fort Sumpter with provisions only; and that, if such attempt be not resisted, no effort to throw in men, arms, or ammunition will be made, without further notice, or in case of an attack on the fort." By eliminating an attempt to send in troops and arms in favor of sending only supplies, Lincoln had positioned his approach perfectly. On the remote chance that the expedition was allowed to land provisions, he had for the first time gained the initiative and forced the Confederacy to make the next move. If, as was far more likely, the expedition was fired on, the Confederacy had fired the first shot and branded itself as the aggressor.[35]

As signs of Union military activity emerged in early April, Confederates accused the Lincoln administration of deliberately misleading them with all the talk of abandoning Fort Sumter and maintaining the status quo at Fort Pickens before turning it over as well. If the Confederate commissioners had been deceived, it was of their own making. Throughout their stay in Washington, they cynically viewed Seward as their naïve pawn and chose to believe Seward was speaking for Lincoln because it served their purpose of buying time for the Confederacy to gain legitimacy and prepare its defenses. As for Davis, he could not have been deceived, for he never placed much credence in Seward's soothing promises. When news of the relief expedition reached Montgomery, he approached it as the military threat he expected.[36]

Shorn of the firepower of the *Powhatan*, the relief expedition had no chance of forcing its way into Sumter. As it turned out, that was a moot point. Davis, making the correct military decision, ordered General Beauregard in Charleston to demand the immediate surrender of the fort. Citing duty and honor, Anderson rejected the demand but said that "to avoid the useless effusion of blood," he would evacuate the fort at noon on April 15 barring "prior to that time controlling instructions from my Government or additional supplies." That was unacceptable to Davis, and Confederate batteries began shelling the fort around 4:30 on the morning of April 12. Anderson's surrender the next day left Charlestonians jubilant. In an impromptu speech on the evening of April 13, Governor Pickens bellowed that for all the "scorn and contempt" heaped on Carolinians, "we have met them and we have conquered. . . . [W]e have lowered [their flag] in humiliation before the Palmetto and the Confederate flags." The war had just started, but Charlestonians felt they had already won it.[37]

Upheaval in the Upper South: The Second Phase of Secession

The shock waves set off by news of the bombardment and surrender of Fort Sumter did not immediately shake loose any more slave states from the Union. In Virginia, the Unionists had been strong enough on March 25 to defeat a secession resolution by the impressive margin of 88 to 45 votes. The news in early April of federal warships heading south with sealed orders was disturbing, but William Rives, a Unionist Whig, brushed it off by asserting that Lincoln was only engaging in a humanitarian act to supply Anderson's garrison with the food denied them by the Charleston authorities. Confirmation on April 13 of the Confederate attack and Anderson's surrender moved another Unionist, Jubal Early, to declare that "that act has done nothing for the cause of the Confederate

States. It has placed a gulf between them and the people of Virginia." Rives prepared to push ahead with plans to convene a conference of the border states to
make demands which, if accepted by the North, could bind the Union together
again.[38]

Everything changed with Lincoln's call on April 15 for the states to contribute
their proportionate share of 75,000 militia to enforce federal laws and repos-
sess US forts and other property in the Confederacy. He emphasized that the
"utmost care" consistent with these objectives would be taken to respect the
property of "peaceful citizens." Congress alone could raise armies, but Lincoln
could not afford to wait as an inflamed North demanded action to sustain the
government and avenge the insult to the flag at Fort Sumter. Calling out the militia was his only immediate military option. He was confident that Congress,
which he summoned to convene on July 4, would sanction any military measures he undertook. He already had bipartisan support when Stephen Douglas
quickly rallied Northern Democrats behind the flag.[39]

For Virginia's secessionists, Lincoln's troop call-up was a godsend. Ever since
their defeat in the February elections, they had labored unsuccessfully to undercut the Unionist majority. Pro-Confederate mobs were organized to demonstrate on the streets of Richmond to intimidate the Unionist delegates. Rives was
among the many Unionists who charged the slave traders with stirring up the
mobs. Forcing Virginia's secession was certainly in the traders' best interests, but
the mobs had their own agenda and were often difficult to control. Although the
Richmond Enquirer encouraged street demonstrations in favor of secession, one
of its editors in late February drew a line when he persuaded a mob not to burn
an effigy and transparency of Samuel McDowell Moore, a Unionist delegate
from Rockingham County. The mob, likely composed of unemployed workers,
then demanded secession speakers but hooted down all calls for the protection
of slave property. In the words of a reporter, the mob seemed to have "no guiding
star except desire for civil revolution and military excitement, and consequent
change in individual fortune."[40]

Outside Richmond, the secessionists kept up the pressure. They broke
up Union meetings, purchased conservative newspapers, and predicted that
eastern Virginians would rise up in a bloody revolution if secession were denied.
A Leesburg paper advertised for sale effigies of John Jenney, the Unionist
president of the convention. Those who accepted patronage appointments
from the Lincoln administration were warned to step down. A committee in
Charlottesville notified the new mail agent for the Alexandria Road that he had
better give up the post "or he would be dealt with according to his deserts as
a Republican, who would never be permitted to scatter his foul teachings over
Virginia soil." Heeding the warnings of a mob in Petersburg that threatened him
with a coat of tar and feathers, George Kueller, a Bell Whig and lifelong resident

Fig. 10.3 The Hercules of the Union. General-in-chief Winfield Scott was hailed as the first savior of the Union in slaying the monster of secession. Library of Congress, LC-USZ62-40070.

of Virginia, resigned his appointment as the mail agent for the Norfolk and Petersburg Railroad.[41]

The secessionists chipped away at the Unionist majority and, judging by the resolutions of county meetings in March, were gaining new converts. Still, the

Unionists defiantly rejected secession even as new pressure from outside the convention was mounting. Vowing never to remain in the Union, Henry Wise began organizing a Southern Rights Party to "train the popular head and heart." A circular went out announcing a convention of the new party in Richmond on April 16. Although Wise likely intended the convention as a pressuring tactic, he rattled off enough loose talk of seizing federal installations with the secessionist-infiltrated militia to raise the suspicions of the Unionists when they learned of the meeting. A Unionist merchant in Alexandria sounded the alarm: "It behooves every good Union man to be on the alert, and . . . to keep up readiness for I can assure you I firmly believe the secession party will if in their power drag us into a civil war."[42]

The reaction to Lincoln's call for troops eliminated the need for any military coup. Unionist ranks dissolved in rage and disbelief. They felt betrayed, but in fact they had badly misjudged Lincoln in allowing themselves to believe he would accept their demands on slavery and sacrifice his party in a national Union coalition that would broker a sectional settlement. They reacted as if Lincoln could ignore the patriotic outcries in the North for a show of force after Sumter's surrender or disregard the responsibilities of his office. As a result, their outrage was all the more intense. In a flash, it swept away all Unionist feeling in Virginia and left Southerners everywhere convinced, in Botts's florid prose, that Lincoln had declared war for "the subjugation of the entire South, and for the extermination of slaves."[43]

After waiting a day for verification of Lincoln's troop requisition, the convention passed a secession ordinance on April 17 by a vote of 88 to 55. The favorable vote was largely pro forma since Wise had already forced their hand by launching his own revolution. Seeing in Lincoln's order the opening salvo in a war in which the "safety" of the people was "about to be destroyed," Wise demanded that Governor Letcher order the seizure of the federal arsenal at Harper's Ferry and the Gosport Navy Yard at Norfolk, the largest in the US Navy. When Letcher refused, citing the fact that Virginia was still in the Union and that only the convention could authorize such military moves, Wise ignored him and assumed the role of the state's chief executive. On April 16, he drew up orders for the seizures by the militia. Confronted by a fait accompli, Letcher gave his approval the next day.[44]

Virginia was woefully unprepared for the emergency into which secession had plunged it. "Where, in fact, are any of the munitions of war, which are indispensable to our security?" asked A. H. Stuart. Sharing a common border in the northwest with free states and exposed to naval attacks via Chesapeake Bay, the state was in danger of being overrun by federal troops, the presence of which would instantly destabilize slavery despite the limited objectives Lincoln set out in his troop request—the retaking of seized federal property and enforcement of the law. The delegates assumed his real aim was the destruction of slavery.[45]

Virginia's manpower and manufacturing resources made the state too vital to be left unsecured in the gap between the passage of the secession ordinance and the required ratification of that ordinance in a popular election scheduled for May 23. Davis immediately responded to Letcher's request for military assistance by ordering thirteen regiments from the Lower South sent to Virginia. He also dispatched Vice-President Stephens to Richmond to forge a military alliance. In his speech before the convention, he warned that the war would be "for our subjugation and the extermination, if possible, of the whole fabric of our civil and social institutions." To clinch the case for a formal alliance, Stephens dangled as a distinct possibility the removal of the Confederate government from Montgomery to Richmond. On April 24, the alliance was signed, and on April 27 the convention offered Richmond as the permanent seat of the Confederate government. Against the wishes of South Carolina, Florida, and Alabama, the offer was accepted in early May. Placing Virginia at the center of the Confederacy before the secession referendum was held trivialized that election into an endorsement of a decision already made.[46]

Tennessee was not far behind. As in Virginia, shock and outrage greeted Lincoln's call for troops. "We are all in a blaze of Excitement," reported a Unionist dry-goods merchant in Nashville. Most Unionists did an abrupt about-face. John Houston Bills, a Unionist throughout the crisis, now proclaimed that the South would be "a unit, however wrong its leaders may have acted, no one will see the South coerced into submission to such a motley Abolition crew as is headed by Lincoln." As if demonstrating their repentance in a revival, on the night of April 15 former Unionists in Memphis marched to the podium of the Exchange building and confessed the error of their ways as they offered their services to the Confederacy.[47]

An estimated 3,000 Northerners in Memphis fled the city in the spring of 1861 to escape the war hysteria and reprisals for their Unionism. Fear as well as Southern patriotism fed into the decision of the residents of Livingston, Tennessee, to heed the demand of the local secessionists to light their homes with candles in celebration of the surrender of Fort Sumter. They had been forewarned that houses not illuminated would be burned down for belonging to "Lincolnites." The revulsion against Lincoln's order was too great to overcome. Emerson Etheridge called off a Unionist speech in Paris when a mob fired into a crowd of his followers, killing one and wounding several. The Unionists in Blountsville, alarmed over the torching of one of their houses, pleaded with Andrew Johnson and fellow Unionist T. A. R. Nelson not to speak in their county.[48]

Armed neutrality and a working alliance with other border states, most notably Kentucky, to act as mediators in the looming war comprised the fallback
position of the remaining Unionists. Always untenable, it collapsed as the pro-
secession governor, Isham Harris, steered Tennessee out of the Union in barely
more than a week. In the absence of a sitting convention, Harris used the legislature as the fulcrum for secession.[49]

Summoned on April 18 into special session by Harris, the legislature passed
a sweeping series of acts between April 25 and May 9 that decided Tennessee's
fate. It began with a proclamation declaring Tennessee out of the Union, a decision subject to the approval of the voters in an election scheduled for June
8. Commissioners were sent to Montgomery to negotiate a military alliance
with the Confederacy, which was ratified by the legislature on May 7. To pay for
a newly created provisional army, the legislature authorized a $5 million bond
issue and levied new taxes. Parson Brownlow, one of the few outspoken critics,
denounced the actions of the legislature as "outrageous, high-handed and infa-
mous." Much of his venom was directed against the empowering of the county
clerks to raise units of home guards "whose duty it shall be to *arrest all suspected
persons* [of disloyalty]." [50]

The collapse of local Unionist leadership in most counties outside of East
Tennessee left persistent Unionists helpless to contest the harsh threats hurled
at them. These Unionists came from the yeoman farmers, tenants, day laborers,
and small slaveholders who were a majority of the population, even in West
and Middle Tennessee. The protection of the slave interests of planters such as
Governor Harris were of no particular concern to them. However, it took real
courage to buck the disunion tide in the formal secession election on June 8. On
the eve of the election in West Tennessee, local secessionist officials and vigilance committees banished Northern newspapers, ransacked private mail to
ferret out the disloyal, and shut down Unionist editors. Secessionists visited the
reputed Unionist William T. Dickens of Gibson County to tell him that "any
man who voted at [his] precinct for the Union would be hung" and any man
who did not vote would be treated the same. Confederate soldiers on patrol
in West Tennessee added their threats as well. Unionists brave enough to vote
came disproportionately from the poorer counties.[51]

Amanda McDowell, a schoolteacher in White County on the edge of the
Cumberland Plateau, felt secession would have been rejected "if the people had
been allowed to vote their true sentiments." She sympathized with the local
Unionists who dared not vote "for fear of their lives." One of them told her
brother Jack that the election was a "hopeless cause," for "all their liberties had
already been taken away by the 'big bugs' of the county." Another schoolteacher
in north central Tennessee, Mary Sproul, noted that the young man who warned

her father of the danger facing him if he voted was, "like many others, afraid to express his opinion boldly, lest he should be beheaded."[52]

Only East Tennessee, the poorest and most commercially isolated region in the state, returned a majority against secession. For all the suppression of the Union vote elsewhere, popular rage to resist was likely strong enough to carry secession even in a fair and open election. The secessionists, however, left nothing to chance as they gained the popular approval they wanted to legitimate what they had already engineered.[53]

The prospects for secession in Arkansas were so bleak in the early spring that Thomas Hindman suggested to Davis that the Confederacy officially request a regiment of Arkansas troops be organized by August 15 in the hope that it might ignite enough military ardor to induce the people to secede. Lincoln's call for troops put an end to Hindman's doubts over secession. In a recollection perhaps embellished by age, N. B. Pearce recalled that "all was changed in a moment" in Bentonville, a Unionist stronghold in the northwestern corner of Arkansas, when a stagecoach dropped off broadsides announcing Lincoln's troop request. A Unionist crowd, which earlier had "hissed and hooted down" a secessionist speaker, was now a unit for resistance. The press announced that "coercion" had begun and called on "the people of Arkansas [to] resist as one." In a public letter, former Unionists emphasized that the adjourned convention was on record in favor of secession in case of coercion. Bowing to popular pressure and the near certainty that the slaveholding counties in the southeast would bolt to the Confederacy, the convention's president, David Walker, summoned it to meet on May 6.[54]

In the meantime, Governor Rector, as a Union officer at Fort Smith put it, was "acting as though the State had already seceded." After the withdrawal of the Union garrison at Fort Smith on April 24 exposed the tribes in the Indian Territory—the Seminoles, Creeks, Choctaws, Chickasaws, and Cherokees—to raids by the Plains Indians, he ordered militia to occupy the fort. In self-defense, as well as to protect their slave property, the tribes aligned with the Confederacy. The main strategic line in Arkansas was the Mississippi River, and Rector ordered a concentration of state troops near Mound City in Crittenden County to guard the river and interdict federal naval traffic. As expected, the convention, after easily defeating an effort by a shrunken Unionist minority to make secession contingent on a popular referendum, voted to secede on May 7.[55]

And so, the slaveholding minority had its way. Governor Rector spelled out their motivation: "That institution [of slavery] is now upon its trial before you, and if you mean to defend and transmit it to our children, let us terminate this northern crusade, by forming a separate government, in which no conflict [threatening slavery] can arise." Slaveholding Unionists such as Samuel

Hempstead, who had previously grasped at the hope that the eight slave states still in the Union could bring about "a reconstruction of the Union, upon fair, just and honorable terms" for the continuance of slavery, now jumped on the secessionist bandwagon.[56]

Angie McRae of Searcy County, the young wife of a captain in the Arkansas militia, left no record of her political leanings, but she was no stranger to the slave-centered concerns of Rector and Hempstead. From the very onset of hostilities, she feared the unsettled wartime conditions would incite the slaves to rebellion. Her husband responded to her "distress of mind" by assuring her that Southern soldiers would protect her. His absence from home, he stressed, had nothing to do with a "thirst for military distinction; my only aim is to keep back the hordes of abandoned ruffians that threaten the home, the peace and the life of our loved ones." In near identical words, Confederate soldiers valorized their military service as their manly duty to preserve domestic peace from an invasion of Northerners intent on a savage war of extermination.[57]

As in the other states of the Upper South, Lincoln's troop proclamation destroyed the Unionist majority in North Carolina. The same scenario— outrage and disbelief, a rush to enlist for the state's defense, the seizure of federal forts and arsenals, and military cooperation with the Confederacy—played itself out. Governor Ellis summed up what had happened when he wrote Davis in late April: "The State is to all intents practically out of the old Union and we are deciding the speediest mode of giving legal sanction to this State of facts." A call was issued for an election on May 13 for a state convention, and on May 20, it easily passed an ordinance of secession.[58]

Unionist leaders, conservative planters with extensive slaveholdings, com- mitted at once to secession. For them, Lincoln had become the great betrayer who had led them on to believe he wanted a peaceful resolution of the crisis, only, in a single stroke, to throw away and crush all they had worked for. Down to April 15, they were confident that a border state conference could exert the pressure for a sectional agreement. Then came the thunderbolt of Lincoln's proc- lamation. Struggling to make sense of what Lincoln had done, Jonathan Worth, concluded that Lincoln was either "a fool" to think that military action could ever restore the Union or "a Devil" whose purpose was "to drive off all the Slave states in order to make war on them and annihilate Slavery." After wavering, Worth leaned toward Lincoln as the abolitionist devil whom he "could fight with a hearty goodwill."[59]

As formerly Unionist planters now backed resistance, Unionist sentiment continued to smolder among poorer North Carolinians. Alarmed citizens of Yadkin County wrote Ellis that Caleb Bohanan, the commander of a local regiment, was telling his men not to fight for the Confederacy but to an- swer any call by Lincoln for volunteers. Writing off Bohanan as an ignorant rabble-rouser, the citizens wanted him "disgraced" by immediately stripping him of his command. Elsewhere, small farmers were threatening to plunder the property of slaveholders they blamed for the war. Reports reached Ellis in May that non-slaveholders in Beaufort County in the east were "willing to sacrifice the slaves to secure other kinds of property." Ellis's informant recommended that slaves be taxed at the same rates as land in order to quell the unrest.[60]

Dissent turned violent in Northampton County, a Piedmont area just south of the Virginia line. An armed band, "a most desperate & lawless gang of white men," was too strong to be put down by the home guard. They had so "corrupted the negroes free & slaves" that a local citizen asked for troops to be sent "to keep them in proper subjection & subordination." In the southwestern county of Henderson in the Blue Ridge Mountains, Ellis learned that a group of "trators" [*sic*] openly declared that "the south was wrong & corrupt & ought to be subdued." They vowed not to fight for the Confederacy and to hold their ground until Lincoln's army arrived to "save them & their property." Homes already had been burned and neighborhoods were hiring night guards.[61]

Desperate economic conditions added fuel to the class resentments exploding into sporadic outbreaks of violence and vengeance. Property values had been sliced in half since November, debtors were being hounded, and no relief was in sight. "Every one is in a panic," wrote David Schenck in March, "and ready for any change which may give them employment." He predicted that "revolution will be the only safety valve if things continue longer as they are." Relieving some of the pressure for the volunteer soldiers in the buildup for war after Lincoln's troop proclamation was the pay for the privates, promises of aid for their families from the planters, and escape from debts. In response to widespread complaints of "unpatriotic and evil disposed persons" serving sheriff's writs for the collection of debts from troops encamped around Raleigh, Ellis called on the legislature for a law "prohibiting the service of any kind of civil process" on any of the military enlistees during the period of their service and for one year thereafter. The legislature complied with a stay law forbidding the collection of all debts whether domestic or foreign.[62]

By late April, North Carolina's secession was a mere formality. Unionism as an organized movement had collapsed, its rank and file were "indifferent and torpid," and its leaders had joined Holden in favor of "resisting to the last extremity the usurpations and aggressions of the federal government." Turnout was light in the election for convention delegates, most of whom were declared secessionists. In a nod to their principled stand against secession as a constitutional right, Whigs introduced a resolution at the convention defining secession as "revolutionary." After defeating the resolution, the convention unanimously

Fig. 10.4 Secession Exploded. As more states seceded in the spring of 1861, Northerners turned to brute force to destroy the demonic secession movement. Library of Congress, LC-USZ62-89738.

passed a secession ordinance on May 20. The Confederacy had its eleventh, and last, state.[63]

The Border States: Shaken but Unmoved

The same resort to federal military action that triggered secession in the Upper South was instrumental in retaining the border slave states in the Union. Slaveholders in all these states were sympathetic to secession, but even after Lincoln's call for troops they were unable to build a political majority. In Delaware and Kentucky, they grimly awaited developments. In Maryland and Missouri, they tried to force their states into the Confederacy through a combination of mob violence and military leverage.

Geographically close to Philadelphia and sharing no border with a Confederate state, Delaware was safe for the Union as long as Maryland did not secede. Still, that did not prevent Governor William Burton, a state's rights Democrat from proslavery southern Delaware, from refusing Lincoln's call to send troops. Burton's dismissal of Lincoln clashed with the acceptance of coercive measures by the conservatives after the loss of Fort Sumter. Reports of the treatment of Unionists in Virginia and armed resistance in Baltimore against federal troops in transit through the city angered the Unionists. "This . . . spitting on the heads of the Union men from the galleries in the Virginia Convention and the anarchy in Maryland has completely disgusted me," wrote Henry A. Dupont. Burton was enough of a pragmatist to appoint Henry's influential father commander of state troops in May. The father used that post to funnel federal arms to pro-Union militia, provide protection for his massive gunpowder works, and in time to disarm the pro-Confederate militias in the southern counties. Delaware would be a solid ally in the Union war effort.[64]

Unlike Burton, Thomas Hicks, Maryland's governor, was committed to the Union. Nonetheless, in mid-April his state teetered on the edge of secession. Most businessmen, notably owners of large firms with markets in the North, backed the Union, but their smaller competitors dependent on trade with the South saw their future in the Confederacy. By late March, William Dorsey Pender, who was in Baltimore as a recruiting agent for the Confederate army, had shipped more than a hundred men southward. He boasted to his wife that he "was backed up by the sympathy of the first men here," including the police. With its large numbers of unemployed, Baltimore served as a fertile recruiting ground. The city had been hit particularly hard in the depression following Lincoln's election. "The suffering among not only the poor but those who have been accustomed to the comforts of life are heartrending," reported resident Mary Pettigrew Brown in March. Letters filled the *Baltimore Sun* with tales of businesses "nearly ruined," one of which was from a clothing firm that had laid off 1,000 of its 1,200 workers. Here was a cauldron of frustrations ready to be mobilized by a call to action in a preemptive strike for secession that would bring membership in the Confederacy and presumed economic relief. Such a call was issued by the State's Rights Party in Baltimore on April 18. Energized by Virginia's secession, the party demanded that all Marylanders unite to "repel . . . any invader who may come to establish a military despotism over us." Merchants and unskilled Irish workers jammed the streets on April 19 to harass and attack Northern troops, infuriating symbols of the Union that had doomed them to economic misery and seemingly were intent on freeing the slaves, thus adding to the competition for jobs.[65]

All rail traffic from the North connected to Baltimore, where a transfer across the city was necessary to reach the Washington-bound trains. Mobs attacked the Sixth Massachusetts Regiment with bricks, paving stones, and scattered gunfire. The troops fired back. Secondary battles erupted between pro-Union, native-born workers aligned with former Know-Nothings and largely unskilled immigrants loyal to the pro-secession Democrats. One recent study placed the death toll at thirteen soldiers and twelve civilians.[66]

Samuel Wethered, a textile manufacturer with extensive business ties in the South, dashed off a frantic letter to his brother-in-law in North Carolina blaming "the vile Black Republicans" for the civilian deaths. "You may depend on it we are out of the Union." Equally confident that Maryland was on the verge of going out, the *Baltimore Sun* praised the rioters for "the organization and efficiency of the excitement and patriotism of the people" and warned Governor Hicks that unless he convened the legislature to take up secession, he would "make necessary those revolutionary proceedings which it is best to avoid."[67]

For the better part of a week, the secessionists moved aggressively to exploit the excitement. The Baltimore police and the Maryland Guard, a militia formed after John Brown's raid, burned rail bridges around the city and in towns to the north. Bands of pro-Confederate militia joined them and destroyed the telegraph line to Washington. To gain time, Lincoln agreed not to route any troops through Baltimore, but as he pointed out to a delegation of Baltimore officials, geography dictated that troops for the protection of Washington had to pass through Maryland. With a touch of sarcasm, he added: "Keep your rowdies in Baltimore, and there will be no bloodshed." Temporary arrangements were made to ferry troops across the Chesapeake Bay to Annapolis, where they could board trains to Washington. In a stark reminder of what Southerners assumed the war was all about, the arrival of the troops in Annapolis set off fears of "an insurrection of the negroes." The commanding Union officer, Benjamin F. Butler, had to assure locals that he stood ready to suppress "any insurrection against the laws of Maryland." Slaves did flee to Union forces but were immediately returned to their owners.[68]

The secession tide ebbed once Union troops were stationed in Maryland. The wanton violence of the Baltimore rioters weakened the secessionists by infuriating Northerners inclined to be conciliatory and solidified Unionism in northern Maryland, where the *Cecil Whig* called for all-out resistance to the "aristocratic military despotism" of the Confederates and their sympathizers. The secessionists did force Hicks to summon the legislature to meet on April 26. If it opted for secession or arming the state against the Union, Lincoln was prepared to use whatever military force was necessary to assert federal authority. His instructions to General Winfield Scott were quite direct. If the legislature decided on armed rebellion, Scott was "to adopt the most prompt, and efficient means to counteract, even, if necessary, to the bombardment of their cities." To impose martial law where conditions warranted, Lincoln on April 27 suspended the writ of habeas corpus on the "military line" between Philadelphia and Washington.[69]

Hicks moved the special session of the legislature from Annapolis to Frederick, a pro-Union site in western Maryland where the presence of federal soldiers would not be an irritant. Secessionists had a slim majority in the legislature, but differences over tactics—calling a convention or seceding by legislative action—and a determined opposition stymied them. Above all, Maryland's exposed position doomed their efforts. The federal troops in the state and large numbers of reinforcements assembling just across the border in Pennsylvania made any bid for secession foolhardy. By early May, the secessionists admitted defeat. Union soldiers never left for the duration of the war and at politically sensitive moments arrested pro-Confederate politicians and editors. Though still secessionists at heart, slaveholders in southern Maryland and their commercial allies in Baltimore could only obstruct, not prevent, the imposition of federal control.[70]

Compounding the Confederacy's failure to gain Maryland was its loss of the trans-Allegheny region of Virginia in the early months of the war. Most delegates from the west were steadfast in their Unionism throughout the Virginia convention, even voting two-to-one against the passage of the secession ordinance. At the root of their opposition was not hostility to slavery, though the vast majority of their constituents were non-slaveholders, but chronic resentments against the political dominance of eastern planters who refused to grant them equality in taxation, representation, and access to funds for internal improvements. Not only did western Virginians reject the planters' agenda for the Confederacy, but those in the Panhandle also identified economically with neighboring Ohioans and Pennsylvanians. Secession meant a war in which they would be militarily crushed and financially ruined. Adding insult to injury, their unequal tax burden would support the eastern slaveholders who would continue to oppress them. "If secession is pleasing and profitable for Eastern Virginia . . . let her go—but let her understand that she goes without the West," declared the *Wheeling Intelligencer*. Staring down death threats for his Unionism in the form of halters hung from trees outside the window of his boarding house in Richmond, William T. Willie, a Morganton lawyer, refused to budge from his belief that secession would "dissever the people of Virginia lying along our North western border from those on the other side of the line." In a last-ditch effort to win over the trans-Allegheny delegates, the easterners capitulated on the issue of ad valorem taxation for slaves four days before the convention adjourned. But it was too late and changed few, if any, minds.[71]

The westerners were as good as their word. Panhandle counties refused to comply with Governor Letcher's call for enlisting in Confederate militia and instead seized arms intended for the militia and organized pro-Union military companies. News of the secession ordinance spurred the formation of vigilance committees pledged to "unequivocal non-conformity to any decree Letcher may issue." As early as April 22, a call went out for a meeting in Wheeling to organize the northwestern counties as a separate state or as part of another Union state.[72]

Confederate efforts to secure the "safety and quiet" of the Panhandle faced insurmountable obstacles, chief of which was the absence of any ready means of sending in men and supplies. Relative to Richmond, the Panhandle was remote and very difficult to reach. Outlining a triangle with Wheeling on the north and Parkersburg and Grafton on the west and east, the Baltimore and Ohio Railroad with its branches served as the only vital rail line. Union troops poured across the Ohio River in May and, assisted by local forces, sealed off the triangle. To Lucy Wood Butler in Charlottesville, it seemed as if northwestern Virginians must be "nearly composed entirely of abolitionists" to allow such a Union advance. A major in the Virginia Volunteers reported from Grafton on May 10 that the area was "verging on a state of actual rebellion," but Confederate measures to put it down effectively ended with the Union victory at Rich Mountain on July 11.[73]

By swiftly gaining control of the Panhandle, Union forces enabled pro-Union politicians to meet in safety. After a series of conventions and highly irregular maneuverings, a "restored" state government, headed by the Wheeling coal magnate Francis Pierpont, claiming to speak for all of Virginia, approved its dismembering by recognizing the new state of West Virginia. Within its boundaries were counties to the southwest of the Panhandle that were not nearly as pro-Union and centers of pro-Confederate guerrilla resistance. As a precondition for its admission to the Union on June 20, 1863, West Virginia had to amend its constitution to provide for the gradual emancipation of its slaves.[74]

Kentucky had none of the Panhandle's early battles and was able to maintain a position of neutrality as long as neither Lincoln nor Davis considered it in their best interests to violate it. Had the legislature been in session when Lincoln's call for troops rocked the state, the secessionists might have succeeded in stampeding the state out of the Union. Certainly, it was their best opportunity. The pro-secession *Louisville Courier* filled its columns with notices seeking volunteers for regiments to repel the "Abolition hordes . . . attempting to subjugate the Southern people." County meetings passed pro-secession resolutions, with former Unionists joining in the public surge in favor of resistance. In the absence, however, of a galvanizing event to focus the outrage, such as the Baltimore riot, the Unionists were able to quell the storm. Led by Bell and Douglas politicians, they came out for neutrality, arguing that since the Confederacy had started the war, Kentuckians had the right to choose their position. While strongly opposing the Union's call for troops, they did likewise with the Confederacy's request for volunteers. As long as the Union engaged in no openly aggressive acts, they pledged their loyalty. For the time being, they counseled an independent stance for Kentucky free of soldiers from either side. Consistent with their prior views, they held that "secession is the remedy for no evils."[75]

Apart from blunting a bid for secession, neutrality had the virtue of temporarily keeping Kentuckians from fighting one another. Edmund Ruffin's daughter, who lived in Kentucky, observed that the state was "so divided & each party so bitter against the other, that there is very great danger of fighting in our midst."

Aware of those divisions and buffeted by both factions, Governor Magoffin laid aside his pro-Confederate leanings and consulted with the governors of Indiana and Ohio to offer the state's service as a mediator seeking a truce. Perhaps then, when the US Congress met on July 4, terms for a settlement could be reached.[76]

Magoffin's neutrality reflected his weak position. Gideon Pillow, who was in Kentucky seeking Magoffin's military cooperation with the Confederacy, recognized the governor's predicament. He valued Magoffin as a Southern "patriot" but conceded the governor was "in a very helpless condition." Having no arms and facing "great peril," he had "for the present made terms with Lincoln by agreeing to occupy neutral ground." Accordingly, Magoffin refused to erect batteries at Columbus, a southwestern Kentucky town overlooking the Mississippi River. At the same time, Louisville bankers spurned Magoffin's request for a large loan. The Unionist bankers, suspecting that Magoffin would use the funds to purchase arms for a pro-Confederate militia, stipulated that any loan was contingent on application by the legislature for purposes of defense.[77]

Magoffin pinned his hopes for secession on the legislature, which he called into special session on May 6. In the weeks leading up to the session, the most committed secessionists left the state in volunteer regiments pledged to Confederate service. The Unionists organized Home Guards and awaited arms to be distributed to them that Lincoln had arranged to be shipped to Cincinnati under the control of William Nelson, a naval lieutenant who served as his liaison. Confederate agents recruited in the state, but Lincoln refused the raising of Union troops on Kentucky soil. The only Kentuckians he would accept were those who could cross over into Ohio for enlistment.[78]

Convinced that Magoffin was "a secessionist and a traitor," Unionists kept him and other state's rights Democrats in check when the legislature met. In his opening message, Magoffin depicted Missouri, Maryland, and Delaware as all moving toward secession in response to "strong public sentiment" and warned that the subjugation of the states that had already seceded would result in "the unlimited slaughter of their citizens." Such a fate could be in store for Kentuckians since the state was defenseless from "invasion from without, or servile insurrection within." Insisting that Kentuckians should decide on how to meet the crisis, he called for "a reference of the question to the people."[79]

Judging by the sixty-five petitions from women to the legislature "praying that Kentucky maintain inviolate an armed neutrality," the citizens had already chosen a course of action. A diluted, politically mandated expression of conditional Unionism, the stance of neutrality kept the secessionists at bay. By a vote of 69 to 26, the House committed to neutrality on May 16. Four days later, Magoffin issued an official proclamation to that effect. The Senate passed its own neutrality resolution on the day the legislature adjourned. The Unionists sealed their triumph by creating and dominating a five-member military board that assumed Magoffin's authority to borrow funds for arms and to direct the state's military preparations.[80]

As measured by the legislative votes on neutrality, the larger, older planters from traditional Whig counties provided the major counterweight to secession. Among slaveholders, they were the most pro-neutrality. The core of the secessionists came out of the Jackson Purchase. Isolated in trading ties from the rest of the state, slaveholders here looked down the Mississippi for the marketing of their tobacco. Their politics followed their economic interests.[81]

The border state conference, of which so much had been expected in the winter and spring, fizzled out in irrelevance. At its gathering in Frankfort on May 27, only Kentucky sent a full delegation. Joined by a handful of representatives from Missouri and Tennessee, it sought what border state conservatives always wanted but could never obtain, mainly some version of the Crittenden Compromise. Failing that, they could only hope that the war would not become one of emancipation.[82]

Contrary to Magoffin, Missouri's Claiborne Jackson tried to force his state's secession under cover of a policy of armed neutrality. Before summoning the legislature into session to prepare the state's defenses, he sent agents to Montgomery requesting artillery for an attack on the St. Louis arsenal, the major source of arms in the state. Davis responded on April 23 that the heavy guns were on the way. He signed off with a fond wish for the day that Missouri seceded.[83]

Jackson was counting on panic-stricken Missourians seeing in Lincoln's troop proclamation the beginning of a war against slavery. Declaring that the "abolition fanatics" had always wanted to "destroy the South," the *St. Louis State Sentinel* now saw them "fomenting and encouraging slave insurrection." It demanded "a second war of Independence." Conditional Unionists also dreaded a sudden, forced emancipation of the slaves, for, as the Reverend S. J. P. Anderson warned, that could be achieved only "by the death of the master or by the death of the slaves." Unlike the secessionists, however, the Unionists believed that neutrality was the only way to prevent military emancipation.[84]

Three days after Jackson spurned Lincoln's call for troops, Clay County secessionists seized the small arsenal in Liberty. In Chariton, another county in the western extension of Little Dixie and one where slavery was growing at the fastest rate in the state, resolutions called on the state legislature to pass a secession ordinance. A new banking law in 1857 had made funds available for the expansion of slavery in these counties. Favored by the area's slaveholding elite, the law shifted capital out of St. Louis and required the establishment of new state banks. Among the beneficiaries was Sterling Price, planter, former governor, and future Confederate general.[85]

The Unionists became alarmed by the rise of secession sentiment in St. Louis, especially when they learned that Governor Jackson was secretly receiving artillery from the Confederacy. Two of their members, Frank Blair Jr. and Nathaniel Lyon, an openly Republican army officer transferred from Kansas to St. Louis in February, mustered recruits at the St. Louis arsenal and claimed its weapons. What arms were not distributed to Unionist home guards were shipped to southern Illinois for safe-keeping. Lyon's preemptive move deprived Governor Jackson of his best chance of seizing the arsenal and its 60,000 small arms desperately needed by the pro-secession Minute Men. In a decision that made little military sense but was politically provocative, Jackson authorized a bivouac of 700 state militia at Camp Jackson on the western outskirts of the city. With an overwhelmingly larger force, composed mostly of German Americans, Lyon forced the surrender of the camp on May 10 with, in his words, its "rabid and violent oppressors of the General Government." As the prisoners were marched through the streets of St. Louis on May 11 on their way to jail, onlookers outraged over their treatment staged a repeat of the Baltimore riots in April. The tally of those killed was thirty-three, most of them civilians.[86]

The St. Louis riot ignited the internal violence that plagued Missouri throughout the war. The legislature granted Jackson all the military power he wanted, but his resources were no match for the Union's control of St. Louis, the state capital of Jefferson City, and the state's railroad and river networks. First Lyon (killed at the battle of Wilson's Creek on August 10, 1861) and then his successor, John C. Frémont, used brute force to impose federal authority. Though reduced to fleeing with his followers, Jackson kept up the resistance. He turned to pro-Confederate bankers to fund his loyal militia, now christened the State Guard. The bankers in Little Dixie extended 2,900 loans totaling $3 million to secessionist families, who then signed off on promissory notes for the purchase of arms. As the Union army extended its control across the state, the notes lost their value, leaving much of the slaveholding elite hopelessly in debt. With nothing to lose once their inheritances were wiped out, the sons of slaveholders joined marauding guerrilla bands.[87]

Most likely, Jackson's dream of a Confederate Missouri was always beyond his reach. Secession had little appeal to the state's large majority of non-slaveholders and St. Louis businessmen, and slaveholders were divided. Many planters blanched at the prospect of losing federal protection for slavery. The most secessionist-minded slaveholders were in the western stretches of Little Dixie, where the acquisition of slaves remained the surest path to social advancement. Jackson, their political hero, did not give up easily. Constantly on the run, he raised troops for the Confederacy, sought assistance from Jefferson Davis, and exhorted the faithful. Ravaged by tuberculosis and stomach cancer, he died in exile in Arkansas in December 1862, eight months after the Union victory at Pea Ridge in northwestern Arkansas eliminated an organized Confederate military presence in Missouri for most of the rest of the war.[88]

Although Kentucky and Missouri would be token members of the Confederacy after rump conventions passed secession ordinances, the slaveholders' republic remained effectively at eleven states. Its inability to win over the border slave states would cost it dearly in the war ahead.

Conclusion

The war came, stamping secession as the most disruptive event in American history. Joseph Cowens, who died for a cause he believed in, and his slave William Robinson, who was freed in a cause he despised, were among the countless whose lives were altered forever. By propelling events that culminated in the Civil War, secession resulted in a staggering national disaster that presented a butcher's bill of 750,000 war deaths. That was the price Confederates were willing to pay for the defense of slavery. Southern whites who favored a war for independence could not have been clearer that slavery was the cause of the war. "The prime cause of this conflict is African slavery in this country," declared South Carolina planter Henry Ravenel. "On the issue of the contest rests its triumph or its complete overthrow." Publicly and privately, others said the same.[1]

Secession was the culmination of rearguard battles slaveholders had fought since the late eighteenth century when the first sustained attack against slavery emerged in the Western world. Reformist currents produced by the Enlightenment, British efforts to reclaim the moral high ground after their mainland colonists decried their political enslavement and mounted a successful revolution grounded in an ideology decrying their political enslavement, and Caribbean slaves' appropriation of the egalitarian promises of the French Revolution all put slavery on the defensive. The Haitian slaves of Sainte-Domingue seized their freedom in a bloody uprising, and their compatriots in the Caribbean launched a series of sporadic, though futile, revolts. Britain abolished the African slave trade in 1807 and the US Congress followed a year later. Except for Brazil, independence movements in Spanish America swept aside slavery, and Spain was left with only the slave colonies of Cuba and Puerto Rico. By the middle of the century, European nations had emancipated the slaves in their New World empires.[2]

Liberalizing currents carried forward by a new middle class and republican-minded workers swept continental Europe into the revolutions of 1848 against the hierarchical old order. Though suppressed, the revolutionaries held fast to their liberal agenda. Italy and Poland joined Ireland in demanding national self-rule.

This was the international context of insurgent liberalism the Confederacy sought to reverse with its bid for a reactionary slaveholders' republic ruled by a landed elite. Its defeat in the Civil War was a setback for conservative regimes in Europe intent on further repression at home and the imposition of new imperial regimes in the Americas, such as Emperor Napoleon III's designs on Mexico and Spain's on Sainte-Domingue. As Lincoln recognized, the Union's cause was the cause of Western liberalism, and the Confederacy's attempt to claim the mantle of national self-determination found no traction among the European masses who backed the Union.[3]

In retrospect, the secessionists' bid for independence appears suicidal, but no proud ruling class engages in the self-abnegation of allowing themselves to be degraded and consigned to the dustbin of history. Once African Americans inspired Northern whites, albeit only a very small minority, to launch a movement for abolition, slavery was under siege at home as well as abroad, and antislavery Northerners never let Southern whites forget it. "You who advocate the perpetuity of slavery," roared Owen Lovejoy on the floor of Congress, "are like a set of madcaps, who should place themselves on the top of an iceberg which has disengaged itself from the frozen regions of the north, and begun to float downward, and downward, through the warm climates."[4]

The most prominent of the "madcaps" were the fire-eaters, the radical state's rights ideologues who preached that the South's salvation was outside the Union. By a strained interpretation of the Constitution, they made secession conceivable as a legal right. Decades of fulminations against the wrongs inflicted on the South by greedy Northern businessmen and fanatical abolitionists normalized secession as a remedy for Southern perceptions of victimization. Yet, despite the propagandizing of the radical vanguard, most Southern whites were unswayed until they saw in Lincoln's election an existential threat to their way of life and the moral foundations on which it rested. "It is not the physical power, but the moral effect I dread," explained a Virginia secessionist. "Let us once enlist under the banner of Lincoln, and the integrity of our institutions is forever lost."[5]

Many whites feared those "institutions" would be lost in a sea of blood. The specter of black vengeance was never far from their thoughts. In the fall of 1860, Rebecca Young felt that specter was about to make her South "as insecure a home as though it were situated at the base of some ever-threatening and never-to-be-trusted volcano." The awful dread earlier sensed by an English visitor to Alabama was now almost tangible. "What will be the end of American slavery?" he asked. "I know that many dare not entertain this question. They tremble when they look at the future. It is like a huge deadly serpeant [sic], which is kept down by incessant vigilance . . . , while the dreadful feeling is ever present, that, some day or other, it will burst the weight that binds it, and take a fearful retribution." In the minds of most whites, Lincoln's call for troops heralded the coming of the day of retribution. Slave insurrections were the last thing that Lincoln wanted, but it made no difference. For Southern whites, his intention to send Northern troops onto their land could have no other effect. "We shall be obliged to fight, and negro insurrections will abound" was one Virginia's woman's matter-of-fact assessment."[6]

The liberty to own slaves, fears of those same slaves, defense of their homes, and a demand for the respect of an outside world that defamed them as sinners were all one and the same as a motive for secession and independence. Faced with the refusal of the Republicans to allow slavery's expansion and obsessed with the decline of slavery in the Border South and its lack of growth in the Upper South, planters imagined a swelling black majority in the Lower South coming to power once the Republicans had breached all constitutional barriers to emancipation. Rather than submit to such a desecration of the white race, they reasoned it was far better to gamble on secession and die honorably if they lost the gamble.

In the Lower South, where slavery infused every aspect of life and slaves were on the verge of outnumbering whites, slaveholders quickly came out for secession once Lincoln was elected. Calls by conservatives to delay secession through unified action by the slave states to gain Northern concessions rang hollow when a congressional compromise on the extension of the Missouri Compromise line collapsed over Republican objections. Older, wealthier planters tended to hang back, while younger slaveholders, especially lawyers and sons of planters whose yearnings for status far outpaced their prospects for success in peacetime, led the charge. South Carolina was the exception. Massive out-migration, depleted soils, and a lack of entrepreneurial innovations had left the state economically stagnant with a proud planter class desperate to regain lost glory once free of the Union's grasp. Slaveholders in the Upper South initially divided along party lines. Democrats in plantation districts pushed for secession, and Whigs continued to look to the Union for the protection of slavery until Lincoln's call for troops in April 1861.

Faced with a singular moment of opportunity, the secessionists forged ahead regardless of the consequences. Their great challenge was winning over enough of the white majority who owned no slaves to enable them to carry the elections for delegates to secession conventions. Popular support for secession emerged in the Lower South in the winter of 1860–61, but it was heavily influenced by the secessionists' command of the governorships and the state legislatures and their control of most of the press and pulpit. Not trusting appeals to class and race alone, they enlisted non-slaveholders into their cause through paramilitary organizations at the local level, which were dedicated to proclaiming white manhood through resisting the imposition of any Republican rule and eliminating any lingering Unionism. They carefully managed the secession elections in the

Lower South so as to follow the forms of democratic politics but not the substance. They limited any real choices and used violence and intimidation to suppress any signs of opposition. Most tellingly, once secession ordinances were passed, they refused (except Texas) to allow them to be submitted to the people in a popular vote. Both the state conventions and the Montgomery convention assumed vast legislative powers on behalf of the new Confederacy but had no direct mandate from the people.

The far larger majorities of non-slaveholders and the organizational strength of the pro-Union Whigs in the Upper South made possible open, fair elections on secession that resulted in its rejection and a hedged commitment to the Union, conditional on further concessions to slavery. It was an unstable position that collapsed in a rush to the Confederacy as Lincoln's call for troops was seen as an invasion to end slavery.

Until Lincoln's call for troops and the identification of secession with the defense of the Southern homeland, secession had gained majority support only in the Lower South. In the slave states as a whole, it lacked a popular mandate. With the exception of South Carolina, whites in the Lower South initially divided along class lines over straight-out secession, especially in Alabama and Georgia where the yeomanry dominated in the northern mountains. Whites in the Upper South were torn by indecision and refused to go out on the issue of slavery alone. In the four slave states of the Border South, comprising nearly one-third of the South's white population, secession was never a real possibility. Secession and Southern independence meant little to the poorest one-third of whites who owned neither land nor slaves. They entered the Confederate army primarily through the forced mechanism of the draft, passed in April 1862.

The pro-secession euphoria in the spring of 1861 evaporated by 1863. The liberties promised by secession were denied by the coercive demands of the Confederate bureaucracy in enforcing war regulations. Congressional elections in the fall of 1863 registered stinging defeats for most of the original secessionists. By then, bands of Unionists, deserters, draft evaders, and impoverished whites, aided by their wives and kin, were waging an internal war against the Confederacy as they rejected the revolution staged by the slaveholding minority.

The war that came exposed the hollowness of the secessionists' claims of peaceable withdrawal sealed by rapid recognition of the Confederacy by the British desperate for Southern cotton. Nor did the North collapse in bankruptcy and class warfare. The enslaved, hailed as a great strength in their loyalty to the Confederacy, escaped to Union armies or ships in liberating themselves wherever they could. The cracks in Southern white unity that the common cause of independence was meant to heal burst open in hatreds and violence that persisted into Reconstruction.

The legacy of secession was the prostrate South at war's end engulfed in an unfathomable tragedy of death, poverty, and broken bodies. Though non-slaveholders were going absent without leave from the army in alarming numbers by 1863, slaveholders continued to fight to the end as valiantly possible. To resist was to engage in a holy war in defense of a providentially ordained way of life and fulfillment of a mission God had assigned them. Steeling his confidence in ultimate victory, Tally Simpson of South Carolina believed, along with other evangelicals, that "God is with us because our people are more conscientious and religious than our enemies." God's will operated differently for antislavery Northerners. "God grant that all the slave-holders may rebel, and remain in rebellion, till the emancipation of their slaves is accomplished!" was the fondest wish of Lydia Maria Child early in the war. She thanked "Jeff. Davis [for] goad[ing] the free States into doing, from policy and revenge, what they have not manhood to do from justice and humanity."[7]

Tally Simpson was killed in the battle of Chickamauga in September 1863, one of the more than 200,000 Confederates who paid the terrible price glorified in postwar Confederate memories as selfless sacrifice on the altar of Southern liberties. Many of the maimed on the battlefield suffered slow, agonizing deaths. Tending to her mortally wounded son in 1864 at the Stuart Hospital in Richmond, Mrs. William Pringle Smith was appalled by what she witnessed. She wrote of how "they bury the dead like animals, without any religious service & without clothes *almost* entirely. They say the Confederacy cannot afford to lose the clothes." Her son, paralyzed from the waist down by a bullet lodged in his pelvis, needed constant attention to brush the flies from his face. She asked him if he would enlist again and come to Virginia now "knowing the results." He answered, "Yes, for I came from a sense of duty in the sight of God, and with the hope of approval of my Uncle & those I love, also of those whose opinion I respect in the community."[8]

John S. Palmer, among the most fervid of the South Carolina secessionists, had no idea of "the horror of this [war]" until he visited the Richmond hospitals in 1862. Already thousands of Confederates had been killed and many more maimed for life. "Great God of Heaven!" he cried out when faced with the awful suffering. His only consolation was his acceptance of the war as "the province of God . . . meant to scourge nations for national sins. If so, we must have incurred the finality and are now expiating in full the calamities of the decree sent forth." The sins were indeed national ones, but contrary to Palmer's expectations, the carnage of the Civil War was only a down payment on their atonement.[9]

NOTES

Introduction

1. This account is based on William H. Robinson, *From Log Cabin to the Pulpit, or Fifteen Years in Slavery* (Eau Claire, Wis.: James H. Tift, 1913), 92–96.
2. See Henry T. Shanks, *The Secession Movement in Virginia, 1847–61* (Richmond, Va.: Garrett and Massie, 1934); Percy Lee Rainwater, *Mississippi: Storm Center of Secession, 1856–61* (Baton Rouge, La.: O. Claitor, 1938); Roger W. Shugg, *Origins of Class Struggle in Louisiana* (Baton Rouge: Louisiana State University Press, 1939); J. Carlyle Sitterson, *The Secession Movement in North Carolina* (Chapel Hill: University of North Carolina Press, 1939).
3. See Steven A. Channing, *Crisis of Fear: Secession in South Carolina* (New York: Simon and Schuster, 1970); William L. Barney, *The Secessionist Impulse: Alabama and Mississippi in 1860* (Princeton, N.J.: Princeton University Press, 1974); Michael P. Johnson, *Toward a Patriarchal Republic: The Secession of Georgia* (Baton Rouge: Louisiana State University Press, 1977).
4. J. Mills Thornton III, *Politics and Power in a Slave Society: Alabama, 1800–1860* (Baton Rouge: Louisiana State University Press, 1978).
5. Bertram Wyatt-Brown, *Southern Honor: Ethics and Behavior in the Old South* (New York: Oxford University Press, 1982).
6. Stephanie McCurry, *Masters of Small Worlds: Yeoman Households, Gender Relations, and the Political Culture of the Antebellum South Carolina Low Country* (New York: Oxford University Press, 1997); Daniel W. Crofts, *Reluctant Confederates: Upper South Unionists in the Secession Crisis* (Chapel Hill: University of North Carolina Press 1989).
7. For a short but powerful work that drives home this point, see Charles B. Dew, *Apostles of Disunion: Southern Secession Commissioners and the Causes of the Civil War*, 2nd ed. (Charlottesville: University Press of Virginia, 2016). It should also be noted that in the 1850s the South sought the national protection of slavery and denounced the efforts of Northern states to interpose their authority against enforcement of the Fugitive Slave Act of 1850.
8. William W. Freehling, *The Road to Disunion*, Vol. 2, *Secessionists Triumphant, 1854–1861* (New York: Oxford University Press, 2007), lays out this argument in exquisite detail.
9. Though dated, Dwight Lowell Dumond, *The Secession Movement, 1860–1861* (New York: Macmillan, 1931), is still a useful political overview of secession in the states that did secede.
10. In addition to the works cited in chapter 1, see the essays collected in Sven Beckert and Seth Rockman, eds., *Slavery's Capitalism: A New History of American Economic Development* (Philadelphia: University of Pennsylvania Press, 2016). For a trenchant critique, see Stephanie McCurry's review essay in *Times Literary Supplement* (May 19, 2017): 23–26.
11. See David Waldstreicher, *Slavery's Constitution: From Revolution to Ratification* (New York: Hill and Wang, 2009), for the role played by slavery in shaping the Constitution. Sean Wilentz, *No Property in Man: Slavery and Antislavery in the Nation's Founding* (Cambridge, Mass.: Harvard

University Press, 2018), presents a counterargument placing freedom, not slavery, at the defining core of the Constitution, but the weight of the evidence points to a decisive refashioning of the Constitution as an antislavery document by the political abolitionists of the 1850s.

12. Matthew Mason's *Slavery and Politics in the Early Republic* (Chapel Hill: University of North Carolina Press, 2006) leaves no doubt that slavery was always a contentious issue in early national politics.

13. Robert Pierce Forbes, *The Missouri Compromise and Its Aftermath: Slavery and the Meaning of America* (Chapel Hill: University of North Carolina Press, 2007), is a masterful account of the Missouri debates and their outcome. William W. Freehling, *Prelude to Civil War: The Nullification Controversy in South Carolina, 1816–1836* (New York: Harper & Row, 1966), demonstrates the centrality of slavery in committing South Carolina to nullification.

14. Christopher Cameron, *To Plead Our Own Cause: African Americans in Massachusetts and the Making of a Antislavery Movement* (Kent, Ohio: Kent State University Press, 2014); Paul Goodman, *Of One Blood: Abolitionism and the Origins of Racial Equality* (Berkeley: University of California Press, 1998); Richard Newman, *The Transformation of American Abolitionism: Fighting Slavery in the Early Republic* (Chapel Hill: University of North Carolina Press, 2002); and *The Mirror of Liberty*, (New York: William S. Dorr, 1841), 2.

15. See the wonderful biography by Peter P. Hinks, *To Awaken My Afflicted Brethren: David Walker and the Problem of Antebellum Slave Resistance* (University Park: Pennsylvania State University Press, 1997).

16. James Brewer Stewart, *Holy Warriors: The Abolitionists and American Society*, rev. ed. (New York: Hill and Wang, 1996). Originally published in 1976, Stewart's study remains among the most readable and informative accounts of the abolitionist movement. Manisha Sinha, *The Slave's Cause: A History of Abolition* (New Haven, Conn.: Yale University Press, 2016), is a recent and very complete study.

17. Quoted in *The Third Annual Report of the American Anti-Slavery Society* (New York: William Dorr, 1836), 47.

18. Quoted in Donald B. Kelley, "Intellectual Isolation: Gateway to Secession in Mississippi," *Journal of Mississippi History* 36 (Feb. 1974): 30.

19. See Aileen S. Kraditor, *Means and Ends in American Abolitionism: Garrison and His Critics on Strategy and Tactics, 1834–1850* (New York: Pantheon Books, 1969), for a perceptive analysis of the core ideas of the movement and how those ideas were distorted and misunderstood then and well into the present. Patricia Roberts-Miller, *Fanatical Schemes: Proslavery Rhetoric and the Tragedy of Consensus* (Tuscaloosa: University of Alabama Press, 2009), shows how and why the abolitionists were scapegoated into murderous agitators threatening all that the South held dear.

20. William W. Freehling, *The Road to Disunion*, Vol. 1, *Secessionists at Bay, 1776–1854* (New York: Oxford University Press, 1990), 487–510.

21. For an overview, see Andrew Delbanco, *The War before the War: Fugitive Slaves and the Struggle for America's Soul from the Revolution to the Civil War* (New York: Penguin Press, 2018), and on the 1850s specifically R. J. M. Blackett, *The Captive's Quest for Freedom: Fugitive Slaves, the 1850 Fugitive Slave Law, and the Politics of Slavery* (New York: Cambridge University Press, 2018). Robert H. Churchill, "When the Slave Catchers Came to Town: Cultures of Violence along the Underground Railroad," *Journal of American History* 105 (Dec. 2018): 514–537, documents the spread of community opposition across the middle states of the North in the late 1850s into 1860. Eric Foner, *Gateway to Freedom: The Hidden History of the Underground Railroad* (New York: Norton, 2015), provides a very readable account of the inner workings of the black underground railroad in New York City.

22. John S. Palmer to Major Edward Manigault, Sept. 15, 1851, in Louis P. Towles, ed., *A World Turned Upside Down: The Palmers of South Santee, 1818–1881* (Columbia: University of South Carolina Press, 1996), 170.

23. David M. Potter, *The Impending Crisis, 1848–1861* (New York: Harper & Row, 1976), completed and edited by Don Fehrenbacher, 151–176. Here, and elsewhere, Potter's probing study remains a wonderful guide to the politics of the 1850s.

24. See Eric Foner, *Free Soil, Free Labor, Free Men* (New York: Oxford University Press, 1970); Nicholas Guyatt, "How Proslavery Was the Constitution?," *New York Review of Books* 66

(June 6, 2019): 45–47; and William E. Gienapp, *The Origins of the Republican Party, 1852–1856* (New York: Oxford University Press, 1987).

25. Don E. Fehrenbacher, *The Dred Scott Case, Its Significance in American Law and Politics* (New York: Oxford University Press, 1978), is the fullest account of the case and the reasoning of the Court.

26. Freehling, *Secessionists Triumphant*, 61–84. Kansas entered the Union as a free state in 1861.

27. Roy Franklin Nichols, *The Disruption of American Democracy* (New York: Macmillan, 1948), remains unsurpassed for its vivid account of the breakdown of Democratic unity and party machinery in the late 1850s. For the Brown and Davis resolutions and the bitter rivalry between these two Mississippi senators, see Freehling, *Secessionists Triumphant*, 275–278.

28. On the "when necessary" qualifier, in effect the position by Davis in his Senate resolutions, see M. Halstead, *Caucuses of 1860. A History of the National Political Conventions . . .* (Columbus, Ohio: Follett, Foster, 1860), 43, and *Proceedings of the Conventions at Charleston and Baltimore: Published by Order of the National Democratic Convention (Maryland Institute, Baltimore) and under the Supervision of the Democratic Executive Committee* (Washington, 1860), 45.

29. William L. Yancey, *Speech of the Hon. William L. Yancey, Delivered in the National Democratic Convention . . .* (Charleston, S.C., 1860), 7, 8, 15, 16. Like most Southern whites, Yancey had lumped together all antislavery political groups in the North into one ominous force labeled abolitionist. In fact, Northern Democrats and most Republicans loathed the abolitionists and shunned any association with them.

30. Lawrence Keitt to William M. Murray, Sept. 22, 1860, *Charleston Mercury*, Sept. 27, 1860; *Anderson* (S.C.) *Intelligencer*, Sept. 4, 1860.

Chapter 1

1. Of the South's major cash crops, only rice did not register a sharp price increase in the 1850s. For slave prices, see *Historical Statistics of the United States: Millennial Edition Online* Table Bb6212 at http://hsus.cambridge.org/HSUSWeb/Search/SearchTabledo?id=Bb209-214. On tenantry and the white poor, see Wilma A. Dunaway, *The First American Frontier: The Transition to Capitalism in Southern Appalachia, 1700–1860* (Chapel Hill: University of North Carolina Press, 1996); Frederick A. Bode and Donald E. Ginter, *Farm Tenancy and the Census in Antebellum Georgia* (Athens: University of Georgia Press, 1986); and Charles C. Bolton, *Poor Whites of the Antebellum South: Tenants and Laborers in Central North Carolina and Northeast Mississippi* (Durham, N.C.: Duke University Press, 1994).

2. *De Bow's Review* 24 (March 1858): 202; *Jackson Semi-Weekly Mississippian*, Aug. 10, 1860.

3. Ted Steinberg, *Down to Earth: Nature's Role in American History* (New York: Oxford University Press, 2002), 81–88; Stoll, *Larding the Lean Earth: Soil and Society in Nineteenth-Century America* (New York: Hill and Wang, 2002), 120–169.

4. *De Bow's Review* 8 (Feb. 1850): 181.

5. Adam Rothman, *Slave Country: American Expansion and the Origins of the Deep South* (Cambridge, Mass.: Harvard University Press, 2005); Brian Schoen, *The Fragile Fabric of Union: Cotton, Federal Politics, and the Global Origins of the Civil* War (Baltimore, Md.: Johns Hopkins University Press, 2009); Walter Johnson, *River of Dark Dreams: Slavery and Empire in the Cotton Kingdom* (Cambridge, Mass.: Harvard University Press, 2013); Edward E. Baptist, *The Half Has Never Been Told: Slavery and the Making of American Capitalism* (New York: Basic Books, 2014); Calvin Schermerhorn, *The Business of Slavery and the Rise of American Capitalism, 1815–1860* (New Haven, Conn.: Yale University Press, 2015). All of these works establish the centrality of slavery and its expansion to the development of capitalism in the United States and on the global stage. Schoen is especially strong on showing why planters were so confident in the power of King Cotton when they bolted from the Union.

6. Smith Lipscomb to his wife and children, Dec. 17, 1860, Lipscomb Family Papers, Southern Historical Collection, University of North Carolina at Chapel Hill, hereafter cited as SHC; George W. Paschal, *Ninety-Four Years, Agnes Paschal* (Washington, D.C.: M'Gill & Witherow, 1871), 290–291; Joseph Jones, *Agricultural Resources of Georgia. Address before the Cotton Planters Convention of Georgia at Macon, Dec. 13, 1860* (Augusta, Ga.: Steam Press of

Chronicle & Sentinel, 1860), 8; James C. Bonner, "Agricultural Adjustment in Ante-Bellum Georgia," in James C. Bonner and Lucien E. Roberts, eds., *Studies in Georgia History and Government* (Athens: University of Georgia Press, 1940); Charles E. Beveridge and Charles Capen McLaughlin, eds., *The Papers of Frederick Law Olmsted*, Vol. 2, *Slavery and the South, 1852–1857* (Baltimore, Md.: Johns Hopkins University Press, 1981), 200; Sarah E. Watkins to her daughter Lettia, June 8, 1857, in E. Grey Diamond and Herman Hattaway, eds., *Letters from Forest Place: A Plantation Family's Correspondence, 1846–1881* (Jackson: University Press of Mississippi, 1994), 104.

7. Steinberg, *Down to Earth*, 86–87; Ulrich Bonnell Phillips, "The Origin and Growth of the Southern Black Belts," in Eugene D. Genovese, ed., *The Slave Economy of the Old South: Selected Essays in Economic and Social History* (Baton Rouge: Louisiana State University Press, 1968), 95–116; William L. Barney, *The Road to Secession: A New Perspective on the Old South* (New York: Praeger, 1972), 6–11.

8. Joseph C. G. Kennedy, *Agriculture of the United States in 1860: Compiled from the . . . Eighth Census . . .* (Washington, D.C.: Government Printing Office, 1864), 184–188; Charles S. Sydnor, *Slavery in Mississippi* (Baton Rouge: Louisiana State University Press, 1961), 189–192; Charles S. Davis, *The Cotton Kingdom in Alabama* (Montgomery: Alabama State Department of Archives and History, 1939), 15; James D. Foust and Dale E. Swan, "Productivity and Profitability of Antebellum Slave Labor: A Micro-Approach," *Agricultural History* 44 (Jan. 1970): 46, 55, 57; John Hebron Moore, *The Emergence of the Cotton Kingdom in the Old Southwest: Mississippi, 1770–1860* (Baton Rouge: Louisiana State University Press, 1988); Alan L. Olmstead and Paul W. Rhode, "Biological Innovation and Productivity Growth in the American Cotton Economy," *Journal of Economic History* 68 (Dec. 2008): 1123–1171.

9. Robert F. W. Allston to Blue Ridge Railroad Committee, Aug. 11, 1859, in J. H. Easterby, ed., *The South Carolina Rice Plantation as Revealed in the Papers of Robert F. W. Allston* (Columbia: University of South Carolina Press, 2004), 162; *De Bow's Review* 28 (Sept. 1860): 263; John K. Bettersworth, *Confederate Mississippi: The People and Policies of a Cotton State in Wartime* (Baton Rouge: Louisiana State University Press, 1943), 97. A thorough study of the role of debt in the cotton economy and how it impacted planters and shaped their behavior is badly needed.

10. Charles L. Pettigrew to Caroline Pettigrew, Sept. 1, 1860, Pettigrew Family Papers, Series J, Part 2, Reel 15, Martin Paul Schipper, Kenneth M. Stampp, and University of North Carolina at Chapel Hill, Southern Historical Collection, *Records of Ante-Bellum Southern Plantations from the Revolution through the Civil War* (Microform) (Frederick, Md.: University Publications of America, 1989–1993), hereafter cited as *Records*, Series J.

11. The figures on debt financed with slave property came from Bobbie Martin, "Slavery's Invisible Engine: Mortgaging Human Property," *Journal of Southern History* 76 (Nov. 2010): 817–866. See also Richard Holcombe Kilbourne Jr., *Debt, Investment, Slaves: Credit Relations in East Feliciana Parish, Louisiana, 1825–1885* (Tuscaloosa: University of Alabama Press, 1995).

12. As quoted in Frederick Law Olmsted, *A Journey in the Seaboard Slave States, with Remarks on Their Economy* (New York: Dix and Edwards, 1856), 661.

13. James M. Clifton, ed., *Life and Labor on Argyle Island: Letters and Documents of a Savannah River Rice Plantation, 1833–1867* (Savannah, Ga.: Beehive Press, 1978), xiv; Dale E. Swan, "The Structure and Profitability of the Antebellum Rice Industry: 1859" (PhD dissertation, University of North Carolina at Chapel Hill, 1972), *passim*; Peter A. Coclanis, *The Shadow of a Dream: Economic Life and Death in the South Carolina Low Country, 1670–1920* (New York: Oxford University Press, 1989), 111–158; Lewis C. Gray, *History of Agriculture in the Southern United States to 1860*, 2 vols. (Washington, D.C.: Carnegie Institute of Washington, 1933), Vol. 2: 731–734.

14. Nathaniel R. Middleton to Anna Middleton, March 2, 6, 1860, Series J, Part 3, Reel 8, *Records*.

15. William Elliott to Ann Elliott, Feb. 22, June 22, 1858, Elliott and Gonzales Family Papers, SHC.; here and elsewhere the emphasis is in the original unless otherwise noted. See also the introduction to *William Elliott's Carolina Sports by Land and Water* (Columbia: University of South Carolina Press, 1994; reprint of the 1846 edition).

16. Edward M. Steel Jr., *T. Butler King of Georgia* (Athens: University of Georgia Press, 1964), *passim*; Anna King to Thomas Butler King, Aug. 9, 1842, Melanie Pavich-Lindsay, ed.,

Anna: The Letters of a St. Simons Island Plantation Mistress, 1817–1859 Athens: University of Georgia Press, 2002), 23; Anna King to Thomas Butler King, May 21, 1855; Anna King to Floyd King, June 22, 1858; Georgia King to Floyd King, May 14, 1860, Thomas Butler King Papers, SHC.

17. The material on these three rice planters was drawn from Clifton, *Life and Labor on Argyle Island*, vii–xlvi. This introduction provides an excellent overview of rice planting in the Carolina-Georgia lowcountry. See also John Brinkley Diary, May 23, Sept. 30, and Nov. 3, 1860, John Brinkley Grimball Diaries, Series 1, Folder 20, SHC.

18. Mary W. Milling to James S. Milling, Oct. 19, Dec. 18, 1860; John R. Milling to James S. Milling, Nov. 2, 1860, James S. Milling Papers, Folder 5, SHC.

19. Richard Eppes Diary, July 11, Aug. 11, 1860, Eppes Family Muniments, Series M, Part 3, Reel 13, Martin Paul Schipper, Kenneth M. Stampp, and Virginia Historical Society, *Records of Ante-bellum Southern Plantations from the Revolution through the Civil War* (Microform) (Frederick, Md.: University Publications of America, 1994–1996), hereafter cited as *Records*, Series M.

20. J. W. W. Kirkland to William M. Otey, Oct. 8, Oct. 29, 1860, Wyche and Otey Family Papers, Subseries 1.3, Folder 16, SHC.

21. Alexander A. Allen to George Washington Allen, Sept. 24, 1860, Jan. 15, 1861, George Washington Allen Papers, Series 1, Folders 7, 8, SHC; Charles C. Jones Jr. to Mrs. Mary Jones, May 25, 1859; Charles C. Jones Jr. to Rev. C. C. Jones, June 3, 1859; Rev. C. C. Jones to Charles C. Jones, June 7, 1859, Robert Manson Myers, ed., *The Children of Pride: A True Story of Georgia and the Civil War* (New Haven, Conn.: Yale University Press 1972), 486–488.

22. Milledge Luke Bonham to Sophia Bonham, Jan. 12, 1847; M. M. Bonham to M. L. Bonham, Aug. 14, 1851; Benjamin Waldo to M. L. Bonham, Jan. 12, 1860; John M. Sandige to M. L. Bonham, Aug. 20, 1861, Milledge Luke Bonham Papers, South Caroliniana Library, University of South Carolina; A. F. Burton to Thomas W. and Nancy Burton, May 4, 1859; A. F. Burton to Thomas W. Burton, March 31, 1861, Thomas W. Burton Papers, SHC.

23. James C. Cobb, *The Most Southern Place on Earth: The Mississippi Delta and the Roots of Regional Identity* (New York: Oxford University Press, 1992), 7–28; Percy L. Rainwater, ed., "Autobiography of Benjamin Grubb Humphreys," *Mississippi Valley Historical Review* 21 (Sept. 1934): 231–255.

24. Martha Jane Brazy, *An American Planter: Stephen Duncan of Antebellum Natchez and New York* (Baton Rouge: Louisiana State University Press, 2006); Randall M. Miller, ed., *"Dear Master": Letters of a Slave* Family (Ithaca, N.Y.: Cornell University Press, 1978), 19, 20; Philip St. George Cocke to John B. Cocke, Nov. 16, Dec. 6, 1860; Philip St. George Cocke to John H. Cocke, Dec. 9, 1860, Cocke Family Papers, Series E, Part 4, Reel 53, Kenneth M. Stampp, Martin Paul Schipper, and University of Virginia Library, *Records of Ante-bellum Southern Plantations from the Revolution through the Civil War* (Microform) (Frederick, Md.: University Publications of America, 1985–1986), hereafter cited as *Records*, Series E; James A. Seddon to Charles Bruce, May 5, 1859, Bruce Family Papers, Series M, Part 5, Reel 12, *Records*, Series M; Cobb, *The Most Southern Place*, 12–13.

25. Rod Andrew Jr., *Wade Hampton: Confederate Warrior to Southern Redeemer* (Chapel Hill: University of North Carolina Press, 2008), 16, 44, 45, 49.

26. George W. Mumford to Charles Ellis Mumford, April 7, 1860, Mumford-Ellis Family Papers, Duke University Library; J. L. Pennington to Thomas W. Watson, Feb. 13, 1860, Watson Family Papers, Series E, Part 1, Reel 28, *Records*; Series E; James M. Willcox to Susanna P. Willcox, Feb. 8, 1860, Series F, Part 4, Reel 23, Martin Paul Schipper, Kenneth M. Stampp, and Duke University Library, Manuscript Dept., *Records of Ante-bellum Southern Plantations from the Revolution through the Civil War* (Microform) (Frederick, Md.: University Publications of America, 1986), hereafter cited as *Records*, Series F. See also the discussion of father-son relations in Bertram Wyatt-Brown, *Southern Honor: Ethics and Behavior in the Old South* (New York: Oxford University Press, 1982), esp. 194–198.

27. Autobiography of Charles A. Hentz, 226–227, 242–247, Hentz Family Papers, Series 7, SHC.

28. Louis Manigault to Charles Manigault, Jan. 10, 22, 1860; Charles Manigault to Louis Manigault, Jan. 17, 19, 26, 1860, Louis Manigault Papers, Series F, Part 2, Reel 6, *Records*, Series F.

29. William Massie to Thomas J. Massie, July 2, 1860, April 1, 2, 3, 1861; Thomas J. Massie to William Massie, July 9, 1860; March 28, April 2, 1861, William Massie Papers, Series G, Part 2, Reel 29, Martin Paul Schipper, Kenneth M. Stampp, University of Texas at Austin, Center for American History, Natchez Trace Collection, and Eugene C. Barker Texas History Center, *Records of Ante-bellum Southern Plantations from the Revolution through the Civil War* (Frederick, Md.: University Publications of America, 1987), hereafter cited as *Records*, Series G.

30. William Elliott to Ralph Elliott, Oct. 17, 1851; Ralph Elliott to William Elliott, Nov. 25, 1859; William C. Bee to William Elliott, Feb. 25, 1860; William Elliott to Ralph Elliott, Sept. 26, 1860, Elliott and Gonzales Family Papers, SHC.

31. Benjamin Waldo to Milledge Luke Bonham, Jan. 12, 1860, Milledge Luke Bonham Papers, South Caroliniana Library.

32. Henry Lord King to Anna King, April 25, 1859; Georgia King to Floyd King, May 14, 1860, Thomas Butler King Papers, SHC.

33. Michael P. Johnson, "Planters and Patriarchy: Charleston, 1800–1865": *Journal of Southern History* 46 (Feb. 1980): 45–72; William L. Barney, "The Ambivalence of Change: From Old South to New in the Alabama Black Belt, 1850–1870," in Walter J. Fraser Jr. and Winfred B. Moore Jr., eds., *From the Old South to the New* (Westport, Conn.: Greenwood Press, 1981), 33–41.

34. Jennifer R. Green, "Born of the Aristocracy? Professionals with Planter and Middle-Class Origins in Antebellum South Carolina," in Jonathan Daniel Wells and Jennifer R. Green, eds., *The Southern Middle Class in the Long Nineteenth Century* (Baton Rouge: Louisiana State University Press, 2011), 157–179.

35. William Elliot to Ralph Elliott, Sept. 19, 1857, Elliott and Gonzalez Family Papers, SHC.

36. Bolton, *Poor Whites of the Antebellum South*, 5; Wilma A. Dunaway, *Slavery in the American Mountain South* (New York: Cambridge University Press, 2003), 139–140. For the most recent assessment of the plight of poor whites, see Keri Leigh Merritt, *Masterless Men: Poor Whites and Slavery in the Antebellum South* (New York: Cambridge University Press, 2017). Following the lead of Bode and Ginter, *Farm Tenancy and the Census in Antebellum Georgia*, recent work on landlessness cuts against an older view that argued for relatively low rates of tenancy and sharecropping and found no significant increase of either in the 1850s. For the previous view, see Frank L. Owsley, *Plain Folk of the Old South* (Baton Rouge: Louisiana State University Press, 1949), Gavin Wright, *The Political Economy of the Cotton South: Households, Markets and Wealth in the Nineteenth Century* (New York: Norton, 1978), and Lacy K. Ford, *Origins of Southern Radicalism: The South Carolina Upcountry, 1800–1860* (New York: Oxford University Press, 1988).

37. Lawrence T. McDonnell, "Bonds, Bonding, Bondage: Debt and Disunion in South Carolina," paper presented at the Fifth Citadel Conference of the South, Charleston, South Carolina, April, 1987; Lori A. Cline, "Something Wrong in South Carolina: A Structural Analysis of Antebellum Agricultural Tenancy and Primitive Accumulation in Three Districts" (Master's thesis, University of Georgia, 1997); Ralph Mann, "Mountains, Land, and Kin Networks: Burkes Garden, Virginia, in the 184s and 1850s," *Journal of Southern History* 58 (Aug. 1992): 423–424; Bolton, *Poor Whites of the Antebellum South*, 75–83; Frederick Law Olmsted, *A Journey in the Back Country, 1853–1854* (New York: Mason Brothers, 1860), 327–328.

38. This sketch of Isham's life is drawn from Charles C. Bolton and Scott P. Culclasure, eds., *The Confessions of Edward Isham: A Poor White Life of the Old South* (Athens: University of Georgia Press, 1998).

39. William L. Barney, "Patterns of Crisis: Alabama White Families and Social Change," *Sociology and Social Research* 63 (April 1979): 540; Bolton, *Poor Whites*, Table 2, p. 14; Table 13, p. 92.

40. Bode and Ginter, *Farm Tenancy and the Census in Antebellum Georgia*, 3–10.

41. Plantation Journal, Jan. 3, 7, 10, 11, 28, Feb. 12, April 6, 1859, George Scarborough Barnsley Papers, SHC.

42. Lettie A. Gordon to Kate Adams, Oct. 21, 1859, Israel L. Adams and Family Papers, Series B, Reel 1, Joseph T. Glatthaar, Louisiana State University (Baton Rouge) Library, and Lower Mississippi Valley Collection, *Confederate Military Manuscripts* (Microform) (Frederick,

Md.: University Publications of America, 2001), hereafter cited as *Confederate Military Manuscripts,* Series B; *De Bow's Review* 14 (June 1853): 222.

43. Duncan McKenzie to Duncan McLaurin, Aug. 23, 1860, Duncan McLaurin Papers, Series F, Part 2, Reel 6, *Records,* Series F.

44. Tryphena Fox to Anna Holder, Jan. 4, 1857, Wilma King, ed., *A Northern Woman in the Plantation South* (Columbia: University of South Carolina Press, 1993), 46; Linton Stephens to Alexander H. Stephens, Feb. 7, 1860, Reel 3, Alexander H. Stephens Papers, microfilm, SHC.

45. William D. Cabell Journal, Nov. 12, 1859, Papers of William D. Cabell and the Cabell and Ellet Families, Series D, Part 1, Reel 10, Martin Paul Schipper, Kenneth M. Stampp, and Maryland Historical Society, *Records of Ante-bellum Southern Plantations from the Revolution through the Civil War* (Microform) (Frederick, Md.: University Publications of America, 1985), hereafter cited as *Records,* Series D.

46. For an excellent account of the trafficking and complexity of poor white–slave relations, see Jeff Forret, *Race Relations at the Margins: Slaves and Poor Whites in the Antebellum Southern Countryside* (Baton Rouge: Louisiana State University Press, 2006).

47. Diane Miller Sommerville, *Rape and Race in the Nineteenth-Century South* (Chapel Hill: University of North Carolina Press, 2004), 19–101.

48. Craig Buettinger, "Masters on Trial: The Enforcement of Laws against Self-Hire by Slaves in Jacksonville and Palatka, Florida," *Civil War History* 46 (June 2000): 91–106. The debate over the use of slave mechanics can be followed in the *Southern Cultivator* for 1860; the quote is from the July issue, 204.

49. Joel Williamson, *The Crucible of Race: Black-White Relations in the American South since Emancipation* (New York: Oxford University Press, 1984), 32; Timothy F. Reilly, "The Louisiana Colonization Society and the Protestant Missionary, 1830–1860," *Louisiana History* 43 (Fall 2002): 441.

50. Bayly E. Marks, "Skilled Blacks in Antebellum St. Mary's County, Maryland," *Journal of Southern History* 53 (Nov. 2013): 537–564.

51. Helen T. Catterall, ed., *Judicial Cases Concerning American Slavery and the Negro,* 5 vols. (Washington, D.C.: Carnegie Institute of Washington, 1926–1937), Vol. 2: 385–386; Teresa Zackodnik, "Fixing the Color Line: The Mulatto, Southern Courts, and Racial Identity," *American Quarterly* 53 (Sept. 2001): 420–451.

52. Sarah E. Watkins to Lettia [Walton], May 25, 1860, Dimond and Hattaway, *Letters from Forest Place,* 169–170; quotation from the Robert H. Cartmell Diary found in Gary T. Edwards, "Negroes . . . and All Other Animals: Slaves and Masters in Antebellum Madison County," *Tennessee Historical Quarterly* 57 (Spring/Summer 1998): 30–32.

53. Ira Berlin, *Slaves without Masters: The Free Negro in the Antebellum South* (New York: Oxford University Press, 1974), 344–380; Freehling, *The Road to Disunion,* Vol. 2: 189–201; Barbara Jeanne Fields, *Slavery and Freedom on the Middle Ground: Maryland during the Nineteenth Century* (New Haven, Conn.: Yale University Press, 1985), 63–89.

54. *Charleston Mercury,* Nov. 26, 1856; for decline in slave ownership, see Lee Soltow, *Men and Wealth in the United States, 1850–1870* (New Haven, Conn.: Yale University Press, 1975), 57.

55. *Yazoo* (Miss.) *Democrat,* quote from 1859 in *Annual Report of the American Anti-Slavery Society . . . for the year ending May 1, 1860* (New York: American Anti-Slavery Society, 1861), 15.

56. *Charleston Daily Courier,* Sept. 24, 1860; Michael Tadman, *Speculators and Slaves: Masters, Traders, and Slaves in the Old South* (Madison: University of Wisconsin Press, 1989), Table 2.1, 12, estimates South Carolina's annual net loss of slaves in the 1850s at 6,500; *Charleston Daily Courier,* Oct. 5, 1860.

57. *De Bow's Review* 22 (June 1857): 663; Robert R. Barrow, letter dated Jan. 10, 1861, *New Orleans True Delta;* Louisiana state senator Edward Delony, *De Bow's Review* 26 (Nov. 1858): 506; Johnson, *River of Dark Dreams,* 395–420, is the best source for the reopening movement in the Mississippi Valley.

58. Edward A. Pollard, *Black Diamonds Gathered in the Darkey Homes of the South* (New York: Pudney & Russell, 1860), 52–57.

59. Freehling, *The Road to Disunion*, Vol. 2: 169–170; Leonidas W. Spratt to John Perkins, *Charleston Mercury*, Feb. 13, 1861; Charleston *Southern Standard*, June 15, 1853, quoted in Ronald T. Takaki, *A Pro-Slavery Crusade: The Agitation to Reopen the African Slave Trade* (New York: Free Press, 1971), 4. For a contemporary's impression of Spratt as an orator, see the *Memphis Daily Appeal*, Sept. 12, 1857.

60. Jim Jordan, "Charles Augustus Lafayette Lamar and the Movement to Reopen the African Slave Trade," *Georgia Historical Quarterly* 93 (Fall 2009): 247–290; Charles A. L. Lamar to G. B. Lamar, Oct. 31, 1857; Charles A. L. Lamar to C. C. Cook, June 20, 1859; Charles A. L. Lamar to B. R. Alden, July 30, 1859, "Anonymous, A Slave-Trader's Letter-Book," *North American Review* 143 (Nov. 1886): 449–450, 459–460.

61. Manisha Sinha, *The Counterrevolution of Slavery: Politics and Ideology in Antebellum South Carolina* (Chapel Hill: University of North Carolina Press, 2000), 154–173.

62. Rev. C. C. Jones to Charles C. Jones Jr., Dec. 30, 1858, Myers, *The Children of Pride*, 468.

63. J. H. Hammond to H. R. Cook, Dec. 31, 1858, Hammond, Bryan, and Cumming Family Papers, Series A, Part 2, Reel 22, Martin Paul Schipper, Kenneth M. Stampp, and South Caroliniana Library, *Records of Ante-bellum Southern Plantations from the Revolution through the Civil War* (Microform) (Frederick, Md.: University Publications of America, 1985), here-after cited as *Records*, Series A.; Freehling, *The Road to Disunion*, Vol. 2: 184.

64. *De Bow's Review* 27 (Sept. 1859): 361; Julian C. Ruffin to Edmund Ruffin, March 14, 1861, Edmund Ruffin Papers, Series M, Part 4, Reel 48, *Records*. Carol Lawrence Paulus, *The Slaveholding Crisis: Fear of Insurrection and the Coming of the Civil War* (Baton Rouge: Louisiana State University Press, 2017), reveals how the memory of the terrors of the Haitian uprising never faded.

65. See Robin Einhorn, *American Taxation, American Slavery* (Chicago: University of Chicago Press, 2006).

66. Marc W. Kruman, *Parties and Politics in North Carolina, 1836–1865* (Baton Rouge: Louisiana State University Press, 1983), 189–195; J. M. Jordan to [Edmund Ruffin, March 1, 1860, Edmund Ruffin Papers, Series M, Part 4, Reel 48, *Records*; Craig M. Simpson, *A Good Southerner: The Life of Henry A. Wise of Virginia* (Chapel Hill: University of North Carolina Press, 1985), 80–85.

67. Michel Cordilott, *Des Hommes Libre Dans Une Societe Esclavagiste: Les Ouvres du Sud des Etats-Unis, 1789–1861* (Paris: Annales Litteraires de l'Universite' de Besancon, 1990).

68. Frank Towers, *The Urban South and the Coming of the Civil War* (Charlottesville: University of Virginia Press, 2004), 7–14; Henry W. Connor to John C. Calhoun, Jan. 12, 1849, J. F. Jameson, "Correspondence of John C. Calhoun," *American Historical Association Annual Report*, Vol. 2, *1899* (Washington, D.C., 1900), 1189.

69. Frank Towers, "Job Busting at Baltimore Shipyards: Racial Violence in the Civil War-Era South," *Journal of Southern History* (May 2000): 221–256.

70. Towers, *The Urban South*, 139, 187–188 193–195. The quote can be found on p. 188.

71. Towers, *The Urban South*, 62–63; L. W. Spratt, *The Philosophy of Secession . . .* (Charleston, 1861), 4.

72. Carol Belser, ed., *Secret and Sacred: The Diaries of James Henry Hammond, A Southern Slaveholder* (New York: Oxford University Press, 1988), 220; Nichols, *The Disruption of American Democracy*, 352–353; Laura A. White, "The National Democrats in South Carolina, 1852–1860," *South Atlantic Quarterly* 28 (Oct. 1929): 370–389. The quote is from Alexander Mazyck, remarks in South Carolina Senate, Dec. 6, 1855, *Charleston Mercury*, Jan. 7, 1856.

73. For the fullest account of the growing radicalization of Alabama politics in the late 1850s, see J. Mills Thornton III, *Politics and Power in a Slave Society: Alabama, 1800–1860* (Baton Rouge: Louisiana State University Press, 1978), 348–382.

74. Diane Neal and Thomas W. Kremm, *The Lion of the South: General Thomas C. Hindman* (Macon, Ga.: Mercer University Press, 1993), 1–77; see also Michael B. Dougan, *Confederate Arkansas: The People and Politics of a Frontier State in Wartime* (University: University of Alabama Press, 1976), 13–14.

75. See Joseph H. Parks, *Joseph E. Brown of Georgia* (Baton Rouge: Louisiana State University Press, 1977), and Robert Dubay, *John Jones Pettus, Mississippi Fire-Eater* (Jackson: University Press of Mississippi, 1975).

Chapter 2

1. *Congressional Globe*, 36th Congress, 1st Session, 510.

2. Robert Lewis Dabney to Charles William Dabney, Jan. 15, 1851, Thomas C. Johnson, ed., *The Life and Letters of Robert Lewis Dabney* (Richmond: Presbyterian Committee of Publication, 1903), 129; Thomas Smyth, "The Sin and the Curse; Or, The Union the True Source of Disunion" (1860), in *The Complete Works of Thomas Smyth*, 10 vols. (Columbia, S.C.: Reprinted by the R. Bryan Company, 1910), Vol. 7: 543.

3. Smyth, "The Sin and the Curse," in *The Complete Works of Thomas Smyth*, Vol. 7: 542.

4. Robert G. Gardner, *A Decade of Debate and Division: Georgia Baptists and the Formation of the Southern Baptist Convention* (Macon, Ga.: Mercer University Press, 1995); Edward L. Bond and Joan R. Gunderson, "Evangelicals Ascendant: Bishop Meade and the High Tide of Evangelical Episcopalianism, 1840–1865," *Virginia Magazine of History and Biography* 115 (Nov. 2, 2007): 263; Jennifer Oast, "'The Worst Kind of Slavery': Slave-Owning Presbyterian Churches in Prince Edward County, Virginia," *Journal of Southern History* 76 (Nov. 2010): 867–900.

5. Quoted in Eugene D. Genovese, "Toward a Kinder and Gentler America: The Southern Lady in the Greening of the Politics of the Old South," in Carol Bleser, ed., *In Joy and Sorrow: Women, Family, and Marriage in the Victorian South* (New York: Oxford University Press, 1991), 127, quoted in Wyatt-Brown, *Southern Honor*, 224; Frederick A. Ross, *Slavery Ordained of God* (Philadelphia: J. B. Lippincott, 1857), 20. On the defiance of poor white women, see Victoria E. Bynum, *Unruly Women: The Politics of Social and Sexual Control in the Old South* (Chapel Hill: University of North Carolina Press, 1992).

6. Hammond coined the "mud-sill" speech in a Senate speech on March 4, 1858; see the *Congressional Globe*, 35th Congress, 1st Session, 961–962.

7. *De Bow's Review* 23 (Oct. 1857): 347; George Fitzhugh, *Cannibals All! Or, Slaves without Masters* (Richmond, Va.: A. Morris, 1857), 294, 296.

8. John Brown, *Slave Life in Georgia: A Narrative of the Life, Sufferings, and Escape of John Brown, a Fugitive Slave Now in England*, ed. Louis Alexis Chamerovzow (London: [W. M. Watts], 1855), 201; William N. Pendleton to Anziolette Elizabeth Page Pendleton, May 5, 1855, William N. Pendleton Papers, SHC; Ross, *Slavery Ordained of God*, 29, 30.

9. Josephine Brown recalled of her father's owner in Missouri: "Quotations from the Bible, and a moral lecture, always accompanied the whip." Josephine Brown, *Biography of an American Bondman, by his Daughter* (Boston: R. F. Wallcut, 1856), 13.

10. Letter of N. R. Middleton, *Proceedings of the Meeting in Charleston, S.C., May 13–15, 1845, on the Religious Instruction of the Negroes, Together with the Report of the Committee and the Address to the Public* (Charleston, S.C.: B. Jenkins, 1845), 42; Whiteford Smith to Wade Hampton II, Sept. 6, 1842, Charles E. Cauthen, ed., *Family Letters of the Three Wade Hamptons, 1782–1901* (Columbia: University of South Carolina Press, 1953), 33.

11. Letter of Richard Griffin, *Proceedings of the Meeting in Charleston, S.C.*, 45; Robert Woodward Barnwell to Robert B. Rhett, May 15, 1841, Robert Barnwell Rhett Papers, SHC; William H. W. Barnwell to Edgar B. Day, April 24, Nov. 7, 1832, Barnwell Family Papers, Lowcountry Digital Library, lowcountrydigital.library.cofc.edu; James W. Patton and Beth G. Crabtree, eds., *"Journal of a Secesh Lady": The Diary of Catherine Anne Devereux, 1860–1866* (Raleigh, N.C.: Division of Archives and History, Dept. of Cultural Resources, 1979), Dec. 21, 1860, 22.

12. Reverend William E. Phillips to John L. Manning, July 31, 1856, Papers of Williams-Chesnut-Manning Families, SCL; E. G. Baker Diary, Oct. 28, 1860, SHC; Isaac Johnson, *Slavery Days in Old Kentucky: A True Story of a Father Who Sold His Wife and Four Children by One of the Children* (Ogdensburg, N.Y.: Republican & Journal Print, 1901), 32; Watson, *Narrative of Henry Watson, A Fugitive Slave*, 31.

13. Quoted in Randy J. Sparks, *On Jordan's Stormy Bank: Evangelicalism in Mississippi, 1773–1876* (Athens: University of Georgia Press, 1994), 67.

14. Quoted in Donald G. Mathews, *Religion in the Old South* (Chicago: University of Chicago Press, 1977), 182.

15. Quoted in Erskine Clarke, *Dwelling Place: A Plantation Epic* (New Haven, Conn.: Yale University Press, 2005), 90; Rev. C. C. Jones to Mrs. Mary Jones, Dec. 10, 1856, Myers, *The Children of Pride*, 271, quoted in Clarke, *Dwelling Place*, 359.

16. Robert L. Dabney to G. Woodson Payne, Jan. 20, 1840, quoted in James Oscar Farmer Jr., *The Metaphysical Confederacy: James Henley Thornwell and the Synthesis of Southern Values* (Macon, Ga.: Mercer University Press, 1986), 206–207.

17. For Nott's views on slavery, see William Howard Russell, *My Diary North and South* (Boston: T.O.H.P. Burnham, 1863), 157, quoted in William Stanton, *The Leopard's Spots: Scientific Attitudes toward Race in America, 1815–59* (Chicago: University of Chicago Press, 1960), 77.

18. For Thornwell's views, see Thornwell to John Adger, Dec. 10, 1856, cited in Framer Jr., *The Metaphysical Confederacy*, 229–230.

19. For estimates on slave church membership, see Robert E. Bonner, *Mastering America: Southern Slaveholders and the Crisis of American Nationhood* (New York: Cambridge University Press, 2009), 124–125.

20. Wilson Lumpkin to John C. Calhoun, Jan. 6, 1847, J. F. Jameson, ed., "Correspondence of John C. Calhoun," *Annual Report of the American Historical Association Annual Report for the Year 1899*, Vol. 2 (Washington, D.C.: Government Printing Office, 1900), 1103; Wilson Lumpkin to John C. Calhoun, Jan. 3, 1849, Chauncey S. Boucher and Robert P. Brooks, eds., "Correspondence Addressed to John C. Calhoun 1837–1849," *Annual Report of the American Historical Association for the Year 1929* (Washington, D.C.: Government Printing Office, 1930), 493; W. D. Mosely to Whitemarsh B. Seabrook, May 18, 1849, Governor's Office Letterbook, 1836–1909, Vol. 5, Record Group 101, Series 32, Florida State Archives, Tallahassee, Fla.; John M. McHenry to Robert M. T. Hunter, Feb. 21, 1850, Charles M. Ambler, ed., "Correspondence of Robert M. T. Hunter, 1826–1876," *Annual Report of the American Historical Association for the Year 1916*, Vol. 2 (Washington, D.C.: Government Printing Office, 1917), 105; James W. Bryan to John H. Bryan, May 30, 1850, Letter Books of James W. Bryan, Box 85, Bryan Family Papers, SHC.

21. Charles C. Colcock to John Branch, Oct. 29, 1851, Branch Family Papers, Folder 7, SHC; Shields is quoted in H. R. Holcombe to John Bragg, July 1, 1852, John Bragg Papers, SHC.

22. James H. Hammond to John C. Calhoun, Sept. 22, 1845, Clyde N. Wilson, ed., *The Papers of John C. Calhoun*, Vol. 22, *1845–1846* (Columbia: University of South Carolina Press, 1995), 172.

23. Robert W. Barnwell to Robert B. Rhett, Nov. 1, 1844, Robert Barnwell Rhett Papers, SHC; David Outlaw to Emily Outlaw, July [28], 1848, Dec. 16, 1847, David Outlaw Papers, SHC.

24. Letitia Dabney Miller Recollections, SHC.

25. Letter from John M. Nelson, Jan. 3, 1839, extracted in [Theodore Dwight [Weld], *American Slavery As It Is: Testimony of a Thousand Witnesses* (New York: American Anti-Slavery Society, 1839), 51–52.

26. Pollard, *Black Diamonds*, 41–47.

27. Charles M. Blackford to Mary Blackford, Jan. 18, 1853, L. Minor Blackford, *Mine Eyes Have Seen the Glory: The Story of a Virginia Lady, Mary Berkeley Minor Blackford, 1802–1896, Who Taught Her Sons to Hate Slavery and to Love the Union* (Cambridge, Mass.: Harvard University Press, 1954), 99–100.

28. Beveridge and McLaughlin, *Papers of Frederick Law Olmsted*, Vol. 2, June 30, 1853, 177; J. B. Scafidel, "The Letters of Augustus Baldwin Longstreet" (PhD dissertation, University of South Carolina, 1976), 609.

29. Quoted in Eugene D. Genovese and Elizabeth Fox-Genovese, *Fatal Self-Deception: Slaveholding Paternalism in the Old South* (New York: Cambridge University Press, 2011), 4.

30. V. Moreau Randolph to Richard Randolph, Oct. 2, 1858, Blackford, *Mine Eyes Have Seen the Glory*, 108–109; for abolitionist praise of black advancements after emancipation in the West Indies, see William Lloyd Garrison to George W. Dorsey, July 31, 1860, Louis Ruchames, ed., *The Letters of William Lloyd Garrison*, Vol. 4, *From Disunion to the Brink of War, 1850–1860* (Cambridge, Mass.: Harvard University Press, 1975), 679–683; Richard C. Rohrs, "The Free Black Experience in Antebellum Wilmington, North Carolina: Refining Generalizations about Race Relations," *Journal of Southern History* 78 (Aug. 2012): 615–638.

31. *Congressional* Globe, 31st Congress, 1st Session, Appendix, 341; Willis Williams to Harriet Williams, Sept. 11, 1860, Willis Williams Papers, SHC.

32. Quoted in Robert Olwell, *Masters, Slaves, and Subjects: The Culture of Power in the South Carolina Low Country, 1740–1790* (Ithaca, N.Y.: Cornell University Press, 1986), 103; Susan Sillers Darden Diary, Sept. 17, 1860, Darden Family Collection, Series N, Reel 6, Kenneth M. Stampp and Mississippi Department of Archives and History, *Records of Ante-bellum Southern Plantations from the Revolution through the Civil War* (Microform) (Frederick, Md.: University Publications of America, 2000), hereafter cited as *Records*, Series N. Joy Ann Viveros, "Slavery's Interior: Intimacy, Violence, and Witness in the Antebellum Slaveholding Relation" (PhD dissertation, University of California, Berkeley, 2003), is quite insightful on the conflicted nature of the slaveholder's mind in dealings with slaves.

33. John L. Manning to Sally Manning, Sept. 21, 1851, Williams-Chesnut-Manning Papers, South Caroliniana Library, University of South Carolina.

34. *William Elliott's Carolina Sports by Land and Water*, with a new introduction by Theodore Rosengarten (Columbia: University of South Carolina Press, 1994), 177. For Elliott's visit to Chee-ha, see 173–191.

35. *Dallas Herald*, March 27, 1861; James W. Bryan to James A. Bryan, Sept. 27, 1859, Bryan Family Papers, SHC.

36. John Brown, *Slave Life in Georgia*, 203–204; Daniel W. Crofts, "Southampton County Diarists in the Civil War Era: Elliott L. Story and Daniel W. Cobb," *Virginia Magazine of History and Biography* 98 (Oct. 1990): 586; Johnson Olive, *One of the Wonders of the Age: Or the Life and Times of Rev. Johnson Olive, Wake County, North Carolina* (Raleigh: Broughton, 1886), 45–46.

37. Mark Thornton, "Slavery, Profitability, and the Market Process," *Review of Austrian Economics* 7 (No. 2, 1994): 41–42.

38. For Virginia, see Eva Sheppard Wolf, *Race and Liberty in the New Nation: Emancipation in Virginia from the Revolution to Nat Turner's Rebellion* (Baton Rouge: Louisiana State University Press, 2006).

39. See Patience Essah, *A House Divided: Slavery and Emancipation in Delaware, 1638–1865* (Charlottesville: University of Virginia Press, 1996).

40. Berlin, *Slaves without Masters*, 140–142, 202–203.

41. Robert J. Turnbull, *The Crisis: or, Essays on the Usurpation of the Federal Government* (Charleston: A. E. Miller, 1827), 131.

42. James G. Birney to Clement C. Clay, [Dec., 1832], Dwight L. Dumond, ed., *Letters of James Gillespie Birney, 1831–1857*, Vol. 1 (Gloucester, Mass.: Peter Smith, 1966), 47; Timothy F. Reilly, "The Louisiana Colonization Society and the Protestant Missionary, 1830–1860," *Louisiana History* 43 (Fall 2002): 433–477; Norwood Allen Kerr, "The Mississippi Colonization Society, 1834–1860," *Journal of Mississippi History* 43 (Feb. 1981): 1–31.

43. Claude A. Clegg III, *The Price of Liberty: African Americans and the Making of Liberia* (Chapel Hill: University of North Carolina Press, 2004); Antonio McDaniel, *Swing Low, Sweet Chariot: The Mortality Cost of Colonizing Liberia in the Nineteenth Century* (Chicago: University of Chicago Press, 1996), quoted in Berlin, *Slaves without Masters*, 204.

44. Eric Burin, *Slavery and the Peculiar Solution: A History of the American Colonization Society* (Gainesville: University of Florida Press, 2005); Marie Tyler-McGraw, *An African Republic: Black and White Virginians in the Making of Liberia* (Chapel Hill: University of North Carolina Press, 2007).

45. Letter from "A Subscriber," *Baton Rouge Gazette*, Oct. 16, 1841; Berlin, *Slaves without Masters*, 144–147.

46. Bernie D. Jones, *Fathers of Conscience: Mixed-Race Inheritance in the Antebellum South* (Athens: University of Georgia Press, 2009), 25–26, quote on p. 26.

47. Jones, *Fathers of Conscience*, 38–40.

48. Jones, *Fathers of Conscience*, 40–42, 125–134, quote on p. 127.

49. Catterall, *Judicial Cases Concerning American Slavery and the Negro*, Vol. 2, 392–393.

50. Mark Tushnet, *The American Law of Slavery, 1810–1860: Considerations of Humanity and Interest* (Princeton, N.J.: Princeton University Press, 1981), 231–232, quote on p. 232.

51. For examples of such masters, see *Annual Report of the American Anti-Slavery Society . . . for the Year ending May 1, 1860*, 44. Correspondent of the *Savannah News*, quoted in the *Florida Peninsular* (Tampa), Nov. 17, 1860.

52. See Suzanne Lebsock, "Complicity and Contention: Women in the Plantation South," *Georgia Historical Quarterly* 74 (Spring 1990): 59–83, a review essay of Elizabeth Fox-Genovese, *Within the Plantation Household: Black and White Women of the Old South* (Chapel Hill: University of North Carolina Press, 1988). Lebsock persuasively argues that Fox-Genovese slighted the inconsistencies in elite women's portrayals of slavery.

53. "A Southern Churchwoman's View of Slavery" by "Filia," *Church Intelligencer* (Nov. 22, 1860).

54. Tryphena Fox to Anna Holder, July 14, 1856, Wilma King, ed., *A Northern Woman in the Plantation South* (Columbia: University of South Carolina Press, 1993), 35; Anna King to Henry Lord King, June 7, 1852, Pavich-Lindsay, *The Letters of a St. Simons Plantation Mistress*, 144.

55. Miriam Hilliard Diary, June 19, 1850, quoted in J. Wayne Jones, "Seeding Chicot: The Issac H. Hilliard Plantation and the Arkansas Delta," *Arkansas Historical Quarterly* 59 (Summer 2000): 159; transcript of letter from Maud C. Fentress to David Fentress, July 2, 1858 (http://texashistory.unt.edu), University of North Texas, Special Collections; *Slave Narratives: A Folk History of Slavery in the United States from Interviews with Former Slaves*, Vol.1, *Alabama Narratives* (Washington, D.C.: Federal Writers Project, 1941), Delia Garlic interview, 102. In a study grounded in "relations of power between women, and contests over that power" (p. 239), Thavolia Glymph in *Out of the House of Bondage: The Transformation of the Plantation Household* (New York: Cambridge University Press, 2008), reveals how extensive was the physical violence of mistresses toward their slaves; for the resistance of the enslaved women that frustrated and enraged the mistresses, see Stephanie M. H. Camp, *Closer to Freedom: Enslaved Women and Everyday Resistance in the Plantation South* (Chapel Hill: University of North Carolina Press, 2004).

56. Diary of Mahala P. Roach, Nov. 7, 1860, Roach and Eggleston Family Papers, SHC; J. D. Green, *Narrative of the Life of J. D. Green, a Runaway Slave, from Kentucky, Containing an Account of His Three Escapes in 1839, 1846 and 1848* (Huddersfield, England: Henry Fielding, Pack Horse Yard, 1864), 27; Malcolm Bell Jr., *Major Butler's Legacy: Five Generations of a Slaveholding Family* (Athens: University of Georgia Press, 1987), 280–281.

57. Loren Schweninger, *Families in Crisis in the Old South* (Chapel Hill: University of North Carolina Press, 2012), quoted in Joan E. Cashin, ed., *Our Common Affairs: Texts from Women in the Old South* (Baltimore, Md.: Johns Hopkins University Press, 1996), 111.

58. Maggie A. Copeland to Mary Bailey, Sept. 2, 1856, James B. Bailey Papers, SHC; Lynette Boney Wrenn, ed., *A Bachelor's Life in Antebellum Mississippi: The Diary of Dr. Elijah Millington Walker, 1849–1852* (Knoxville: University of Tennessee Press, 2004), Aug. 2, 1850, 71.

59. Ann Barnes Archer to Abram Archer, May 2, 1860, Richard Thompson Archer Family Papers, Series G, Part 5, Reel 3, *Records*.

60. Henry Watson, *Narrative of Henry Watson, a Fugitive Slave* (Boston: Bela Marsh, 1848), 13–14; *Slave Narratives*, Vol. 11, Part 2, *North Carolina Narratives*, James Manson interview, 98.

61. E. G. Baker Diary, June 15, 1861, SHC; V. Lynne Kennedy, *Born Southern: Childbirth, Motherhood, and Social Networks in the Old South* (Baltimore, Md.: Johns Hopkins University Press, 2010), 122.

62. C. Vann Woodward, ed., *Mary Chesnut's Civil War* (New Haven, Conn.: Yale University Press, 1981), 29.

63. Virginia Ingram Burr, ed., *The Secret Eye: The Journal of Ella Gertrude Clanton Thomas, 1848–1889* (Chapel Hill: University of North Carolina Press, 1990), 168–169, 236.

64. Diaries of Lucila Agnes McCorkle, 1858–1860, n.d., Series 3.1, Folder 160; Diaries of Lucila Agnes McCorkle, 1846–1858, June 14, 1846, Series 3.1, Folder 159, William P. McCorkle Papers, SHC.

65. Mary B. Carter to Mildred Walker Campbell, March 10, 1849, quoted in Cashin, *Our Common Affairs*, 191; Cashin, *Our Common Affairs*, 198–199; Dairy of Susan Eppes, Jan. 1861, 138, SHC; Mary Elliott Johnstone to Ann Elliott, ca. 1856, Elliott and Gonzales Family Papers, SHC.

66. Rogene Scott to her mother, Oct. 29, 1859, Scott Family Papers, SHC; diary entry of Nov. 17, 1859, quoted in Brenda E. Stevenson, *Life in Black and White: Family and Community in the Slave South* (New York: Oxford University Press, 1996), 322.

67. Marion Harland, *Marion Harland's Autobiography: The Story of a Long Life* (New York: Harper & Brothers, 1910), 187; Christian Bell to her father and mother, June 20, 1854, Major Bell Papers, Series F, Reel 7, *Records.*

68. Cashin, *Our Common Affairs*, 206.

69. For examples of such relief, see King, *A Northern Woman*, 139; Burr, *The Secret Eye*, 265.

70. Henry Clay to William Henry Russell, July 18, 1835, James F. Hopkins et al., eds., *The Papers of Henry Clay*, 10 vols. (Lexington: University of Kentucky Press, 1959–1992), Vol. 8: 789, quoted in Freehling, *Secessionists at Bay*, 467.

71. For the most recent examination of Nat Turner and his local world, see David F. Allmendinger Jr., *Nat Turner and the Rising in Southampton County* (Baltimore, Md.: Johns Hopkins University Press, 2014); David T. Bailey, *Shadow on the Church: Southwestern Evangelical Religion and the Issue of Slavery* (Ithaca, N.Y.: Cornell University Press, 1985), 253–257. x

72. Richard Fuller and Francis Wayland, *Domestic Slavery Considered as a Domestic Institution* (New York: Lewis Colby, 1845), 170, quoted in David B. Cheseborough, *Clergy Dissent in the Old South* (Carbondale: Southern Illinois University Press, 1968), 31.

73. Quoted in Freehling, *Secessionists Triumphant*, 33.

74. Quoted in Francis R. Flournoy, *Benjamin Mosby Smith, 1811–1893* (Richmond: Richmond Press, 1947), 74; Martha Griffith Browne, *Autobiography of a Female Slave* (New York: Redfield, 1857), 130; Caroline Pettigrew to James Lewis Petigru, Dec. 2, [1858], Pettigrew Family Papers, SHC; Browne, *Autobiography of a Female Slave*, 130.

75. Frederick Lewis Olmsted, *A Journey in the Seaboard Slave States* (New York: Dix & Edwards, 1856), 675–676; Parish, *Richard Taylor*, 46; Frederick Lewis Olmsted, *The Cotton Kingdom*, ed. Arthur M. Schlesinger Sr. (New York: Alfred A. Knopf, 1953), 370.

76. *American Colonization Society v. Gartrell*, 23 Georgia, Atlanta, August Term, 1857, p. 464, *Reports of Cases in Law and Equity, Argued and Determined in the Supreme Court of the State of Georgia . . . , Vol. 23*, B. Y. Martin Reporter (Columbus, Ga., 1858).

77. Timothy F. Reilly, "Slavery and the Southwestern Evangelist in New Orleans (1800–1861)," *Journal of Mississippi History* 41 (Nov. 1979): 314–315; see also Reilly, "The Louisiana Colonization Society and the Protestant Missionary, 1830–1860," *Louisiana History* 43 (Fall 2002): 433–477.

78. Hinton Rowan Helper, *The Impending Crisis of the South* (New York: Burdick Brothers, 1857), 25.

79. John C. Calhoun, "Speech on the Oregon Bill," June 27, 1848, in Clyde N. Wilson and Shirley Bright Cook, eds., *The Papers of John C. Calhoun, Vol. 25: 1847–1848* (Columbia: University of South Carolina Press, 1999), 533; Helper, *The Impending Crisis*, 42, 41, 300.

80. For an insightful examination of what motivated Brown and his impact, see Robert E. McGlone, *John Brown's War against Slavery* (New York: Cambridge University Press, 2009).

81. Catterall, *Judicial Cases Concerning American Slavery and the Negro*, Vol. 2, 238.

Chapter 3

1. Franc M. Carmack Diary, Jan. 1, 1860, SHC; Jane Allen Stuart to Robert M. Tunnell, Jan. 9, 1860, Chapin-Tunnell Family Papers, SHC, quoted in Walter Kyle Planitzer, "A Dangerous Class of Men, without Direct Interest in Slavery: Proslavery Concern about Southern Nonslaveholders in the Late Antebellum Era" (PhD dissertation, Johns Hopkins University, 2008), 45.

2. *Charleston Mercury*, Jan. 2, 1860; *Charleston Daily Courier*, Jan. 30, 1860.

3. Letter from "A Vigilant," *Charleston Mercury*, Jan. 25, 1860; *Charleston Mercury*, Jan. 20, 1860.

4. *Enterprise* (Miss.) *News*, Feb. 2, 1860, cited in *Charleston Mercury*, Feb. 10, 1860; *Edgefield* (S.C.) *Advertiser*, Feb. 6, 1860, cited in *Charleston Mercury*, Feb. 13, 1860.

5. A. C. McEwen to Governor Pettus, Feb. 29, 1860, Series E, Governor's Records, Vol. 49, Administration of Governor John J. Pettus: Correspondence for the Year 1860, Mississippi Department of Archives and History, hereafter cited as MDAH; *New York Sun*, cited in *Charleston Mercury*, Jan. 13, 1860.

6. C. G. Memminger to William P. Miles, Jan. 3, [1860], D. H. Hamilton to Miles, Jan. 23, 1860, William Porcher Miles Papers, SHC.

7. For a cogently argued statement on the strategy of the radicals, see R. B. Rhett Jr. to Miles, Jan. 29, 1860, William Porcher Miles Papers, SHC.
8. William Henry Trescot to Miles, Feb. 22, 1860, Alfred Huger to Miles, April 4, 1860, D. H. Hamilton to Miles, April 4, 1860, William Porcher Miles Papers, SHC.
9. Edward Spann Hammond to James Henry Hammond, April 21, 1860, James Henry Hammond Papers, Series A, Part 1, Reel 10, *Records*; S. D. Moore to [Edmund Ruffin], Jan. 30, Feb. 28, 1860, Ruffin Family Papers, Series M, Part 4, Reel 48, *Records*.
10. The journalist Murat Halstead, whose reporting on the 1860 presidential election was both colorful and informative, called Yancey the "prince of the fire-eaters" in his *Caucuses of 1860 . . .* (Columbus, Ohio, 1860), 5. Henry Craft, a Tennessean, was amazed at the reach of Yancey's voice when he heard him speak before a crowd estimated at 3,000 in Memphis in August 1860. He "held the crowd better than any speaker I ever saw address a crowd." Henry Craft Diary, Aug. 19, 1860, SHC.
11. For an excellent biography, see Eric H. Walther, *William Lowndes Yancey and the Coming of the Civil War* (Chapel Hill: University of North Carolina Press, 2006). Though fulsome in its praise, John DuBose, *The Life and Times of William Lowndes Yancey* (Birmingham, Ala.: Roberts & Son, 1892) is still valuable for its inclusion of many of Yancey's speeches.
12. *Speech of the Hon. William Lowndes Yancey of Alabama: Delivered in the National Democratic Convention, Charleston, April 28th 1860*, 4; Halstead, *Causes of 1860*, 76, 75. Nichols, *The Disruption of American Democracy*, 288–308, is unsurpassed on the atmosphere in Charleston and the frantic activity in the convention.
13. Halstead, *Caucuses of 1860*, 82–91.
14. For the fears of the radicals, see Robert N. Gourdin to William Porcher Miles, April 4, May 12, 1860,Philip D. Racine, ed., *Gentlemen Merchants: A Charleston Family's Odyssey, 1828–1870* (Knoxville: University of Tennessee Press, 2008), 384, 387; L. Q. C. Lamar to C. H. Mott, May 29, 1860, Edward Mayes, *Lucius Q. C. Lamar: His Life, Times, and Speeches, 1825–1893* (Nashville, Tenn.: Publishing House of the Methodist Episcopal Church, South, 1896), 83.
15. Georgia King to Henry Lord King, May 9, 1860, Thomas Butler King Papers, SHC; F. L. Claiborne to William N. Whitehurst, May 12, 1860, William N. Whitehurst Papers, Box 1, Folder 5, MDAH.
16. Halstead, *Caucuses of 1860*, 109.
17. Halstead, *Causes of 1860*, 225–226, 230; *Charleston Mercury*, July 2, 1860.
18. *Natchez Mississippi Free Trader*, July 30, 1860; *Montgomery Weekly Mail*, cited in *Mobile Daily Advertiser*, May 29, 1860; Dunbar Rowland, ed., *Jefferson Davis, Constitutionalist, His Letters, Papers, and Speeches*, Vol. 4 (Jackson: Mississippi Department of Archives and History, 1923), 174.
19. *Congressional Globe*, 36th Congress, 1st Session, Appendix, 53; M. W. Cluskey, ed., *Speeches, Messages, and Other Writings of the Hon. Albert G. Brown, a Senator in Congress from the State of Mississippi* (Philadelphia: Smith and Peters, 1859), 595.
20. For more on how the political economies of the Northeast and West contributed to an anti-Southern voting bloc by the 1850s, see Barrington Moore Jr., *Social Origins of Dictatorship and Democracy: Lord and Peasant in the Making of the Modern World* (Boston: Beacon Press, 1966), 111–140 and Marc Egnal, *Clash of Extremes: The Economic Origins of the Civil War* (New York: Hill and Wang, 2009).
21. *Huntsville Southern Advocate*, May 9, 1860; *New Orleans Bee*, May 4, 1860; Wade Pugh to W. W. Pugh, Sept. 23, 1860, Pugh Family Papers, Series G, Part 1, Reel 6, *Records*; John A. Campbell to Lucius Q. C. Lamar, Jan. 5, 1861, "Notes and Documents: James Murphy, 'Justice John Archibald Campbell on Secession,'" *Alabama Review* 28 (Jan. 1975): 51; *Memphis Daily Appeal*, Oct. 2, 1860.
22. *Speech of William C. Smedes, Esq. . . .* (Vicksburg: Job Office of M. Shannon, 1860), 36–37; David E. Meerse, "Buchanan, Corruption, and the Election of 1860," *Civil War History* 12 (June 1966): 116–131.
23. *Mobile Daily Register*, March 29, 1860
24. *Paulding* (Miss.) *Eastern Clarion*, Aug. 29, 1860; *Port Gibson* (Miss.) *Tri-Weekly Reveille*, Aug. 16, 1860; the first quote is from *Speech of Hon. Albert G. Brown, delivered at Crystal Springs,*

Copiah Co., Miss., Sept. 6, 1860 (Jackson: n.p., 1860), 5–6; *Charleston Daily Courier*, May 21, 1860.

25. *Columbus* (Ga.) *Enquirer*, cited in *Augusta Weekly Chronicle and Sentinel*, Aug. 10, 1859; *Brownlow's Knoxville Whig*, June 16, 1860.

26. H. J. Harris to Jefferson Davis, June 7, 1859, Rowland, *Jefferson Davis, Constitutionalist*, Vol. 4, 56.

27. *Hayneville* (Ala.) *Watchman*, cited in *Mobile Daily Advertiser*, July 17, 1860; *Natchez Daily Courier*, Aug. 16, 1860.

28. William M. Lawton to William P. Miles, May 6, 1860, William P. Miles Papers, SHC.

29. Powhatan Ellis to Charles Ellis, May 26, 1860, Mumford-Ellis Family Papers, SHC; William P. Miles to [?] [May 6, 1860], William P. Miles Papers, SHC. Had Lincoln lost New York's electoral votes or those of Pennsylvania and New Jersey, he would have fallen short of the 152 votes he needed to win.

30. *Montgomery Weekly Mail*, June 8, 1860; *Natchez Mississippi Free Trader*, Aug. 6, 1860; *Louisville Daily Courier*, Sept. 8, 1860.

31. *Hayneville* (Ala.) *Democratic Watchman*, July 11, 1860; *Weekly Vicksburg Whig*, Oct. 31, 1860; *Eutaw* (Ala.) *Whig*, cited in the *Mobile Daily Advertiser*, April 18, 1860.

32. *Montgomery Advertiser*, cited in *Hayneville* (Ala.) *Democratic Watchman*, July 11, 1860.

33. *Claiborne* (Ala.) *Southern Champion*, June 29, Aug. 10, 1860; Grant quoted in the (Ala.) *Clarke County Democrat*, July 5, 1860.

34. Laurence Keitt to Miles, Oct. 3, 1860, William P. Miles Papers, SHC.

35. Jonathan Worth to John A. Gilmer, March 9, 1858, J. G. deRoulhac Hamilton, ed., *The Correspondence of Jonathan Worth*, Vol. 1 (Raleigh, N.C.: Edwards & Broughton Printing, 1909), 55.

36. Robert Barnwell Rhett Jr. to William Henry Branch, May 23, 1857, Branch Family Papers, SHC.

37. *Wheeling Daily Intelligencer*, Oct. 1, 1860.

38. There is no biography of Underwood, but see Freehling, *Road to Disunion*, Vol. 2, 236–240, for a concise and shrewd summary of his career as a gadfly to Southerners.

39. For a solid biography of Clay that underplays his commitment to white supremacy, see H. Edward Robinson, *Cassius Marcellus Clay: Firebrand of Freedom* (Lexington: University of Kentucky Press, 1976).

40. Francis P. Blair Jr., *Speech of Hon. F. P. Blair, Jr., of Missouri at the Cooper Institute . . . Jan. 25, 1860* (Washington, D.C.: Buell & Blanchard, 1860), 7–8, 11.

41. *Charleston Mercury*, Oct. 11, 1860; *New Orleans Delta*, Nov. 1, 1860, quoted in Dwight Lowell Dumond, ed., *Southern Editorials on Secession* (New York: Century, 1931), 202.

42. Because of its high moisture requirement during the tasseling stage, corn was especially vulnerable to droughts. On the importance of corn in the Southern diet, see Donald L. Kemmerer, "The Pre-Civil War South's Leading Crop, Corn," *Agricultural History* 23 (Oct. 1949): 236–239.

43. O'Neal cited in *Newberry* (S.C.) *Rising Sun*, Aug. 8, 1860; *Savannah Daily Republican*, July 13, 23 (letter from "H.L.M."); *Augusta Chronicle and Sentinel*, cited in *Charleston Daily Courier*, July 30, 1860.

44. *Jackson Semi-Weekly Mississippian*, July 10, 17, Aug. 1, 1860; *Wedowee* (Ala.) *Mercury*, cited in *Huntsville Southern Advocate*, May 23, 1860; *Montgomery Weekly Mail*, July 27, 20, 1860; *Selma* (Ala.) *Sentinel*, cited in *Savannah Daily Republican*, Aug. 17, 1860; *Alexandria* (La.) *Constitutional*, Aug. 20, 1860; Natchitoches Chronicle, cited in *New Orleans Bee*, Aug. 31, 1860.

45. W. F. Weeks to Mary C. Moore, Sept. 30, 1860, David Weeks and Family Papers, Series I, Part 6, Reel 16, Martin Paul Schipper, Kenneth M. Stampp, and Louisiana State University Library, *Records of Ante-bellum Southern Plantations from the Revolution through the Civil War* (Microform) (Frederick, Md.: University Publications of America, 1988), hereafter cited as *Records*, Series I: Vermillionville (La.) *Echo*, Oct. 5, cited in *New Orleans Daily Picayune*, Oct. 9, 1860; *Eufaula* (Ala.) *Spirit*, Oct. 27, cited in *Tallahassee Floridian and Journal*, Nov. 10, 1860; for the tobacco planters, see Philip St. George Cocke to John Hartwell Cocke, Aug. 8, 1860, Cocke Family Papers, Series E, Part 4, Reel 53; William D. Cabell to Dr. Arthur Lee Brent, July 30, 1860, Bremo Recess Papers, Series E, Part 4, Reel 71; Richard Eppes Diary, July 8,

Aug. 13, 1860, Series M, Part 3, Reel 13, *Records*; for sugar planters, *Point Coupeé Democrat*, cited in *New Orleans Bee*, Oct. 6, 1860; John D. Slack to Henry R. Slack, Sept. 22, 30, 1860, Slack Family Papers, Series J, Part 5, Reel 13; Pitts Diary, Nov. 12, 1860, Philip Henry Pitts Diary, Series J, Part 7, Reel 6, *Records*; Letter from "Ozan," *Southern Cultivator*, Vol. 18, Dec., 1860, 364.

46. *Montgomery Weekly Mail*, July 27, 1860; on the rush of small farmers in Georgia into cotton production, see George B. Crawford, "Cotton, Land, and Sustenance: Towards the Limits of Abundance in Late Antebellum Georgia," *Georgia Historical Quarterly* 72 (Summer 1988): 215–247.

47. *Mobile Daily Advertiser*, May 27, 1860; *Paulding* (Miss.) *Eastern Clarion*, Aug. 8, 1860; *Weekly Montgomery Confederation*, July 27, 1860; on conditions in Marietta, Georgia, see Mrs. Eliza G. Robarts to Rev. C. C. Jones, Aug. 25,1860, Myers, *Children of Pride*, 606; cited in the *Montgomery Weekly Mail*, June 1, 1860.

48. *Clayton Banner*, July 26, 1860; *Missouri Advertiser*, cited in the *Pickens* (Ala.) *Republican*, Aug. 2, 1860.

49. For the calming tone of the Breckinridge press, see the *Clayton Banner*, Aug. 30, 1860; letter from "X," *Mobile Daily Advertiser*, Aug. 16 , 1860; *Huntsville Southern Advocate*, July 25, 1860; *Talladega Alabama Reporter*, Aug. 16, 1860; William Henry Tayloe to Henry A. Tayloe, Jan. 12, 1860, Tayloe Family Papers, Series M, Part 1, Reel 22, *Records*.

50. Thomas D. Gray to Brack [C. B. Johnson], Aug. 25, 1860, Hubbard S. Bosley Papers, Series I, Part 2, Reel 19, *Records; De Bow's Review* 29 (July 1860): 70.

51. On the fears of famine, see the reports in the *Newberry Rising Sun*, Aug. 8, 1860, and *Athens Southern Banner*, Aug. 9, 1860; [John L. Hull] to Ingram A. Holland, June 19, 1860, Martha Holland Papers, SHC.

52. For Pryor's conspiratorial explanation for the Texas fires, see the report from the *Houston Telegraph* cited in the *Alexandria Constitutional*, Aug. 13, 1860.

53. The course of the panic can be followed in the accounts in the *New Orleans Bee*, Aug. 3, 6, 13, 24, 27, 1860, and the *Houston Telegraph*, cited in the *Alexandria Constitutional*, Aug. 13, 1860; Mary E. Starnes to Sarah J. Thompson, Sept. 20, 1860, quoted in Cashin, *Our Common Affairs*, 259.

54. Donald E. Reynolds, *Texas Terror: The Slave Insurrection Panic of 1860 and the Secession of the Lower South* (Baton Rouge: Louisiana State University Press, 2007), is indispensable for understanding the Texas panic and the political uses to which it was put.

55. Sarah R. Espy Diary, Aug. 11, 1860, Alabama Department of Archives and History, hereafter cited as ADAH; *Sumter Democrat*, cited in *Montgomery Weekly Advertiser*, Sept. 19, 1860; *Montgomery Weekly Advertiser*, Oct. 10, 1860.

56. *Weekly Vicksburg Whig*, Oct. 10, 1860; *Mississippi Meridian*, cited in *Anderson* (S.C.) *Intelligencer*, Sept. 4, 1860; *Jackson Semi-Weekly Mississippian*, Oct. 9, 1860; *Lawrenceville* (Ga.) *Air Line Eagle*, cited in *Athens Southern Banner*, Nov. 8, 1860.

57. *Oxford Mercury*, cited in the *Carrollton* (La.) *Sun*, Oct. 4, 1860; *Weekly Vicksburg Whig*, Oct. 10, 1860.

58. *Selma* (Ala.) *Issue*, cited in *Charleston Daily Courier*, Aug. 28, 1860, and *Montecello* (Fla.) *Family Friend*, Sept. 15, for the tale of the gypsies; *Selma Alabama Reporter*, Aug. 30, 1860, and letter from "G.A.P." Aug. 29, 1860, *Macon* (Ga.) *Daily Telegram*, cited in *Monticello Family Friend*, Sept. 8, 1860, for the Selma episode; Lucila Agnes Diary, Sept. 9, 1860, SHC; George Knox Miller to Celestine McCann, Sept. 8, 1860, George Knox Miller Papers, SHC.

59. *Anderson Intelligencer*, Sept. 11, 1860; Sereno Watson to Henry Watson, Sept. 4, 1860, Henry Watson Jr. Papers, Duke University.

60. On the Georgia panics, see the Barnsley Plantation Journal, Aug. 18, 1860, SHC, the *New Orleans Bee*, Sept. 7, 1860, *Newberry Rising Sun*, Sept. 7, 1860, the *Anderson Intelligencer*, Sept. 11, 1860, and the letter of Oct. 20, 1860, from a resident of Leon County, Florida, *Thomasville* (Ga.) *Enterprise*, cited in *Tallahassee Floridian and Journal*, Nov. 10, 1860. For South Carolina, Caroline Pettigrew to William S. Pettigrew, Sept. 17, 1860, and Jane North to William S. Pettigrew, Pettigrew Family Papers, Series J, Part 2, Reel 15, *Records; Henry* W. Ravenel Journal, Oct. 31, 1860, SHC, and James J. Palmer to John S. Palmer, Sept. 30, 1860, Louis P. Towles, ed., *A World Turned Upside Down: The Palmers of South Santee, 1818–1881*

(Columbia: University of South Carolina Press, 1996), 267. On Tyrel and Washington counties, see William S. Pettigrew to James C. Johnston, Oct. 25, Charles L. Pettigrew to Caroline Pettigrew, Nov. 14, 1860, Pettigrew Family Papers, Series J, Part 2, Reel 15, *Records; Richmond Dispatch*, Oct. 8, 11, 13, and Norfolk *Herald*, cited in *New Orleans Daily Picayune*, Oct. 14, 1860.

61. *Augusta Chronicle*, cited in *Charleston Mercury*, June 13, 1860; *Augusta Dispatch*, cited in *Savannah Republican*, Aug. 13, 1860; *Barnwell* (S.C.) *Sentinel*, cited in *Charleston Daily Courier*, Aug. 13, 1860.

62. For the dominance of non- and small slaveholders in the vigilance committees in the lowcountry districts of South Carolina, see McCurry, *Masters of Small Worlds*, 293–300. A. S. Kirk to Samuel M. Meek, Sept. 29, 1860, Samuel M. Meek Papers, MDAH; J. E. Taliaferro to Gov. Pettus, Aug. 21, 1860, Governors' Records, MDAH.

63. *Newberry Rising Sun*, Nov. 7, 1860; Malachi J. White to [William S. Pettigrew, late Oct. 1860], Pettigrew Family Papers, Series J, Part 2, Reel 15, *Records*. For a fascinating history of Pettigrew and his relations with his neighbors, see Wayne K. Durrill, *War of Another Kind: A Southern Community in the Great Rebellion* (New York: Oxford University Press, 1990).

64. *Montgomery Weekly Mail*, Aug. 31, 1860; *Clayton Banner*, Aug. 9, 1860.

65. *Montgomery Weekly Post*, Aug. 1, 1860; *Weekly Montgomery Confederation*, Sept. 28, 1860.

66. *Weekly Vicksburg Whig*, Oct. 31, 1860.

67. Anna Rebecca Young to Robert N. Gourdin, Oct. 12, Racine, *Gentlemen Merchants*, 395; R. S. Holt to Joseph S. Holt, Nov. 10, 1860, quoted in Nichols, *Disruption of American Democracy*, 363–364.

68. John Townsend, *The Doom of Slavery in the Union: Its Safety Out of It* (Charleston: Evans & Cogswell, 1860).

69. E. C. Anderson to Robert N. Gourdin, Sept. 30, 1860, Racine, *Gentlemen Merchants*, 393.

70. John G. Nicolay and John Hay, *Abraham Lincoln*, 29 vols. (New York: Century, 1890), Vol. 2: 252–260, includes Gist's letter and the responses. For the quotes, see 252, 255, 256.

71. Jefferson Davis to Robert Barnwell Rhett Jr., Nov. 10, 1860, Lynda Lasswell Crist and Mary Seaton Dix, eds., *Papers of Jefferson Davis* (Baton Rouge: Louisiana State University Press, 1989), Vol. 6: 368–371.

72. *Newberry Rising Sun*, Oct. 3, 1860; *Natchez Mississippi Free Trader*, Oct. 1, Nov. 12, 1860, for quotes on pillage and free blacks; *Jackson Semi-Weekly Mississippian*, Sept. 28, 1860.

73. *Natchez Mississippi Free Trader*, cited in *New York Times*, Sept. 12, 1860.

74. Linton Stephens to A. H. Stephens, Oct. 16, 1860, Alexander H. Stephens Papers, microfilm copy, SHC; Philip St. George Cocke to John B. Cocke, Nov. 6, 1860, Cocke Family Papers, Series E, Part 4, Reel 53, *Records*.

75. *New Orleans Bee*, Sept. 3, 1860; Hunt and James to William Massie, Oct. 4, 1860, William Massie Papers, Series G, Part 2, Reel 29, *Records*; William Elliott to Ralph Elliott, Sept. 26, Elliott and Gonzales Family Papers, SHC.

76. Rogene Scott to her mother, Oct. 27, 1860, Scott Family Papers, SHC.

Chapter 4

1. Robin Edward Baker, "Class and Party: Voting Behavior in the late Antebellum South, Volumes I and II" (PhD. dissertation, Texas A & M University, 1989), 22, 223, 227–228, 276; for the breakdown of the vote in an agriculturally mixed county that underscores the relationship between partisanship, economic status, and age, see Michael J. Daniel, "The Secession Crisis in Butler County, Alabama, 1860–1861," *Alabama Review* 42 (Apr. 1989): 97–124.

2. Voting returns for Mobile taken from *Mobile Daily Advertiser*, Nov. 11; Richmond and Norfolk, *Richmond Daily Examiner*, Dec. 24; New Orleans, *New Orleans Daily Picayune*, Nov. 7; Memphis, *Baton Rouge Daily Gazette and Comet*, Nov. 17; Louisville, *Louisville Daily Courier*, Nov. 9; and St. Louis, *Glasgow* (Mo.) *Weekly Times*, Nov. 15, 1860. On Baltimore, see Towers, *The Urban South and the Coming of the Civil War*, 160.

3. Quoted in Roger W. Shugg, *Origins of Class Struggle in Louisiana*, 145–146.

4. On the link between growth and Breckinridge support, see William L. Barney, *The Secessionist Impulse: Alabama and Mississippi in 1860* (Princeton, N.J.: Princeton University Press, 1974), esp., the tables at 134–135.

5. For the preponderance of younger slaveholders and lawyers in the Breckinridge coalition, see Barney, *The Secessionist Impulse*, 55–100.

6. *Jackson Semi-Weekly Mississippian*, Oct. 9, 1860.

7. *Congressional Globe*, 35th Congress, 2nd Session, 1059. For Whig arguments against expansion, see *Congressional Globe*, 35th Congress, 2nd Session, 1058–1063 and 1344–1361.

8. Woodward, *Mary Chesnut's Civil War*, 3.

9. William H. Ogbourne to his sister, Dec. 14, 1860, James B. Bailey Papers, SHC; George Gilmer Smith, Autobiography, 68, SHC; *Micanopy* (Fla.) *Peninsular Gazette*, cited in *Tampa Florida Peninsular*, Nov. 24, 1860; Sereno Watson to Henry Watson, Nov. 17, 1860, Henry Watson Jr. Papers, Series F, Part 1, Reel 9, *Records*.

10. Linton Stephens to Alexander H. Stephens, Oct. 16, 1860, Alexander H. Stephens Papers, microfilm copy, SHC; *Richmond Examiner*, Oct. 22, cited in *Macon Weekly Georgia Telegraph*, Oct. 25, 1860; Linton Stephens to Alexander H. Stephens, Oct. 16, 1860, Alexander H. Stephens Papers, microfilm copy, SHC.

11. *Keowee* (S.C.) *Courier*, Dec. 8; *Plaquemine* (La.) *Gazette and Sentinel*, Nov. 17; Message of Governor A. B. Moore, Nov. 14, 1860, reprinted in William R. Smith, *The History and Debates of the Convention of the People of Alabama Begun and Held in the City of Montgomery, on the seventh Day of January, 1861* ... (Montgomery: White, Pfister & Co., 1861), 13–18; David Schenck Diary, Vol. 3, Nov. 5, 1860, SHC.

12. *Albany Patriot*, Dec. 27, 1860; Philip St. George Cocke to John B. Cocke, Nov. 16, 1860, Cocke Family Papers, Series E, Part 4, Reel 53, *Records*; Susan Cornwall Diary, Jan. 31, 1861, SHC; David Clopton to C. C. Clay Jr., Dec. 13, 1860, Clement Claiborne Clay Papers, Series F, Part 1, Reel 20, *Records*.

13. Wash. Smith to Chief [De Bow], May 14, 1860, James D. B. De Bow Papers, Duke University.

14. Philip St. George Cocke to John B. Cocke, Nov. 16, 1860, Cocke Family Papers, Series E, Part 4, Reel 53, *Records*; *Charleston Mercury*, Nov. 13, 1860.

15. For the secessionist case for prosperity, see letter of John Cunningham to his fellow citizens of Lexington District, South Carolina, Dec.1, *Charleston Daily Courier*, Dec. 4; *Charleston Mercury*, June 14, 1860.

16. Speech of Jefferson Davis at Atlanta, Feb. 16, 1861, Crist and Dix, *Papers of Jefferson Davis*, Vol. 7, 44; letter of A. B. Longstreet, *Southern Guardian*, cited in *Milledgeville* (Ga.) *Daily Federal Union*, Dec. 2, 1860; James H. Hammond, undated memorandum [c. Nov. 1860], James Henry Hammond Papers, Series A, Part 1, Reel 10, *Records*.

17. *Newberry Rising Sun*, Aug. 1, 1860; *Charleston Mercury*, Jan. 30, 1861; *Milledgeville* (Ga.) *Southern Union*, Feb. 5, 1861; *Dallas Herald*, Dec. 19, 1860. Brian D. Schoen, *The Fragile Fabric of Union: Cotton, Federal Politics, and the Global Origins of the Civil War* (Baltimore, Md.: Johns Hopkins University Press, 2009), makes a powerful case for the confidence placed in King Cotton.

18. *New Orleans Bee*, Nov. 12, 13, 19; on a national convention, see *Savannah Daily Republican*, Nov. 14; and for cooperation, *Mobile Daily Advertiser*, Nov. 20, 1860.

19. *Athens* (Tenn.) *Post*, Dec. 14, 1860.

20. James C. Johnston to William S. Pettigrew, Jan. 1, 1861, Pettigrew Family Papers, SHC; letter of Nov. 13, Benjamin F. Perry, *Charleston Daily Courier*, Nov. 20, 1860.

21. *Augusta Weekly Chronicle and Sentinel*, Feb. 20, 1861; *Savannah Daily Republican*, July 11, 1860, citing the *New York World*; *Brownlow's Knoxville Whig*, Feb. 9, March 2, 1861.

22. *Alexandria* (La.) *Constitutionalist*, Oct. 13, 27, 1860.

23. Letter from "Virginia," Nov. 15, printed in *New Orleans Picayune*, Nov. 20; *Alexandria Constitutionalist*, Oct. 13, 1860.

24. Letter from "A UNION MAN," *Memphis Daily Appeal*, Dec. 9, 1860; letter from "THE LAST WORD," *Charleston Daily Courier*, Nov. 30, 1860, citing the *New Bern* (N.C.) *Progress*.

25. *Clarksville* (Tenn.) *Chronicle*, Nov. 16; *Vicksburg Whig*, Nov. 23, cited in *Clarksville Chronicle*, Nov. 30; letter of R. W. Phillips, *Savannah Republican*, Dec. 27; letter of Richard Call, *Tallahassee Floridian and Journal*, Nov. 10, 1860.

26. *Charleston Daily Courier*, Oct. 15, 22, 1860.

27. The *Charleston Mercury* made explicit the reference to the Wide-Awakes, cited in *Macon* (Ga.) *Daily Telegraph*, Oct. 19, 1860; *Columbia Guardian*, cited in *Charleston Mercury*, Oct. 15, 1860.

28. *Darlington Southerner*, cited in *Newberry Rising Sun*, Oct. 24, 1860; Stephen A. West, "Minute Men, Yeomen, and the Mobilization for Secession in the South Carolina Upcountry," *Journal of Southern History* 71 (Feb. 2005): 75–104.

29. McCurry, *Masters of Small Worlds*, 265–271, 292–293, very effectively makes the case for the political importance of the linkage between paramilitary groups and the militia in the Carolina lowcountry; Selma *Alabama State Sentinel*, Nov. 21; *Jackson Daily Mississippian*, Dec. 1; *Weekly Vicksburg Whig*, Nov. 18, 1860.

30. *Memphis Avalanche*, quoted in *Memphis Daily Appeal*, Dec. 1, 1860.

31. *Newberry Rising Sun*, Dec. 5, 1860; *Weekly Panola Star*, Jan. 10, 1861.

32. *Albany Patriot*, Nov. 22, 1860, citing *Columbus Times*, Nov. 15, 1860; *Savannah Daily Republican*, Nov. 19, 1860; *Carrolton* (La.) *Sun*, Nov. 28, citing a Texas report; *Savannah Daily Republican*, Nov. 28, 1860, for lowcountry vigilantes; Mobile *Daily Advertiser*, Dec. 13, 1860.

33. *Carrolton Sun*, Dec. 19, 1860, citing letter from Samuel J. Halle in *Memphis Daily Argus*, Dec. 11, 1860. Citizens from Friar's Point quickly refuted the account as "false from beginning to end" in a letter to the *Memphis Daily Appeal*, Dec. 14, 1860, admitting only to having roughed up the carpenters and ordered them out. The Friar's Point incident and many others were picked up from the Southern press by the abolitionists and published in *A Fresh Catalogue of Southern Outrages upon Northern Citizens* (New York: American Anti-Slavery Society, 1860). For the produce dealer, see *Placquemine Gazette and Sentinel*, Nov. 17, 1860, citing *Montgomery Mail*. For the incident of the sea captain, see Charles Manigault to Louis Manigault, Feb. 10, 1861, Louis Manigault Papers, Series F, Part 2, Reel 14, *Records*.

34. Mrs. Clara Young to Robert Tweed, Dec. 15, Robert Tweed Papers, SHC; James H. Hammond to William G. Simms, Nov. 10, Hammond Papers, Series A, Part 1, Reel 10, *Records*; for the efforts of the mayors to quell the violence, see *Savannah Daily Republican*, Dec. 3, *Mobile Daily Register*, Dec. 9, *New Orleans Bee*, Dec. 11, 1860.

35. *Paulding* (Miss.) *Eastern Clarion*, Dec. 26, quoting *Independent Monitor*, Nov. 16, 1860.

36. William P. Gould Diary, Nov. 12, 13, ADAH; *Weekly Montgomery Confederation*, Nov. 16; John E. Hall to Bolling Hall, Nov. 11, 1860, Bolling Hall Letters, ADAH; *Brownlow's Knoxville Whig*, Feb. 2, 1861, asserted that the secessionists controlled all the major telegraph companies and colored the news to bolster secession.

37. Alonzo B. Cohen to his sister Irene, Jan. 12, 1861, Alonzo Boyer Cohen Letters, ADAH, captures the bravado of the volunteers; *Richmond Dispatch*, March 9, 1861, citing the *Memphis Avalanche*.

38. For a subscription drive, see Henry W. Ravenel Journal, p. 54, Feb. 28, 1861, SHC; *Newberry Rising Sun*, Jan. 16, 1861.

39. T. F. Murphy to A. B. Moore, Nov. 24, 1860, Moore Correspondence, ADAH; *Clayton Banner*, Nov. 19, 22, 1860. The estimate on the crowd size came from Lewry Dorman, "Barbour County History," MS, 507, University of Alabama Library.

40. *Newberry Rising Sun*, Nov. 21, 1860.

41. *Augusta Weekly Chronicle and Sentinel*, June 15, 1859, citing *New Orleans Picayune*; *Milledgeville Federal Union*, June 17, 1860, Ulrich B. Phillips, ed., *Plantation and Frontier Documents, 1649–1863: Illustrative of Industrial History in the Colonial and Ante-bellum South* (Cleveland: A. H. Clark, 1909), Vol. 2, 73.

42. Sarah Hamilton to her daughter Sarah Hamilton, Dec. 7, 1858; M. C. Fulton to Benjamin C. Yancey, April 11, 1859, Benjamin Cudsworth Yancey Papers, SHC.

43. A. F. Burton to Thomas W. and Nancy Burton, May 4, 1859, Thomas W. Burton Papers, SHC.

44. John A. Civitis to John C. James, June 27, 1857; List of Accounts Due, Jan., 1858; G. W. Thornton to James, March 30, 1859; Agreement between William Drake and John C. James, June 1, 1860, John C. James Papers, SHC.

45. Letter from "Domestic Industry," *Charleston Daily Courier*, Feb. 4, March 6, 1860; *Savannah Daily Republican*, Jan. 11, 1860, quoting the *New York World*.

46. See Harold D. Woodman, *King Cotton and His Retainers: Financing and Marketing the Cotton Crop of the South, 1800–1925* (Lexington: University of Kentucky Press, 1968), and Johnson, *River of Dark Dreams*, 257–262. For a critique by a contemporary Southerner, see Thomas P. Kettel, *Southern Wealth and Northern Profits, as Exhibited in Statistical Facts and Official Figures* (New York: George W. & John A. Wood, 1860). In the absence of a national currency, each state had its own money in the form of the banknotes issued by its banks. South Carolina money, for example, had to be converted (at the cost of the prevailing exchange rate) into New York money to pay for goods bought in New York.

47. *Memphis Daily Appeal*, Nov. 20, 1860, quoting the *Montgomery Mail*.

48. See *Savannah Republican*, Dec. 28, 1860, for the estimate on the drop in receipts; Susan Sellers Darden Diary, Dec. 6, 1860, Darden Family Collection, Series N, Reel 6, *Records*; C. Fitzsimmons to J. H. Hammond, Oct. 19, 1860, Hammond Papers, Series A, Part 1, Reel 10, *Records*, for depressed market for slaves in Charleston; Roscoe Briggs Heath to Lewis E. Mason, Oct. 5, 1860, Lewis Edmunds Mason Correspondence, SHC, on conditions in Richmond in the fall of 1860; John S. Haywood to George W. Haywood, Nov. 21, 1860, Ernest Haywood Papers, Series J, Part 7, Reel 19, *Records*, on the sheriff's sale; *Athens* (Tenn.) *Post*, Dec. 14, 1860, quoting a private letter from New Orleans, dated Dec. 8, 1860; William J. Palmore to Lucy A. Palmore, Jan. 21, 1861, Palmore Family Papers, Series E, Part 1, Reel 36, *Records*; Eliza DeRosset to Katherine Meares, Jan. 6, 1861, DeRosset Family Papers, SHC.

49. Susan Currie to Henry W. Jones, Feb. 10, 1861, Henry W. Jones Papers, Series F, Part 3, Reel 3, *Records*; B. M. Dewitt to Doctor [Iverson L. Twyman], Jan. 12, 1861, Austin-Twyman Papers, Series I, Part 4, Reel 3, *Records*; *Richmond Dispatch*, Dec. 12, 1860; Alexander Franklin Pugh Plantation Diaries, Dec. 26, 1860, March 20, 1861, Series I, Part I, Reel 7, *Records*; *Richmond Dispatch*, March 28, 1861, quoting item from *Aberdeen* (Miss.) *Conservative* (n.d.); letter from "A Southerner," *Richmond Dispatch*, Jan. 3, 1861.

50. Letter from "CHAW," *Athens Southern Watchman*, Jan. 30, 1861.

51. Mary E. Thompson to Elias, Jan. 2, 1861, Benson-Thompson Family Letters, Duke University; Alexander H. Stephens to Linton Stephens, Dec. 27, 1860, A. H. Stephens Papers, microfilm copy, SHC; William H. Ogbourne to his sister, Dec. 14, 1860, James B. Bailey Papers, SHC; T. C. Howard to B. C. Yancey, Dec. 29, 1860, B. C. Yancey Papers, SHC; John B. Cherry to George W. Mordecai, Jan. 13, 1861, Cameron Family Papers, Series J, Part 1, Reel 37, *Records*.

52. *Richmond Dispatch*, Dec. 21, quoting a letter in *Mobile Register*, Dec. 18, 1860; Governor's Message, Jan. 14, 1861, p. 11, *Journal for the Senate of Alabama, 1861* (Montgomery: Shorter & Reid 1861); *Columbus* (Ga.) *Enquirer*, Dec. 25, 1860.

53. *Savannah Daily Republican*, Dec. 3, quoting *Atlanta Locomotive*, Dec. 1, 1860; *New Orleans Bee*, Dec. 27; *New Orleans Daily Picayune*, Dec. 28, 1860; *Alexandria Constitutional*, Dec. 15, 1860; *Richmond Dispatch*, Nov. 21, 1860, Jan. 3, 1861, report from Norfolk correspondent; Rogene Scott to her mother, Jan. 6, 1861, Scott Family Papers, SHC.

54. See *Brownlow's Weekly Knoxville Whig*, Nov. 24, 1860, for a particularly scathing indictment of the secessionists for bringing on the crisis; *Macon Daily Telegraph*, Dec. 12, 1860.

55. Henry Wise to William Samford, Oct. 21, 1860, William F. Samford Papers, SHC; Frank Valliant to Marion Rucks, Dec. 14, 1860, Folder 13, Rucks-Valliant Family Papers, MDAH; J. B. Sharpe & Co. to William T. Sutherlin, Feb. 26, 1861, Box 2, Folder 9, William T. Sutherlin Papers, SHC.

56. *Athens* (Ga.) *Southern Banner*, Aug. 16, 1860; J. W. Walton to his granddaughter, Nov. 21, 1860, James L. Alcorn and Family Papers, MDAH; *Charleston Daily Courier*, Nov. 15, 1860.

57. William Webb, *The History of William Webb, Composed by Himself* (Detroit: Egbert Hoekstra, 1873), 13.

58. On slave literacy and the value slaves placed on learning, see Janet D. Cornelius, *When I Can Read My Title Clear: Literacy, Slavery, and Religion in the Antebellum South* (Columbia: University of South Carolina Press, 1991); Henry Clay Bruce, *The New Man: Twenty-Nine Years a Slave, Twenty-Nine Years a Free Man* (York, Pa.: P. Anstadst & Sons, 1895), 86, 99; Lewis Garrard Clarke, *Narrative of the Sufferings of Lewis Clarke . . .* (Boston: David H. Ela, Printer, 1845), 81; Henry Watson, *Narrative of Henry Watson*, 34.

59. See Thomas C. Buchanan, *Black Life on the Mississippi: Slaves, Free Blacks, and the Western Steamboat World* (Chapel Hill: University of North Carolina Press, 2000) and David S.

Cecelski, *The Waterman's Song: Slavery and Freedom in Maritime North Carolina* (Chapel Hill: University of North Carolina Press, 2001).

60. James H. Hammond to John C. Calhoun, May 10, 1844, Jameson, *Correspondence of John C. Calhoun*, 955; Beveridge and McLaughlin, *Papers of Frederick Law Olmsted: Slavery and the South*, April, 1853, p. 122.

61. Caroline Pettigrew to Charles L. Pettigrew, Nov. 7, 17, 1860, Pettigrew Family Papers, Series J, Part 2, Reel 15, *Records*.

62. *Macon* (Ga.) *Daily Telegraph*, Dec. 20, 1860, citing a letter from Ramer Post Office; *Montgomery Mail*, Dec. 13, 1860; *Carrolton* (La.) *Sun*, Dec. 18, 1860, citing *Montgomery Mail*, Dec. 17, 1860.

63. *Weekly Panola Star*, Dec. 20, 27, 1860; *Athens* (Tenn.) *Post*, Feb. 15, 1861, quoting *Aberdeen Conservative*, Feb. 2, 1861.

64. For Cobb's speech, see Allen D. Chandler, ed., *The Confederate Records of the State of Georgia*, 6 vols. (Atlanta: C. P. Byrd, 1909–11), Vol. 1: 163–164.

65. *Macon Weekly Georgia Telegraph*, Nov. 8, 15, 22, 1860 (quote); on Nov. 22, the *Telegram* published an account of the Habersham affair taken from the *Clarksville Herald*; Rebecca L Felton, *Country Life in Georgia in the Days of My Youth* (Atlanta: Index Printing, 1919), 87.

66. James Hammond Moore, ed., *A Plantation Mistress on the Eve of the Civil War: The Diary of Keziah Goodwyn Brevard, 1860–1861* (Columbia: University of South Carolina Press, 1993), Oct. 13, 1860; Jan. 8, Feb. 13, 1861.

67. *Richmond Dispatch*, Nov. 19, 1860, citing *Fredericksburg Herald; Daily Richmond Examiner*, March 2, 1861; *Richmond Dispatch*, March 4, 1861; Crofts, "Southampton County Diarists," 593.

68. *Vicksburg Daily Evening Citizen*, Dec. 28, 1860, quoting *Coffeeville Intelligencer*.

69. *St. Augustine Examiner*, Jan. 19, 1861, citing *Bolivar* (Tenn.) *Southern*; Jane North to Caroline Pettigrew, Jan. 10, 1861, Pettigrew Family Papers, Series J, Part 2, Reel 15, *Records*; "More Anon," *Charleston Daily Courier*, Dec. 25, 1860; *New Orleans Daily Picayune*, Feb. 27, 1861.

70. *Keowee* (S.C.) *Courier*, Sept. 15, 1860, citing a letter sent to the *Sumter* (S.C.) *Dispatch* on the killing of Keely, a South Carolina native; *Macon* (Miss.) *Beacon*, Nov. 21, 1860; *Carrolton* (La.) *Sun*, Nov. 28, 1860, citing *Brandon* (Miss.) *Republican* (n.d.); *Richmond Dispatch*, April 1, 1861.

71. *Carrolton Sun*, Nov. 21, 1860, citing *Terrebonne Civic Guard*, Nov. 15, 1860; *Richmond Dispatch*, Nov. 8, Dec. 21, 1860, citing *Jackson West Tennessee Whig; Macon Daily Telegraph*, March 12, 1861, citing *Columbus* (Ga.) *Times; Augusta Weekly Chronicle and Sentinel*, April 10, 1861; *Richmond Dispatch*, March 29, 1861; Rogene Scott to her mother, May 28, 1861, Scott Family Papers, SHC.

72. See *New Orleans Bee*, Jan. 12, 1861, citing *Baltimore American* for an account of the murder and its aftermath.

73. *Richmond Dispatch*, Oct. 15, Dec. 5, 1860, Feb. 22, 1861, letter from "Pen"; Sue H. Burbridge to Abraham Lincoln, Jan. 20, 1861, Abraham Lincoln Papers, Library of Congress, accessed at http://memory.loc.gov/ammem/alhtml/alhome.html.

74. See John Hope Franklin and Loren Schweninger, *Runaway Slaves: Rebels on the Plantation* (New York: Oxford University Press, 1999), 279–282; Charles Manigault to Louis Manigault, Jan. 19, 1861, Louis Manigault Papers, Series A, Part 1, Reel 14, *Records*; J. J. Pringle Smith to Robert N. Gourdin, Jan. 19, 1861, Racine, *Gentlemen Merchants*, 431.

75. Jane E. Johnston to Mary Jane Hazlehurst, March 21, 1861, Leighton Wilson Hazlehurst Papers, Duke University; Sarah F. Williams to her parents, Dec. 3, 1860, Sarah F. Williams Papers, SHC; *Carrolton* (La.) *Sun*, March 6, 1861.

76. *Augusta Weekly Chronicle and Sentinel*, April 10, 1861, citing a report from Chicago; *Staunton* (Va.) *Spectator*, April 16, 1861; *Chicago Daily Tribune*, April 6, 1861; *New Orleans Daily Picayune*, Dec. 27, 1860, citing *St. Joseph* (Mo.) *Gazette*, Dec. 19, 1860.

77. *Newberry Rising Sun*, April 4, 1860; see *Macon Daily Telegraph* in early April, and Clarence L. Mohr, *On the Threshold of Freedom: Masters and Slaves in Civil War Georgia* (Athens: University of Georgia Press, 1986), 22–25; *Natchez Mississippi Free Trader*, May 28, 1860; *Weekly Vicksburg Whig*, May 9, 1860; J. A. Turner, "What Are We to Do?" *De Bow's Review* 29 (July 1860): 70–77, quotes 70,71.

78. B. L. C. Wailes Diary, Oct. 31, 1860, Duke University; *Natchez Mississippi Free Trader,* Oct. 29; *New Orleans Daily Picayune,* Oct. 9; *Albany Patriot,* Oct. 25, citing *Tallahassee Floridian Journal; Keowee Courier,* Oct. 20, citing *Spartanburg Spartan; New Orleans Daily Picayune,* Oct. 15, 19, 30, quoting *Coahoma* (Miss.) *Citizen,* Oct. 20; for Opelika fire, *Richmond Dispatch,* Oct. 30, *New Orleans Daily Picayune,* Oct. 31. All dates are 1860.

79. *Newberry Rising Sun,* Nov. 14; *Richmond Dispatch,* Nov. 7; *Macon Daily Telegraph,* Nov. 21; *New Orleans Daily Picayune,* Nov. 24, 30, Dec. 9. All dates are 1860.

80. John S. Haywood to George W. Haywood, Nov. 21, 1860, Ernest Haywood Papers, Series I, Part 7, Reel 19, *Records; Carrolton Sun,* Nov. 10, citing *Panola Star,* Nov. 3, 28; *New Orleans Daily Picayune,* Dec. 8, citing *Coahoma* (Miss.) *Citizen,* Nov. 28; *Alexandria Constitutional,* Nov. 24. All dates are 1860.

81. *Carrolton Sun,* Jan. 5, 1861; *New Orleans Daily Picayune,* Dec. 25, 1860, April 5, 1861; *Newberry Rising Sun,* March 13; *Edgefield Advertiser,* April 10, 1861.

82. Craft Diary, Dec. 16, 1860, Henry Craft Papers, SHC; *Richmond Dispatch,* Jan. 16, April 5, 1861; *Macon Daily Telegraph,* Feb. 26, March 26; *Richmond Dispatch,* Feb. 2, 26.

83. *Richmond Dispatch,* correspondent from Suffolk, Dec. 29, 1860; from Caroline, Jan. 1; from Amelia, Jan. 25, 1861.

Chapter 5

1. Stoll, *Larding the Lean Earth,* 134–136; *De Bow's Review* 19 (Aug. 1855): 223.

2. On efforts to create a Southern nationalism, see John McCardell, *The Idea of a Southern Nation: Southern Nationalists and Southern Nationalism* (New York: Norton, 1979), and more recently and in more depth, Robert E. Bonner, *Mastering America: Southern Slaveholders and the Crisis of American Nationhood* (New York: Cambridge University Press, 2009) and Paul Quigley, *Shifting Grounds: Nationalism and the American South, 1848–1865* (New York: Oxford University Press, 2012).

3. William H. Trescot, *The Position and Course of the South* (Charleston: Walker & James, 1850), 6, 7, 19.

4. [David F. Jemison] "The National Anniversary," *Southern Quarterly Review* 2 (Sept. 1850): 172, 174, 190–191.

5. *New Orleans Bee,* Oct. 15, 1860, quoted in William Kauffman Scarborough, *Masters of the Big House: Elite Slaveholders of the Mid-Nineteenth-Century South* (Baton Rouge: Louisiana State University Press, 2003), 238, 264.

6. Mary Elliott Pinckney to Phoebe Elliott, Dec. 14, 1860, Ann Habersham Wright, ed., *A Savannah Family, 1830–1901: Papers from the Clermont Huger Lee Collection* (Milledgeville, Ga.: Boyd, 1999), 65.

7. This account of the Pinckneys is drawn from the compelling analysis in Barbara Bellow, "Of Time and City: Charleston in 1860," *South Carolina Historical Magazine* 12 (July–Oct. 2011): 157–172.

8. *Charleston Daily Courier,* Nov. 6–8, 1860; Samuel W. Crawford, *The Genesis of the Civil War: The Story of Sumter, 1860–1861* (New York: C. L. Webster, 1887), 12–13.

9. *Charleston Mercury,* Nov. 8, 1860; for the duel, see Freehling, *Secessionists Triumphant,* 399–400.

10. *Charleston Daily Courier,* Nov. 9, 1860; Freehling, *Secessionists Triumphant,* 401–403.

11. James H. Hammond to the Legislature, Nov. 8, 1860, James H. Hammond Papers, Library of Congress.

12. *Charleston Mercury,* Nov. 10, 1860.

13. *Charleston Mercury,* Nov. 12, 1860.

14. *Charleston Daily Courier,* Nov. 12, 1860.

15. For a sketch of Hampton's life, see Ann Fripp Hampton, ed., *A Divided Heart: Letters of Sally Baxter Hampton, 1853–1862* (Spartanburg, S.C.: Reprint Company, 1980), xi–xx; quotes from Sally Hampton to Samuel Bulkley Ruggles, Dec. 14, 1860, pp. 74–75.

16. James H. Hammond to Marcus C. M. Hammond, Nov. 12, 1860, Carol Bleser, ed., *The Hammonds of Redcliffe* (New York: Oxford University Press, 1981), 88.

17. John S. Palmer to James J. Palmer, Nov. 16, James J. Palmer to Harriet R. Palmer, Nov. 26, 1860, Towles, *A World Turned Upside Down,* 272–273, 277.

18. Caroline Pettigrew to Charles L. Pettigrew, Nov. 26, 1860, Pettigrew Family Papers, Series J, Part 2, Reel 15, *Records*; Meta Grimball Diary, Dec. 10, 1860, SHC; Jane G. North to Caroline Pettigrew, Dec. 3, 1860, Pettigrew Family Papers, Series J, Part 2, Reel 15, *Records*; A. G. Guskins to his cousin, Dec. 30, 1860, The Valley of the Shadow: Cochran Family Letters, valley.lib.virginia.edu/papers/AO574; Stephen W. Berry II, *All That Makes a Man: Love and Ambition in the Civil War South* (New York: Oxford University Press, 2005), shows how primal needs to demonstrate their loving protection of women and achieve glory for themselves drove young men to enlist.

19. *Charleston Mercury*, Nov. 13, 1860.

20. *Charleston Mercury*, Nov. 17, 16, 1860.

21. *Charleston Mercury*, Nov. 13, 1860; Scarborough, *Masters of the Big House*, 347; Sally Baxter Hampton to George Baxter, Dec. 22, 23, 1860, Hampton, *A Divided Heart*, 83.

22. Anna E. Kirkland to Harriet R. Palmer, Nov. 24, 1860, and Leora Sims to Palmer, Dec. 10, 1860, Towles, *A World Turned Upside Down*, 274, 278.

23. Sally Baxter Hampton to the Baxter family, Dec. [10?], 1860, Hampton, *A Divided Heart*, 73; Emmie Holmes to Lizzie Green, Nov. 10, 1860, Green Family Papers, Series D, Part 1, Reel 15, typed copy, *Records*.

24. On women's religiosity, see the disappointment of Clemmentina G. Legge over the cancelation of Bishop Thomas Davis's sermon in Spartanburg in November and her frustration over the lack of a regular minister at the local church, in Clemmentina G. Legge to Harriet R. Palmer, Nov. 15, 1860, Towles, *A World Turned Upside Down*, 271; Rev. J. H. Thornwell, *National Sins: A Fast-Day Sermon, Preached in the Presbyterian Church, Columbia, Wednesday, November 21, 1860* (Columbia: Southern Guardian Steam-Power Press, 1861), 8, 16, 11, 42.

25. Quotes from Townsend's speech at St. John's Colleton, *Charleston Mercury*, June 14, 1860.

26. Letter from H. Judge Moore, *Charleston Daily Courier*, Dec. 8, 1860. Employing a microcultural approach, Lawrence T. McDonnell, *Performing Disunion*, explains how ordinary Charlestonians experienced joining a Minute Man company and marching in the streets in support of secession as an affirmation of their social worth and manly independence.

27. See the notices in *Charleston Daily Courier*, Nov. 16, 1860.

28. Madame Baptiste to Bishop Patrick Lynch, Jan. 8, 1861, Lynch Family Papers, Diocese of Charleston Archives, accessed at lcdl.library.cofc.edu/content/lynch-family-letters-1858-1866.

29. *Charleston Daily Courier*, Nov. 16; *Charleston Mercury*, Nov. 15, 1860.

30. *Charleston Mercury*, Nov. 13, 1860.

31. *Charleston Daily Courier*, Nov. 16, 19, 1860.

32. *Charleston Mercury*, Nov. 23, 1860; *Charleston Daily Courier*, Nov. 20, 23, 7, 1860.

33. *Charleston Daily Courier*, Dec. 24, 1860; cited in *Richmond Dispatch*, Dec. 11, 1860.

34. Alfred P. Aldrich to James H. Hammond, Nov. 25, 1860, Hammond Papers, Library of Congress; *Charleston Daily Courier*, Nov. 16, 1860.

35. Caroline Pettigrew to Charles L. Pettigrew, Nov. 7, 1860, Pettigrew Family Papers, Series J, Part 2, Reel 15, *Records*; *Charleston Daily* Courier, Nov. 29, 1860; see the *Courier*, Dec. 22, 1860, for the item from the South Carolina House Journal of Dec. 21, 1860, on the striking out of such authorization in a new bill on slave patrols.

36. *Charleston Daily Courier*, Nov. 13, 1860; Cornish Diary, Nov. 8, 1860, John Hamilton Cornish Papers, SHC.

37. Jane North to Charles L. Pettigrew, Nov. 29, 1860, Pettigrew Family Papers, Series J, Part 2, Reel 15, *Records*; letter from "X.Y.Z.," *Charleston Daily Courier*, Nov. 24, 1860; Manisha Sinha, *The Counterrevolution of Slavery: Politics and Ideology in Antebellum South Carolina* (Chapel Hill: University of North Carolina Press, 2000), 235; claim of Albert M. Boozer, Lexington, Southern Claims Commission, file # 3205, accessed via Fold3.com, hereafter cited as SCC (Albert was the administrator for the estate of Lemuel Boozer); claim of James Beverly, Marlboro, SCC, file # 275 (Pearson testified as a witness); Philip N. Racine, ed., *Piedmont Farmer: The Journals of David Golightly Harris, 1855–1870* (Knoxville: University of Tennessee Press, 1990), Jan. 5, 1861, p. 173.

38. *The Negro Law of South Carolina, Collected and Digested by Judge Belton O'Neal* (Columbia, S.C.: J. G. Bowman, 1848), 11; Robert S. Starobin, ed., *Denmark Vesey: The Slave Conspiracy of 1822* (Englewood Cliffs, N.J.: Prentice-Hall, 1970), 149–151.

39. Bernard Edward Powers Jr., "Black Charleston: A Social History, 1822–1885" (PhD dissertation, Northwestern University, 1982), 15–17.

40. For an overview of the brown aristocracy and its origins, see Michael P. Johnson and James L. Roark, eds., *No Chariot Let Down: Charleston's Free People of Color on the Eve of the Civil War* (Chapel Hill: University of North Carolina Press, 1984), 3–7.

41. Michael Eggart, "Annual Address," Minutes of the Friendly Moralist Society, June 11, 1848, cited in Michael P. Johnson and James L. Roark, *Black Masters: A Free Family of Color in the Old South* (New York: Norton, 1984), 215.

42. Ira Berlin and Herbert G. Gutman, "Natives and Immigrants, Free Men and Slaves: Urban Workingmen in the Antebellum South," *American Historical Review* 88 (Dec. 1983): 1175–1200, Tables 6 and 7; on the highly stratified wealth holdings in Charleston, see Michael P. Johnson, "Wealth and Class in Charleston in 1860," in Walter J. Fraser Jr. and Winfred B. Moore Jr., eds., *From the Old South to the New: Essays on the Transitional South* (Westport, Conn.: Greenwood Press, 1981), 65–80.

43. Letter from "Stevedores," *Charleston Daily Courier*, Jan. 30, 1860.

44. On the arrests and the capitation tax, see Johnson and Roark, *No Chariot Let Down*, note 22, pp. 94–95, note 5, p. 90.

45. The *Charleston Courier*, Aug. 9, carried a notice on the spike in the sale of slave badges.

46. J. M. Johnson to Henry Ellison, Aug. 20, 28, 1860, Johnson and Roark, *No Chariot Let Down*, 85–86, 101; correspondent from Philadelphia, *New York Tribune*, Nov. 10, 1860.

47. J. M. Johnson to Henry Ellison, Aug. 20, 1860, Johnson and Roark, *No Chariot Let Down*, 85–86.

48. *Charleston Mercury*, Sept. 25, Nov. 30, 1860.

49. William Ellison Jr. to Henry Ellison, Oct. 31, 1860, Johnson and Roark, *No Chariot Let Down*, 128.

50. *Charleston Mercury*, Nov. 14, 1860; John Belton O'Neal and John A. Chapman, *The Annals of Newberry in Two Parts* (Newberry, S.C.: Aull & Houseal, 1892), 373; Charles E. Cauthen, *South Carolina Goes to War, 1860–1865* (Chapel Hill, N.C., 1950), 62–63.

51. Claim of Ransom P. Pigg, Chesterfield, SCC, file # 10365; claim of Hugh L. Belk, Lancaster, SCC, file # 12644; claim of John Herndon, Marlboro, SCC, file # 267.

52. J. A. Rice, quoted in claim of Charles Brent, Barnwell, SCC, file # 7998, and Joseph Rozier, quoted in claim of Catharine R. Belton, Beaufort, SCC, file # 9366; William V. Harvey, quoted in claim of Ezekiel Stokes, Beaufort, SCC, file # 6662; claim of Elizabeth Avio, Beaufort, SCC, file # 9364.

53. The story is related in Crabtree and Patton, *"Journal of a Secesh Lady,"* Dec. 22, 1860, p. 26, quoted in Scarborough, *Masters of the Big House*, 306.

54. James L. Petigru to Edward Everett, Jan. 20, 1861, James Petigru Carson, ed., *Life, Letters and Speeches of James Louis Petigru: The Union Man of South Carolina* (Washington, D.C.: W. H. Lowdermilk, 1920), 367; for an excellent biography, see William H. Pease and Jane H. Pease, *James Louis Petigru: Southern Conservative, Southern Dissenter* (Athens: University of Georgia Press, 1995).

55. Sally Hampton to the Baxter family, [Dec. 9], 1860, Hampton, *A Divided Heart*, 71–72.

56. D. H. Hamilton to Robert N. Gourdin, Nov. 26, 1860, Racine, *Gentlemen Merchants*, 401.

57. Correspondence of *Baltimore American*, Dec. 3, cited in *New York Daily Tribune*, Dec. 7, 1860; on Rhett's urging of Governor Means in 1851 to seize Fort Moultrie, see John Barnwell, *Love of Order: South Carolina's First Secession Crisis* (Chapel Hill: University of North Carolina Press, 1982), 170–171.

58. Rhett's speech at Institute Hall, Nov. 12, *Charleston Daily Courier*, Nov. 21, 1860; William Frazier to James D. Davidson, Jan. 8, 1861, Bruce S. Greenawalt, ed., "Unionists in Rockbridge County: The Correspondence of James Dorman Davidson Concerning the Virginia Secession Convention of 1861," *Virginia Magazine of History and Biography* 73 (Jan. 1965): 82; M. Harvey Effinger to William Massie, Dec. 11, 1860, William Massie Papers, Series G, Part 2, Reel 29, *Records*.

59. Philip S. Klein, *President James Buchanan: A Biography* (University Park: Pennsylvania State University Press, 1962) is the fullest and best-balanced treatment of Buchanan; Philip G. Auchampaugh, *James Buchanan and His Cabinet on the Eve of Secession* (Boston: privately

printed, 1926), the most sympathetic; and Jean Baker, *James Buchanan* (New York: Times Books, 2000), the most damning. Buchanan provided his own defense in *Mr. Buchanan's Administration on the Eve of the Rebellion* (New York: D. Appleton, 1866).

60. Quoted in James Ford Rhodes, *History of the United States from the Compromise of 1850 to the McKinley-Bryan Campaign of 1896*, 8 vols. (New York: Macmillan, 1920), Vol. 3: 137.

61. "Narrative and Letter of William Henry Trescot, concerning the Negotiations between South Carolina and President Buchanan in December, 1860," *American Historical Review* 13 (April, 1908): 533. Here, and elsewhere, Trescot is a reliable source for the workings of Buchanan's cabinet in the crisis.

62. Winfield Scott, "Views Suggested by the Imminent Danger . . . of a Disruption of the Union . . . ," John Bassett Moore, ed., *The Works of James Buchanan, Comprising His Speeches, State Papers, and Private Correspondence*, 12 vols. (Philadelphia: J. B. Lippincott, 1910), Vol. 11: 301–303; Trescot, "Narrative," 535–536.

63. William T. Sherman to George Mason Graham, Dec. 25, 1860, Walter L. Fleming, ed., *General W. T. Sherman as College President: A Collection of Letters, Documents, and Other Material . . .* (Cleveland: Arthur M. Clarke, 1912), 318–319.

64. For the circulation figures, see correspondence from Charleston, Nov. 7, *New York Daily Tribune*, Nov. 10. Though superseded by William C. Davis, *Rhett: The Turbulent Life and Times of a Fire-Eater* (Columbia: University of South Carolina Press 2001), Laura A. White, *Robert Barnwell Rhett, Father of Secession* (New York: Century, 1931), remains valuable for its insights into Rhett's character.

65. *Journal of the Convention of the People of South Carolina, Held in 1860, 1861 and 1862 . . .* (Columbia, S.C.: R. W. Gibbes, printer to the Convention, 1862), 4.

66. John S. Palmer to Esther Palmer, Dec. 19, 1860, Towles, *A World Turned Upside Down*, 279.

67. *Charleston Mercury*, Dec. 21, 1860.

68. *Charleston Daily Courier*, Dec. 22, 1860; the address Keitt mentioned was the "Declaration of the Immediate Causes Which Induce and Justify the Secession of South Carolina from the Federal Union," issued on Dec. 24, 1860.

Chapter 6

1. *Randolph* (Ind.) *County Journal*, Nov. 22, 1860; *Wilmington* (Del.) *Journal*, Nov. 16, quoted in *Hartford* (Conn.) *Courant*, Nov. 18; *Wabash Express*, Nov. 14. All dates are 1860.

2. *Randolph* (Ind.) *County Journal*, Nov. 22, 1860; *Chicago Daily Tribune*, Nov. 16, 1860.

3. *Ottawa* (Mich.)*Free Trader*, Nov. 20, 1860; *Detroit Free Press*, Nov. 10, 11, 13, 15, 1860.

4. *Detroit Free Press*, Nov. 13, 1860.

5. On the South as a proponent of consolidated national power on behalf of slavery and against the state's rights position of Northern states, see Arthur Bestor, "State Sovereignty and Slavery: A Reinterpretation of Proslavery Constitutional Doctrine, 1846–1860," *Journal of the Illinois State Historical Society* 54 (Summer 1961): 117–180 and Paul Finkleman, "States' Rights, Southern Hypocrisy, and the Crisis of the Union," *Akron Law Review* 45, no. 2 (2012): 449–478.

6. John G. Tappan to John H. Cocke, [Nov. 10? 1860], Cocke Family Papers, Series E, Part 4, Reel 53, *Records*; Emory Washburn to A. A. Echols, Nov. 17, 1860, T. Butler King Papers, SHC.

7. G. C. Norton to Abraham Lincoln, Dec. 11, 1860, Abraham Lincoln Papers, Library of Congress.

8. P. V. Wise to Abraham Lincoln, Dec. 13, 1861, Lincoln Papers, Library of Congress.

9. William C. Smedes to Lincoln, Feb. 4, 1861, Lincoln Papers, Library of Congress.

10. *Charleston Daily Courier*, Nov. 21, 1860; William P. Miles to Howell Cobb, Jan. 14, 1861, Ulrich B. Phillips, ed., "The Correspondence of Robert Toombs, A. H. Stephens, and Howell Cobb," *American Historical Association*, Vol. 2 (Washington, D.C.: Government Printing Office, 1913), 529; J. L. Pugh to Miles, Jan. 24, 1861, William Porcher Miles Papers, SHC.

11. *Congressional Globe*, 36th Congress, 2nd Session, 332; Daniel W. Crofts, *Reluctant Confederates: Upper South Unionists in the Secession Crisis* (Chapel Hill: University of North Carolina Press, 1989), 135.

12. Governor's Message, Nov. 16, *The Weekly* (Jackson) *Mississippian*, Nov. 28, 1860; Lamar to Augustus B. Longstreet, Nov. 13, Edward Mayes, *Lucius Q. C. Lamar, His Life, Times,*

and Speeches, 1825–1893 (Nashville, Tenn.: Publishing House of the Methodist Episcopal Church, South, 1896), 86; Davis, cited in Percy Lee Rainwater, *Mississippi: Storm Center of Secession*, 171; Sally Hampton to Anna Baxter, Jan. 11, 1861, Hampton, *A Divided Heart*, 98.

13. *Macon Daily Telegraph*, Dec. 12, 1860; *New Orleans Bee*, Dec. 7, 1860; *Memphis Daily Appeal*, Dec. 13, 1860.

14. A. Henderson to William T. Sutherlin, Jan. 28, 1861, Sutherlin Papers, Box 2, Folder 9, SHC; William A. Graham to Alfred M. Waddell, Feb. 5, 1861, J. G. deRoulhac Hamilton, ed., *The Papers of William Alexander Graham*, 7 vols. (Raleigh, N.C.: State Department of Archives and History, 1957–92), Vol. 5: 224.

15. *Douglass' Monthly*, Dec. 1, 1860; *Congressional Globe*, 36th Congress, 2nd Session, 7.

16. *Congressional Globe*, 36th Congress, 2nd Session, 11; *New York Times*, Dec. 5, 1860.

17. See *United States Congress Serial Set*, No. 10, Senate Report # 288, 36th Congress, 2nd Session (Washington, D.C.: Government printing Office, 1860) for Douglas's compromise measures.

18. Horatio King to John Dix, Dec. 10, 1860, Horatio King, *Turning on the Light: A Dispassionate Survey of President Buchanan's Administration from 1860 to Its Close* (Philadelphia: J. B. Lippincott, 1895), 32; *New York Herald*, Dec. 14.

19. Lincoln to Lyman Trumbull, Dec. 10; Lincoln to William Kellogg, Dec. 11, 1860, Roy P. Basler, *The Collected Works of Abraham Lincoln*, 9 vols. (New Brunswick, N.J.: Rutgers University Press, 1953–55),Vol. 4: 148–149.

20. For Adams's thinking, see David M. Potter, *The Impending Crisis, 1848–1861*, compiled and edited by Don E. Fehrenbacher (New York: Harper & Row, 1976), 529–530.

21. John A. Campbell to Daniel Chandler, Dec. 4, 1860, *Southern Historical Society Papers* (Richmond: Virginia Historical Society, 1917), 42: 24–26.

22. Philip S. Foner, *Businessmen and Slavery: The New York Merchants and the Irrepressible Conflict* (Chapel Hill: University of North Carolina Press, 1941), 227–232; for Lathers and the Pine Street meeting, see the *New York Herald*, Dec.16, 1860.

23. On the confidence that the North would yield, see *New Orleans Bee*, Nov. 14, 1860, and *Athens* (Tenn.) *Pose*, Dec. 14, 1860; quote is from the resolutions of a meeting in Marion County, Kentucky, on December 10, 1860, *Louisville Daily Courier*, Dec. 14, 1860; Henry G. Smith to Andrew Johnson, Dec. 23, 1860, Leroy P. Graf and Ralph W. Haskins, eds., *The Papers of Andrew Johnson*, 16 vols. (Knoxville: University of Tennessee Press, 1967–2000), Vol. 4: 80.

24. For calls for a middle confederacy, see M. Harvey Effinger to William Massie, Dec. 11, 1860, and William M. Massie to William C. Rives, Feb. 8, 1861, William Massie Papers, Series G, Part 2, Reel 29, *Records; Memphis Enquirer*, cited in *Baltimore Daily Exchange*, Nov. 16, 1860; Crofts, *Reluctant Confederates*, 109. Baltimore *American and Commercial Advertiser*, Jan. 15, 1861.

25. Julian C. Ruffin to his father, Dec. 22, 1860, Ruffin Family Papers, Series M, Part 4, Reel 48, *Records.*

26. Cited in *Athens* (Tenn.) *Post*, Dec. 21, 1860.

27. *Congressional Globe*, 36th Congress, 2nd Session, 112–114.

28. *Congressional Globe*, 36th Congress, 2nd Session, 114; *Philadelphia Press*, Dec. 22; *New York Herald*, Dec. 23, 1860.

29. Justin S. Morrill to his wife Ruth, Dec. 7, 1860, George Weston Smith and Charles Judah, eds., *Life in the North during the Civil War* (Albuquerque: University of New Mexico Press, 1966), 16; *Congressional Globe*, 36th Congress, 2nd Session, 1005.

30. Abby Howland Woolsey to "my dear cousin," [Jan. 1861], Eliza Woolsey Howland, ed., *Letters of a Family during the War for the Union*, 2 vols. (New Haven, Conn., 1899), Vol. 1: 30.

31. For critical accounts of Lincoln's handling of the crisis, see Russell McClintock, *Lincoln and the Decision for War: The Northern Response to Secession* (Chapel Hill: University of North Carolina Press, 2009) and William J. Cooper, *We Have the War upon Us: The Onset of the Civil War, November 1860–April 1861* (New York: Alfred A. Knopf, 2012); *Congressional Globe*, 36th Congress, 1st Session, Appendix, 388.

32. *Congressional Globe*, 36th Congress, 2nd Session, 270; Appendix, 132. For the constant pressure Southerners had exerted in Congress and the State Department for more territory and protection for slavery, see Matthew Karp, *The Vast Southern Empire: Slaveholders at the Helm of American Foreign Policy* (Cambridge, Mass.: Harvard University Press, 2016).

33. *Congressional Globe*, 36th Congress, 2nd Session, 403; Lincoln to Lyman Trumbull, Dec. 10, 1860, Basler, *Collected Works of Lincoln*, Vol. 4: 150. Lincoln used the same phrase in his letter to William Kellogg on Dec. 11, 1860.

34. *New Orleans Bee*, Jan. 16, 25, 1861; *Richmond Dispatch*, Dec. 27, 1860.

35. See the correspondence between Washington and Anderson in *The War of the Rebellion: A Compilation of the Official Records of the Union and Confederate Armies*, 128 vols. (Washington, D.C.: Government Printing Office, 1888–1901), Series 1, Vol. 1, 79–105, hereafter cited as *O.R.*; see 89–90 for Memorandum of Verbal Instructions to Anderson from D. C. Buell, Dec. 11, 1860.

36. Floyd to Anderson, Dec. 21, 1860, *O.R.*, Series 1, Vol. 1, 103; Anderson to S. Cooper, Dec. 21, 1860, *O.R..*, Series 1, Vol. 1, 105; Crawford, *The Genesis of the Civil War*, 101.

37. Abner Doubleday, *Reminiscences of Fort Sumter and Moultrie in 1860–'61* (New York: Harper & Brothers, 1876), 59–67; Crawford, *Genesis*, 102–108; John G. Nicolay and John Hay, *Abraham Lincoln: A History*, 10 vols. (New York: Century, 1890), Vol. 3: 47–56.

38. *Charleston Mercury*, Dec. 28, 1860; Pickens to Miles, Dec. 25, 1860, William Porcher Miles Papers, Box 3, Folder 34, SHC.

39. *Journal of the Convention of the People of South Carolina*, 53.

40. Trescot, *Narrative and Letter*, 544; Nichols, *Disruption of American Democracy*, 423.

41. Moore, *Works of Buchanan*, Vol. 11: 77; Nicolay and Hay, *Abraham Lincoln*, Vol. 3: 70–72.

42. Nichols, *Disruption of American Democracy*, 425–426; *O.R.*, Series 1, Vol. 1, 116–118, 120–125.

43. *Macon Daily Telegraph*, Dec. 29, 1860; A. L. Lamar to Robert N. Gourdin, Dec. 29, 1860, Racine, *Gentlemen Merchants*, 420; Freehling, *Secessionists Triumphant*, 481–482.

44. Governor Moore to Colonel J. B. Todd, General Order No. 1, Jan. 3, 1861, John B. Todd Papers, ADAH; A. B. Moore to the President of the United States, Jan. 4 [?], 1861, *O.R.*, Series 1, Vol. 1, 327–328; T. J. McClellan to his wife, Jan. 6, 1861, Thomas Joyce McClellan Papers, ADAH.

45. Stephens to Linton Stephens, Jan. 7, 1861, A. H. Stephens Papers, microfilm copy, SHC.

46. Joseph P. Thomas, *The President's Fast: A Discourse upon the Nation's Crisis and Follies* (New York: T. Holman, 1861), 18, 20.

47. *Cincinnati Enquirer*, Jan. 4, 5, 1861; *Evansville* (Ind.) *Daily Journal*, Jan. 7, 1861; *Randolph County Journal* (Ind.), Jan. 10, 1861.

48. James D. Richardson, compiler, *A Compilation of the Messages and Papers of the Presidents, 1789–1897*, 10 vols. (New York: Bureau of National Literature, 1896–99), Vol. 5: 656; *O.R.*, Series 1, Vol. 1, 445–446.

49. *New York Herald*, Jan. 6, 1861.

50. *New York Herald*, Jan. 6, 1861; quote is from A. G. Brown's telegram, *O.R.*, Series 1, Vol. 52, part 2:3.

51. *New York Herald*, Jan. 6, 1861; *Chicago Daily Tribune*, Jan. 4, 1861, citing a Philadelphia correspondent of the *New York Times*.

52. Cited in *Charleston* Mercury, Jan. 19, 1861; Chicago *Daily Tribune*, Jan. 9, 1861.

53. *O.R.*, Series 1, Vol. 1, 120.

54. Crawford, *Genesis*, 174–175; Wigfall to M. L. Bonham, Jan. 2, 1861, *O.R.*, Series 1, Vol. 1, 252.

55. Doubleday, *Reminiscences*, 102–104; Crawford, *Genesis*, 186, for the quote.

56. *Executive Documents No. 2, Correspondence and Other Papers Relating to Fort Sumter, Including Correspondence of Hon. Isaac W. Hayne with the President* (Charleston: Evans & Cogswell, 1861), 3–6.

57. For the letter from the ten senators to Hayne on January 15, 1861, see *Executive Documents No. 2*, 12–13.

58. Moore, *Works of James Buchanan*, Vol. 11: 128–131.

59. Report from Richmond correspondent, Jan. 19, 1861, *Charleston Mercury*, Jan. 24, 1861.

60. *Detroit Free Press*, Jan. 12, 1861; *New York Daily Tribune*, Jan. 11, 1861.

61. Andrew Johnson to John Trimble, Jan. 13, 1861, Graf and Haskins, *Papers of Andrew Johnson*, Vol. 4: 163; *Congressional Globe*, 36th Congress, 2nd Session, 412–414?

62. *House Reports*, 36th Congress, 2nd Session, No. 31, Serial 104, 35–40. For the story of the proposed thirteenth amendment, see Daniel W. Crofts, *Lincoln and the Politics of Slavery: The*

Other Thirteenth Amendment and the Struggle to Save the Union (Chapel Hill: University of North Carolina Press, 2016).

63. Davis to C .C. Clay Jr., Jan. 19, 1861, Clement Claiborne Clay Papers, Series F, Part 1, Reel 20, *Records*; Yulee to Joseph Finegan, Jan. 5, 1861, *O.R.*, Series 1, Vol. 1, 442.

Chapter 7

1. J. L. Power, *Proceedings of the Mississippi State Convention, Held Jan. 7th to 28th A.D. 1861 ...* (Jackson: Power & Cadwallader, 1861), 47.

2. On the Delta elite's conservatism, see Scarborough, *Masters of the Big House*, 307, 338–342; William Banks Taylor, "Southern Yankees: Wealth, High Society, and Political Economy in the Late Antebellum Natchez Region," *Journal of Mississippi History* 59 (Summer 1997): 79–121; and Rebecca M. Dresser, "Kate and John Minor: Confederate Unionists of Natchez," *Journal of Mississippi History* 64 (Fall 2001): 189–216. On the very localized world of Mississippi politics and voters, see Christopher J. Olsen, *Political Culture and Secession in Mississippi: Masculinity, Honor, and the Antiparty Tradition, 1830–1860* (New York: Oxford University Press, 2000).

3. *Canton American Citizen*, Nov. 10, 1860; *Vicksburg Daily Whig*, Nov. 8, 20, 1860.

4. David Clopton to C .C. Clay Jr., Dec. 13, 1860, Clement Claiborne Clay Papers, Series F, Part 1, Reel 20, *Records*; S. R. Gist to Gov. Pettus, Nov. 8, 1860, Governor's Records, MDAH.

5. Mayes, *Lamar*, 86–87; Reuben Davis, *Recollections of Mississippi and Mississippians* (Boston: Houghton Mifflin, 1889), 391–392; O. R. Singleton to W. T. Walthall, July 14, 1877, Rowland, *Jefferson Davis*, Vol. 7, 560–562; William Howard Russell, *My Diary North and South* (Boston: T.O.H.P. Burnham, 1863), 299.

6. R. L. Dixon to Harry Dixon, Nov. 27, Dec. 8, 1860, Harry St. John Dixon Papers, SHC.

7. Jackson *Semi-Weekly Mississippian*, Dec. 11, 1860; Flavellus G. Nicholson Diary-Journal, Nov. 6, 1860, MDAH; Fontaine to Gov. Pettus, Nov. 12, 1860, Governor's Records, MDAH; John H. Aughey, *Tupelo* (Lincoln, Neb.: State Journal Company, 1888), 30–31.

8. Claim of John C. Kirk, Bolivar, SCC, file # 2743; claim of William A. Brown, Alcorn, SCC, file # 8173, testimony of James A. Brown; Aughey, *Tupelo*, 46.

9. See *Jackson Weekly Mississippian*, Jan. 2, 1861, for a classification of the convention delegates.

10. Power, *Proceedings*, 5, 10–12; Alexander M. Clayton and J. F. H. Claiborne, "The Secession Convention," Claiborne Papers, Folder 35, p. 4, SHC; for the Alcorn quote, see Percy Lee Rainwater, ed., H. S. Fulkerson, *A Civilian's Recollections of the War between the States* (Baton Rouge, La.: O. Claitor, 1939), 8.

11. For Alcorn's career, see Lillian A. Pereyra, *James Lusk Alcorn: Persistent Whig* (Baton Rouge: Louisiana State University Press, 1966). Glenn left few papers and has found no biographer.

12. Power's account of the convention, Jan. 15–17, 22, 1861, Claiborne Papers, D. C. Glenn, "Memoranda," Claiborne Papers, Folder 39, SHC.

13. Edward E. Baptist, *Creating an Old South: Middle Florida's Plantation Frontier before the Civil War* (Chapel Hill: University of North Carolina Press, 2002); Ralph A. Wooster, *The People in Power: Courthouse and State House in the Lower South, 1850–1860* (Knoxville: University of Tennessee Press, 1969), Table 1, p. 29.

14. William W. Davis, *The Civil War and Reconstruction in Florida* (New York: Columbia University, 1913), 31–39; for the Calhoun War, see *Apalachicola Times*, cited in *Tampa Florida Peninsular*, Nov. 10, 1860.

15. *Monticello Family Friend*, Nov. 17, 1860; *Fernandina East Floridian*, Dec. 1, 1860; *Family Friend*, Jan. 19, 1861; *East Floridian*, Dec. 19, 1860.

16. *Tampa Florida Peninsular*, Nov. 10, 1860; *Gainesville Micanopy Gazette*, Nov. 3, 1860, noted that the burning of Perry's gin was "supposed to be the work of an incendiary."

17. On the Baptists, see *Monticello Family Friend*, Dec. 8, 1860; *Ocala Companion*, Dec. 1, 1860; Governor's Message, *A Journal of the Proceedings of the House of Representatives ... of the State of Florida ... on November 26, 1860* (Tallahassee; Office of the Floridian and Journal, printed by Dyke and Carlisle, 1860), 9; *St. Augustine Examiner*, Dec. 8, 1860.

18. Diary of Susan Bradford Eppes, Richard Eppes, ed., *Through Some Eventful Years* (Macon, Ga.: Press of the J.W. Burke Company, 1926), 141.

19. Henry Erben, "Surrender of the Navy Yard at Pensacola, Florida, January 12, 1861," A. Noel Blakeman, ed., *Personal Recollections of the War of the Rebellion* (New York: G. P. Putnam's Sons, 1897), 212; Ellen Call Long, *Florida Breezes; or, Florida, New and Old. A Facsimile Reproduction of the 1883 ed.* (Gainesville: University Press of Florida, 1962), 282.

20. Quoted in Davis, *Civil War*, 50; Ethelred Philips to J. J. Philips, Dec. 20, 1860, James Jones Philips Papers, SHC; *New York Daily Tribune*, Feb. 20, 1864, for claims of intimidation by Unionist refugees; Allen Turner Davidson to his wife, April 4, 1861, Allen Turner Davidson Letters, SHC; *St. Augustine Examiner*, Nov. 24, 1860. My thanks to Robert Colby for alerting me to the Philips collection.

21. Charles B. Dew, *Apostles of Disunion*, is the best source on the commissioners and their uniform message of the need to protect slavery and white supremacy. Diary of Eppes, Jan. 7, 8, 1861, *Through Some Eventful Years*, 141–142; *Journal of the Proceedings of the Convention of the People of Florida . . . on January 3, A.D., 1861* (Tallahassee: Office of the Floridian and Journal, printed by Dyke and Carlisle, 1861), 28–30.

22. John W. Pratt to Robert N. Gourdin, Dec. 12, 1860, Racine, *Gentlemen Merchants*, 411; L. T. Tichenor to Gov. A. B. Moore, Nov. 14; *Hayneville* (Ala.) *Chronicle*, Nov. 22, 1860; *Montgomery Post*, Nov. 14; *Mobile Daily Advertiser*, Nov. 18.

23. *Hayneville* (Ala.) *Chronicle*, Nov. 15, 1860.

24. *Autauga Citizen* (Pratteville), Nov. 22, 1860; *Mobile Register*, cited in *Weekly Montgomery Confederation*, Nov. 23, 1860; speech of Daniel Chandler, *Mobile Daily Advertiser*, Dec. 18, 1860. Chandler was a prominent Mobile lawyer.

25. Clemens to John J. Crittenden, Dec. 25, 1860, Crittenden Papers, Library of Congress.

26. *Alabama Beacon* (Greensboro), Nov. 30, 1860.

27. Barney, *Secessionist Impulse*, 276, 252–255.

28. William P. Gould Diary, Oct. 16, Nov. 24, Dec. 23, 1860, ADAH.

29. *Clayton Banner*, Dec. 13, 1860.

30. *St. Clair Diamond*, Dec. 5, 1860.

31. *St. Clair* Diamond, Dec. 5, 1860; *Tuscumbia States' Rights Democrat*, Dec. 7, 1860; Barney, *Secessionist Impulse*, 258–259; Clemens to William B. Wood, Nov. 26, 1860, Samuel Alexander Martin Wood Papers, ADAH.

32. John W. Inzer, "Alabama's Secession Convention," *Confederate Veteran* 31 (Jan. 1923): 7–9; Thomas Joyce McClellan to John Beattie McClellan, Jan. 7, 1861, Robert A. McClellan Papers, Duke University; William R. Smith, *The History and Debates of the Convention of the People of Alabama, Begun and Held in the City of Montgomery, on the Seventh Day of January, 1861* (Montgomery: White, Pfister, 1861), 22, 45.

33. T. J. McClellan to J. B. McClellan, Jan. 7, 1861, Robert A. McClellan Papers, Duke University; Clarence P. Denman, *The Secession Movement in Alabama* (Montgomery: Alabama State Department of Archives and History, 1933); Smith, *Convention*, 23.

34. Smith, *Convention*, 50–57, 34, 42, 63–64.

35. Smith, *Convention*, 69–74.

36. Smith, *Convention*, 69–93; Rev. Wm. H. Mitchell to his wife, Jan. 11, 1861, Reverend William H. Mitchell Letters, ADAH.

37. Davis to John B. McClellan, Jan. 13, 1861; T. J. McClellan to his wife, Jan. 14, 1861, Robert A. McClellan Papers, Duke University.

38. Hugh Lawson Clay to C. C. Clay, Jan. 11, 1861, Clay Papers, Duke University; Elbert J. Watson, "The Story of Nickajack," *Alabama Review* 20 (Jan. 1967): 34–44, notes that the chances of creating a new state were always remote.

39. For calls for a referendum, see Tuscaloosa *Independent Monitor*, Feb. 1, 1861; Smith, *Convention*, 323–325, 334–341, 361–363.

40. Stephens, quoted in William B. McCash, *Thomas R. R. Cobb (1823–1862): The Making of a Southern Nationalist* (Macon, Ga.: Mercer University Press, 1983), 65; "Substance of Remarks Made by Thomas R. R. Cobb, Esq., Before the General Assembly of Georgia, November 12th, 1860," Chandler, *Confederate Records of Georgia*, Vol. 1, 171–172; *Athens Southern Banner*, Nov. 15, 1860.

41. James C. Cobb, "The Making of a Secessionist: Henry L. Benning and the Coming of the Civil War," *Georgia Historical Quarterly* 60 (Winter 1976): 313–323.

42. *Special Message of Gov. Joseph E. Brown, to the Legislature of Georgia . . . on November 7th, 1860* (Milledgeville, Ga.: Boughton, Nisbet & Barnes, State Printers, 1860).

43. "Substance of Remarks Made by Thomas R. R. Cobb," Chandler, *Confederate Records of Georgia*, Vol. 1, 182.

44. Georgia King to Henry Lord King, Nov. 15, 1860, Thomas Butler King Papers, SHC; William W. Freehling and Craig M. Simpson, eds., *Secession Debated: Georgia's Showdown in 1860* (New York: Oxford University Press, 1992), xvii–xviii.

45. C. W. Howard to Robert N. Gourdin, Dec. 3, 1860; John M. Richardson to Gourdin, Dec. 5, 14, 1860, Racine, *Gentlemen Merchants*, 402, 405–406, 412.

46. *Milledgeville Weekly Federal Union*, Dec. 11, 1860.

47. John B. Lamar to Howell Cobb, Dec. 11, 1860; J.B. Guthrie to Philip Clayton, Dec. 27, 1860, R. P. Brooks, ed., "Howell Cobb Papers," *Georgia Historical Quarterly* 6 (Sept. 1922): 263–264; Hershel Johnson to Alexander Stephens, Nov. 30, 1860, Percy Scott Flippin, *Hershel V. Johnson: State Unionist* (Richmond: Dietz Printing, 1931), 159.

48. Alexander Stephens to J. Henly Smith, Nov. 23, 1860, Phillips, *Correspondence of Toombs, Stephens, and Cobb*, 630; *Augusta Weekly Chronicle & Sentinel*, Dec. 23, 1860.

49. Letter from "Georgia," *Athens Southern Banner*, Nov. 29, 1860; "Nullifier of 1833," *Augusta Weekly Chronicle & Sentinel*, Nov. 21, 1860; Alexander Stephens to Linton Stephens, Dec. 24, 1860, Alexander H. Stephens Papers, microfilm, SHC.

50. Letter from "Observer," *Augusta Weekly Chronicle & Sentinel*, Jan. 16, 1861; George Hall to H. V. Johnson, Jan. 7, 1861, Flippin, *Hershel V. Johnson*, 173.

51. For the pronounced support of town leaders for secession, see Johnson, *Toward a Patriarchal Republic*, 96–101; on the shift of small farmers into cotton, George B. Crawford, "Cotton, Land, and Sustenance: Toward the Limits of Abundance in Late Antebellum Georgia," *Georgia Historical Quarterly* 72 (Summer 1988): 215–247; Frank J. Byrne, "Rebellion and Retail: A Tale of Two Merchants in Confederate Georgia," *Georgia Historical Quarterly* 79 (Spring 1955): 30–56, quote on p. 37.

52. Michael P. Johnson, "A New Look at the Popular Vote for Delegates to the Georgia Secession Convention," *Georgia Historical Quarterly* 56 (Summer 1972): 259–275; *Augusta Weekly Chronicle & Sentinel*, Jan. 9, 1861.

53. *Macon Daily Telegraph*, Dec. 12, 1860, reporting on Nisbet's speech of Dec. 8, 1860; *Journal of the Public and Secret Proceedings of the People of Georgia: Held in Milledgeville and Savannah in 1861, Together with the Ordinances Adopted* (Milledgeville, Ga.: Boughton, Nisbet & Barnes, State Printers, 1861), 15–23, 26–32.

54. *Journal of . . . the Convention of the People of Georgia*, 45–46; Johnson, *Toward a Patriarchal Republic*, 120–121; Ralph A. Wooster, *The Secession Conventions of the South* (Princeton, N.J.: Princeton University Press, 1962), 91.

55. *Augusta Weekly Chronicle & Sentinel*, Jan. 23, 1861; James W. Allen to Joseph E. Brown, Feb. 15, 1861, quoted in Donald A. DeBats, "Elites and Masses: Political Structure, Communication and Behavior in Ante-Bellum Georgia" (PhD Thesis, University of Wisconsin, 1973), 547.

56. Quoted in Louis M. Sears, *John Slidell* (Durham, N.C.: Duke University Press, 1925), 194; *Caddo Gazette*, cited in *New Orleans Bee*, Jan. 20, 1861, for expulsion of Lemuel Gilbert of Boston; *New Orleans Daily Picayune*, Feb. 14, 1861, for arrest of Catholic priest; Charles G. Schultz, ed., "New Orleans, 1860," *Louisiana History* 9 (Winter 1968): 59–60.

57. Rev. Benjamin Morgan Palmer, "The South: Her Peril and Her Duty," Jon L. Wakelyn, ed., *Southern Pamphlets on Secession, November 1860–April 1861* (Chapel Hill: University of North Carolina Press, 1996), 66–67, 71, 69, 77.

58. W. H. Pearson to John W. Gurley, Dec. 3, 1860, John W. Gurley Papers, Series I, Part 2, Reel 13, *Records*; Robert A. Grinnan to Beverly R. W. Wellford, Dec. 3, 1860, Jan. 2, 24, 1861, White, Wellford, Taliaferro, and Marshall Family Papers, microfilm, SHC.

59. Ann Davison to Ann Maria Jennings, Feb. 14, 1861, Hennen-Jennings Family Papers, Confederate Military Manuscripts, Series B, Reel 7, *Records*.

60. Scott P. Marler, *The Merchants' Capital: New Orleans and the Political Economy of the Nineteenth-Century South* (New York: Cambridge University Press, 2013), 12–23; for prosperity in an independent South, see *New Orleans Daily Crescent*, Nov. 10, 1860.

61. *New Orleans Bee*, Dec. 20, 28, 1860; letter of "A Citizen," Jan. 14, 1861, was a lonely voice for Louisiana to establish its own independent republic.

62. Thomas Pollock to his parents, [Nov.], Oct. 7, Nov. 20, 1860, Abram David Pollock Papers, SHC.

63. Shugg, *Origins of Class Struggle in Louisiana*, 161–162; William Tecumseh Sherman to Ellen Sherman, Nov. 3, 23, 1860, Walter L. Fleming, ed., *General W. T. Sherman as College President: A Collection of Letters, Documents, and Other Material, Chiefly from Private Sources, Relating to . . . the Stirring Conditions, Existing in the South on the Eve of the Civil War, 1859–1861* (Cleveland: Arthur M. Clark, 1912), 301, 305; Edward J. Gay to L. Janin, Jan. 17, 1861, Edward J. Gay and Family Papers, Louisiana and Lower Mississippi Valley Collections, LSU Libraries.

64. The official returns were never published, but the immediate secessionists undoubtedly won a slight majority: see Charles B. Dew, "The Long Lost Returns: The Candidates and Their Totals in Louisiana's Secession Election," *Louisiana History* 10 (Winter 1969): 358–369; Pugh is quoted in Christopher G. Peña, *Scarred by War: Civil War in Southeast Louisiana* (Bloomington, Ind.: Authorhouse, 2004), 34.

65. *Official Journal of the Proceedings of the Convention of the State of Louisiana* (New Orleans: J. O. Nixon, 1861), 10–12, 15–16; Shugg, *Origins of Class Struggle*, 166–167; Wooster, *Secession Conventions of the South*, 119–120; *New Orleans Daily Crescent*, Jan. 28, 1861.

66. Kenneth Michael Stickney, "Silenced: The Abrupt Demise of Catahoula Parish's Unionist Newspaper" (Master's Thesis, University of Louisiana at Monroe, 2007); Roger W. Shugg, "A Suppressed Co-operationist Protest against Secession," *Louisiana Historical Quarterly* 19 (No. 1, 1936): 199–203; for the protest, see *New Orleans Daily Crescent*, Jan. 31, 1861.

67. Sam Houston to Sam Houston Jr., Nov. 6, 1860, Amelia W. Williams and Eugene C. Barker, eds., *The Writings of Sam Houston, 1813–1863*, 8 vols. (Austin: University of Texas Press, 1938–1943), Vol. 8: 184–185. Llerena Friend, *Sam Houston: The Great Designer* (Austin: University of Texas Press, 1954), provides a solid biography.

68. Walter L. Buenger, *Secession and the Union in Texas* (Austin: University of Texas Press, 1984), 17, 19–20, 37–40, 94–95; letter from J. W. Ferris, *Dallas Herald*, Dec. 12, 1860.

69. Cited in *New Orleans Bee*, Jan. 7, 1861. On relations between the army and frontier Texans, see Buenger, *Secession and the Union*, 106–112, and for the persistence and destructiveness of the raids, Brian DeLay, *War of a Thousand Deserts: Indian Raids and the U.S.-Mexican War* (New Haven, Conn.: Yale University Press, 2008).

70. Andrew F. Muir, ed., "William P. Johnson, Southern Proletarian and Unionist," *Tennessee Historical Quarterly* 15 (Dec. 1956): 330–338; quotes are from William P. Johnson to Andrew Johnson, Dec. 2, 1860, *Papers of Andrew Johnson*, Vol. 3, 682–683.

71. Alwyn Barr, "The Making of a Secessionist: The Antebellum Career of Roger Q. Mills," *Southwestern Historical Quarterly* 79 (Oct. 1975): 129–144, quote on 142.

72. Petition from Houston County, Nov. 24, 1860, Records of the Governor, Archives Division, Texas State Library; Anna Irene Sandbo, "The First Session of the Secession Convention of Texas," *Southwestern Historical Quarterly* 18 (Oct. 1914): 179–180; Guy M. Bryan to Miles Bonham and William P. Mills, Dec. 18, 1860, William Porcher Mills Papers, SHC.

73. R. T. Wheeler to O. M. Roberts, Jan. 6, 1861; N. B. Ellis to O. M. Roberts, Jan. 4, 1861, O. M. Roberts Letterbook, Center for American History, University of Texas at Austin; Buenger, *Secession and the Union*, 174–175.

74. Diary of William Pitt Ballinger, Dec. 30, 1860, Center for American History, University of Texas at Austin; John A. Moretta, *William Pitt Ballinger, Texas Lawyer, Southern Statesman, 1825–1888* (Austin: Texas State Historical Association, 2000), 129–132.

75. Wooster, *Secession and the Union*, 125–129; Ernest W. Winkler, ed., *Journal of the Secession Convention of Texas, 1861* (Austin, Tx.: Austin Printing Company, 1912), 42–44; Buenger, *Secession and the Union*, 174. For Houston's argument for an independent Texas, see Sam Houston to J. M. Calhoun, Jan. 7, 1861, *Journal of the House of Representatives of the State of Texas, Extra Session of the Eighth Legislature, 1861* (Austin, Tx.: John Marshall, State Printer, 1861), 37–40.

76. Baker, "Class and Party," 254–256, 282.

Chapter 8

1. See William G. Shade, *Democratizing the Old Dominion: Virginia and the Second Party System, 1824–1861* (Charlottesville: University Press of Virginia, 1996), 30–49, and William A. Link, *Roots of Secession: Slavery and Politics in Antebellum Virginia* (Chapel Hill: University of North Carolina Press, 2003), 29–36.

2. Crofts, *Reluctant Confederate*, 45–49, 54–60, and "Late Antebellum Virginia Reconsidered," *Virginia Magazine of History and Biography* 107 (Summer 1999): 254–286. For a wonderful biography on a central figure in the state's economic and social cross currents, see Craig M. Simpson, *A Good Southerner: The Life of Henry A. Wise of Virginia* (Chapel Hill: University of North Carolina Press, 1985).

3. Link, *Roots of Secession*, 38–43.

4. William Kaufman Scarborough, ed., *The Diary of Edmund Ruffin*, 3 vols. (Baton Rouge: Louisiana State University Press, 1972–1989), Vol. 1, Oct. 31, 1860, p. 481. For attempts to understand this driven secessionist, see Avery Craven, *Edmund Ruffin, Southerner: A Study in Secession* (New York: D. Appleton, 1932), Betty L. Mitchell, *Edmund Ruffin: A Biography* (Bloomington.: Indiana University Press, 1981), and David F. Allmendinger, *Ruffin: Family and Reform in the Old South* (New York: Oxford University Press, 1990).

5. Philip St. George Cocke to John B. Cocke, Dec. 6, 1860, Cocke Family Papers, Series E, Part 4, Reel 53, *Records*.

6. R. M. T. Hunter to James R. Micou, Thomas Croxton, and others, Dec. 10, 1860, Charles Henry Ambler, ed., *Correspondence of Robert M. T. Hunter, 1826–1876* (Washington, D.C.: Government Printing Office, 1918), 347.

7. *Richmond Dispatch*, Jan. 31, 1861; Charles Bruce to Sarah Bruce, Dec. 9, 1860, Bruce Family Papers, Series M, Part 5, Reel 11, *Records*.

8. Peter S. Carmichael, *The Last Generation: Young Virginians in Peace, War, and Reunion* (Chapel Hill: University of North Carolina Press, 2005), 19–35; Charles Blackford to Mrs. Mary B. Blackford, Christmas Eve, 1859, Blackford Family Correspondence, Vol. 5, Typed Transcription, SHC; Freehling, *Secessionists Triumphant*, 509–510; quote from speech of Holcombe in George H. Reese, ed., *Proceedings of the Virginia State Convention of 1861*, 4 vols. (Richmond: Virginia State Library, 1965), Vol. 2: 79

9. William I. Anson to Edmund Ruffin, Nov. 28, 1860, Edmund Ruffin Papers, Series M, Part 4, Reel 48, F. W. Pendleton to R. W. Carter, Feb. 21, 1861, Carter Papers, Series L, Part 1, Reel 7, *Records*.

10. John H. Cocke to Cary Charles Cocke, Oct. 11, 1860, Jan. 14, 1861, Cocke Family Papers, Series E, Part 4, Reel 53, *Records*.

11. Patrick Sowle, "The Trials of a Virginia Unionist: William Cabell Rives and the Secession Crisis, 1860–1861," *Virginia Magazine of History and Biography* 80 (Jan. 1972): 3–20; Link, *Roots of Secession*, 221; *Alexandria Constitutional*, Nov. 17, 1860, for Scott's speech at Alexandria.

12. Letter from Botts, Nov. 27, 1860, *New York Times*, Dec. 11, 1860. Botts's forceful personality comes across in his *The Great Rebellion, Its Secret History, Rise, Progress, and Disastrous Failure* (New York: Harper & Brothers, 1866).

13. Letter from "Alex H. H. Stuart," *Staunton Spectator*, Jan. 22, 1861. For a typical linkage of saving the Union with additional guarantees for the South, see Richard Eppes Diary, Feb. 14, 1860, Eppes Family Munements, Series M, Part 3, Reel 13, and Harrison Robertson to Robert Douhat, Dec. 15, 1860, Douhat Family Papers, Series M, Part 3, Reel 8, *Records*.

14. *Congressional Globe*, 36th Congress, 2nd Session, Appendix, 103–106.

15. Howard C. Perkins, *Northern Editorials on Secession* 2, vols. (New York: D. Appleton-Century, 1942), Vol. 2: 900–903.

16. Shanks, *The Secession Movement in Virginia*, 150–151.

17. John Owen Allen, "Tobacco, Slaves, and Secession: Southside Virginia on the Brink of the Great Rebellion" (PhD Thesis, Catholic University of America, 2003), 271–273; *Richmond Enquirer*, Feb. 8, 1861.

18. Crofts, *Reluctant Confederates*, 140–142, 164–194, provides the closest analysis of the returns; Junius Hillyer to Howell Cobb, Jan. 30, Feb. 11, 1861, Phillips, *Correspondence of Toombs,*

Cobb, and Stephens, 535, 542; Robert T. Hubbard Jr. to Robert T. Hubbard, Feb. 7, 1861, Hubbard Family Papers, Series E, Part 1, Reel 29, *Records*.

19. William M. Blackford to Launcelot Blackford, Feb. 17, 1861, Blackford Family Correspondence, Series D, Part 1, Reel 3; John Critcher to Robert W. Carter, Carter Papers, Series L, Part 1, Reel 7, Martin Paul Schipper, Kenneth M. Stampp, and College of William and Mary, Swem Library, *Records of Ante-bellum Southern Plantations from the Revolution through the Civil War* (Microform) (Bethesda, Md.: University Publications of America, 1994), hereafter cited as *Records*, Series L.

20. Crofts, *Reluctant Confederates*, 45, 62–63.

21. Jonathan M. Atkins, *Parties, Politics, and the Sectional Conflict in Tennessee, 1832–1861* (Knoxville: University of Tennessee Press, 1987), 227–228; *Athens Post*, Nov. 23, 1860; *Clarksville Chronicle*, Nov. 16, 1860.

22. Sam Davis Elliott, *Isham G. Harris of Tennessee: Confederate Governor and United States Senator* (Baton Rouge: Louisiana State University Press, 2010).

23. Robert H. White and Stephen V. Ash, eds., *Messages of the Governors of Tennessee*, 11 vols. (Nashville: Tennessee Historical Commission, 1952–[1990]), Vol. 5 (1959): 255; Crofts, *Reluctant Confederates*, 144.

24. Hans L. Trefousse, *Andrew Johnson: A Biography* (New York: Norton, 1989), provides the fullest political account; Annette Gordon-Reid, *Andrew Johnson* (New York: Times Books, 2011), focuses on the psychological factors that drove Johnson; E. Merton Coulter, *William G. Brownlow: Fighting Parson of the Southern Highlands* (Chapel Hill: University of North Carolina Press, 1937).

25. Andrew Johnson to John Trimble, Jan. 13, 1861, *Papers of Andrew Johnson*, Vol. 4: 164; *Brownlow's Knoxville Whig*, Feb. 2, 9, 1861.

26. *Congressional Globe*, 36th Congress, 2nd Session, Appendix, 11–12, 106, 108.

27. *Clarksville Chronicle*, Nov. 2, 9, 1860; Jan. 4, 1861.

28. Diary of John H. Bills, Jan. 2, March 23, Feb. 6, Jan. 8, 1861, John Houston Bills Papers, SHC.

29. *Brownlow's Knoxville Whig*, Feb. 2, 1861.

30. Rogene Scott to her mother, Dec. 16, 25, 1860, Scott Family Papers, SHC; *Nashville Union and American*, Jan. 13, 1861.

31. Derek William Frisby, "'Homemade Yankees': West Tennessee Unionism in the Civil War Era" (PhD Thesis, University of Alabama, 2004), 54, 56; John F. Henry to Marion Henry, Dec. 13, 1860, Gustavus A. Henry Papers, Subseries 3, Folder 1, SHC; *Memphis Daily Appeal*, Nov. 27 (letter from "Memphis Mechanic"), 10, 28, Dec. 5, 1860.

32. Thomas M. Brennan to Andrew Johnson, Jan. 7, 1861, *Papers of Johnson*, Vol. 4: 128–129.

33. William Crutchfield to Andrew Johnson, Jan. 7, 1861, *Papers of Johnson*, Vol. 4: 128–129; *Brownlow's Knoxville Whig*, Feb. 2, 1861; Oliver M. Temple, *East Tennessee and the Civil War* (Cincinnati, Ohio: Robert Clarke, 1899), 133–135.

34. *Nashville Union and American*, Feb. 5, 1861; Crofts, *Reluctant Confederates*, 149, 166–173; for the results of the election broken down by sections, see Atkins, *Parties, Politics, and the Sectional Conflict*, Table 11, p. 241.

35. *Nashville Union and American*, Feb. 12, 1861; *Daily Nashville Patriot*, Feb. 11, 1861.

36. Joseph C. Robert, *The Tobacco Kingdom: Plantation, Market, and Factory in Virginia and North Carolina, 1800–1860* (Durham, N.C.: Duke University Press, 1939); Robert B. Outland, "Slavery, Work, and the Geography of the North Carolina Naval Stores Industry, 1835–1860," *Journal of Southern History* 62 (Feb. 1996): 27–56.

37. Marc W. Kruman, *Parties and Politics in North Carolina, 1836–1865* (Baton Rouge: Louisiana State University Press, 1983), 12.

38. Kruman, *Parties and Politics*, 47–52; Crofts, *Reluctant Confederates*, 45–49, 60–62.

39. Crofts, *Reluctant Confederates*, 81–87; Speech of John W. Ellis, March 7, 1860; Ellis to William H. Gist, Oct. 19, 1860, Noble J. Tolbert, *The Papers of John Willis Ellis*, 2 vols. (Raleigh, N.C.: State Department of Archives and History, 1969), Vol. 2: 387, 469.

40. Message to the General Assembly of North Carolina, Nov. 20, 1860, Personal Journal of John W. Ellis, Jan. 1, 1861, Tolbert, *Papers of Ellis*, Vol. 2: 508–509, 514–515, 477; Samuel A. Ashe, Stephen B. Weeks and Charles L. Van Noppen, eds., *Biographical History of North Carolina*, 8 vols. (Greensboro, N.C.: C. L. Van Noppen 1905–17), Vol. 8: 30–36.

41. Robert N. Gourdin to Ellis, Dec. 12, 1860; Ellis to Gourdin, Dec. 17, 1860; Ellis to Joseph E. Brown, Jan. 14, 1861, Tolbert, *Papers of Ellis*, Vol. 2: 529, 534, 558.

42. Crofts, *Reluctant Confederates*, 45–46; J. Carlyle Sitterson, *The Secession Movement in North Carolina* (Chapel Hill, N.C.: University Press, 1939), 209–210.

43. Henry W. Miller to William A. Graham, Dec. 29, 1860, Max R. Williams and J. G. de Roulhac Hamilton, eds., *The Papers of William Alexander Graham*, 8 vols. (Raleigh, N.C.: State Department of Archives and History, 1957–1992), Vol. 5: 204; William S. Pettigrew to James C. Johnston, Dec. 27, 1860, Hayes Collection, James Cathcart Johnston Papers, Box 27, Folder 652, SHC; Zebulon Vance to William Dickson, Dec. 11, 1860, Frontis W. Johnston, ed., *The Papers of Zebulon Baird Vance*, 2 vols. (Raleigh, N.C.: State Department of Archives and History, 1963–), Vol. 1: 72; Vance's letter, *Raleigh Register*, Jan. 16, 1861.

44. Horace W. Raper, *William W. Holden: North Carolina's Political Enigma* (Chapel Hill: University of North Carolina Press, 1985) and William C. Harris, *William Woods Holden: Firebrand of North Carolina Politics* (Baton Rouge: Louisiana State University Press, 1987) are solid biographies.

45. Vance to C. C. Jones, Feb. 11, 1861, Zebulon Baird Vance Papers, SHC.

46. On the Quaker Belt, see Hiram H. Hilty, *Toward Freedom for All: North Carolina Quakers and Slavery* (Richmond, Ind.: Friends United Press, 1984); "Mr. Worth's Address to the People of Randolph and Alamance," J. G. de Roulhac Hamilton, ed., *The Correspondence of Jonathan Worth*, 2 vols. (Raleigh: Edwards & Broughton, 1909), Vol. 1: 130, 132.

47. *Raleigh Semi-Weekly Standard*, March 9, 1861; Kenneth Rayner to Thomas Ruffin, Dec. 25, 1860, J. G. de Roulhac Hamilton, ed., *The Papers of Thomas Ruffin*, 4 vols. (Raleigh: Edwards & Broughton, 1918–20), Vol. 3: 109; Charles Pettigrew to Caroline Pettigrew, Dec. 4, 1860, Caroline Pettigrew to J. Johnston Pettigrew, Feb. 23, 1861, William S. Pettigrew to James C. Johnston, March 12, 1861, Pettigrew Family Papers, Series J, Part 2, Reel 15, *Records*. For an account of the Pettigrew-Latham encounter and what it foreshadowed for the region in the upcoming war, see Wayne K. Durrill, *War of Another Kind: A Southern Community in the Great Rebellion* (New York: Oxford University Press, 1990), 23–32.

48. *Salisbury Banner*, Feb. 19, 1861; William K. Ruffin to Paul C. Cameron, [Dec. 1860?], Cameron Family Papers, Series J, Part 1, Reel 37, *Records*.

49. *Raleigh Standard*, Feb. 6, 1861; John C. Inscoe, *Mountain Masters, Slavery, and the Sectional Crisis in Western North Carolina* (Knoxville: University of Tennessee Press, 1989), 243–248, has the closest analysis of the election returns in the mountains.

50. On the Unionist majority, see Crofts, *Reluctant Confederates*, 164–194; Sitterson, *Secession Movement in North Carolina*, 226, sees the Peace Conference as the key to the Unionist victory.

51. For Gilmer and the cabinet offer, see Crofts, *Reluctant Confederates*, 225–226, 245–247; *Salisbury Banner*, March 19, 1861; Schenck Diary, Vol. 3, [March 1861], 463, SHC; *Goldsboro Rough Notes*, cited in *Salisbury Banner*, March 19, 1861.

52. *New Orleans Picayune*, cited in *De Bow's Review*, 29 (Dec. 1860): 794; John M. Woods, *Rebellion and Realignment: Arkansas's Road to Secession* (Fayetteville: University of Arkansas Press, 1987), 5–31.

53. Tommy R. Thompson, ed., "Searching for the American Dream in Arkansas: Letters of a Pioneer Family," *Arkansas Historical Quarterly* 38 (Summer 1979): 167–181, quotes on 176–177.

54. Neal and Krimm, *Lion of the South*, 21–64.

55. Woods, *Rebellion and Realignment*, 110, 114–115; for Rector's speech, Little Rock *Arkansas Gazette*, Nov. 24, 1860; Michael P. Dougan, *Confederate Arkansas: The People and Policies of a Frontier State in Wartime* (University: University of Alabama Press, 1976), 17–18.

56. Little Rock *Arkansas Gazette*, Dec. 22, 1860; for the petitions, see *Journal of the Senate of Arkansas, 1861* (Little Rock, Ark.: Little Rock Printing and Publishing, 1861), Dec. 3, 7, 15, 1860, pp. 189, 216, 280.

57. Little Rock *Arkansas Gazette*, Dec. 22, 1860.

58. Dougan, *Confederate Arkansas*, 38–39; Little Rock *Arkansas Gazette*, Dec. 29, 1860.

59. Clifford Dale Whitman, ed., "Private Journal of Mary Ann Owen Simms, Part II," Jan. 13, 1961, *Arkansas Historical Quarterly* 35 (Autumn 1976): 289; J. Wayne Jones, "Seeding

Chicot: The Isaac H. Hilliard Plantation and the Arkansas Delta," *Arkansas Historical Quarterly* 59 (Summer 2000): 163.

60. Resolutions from Union County, cited in James J. Gigantino II, ed., *Slavery and Secession in Arkansas: A Documentary History* (Fayetteville: University of Arkansas Press, 2015), 88; Dougan, *Confederate Arkansas*, 38, 135, n. 14 (quote from Brown).

61. For the fears of a conspiracy in northern Arkansas, see "Let the People Be Heard!" *Fayetteville Democrat*, Dec. 15, 1860; John Smith, "To the Voters of Benton County, February 18, 1861," quoted in Woods, *Rebellion and Realignment*, 125–126; *Journal of Both Sessions of the Convention of the State of Arkansas* (Fayetteville, Ark.: Johnson & Yerkes, state printers, 1861), 63; Benton resolution cited in Gigantino, *Slavery and Secession in Arkansas*, 70.

62. Jack B. Scroggs, "Arkansas in the Secession Crisis," *Arkansas Historical Quarterly* 12 (Autumn 1953): 200–203; *Arkansas Gazette*, Feb. 19, 1861.

63. Henry C. Lay to his wife, Feb. 20, 1861, Henry C. Lay Papers, SHC; claim of Jeremiah Harris, Phillips, SCC, file # 14411; claim of Thomas Barrow, Phillips, SCC, file # 15265, testimony of the former slave Benjamin Barrow; claim of Thomas J. Atwood, Arkansas, SCC, file #11413, testimony of Charles B. Brinkley; Dorsey D. Jones, "He Taught Near Eudora, Arkansas in the Early 1860s," *Arkansas Historical Quarterly* 18 (Autumn 1959): 223–236.

64. Woods, *Rebellion and Realignment*, 130–131; Jones, "Seeding Chicot," 167.

65. Wooster, *Secession Conventions*, 58; *Arkansas Gazette*, March 2, 1861; Alfred Holt Carrigan and James N. Cypert, "Reminiscences of the Secession Convention," *Publications of the Arkansas Historical Association*, 4 vols. (Fayetteville: Arkansas Historical Association, 1906–18), Vol. 1: 306.

66. *Journal of Both Sessions of the Convention*, 10–11; Ted J. Smith, "Mastering Farm and Family: David Walker as Slaveholder," *Arkansas Historical Quarterly* 38 (Spring 1998): 61–79.

67. *Journal of Both Sessions of the Convention*, 82, 90–93; *Arkansas Gazette*, March 16, 1861.

68. The linkage of the Union with defending slavery is the main theme of a fine recent study, Michael D. Robinson, *A Union Indivisible: Secession and the Politics of Slavery in the Border South* (Chapel Hill: University of North Carolina Press, 2017).

69. Essah, *A House Divided*, 78, 83–84; Charles L. Wagandt, *The Mighty Revolution: Negro Emancipation in Maryland, 1862–1864* (Baltimore, Md.: Johns Hopkins University Press, 1964), 1–4.

70. Stephen Aaron, *How the West Was Lost: The Transformation of Kentucky from Daniel Boone to Henry Clay* (Baltimore, Md.: Johns Hopkins University Press, 1996); R. Douglas Hurt, *Agriculture and Slavery in Missouri's Little Dixie* (Columbia: University of Missouri Press, 1992).

71. Essah, *A House Divided*, 158–161; James Warner Harry, *The Maryland Constitution of 1851* (Baltimore, Md.: Johns Hopkins University Press, 1902); Harrold Tallant, *Evil Necessity: Slavery and Political Culture in Antebellum Kentucky* (Lexington: University Press of Kentucky, 2003), 158–159, 95–97; Christopher Phillips, *Missouri's Confederate: Claiborne Fox Jackson and the Creation of Southern Identity in the Border West* (Columbia: University of Missouri Press, 2000), 220–233.

72. Population figures taken from Robinson, *A Union Indivisible*, Table A-3, Appendix, 210.

73. For the often-violent friction over slavery along the border, see Stanley Harrold, *Border War: Fighting over Slavery before the Civil War* (Chapel Hill: University of North Carolina Press, 2000).

74. *Louisville Journal*, cited in *Wheeling* (Va.) *Daily Intelligencer*, April 1, 1861; S. C. Brickensten to Robert B. Davis, Jan. 16, 1861, Beale and Davis Family Papers, SHC; C. F. Mitchell to Abraham Lincoln, Jan. 27, 1861, Abraham Lincoln Papers, Library of Congress.

75. *Monticello Family and Friend*, March 16, 1861; *Tallahassee Floridian and Journal*, Dec. 15, 1860; *The* (Lexington) *Kentucky Statesman*, Dec. 25, 1860, Dwight L. Dumond, ed., *Southern Editorials on Secession* (New York: Century, 1931), 370–371.

76. *Discourse of Dr. Breckinridge, Delivered on the Day of National Humiliation, January 4, 1861, at Lexington, Ky.* (Baltimore, Md.: John W. Woods, printer, 1861?), 2, 13–15; Joseph Pendleton Kennedy, *The Border States: Their Power and Duty in the Present Disordered Condition of the Country* (Philadelphia: J. B. Lippincott, 1861).

77. Kennedy, *The Border States*, 29–30.

78. Robert G. Gunderson, *Old Gentlemen's Convention: The Washington Peace Conference of 1861* (Madison: University of Wisconsin Press, 1961).

79. R. L. Dixon to Harry Dixon, March 2, 1861, Henry St. John Dixon Papers, SHC.

80. Jonathan Worth to his brother, March 16, 1861, Hamilton, *Correspondence of Jonathan Worth*, Vol. 1: 133–134; *Richmond Daily Enquirer*, March 2, 1861; *Louisville Daily Courier*, March 1, 1861.

81. Essah, *A House Divided*, 161; Robinson, *A Union Indivisible*, 119–123; on Jackson Purchase, see James E. Copeland, "Where Were the Kentucky Unionists and Secessionists?" *Register of the Kentucky Historical Society* 71 (Oct. 1973): 350.

82. Phillips, *Missouri's Confederate* is superb as a biography and a political history.

83. Phillips, *Missouri's Confederate*, 236–240.

84. Nancy D. Baird, ed., *Josie Underwood's Civil War Diary* (Lexington: University Press of Kentucky, 2009), Feb. 5, 1861, p. 58.

Chapter 9

1. For a description of Montgomery and its setting, see Thomas C. De Leon, *Four Years in Confederate Capitals: An Inside View of Life in the Confederacy from Birth to Death* (Mobile: Gossip Printing Co., 1890), 23–24; *New York Times*, Feb. 9, 1861.

2. *Charleston Mercury*, Dec. 21, 1860; *Journal of the Convention of the People of South Carolina*, 92–93; William Henry Trescot to Howell Cobb, Jan. 14, 1861, *Correspondence of Toombs*, 531.

3. *Charleston Mercury*, Feb. 5, 8, 1861.

4. *Charleston Mercury*, Feb. 6, 1861; Cauthen, *South Carolina Goes to War*, 85.

5. For a profile of the delegates, see William C. Davis, *"A Government of Our Own:" The Making of the Confederacy* (New York: Free Press, 1994), 74–75.

6. *Journal of the Congress of the Confederate States of America, 1861–1865*, 7 vols. (Washington, D.C.: Government Printing Office, 1904–09), Vol. 1: 16; *An Address to the Citizens of Alabama, on the Constitution and Laws of the Confederate States of America by the Hon. Robert H. Smith at Temperance Hall, on the 30th of March, 1861* (Mobile: Mobile Daily Register Print, 1861), 5.

7. For the text of the provisional constitution, see James D. Richardson, *A Compilation of the Messages and Papers of the Confederacy, including the Diplomatic Correspondence, 1861–1865*, 2 vols. (Nashville: United States Printing Co., 1906), Vol. 1: 3–14.

8. *Jacksonville* (Ala.) *Republican*, March 7, 1861, citing a reporter's pen-sketch; on Toombs, see Davis, *The Making of the Confederacy*, 52–53, 91–93; Alexander Stephens to Linton Stephens, Feb. 23, 1861, A. H. Stephens Papers, microfilm, SHC.

9. Reporter's description in *Richmond Dispatch*, Feb. 13, 1861; Sarah Knox Taylor to Margaret Mackall Smith Taylor, June 17, 1835, Haskell M. Monroe Jr. and James T. McIntosh, eds., *The Papers of Jefferson Davis*, Vol. 1, *1808–1840* (Baton Rouge: Louisiana State University Press), 406–407; for the persistence of the account of a runaway marriage, see Laura Carter Holloway, *The Ladies of the White House* (Philadelphia: Bradley & Company, 1883), 440–441.

10. William C. Davis, *Jefferson Davis: The Man and His Hour* (Baton Rouge: Louisiana State University Press, 1991), is thorough and reliable, but William C. Cooper Jr., *Jefferson Davis, American* (New York: Alfred A. Knopf, 2000) probes more deeply into Davis's private life.

11. Davis, *The Making of the Confederacy*, 116–117; *Augusta Chronicle*, n.d.; Moore, *The Rebellion Record*, Vol. 1, Doc. 34, p. 30.

12. Smith, *An Address to the Citizens*, 19; Richardson, *Messages and Papers*, Vol. 1: 43; for Hill's speech, see *New York Times*, April 11, 1861.

13. T. R. R. Cobb to Howell Cobb, Aug. 24, 1859, R. P. Brooks, "Howell Cobb Papers," *Georgia Historical Quarterly* 6 (Sept. 1922): 243; Smith, *Address to the Citizens*, 19; *Journal of the Congress*, Vol. 1: 74, 78–79.

14. *Journal of the Congress*, Vol. 1: 84, 95, 98; Thomas Cobb to Marion Cobb, Feb. 28, 1861, Augustus Longstreet Hull, ed., "The Correspondence of Thomas Reade Root Cobb, 1860–1862," *Publications of the Southern Historical Association* (Washington, D.C.: Southern Historical Association), 11 (May 1907): 234.

15. Confederate Constitution, Article 1, Section 8 (3), Richardson, *Messages and Papers*, 41; *New York Times*, April 11, 1861.

16. *New York Times*, April 11, 1861; Confederate Constitution, Article 2, Section 2 (3), Richardson, *Messages and Papers*, Vol. 1: 148–149; for the best study of the goal of uprooting political parties, see George C. Rable, *The Confederate Republic: A Revolution against Politics* (Chapel Hill: University of North Carolina Press, 1994).

17. For a strongly argued nationalist reading of the Confederate Constitution, see Aaron R. Hall, "Reframing the Fathers' Constitution: The Centralist State and Centrality of Slavery in the Confederate Constitutional Order," *Journal of Southern History* 83 (May 2017): 255–296.

18. *Journal of the Congress*, 1: 883–886; Smith, *Address to the Citizens*, 19–20; Power, *Proceedings of the Mississippi State Convention*, 97; Alexander Stephens to Linton Stephens, March 8, 1861, Alexander H. Stephens Papers, microfilm, SHC.

19. Smith, *History and Debates of the Convention . . . of Alabama*, 326–327, 334, 342, 362–364.

20. *Charleston Mercury*, Feb. 20, 1861.

21. L. W. Spratt, *The Philosophy of Secession: A Southern View, Presented in a Letter addressed to the Hon. Mr. Perkins of Louisiana, in criticism on the Provisional Constitution adopted by the Southern Congress at Montgomery, Alabama* (Charleston: s.n.), 1–4.

22. *Montgomery Post*, Feb. 16, 1861; *Journal of the Convention . . . of South Carolina*, 236; Smith, *Address to the Citizens*, 18.

23. Alexander Stephens to Linton Stephens, March 3, 1861, Alexander H. Stephens Papers, microfilm, SHC; Thomas Cobb to Marion Cobb, Feb. 20, 1861, Hull, "Correspondence of Thomas Cobb," 234; Cauthen, *South Carolina Goes to War*, 85–87.

24. "Mercator," *Charleston Mercury*, Feb. 5, 1861; Gazaway B. Lamar to Howell Cobb, Feb. 22, March 9, 25, 1861, Phillips, "Correspondence of Toombs," 545, 549, 552.

25. Lawrence Keitt to James H. Hammond, Feb. 13, 1861, Elmer Don Herd Jr., ed., "Lawrence M. Keitt's Letters from the Provisional Congress of the Confederacy, 1861," *South Carolina Historical Magazine* 61 (Jan. 1960): 20; Gazaway B. Lamar to Howell Cobb, Feb. 22, 1861, Phillips, "Correspondence of Toombs," 546.

26. For pro-diversification views, see *Athens Southern Watchman*, Feb. 13, 1861; *Augusta Weekly Chronicle and Sentinel*, Jan. 23, Feb. 13, 27, March 20, 1861; *Memphis Daily Appeal*, March 7, 1861, citing the *New Orleans Delta* on the tariff debate.

27. *Charleston Mercury*, Feb. 3, 6, 1861; Gazaway B. Lamar to Howell Cobb, March 25, 1861, Phillips, *Correspondence of Toombs*, 542; *Augusta Weekly Chronicle and Sentinel*, March 20, 1861.

28. *De Bow's Review* 30 (Feb. 1861): 163; William G. Simms to William P. Miles, Nov. 12, 1860, William P. Miles Papers, SHC; *De Bow's Review* 30 (Feb. 1861): 196; *Augusta Weekly Chronicle and Sentinel*, Jan. 21, Feb. 27, 1861.

29. *Natchez Courier*, cited in *Augusta Weekly Chronicle and Sentinel*, Feb. 27, 1861; *Journal of the Congress*, Vol. 1: 861; preamble, Article 1, Section 8 (4), Richardson, *Messages*, Vol. 1: 37, 42; Stephanie McCurry, *Confederate Reckoning: Power and Politics in the Civil War South* (Cambridge, Mass.: Harvard University Press, 2010), 79–80.

30. First quote from speech at Cartersville, Georgia, Crist, *Papers of Davis*, Vol. 7: 42; second on reconstruction, *Charleston Daily Courier*, Feb. 20, 1861.

31. Inaugural Address, Crist, *Papers of Davis*, Vol. 7: 48, 47.

32. *Augusta Constitutionalist*, March 30, 1861; *Athens* (Tenn.) *Post*, April 5, 1861, for the Augusta speech.

33. James P. Jones and William Warren Rogers, eds., "Montgomery as the Confederate Capital: View of a New Nation," *Alabama Historical Quarterly* 26 (Spring 1964): 35–36. "Sigma," a newspaper correspondent, wrote the account comprising the article.

34. Pickens to Howell Cobb, Feb. 12, 1861, John Tyler to Governor Pickens, Feb. 18, 1861, *O.R.*, Series 1, Vol. 1, 257.

35. Jefferson Davis to Francis Pickens, Feb. 20, 22, 1861, Crist, *Papers of Davis*, Vol. 7: 55, 57–58; Thomas R. R. Cobb to Marion Cobb, Feb. 25, 1861, Hull, "Correspondence of Thomas Cobb," 241.

36. Richardson, *Messages*, Vol. 2: 1–8 (p. 8 for veiled reference to withholding cotton).

37. *London Times*, Feb. 19, 1861, cited in *Charleston Daily Courier*, March 12, 1861; De Leon, *Four Years*, 34.

38. For the sharpest and most detailed critique of Confederate finances, see Douglas B. Ball, *Financial Failure and Confederate Defeat* (Urbana: University of Illinois Press, 1991).

39. John H. Reagan, *Memoirs with Special Reference to Secession and the Civil War* (New York: Neale Publishing, 1906), 117.

40. Emory M. Thomas, *The Confederate Nation: 1861–1865* (New York: Harper and Row, 1979), 74–75.

41. On sending commissioners to Europe, see Cauthen, *South Carolina Goes to War*, 83–84, and Paul D. Escott, "Georgia," in Wilfred Bick Yearns, ed., *The Confederate Governors* (Athens: University of Georgia Press, 1985), 72.

42. Malcolm C. McMillan, *The Disintegration of a Confederate State: Three Governors and Alabama's Wartime Home Front, 1861–1865* (Macon, Ga.: Mercer University Press, 1986), 16; Memorandum, dated 1861, J. R. Powell Folder, 1860, Moore Correspondence, ADAH; William T. Martin to Governor Pettus, Jan. 8, 1861, Governors' Records, MDAH.

43. For Walker's circular, see *O.R.*, Series 4, Vol. 1, 119; A. B. Moore to Walker, March 4, 1861, *O.R.*, Series 4, Vol. 1, 121; report of Georgia convention, March 15, 1861, *O.R.*, Series 4, Vol. 1, 269–270.

44. See *O.R.*, Series 4, Vol. 1, 134–135, for Walker's request; the wrangling between Brown and Walker can be followed in Chandler, *Confederate Records of Georgia*, 3: 20–39.

45. A. B. Moore to Walker, March 19, 1861, *O.R.*, Series 4, Vol. 1, 452; Pickens to Davis, March 17, 1861, Crist, *Papers of Davis*, Vol. 7: 70–71.

46. Chandler, *Confederate Records of Georgia*, Vol. 3: 3–39; Alexander H. Stephens to Lewis P. Walker, April 18, 1861, *O.R.*, Series 4, Vol. 1, 224–225; A. B. Moore to Walker, March 4, 1861, *O.R.*, Series 4, Vol. 1, 120–122; Pickens to Walker, March 23, 1861, *O.R.*, Series 4, Vol. 1, 185–186; Walker to Pickens, March 26, 1861, *O.R.*, Series 4, Vol. 1, 189–190.

47. Pickens to Walker, March 23, 1861, *O.R.*, Series 4, Vol. 1, 186; Brown, communication to Georgia convention, March 15, 1861, *O.R.*, Series 4, Vol. 1, 168; Robert W. Dubay, "Mississippi," in Wilfred Bick Yearns, ed., *The Confederate Governors* (Athens: University of Georgia Press, 1985), 114.

48. Brown, communication to Georgia convention, March 15, 1861, *O.R.*, Series 4, Vol. 1, 167–168; Paul Jones Semmes to Joseph E. Brown, Jan. 30, 1861, Brown Papers, Duke University.

49. Henry W. Ravenal Journal, Feb. 28, 1861, SHC; Susan Sellers Darden Diary, March 19, 1861, Duncan Family Collection, Series N, Reel 8, *Records; Monticello Family and Friend*, Feb. 9, 1961; *Macon Daily Telegraph*, March 6, 1861.

50. On Toombs's assurances, see T. Conn Bryan, *Confederate Georgia* (Athens: University of Georgia Press, 1953), 16, and for Walker, William C. Harris, *Leroy Pope Walker, Confederate Secretary of War* (Tuscaloosa: University of Alabama Press,1962), 26–27; Holden's *Raleigh Weekly Standard*, Feb. 27, 1861, was among those warning of "terrorism."

51. *Albany* (Ga.) *Patriot*, March 7, 1861; J. Quitman Moore, "The Belligerents," *De Bow's Review* 31 (July 1861): 71. Along the same lines, see Moore, "Feudalism in America," *De Bow's Review* 29 (June 1860): 615–624, and "The Conflict of Northern and Southern Races," *De Bow's Review* 31 (Oct.–Nov. 1861): 391–395; Robert B. Bonner, "Roundheaded Cavaliers? The Context and Limits of a Confederate Racial Project," *Civil War History* 48 (March 2002): 34–59, explains the rise and permutation of the fanciful Norman/Saxon theme.

52. Moore, "The Belligerents," 75; Ball, *Financial Failure*, 12–13.

53. William F. Hutson, "The History of the Girondists, or Personal Memoirs of the Patriots of the French Revolution," *Southern Presbyterian Review* 2 (1848): 389–391; George W. Bagby, "The Union: Its Benefits and Dangers," *Southern Literary Messenger* 32 (Jan. 1861): 1–3.

54. William Henry Holcombe, *Suggestions as to the Spiritual Philosophy of African Slavery* (New York: Mason Brothers, 1861), 1–3.

55. James W. C. Pennington, *A Narrative of Events of the Life of J .H. Banks, an Escaped Slave, from the Cotton State, Alabama, in America* (Liverpool, England: M. Rourke, Printer, 1861), 33; William S. Pettigrew to Ebenezer Pettigrew, Sept. 5, 1838, Sarah McCulloh Lemmon, ed., *The Pettigrew Papers*, 2 vols. (Raleigh, N.C.: State Department of Archives and History, 1971–[1988]), Vol. 2: 385; *Newberry Rising Sun*, Nov. 14, 1860.

56. For the black flight, see *Baltimore Daily Exchange*, Nov. 16, 1860, and *Richmond Dispatch*, Nov. 23, 1860, Jan. 31, Feb. 7, 1861; for the mayor's order, *Richmond Dispatch*, Nov. 24, 1860, and the cases of Logan and Albert, Oct. 27, 1860, and March 7, 1861.

57. Mrs. Burton [Constance Cary Harrison], "A Virginia Girl in the First Year of the War," *Century Illustrated Monthly Magazine* 30 (May 1885 to October 1885): 606.

58. *Athens Southern Banner*, April 10, 1861; Harvey Tolliver Cook, ed., *The Life Work of James Clement Furman* (Greenville, S.C.: Private Printing, 1926), 199–201.

59. *Keowee Courier*, Jan. 26, 1861.

60. Edwin T. Winkler, "*Duties of the Christian Soldier: A Sermon, Delivered in the First Baptist Church of Charleston, S.C. . . . before the Moultrie Guards* (Charleston: A. J. Burke, 1861), 6–7.

61. Mrs. Mary Nisbet to Mrs. Mary C. Jones, Jan. 17, 1861; Mrs. Mary Jones to Ruth B. Jones, Jan. 22, 1861, Myers, *Children of Pride*, 642, 644.

62. (Nashville) *Tennessee Baptist*, Feb. 9, 1861; Ebenezer W. Warren, "Scriptural Vindication of Slavery," *Macon Weekly Georgia Telegraph*, Feb. 7, 1861.

63. Thornwell, *A Fast-Day Sermon*, 23, 35, 33.

64. Simeon Colton Diary, Apr. 20, 1861, SHC; [Frederick A. Porcher], "The Prospects and Policy of the South," *Southern Quarterly Review* 26 (Oct. 1854): 454; James L. Petigru to William Carson, March 2, 1861, Carson, *Life, Letters, and Speeches of Petigru*, 372, 371.

65. Petigru to William Carson, March 2, 1861, Carson, *Life, Letters, and Speeches of Petigru*, 370; Sallie Douglas McDowell and Susan Witherspoon McDowell Notebooks, SHC; Susan Cornwall Diary, Feb. 12, 1861, SHC; *Dallas Herald*, Dec. 26, 1860.

Chapter 10

1. *Daily Richmond Examiner*, Feb. 28, March 4, 1861; George Miller to Celestine McCann, Feb. 24, 1861, George Knox Miller Papers, SHC; M. D. . Taylor, Jan. 12, 1861, *Journal of the House of Representatives of the State of Texas, Extra Session of the Legislature, 1861* (Austin, 1861), 5.

2. For his anger, see Remarks Concerning Concessions to Secession [c. Jan. 19–21, 1861], Basler, *Works of Lincoln*, 4: 176.

3. *Douglass' Monthly*, April 1861, 434; *New Orleans Bee*, March 6, 1861; *Brownlow's Knoxville Whig*, March 22, 1861.

4. *Douglass' Monthly*, April, 1861, 433; Charles C. Jones Jr. to Rev. C. C. Jones, March 5, 1861, Myers, *Children of Pride*, 655.

5. Joseph Holt and Winfield Scott to Lincoln, March 5, 1861, Abraham Lincoln Papers, Library of Congress; for Anderson's letter, see David C. Mearns, ed., *The Lincoln Papers: The Story of the Collection, with Selections to July 4, 1861*, 2 vols. (New York: Doubleday, 1948), Vol. 2: 450–451.

6. Message to Congress in Special Session, July 4, 1861, Basler, *Works of Lincoln*, Vol. 4: 424; Potter, *The Impending Crisis*, 571–572.

7. *New Orleans Bee*, March 9, 1861.

8. Henry Gourdin to Langdon Cheves, Jan. 12, 1861, Larz Anderson to Robert Gourdin, Feb. 1, Robert Gourdin to Langdon Cheves, Feb. 3, Robert Gourdin to Robert Anderson, Feb. 9, 1861, Racine, *Gentlemen Merchants*, 426–427, 435, 437, 441.

9. "Ariel," *Daily Richmond Examiner*, March 19, 1861; *New Orleans Daily Picayune*, March 27, 1861.

10. Frederick L. Roberts to William H. Seward, March 18, 1861, quoted in Doris Kearns Goodwin, *Team of Rivals: The Political Genius of Abraham Lincoln* (New York: Simon & Schuster, 2005), 341; Donn Piatt, *Memories of the Men Who Saved the Union* (New York: Belford, Clarke, 1887), 139.

11. Smith, *Convention of Alabama*, 46.

12. H. G. Eachin to S. O. Wood, March 4, 1861, Samuel O. Wood Papers, Series F, Part 1, Reel 9, *Records*; Anne Gordon Finley to Carolina Gordon Hackett, April 4, 1861, Gordon and Hackett Family Papers, SHC; *Augusta Weekly Chronicle and Sentinel*, cited in *Douglass' Monthly*, March 1861, along with accounts of depressed slave prices in Florida; on complaints of high prices for provisions, see Mrs. Eliza G. Roberts to Rev. C. C. Jones, Jan. 26, 1861, Myers, *Children of Pride*, 647; "Ariel," *Daily Richmond Examiner*, March 19, 1861.

13. Robert F. W. Allston to Benjamin Allston, March 24,1861, Benjamin Allston to Robert F. W. Allston, March 31, 1861, J. H. Easterby, ed., *The South Carolina Rice Plantation as Revealed in the Papers of Robert F. W. Allston* (Chicago: University of Chicago Press, 1945), 172–173.

14. G. W. Lewis to R. W. Carter, March 16, 1861, Robert W. Carter Correspondence, Series L, Part 1, Reel 7, T. F. Nelson to William Massie, April 4, 1861, William Massie Papers, Series G, Part 2, *Records.*

15. Jeptha M. Fowlkes to Andrew Johnson March 10, 1861, William S. Speer to Johnson, March 12, 1861, Graf and Haskins, eds., *Papers of Andrew Johnson*, Vol. 4: 378–379, 385–386; Crofts, *Reluctant Confederates*, 264–267; John H. Gilmer to Lincoln, Dec. 29, 1860, Abraham Lincoln Papers, Library of Congress.

16. Washington report of Feb. 25, 1861, *New York Times*, Feb. 26, 1861.

17. Winfield Scott to William H. Seward, March 3, 1861, Moore, *Works of James Buchanan*, Vol. 11: 300–301.

18. *Journal of the Confederate Congress*, Vol. 1: 55; Ludwell H. Johnson, "Fort Sumter and Confederate Diplomacy," *Journal of Southern History*26 (Nov. 1960): 441–477, remains the best account of the commissioners and their dealings in Washington.

19. Samuel Ward, Memoranda, [March 4, 1861?], Frederic Bancroft, *The Life of William H. Seward*, 2 vols. (New York: Harper and Brothers, 1900), Vol. 2: Appendix, 544, and, for what Crawford heard of Seward's comments, 109–110.

20. Johnson, "Fort Sumter," 450–452; John Forsyth to Leroy P. Walker, March 14, 1861, *O.R.*, Series 4, Vol. 1: 165.

21. Johnson, "Fort Sumter," 455–459; for Campbell's message sent on March 15 to Montgomery, see Crawford, *Genesis of the Civil War*, 330; John A. Campbell to Jefferson Davis, April 3, 1861, Crist, *Papers of Jefferson Davis*, Vol. 7: 788–789.

22. Johnson, "Fort Sumter," 461.

23. For Fox's plan, see Robert M. Thompson and Richard Wainwright, eds., *Confidential Correspondence of Gustavus Vasa Fox*, 2 vols. (New York: Printed for the Naval History Society by De Vinne Press, 1918–1920), Vol. 1: 809. He had first presented his plan to the Buchanan administration in early February.

24. For a summary of the cabinet's thinking, see Lincoln to William H. Seward, March 15, 1861, Basler, *Collected Works*, Vol. 4: 284–285.

25. G. V. Fox to Mrs. Fox, March 19, 1861, Thompson and Wainwright, eds., *Correspondence of Fox*, Vol. 1: 9–10; Simon Cameron to Winfield Scott, March 19, Robert Anderson to Colonel L. Thomas, March 22, 1861, *O.R.*, Series 1, Vol. 1, 208–209, 211; Nicolay and Hay, *Abraham Lincoln*, Vol. 3: 389–390.

26. Nicolay and Hay, *Abraham Lincoln*, Vol.3: 391; Bancroft, *Life of Seward*, Vol. 2: 107.

27. Scott's memorandum, *O.R.*, Series 1, Vol. 1: 200–201; for Lincoln's reaction, see Erasmus Darwin Keyes, *Fifty Years' Observations of Men, Civil and Military* (New York: C. Scribner's Sons, 1884), 378; Nicolay and Hay, *Abraham Lincoln*, Vol. 3: 429–433.

28. "Some Thoughts for the President's Consideration," April 1, 1861, Nicolay and Hay, *Abraham Lincoln*, Vol. 3: 445–447; Lincoln's written response, in Basler, *Collected Works*, Vol. 4: 316–317, was likely never sent as Lincoln spoke directly to Seward.

29. *Philadelphia Public Ledger*, March 23 (for the quote), March 21, 1861; Kenneth M. Stampp, *And the War Came: The North and the Secession Crisis* (Baton Rouge: Louisiana State University Press, 1950), 224–230; for the Confederate legislation on Northern debts, see *Athens* (Tenn.) *Post*, March 22, 1861.

30. *New York Times*, March 29, 1861; *New York Herald*, March 23, 1861.

31. *Chicago Daily Tribune*, March 27, 1861; report from Washington, *New York Times*, March 22, 1861; Joseph Blanchard to Abraham Lincoln, March 28, 1861; W. H. West to Lincoln, April 3, 1861, Abraham Lincoln Papers, Library of Congress.

32. See "Papers of John A. Campbell, 1861–1865," *Southern Historical Society Papers*, (New Series, Vol. 4, 1917), 34–35, for the exchange of letters between Campbell and Seward on March 30 and April 1.

33. Cooper, *We Have the War upon Us*, 251–252.

34. John B. Baldwin, *Interview between President Lincoln and Col. John B. Baldwin, April 4, 1861* (Staunton, Va.: D. E. Strasburg, Printer,1866). John Minor Botts, a Virginia Unionist who

had an interview with Lincoln on April 5, 1861, presented a different account of what Lincoln had said to Baldwin. Crofts, *Reluctant Confederates*, 301–306, has the best analysis of the two interviews and persuasively makes the case for the veracity of Baldwin's account.

35. Brian Holden Reid, *The Origins of the American Civil War* (New York: Longman, 1996), 345; Simon Cameron to Robert Chew, April 6, 1861, Basler, *Collected Works*, Vol. 4: 323.

36. See the correspondence between the Confederate commissioners and Toombs in Bancroft, *Seward*, Vol. 2: 118–119; Johnson, "Fort Sumter," 468–469.

37. Robert Anderson to General Beauregard, April 12, 1861, *O.R.*, Series 1, Vol. 1: 14. Maury Klein, *Days of Defiance: Sumter, Secession, and the Coming of the Civil War* (New York: Alfred A. Knopf, 1957), 403–420, provides a fine account of Anderson's last days in Fort Sumter. *Charleston Daily Courier*, April 15, 1861.

38. Reese, *Proceedings of the Virginia State Convention of 1861*, Vol. 3: 480, 723; Crofts, *Reluctant Confederates*, 313.

39. "Proclamation Calling Militia and Convening Congress," April 15, 1861, Basler, *Collected Works*, Vol. 4: 332–333; Robert W. Johannsen, *Stephen A. Douglas* (New York: Oxford University Press, 1973), 868–869.

40. Soule, "The Trails of a Virginia Unionist," 18; Frederic Bancroft, *Slave Trading in the Old South* (Baltimore, Md.: J. H. Furst, 1931) 96, 116–117; Tadman, *Speculators and Slaves*, 63–64; Wheeling *Daily Intelligencer*, March 2, 1861, report from Richmond, Feb. 26, 1861.

41. Shanks, *Secession Movement in Virginia*, 186; John H. Cochran to his mother, March 19, 1861, The Valley of the Shadow: Cochran Family Letters, valley.lib.virginia.edu/papers/AO578; Ann Sarah Rubin, "Between Union and Chaos: The Political Life of John Janney," *Virginia Magazine of History and Biography* 102 (July 1994): 411; *Charles Town Spirit*, March 29, 1861, citing the *Lynchburg Republic*; *Richmond Dispatch*, April 2, 5, 1861.

42. Henry A. Wise to Andrew Hunter, April 2, 1861, *Proceedings of the Massachusetts Historical Society*, 46 (Boston: The Society, Dec. 1912): 248; Crofts, *Reluctant Confederates*, 312–313, 317; Simpson, *A Good Southerner*, 220, 230; Reese, *Proceedings*, Vol. 3: 460–462; Samuel Hefelboner to William Massie, April 6, 1861, William Massie Papers, Series G, Part 2, *Records*.

43. See Reese, *Proceedings*, Vol. 3: 659–675, for the debates on April 12 that made it clear that some form of the Crittenden Compromise for dividing the territories between free and slave labor was Virginia's price for staying in the Union; John B. Botts to Dr. Michael Burton et al., April 19, 1861, *Daily Richmond Examiner*, April 26, 1861.

44. Reese, *Proceedings*, Vol. 4: 144, for the roll call on the secession ordinance and Vol. 3: 758, for the Wise quote; Crofts, *Reluctant Confederates*, 321–322; Simpson, *A Good Southerner*, 249–250.

45. Reese, *Proceedings*, Vol. 4: 15, 427.

46. Thomas, *The Confederate Nation*, 99–100; "Speech of the Honorable Alex H. Stephens," Reese, *Proceedings*, Vol. 4: 373.

47. Alexander J. D. Thurston to Andrew Johnson, April 20, 1861, Graf and Haskins, eds., *Papers of Johnson*, Vol. 4:472; Bills Diary, April 16, 1861, John Houston Bills Papers, SHC; Charles L. Lufkin, "Secession and Coercion in Tennessee, the Spring of 1861," *Tennessee Historical Quarterly* 50 (Summer 1991): 103.

48. Lufkin, "Secession and Coercion," 104; Albert W. Schroeder Jr., "Writings of a Tennessee Unionist," Notes and Documents, *Tennessee Historical Quarterly* 9 (Sept. 1950): 251; Gideon J. Pillow to L. P. Walker, April 24, 1861, *O.R.*, Series 1, Vol. 52, Part 2, p. 69, related the incident in Paris and praised "the people" for blocking Etheridge's speech; *Brownlow's Knoxville Whig*, May 18, 1861.

49. For the call for neutrality, see *Nashville Republican Banner*, April 17, 1861, and *Daily Nashville Patriot*, April 19, 1861.

50. Atkins, *Sectional Conflict in Tennessee*, 246–247; *Brownlow's Knoxville Whig*, May 18, 1861.

51. Frisby, "Homemade Yankees," 59–60, 72–73; Charles Lufkin, "Divided Loyalties: Sectionalism in Civil War McNairy County, Tennessee," *Tennessee Historical Quarterly* 47 (Fall 1989): 176.

52. Diary of Amanda McDowell, June 9, 1861, Cashin, *Our Common Affairs*, 284; Schroeder, "Writings of a Tennessee Unionist," 248.

53. For the secession vote by region, see Atkins, *Sectional Conflict in Tennessee*, Table 12, p. 248.

54. Thomas Hindman to Jefferson Davis, April 11, 1861, Crist, *Papers of Davis*, Vol. 7: 101; N. B. Pearce, "Price's Campaign of 1861," *Publications of the Arkansas Historical Association* 4 (Fayetteville, Ark.: The Association, 1917): 332–333; *Little Rock Weekly Gazette*, April 20, 1861.

55. R. C. Gatlin to Colonel L. Thomas, April 24, 1861, *O.R.*, Series 1, Vol. 1: 650; on the troop concentration, see D. McRae to Angie McRae, April 25, 1861, Alan Thompson, " 'Frank and outspoken in my Disposition': The Wartime Letters of Confederate General Dandridge McRae," *Arkansas Historical Quarterly* 72 (Winter 2013), 334–335; Woods, *Rebellion and Realignment*, 158–159.

56. Governor's Message, March 2, 1861, *Journal of Both Sessions of the Convention of the State of Arkansas*, 44; S. H. Hempstead to David Walker, May 6, 1861, *Journal of Both Sessions*, 119.

57. D. McRae to Angie McRae, May 6, 10, 1861, Thompson, " 'Frank and outspoken,' " 335, 337. See the *Arkansas Weekly Gazette*, May 11, 1861, for the reports of a slave uprising in Searcy plotted by Charles Cavender, a Methodist preacher, and four African Americans. Whether an uprising was planned is debatable, but Cavender and two slaves were rounded up by excited vigilantes and hanged in Searcy on May 10.

58. John W. Ellis to Jefferson Davis, April 27, 1860, Tolbert, *Papers of Ellis*, Vol. 2: 689; Crofts, *Reluctant Confederates*, 338–340.

59. Jonathan Worth to T. C. and D. G. Worth, May 13, July 13, 1861, Hamilton, *Worth Correspondence*, 142, 155.

60. Yadkin County Citizens to John W. Ellis, April 22, 1861, William B. Gulick to Ellis, May 2, 1861, Tolbert, *Papers of Ellis*, Vol. 2: 662, 710.

61. Thomas Goode Tucker to Ellis, May 7, 1861, Balis M. Edney to Ellis, May 20, 1861, Tolbert, *Papers of Ellis*, Vol. 2: 728–729, 766.

62. See William L. Brookes to Iveson L. Brookes, Feb. 12, 1861, Iveson Lewis Brookes Papers, Series J, Part 4, Reel 37, *Records*, for a typical commentary on the hard times; Schenck Diary, Vol. 3, March 18, 1861, p. 463, SHC; John W. Ellis to the General Assembly, May 3, 1861, Tolbert, *Papers of Ellis*, Vol. 2: 715–716.

63. Robert B. Gilliam to William Graham, May 16, 1861, Williams and de Roulhac Hamilton, *The Papers of William Alexander Graham*, Vol. 4: 255; card of W. W. Holden, *Raleigh Weekly Standard*, May 8, 1861; Crofts, *Reluctant Confederates*, 341.

64. Henry Algernon duPont to Louisa G. duPont, April 21, 1861, HADP_18610421b, Group 8, Series A, Box 2, Folder "Correspondence, 1861," Winterthur Manuscript (Accession WMSS), Manuscript and Research Department, Hagley Museum and Library, Wilmington, Del.; John Thomas Scharf, *History of Delaware, 1608–1888*, 2 vols. (Philadelphia: L.J. Richards & Co., 1888), Vol.1: 332, 339.

65. William Dorsey Pender to Mary Frances Pender, March 26, April 3, 1861, William Dorsey Pender Papers, SHC; Mary B. Pettigrew Browne to Caroline Pettigrew, March 1, 1861, Pettigrew Family Papers, Series J, Part 2, Reel 27, *Records*; *Richmond Dispatch*, March 26, 1861, citing letters in *Baltimore Sun*; for the State Rights convention and its resolutions, see *Baltimore Sun*, April 20, 1861; Towers, *The Urban South*, 169–171.

66. See Towers, *The Urban South*, 174–175, for a profile of the Unionists in the riot and for the estimate of those killed, 166; Report of Colonel Edward F. Jones, Sixth Massachusetts Militia, *O.R.*, Series 1, Vol. 2: 7–9, provides a Northern, and the *Baltimore Sun*, April 20, 1861, a Southern account of the riot.

67. Samuel Wethered to "Beloved Ones" (the Barringers of North Carolina), April [19, 1861], Daniel Moreau Barringer Papers, SHC; *Baltimore Sun*, April 22, 1861.

68. Reply to Baltimore Committee, April 22, 1861, Basler, *Works of Lincoln*, Vol. 4: 342; B. F. Butler to Thomas H. Hicks, April 23, 1861, *O.R.*, Series 1, Vol. 2: 593. A North Carolinian was happy to report that the fleeing slaves were "driven back to their masters." See William B. Gullick to John W. Ellis, May 2, 1861, Tolbert, *Papers of Ellis*, Vol. 2: 709.

69. *Cecil Whig* (Elkton, Md.), April 20, 1861; Lincoln to Winfield Scott, April 25, 27, 1861, Basler, *Works of Lincoln*, Vol. 4: 344, 347.

70. Robinson, *A Union Indivisible*, 165–169.

71. For a regional breakdown of the vote on the secession ordinance, see Shanks, *Secession Movement in Virginia*, 205; *Wheeling Daily Intelligencer*, Dec. 28, 1860, and, for the threats against Unionists, April 20, 1861; Reese, *Proceedings*, Vol. 4: 51, 545–546.
72. *Wheeling Daily Intelligencer*, April 22,1861, and, for the quote, April 23, 1861.
73. R. S. Garnett to Colonel C. B. Tompkins, May 3, 1861, *O.R.*, Series 1, Vol. 2: 800; Lucy Wood Butler Diary, June 7, 1861, microfilm of transcript, 4, SHC; Francis M. Boykin Jr. to General R. E. Lee, May 10, 1861, *O.R.*, Series 1, Vol. 2: 827.
74. Charles H. Ambler, *Francis H. Pierpont: Union War Governor of Virginia and Father of West Virginia* (Chapel Hill: University of North Carolina Press, 1937); Richard O. Curry, *A House Divided: A Study of Statehood Politics and the Copperhead Movement in West Virginia* (Pittsburgh, Pa.: University of Pittsburgh Press, 1964). For the age-segmented steps by which slavery was to be ended, see *Amended Constitution of West Virginia, Adopted by the Convention February 18th, 1863* (Wheeling: n.p., 1863), Article XI (7), p. 21.
75. Reference to "Abolition hordes" from card of John Allen seeking recruits, "Kentucky to Arms!" *Louisville Daily Courier*, April 18, 1861; for the Unionists' call for neutrality, see A. C. Quisinberry, "Kentucky's Neutrality in 1861," *Register of Kentucky State Historical Society* 15 (Jan. 1917): 15–16.
76. Mildred C. Sayre to Edmund Ruffin, March 8, 1861, Edmund Ruffin Papers, Series M, Part 4, Reel 48, *Records*; Robinson, *A Union Indivisible*, 159–160.
77. Gideon J. Pillow to L. P. Walker, April 24, 1861, Leslie Coombs to Green Adams, April 24, 1861, *O.R.*, Series 1, Vol. 52, Part 1: 68–69, 137.
78. For the Confederate regiments, see *O.R.*, Series 1, Vol. 52, Part 2: 43–44, 46–47, 50, 53–54, 56–57; Garrett Davis to Simon Cameron, May 3, 1861, C. F. Beyland and others to Simon Cameron, May 10, 1861, *O.R.*, Series 1, Vol. 52, Part 1: 138, 141–142; Thomas Speed, *The Union Cause in Kentucky, 1860–1865* (New York: G.P. Putnam's Sons, 1907), 99–102, 129–132; Abraham Lincoln to all who shall see these presents, [May 7, 1861], *O.R.*, Series 1, Vol. 52, Part 1: 140–141.
79. Garrett Davis to Simon Cameron, May 3, 1861, *O.R.*, Series 1, Vol. 52, Part 2: 138; *Journal of the House of Representatives of the Commonwealth of Kentucky, May 6, 1861–May 24, 1861* (Frankfort: John B. Major, State printer, 1861), 6–8.
80. For the petitions, see *Journal of the House of Kentucky*, 22, 24–25, 34; Robinson, *A Union Indivisible*, 171–173.
81. Wooster, *Secession Conventions*, 217–221; Berry Craig, *Kentucky Confederates: Secession, Civil War, and the Jackson Purchase* (Lexington: University Press of Kentucky, 2014).
82. Robinson, *A Union Indivisible*, 180–181.
83. Davis to C. F. Jackson, April 23, 1861, *O.R.*, Series 1, Vol. 1: 688.
84. *St. Louis State Sentinel*, cited in *Charleston* (Mo.) *Courier*, April 26, 1861; S. J. P. Anderson, *"The Dangers and Duties of the Present Crisis!" A Discourse Delivered in the Union Church, St. Louis, Jan. 4, 1861* (St. Louis: Schenck & Co., 1861), 15.
85. *Glasgow* (Mo.)*Weekly Times*, May 9, 1861; Mark W. Geiger, *Financial Fraud and Guerrilla Violence in Missouri's Civil War, 1861–1865* (New Haven, Conn.: Yale University Press, 2010), 30.
86. James Peckham, *General Nathaniel Lyon and Missouri in 1861* (New York: American News Company, 1866), 56; Phillips, *Missouri's Confederate*, 246–248, 251–252; quote is from Lyon's report, May 11, 1861, *O.R.*, Series 1, Vol. 3: 4; Thomas L. Snead, *The Fight for Missouri from the Election of Lincoln to the Death of Lyon* (New York: C. Scribner's Sons, 1886), 168–172; Louis S. Gerteis, *Civil War St. Louis* (Lawrence: University Press of Kansas, 2001), 114.
87. Robinson, *A Union Indivisible*, 175–176; Geiger, *Financial Fraud*, 3.
88. On divisions between Unionists and secessionists, see Wooster, *Secession Conventions*, 236–238; Phillips, *Missouri's Confederate*, 253–273.

Conclusion

1. J. David Hacker, "A Census-Based Count of the Civil War Dead," *Civil War History* 57 (Dec. 2011): 306–347; Childs, *Private Journal of Henry Ravenel*, 181–182; Chandra Manning, *What This Cruel War Was Over: Soldiers, Slavery, and the Civil War* (New York: Alfred A. Knopf,

2007) makes a very strong case for the centrality of slavery in the motivations of the soldiers on both sides.

2. David Brion Davis, *The Problem of Slavery in the Age of Revolution, 1770–1823* (Ithaca, N.Y.: Cornell University Press, 1975); Christopher Leslie Brown, *Moral Capital: Foundations of British Abolitionism* (Chapel Hill: University of North Carolina Press, 2006); *The Common Wind: Afro-American Currents in the Age of the Haitian Revolution* (New York: Verso, 2018).

3. For an insightful, transnational study of the ideological stakes involved in the American Civil War, see Don H. Doyle, *The Cause of All Nations: A New International History of the Civil War* (New York: Basic Books, 2015). Also consult the essays in David T. Gleeson and Simon Lewis, eds., *The Civil War as Global Conflict: Transnational Meanings of the American Civil War* (Columbia: University of South Carolina Press, 2014) and the groundbreaking article by David M. Potter in C. Vann Woodward, ed., *The Comparative Approach to American History* (New York: Basic Books, 1968).

4. *Congressional Globe*, 36th Congress, 1st Session, Appendix, 206.

5. Dr. Robert Randolph to Beverly R. Wellford, Jan. 26, 1861, White-Welford-Taliaferro-Marshall Papers, Microfilm M-1300, Reel 1, SHC.

6. Anna Rebecca Gourdin Young to Robert N. Gourdin, Oct. 12, 1860, Racine, *Gentlemen Merchants*, 395; Philip Henry Gosse, *Letters from Alabama, (U.S.A.) Chiefly Relating to Natural History* (London: Morgan and Chase, 1859), 253; Mary Ann Whittle to Lewis N. Whittle, Dec. [?], 1860, Lewis Neale Whittle Papers, SHC. For an overview of insurrectionary scares after the 1790s, see Carl Lawrence Paulus, *The Slaveholding Crisis: Fear of Insurrection and the Coming of the Civil War* (Baton Rouge: Louisiana State University Press, 2017).

7. T. N. Simpson to Caroline Virginia Taliaferro Miller, July 14, 1862, Guy R. Everson and Edward H. Simpson Jr., eds., *"Far, Far from Home": The Wartime Letters of Dick and Tally Simpson, 3rd South Carolina Volunteers* (New York: Oxford University Press, 1994), 136. For the evangelical beliefs Simpson drew upon, see Pearl J. Young, "Secession as a Moral Imperative: White Southerners and Evangelical Theology" (PhD thesis, University of North Carolina at Chapel Hill, 2018). Lydia Maria Child to Lucy Searle, June 8, 1861, *Letters of Lydia Maria Child with a Biographical Introduction by John G. Whittier and Appendix by Wendell Phillips* (Boston: Houghton, Mifflin, 1883), 280.

8. Mrs. William Pringle Smith to J. J. Pringle Smith, July 4, 10, 1864, Daniel E. Huger Smith, Alice R. Huger Smith, and Arney R. Childs, eds., *Mason Smith Family Letters, 1860–1868* (Columbia: University of South Carolina Press, 1950), 108–110.

9. John S. Palmer to Esther Simmons Palmer, July 9, 10, 1860, Towles, *A World Turned Upside Down*, 328–329.

INDEX

Page numbers followed by *f* indicate figures. Numbers followed by n indicate footnotes.

For the benefit of digital users, indexed terms that span two pages (e.g., 52–53) may, on occasion, appear on only one of those pages.